Applied Psychology

For Civil Services Main Examination

Applied Psychology

For Civil Services Main Examination

Third Edition
2019

Smarak Swain

B.Tech, IIT Kharagpur

Published by
OakBridge Publishing Pvt. Ltd.
M 35, 1st Floor, Old DLF, Gurugram, 122001, Haryana, India
Tel.: +91 124 4305970, E-mail: info@oakbridge.in
www.oakbridge.in

ISBN: 978-81-940312-3-9

Printed and bound at Saurabh Printers Pvt.Ltd.

Foreword to the First Edition

Psychology in its various manifestations has grown over the years. Though it has maintained its traditional approach gradually, its relevance and applicability in a sphere of life is worth noticing. Among the social sciences, it has a distinct and unique place and over the years it has obtained more and more market value.

Observation analysis and interpretation of human behaviour is facilitated using various tests and techniques - for instance while dealing with educational issues one must know that each person has an individual profile of characteristics, abilities which result in discrepancies in intelligence, creativity, cognitive style motivation, and capacity to process information. The 'what, how, and why' principle of acquisition and processing application of knowledge is very important for teaching-learning process In organization formulation of organizational effectiveness strategies, reduction of stress and burnout syndrome, improvement of morale and job satisfaction through intervention strategies is very important. Principles of psychology are of great use in selection of personnel in various sphere like sports, defence, and creation of a positive environment for work. A psychologist is always there for a person in need, be it a "six hour retarded" child, a psychotic, neurotic or psychosomatic. The diagnosis-treatment process gives emphasis on coping with stress and development of positive mental health through behaviour modification. Rehabilitation aspect deals with services like counseling wellness promotion and compensatory strategies to clients etc. The emerging field of media psychology is closely related with media based on the ability to understand how people perceive, interpret, and respond.

In this book, the author has given a simple and consolidated analysis of psychological principles and application in controlling, maintaining, and modifying human behaviour. The relevance of psychological principles in dealing with various issues and concerns of life are well explained in each chapter. This book will be of great use to the students appearing in various competitive examinations as well as to postgraduate students in Psychology.

Dr Namita Panda

Head, Department of Psychology

Ravenshaw University, Cuttack

Preface

When I had started preparing for civil services, I had taken mathematics and physics as my options. I had, in fact, given my preliminary examination with mathematics as an optional. But owing to various reasons, I decided to take psychology and sociology as my options for mains. Now, being a student from engineering background, I was new to psychology as a subject. And I had extremely less time between prelims and mains. On top of that, I experienced great difficulty in obtaining good source materials on paper 2. This was because paper 2 was about applications and issues of psychology. The topics are contemporary and a single source covering most of the topics wasn't available. Besides, this paper deals with a wide array of issues. So, to deal with the problem, I relied heavily on scholarly books and journal articles I got access to in various libraries of Delhi. I also got involved in meticulous notes making. By the time I got my result (I had secured 196th rank on the merit list), had very solid notes on psychology paper 2. With encouragement from friends, I finally decided to rewrite my notes in book form with additional material.

Now, I would like to put some suggestions about how to use this book. Please remember that as the name suggests, Applied Psychology is an advanced level course in most of the universities. To understand the contents in this book, a basic prerequisite is to know the basics of psychology. For civil service aspirants, a thorough grasp of paper 1 is a must before reading this book. Reading this book without proper grasp of basic psychology can be dangerous, as it may lead to learning of incorrect concepts which you will later have to unlearn. Hence, I suggest that you read it only after having a grasp over paper 1 syllabus of psychology. Also, it will be better to read the chapters in the order mentioned in the contents of this book. This is because, some chapters (such as gender psychology, rehabilitation psychology, military psychology etc) are better understood after reading chapters such as organizational psychology and psychological well-being.

Applied psychology is a vast and contemporary field. Hence, this book can never claim to be extensive enough to be a single exhaustive source. At the same time, you readers are the best judge of what this book lacks and how it could be improved further. I invite your kind suggestions and feedback on the book.

Smarak Swain

Email: smarak@gmail.com

Preface

Preface to the Third Edition

This book was first published in 2010. I have been receiving constructive feedback on the book ever since. The second edition of the book had a dream run of five years with multiple reprints. From the feedback I received, it appeared that students did like the book.

This book's content is based on the syllabus of Psychology Paper II in the Civil Service Examinations conducted by the Union Public Service Commission (UPSC). However, over time, many regular psychology students in various Indian Universities started using the book. The book's key strength is the focus on application of psychology to public policy and stressors. Public policy is one key area of implementation in which Indian psychologists have left their mark. Indian psychologists have provided empirical data on entrepreneurship, deprivation, alleviation, and interventions, which policymakers have used to take informed decisions. Studies of Indian psychologists into group processes and inter-group relations has helped administrators in India in forging amity between various social groups. It has helped administrators and policymakers in devising strategies for social integration and social inclusion. Study of group processes and psyche of individuals joining deviant groups has helped investigating agencies in understanding deviance, organised crime and terrorism.

The contribution of Indian psychologists to nation-building and social change is tremendous. Psychological theories place inordinate focus on Western societies, because most early theories and findings were made in universities of America and Europe. Such theories cannot be directly (or blindly) applied to the Indian context. This is where Indian psychologists pitched in and contributed. The legacy of hard empirical evidences established by them have helped India drive its policies.

Second major contribution of Indian psychologists has been in the area of stressors. Classical theories of psychology have informed us of the impact of stressors on human health and performance. However, these theories could not be applied in a cross-cultural context blindly. Indian psychologists have chipped in here too and have demonstrated the impact of stressors, like work pressure, pollution, noise, trauma, etc. on well-being.

This book has tried to narrate the success story of Indian psychologists within the framework of syllabus prescribed for Psychology Paper II in the Civil Service Examinations.

Although the first two editions received positive feedback, a need was felt for updating the content. Recent researches and few relevant theories that can help in better understanding of the applications of psychology have been added in this updated edition. I heartily thank the readers who gave their feedback and helped enrich the book. I also thank Shreesh Chandra, Vikesh Dhyani and Sulekh Varma of OakBridge Publishing for keeping me motivated and for bringing the book out in its current form.

Smarak Swain
Email: smarak@gmail.com

Preface to the Third Edition

Contents

CHAPTERS

PSYCHOLOGY APPLIED TO HUMAN PROBLEMS

PSYCHOLOGY APPLIED TO HUMAN RESOURCE DEVELOPMENT

PSYCHOLOGY APPLIED TO SOCIO-ECONOMIC PROBLEMS

PSYCHOLOGY APPLIED TO SOCIO-ECONOMIC DEVELOPMENT

PSYCHOLOGY APPLIED TO TECHNOLOGY RELATED ISSUES

APPENDIX

REFERENCES

Psychology Applied to Human Problems

Chapter 1. Psychological Well-being and Mental Disorders

Chapter 2. Disorders Therapies

Chapter 3. Rehabilitation Psychology

1

PSYCHOLOGICAL WELL-BEING AND MENTAL DISORDERS

Chapter outline

1.1 The Concept of Health and Ill-health

It is tough to define health, as it is not a single concept. Rather, health refers to a philosophical construct which has been variously inferred by various schools of study. When the term 'health' originated, it was associated with both- physiological functioning and mental and moral soundness, as well as spiritual salvation. These were, of course, only philosophical theories of health. Many supernatural phenomena too, were attached to health. In few cultures, health was a divine responsibility and ill-health, a supernatural phenomenon where the forces of darkness had taken over a man.

With advances in scientific fields of medicine, psychology, science and sociology, these philosophical theories have given way to more scientific ideas. Yet, health is but a collection of ideas rather than an integrated idea. This is because the concept of health varies from culture to culture. Also, individuals differ in their ideas of health. The only agreement is that as a concept, health is multi-dimensional and subjective in nature. An individual may suffer from physical disability and yet be healthy. Another individual with no medical disorder may not be.

Here, we will understand the concept of health, positive health and ill-health, as they have evolved in modern western psychology. Beyond this, we will also investigate into notice of health in Indian culture. These ideas can be dealt under the following heads:

1. Traditional medical concept
2. WHO concept of health
3. Ecological concept of health
4. Positive Psychology Movement
5. Concepts of health in Yogic Psychology

The traditional medical concept of health is the earliest scientific notion of health. It conceptualizes health as a disease-free state. This view was very popular among physicians and medical personnel in the first half of the twentieth century. A major flaw with this view is that it works on the assumption that health and disease are objective phenomena that can be observed and quantified. A second flaw was that rather than representing the presence of certain attributes, it defines health solely in terms of lack of ill-health. Thus, according to the medical concept, there is a dichotomy between health and illness. What is not illness is health! Truth is, there is a continuum between absolute illness and absolute health. One can have some disease, yet be healthy. Hence, it is flawed to take health as the absence of disease.

A third flaw of the traditional medical concept was that it neglected the individual as a whole when it focused its attention on specific diseases. Any workable concept of health necessarily has to be a holistic concept. An attempt to define health more holistically was made by the World Health Organization (WHO). WHO conceptualizes health as, "a state of complete physical, mental and social well-being and not merely as the absence of disease or infirmity". This concept was a radical departure from the medical concept in that it defines health in terms of presence of some positive attributes. It conceptualizes health as a positive state of well-being in which not only physical health, but also social, psychological, economic and political aspects of health are incorporated into a single definition.

Yet, there are certain grave problems with the WHO concept of health. Some important ones are:

1. Being so broad and vague, the WHO concept has low utilitarian value. Any concept needs to be specific to be defined operationally and to be applied to practical situations.
2. Though words, like 'well-being' and 'wellness' are used freely, these concepts haven't been clearly defined.
3. It is a utopian view of health. The WTO definition, it seems, tries to paint a perfectly healthy state which is unrealistic and unreachable.

The ecological concept of health emerged in reaction to the previous medical and holistic approaches discussed above. The concept is different from the earlier concepts in two aspects- 'first, by conceiving health as a more relative sort of concept and second, by placing a greater emphasis on the interrelationship between the environment and the individual's quality of life. These ecological and relative definitions of health were heavily based on an evaluation of the person's level of functioning and adaptation to the environment' (Boruchovitch and Mednick, 2002).

This view has immense utilitarian value in the sense that (1) it conceptualizes health as a relative concept, (2) it focuses on the functional adaptation of the individual to her environment, hence includes issues like, quality of life as well as maladaptation, and lastly (3) it is a specific definition. Hence, it can be used to operationally define health.

Some attempts to integrate various ideas of health have been made. However, other psychologists argue that health refers to a number of entities and therefore, is a multi-dimensional concept. Smith (1981) has tried to organize (not integrate) multiple views of health into four distinct models:

(a) Clinical

(c) Adaptive

(d) Eudaimonistic

Smith reiterates that these four models are not exclusive, but are progressively wider conceptualizations of health. For instance, the clinical model defines health minimally as the absence of diseases. On the other end, the eudaimonistic model is the broadest concept. It includes the basic ideas of the three earlier models and also, issues of self-actualization and self-fulfillment.

Positive Psychology is the branch of psychology that focuses on positive experiences rather than negative ones. Positive psychology has not contributed to the concept of health in a big way; yet it has helped shift the focus of attention towards well-being. Central to positive psychology is the idea that the individual's experience matters. It defines health in terms of the individual's perception of how healthy she is. While earlier ideas of health were from academic and professional perspective, positive psychology states that the health of an individual is how healthy he/ she feels! This is radical in the sense that how one feels also determines her health. If suppose, a man has good functional adaption to his surrounding and is not diseased, yet is pessimistic and unhappy with life. Can this man be called healthy?

After discussing the various conceptualizations of health in modern western psychology, let us now take a look at cross-cultural variations in the idea of health. It would amaze you to know that spiritual health is a part of the concept of health in many cultures. Yet, this concept was largely absent in western psychology before Maslow. Here, I will deal with a single cross-cultural definition of health, that is of yogic psychology.

Health in Yogic Psychology

While a holistic concept of health has evolved in the West only lately, an equally holistic concept of health can be found in yoga literature of ancient India. Yoga doesn't belief in dichotomies of positive health and illness; nor does it recognize divisions on the lines of physical, mental and spiritual dimensions. Rather, all these ideas are integrated in a model called the Anasakti-Asakti model.

Asakti referes to attachment, that is, attraction towards individuals or objects with expectations. This attachment leads to cathartic fixation, to use the Freudian terminology and may lead to frustration and mental problems if the need is not fulfilled. Asakti leads to anxiety, depression, fear and insecurities. Asakti manifests itself in three important psychological aspects:

1. *Raga:* It is the attraction towards selected persons and objects with expectations and ego involvement.
2. *Dwesha:* It is a feeling of hatred and a tendency to cause harm. Dwesha leads to negative emotions, violence, aggression etc..
3. *Ahamkara:* It refers to the need for recognition, egoism and arrogance.

Anasakti is detachment. Only detachment from the material world can help one to pursue self-actualization. Inherent here is also the notion of spiritual health. An anasakt individual experiences spiritual unity of atman (herself) with the Brahman (the supreme one). As a result, the anasakt individual is free from pain and sufferings.

Asakti and Anasakti are not dichotomies. Rather, they are polar opposites on a continuum. No person is 100% detached or 100% attached.

To conclude, health is a multi-dimensional concept that means not only the absence of diseases, but also proper functional adaptation to environment. Health doesn't refer to dichotomous states, but to a continuum as under:

Absolute Positive Health —————————— **Absolute ill-health**

Today, the concept of health is being reinvented to include well-being, feeling of happiness, a sense of satisfaction and harmony between the mind and body.

1.2 Conceptualizing Health in India

Clearly, the concept of health varies from society to society. The Anasakti-Asakti model is one of the many definitions of health forwarded in Indian philosophical texts. There are many more conceptualizations that make the Indian concept of health broad-based and affirmative (D. Sinha, 1990).

For instance, Sushruta, the father of medicine and surgery in ancient India, defined health as prassannanmendriyanamah Swastha, i.e., health as a state of delight with feelings of spiritual, physical and mental well-being. The essential features for a healthy person are possessing in the right quantity (Sama), the-

1. Defects or weaknesses (Samadosah)
2. Digestive quality (Samaagni)
3. Semen (Samadhatu)
4. Normal bodily functions (Malakriya)
(D. Sinha, 1990)

But then, you may say these are only definitions mentioned in ancient scriptures. How do the people define and conceptualize health today? Some empirical studies have thrown light on this. For instance, Tripathi (1993) conducted a study of the meaning of health and sickness in rural areas of Allahabad. Using statistical tools, he derived three factors which explained 62.5% of the total variance.

These are:

1. *Vitality:* powerful, untiring, physically strong, good digestion, etc.
2. *Hardiness:* Rarely fall sick, high immunity, not lazy, etc.
3. *Fitness:* Energetic, strong, carefree

A study that throws light on the superstitions attached to health beliefs was by Rizvi (1991). He studied the health beliefs of the Jaunsaris of the Himalayan region and found that health for Jaunasaris means proper functioning of the body. These had a muscular body, were able to work hard and could digest good food and therefore, were considered healthy. On the other hand, ill-health was defined as not feeling well. Most of the diseases were attributed to sins, crimes, non-observance of religious laws, etc. Hence, the cure prescribed was to appease supernatural entities with prayers, vows, holy baths and sacrifices.

1.3 Well-being: The Concept

Well-being can mean two concepts at the same time- economic well-being, which is an objective measure of economic standing of an individual; alternately, it also refers to subjective well-being, i.e., an individual's degree of satisfaction with various facets of life. It is subjective because it is the individual's perspective of her satisfaction with life.

Subjective well-being (SWB) is defined as an individual's cognitive and affective evaluations of her life (Diener et al, 2002). Simply stated, it is a technical term for happiness. The more satisfied you are with life, happier you are. The focus of this section is on subjective well-being, which is now touted as the best measure of health of an individual.

For many years, the focus of researchers was primarily on negative motions, such as anxiety, depression and anger. The school of positive psychology seeks to shift the focus to positive emotions of happiness and satisfaction. Well-being refers not just positive health, but also to aspects of emotions that make life more satisfying.

So, what constitutes SWB? According to Seligman (2004), there are three components of SWB:

1. Pleasure
2. Engagement
3. Meaning

The pleasure route to greater happiness (i.e., SWB) is hedonic, increasing positive emotion. Within limits, this route leads to positive emotions. However, there are limits set on positive emotions by genetic factors. Heredity determines a certain band in which positive emotions vary. Most modern researchers agree that there is a ***happiness disposition,*** i.e., some individuals are hereditarily more pre-disposed to have better positive emotions. Fortunately, positive emotion is not the sole determinant of happiness and those with lower positive emotions (based on their hereditary codes) can still achieve higher levels of happiness (Seligman, 2002).

Engagement refers to the pursuit of activities that lead to intrinsic gratifications. We are often intrinsically motivated to do certain things over others. One may find gratification in watching movies, another in writing, still another in reading psychology (though I am not sure how psychology can help gratify one!) and yet another in arts. There is no short-cut to gratification. We can take short-cuts to pleasure (e.g., masturbating, taking drugs, watching pornography, taking good food etc.). But, there is no short-cut to gratification. It demands ego-involvement.

The third route of SWB is that of finding a meaning in life. How does one make her life meaningful? Knowledge, altruism, family and community welfare, and spirituality are certain elements, the pursuit of which leads to happiness. Basically, these are some activities that help us realize something higher than self, a 'meaningful life', for example, altruism helps the individual self to connect to the society at large. Spirituality helps the self to connect in harmony with the divine. Whether divine exists or not, this leads to harmony.

Peterson et al. (2005) have developed some measures of happiness to assess how people use the three routes to happiness. They have found that people tend to rely on one route rather than another. Following this finding, they have given a typology:

1. *The pleasant life:* Tendency to pursue happiness by boosting positive emotion.
2. *The good life:* Tendency to pursue happiness via gratifications.
3. *The meaningful life:* The tendency to pursue happiness via using our strengths towards something larger than ourselves.
4. *The full life:* A person who uses all three routes to happiness is said to lead a full life.

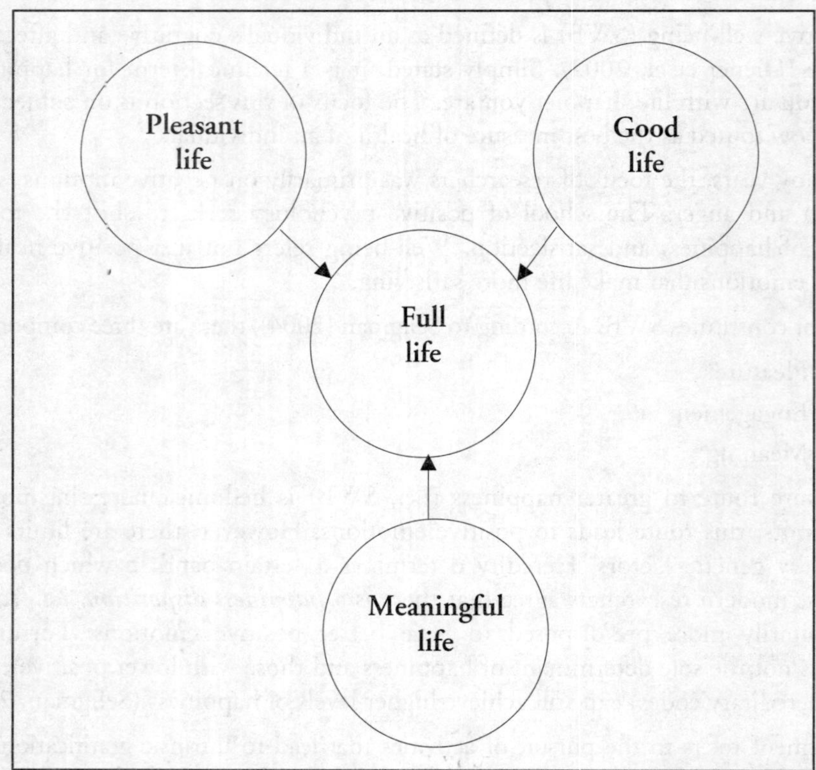

Fig. 1.1 : Concept of well-being

The pursuit of happiness is of paramount importance in modern health psychology because of its importance to human beings. It is so important to humans that 'The Pursuit of Happiness' is an academy award winning movie starring Will Smith. The concept of SWB helps us to understand factors that make us happy and satisfied beyond material consumption.

Factors affecting Positive Health

Many models explaining the nature of positive health have been forwarded by psychologists. For example, the stress-model believes that how one deals with external stressors determines how healthy she is. Many other models look into many other factors that affect positive health.

A few factors that affect positive health can be listed here:

1. Stress coping style
2. Resilience
3. Beliefs and attitude
4. Lifestyle
5. Social support
6. Finding meaning in life
7. Anasakti
8. Sense of humour

Some of these factors are elaborated below.

Stress Coping Style

There are countless ways in which people may respond to a stressful event; yet broadly there are three coping styles:

1. Problem-focused coping
2. Emotion-focused coping
3. Seeking social support

Problem-focused coping refers to strategies to directly confront and deal with the demands of the situation. For example, if I have misunderstandings about a person and it is causing me anxiety, I would directly approach the person. If, on the other hand, I don't directly deal with the stressful situation, but attempt to manage the emotional response that results from it, it is emotion-focused coping. This style may take many forms – denial, avoidance, etc. I may deny that there is any misunderstanding or I may avoid stressful situations. The third class is seeking support, i.e., turning to others for assistance and emotional support.

It has been found that problem-focused coping and seeking social support leads to favorable adjustment to stressors. On the other hand, emotion-focused coping strategies that involve avoiding feelings leads to poor adjustment. In one study (Holahan and Moos, 1991), coping patterns in more than 400 Californian adults were studied over a period of one year. The results confirm the above conclusion. The study further found that emotion-focused strategies lead to depression and poor adjustment to stressors.

Resilience

Resilience is the ability to bounce back from adversity. Resilience shows the unusual ability of some to manage extremely stressful situations. The research on resilience has mostly focused on resilient children. For instance, Priscilla was a child who grew up in a terrible home environment with a psychotic mother and a father who abused her and committed suicide in her presence. Despite these experiments, Prescilla grew up into a highly successful woman (narrated in Passer and Smith, 2007, p.500)

The above example shows that some individuals have better ability to cope with stress than others. It has been found that resilient kids have certain unique characteristics, like adequate intellectual functioning, social skills, self-efficacy, faith, optimism and hope.

Beliefs and Attitude

Great therapists, like Ellis and Beck have observed that many negative emotions are the result of incorrect cognitions and beliefs. Attitudes and cognitions are important factors influencing positive health. It has been empirically proved that optimistic expectations and positive attitudes lead to better health. On the other hand, rigid expectations from life lead to extreme stress. Pessimism leads to unnecessary anxiety and depression.

In one study, women suffering from cancer were studied over a period of five years (Levy et al., 1988). It was found that women who were optimistic lived longer on average than pessimistic women. This shows the direct correlation between health and optimism. In a year-long study conducted by Peterson and Seligman (1987), optimists were found to have half as many infectious illnesses and visits to doctors as the pessimists.

Finding Meaning in Stressful Life

Humanistic theorists have emphasized that human beings are motivated to find meaning in life. There are many routes to explore meaning in life that includes creativity, artistic work, spirituality, altruism, etc. Some people turn to spirituality and find meaning of life in divinity. Surprisingly, spirituality has been positively correlated with positive health. Spiritual beliefs provide personal beliefs that are a source of comfort in times of crisis.

A behaviour that peculiarly leads to positive health is altruism. Many researchers have shown that by helping others, the altruist basically helps himself. It gives a meaning to life, but how? Altruism helps oneself become part of the larger, undivided self. In an analysis of 1700 women who were regularly involved in helping others, it was found that there was considerable improvement in the physical health of the helpers. Disorders, such as headaches, multiple sclerosis and depression suffered by the helpers showed improvement. This was in addition to the positive sense of having done some good which enhances one's self-concept. (See Pandya, 1997). Hence, 'altruism behaves like a miracle drug and a strange one at that. It has beneficial effects on the person doing the helping – the ***helper's high***. It benefits the person to whom help is directed; and it can stimulate healthy responses in persons at a distance who may view it only obliquely…. Part of the warm feeling may be due to coming home – returning to our original, undivided, larger self, the part of us that connects, that knows no divisions in space and time' (Dossey, 1991, p.290).

Sense of Humour

Laughter is the best medicine and its therapeutic uses have been well documented. The value of laughter has been documented even in our ancient text ***Hasya Rasya***. How is humour related to positive health? Basically, humour leads to unparalleled relaxation. Hence, a person with a sense of humour affords better and more positive affect, even in stressful situations.

This is the reason why many psychologists recommend patients of depression and anxiety to join laughter clubs. In a typical laughter exercise, a regular group gathers early in the morning. 'After initial warming up exercises, aimed at expanding the lungs, a leader starts off a round of laughter. Initially, this happens through jokes, but the group learns that a single person bursting into laughter soon infects the rest of the group. Variations on the theme have been devised – laughing with the mouth shut, laughing with the mouth wide open, but without creating any sound. These are said to expand the lungs and ensure better oxygenation of the blood in addition to releasing tension'. (Pandya, 1997, p.194-195).

Factors affecting Subjective Well-Being

To assess the factors affecting subjective well-being, researchers typically study factors that predict satisfaction and happiness. Based on an array of research on various factors, the following list can be drawn (Weitten, p.422):

1. Factors that do not predict satisfaction and happiness
   (a) Money
   (b) Age
   (c) Physical attractiveness
2. Factors that moderately predict satisfaction and happiness
   (a) Health
   (b) Social network
   (c) Religion
   (d) Culture
3. Strong predictors of Subjective Well-Being (SWB)
   (a) Work
   (b) Love and marriage
   (c) Personality

1.4 Factor that do not predict SWB

Money, beauty and physical attractiveness are certain factors that we often believe, lead to happiness. Especially in our modern consumerist culture, money is said to satisfy the wants of the consumer. And, it is believed that the more you consume, the happier you are. However, psychological studies have provided certain counter-intuitive results. Obviously, being very poor makes people unhappy and reduces their SWB. But, once people rise above the poverty level, little relation is seen between income and SWB. For instance, one study found a correlation of only 0.12 between income and SWB in USA, an affluent country (Diener et al., 1993). Empirical surveys have consistently found that even those who are poor or disabled characterize themselves as fairly happy (Diener and Diener, 1996). Similarly, even though good-looking people enjoy a variety of advantages in comparison to unattractive people, it doesn't mean that they have better SWB.

Finally, it is generally believed that SWB decreases in old age. But, empirical findings have shown that age accounts for less than 1% of the variation in people's sense of satisfaction with life (Inglehart, 1990).

Moderately Good Predicators of Health

Good physical health is obviously a factor influencing happiness. But, it doesn't mean that people with health problems cannot be happy. Research reveals that individuals who develop serious, disabling health problems aren't as unsatisfied with life as we would like to believe (Myers, 1992). Rather, good health may not lead to happiness as people tend to take good health for granted (Freedman, 1978).

Social networks, like social support, family and friendship networks contribute to SWB. Good interpersonal relations with others lends a sense of satisfaction. Also, spirituality and religious beliefs seem to foster happiness. Researchers haven't yet established the exact link, but many large-scale surveys suggest that people with religious convictions are happier than people who label themselves as non-religious. Myers (1992) argues that this is because religion gives people a sense of purpose and meaning in life.

Cross-cultural variations in SWB have been noted. These variations have mostly been related to individualistic versus collectivistic orientation. In individualistic cultures, *the individual puts personal goal ahead of group goals and defines her identity in terms of her personal attributes.* In contrast, individuals of collectivistic cultures *put group goals ahead of personal goals and define her identity in terms of the group she belongs to (*Weitten, P.424). Interestingly, people from individualistic cultures report somewhat higher SWB than that of collectivistic cultures (Diener and Suh, 1999). No conclusion should be drawn from this, however, because of presence of many other variables (for example, western countries are both rich and individualistic. Though wealth doesn't predict SWB, poverty does. Countries of the east with collectivistic orientation are mired by larger-scale poverty).

Strong Predicators of SWB

Though people in romantic relations and marriages often complain a lot, they have been found to be happier than those who aren't involved in a romantic relation or marriage. Married people are happier than those who are single or divorced (Myers and Diener, 1995). Another strong predictors of SWB is work. Humanistic theorists have emphasized that job satisfaction helps the individual realize her potential and actualize herself. No wonder, studies have shown that job satisfaction leads to SWB (Warr, 1999), whereas unemployment has strong negative effects on SWB (Argyle, 1999).

Finally, there are some dispositional factors in the level of happiness. Personality is a strong causal factor of SWB. Some people seem to be happy regardless of triumphs or setbacks; others seem to be unhappy no matter what. For instance, in one study it was found that winning lottery tickets or being victims of accidents only marginally changes level of happiness (Brickman et al., 1978). Many scholars today agree that happiness is more due to internal factors than external factors. Strong correlations have been found between SWB and personality traits like, extraversion, self-esteem and optimism. For example, people who are outgoing, upbeat and sociable, tend to be happier than others (Also see the section on 'Happiness Disposition').

Conclusion

This section just gave an overview of certain factors that affect subjective well-being. However, one must understand that subjective will-being is subjective, i.e., it is about how one feels. I have discussed research findings that money doesn't lead to happiness beyond a limit. But, a miser may feel utmost happiness on being able to hoard money! When it comes to happiness, everything is relative (Argyle, 1999). The above factors are only indicative of the general population. Causality for SWB vary across individuals and across contexts.

1.5 Happiness Disposition

Some people seem to be destined to be happy, while others are unhappy, whatever be their personal achievements or setbacks. Back in my graduation days, some students were never happy with life. A student I knew did not show any enthusiasm after his application for higher education in a top US university was accepted. On the other hand, I would be ready for parties even on days my research guide scolded me for my lousy project work. My guide believed that I am shameless, but the reality is that I am predisposed to be a happy person!

Disposition is the tendency in an individual to react to a given situation in a specific way. Hence, it includes inherent personality trait or biological attribute. Happiness refers to the ability to cope with situations with positive emotions and getting satisfaction from life. Happiness disposition refers to the natural tendency of some people to deal with a stressful situation more positively than others. From the previous section, we know that many factors affect a person's subjective well-being (SWB). These factors can be external or internal. Happiness disposition concentrates on the factors internal to the individual that affect happiness and SWB.

There are two major internal factors that may predispose us towards happiness:

1. Personality factors
2. Biological and genetic factors

Personality factors have shown strong correlation to happiness. Extroverts, for instance, have been found to be happier than introverts. People who are outgoing and sociable tend to be happier than others (Lucas, Diener and Suh, 1996). Other traits like, self-esteem and optimism also are good predictors of happiness.

Biological factors also seem to affect happiness disposition. A study of 2,310 identical and fraternal twins found that identical twins are far more similar in subjective well-being, whatever their life circumstances be (Lykken and Tellegen, 1996). The underlying mechanism is not clear, though it may be because of genetic factors that control right-hemisphere and left-hemisphere activation of brain. It is also possible that neurotransmitters that lead to positive and negative emotions are genetically different in people.

Indeed, Eysenck (1967) has tried to link the two factors discussed above- personality and biological factors. He had made a distinction between neuroticism and emotional stability as a trait in people. In neurotics, sudden change in arousal of autonomic nervous system takes place.

Today, it is accepted that individual differences in happiness exist. Happiness disposition refers to the internal factors that cause these individual differences. Subjective well-being is the result of interaction between happiness disposition and external factors.

Lifestyle Factors in Health

Health of an individual is a product of her genes and environment. While genes predispose her towards some diseases, environmental factors like, life stress, lifestyle, bacteria, virus, success and failure have an important role to play in the incidence of diseases. Of these environmental factors, lifestyle is a singularly important factor that is leading to an increased prevalence of psychosomatic diseases. The aim of this section is to discuss the modern lifestyle and its demerits; lastly, a normative model of lifestyle for perfect health is provided.

The Modern Lifestyle

The modern lifestyle is a complex whole of learned habits in urban India which is responsible for various ill-health. Let us take certain examples:

- *Eating habits:* In the name of modernization, various unhealthy eating styles are promoted. Partly, this is because of consumerism, i.e., advertisements that create a perception that larger the consumption of food, greater the happiness. Secondly, the consumption of junk food, like burgers, pizzas, etc. with high fat content is increasing. This leads to problems of obesity, coronary heart diseases and other ailments. The per capita consumption of alcohol, tobacco and fats is rising by the day. About 53% of adult males and 3% of adult female smoke bidi or cigarette.

  Also our eating preferences are shifting from fresh and fibrous food to heavy, oily, spicy and processed foods, which we can't digest easily (Parashar, 2000).

- *Exercise:* Previously, people used to get sufficient physical exercise owing to low development of transport and certain healthy lifestyles. But, the situation has changed. For example, the prevalence of elevators in most modern buildings and preferred usage of these elevators has decreased the use of staircase. In an article in the Times of India, psycho-analyst Sudhir Kakkar had opined that television (TV) has led to a lifestyle, where obesity increases and scope of physical exercise is low.

- *Increased stressors:* In today's times, wants are unlimited. To fulfil these wants, the income desired is unlimited. Aspirations are high. Hence, there is always tension to earn more. If a person earns more, she is tensed that she has to spend more. She hits the shopping mall and finds that what she earns is still to meet her consumerist wants. The tension in offices is also more. Individuals hardly get job satisfaction as the only factor that motivates them is the salary which never seems to be sufficient.

There are other stressors working in modern cultures. In urban India, for instance, the social support and friendship network is low. Even divorce rate is high. As a result, a major factor behind stress reduction is absent.

The uneven and odd time at which people in metros sleep is also an issue. Many BPO employees work in night-shifts and hence, face many psychological problems.

From above, we see that modern lifestyle leads to both physical and psychological problems. Parashar (2000) is so frustrated with the lifestyle that he opines, 'Our present lifestyle has forced us to become materialistic, selfish, egoistic and self-centered. We have restricted ourselves only to physical health and we have forgotten about the mental, social and spiritual health. Materialism is indeed the original cause of all misery, including diseases and a loss of a balanced state of mind'. He has made certain amazing revelations about how our lifestyle is linked to diseases- 'Unmindful modernization is providing to be a curse for the health of Indian people. Almost half of the Indian population is suffering from some physical disease or mental disorder. Presently, 50 million Indians are suffering from blood pressure and other cardiac disorders. The number of diabetic patients is 30 million. About 8 lac people die every year due to tobacco consumption and India tops the list of patients having mouth cancer worldwide ... the number of patients suffering from anxiety, depression, insomnia and addiction is rising sharply.... One of the main factors responsible for this situation is the faulty lifestyle we have chosen in the name of modernization. The urban population has forgotten the basic principles of healthy living, like, early to bed and early to rise, physical exercise, diligence, contentment, endurance, cooperation etc.' (I bid).

Ayurveda: Normative Model for Perfect Health

The modern lifestyle is harmful for health. Then, which lifestyle should we follow for a better health? While western psychologists are researching on various alternative lifestyles, Parashar (2000) proposes that we use the lifestyle advocated in Ayurveda. The lifestyle advocated by Ayurveda is based on four fundamental principles:

1. Ahara (food)
2. Vihara (Recreation)

3. Achara (Routine)
4. Vichara (Thinking)

Ayurveda had recognized that a healthy lifestyle should lead to both physical and psychological well-being. Hence, it tries to fuse Vichara (thinking) and Vihara (recreation) with Ahara and Achara.

Ahara

Ayurveda advises that vegetarian food should be preferred over non-vegetarian food. For better health, our food should contain fresh vegetables and sufficient fiber contents. As already discussed, spicy and junk food causes obesity, diabetes, gastric ulcers and hypertension. The oil that we use should be wisely selected. Saturated fats derived from animal food, coconut oil and palm can clog arteries if consumed in excess. South Indian people suffer from a number of diseases related to saturated fats due to excess consumption of coconut oil (Parashar, 2000). Rather, polyunsaturated fats found in the oils of corn, sunflower, fatty fish and cotton seeds actually reduce blood cholesterol level. Similarly, monounsaturated fats found in olive peanuts help protect against incidence of heart diseases.

Ayurveda further advocates that the principle of "Virudha Bhojana" should be followed. "Virudha Bhojana" or opposite food means one must not consume two food items with opposite effects at the same time. For example, items like ice cream shouldn't be taken with hot tea or coffee. Similarly, it is not advised to take meat with milk; curd with milk, etc. If taken so, it may lead to stomach imbalances and problems such as gastric upsets and food poisoning.

Achara

Ayurveda has distinguished three types of routines:

1. Ritucharya (Season routine)
2. Dincharya (Day routine)
3. Ratricharya (Night routine)

Ritucharya means to follow a lifestyle in accordance with the six seasons of a year. For example, during summer season, we should take light food containing plenty of fluids, brisk exercises should be avoided. Similarly, Dincharya and Ratricharya specify that one should eat and act according to the time of the day. One should wake up early in the morning. 'Dawn drinking' should be the first act after waking. It refers to drinking of water kept overnight. Dawn drinking ensures smooth excretion of body waste and is a remedy for constipation (Parasher, 2000). This should be followed by the following routine:

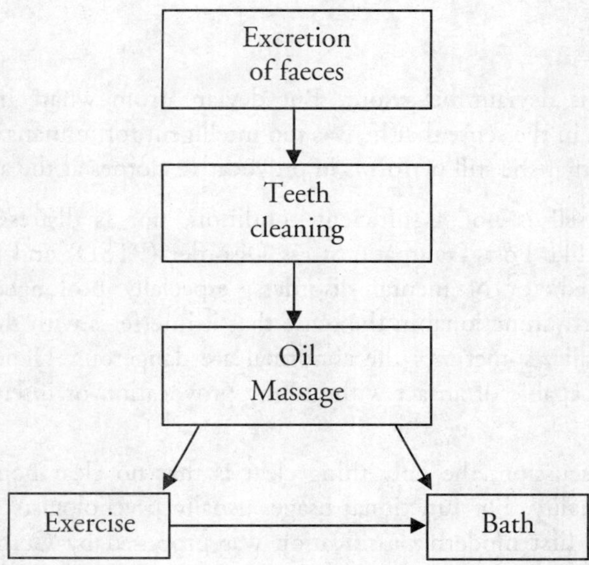

Fig. 1.2 : Illustration of Dincharya

Ratricharya

These norms advise to take dinner 2-3 hours before sleep. It also prescribes that people should engage in sexual intercourse only during the night as a rest of few hours is necessary after sexual intercourse for the body muscles to come back to the relaxed state.

Vihara and Vichara

While Ahara and Achara refer purely to the physical and physiological aspects, Vihara (recreation) refers to psycho-physiological aspects and Vichara (thinking) refers to mental aspects (Parasher, 2000). Vichara norms specify that one should neither be driven by greed nor be dominated by emotions of fear, anger, jealousy, guild or worry. Anasakti is a related concept. Detachment from hatred or greed forms part of the thinking process of a healthy lifestyle.

Normality and Abnormality

Abnormal is what is not normal and normal refers to a behaviour that doesn't violate the norm. My purpose in making this ambiguous and confusing statement is to show that there is no agreement regarding what is normal and what is abnormal. Usually the definitions of abnormality include the following concepts, called the 4-Ds (Christensen et al., 2001):

1. Deviance
2. Distress

3. Dysfunction
4. Dangerousness

Abnormal behaviour is deviant behaviour. But deviant from what? In what sense? Albert Einstein was abnormal in the sense that he was too intelligent for humans. Pop queen Madonna is deviant in the sense that she still performs in provocative clothes at the age of fifty.

Hence, deviance itself is not a sufficient condition, nor is distress. Distress is seen in abnormal behaviours, like Post-Traumatic Stress Disorder (PTSD) and panic attacks. Hence, distress is a good predictor of mental disorders, especially prolonged distress. Abnormal behaviour may also be dysfunctional in the sense that it interferes with the normal functioning of the individual. Finally, sometimes the abnormal are dangerous. Hence, if an individual is dangerous and she is capable of an act without any provocation or intentionality, she may be suffering from insanity.

From the above discussion, the only thing clear is that no clear boundary exists between normality and abnormality. For functional usage, usually psychologists use a classification of mental disorders. The first modern classification was proposed by German psychiatrist Emil Kraeplin (1883). Kraeplin had proposed that the professional should identify symptoms (what the person complains of) and signs (indications of abnormal function from behavioural observation or otherwise) and finally establish the problem's onset and course (how the disorder has developed). Together, these factors should be able to help the clinician to diagnose the patient as suffering from a particular illness. Kraeplin's system of classification is no longer in use, but it forms the basis of all modern classifications, like the World Health Organization's International Classification of Disorders (ICD) and the American Psychiatric Association's (APA) Diagnostic and Statistical Manual of Mental Disorders (DSM). The latest version of APA's manual, DSM-IV, is the most popular system of classification.

The DSM-IV adopts a system of diagnosis that is multiaxial and proceeds by resolving all these axes:

- What are the symptoms? (Axis I)
- Are there any abnormal functions that the individual is predisposed to? For example, are there any personality disorders or developmental disorders? (Axis 2)
- Are there any relevant physical disorders? (Axis 3)
- What is the intensity of stressors? (Axis 4)
- What is the individual's ability to adapt to the stressors? (Axis 5)

Causal Factors in Mental Disorders

In this section, we will investigate into various factors responsible for mental disorders, like schizophrenia, delusional disorder, anxiety and mood disorders. The factors are primarily of three types- biological, psychological and socio-cultural factors. Many of the proposed causal factors have been proved beyond doubt, while others are lacking in empirical validity (for example, Freudian explanations of schizophrenia). We must respect the fact that multiple factors act together to produce effects like mental disorders. Hence, I attempt to integrate various perspectives in explaining the causality of mental disorders.

There are three factors that lead to disorders:

1. *Predisposing factors or vulnerability factors* that do not themselves lead to disorder, but increase the vulnerability of the individual to the disorder. Biological dispositions, occurrences in childhood (usually used by psychoanalysts to explain disorders) and personality factors are important predisposing factors.
2. *Precipitating factors* or stressors are the immediate conditions that trigger the disorder. This includes cognitive factors, environmental stressors and socio-cultural factors.
3. *Reinforcing factors:* Factors that reinforce a past disorder; such as the reinforcing mechanisms highlighted by the behaviourist school.

These factors can be represented as under:

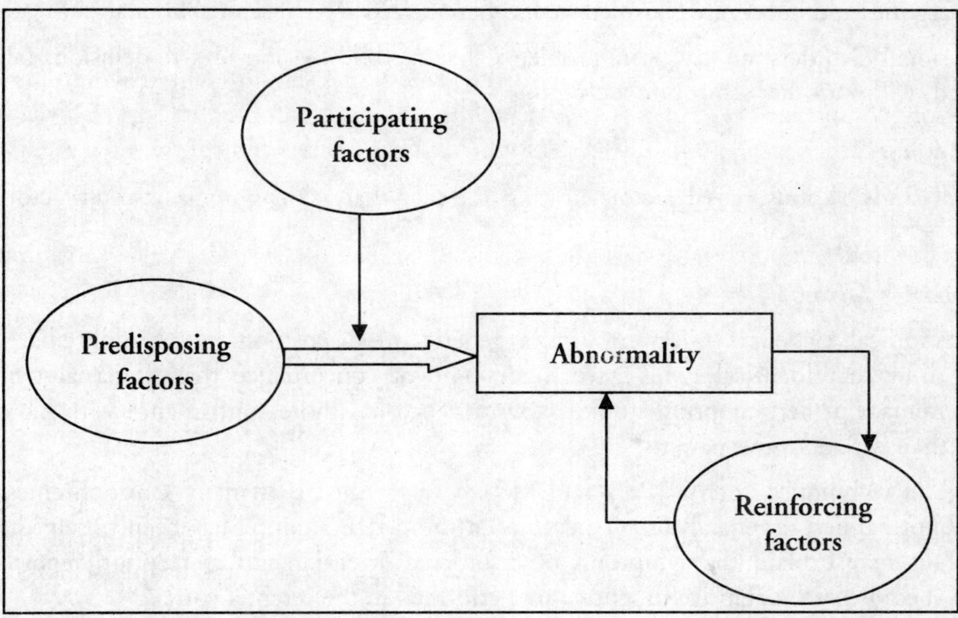

Fig. 1.3 : Factors leading to disorders

Schizophrenia and Delusional Disorders

Disorders that pertain to loss of contact with reality are called psychosis. Typically, the psychotic people may have hallucinations (false sensory perceptions) or delusions (false beliefs) or both.

Schizophrenia literally means "split mind". It is a particular psychotic condition that fulfils certain criteria. Typically, schizophrenia suffers from four types of delusions:

1. *Delusion* of grandeur: Belief that one is of great importance.
2. *Delusion of persecution:* Delusion that one is the victim of enemy plots.
3. *Delusion of reference:* Belief that the actions of others or world events are conspiracies against her.
4. *Delusions of control:* A belief that other people are controlling one's actions.

Delusions are most prominent among the paranoid-type schizophrenics. The catatonic type schizophrenia on the other hand, is characterized by immobility or repetitive movements like echolalia (reception of words) or echopraxia (repetition of observed behaviour).

A third variety of schizophrenia, the disorganized type, is characterized by inappropriate affect (for instance laughing at a tragic news or crying on hearing a joke), together with incoherent speech and confused behaviour. Many other schizophrenics can't be put into any of these categories and hence, are classified as undifferentiated type of schizophrenia.

Delusional disorders are psychotic problems characterized by non-bizarre delusions (already discussed) without other schizophrenic signs.

Causal factors

We shall study various causal factors bearing the fact that schizophrenia is multifactorial in origin:

Pre-disposing factors

Many empirical evidences point towards a genetic pre-disposition in schizophrenia. Twin studies show that identical twins have higher rate of concordance than fraternal twins in schizophrenia. Further, adoption studies show that ego has more concordance with biological parents than with adoptive parents.

Usage of techniques, such as PET and MRI have revealed that many schizophrenics have brain abnormalities; a general loss of neurons in the cerebral cortex has been observed using MRI. This may explain the symptoms of disordered attention and perception reported by patients, because such cognitive functions are performed in the cerebral cortex.

The dopamine hypothesis states that the cause for schizophrenia is an increase in activity of the dopamine system in the brain. People diagnosed with schizophrenia seem to have more dopamine receptors on neurons than non-schizophrenics. It has also been seen that injecting schizophrenics with drugs that increase dopamine activity in the brain increases their symptoms. However, the exact mechanism of dopamine activity is not known. The neurons affected by excess dopamine secretions extend from the midbrain to limbic system and these play crucial function in linking perception with memory. May be dopamine-caused hyperactivity lead to a situation in which the brain cannot relate sensory input with memory, nor can it ignore the sensory input.

Precipitating factors

Many stressors have been identified that may precipitate the condition to lead to schizophrenia. Freud believed that to escape from unbearable stress and conflict, the schizophrenic uses the defence mechanism of regression, in which she retreats to an earlier stage of psychosocial development.

Some cognitive theorists reason that when people develop a defect in the attentional mechanism that filters out irrelevant stimuli, they are overwhelmed by external stimuli. There is a stimulus overload that leads to disorganized thought pattern, hallucinations and delusions.

The incidence of schizophrenia is five times as high in lowest socio-economic groups as in the highest. Owing to this finding, it is reasoned that the higher level of stress that low-income people experience may lead to higher prevalence of schizophrenia.

Even the family is said to act as a source of precipitator (stressor). According to the double-bind hypothesis, the parents of schizophrenic patients behave towards them in self-contradictory ways (double-binds). For instance, a mother may encourage an unemployed son verbally but through non-verbal cues, which shows that she thinks he is a loser. Repeated exposure to these double-binds leads to abnormal ways of coping that finally leads to schizophrenia.

Reinforcing factors: Once the label of schizophrenic is put on a patient, she faces social stigma. This stigma acts as a self-fulfilling prophecy in reinforcing schizophrenia. In a study conducted in the 1970s, Rosenhan got eight normal people to report hallucinations in different hospitals. All were diagnosed as psychotic and admitted as patients. After admission, they tried to behave normally, but it became increasingly difficult for them to do so due to the hospital staff's self-fulfilling prophecies. Their normal behaviour was labelled as schizophrenic. For example, if a patient wrote a poem, the staff reported that they engaged in writing behaviour! Finally, they became bored, listless and apathetic (these are the symptoms of schizophrenia!).

Mood Disorders

Mood disorders are emotion-based disorders. There are two types of mood disorders- unipolar disorder and bipolar disorder. Unipolar disorder or depression refers to an abnormal condition where the individual is in an intensely depressed state, owing to which she cannot function effectively.

Emotional symptoms of depression include sadness, anxiety, inability to enjoy and hopelessness. Depression is primarily a disorder of emotions or mood; but there are other types of symptoms also. Some other symptoms can be summarized as:

- ❖ Motivational symptoms
    - o Loss of interest
    - o Lack of drive
    - o Difficulty in taking any initiative
- ❖ Cognitive symptoms
    - o Negative cognitions about self, world and future
    - o Incorrect attributions
    - o Automatic thoughts

- Somatic symptoms
  - Lack of energy
  - Loss of appetite
  - Sleep difficulties

In bipolar disorders, depression alternates with periods of mania, an emotional state in which the individual is very excited and shows behaviour that is quite opposite to depression. In the manic state, the individual turns megalomaniac. She has grandiose cognitions and doesn't consider the negative consequences before acting on these grandiose plans. Speech is often rapid, as if she has to say as many words as possible in the time allotted.

Causal Factors in Depression

Therapists often differentiate between two kinds of unipolar disorders – endogenous depression (which happen without any trigger) and reactive depression (which is triggered by 'stressors'). Owing to this distinction, researchers are investigating into various external and internal factors that result in prolonged depression. While stressful events seem to trigger depression, internal factors, like cognitions and neurochemicals also play a significant role.

Internal factors

The most dominant view about depression is that of cognitive theorists. Aaron Beck (1976) argues that the emotional state of depression is a product of incorrect cognitions. He has proposed a number of negative thoughts that the depressed have, as mentioned below:

- *Cognitive triad of depression:* Interpreting one's self, experiences and future in a negative way.
- *Automatic thoughts:* Persistent and automatic thoughts that pop up into the conscience automatically and remind the patient of her inadequacies.
- *Errors in thinking:* Manifested in many forms, for example blaming oneself for bad weather.

The errors in thinking are a result of a depressive attributional pattern, attributing successes to factors external to self and blaming self for negative outcomes. Another cognitive dynamic forwarded by Martin Seligman is 'learned helplessness'. He conducted a study of dogs in situations from where they couldn't escape any negative consequences. Finally, the dogs learned to be helpless, i.e., they didn't escape the negative consequences even when given the chance. It is reasoned on this basis that depressed people believe bad events will occur and there is nothing they could do to prevent these or cope with these events.

A problem with the cognitive approach is that it confuses cause and effect. Does depression lead to such negative thoughts or do the negative thoughts lead to depression? Cognitive theorists use incorrect cognitions to explain depression, whereas, it may be that incorrect cognitions are the consequence of a depressive state. Secondly, they don't say why some people become depressive and other don't. This difference, however, can be explained by genetic and neurochemical factors.

Neurological research has shown that depression is associated with low levels of a neurotransmitter called norepinephrine. There is also evidence that another neurotransmitter, serotonin, may be low in quantity in the brain. This view is supported by the fact that drugs that increase the level of norepinephrine (like Tricyclics) and serotonin (like Prozac) act as antidepressants. Taking these drugs can help one out of depression.

External factors

It is generally agreed that an extremely stressful condition acts as the trigger (or precipitating factor) in depression. For instance, it has been seen that depression runs in families. A reason for that may be genetic. But, Hammen (1991) believes that an even greater factor is that children of depressed people often experience poor parenting and many get stress as they grow up. As a result, they may fail to develop a positive self-concept or proper coping skills; this makes them quite vulnerable to depression.

Once depression starts, it becomes a vicious circle due to a self-reinforcing mechanism. This mechanism is explained by behaviourists. They reason that depressed people show decreased reward-seeking behaviour and avoid others. Owing to this, their social support decreases and others get alienated from them. This further increases depression. This can be represented as under:

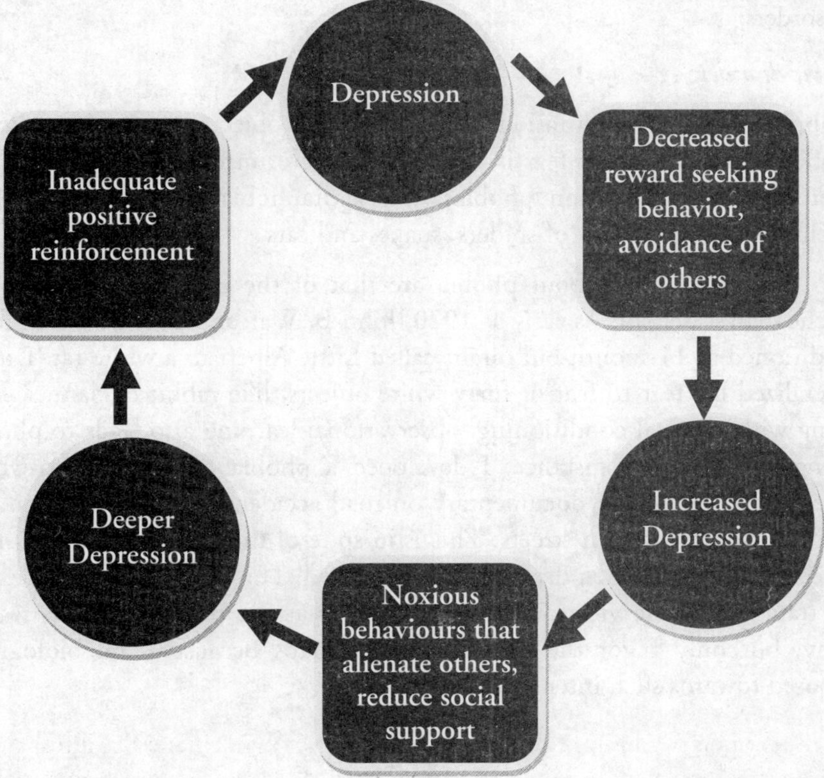

Fig. 1.4 : Vicious cycle of depression Adapted from Passer and Smith (2007, p. 551)

Causal Factors in Bipolar Disorders

Genetic factors have been found to have greater influence on bipolar disorder than depression. It is also reasoned that norepinephrine is low in depressed episodes and higher than normal in manic episodes. Lithium, which is considered the most effective treatment for manic states, reduces norepinephrine activity in the brain. However, the exact nature of mania and the exact role of neurochemicals in it hasn't yet been known.

Anxiety Disorders

Sigmund Freud believed that there are three kinds of anxieties- normal, realistic and neurotic. At some point of time, we all become anxious. However, anxiety disorder is a form of neurotic anxiety wherein the frequency and intensity of anxiety responses are out of proportion to the situations that trigger them (Passer and Smitha, 2007). Anxiety disorder manifests itself in many forms, like phobic disorder, Generalized Anxiety Disorder (GAD), panic disorder, Obsessive-Compulsive disorders (OCD) and Post-Traumatic Stress Disorder (PTSD).

In this section, I seek to discuss these disorders along with dominant views about factors that cause these disorders:

- *Phobic disorder*

  Phobias are strong and irrational fears of certain objects or situations. People with phobia realize that their fear is irrational, yet are impotent in dealing with them. There are many common phobias, like agoraphobia (fear of open spaces) and specific phobias, like fear of spiders, snakes and cats.

  Two dominant views about phobia are that of the Behaviourist School and the Psychoanalyst School. As early as 1920, John B. Watson had shown that fear can be conditioned as 11-month-old infant called Little Albert to a white rat. Later, Albert generalized his fear to fear of furry white objects, like rabbit or Santa Claus mask. Along with classical conditioning, observational learning also leads to phobia about sitting in bikes. For instance, I developed a phobia of driving two-wheelers on streets after watching a documentary on road accidents. As a result, I am generally afraid of riding bikes on streets. This is in spite of the fact that I know the chances of accident are low when driven at average speed! This may be because I experienced the traumatic scene vicariously. Please note that the television event was seen by many, but only I got the phobia. It is perhaps because I am biologically pre-disposed towards such intense fear.

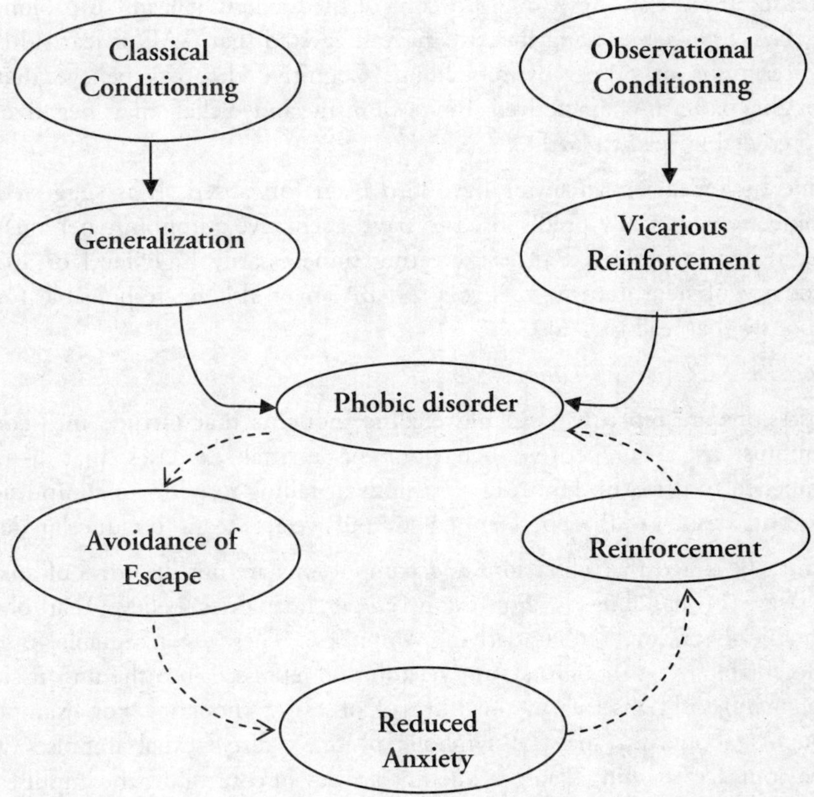

Fig. 1.5 : Phobic Disorders

Once phobia is learned through classical conditioning or observational learning, people are motivated to avoid or escape any phobia arousing situation. Avoidance and escape are reinforced by a reduction of anxiety, i.e., operant conditioning reinforces phobia.

Another major explanation is the Freudian one. In one of Freud's most celebrated case studies, a 5-year old boy Hans suddenly developed a fear of horses. He was afraid that a horse may bite him. Freud explained this phobia in this way- the powerful horse represented Hans's father and the fear of being bitten symbolized Hans's unconscious fear of being castrated by his father for harbouring sexual desires for his mother.

- *Generalized Anxiety Disorder (GAD)*

GAD refers to a case where anxiety and worry are prolonged, but are not focused on specific issue or occurrence. Rather, the anxiety is free-floating. Little is known about the causality of this disorder and most proposed explanations are lacking in some respects. According to Freud, when unacceptable impulses (existing in the unconscious) try to break through the defenses, it leads to neurotic anxiety. If the defenses are not strong enough to control the anxiety, it leads to prolonged anxiety, i.e., GAD. Social learning theorists have suggested that GAD is learned by observing the reactions of others by modelling. Cognitive theorists believe that a definite thought pattern characterized by pessimism and belief that negative events are unpredictable, lead to GAD.

Some biological explanations have also been forwarded. It is suggested that some people are genetically predisposed to have a sensitive autonomic nervous system that over reacts to perceived threat, creating unnecessarily high level of arousal. Over-reactivity of neurotransmitters, like GABA, may also be responsible for emotional responses that lead to GAD.

- *Obsessive – Compulsive Disorder (OCD)*

  Obsessions are repetitive and unwelcome thoughts that intrude into consciousness. Compulsions are repetitive behaviour or mental exercises that a person feels compelled to perform. Ignoring obsessions or failing to perform compulsions leads to anxiety, so much so that, performing compulsive acts seem to reduce anxiety.

  It must be noted that obsessions and compulsions are not disorders of anxiety but are the ways of handling it. For example, psychoanalysts believe that obsessions are symbolically related to underlying impulses. These unacceptable urges are too unacceptable to be thought about, yet can't be repressed into the unconscious. Hence, they manifest themselves in the form of obsessive thoughts. For example, obsessive thoughts about dirt may be symbolic of one's dirty sexual impulses. Compulsive behaviour, like washing hands frequently is a way of controlling the impulses.

  Cognitive theorists argue that we people usually get repetitive, but unwanted thoughts. In case of patients of OCD, these thoughts cannot be controlled and the repetition becomes chronic. In an attempt to dispel these thoughts, the OCD patient uses certain mental and behavioural strategies that lead to OCD. A physiological explanation has been suggested on the basis of findings that OCD patients have low levels of the neurotransmitter serotonin.

  Once OCD occurs, it is reinforced by the obsessions and compulsions. Compulsive behaviour provides negative reinforcement by reducing anxiety. For example, if I get obsessive about cleanliness, it arouses anxiety in me. When I engage in compulsive behaviour, i.e., washing my hands every now and then, it reduces anxiety and so the behaviour is reinforced.

- *Panic Disorder*

  Panic disorder are disorders wherein anxiety occurs suddenly and unpredictably and is much more intense than that of any other anxiety disorder. Panic attacks usually happen suddenly and without any visible reason. Panic attacks often lead to agoraphobia (fear of public places) because the victim often fears that she may get panic attacks in public places.

Explanations of cognitive theorists have been by far most conclusive about panic disorder. David Barlow (2002) reasons that panic attacks are triggered by exaggerated misinterpretations of normal bodily arousal relating to heart palpitations, dizziness and breathlessness. Basically, the victims of panic attack catastrophize bodily sensations and magnify the threat perceptions.

- *Post-Traumatic Stress Disorders (PTSD)*

  PTSD is 'an anxiety disorder arising as a delayed and protracted response after experiencing or witnessing a traumatic event, involving actual or threatened death or serious injury to self or others. It is characterized by intense fear, helplessness or horror, lasting more than four weeks; the traumatic event being persistently re-experienced in the form of distressing recollections, recurrent dreams, sensations of reliving the experience, hallucinations, or flashbacks, intense distress and physiological reactions in response to anything reminiscent of the traumatic event' (Oxford Dictionary of Psychology, 2006).

  Undoubtedly, the stressful event acts as the precipitating factors in causing FTSD. The traumatic event can be rape, violence, combat situations, a natural disaster or a serious accident. Today, it is generally accepted that PTSD is natural, especially among children and the old. However, the one question that remains unanswered is- why do some people develop PTSD while others who have experienced the same situation don't? Some recent researches have shown that vulnerability to PTSD develops in childhood when one is exposed to violence or mental disorders. The way one copes with stressors (coping style) and personality type are also factors that affect the vulnerability to PTSD.

Personality Disorders

Personality disorders are inflexible and long-term patterns of behaviour and thinking that lead to maladaptive ways in which one relates to social environment. As per the DSM definition, there are ten different types of personality disorders. There are different characteristics of these disorders, but some common characteristics can be identified as:

1. Personality disorders differ from other disorders discussed here in the way that these disorders begin in childhood and remain relatively unchanged till late in life. There is hardly any change in intensity or nature of the disorder.

2. They have maladaptive ways of thinking, feeling and behaving.

3. They have inappropriate emotional responses and impulse control.

There are ten types of personality disorders, which are discussed in the following table

Personality disorder	Features
Antisocial	• pattern of disregarding or violating the rights of others. • Marked by non-conformity to social norms, habitual lying or deception • Impulsive behaviour
Histrionic	• pattern of excessive emotion and attention seeking • Uneasy feeling when they are not the center of attention, may use physical appearance to draw attention to themselves or have rapidly shifting or exaggerated emotions.
Narcissistic	• pattern of need for admiration and lack of empathy for others. • grandiose sense of self-importance, a sense of entitlement, taking advantage of others or lack empathy.
Borderline	• pattern of instability in personal relationships, intense emotions, poor self-image and impulsivity • Person with borderline disorder may go to great lengths to avoid being abandoned, • Display of inappropriate intense anger or ongoing feelings of emptiness.
Avoidant	• Pattern of extreme shyness, feelings of inadequacy and extreme sensitivity to criticism. • Unwillingness to get involved with people unless they are certain of being liked • Preoccupation with thoughts of being criticized or rejected
Dependent	• pattern of needing to be taken care of and submissive and clingy behavior. • Difficulty in making daily decisions without reassurance from others • Feeling of helpless when alone because of fear of inability to take care of themselves.
Obsessive-compulsive	• This is not the same as Obsessive Compulsive Disorder (OCD) • pattern of preoccupation with orderliness, perfection and control • Too much of focus on details or schedules • Workaholic behaviour, not allowing time for leisure or friends • Inflexibility in morality and values.
Schizoid	• Detachment from social relationships and expressing little emotions • Typically do not seek close relationships, choose to be alone and seem to not care about praise or criticism from others.

Personality disorder	Features
Schizotypal	• pattern of being very uncomfortable in close relationships, having distorted thinking and eccentric behavior. • May have odd beliefs or odd or peculiar behavior or speech or may have excessive social anxiety.
Paranoid	• Pattern of paranoia • Pervasive, long-standing suspiciousness and generalized mistrust of others

These ten types can be divided into three clusters that capture commonalities of characteristics as:

1. Dramatic/Impulsive cluster: Antisocial, Histrionic, Narcissistic, Borderline
2. Anxious/Fearful cluster: Avoidant, Dependent, Obsessive-compulsive
3. Eccentric cluster: Schizoid, Schizotypal, Paranoid

Among the personality disorders, the most dangerous to society is the anti-social personality disorder. This has also received the maximum research interests. Hence, I will discuss this disorder, and its causal factors in detail.

Anti-social Personality Disorders

Also called psychopaths and sociopaths, people with anti-social personality disorder seem to lack any conscience, due to which they are capable of doing acts that are considered socially deviant and morally unacceptable. Some famous examples are Charles Shobraj and Mithilesh Kumar Shrivastav, popularly called 'Natwarlal'.

Some typical characteristics of people with antisocial personality disorders are:

1. They have a very weak conscience, if at all they have.
2. They exhibit little anxiety and guild.
3. They are impulsive and can't delay gratification. Hence, they have short-term objectives and are oriented towards getting pleasure.
4. They often appear very charming and innocent, and can effectively rationalize their inappropriate behaviour, so that it appears reasonable (Passer and Smith, 2007).
5. They don't learn from punishments. The treat of punishment doesn't deter them from engaging in anti-social acts again and again.

Causal Factors

Biological explanations

Both twin studies and adoption studies have shown consistent results that point towards a genetic pre-disposition in anti-social personality disorder. But, how can a lack of conscience be genetically inherited? Some researchers argue that psychopaths show a relative absence of anxiety and guild. The disorder might be because of some dysfunction in brain structures that govern emotional arousal and anxiety responses. This results in a chronically under aroused state due to which-

(1) They don't become anxious, or feel guilty.

(2) Their avoidance learning is impaired and they don't learn from punishments, and

(3) The under arousal drives them to seek for pleasure and excitement. The drive is so much that they go for instant, hedonic gratification.

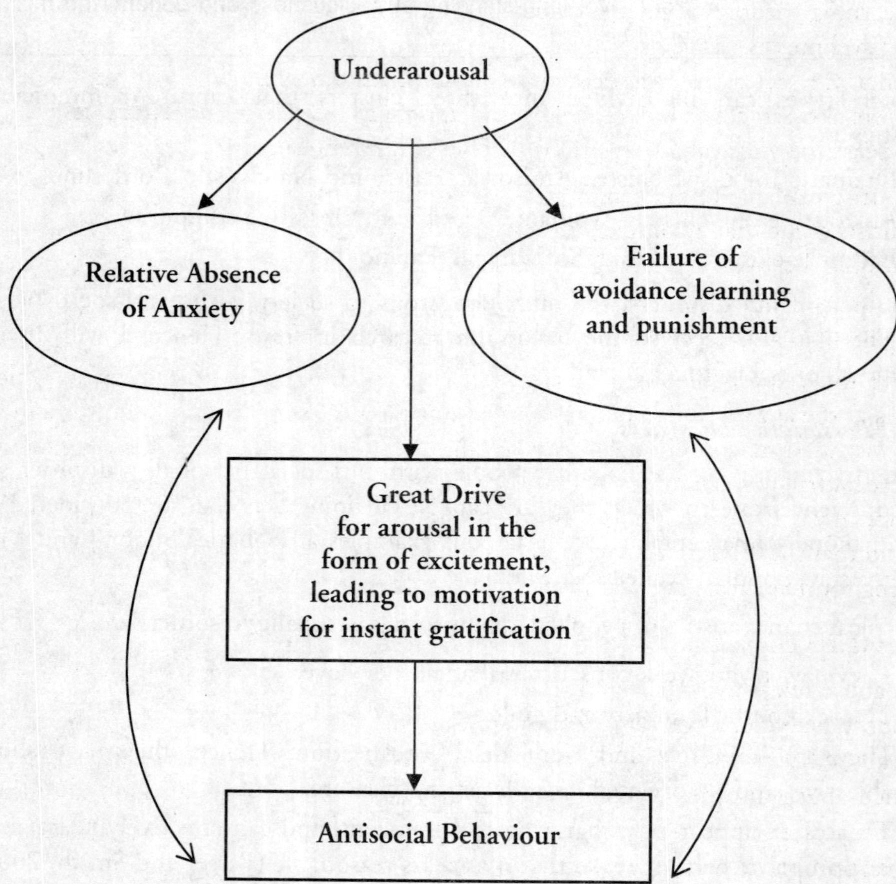

Fig. 1.6 : Undersrousal and its impact

Psychological explanations

Psychodynamic theorists argue that conscience develops when superego develops. This superego is the result of proper socialization during childhood. The persons with anti-social personality disorder do not develop a well-defined superego. Ego tries to balance the demands of id and restraints of the superego. The demands of id dominate, resulting in impulsive and hedonic behaviour. Why could the superego not develop properly? The dominant explanation is: the psychic problems of phallic stage (sexually desiring the parent of opposite sex) are resolved by identification with parent of the same sex. But, if the parent is not available for identification, or if the psychological distance from parent is too much, there are problems in developing a strong superego.

Cognitive theorists argue that anti-social individuals consistently fail to anticipate the long-term negative consequences of their behaviour. Hence, incorrect cognitions and beliefs are at the root of anti-social behaviour of these people.

Social learning theorists argue that modelling may play an important role. It has been found that most psychopaths come from families where parents exhibit a high degree of aggression. Such parents may act as role models for aggressive behaviour and to disregard social norms. Deviant peers also can act as role models. However, these role models most probably contribute only to increase the vulnerability in childhood.

Behaviourist explanations are one of the dominant explanations of anti-social behaviour. These theorists argue that a conscience develops when one learns fears and avoidance responses. I avoid stealing behaviour because I fear that it may lead to punishment. Such avoidance learning is the basis of conscience. Unfortunately, these individuals are incapable of conditioned fear responses and hence, they don't develop a conscience.

To prove this hypothesis, Adrian Paine and co-workers (1996) did a study in which male participants at the age of 15 had been subjected to a classical conditioning procedure in which a soft tone was used as conditioned stimulus and a loud, aversive tone as the unconditioned stimulus. Fear that was conditioned by this procedure was measured by the participants' skin conductance. After 14 years, a follow-up study was done on the (now 29 years old) participants. It was found that those who had a criminal record in the follow-up study had shown poorer fear conditioning fourteen years back, than those with no criminal record.

Substance-Abuse Disorders

Substance abuse refers to a maladaptive use of a drug, leading to impairment of functioning or distress. Substance abuse disorder refers to a class of mental disorders when the problem of substance abuse becomes clinically significant. There are 11 groups of substances that can lead to substance abuse disorder (SAD), as per DSM-IV. This includes alcohol, amphetamines, caffeine, cannabis, cocaine, hallucinogens, inhalants, nicotine, opiates, phencyclidine, sedatives, hypnotics and anxiolytics.

Psychology Applied to Human Problems

Certain characteristics features of substance dependence are:

1. *Tolerance:* Drugs are used because of the desirable physiological response that they provide. However, with regular use, the body develops a tolerance towards the drug, necessitating greater dose of the drug for the same effect.
2. *Withdrawal:* If the supply of drugs is stopped, the body's response (which had become accustomed to the drug) is such that there is an extreme craning for the drug.

3. Persons suffering from substance-abuse disorders spend excess time on activities related to getting drugs and using drugs. Due to this, their social, occupational and family life are neglected.

Further, substance abuse disorders are a joint result of physiological and psychological dependence. Physiological dependence refers to withdrawal symptoms, i.e., the excessive dependence of the body on drugs. Psychological dependence on the other hand, refers to the strong craving for a drug because of its pleasurable effects.

Causal Factors

Drugs, no doubt, lead to physiological changes, but drug-abuse disorder, as such, is a combination of multiple factors. Let us study these in detail:

Biological causation

As you must have read in the chapter on motivation in basic psychology, the human body tries to maintain a homeostasis. There is a set point of hormones and neurotransmitters in human body. When you take drugs, the hormonal response and neurotransmitter secretion change. But this is momentary. On regular use, however, the set point changes. Suppose the set point for a neurotransmitter is X, drug use increases the neurotransmitter secretion. To keep the set-point at X, the body tries to decrease the normal secretion of the neurotransmitter. This attempt to restore balance is called 'compensating response of the body'. Due to compensatory response, the use of the drug in the same amount doesn't lead to any extra pleasure. (The pleasure comes when the level of neurotransmitter is more than X. But when regularly used, the level with drugs automatically readjusts to X). This phenomenon is basically tolerance. Due to tolerance, the individual has to take greater dose to have the same effect. This way, tolerance and compensatory response become a vicious circle and the individual has to increase the intake of drugs every time.

Now, what happens when drug intake is suddenly stopped? The present level of the neurotransmitter (in our example) is X with drug use. When drug use is stopped, the level of neurotransmitter abruptly falls much below the level X. Body's set point needs time to adjust. Owing to this, withdrawal symptoms happen. The individual is in a distress because at such low levels of hormones and neurotransmitters, she experiences extremely negative emotions.

Role of Learning

The setting in which drug is usually taken has a significant role to play in drug use. By classical conditioning, the environmental stimuli are conditioned to secretion of stronger compensatory responses. Hence, a strong dose of drug can be handled by the body. This conditioning also explains why certain settings increase the craving for drugs for addicts and for rehabilitated individuals.

Now, consider a case when the same dose of drug is taken in an environment not similar to the environment where usually the drug is taken. The new environment can't act as a cue for stronger compensatory response. Hence, the body may not be able to tackle even the same dose. This leads to death. You must have heard about some celebrity or member of rock band die of drug overdose. Actually, it is not overdose, but regular dose in unfamiliar environment.

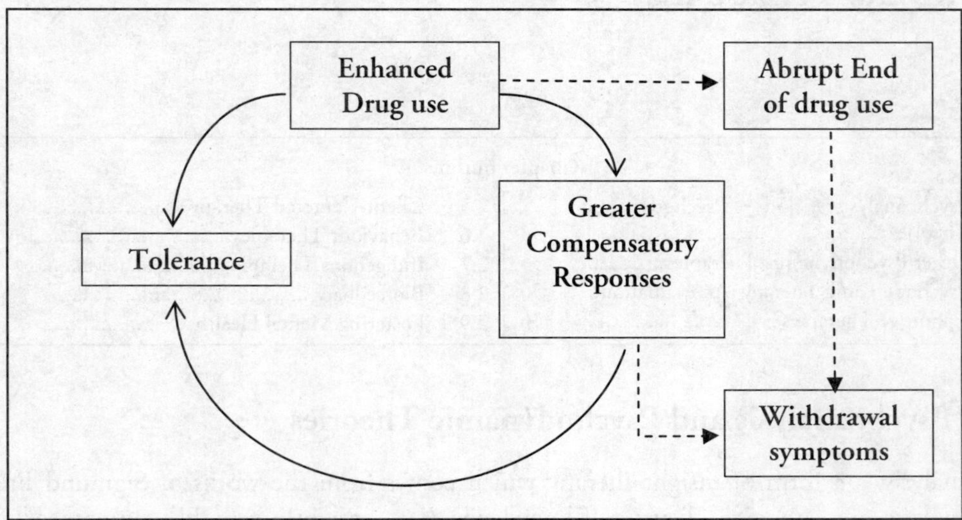

Fig. 1.7 : Vicious circle of increasing dosage of drug intake

This is proved from a study by Shephard Siegel (1984). Siegel interviewed heroin-addicts who had experienced near-fatal overdoses. He found that in most cases, they hadn't taken a dose more than they normally do. Rather, they had injected a regular amount in an unfamiliar situation.

Other Explanations

The psychoanalytic approach assumes that the main cause of addiction is an unconscious need to entertain and to enact various kinds of homosexual and perverse fantasies, while at the same time fearing social retribution for actually trying out the fantasies. Since drug use is a better substitute for masturbation to entertain these fantasies, the addicts prefer drugs to experience their perverse fantasies.

Cognitivists explain substance-abuse disorder in terms of certain core beliefs that are incorrect. The addict may not be even aware of the core beliefs (e.g., "I am useless"). This triggers a system of addictive beliefs (imagined benefits of substance use) and consequent craning.

■ ■ ■

2

Disorders Therapies

Chapter outline

2.1 Psychoanalysis and Psychodynamic Theories

Psychoanalysis is a form of insight therapy which comes from the works of Sigmund Freud. Psychoanalysis aims to give clients self-knowledge (i.e., insight) into the contents of their unconscious mind. Freud believed that there is a hidden reservoir in our minds that is filled with primitive urges and desires, conflictual memories and repressed thoughts. Most forms of maladaptive behaviour are an expression of these unconscious processes expressed through defence mechanisms.

Freud developed his theory as a result of case studies of patients he met in the course of his private practice. He found that he could help these people by just getting them to recall and relive the experiences that have been repressed. Freud was particularly interested in finding significant childhood experiences, because he believed that traumatic experiences of the childhood are tough for the growing mind to deal with. So, children bury these in the unconscious.

Tools of Psychoanalysis

The goal of psychoanalysis is to help the client uncover various unconscious, conflict arousing memories. Since these memories are unconscious, even the client is not aware of this. Hence, the therapist has to use certain tools to uncover these repressed thoughts. One such tool is 'free association'. In free association, clients are asked to relax on a couch and asked to freely express whatever thoughts and feelings come to their minds. The psychoanalyst doesn't sit facing the client; rather he/ she sits out of sight of the client, so that the client's thought processes aren't interrupted by his presence. The client is encouraged to talk about anything that she wishes to.

What the client speaks may sound meaningful and haphazard. But, the meaningless and unrelated thoughts provide symbolic cues to understand the contents of the unconscious.

Another important therapeutic tool used by psychoanalysts is 'dream analysis'. Dreams are, according to Freud, the royal road to the unconscious. He believed that dreams are a mechanism of wish-fulfillment; dreams provide a channel to live out and experience one's hidden impulses and fantasies. Even in dreams, such desires can produce considerable anxiety. Yet, dreams don't explicitly show unconscious desires. Hence, dreams are symbolic of unconscious desires. The latent content of these dreams need to be analyzed and interpreted to understand the unconscious.

Resistance and Transference

The patient shows certain unconsciously motivated behaviours in the course of psychoanalysis. One of these behaviours is resistance. In the course of therapy, the client has to relive her emotional conflicts and unconscious memories that produce anxiety. It is necessary for getting insight that the client face such conflictual emotions. During this process, the client may show resistance, an attempt to subvert or hinder the therapy in order to avoid facing the anxiety provoking thoughts. For example, the client may state that she can't come to the therapeutic session because of a common cold or headache. Even the client doesn't know that she is resorting to these behaviours because of resistance.

There are many types of resistances that the client shows during therapy. Freud believed that a turning point in the therapy comes when the client shows a type of resistance called 'transference'. In transference, the client expresses thoughts and feelings towards the therapist that are representative of feelings towards someone else. For example, suppose a woman had unconscious desires to have sex with her brother-in-law; she had emotions and feelings towards her brother-in-law and desired that her sister would die so that she could possess her sister's husband for herself. Such amoral feelings create anxiety; in her case it was repressed into the unconscious. Now during therapy, she has to face these feelings and thoughts. Finding these feelings towards her brother-in-law anxiety provoking, she 'transfers' the feelings towards the therapist. Whatever be the nature of original feelings (love, hate or dependence), she transfers these towards a substitute figure, who usually is the therapist.

Freud calls transference a turning point of psychoanalysis, because the patient no longer is in denial of powerful emotional urges. These urges have been recovered from the unconscious. The woman in our example may flirt with the therapist, or seduce him to possess him physically. Now, the only job that remains is interpretation of these feelings and thoughts in order to get insight.

2.2 Other Psychodynamic Therapies

Classical psychoanalysis is a very time-consuming and costly process. It may take years for the analyst to uncover the hidden, unconscious thoughts. Usually, the client is in need of immediate help. Hence, modern practitioners of psychodynamic therapy try to make the process brief and take an active role in the therapy. Rather than waiting for the client to get her own insight, these analysts provide their own interpretations in early stages of the therapeutic process. Also, rather than waiting for transference to occur, they encourage ***role playing*** in order to help the client experience her unconscious motives.

One popular psychodynamic therapy is the interpersonal therapy, in which focus is almost exclusively on the client's current relationship with significant others. This therapy is highly structured and usually takes 15 to 20 sessions. The goal of this therapy is to resolve role disputes and interpersonal issues, such as marital conflict, death of a closed one, a change in relationships, etc.

2.3 Psychodynamic Therapy: An evaluation

Classical psychoanalysis has been heavily criticized for a number of reasons, such as:

1. It is relatively time-consuming and expensive.
2. It is based on a questionable approach to human nature. This approach has no scientific basis.
3. It neglects the client's immediate needs in its obsession with childhood and experiences of the remote past.
4. There is an inadequate proof of its effectiveness. Some studies conducted on the effectiveness of psychoanalysis haven't given encouraging results (See Wallerstein, 1989).

Yet, many people who have undergone psychoanalysis have opined that the therapy helps them get an insight into their personality and provides them relief from inner conflict.

Modern psychodynamic therapies have been found to be quite effective in relation to classical psychophysics. For instance, interpersonal therapy has been found to be effective for serval disorders, particularly depression.

2.4 Cognitive Therapies

Cognitive psychologists believe that maladaptive behaviour is the result of irrational beliefs and negative thoughts. Hence, mental health can be fostered by teaching people to more accurately think about their goals and behaviour. Cognitive therapies typically try to restructure the client's cognitions. But, before dealing with that, let us analyze the cognitive point of view in detail.

The Cognitive Point of View

There are many typical cognitive processes and thinking patterns that are responsible for different types of disorders. Rosenhan and Seligman (1989) divide these processes into two categories:

1. Short-term conscious cognitive processes
2. Long-term and unconscious cognitive processes

Short-term cognitive processes

Three primary short-term cognitive processes which, if inaccurate, lead to mental disorders are- expectations, appraisals and attributions. Expectations refer to the expectancy that a behaviour would lead to a desirable outcome. After Bandura (1977), we can in fact say that there are two kinds of expectations a person can have- outcome expectations and efficacy expectations. Negative outcome and efficacy expectations have been linked to phobias and anxiety (Lang, 1967). Individuals who are anxious or phobic have incorrect cognitions in the sense that they expect something undesirable to happen.

Appraisals are evaluations about various events and behaviours of self. These self-evaluations are not always obvious and sometimes occur automatically. Beck (1964) has outlined many assumptions that predispose a person to negative appraisals:

1. To be happy, I have to be successful.
2. To be happy, I must be accepted by others at all times.
3. My value as a person depends on how others evaluate me.

Beck argues that when appraisals are based on these assumptions, they are bound to be negative, causing extreme sadness and hopelessness.

Attributions are our concept about why things happen to us. For example, if a student fails in the exam, whom does she blame for the failure? If she blames the teacher, it is an external attribution, but if she blames herself it is an internal attribution. There are three dimensions of attributions:

1. External-internal
2. Stable-unstable
3. Global-specific

A stable cause is one that is maintained over time. For example, if the student thinks that she will never be able to get good marks, she is making a stable attribution; but if she believes that not studying well for this exam led to failure, the attribution is unstable. Global attributions are displayed across situations, whereas specific attributions are specific to a task. If the student thinks that she is a loser and she won't be able to do anything in life because she failed a psychology exam, it is global attribution.

Cognitive psychologists state that the attribution style determines whether anyone is prone to certain disorders, like depression. The clinically deprived make internal, stable and global attributions. If there is extreme cold, they blame themselves for it. If Barack Obama dies, they will blame themselves for the bad news.

Long-term Cognitive Processes

We people tend to have some core beliefs based on hypothetical constructs. Ellis (1962) argues that psychological disorders result when these core beliefs are irrational. Usually, we are not conscious of these core beliefs; hence they are unconscious processes that affect our short-term expectations, appraisals and attributions.

How do core beliefs lead to maladaptive behaviour? Ellis forwards the **ABC Model** to explain this. He states that A is an activating event which is unpleasant and bothersome. There are consequences C which are direct result of the event A; however, there is an intermediate step called B which represents the beliefs one holds about the event. Irrational beliefs in the second step B actually lead to such emotional consequences. For example, if a person is phobic to dogs, she thinks that she becomes anxious (emotional consequence C) when she confronts a dog (event A). Actually, there are irrational beliefs (B) that are unconscious and lead to C.

Rational-Emotive Therapy

The rational-emotive therapy forwarded by Ellis is based on the idea that to change maladaptive behaviour, we need to change incorrect cognitions. Hence, while he explains disorders using the ABC Model, he proposes that disorders can be treated using the ABCD Models, where D stands for the process of disputing and changing B.

In rational-emotive therapy (RET), the therapist acts as cross-examiner of irrational beliefs of the client. The therapist is an active part of the therapy and aggressively confronts the client about her irrational beliefs. Ultimately, it is cognitive restructuring- the therapist introduces the client to commonly held irrational beliefs and then trains her by aggressive confrontation to change her irrational beliefs.

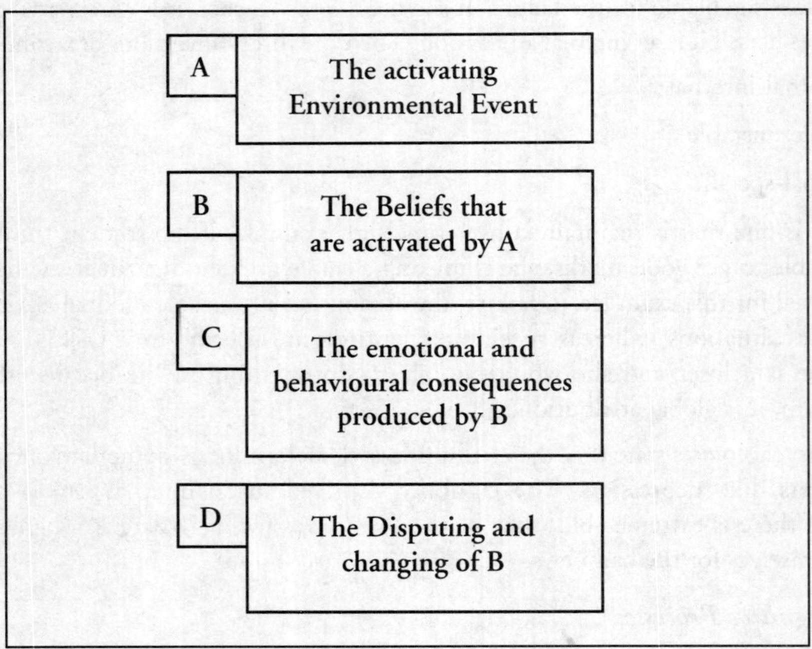

Fig. 2.1: ABCD Model of Ellis. Adapted from Passer and Smith (2007)

Beck's Cognitive Therapy

Although all forms of cognitive therapy concentrate on cognitive restructuring, not all treatments are as direct and confrontational as the rational-emotive therapy. In Aaron Beck's cognitive therapy, the therapist is suggestive, helping the client discover her own unique kinds of faulty beliefs, while the task of identification of irrational belief is with the client. In a sense, the clients are made to act as psychological detectives. Clients are asked to note their automatic thoughts and emotions in a notebook and then write rational responses to such thoughts and emotions. Beck believed that a successful client of his therapy passes through four stages:

1. Become aware of what she is thinking.
2. Recognize what thoughts are inaccurate.
3. Substitute accurate for inaccurate judgments.
4. Take feedback from the therapist to inform her where her changes are correct.

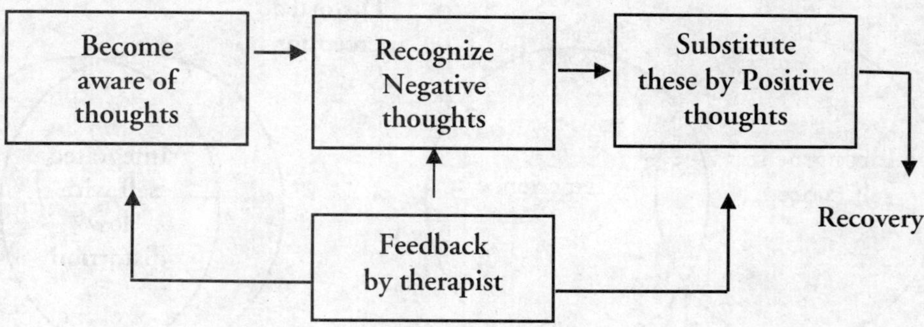

Fig. 2.2 : Four stages of Beck's Therapy

Cognitive Therapies: An Evaluation

Rational Emotive Therapy (RET) has been found to be useful in reducing disorders, such as test anxiety and speech anxiety quite effectively. Researchers have also found that RET is quite effective for depressive disorders. However, it seems to be most effective in helping generally healthy people to cope with everyday stress and prevent them from developing clinical anxiety or depression.

Beck's therapy seems to be extremely effective in alleviating many different kinds of disorders. Its effect in the case of depression is comparable to drug treatment and indeed often better. Moreover, it has superior long-term benefits; relapse chances in the case of drug addiction are low in case of Beck's therapy. Beck's therapy has shown promising results in the treatment of certain personality disorders and substance-abuse disorders also.

2.5 Client-Centered Therapy

Client-centered therapy is the most popular humanistic therapy. Carl Rogers developed this therapy in reaction to the psychoanalytic method of treatment. He reasoned that in the therapy process, most important element is the therapist-client relationship. It is not the therapist, but the client who ultimately holds the key to psychological health and well-being. Hence, therapy should be client-centered; the role of the therapist is to provide a therapeutic environment that fosters self-exploration and personal growth.

The Idea

Before getting into the nature and assumptions of client-centered therapy, it is important to understand Rogers' view of abnormality. Rogers believed that most psychological problems originate from incongruence between self-perceptions and experience. The self, according to him, refers to an organized, consistent set of perceptions and beliefs about oneself. Any experience which is inconsistent with our concept evokes anxiety. Well-adjusted people respond to the anxiety adaptively by modifying the self-concept. But, individuals with abnormality have rigid and inflexible self-concepts, owing to which they are less open to experiences and hence, are maladjusted.

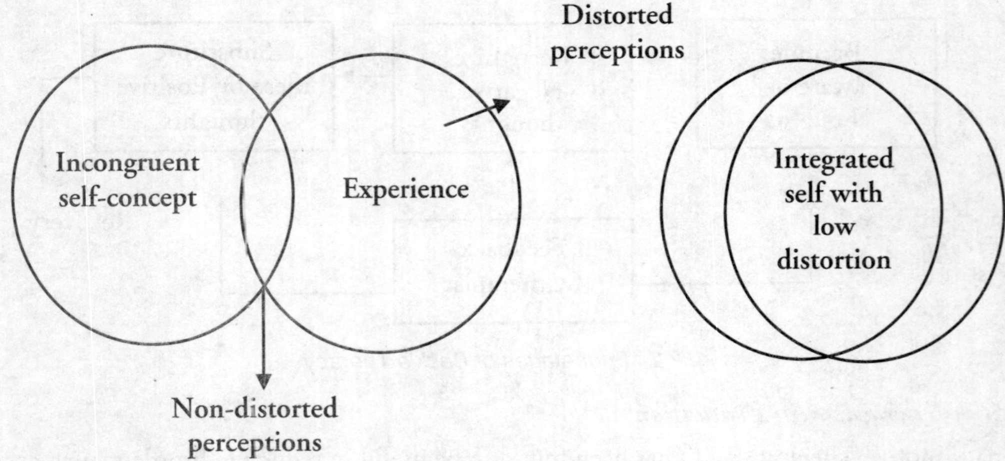

Fig. 2.3 : Degree of congruence between self concept and experience; Adapted by Passer and Smith (2007)

The Therapy

Based on his research and experiences as a therapist, Rogers identified three attributes of a therapist in client-centered therapy:

1. *Unconditioned positive regards:* We humans have an ingrained need for positive regards (i.e., approval, love and companionship) of significant others in our life. But, these significant others (father, mother, siblings, friends, etc.) attach conditions of worth when giving positive regards, that is, you are positively regarded only if you act and think in certain ways. Such conditioned positive regards become problematic when the ways in which we are supposed to behave, are incongruent to our true inner feelings.

Hence, Rogers argues that the therapist should show conditioned positive regards therapy. The therapist should accept the client, without judgment or evaluation. The therapist trusts that the client has the ability to work through her problems. This is also the reason why the therapy is non-directive, that is, the therapist doesn't offer advice or guidance.

2. *Empathy* is the willingness and ability to take on the client's perspective and view the world from the client's perspective. Not only this, the therapist communicates to the client that he empathetically feels about her, by reflecting back to the client what the client says in their conversation.
3. *Genuineness* is also an important attribute of the therapist. The therapist must be open enough to express her own feelings honestly, whether the feelings are positive or negative. You may wonder how the therapist can show unconditioned positive regard and still express negative feelings? This seems contradictory, but is not necessarily so. It is the skill of the therapist to accept the client even while expressing displeasure with the client's behaviour. For example, the therapist may observe, "I feel frustrated that you did not give the exams because I want things to work out for you".

Roger believed that these three attributes of the therapist creates a climate in which the client feels free to explore basic attitudes and beliefs without fear of being rejected or judged. This climate facilitates the client's innate potentialities to explore her feelings and strive for personal growth.

Client-Centered Therapy: An Evaluation

Client-centered therapy has often been criticized for the lack of any systematized model of human behaviour. The way that Rogers believes a therapy should progress, some critics fear that even a layman can become a therapist. That is exactly what Rogers believed! The therapy is similar to the way a very close friend of yours behaves with you. Yet, many skills are necessary to become a therapist in Rogerian therapy. Not every stranger can behave with you the way your best friend does.

Research on client-centered therapy, chiefly involving clients with mild problems, have shown encouraging results (e.g., Rogers and Dymond, 1954). However, a later trial of this therapy by Rogers and his colleagues (1967), proved disapproving many concepts introduced by client-centered therapy (such as, importance of therapist empathy, human potential for self-direction, motivation to search for meaning in life, etc.) have deeply influenced contemporary views on psychotherapy.

2.6 Behaviour Therapies

Psychodynamic, humanistic and cognitive therapy- all are based on the idea that disorders are due to inner dynamics. Hence, all these types of therapies focus on insight. Behaviour therapies are radically different, in that they believe that maladaptive behaviours aren't symptoms of inner disorder; rather they are the disorders. Maladaptive behaviours are learnt very much the same way normal behaviours are, on the principles of classical conditioning, operant conditioning and modelling. Hence, therapy should focus on charging these maladaptive behaviours using the principles of behavioural approach.

Classical conditioning is one in which a conditioned stimulus (CS) is paired with an unconditioned stimulus (UCS). Due to this, the CS starts eliciting response (conditional response: CR) that is otherwise omitted in response to the unconditioned stimulus. In therapies, this principle is used either to decondition (i.e., reverse maladaptive behaviours that result due to classical conditioning) or to condition aversive emotional response to some stimuli (for e.g., condition avoidance in response to stimuli, such as, alcohol for alcoholics, children for pedophiles). Most common classical conditioning approaches are systematic desensitization, implosive therapy and flooding and aversion therapy. Operant conditioning refers to conditioning a behaviour that is emitted more often when rewarded and less often when punished. Many positive-reinforcement techniques and punishment techniques are based on this. Modelling is used in techniques like, assertive therapy and social skills training. Let us discuss the above mentioned therapies in greater detail:

1. Systematic desensitization

This is the most popular behavioural therapy used in the treatment of phobias and other anxiety-related disorders. Developed by Wolpe, it uses a procedure called 'counter conditioning', in which a new response incompatible with anxiety is conditioned to an anxiety arousing CS. The new response usually is relaxation. The logic is that one cannot be anxious and relaxed at the same time. For example, suppose an individual gets anxious on approaching a dog (she suffers from a phobia). That means, dog is a CS that elicits anxiety as a CR. If dog as a CS is paired with relaxation as CR, anxiety as a CR fails; all because one can't be anxious and relaxed at the same time.

A desensitization training typically passes through four stages:

(a) Interview
(b) Training in relaxation
(c) Construction of anxiety hierarchies
(d) Desensitization proper

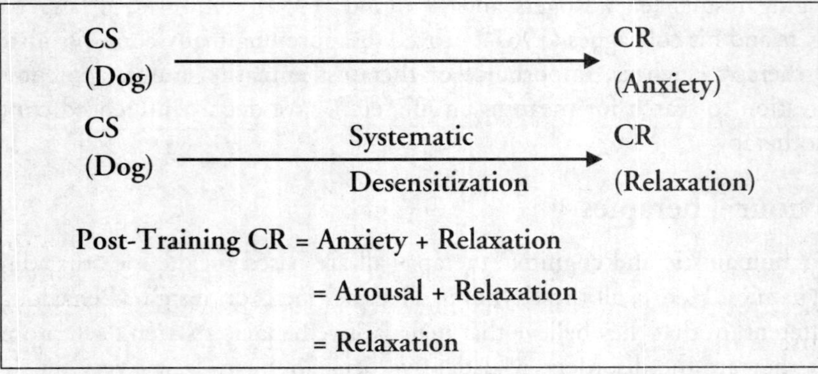

Fig. 2.4 : Stages of desensitization training

The therapy starts with an interview and a few tests to assess the type and nature of anxiety. The prime purpose here is to determine the sources of anxiety, i.e., CS that leads to anxiety. Then the client is trained in skills of voluntary muscle relaxation. A stimulus hierarchy is then constructed, consisting of some 10 to 20 scenes that have a gradient from being low-anxiety provoking stimulus to high-anxiety providing stimulus. For example, suppose a girl is afraid of frogs. Frogs are placed at different distances in every scene with even a scene in which a frog is placed on the girl's lap. After this, starts the desensitization proper. The client has to move from the bottom of the hierarchy (low-anxiety producing stimuli) to the top (high-anxiety producing stimuli). In every step, relaxation is taught to substitute anxiety as a CR. As the relaxation becomes strong enough to counter anxiety at one stage, the client moves on to the next stage in the hierarchy.

2. Implosive therapy and flooding

While systematic desensitization tried counter-conditioning (i.e., conditioning an incompatible CR to counter the original CR), there are other techniques that can uncondition the original CR. These techniques are based on the concept of extinction. If a CS is not paired with an UCS for a long time, it leads to extinction.

What happens in the case of phobias? Usually, phobia happens due to conditioning of the object of phobia (say a frog) with an unconditioned stimulus (UCS). After that, even in the absence of UCS, the CS (frog) leads to CR (anxiety). Why doesn't extinction take place? Because the CR (anxiety) motivates the individual to avoid the frog. Avoidance leads to reduction of fear and hence avoidance becomes an operant conditioned response that is reinforced of fear and hence avoidance becomes an operant conditioned response that is reinforced by a reduction of fear.

Phobia = Classical conditioning + Operant Conditioning

= Fear of an object + Reinforcement of the fear by avoidance

Avoidance behaviour is difficult to extinguish because one never gets to realize that the conditioned stimulus (frog) is no longer paired with the UCS, the real anxiety-causing stimulus.

Implosive therapy is based on an approach of extinction. In order for extinction to occur, it uses the following strategies:

1. Flooding of CS without UCS, so that the strength of conditioning decreases.
2. Preventing the client from avoiding or escaping the stimulus.

   Implosive therapy has been found to be quite effective in the treatment of phobias and certain anxiety-related disorders. However, critics remain concerned that initially, such flooding leads to intense anxiety and fear in the clients. Systematic desensitization is sometimes preferred over implosive therapy, as it produces far less anxiety for the client. However, implosive therapy provides better results in briefer course of the therapy.

3. Aversion therapy

Suppose, some pedophile offenders (child molesters) are brought up to you and you are asked to rehabilitate them, what do you do? You know that if left without any supervision, they may be dangerous to children in the society. So, the only solution is to treat them for their sick, perverse desire for children.

Aversion therapy does exactly the opposite of what implosive therapy does. An undesirable noxious stimuli (UCS) is paired with something you want the individual to avoid (CS), so that the CS also becomes anxious stimuli. For example, in case of pedophiles, show them pictures of children and condition it with electric shock. Make an alcoholic drink alcohol while injecting a nausea-arousing drug. The nausea is paired with alcohol and the individual avoids drinking alcohol.

A major shortcoming of this therapy is that the results of treatment often don't get generalized from treatment conditions to the real world. A reason for this may be expectancy; the client understands that children she is sexually attracted to in real life don't give shock if molested. Hence, discrimination takes place between the stimuli in treatment conditions and real-life conditions. Some experts believe that if aversive therapy is part of a larger treatment program that makes use of multiple approaches, it is more effective.

4. Token economy

This is based on the concepts of operant conditioning. This training has been of immense use in changing behaviours of hospitalized patients, specifically schizophrenic patients. A token is paid to a patient for performance of desired behaviour. This token can be used by the patient for a wide range of reinforces, such as private room, opportunity to watch a movie, recreational facilities. Token economy has proved to be quite effective in treating even the most challenging patients. In a study spanning four years, Paul and Leniz (1977) studied severely disturbed schizophrenic patients. An experimental group was provided token economy, while a control group was not. It was found that after the behavioural training programme, about 98% of the experimental group had been discharged from hospital. In contrast, only 45% of the control group were discharged.

5. Punishment

Punishment is usually avoided as a therapy technique as it has potential negatives side effects. It can be used as a measure of last resort, when less painful alternatives are not available. Even then, the consent of the patient or a guardian (in case the patient is a minor or mentally incompetent to give consent) is needed.

Punishment has been found to be quite effective in treating severely disturbed autistic children. Autistic children often indulge in repetitive, self-destructive behaviour, such as banging their head on sharp objects or tear pieces of flesh from their body. Lovaas (1977), a pioneer in the treatment of operant conditioning techniques, had conducted a training in which a severely disturbed girl (who banged her head against objects) was given electric shocks every time she indulged in self-destructive behaviour. In 15 shocks, her self-destructive behaviour was eliminated.

6. Modelling techniques

In social skill training, clients learn new skills by observing and imitating a model. This has been effectively used in inculcating social skills among populations, ranging from those who fear to talk to girls, to delinquents who have to resist peer pressure to severely disturbed schizophrenic patients.

Another modeling technique is the assertiveness training in which the client is asked to try out new behaviour, keeping a person who is more assertive as role model. Role Model is used in assertive therapy to develop such skills.

2.7 Indigenous Therapies

All the therapies we have discussed till now are based on theoretical constructs of psychology and medical science. However, there are certain traditional exercises and practices that have therapeutic value. Some of the popular traditional therapies have been indigenously developed and used in eastern traditions, for instance yoga, meditation and reiki.

Indigenous therapies have been in use for centuries in our tradition. Their therapeutic value has been documented in many documents. For example, Patanjali had forwarded various constructs of Yoga. Since then, many students of yoga have benefited from its therapeutic value. The real interest for indigenous therapies in scientific circles of psychology came when it was found that meditation and yoga lead to certain physiological changes that foster mental health and have the ability to help deal with mental disorders.

It has been found from electroencephalogram (EEG) studies that numerous brain-waves exist, each wave active in a different state of consciousness. Alpha waves are active when the individual experiences tranquility. Beta waves are of high frequency and are active when the individual undertakes cognitive tasks. It is usually accompanied by tension. Delta waves and Theta waves are active when the individual is asleep. EEG studies have shown that meditation and yoga practitioners are able to control their brain waves. Alpha waves noticeably increase during meditation. The implications of these finding are profound. It means that meditation and yoga take you to a different state of consciousness, where you experience tranquility. Indigenous therapies also influence other physiological functions. The rate of metabolism lowers (as evidences from the fact that oxygen consumption decreases and carbon dioxide is eliminated) and there is a decrease in blood lactate, a chemical that is related to stress.

Yoga

Yoga means union. It is based on the ancient Indian philosophy of uniting the individual spirit with universal spirit. Yoga is touted to be a state of super consciousness in our traditional literature. In this section, we will concentrate on therapeutic applications of yoga.

Ramamurthi (1977) has studied yogis under states of relaxation, concentration and meditation. He found changes in the brain which had a beneficial effect on the activity of nervous system. These changes also affected the way the heart, the lungs, the digestive system as well as the endocrine system functions. These physiological changes, contends Ramamurthi, foster positive health.

An obvious utility of yoga is in tackling stress and fostering relaxation. Dr. Cabot-Zinn of University of Massachusetts had designed Stress Reduction and Relaxation Programme (SRRP) based on Hatha Yoga around twenty years back. A slew of peer-reviewed journal papers have verified the therapeutic usage of this program and other such programs based on yoga.

Relaxation is also linked to anxiety. A relaxed person can't be anxious at the same time. Does it mean that yoga affects anxiety also? Many studies have shown that yoga is an effective tool to reduce anxiety. For instance, after the disastrous tsunami struck South India in 2006, many survivors suffered from Post-Traumatic Stress Disorder (PTSD). Dr. Gerbarg who teaches psychiatry at New York Medical College, conducted a study on these victims in which three groups were taken. One group of 60 victims were given 4-day yoga training. Another group of 60 acted as control. The researcher found that yoga had significant effect on PTSD. Counselling didn't seem to have as substantial effect as yoga, as the results for first two groups were similar. Other studies have explored the therapeutic value of controlled breathing in yoga. I. Sharma and Agnihotri (1982) had investigated the effect of controlled breathing on 20 persons who were diagnosed high on anxiety. After 4 weeks of practice, there was definite reduction in anxiety in 10 out of the 20 patients.

The benefits of Yoga in handling stress, anxiety depression and hypertension have been verified. But, do you know that yoga helps treat physiological disorders such as cancer, diabetes and heart diseases also? Take, for instance, Divakar's (1982) study of diabetic patients. He found that in a majority of cases, there was a fall of blood sugar level among these patients after practicing yoga for a specific period. Nagarathna and Nagendra (1981) have given similar reports.

Transcendental Meditation

Almost all forms of meditation involved an attempt to direct the focus of attention away from the world of stimuli (i.e., outside world) by using intense concentration. In the case of transcendental meditation (TM), subjects sit quietly in comfortable position with their eyes closed. They exclusively concentrate on the sound of a mantra, that they repeat to themselves silently. Participants are discouraged from thinking logically or concentrate on any specific idea; rather, the mind should be allowed to experience freely the thoughts elicited by the mantra. During TM, the mind 'transcends' normal consciousness to arrive at a state of nothingness.

EEG activity has shown that brain-wave activity during meditation resemble that of a drowsy state superficially. The difference lies in the fact that during meditation, one is not inattentive. Rather, the attention is inwardly directed. The decrease in body metabolism is greater in meditation than in a drowsy state or deep sleep. Hence, Wallace (1970) is justified in calling meditation a unique "fourth state of consciousness".

There are significant health changes due to TM. For example, Bharadwaj, Upadhyaya and Gaur (1979) have examined the effects of TM, drugs and placebo on three groups of neurotic patients. Their anxiety level was assessed before and after the treatments. The conclusion was that maximum reduction in total anxiety was in the TM group, followed by the drug treatment group. Hence, TM seems to be more effective than drugs in case of anxiety. On top of that, drugs, like Prozac (used to treat anxiety) are costlier and have side-effects.

TM also seems to change one's personality. For instance, Schwartz and Coleman (1973) observed that practitioners of meditations are less anxious and less neurotic when measured by Eysenck's Personality Inventory. They are also low on aggression.

Criticisms

It seems that all forms of yoga don't have the same benefit on all people. This is the reason why many studies on yoga have got inconclusive results. If you conduct a test on psychologically heterogeneous population and the results show that yoga has beneficial effects on some while no effect on others, it means that yogic practice doesn't benefit all people alike.

In a review article, I Sharma and Agnihotri (1982) make the revelation that yoga and TM have side-effects also. There are possibilities of subject developing dissociative states, de-personalization and de-realization experiences. Anxiety may increase in some individuals due to meditation, because during meditation the individual gets to confront emotionally charged memories. These emotionally charged memories may overwhelm the individual. Hence, I. Sharma and Agnihotri have warned against the indiscriminate use of yoga.

2.8 Biofeedback

Biofeedback is essentially a type of behavioural therapy. The development of sensitive electronic equipment that could tell us about our physiological responses has enabled us to take feedback from our biological system. This feedback helps us to develop operant learning procedures to voluntarily control our physiological processes, such as heart rate, penile erection, blood pressure, etc. Feedback acts as the knowledge of results (KR), important for operant learning.

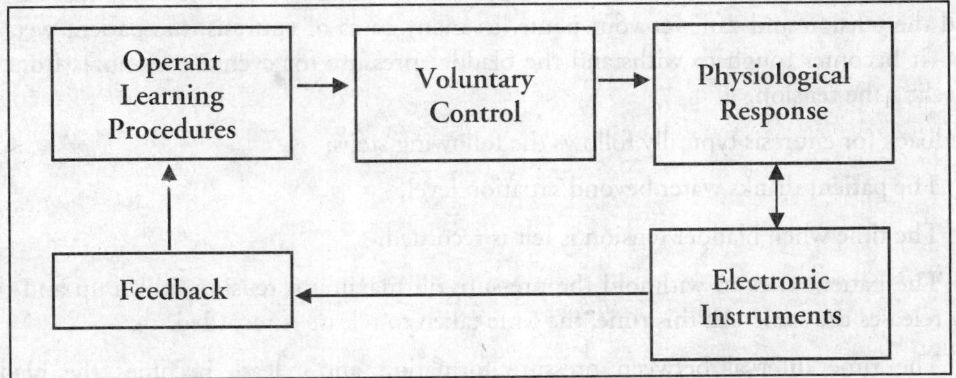

Fig. 2.5 : Mechanism of biofeedback

To illustrate biofeedback, some specific examples will be taken here. Here, I will borrow heavily from results of a study conducted by H. Mishra and S.K. Kiran Kumar (1993).

Secondary Sexual Impotence

Primary sexual impotence is one where penile erection does not happen. Biofeedback cannot be used in this case, as the individual can't make physiological changes (penile erection) on sexual arousal in any way. In secondary sexual impotence, penile erection is present, but the clients wouldn't maintain it for sufficient period to have vaginal penetration and satisfactory intercourse. The feedback procedure in this case typically follows the following steps:

1. Relaxation training.
2. An electronic instrument is arranged to take biofeedback. Plethysmograph is an instrument that records penile (erection) responses. It can be used to take biofeedback.
3. The client is presented with pictures of nude females of his choice. He is asked to fantasize and relive the sexual intercourse and sex play when viewing the pictures. This he has to do for a 45 minute session. The pictures are regularly changed to avoid satiation.
4. After 45 minutes, the results of plethysmograph are taken. The graph between maintenance of penile volume and duration of erection is provided to the client for analysis, so that he could make informed attempts in the next session.

In the study by Misra and Kiran Kumar, it was found that the feedback received from the plethysmograph along with relaxation, can improve penile response in about 27 sessions. Relaxation is important, because it reduces any anxiety one has during the intercourse process. Anxiety affects performance and penile volume. If you are unable to consummate your conjugal life, I recommend you try out biofeedback. Medications only provide temporary help.

Enuresis

Enuresis is a disorder in which if you drink water beyond a satiation level, your bladder can not withstand the tension and can wet your pants. In many cases of enuresis, the patient wets the bed daily. It becomes tough to withstand the bladder pressure for even 2-3 minutes from the time of feeling the tension.

Biofeedback for enuresis typically follows the following steps:

1. The patient drinks water beyond satiation level.
2. The time when bladder tension is felt is recorded.
3. The patient tries to withhold the pressure till maximum tension builds up and then releases the same. All this time, the time taken to release is recorded.
4. The time interval between pressure formation and release becomes the bladder tension feedback. This is monitored in every trail.

In every trail, effort is made to lengthen the interval of withholding pressure. A twice-a-day practice, once in the forenoon and once in the afternoon are recommended. Mishra and Kiran Kumar (1993) had worked with a patient with enuresis. This patient had been suffering from the problem for the past 13 years. He had earlier been treated with drugs, psychotherapy and behaviour therapy, but to no avail. He used to wet his bed daily at night one or two times. In the biofeedback exercise, this enuretic patient took 272 days to achieve complete dry nights. It is quite an encouraging result, given that other treatments didn't work in the past 13 years.

Phobia

Biofeedback can be coupled with systematic desensitization therapy in treating phobia. The biofeedback instrument used here is a galvanometer that measures Galvanic Skin Response (GSR). Changes in GSR show the pattern of anxiety response to phobia-arousing stimuli. A biofeedback procedure to treat phobia can follow the following steps:

1. Construction of an anxiety hierarchy.
2. Client education, in which the client is educated about how deflection in the galvanometer indicates physiological changes.
3. Presentation of items from the anxiety hierarchy for visualization. All this time, the client monitors GSR changes through visual and auditory modalities.

Chronic Anxiety and Tension

In a series of pioneering studies on brain-wave activity, Dr. Kamiya found that conscious control of alpha waves is possible. Biofeedback can be used to get feedback about alpha wave activity and muscle tension, and then voluntarily trying to change alpha wave activity. This technique is also referred to as "electronic yoga", because it seeks to do the same thing that yoga and meditation do, making use of electronic feedback of EEG and other instruments. This use of biofeedback has been particularly helpful in overcoming chronic anxiety and tension.

Biofeedback: An Appraisal

As already seen, biofeedback is a modern therapeutic tool. But what is its efficacy? Some concerns regarding biofeedback are:

1. The effects of biofeedback procedures are generally small.
2. Many of the effects of biofeedback procedure do-not generalize to situations outside the laboratory, where feedback devices are not present.
3. It is quite a costly method, involving costly electronic equipments for feedback.

2.9 Fostering Mental Health

In most of the therapies we have discussed in this chapter, the focus has been on treating a mental disorder. An alternative is to prevent the incidence of mental disorder. Hence, many psychologists, especially community mental health workers and school psychologists are now concentrating on attempts to foster mental health. In this section, we will discuss certain interventions to foster mental health in children and then move on to certain general psychological interventions.

Interventions to foster mental health in children

The most important aspect of fostering mental health is to help the individual develop a correct frame of reference in childhood. This can be done in the following ways:

1. *Nutrition:* Sufficient and healthy nutritious food is not only necessary for physical health, but also for mental health. Many studies on deprived groups in India has shown that malnutrition is linked with impaired cognitive development, and with mental ill-health. Agarwal et al. (1987) have found from a large-scale study on 6-8 years old rural children in Varanasi that severity of malnutrition is proportional to impairment of intelligence, verbal reasoning, short term memory and perceptual and spatial skills.

2. *Rich environment:* The human child is in need of a rich environment for stimulation of its mental faculties, in order to develop a strong self-concept. Hence, schools should try to provide an intellectual environment, rich in problem-solving tasks and logical reasoning.

3. *Realistic aspirations:* Those with unrealistic goals often face frustration in life. They also tend to develop a rigid self-concept. Often, failure is following by incorrect attributions and appraisals. For example, many students with poor mental health attribute success to external factors and failure to internal factors. Hence, there is a need to develop in children realistic perceptions about what they can aim for and achieve. Correct training in school prevents negative attributions of events.

4. *Core beliefs:* Cognitive theorists believe that underlying most mental health problems are certain irrational core beliefs. The individual is not conscious of these core beliefs; indeed, these beliefs often develop early in life and effect other cognitive processes. Hence, an important strategy to foster mental health in children is to make interventions to change irrational core beliefs.

General Intervention Strategies

The strategy used by psychological interventions to foster mental health is to reduce the factors that increase vulnerability of mental disorders. These factors, that can increase or decrease mental health, are of two types- situational factors and personal factors. Hence, interventions are also of two types- situation-focused interventions and competency-focused interventions.

Some prominent situation-focused interventions are those that try to enhance interpersonal relations in families, reduce stress within organizations and provide social support by developing a sense of connection to the community at large. Many mental health problems develop, for instance, because of improper child-rearing practices in the family. Parents make conditioned positive regard and have contradictory expectations form the child. This creates a double bind for the child and may lead to split mind (causal factor in schizophrenia) or depression.

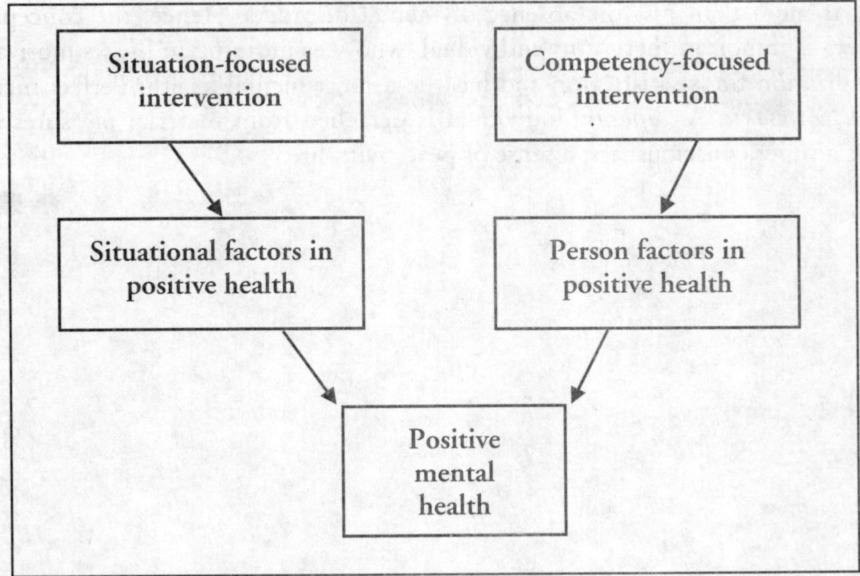

Fig. 2.6.: General Intervention Strategies

Here, we shall discuss a successful community intervention programme to prevent mental disorder and thereby, to promote mental health. Raine and co-workers (2003) designed a program to prevent the development of an anti-social personality disorder in a high-risk slum environment in the inner-city. Children in the age group 3-5 years were randomly assigned to an experimental group that was given an intensive nutritional, physical exercise and educational program. At the age of 17, the children who were part of the experimental group had lower scores on measures of anti-social personality disorder than the control group-members.

Competency-focused interventions are concerned with the person factors in mental health. Hence, these programs seek to increase the competency of people, i.e., increase personal resources and coping skills. For instance, Rath (1992) had studied the effect of verbal self-instructional training and operant manipulation of response and reward on children from tribal families in Orissa. He found that both kinds of trainings were effective in remediation of impulsive tempo in children. Many other studies have reported that high self-efficacy treatment helps to develop better stress-coping skills.

Lifestyle and Well-being

Till now, we have been discussing various psychological interventions to foster better mental health, but there are certain measures that the individual can take (and should take) to foster mental health. We have discussed of lifestyle and how a flawed lifestyle affects mental health in the chapter on psychological well-being. A lifestyle model for perfect health proposed by Parashar (2000) has also been included in the discussion. Healthy lifestyles lead to not only physical well-being, but also mental well-being.

Mental health is more than just the absence of mental disorders. Hence, the concept of *subjective well-being* is important here. Any individual, who sees meaning in life, is motivated towards self-actualization finds satisfaction and has the utmost mental health. Perfect mental health is found in *Anasakti*. An *anasakt* individual is detached from material pleasures and hence experiences a super consciousness; a sense of peace with life.

■ ■ ■

3

Rehabilitation Psychology

Chapter outline

3.1 Prevention

The major focus of mental health efforts has traditionally been restorative, that is, helping people only after they develop disorders. A more effective strategy is to try to provide support and help at early stages, or better yet, to focus on preventing psychological disorders. The concept of prevention is based on this philosophy. Broadly, various strategies for prevention used in public health can be categorized as:

- o Primary Prevention (PP)
- o Secondary Prevention (SP)
- o Tertiary Prevention (TP)

PP refers to efforts aimed at reducing the possibility of disorders and fostering positive health. Once disease or disorder develops, SR is used as an emergency step to reduce the impact and spread of the disorder. TP seeks to reduce the long-term consequences of disorders.

Primary Prevention

Primary Prevention (PP) includes a variety of strategies aimed at reducing the possibility of disorders and fostering good health. Psychologists involved in PP undertake epidemiological studies to obtain information about incidence and distribution of various maladaptive behaviours. Epidemiological studies provide information regarding the incidence of maladaptive behaviours and diseases in various sections of the population. The results of these studies are used to define target groups – groups that have greater vulnerability for a disorder. For example, it has been found that divorced people and elderly people living alone are at high risk for delusional disorders. They become the target group for preventive intervention programmes aimed at preventing delusional disorders.

After this, psychologists study the factors affecting the vulnerability of these groups. There are two types of factors- ***risk factors and protective factors***. Psychologists try to alter conditions that contribute to disorders and establish conditions that foster well-being. Risk factors are those conditions that contribute to disorders, while protective factors are those that foster well-being. For example, in the case of preventing spread of HIV/AIDS, having sex with multiple partners is a risk factor, while using condoms (doing safe sex) is a protective factor.

Strategies used in prevention programmes are numerous and varied. Yet, they can be studied under the following three heads:

(a) Biological measures of prevention

A major reason for mental retardation is defect in the fetus due to genetic causes or due to teratogens (environmental agents that alter the genetic structure of the baby in the uterus). PP workers provide ***genetic counselling*** to couples on the status of the fetus. If genetic defects can be identified in advance, abortion may be considered an option.

Before the birth of the baby, PP workers provide ***pre-natal care***. After the birth, post-natal care is provided for the healthy development of infants. Special care is taken to ascertain that the baby gets necessary vaccines; that the infant gets adequate nutritional inputs, etc.

Beyond childhood, PP also looks into factors, such as lifestyle, that fosters both physical and mental well-being and prevents mental disorders.

(b) Psychosocial measures

Optimal development and functioning of an individual depends on both maturational factors (nature) and learning (nurture). Hence, learning of physical, intellectual, emotional and social competencies is a psychosocial process. To develop these competencies effectively, the individual needs to be exposed to sufficient stimulants. Proper socialization in a rich environment fosters psychosocial health. We have seen in the chapter on disadvantaged groups the consequence, both mental and physical, of prolonged deprivation from stimulation. PP seeks to provide adequate stimulants to the growing child in the crucial, formative stages.

Also necessary for psychosocial health is that the person acquires an accurate frame of reference; when an individual's perceptions of the world are far from reality, she is more vulnerable to mental disorders. For instance, as Kakar has pointed, socialization process in Indian families leaves an individual with a narcissistic self-concept (Kakar's theory is discussed in detail in the chapter on psychology of terrorism). Such identity distortion leads to maladaptive development. Hence, primary prevention measures should include interventions for correct socialization.

Erik Erikson, among others, had stressed that development is a life-long process and we face problems in every life-stage. Primary prevention looks into problems and crisis during the ***whole life span***. For example, parenthood, marriage, career choices, etc. are problems faced in adulthood. PP in these stages includes guidance to parents and couples and career counselling. Geriatric care is provided to people at the age of retirement. These are some important measures of PP throughout the life span.

(c) Socio-cultural measures

In many cases, pathological social conditions lead to maladaptive behaviour. For example, it has been seen that most juvenile delinquents belong to low socio-economic status (SES) groups. Sometimes, individuals may be genetically predisposed for maladaptive behaviour, but precipitating factors (stressors) are provided by social conditions. For example, a schizophrenic's son faces social stigma due to the wrong belief that madness is genetic. The social stigma acts as a stressor to increase the chances of the son becoming schizophrenic.

PP entails the removal of above risk factors. Some popular PP strategies to prevent the occurrence of socio-cultural problems (such as drug abuse, alcoholism, violence) are:

1. Intervention for high-risk groups
2. Intervention for adolescents
   (a) Educational programs
   (b) Family-based programs
   (c) Peer group influence programs
3. Modelling and awareness through mass-media

   High risk groups include individuals who, owing to their social situation or nature of work, are more vulnerable than others. For example, Female Sex Workers (FSW) and men having sex with men (MSM) are especially prone to HIV/AIDS. In India, NACO is promoting safe sex practices and regular medical check-up of these groups.

Adolescence is a period of identity confusion. In this stage, people are especially vulnerable to drug abuse and unsafe sex. Hence, primary prevention includes ***educational programs*** to educate them. Parents are also educated, so that they can recognize the symptoms of, say, drug abuse in teens. Owing to the important role played by peer groups in adolescence, there is a pressure for conformity. Interventions, such as ***assertiveness training*** in schools, help students resist negative peer pressure.

Modelling is used through the medium of mass media or street dramas to foster positive attitude towards health and well-being and to develop negative attitudes towards drug abuse and anti-social behaviour.

Secondary Prevention

Secondary prevention emphasizes the early detection and prompt treatment of disorders. It is based on the philosophy that early detection and intervention makes treatment easier. For example, victims of violence show acute responses, like shock and denial. If not immediately treated, they show delayed responses, such as regression to an earlier psychosocial stage (for instance, anal stage or phallic stage) or Post-traumatic Stress Disorders (PTSD). Most contemporary psychologists agree that PTSD is a natural response to traumatic events, yet the severity may be high if immediate help is not provided.

Two popular modes of secondary prevention are ***short-term crisis therapy and telephone hot line. Nowadays,*** even internet is being used as a means to get immediate therapeutic help from experts. Taking the earlier example of victims of violence, short-term crisis therapy includes debriefing sessions. If the number of victims are too many, everyone may not be able to get help from counsellors. Here, telephone hotline or internet may be used; for example, victims of terrorist attacks in Jammu and Kashmir can be connected to counsellors in Kerala!

Some other secondary prevention approaches are called ***harm reduction approaches.*** After an individual starts engaging in a high-risk behaviour, the attempt is to reduce the harmful effects of that behaviour. For example, having sex with sex workers is a high risk behaviour. Primary prevention approach is to discourage people from showing such behaviour. But, when people start engaging in this behaviour, the secondary prevention strategy is to motivate them to engage in safe sex. Similarly, drug addicts are given new needle and syringe by secondary prevention workers. A major reason for spread of AIDS is the use of infected syringe again and again by drug addicts. SP worker provides new needle and syringe, so that the addicts don't get AIDS.

Tertiary Prevention

Tertiary prevention involves efforts aimed at reducing the long-term impact of a disorder. Two major modes of tertiary prevention (TP) are:

1. Providing therapeutic climate in mental hospitals, and
2. Aftercare

Traditionally, mental hospitals have focused on treatment rather than prevention or rehabilitation. It has, however, been found that the hospital environment can influence the patient's mental health. Hence, TP looks at the hospital as a therapeutic community. This approach, called ***milieu therapy***, is based on three general principles:

1. Staff expectations are closely communicated to mentally challenged patients.
2. Patients are encouraged to get involved in daily decision-making of the hospital.
3. All patients form a small group. Group cohesiveness gives patients support and a sense of social efficacy; group pressure exerts pressure on the patients to exercise control over their behaviour (Carson et al., 1998).

Even after successful treatment in hospitals, readjustment in the community is difficult. Many studies have shown that as much as 45% of schizophrenic patients have relapsed. So, what is the solution? TP provides a solution in the form of ***aftercare***. Aftercare programmes smoothen the transition from institutional to community life and reduce the number of relapses. ***Halfway homes*** are health facilities managed by the community, where patients stay for a while after leaving hospital. Here, community and family play proactive roles to teach social skills for readjustment to community.

The role of TP doesn't end after the patient starts her normal life. Relapse can occur even now.Relapse occurs when the treated patient faces high-risk situations. People with high coping skills can resist relapse, but many can't. For them, relapse prevention training and regular follow-up sessions are necessary.

3.2 Rehabilitation

Rehabilitation refers to all attempts made at training and retraining an individual (usually with some kind of disability), so as to enable the individual achieve maximum possible functional capability. Due to various environmental and personal factors, an individual may face a situation of crisis, a disability or to say inability, to properly integrate with her social environment. For example, an accident may lead to physical disability. A physically disabled person is no longer the same person. If one has lost a hand, she finds it tough to work in office to the same capacity as she earlier could. She finds it tough to adjust to her daily lifestyle and social life. But, if she is trained, she can attain maximum skills that could be attained with one hand lost. Hence, the need for rehabilitation is there. The role of rehabilitation, in a broad sense, is to ***restore status*** of an individual who has met with a ***disabling crisis***.

Rehabilitation is different from treatment in the sense that treatment is based on the medical model, while rehabilitation draws from many social and physical sciences. If an individual tries to commit suicide by taking poison, the doctors try to save her life. They don't enquire into what caused suicidal behaviour and whether the individual will be prone to suicide again! Similarly, in the case of a physical disability, doctors provide only surgical help. A person who has lost a limb in an accident naturally feels depressed, may lose ***subjective efficacy***, may feel ***powerless*** and ***helpless.*** These are serious problems; these psychological problems may in fact be more serious than physical disability. You can easily lead a life of dignity without a limb. You may even get a good job. But, if after your disability, you get self-defeating, negative thoughts or perceive an ***external locus of control,*** the doctors don't cater to these. On the other hand, rehabilitation workers look into all aspects of the individual's problems- physical, psychological and social. The ultimate aim of rehabilitation is to bring about a proper person-environment (PE) fit. To put it without psychological jargon, the aim of rehabilitation is to ***reintegrate the individual to her community and to ensure that she can perform to her maximum ability possible.***

Role of Psychologists in Rehabilitation

The role of a psychologist spans over the three stages of rehabilitation- assessment, intervention and aftercare. Also, it needs to be emphasized that a rehabilitation psychologist is both a scientist and an artist. She works within the theoretical framework of psychological research. At the same time, she tailors her rehabilitation programme to the needs of the specific client. Every client has problems unique to him, which the psychologist has to deal with. Hence, she is both a scientist and an artist.

The role of a psychologist varies as per the individual needs and problems of the client, yet a general analysis of the role of psychologists can be made as under:

Mentally challenged persons

Mentally challenged persons are the ones who have developed maladaptive behaviour due to a complex interaction between environmental stressors and genetic factors.

Previously, the medical model was followed in treating mentally challenged persons. As a result, persons with mental disorder were institutionalized in mental hospitals. They were given drugs and medicines that supposedly cured mental disorders. But lately, there has been a movement for deinstitutionalization. Many recent researchers have found that medicines and drugs have side-effects. Besides, they only provide temporary cure to any abnormal behaviour. Other studies have confirmed that a mental patient needs her family and friends the most for recovery and institutionalization simply cuts the patient from her social support. Hence, rather than helping mental patients, institutionalization worsens their condition. Hence, a focus on rehabilitation over treatment is preferred. Rehabilitation workers see individuals with disorders as "clients" rather than "patients". Now, let us turn our attention towards the role of psychologists in rehabilitation of mentally challenged persons:

(a) *Crisis intervention*

Some psychological help may be needed immediately after a crisis. It is always not necessary but may be necessary in certain cases, such as, for the victims of a terrorist attack. The immediate response of victims of such traumatic violence is shock and denial. If these are not dealt by a psychologist (usually the psychologist does a debriefing session to bring the victim out of the state of shock) immediately, the victim may experience severe PTSD or may go to a state of deeper psychological regression.

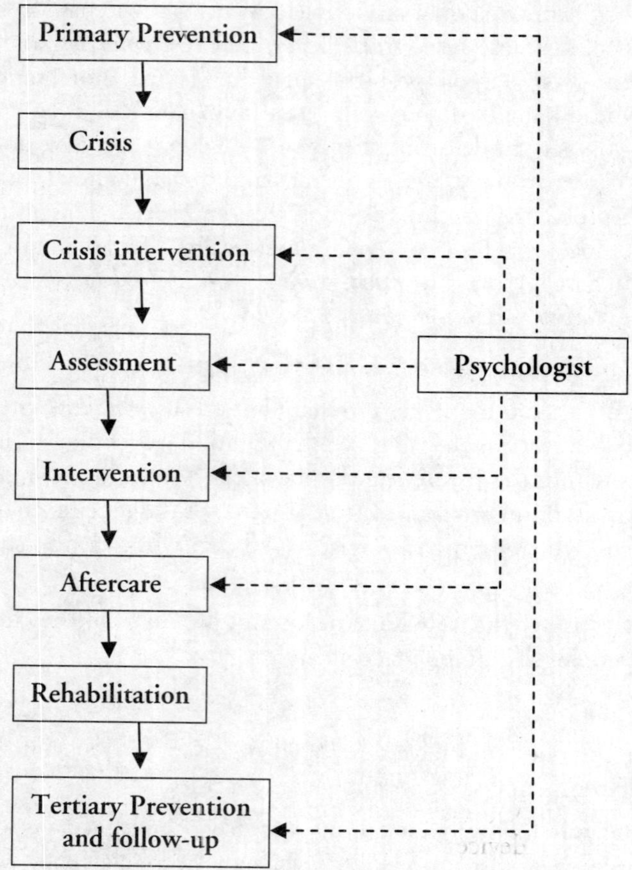

Fig. 3.1 : Steps in Prevention and scope of psychologist's role

(b) *Assessment*

The nature of problem varies from person to person. Hence, there is a need to assess the situation of the client, to understand his problem holistically. To do so, the psychologist makes various assessments, such as:

1. Study of client's social history
2. Interviews and clinical observation
3. Personality tests, such as MMPI
4. Projective tests (e.g. TAT)
5. Neurological examination using EEG, PET, and MRI scans
6. Neuropsychological tests measuring cognitive, perceptual and motor abilities

Let us take the hypothetical case of Hari to understand the job of a rehabilitation psychologist better. Hari is a student of electrical engineering and has attempted to commit suicide. The psychologist tries to understand the client's ***social history.*** She finds that Hari was good at music and wanted to make a career in it. However his parents forced him to study electrical engineering. Since he did not have the aptitude for it or interest in the subject, he regularly failed in exams. Did it lead to depression? Did it hurt his self-esteem?

To know the answers to these questions, the psychologist interviews him and his family members. She also makes use of ***clinical observation*** method to check psychological responses, such as emotions, aggression, anxiety, hallucinations or delusions. Clinical observation refers to detailed observation of the client when he/she is admitted in the hospital. This is usually done through hospital staff or by video recording.To understand Hari's self-concept, she tests Hari on personality tests, like MMPI and Eysenck Personality Inventory (EPI). Was Hari introvert? How good a friends' circle did he have? Was he evasive? Or neurotic? Many students who commit suicide often show introversion, social withdrawal and neuroticism.

What were the environmental stressors for Hari? The psychologist also studies Hari's peer group, family relations and his relations with his professors to understand the social context; often social contexts are precipitation factors for maladaptive behaviour.

Lastly, could the suicide attempt be an instinctive behaviour due to some genetic or biological factor? The psychologist takes the help of neurologists and neuropsychologists. Neurologists use MRI, EEG and other such instruments. An Electroencephalogram (EEG) can assess brainwave patterns; Magnetic Resonance Imaging (MRI) can-detect structural anomalies in the central nervous system, Position Emission Tomography (PET) scan throws light on brain activity. Neuro-psychologists provide testing devices to measure Hari's cognitive, perceptual and motor performance.

After doing assessment, the psychologist has the option of making a formal diagnosis on the basis of DSM-IV classification of disorders. However, the psychologist tries to avoid formal classification as much as possible; as such a classification is associated with social stigma. DSM-IV classification becomes necessary when (a) the client is so disturbed mentally that she has become a danger to society, or (b) when the condition is so severe that there is a need for admitting the client to a mental hospital.

(c) *Intervention*

The medical model advocated medication as the route to treatment. However, psychologists believe that therapy and counselling are better and more durable strategies of intervention. Indeed, the rehabilitation psychologist decides if hospitalization is at all necessary. Many schizophrenics, for instance, have been found to recover by use of cognitive behavioural therapies, self-help and family intervention.

Next, the psychologist determines the nature of mental disorder and the therapy best suited for the disorder. Generally, psychologists make a wise combination of many different therapies in their rehabilitation program (this is called eclectic approach). For example, cognitive therapy is best for dealing with depression and psychoanalytic approach is quite effective in dealing with anxiety-related problems. So, a combination may be needed for a military person who has tested high on both.

In the case of brain disorders affecting cognitive functions, the psychologist targets skills lost by brain dysfunction. She may develop compensatory strategies for the client; for example, if a client faces memory problem, she may train him in using a laptop as long book to organize information. Social skill training using behavioural techniques of positive reinforcement and modeling have been found to be quite effective in treating schizophrenia and other mental disorders. Application of these simple learning principles leads to significant improvements in social functioning and in the quality of life of patients suffering from disorders.

(d) *Aftercare*

After intervention succeeds in developing functional autonomy in a person with mental disorder, she is taught social skills, so that she can be adequately rehabilitated back to society. Aftercare happens in halfway homes. The client released from mental hospital has a gradual return to the outside world through halfway homes. At the halfway home, the individual's interaction with family and peer groups is increased. She is trained to develop functional skills for employment also.

Physically challenged persons

Physical disability produces stressors that are cumulative. These stressors lead to psychological ill-health. For instance, a person who loses a limb in an accident perceives an external locus of control. Her ***self-efficacy*** gets a beating and she may become depressed. Her emotional reactions may range from anxiety to learned helplessness. Also, status in family and peer group decreases. This leads to a ***lowered self-concept.***

A depressed person feeling learned helplessness, may not even try to adjust to her new condition. ***Denial or avoidance*** are defensive styles that may be used by the person.

The psychologist uses various stress management techniques to reduce the effect of stressors.

She can counsel the client in Rogerian therapy to increase her self-concept; cognitive approach is effective for anxiety and depression. Techniques, such as biofeedback, have been used in novel ways to improve aspects of motor control.

Not just therapy, the psychologist helps the client in many other ways. For instance, she suggests adaptive technologies for the client and ergonomics for places the client frequently visits (for example, facilities in the toilet, so that the client feels comfortable and is not reminded of her disability).

Socially challenged persons

Socially challenged individuals are those who have become marginalized in society because of their inability to follow social norms. Juvenile delinquents, individuals involved in criminal activities, drug addicts and alcoholics are examples of socially challenged persons. Not just deviant behaviour, developmental challenges in the life span also may lead to social challenges. For example, old age problems are certain problems that make the elderly citizens socially challenged.

The role of psychologists in rehabilitation of socially challenged persons begins with early detection of problems. Epidemiology is the study of distribution of disorders in a given population. Psychologists make epidemiological studies to assess the distribution of social problem and to find groups where incidence of social challenges is high. The intervention technique differs widely for different cases of social challenges. However, it is generally agreed that the social deviants are deviants because of lack of proper small group. There may be other causal factors also, but the best intervention is provided by small groups. Hence, role of community and family is paramount here. Many field psychologists working in the area of community welfare develop community-based interventions to rehabilitate victims of substance abuse disorder and alcoholism.

The socially deviant individuals are deviants because they don't conform to social norms. They don't conform to social norms because they are not properly socialized. Hence, ***resocialization*** is seen as an effective strategy to rehabilitate them. This, again, is most effectively done in small groups. Group therapy approaches, such as alcoholic anonymous (AA) have been found to be effective. Psychologists are also using innovative strategies to treat drug addicts, alcoholics, pedophiles, etc. For example, a picture of a child (conditioned stimulus) is paired with shock to treat pedophiles. Nausea producing drugs are mixed with alcohol in some therapies to condition an avoidance towards it.

Aftercare is the last stage of rehabilitation. Here also, there is a high chance of relapse. We will deal with rehabilitation of victims of alcoholism, substance abuse disorder, juvenile delinquency, etc. in greater detail in other sections in this chapter.

3.3 Substance Abuse Disorder

Substance abuse disorder is a major problem being faced at various levels- society, family and the individual. Harmful for personal health, it is also dysfunctional to family and society. Many drug-abusers resort to crime in order to maintain their supply of drugs. Drug abuse is also related to incidence of HIV/AIDS. Use of infected syringe for drug intake increases the risk of getting HIV/AIDS. Drug overdose kills. Hence, there is a need for prevention of drug abuse and rehabilitation of victims of substance abuse disorder.

Prevention

The first step to preventive interventions is identification of ***target groups***. Teens are the most vulnerable group of population when it comes to substance abuse. Hence, awareness programmes must be directed towards teens. These programmess usually use 'fear' to induce a negative attitude towards substance abuse in adolescents. However, it has been found that just appealing to teens is not enough. Teens who get involved in high risk behaviour usually selectively don't attend to such messages. Hence, there is a need to educate parents too. Very few parents are aware of the symptoms of substance abuse. Hence, they can't detect the high risk behaviours of their children. There is a need to educate them through messages sent via mass media.

The peer group has a significant role to play in influencing substance use behaviour. This is because, peer groups have great influence on an individual during adolescence. There is always the pressure to conform to group norms. ***Assertiveness training***, among other forms of training, helps the individual to resist group pressure.

Rehabilitation

Rehabilitation of substance abuse disorder follows the following steps:

1. Assessment of dependency
2. Intervention and counselling
3. Aftercare and relapse prevention

Assessment of dependency

Drug dependency has two broad dimensions – ***physical dependency*** and ***psychological dependency.*** With regular use of drugs, tolerance level of the body towards the particular drugs increases. Owing to this, the same amount of drugs that previously gave the 'kick' doesn't show desired effects. The abuser starts taking more amount to keep up the 'kick' (see the chapter on disorders). This leads to physical dependency. Such is the dependency that disuse of the drug leads to withdrawal symptoms.

Another form of dependency is psychological. What is the ability (or efficacy) of the abuser to resist the use of drugs? What coping style does he use if drug supply is stopped? What are the cognitions/beliefs behind the craving for drugs? The answer to these questions vary from individual to individual. Those with high psychological dependence on drugs believe that they can't live without drugs. They have low self-efficacy and an external locus of control.

The rehabilitation worker has to assess both physical and psychological dependency. This is because sometimes substance abuse is due to physical dependency; in other cases, due to psychological dependency. In still other cases, both dependency interact to produce complex forms of the disorder. The goal of rehabilitations is to counter both forms of dependency.

So, how do you assess extent of drug abuse? Biological testing is used to check whether drug has been consumed. In biological testing, the specific drug in a blood sample can be assessed. But, biological testing cannot assess (a) the duration of time since when drugs are being consumed, (b) the amount and frequency of drug consumption, (c) the means of drug consumption (smoke through nostrils, or directly injected to blood), and (d) the extent of dependence. Biological test is, hence useful as proof of drug abuse in courts, but of not much use in assessment of substantial abuse disorder.

Therefore, the primary method of assessment of substance abuse disorder is interview. The diagnostic interview is conducted with the substance abuser, as well as family members and close friends. In addition, information about the disorder is obtained from self-report and paper-and-pencil tests (Dodgen, 2004). The psychologist typically searches for the following information in a drug abuse assessment (Dodgen, 2004):

1. List of all drugs ever used.
2. Age of first use of these drugs.
3. How have each of these drugs been used, did the abuser smoke, drink, snort, or directly inject into the blood stream? (Note that the way a drug is taken into the body is important. When it comes to the effect of drug taken, snorting is more effective and faster than smoking; and injecting into blood is more effective than snorting. A drug abuser who has acquired tolerance due to regular use steadily moves from smoking to snorting and finally to direct injection into blood).
4. Age of peers, and amount of the drug used.
5. Amount of drugs used in a day typically.
6. List all negative consequences of using various drugs.

Intervention and counselling

The steps that rehabilitation of an individual suffering from substance abuse disorder goes through can be understood from the transtheoretical model. This model states that behavioural change proceeds through six steps (Prochaska and Narcross, 1994):

1. Precontemplation: No intention to make change.
2. Contemplation: Contemplating a behavioural change, but not actively doing it.
3. Preparation: Making small changes.

4. Action: Actively following new behavioural patterns to overcome the problem.
5. Maintenance: Sustaining the change over time.
6. Relapse and termination.

The model states that these steps don't follow a linear path; rather they follow a rehabilitation path as shown in the figure.

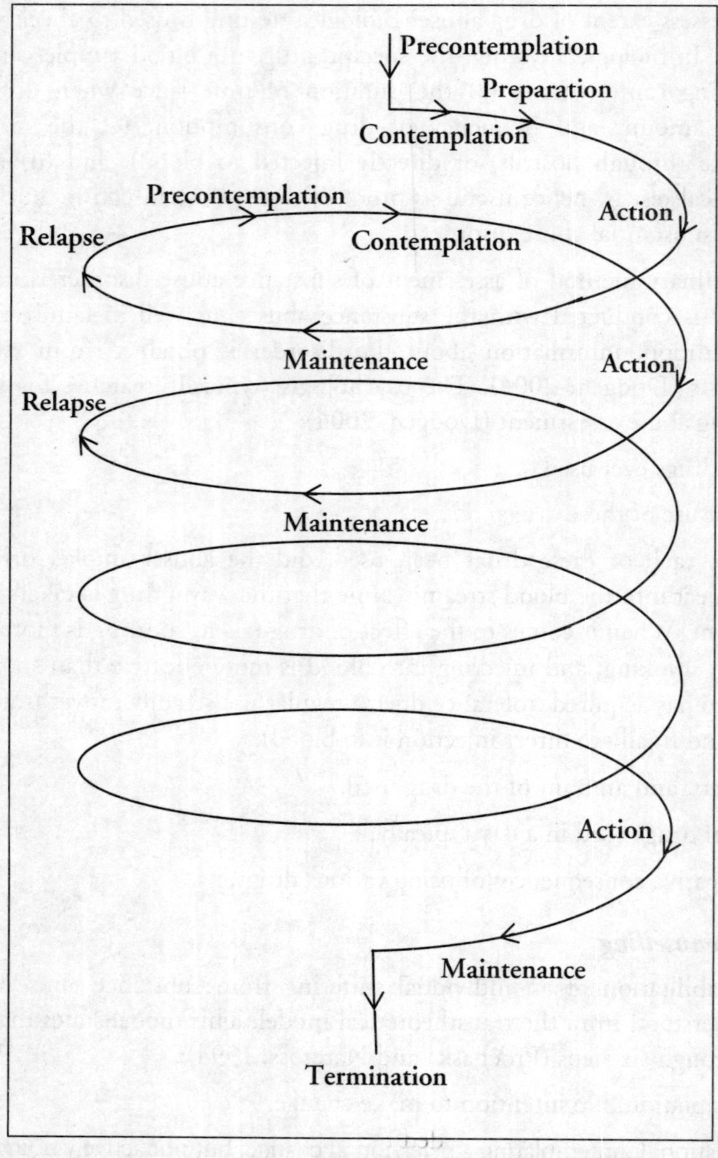

Fig. 3.2 : The transtheoretical model; Bas on Prochaska and Narcross (1994).

A variety of intervention strategies are used to reduce (or eliminate) the dependency on drugs – ranging from medical solutions to psychotherapies. These can be summarized as:

1. Pharmacotherapies
2. Disease model and 12-steps process
3. Client-centered therapy
4. Psychoanalytic therapy
5. Cognitive therapy
6. Motivational interviewing
7. Behaviourist therapies
8. Group therapy

Pharmacotherapy refers to the use of certain medicinal drugs to treat addiction. For example, methadone is a drug that gives effects similar to substance abuse drugs, but is not as harmful. Methadone can be used as a substitute to the drugs taken by the patient in a rehabilitation centre. This way the withdrawal symptoms could be avoided during treatment. However, pharmacotherapies only give temporary solutions, not permanent rehabilitation. They are effective in controlling withdrawal symptoms in the patients; hence can be used for temporary relief to the patient while a longer rehabilitation program is underway.

The disease model of addiction argues that addicted individuals are predisposed to drug addiction (due to genetic, biological, or trait factors). Hence, the individual is powerless on the face of her addiction. Naturally, the treatment considers the client as a 'patient'. A behavioural treatment strategy called 'Twelve Step Programs' is used where the addict is forced to renounce her former lifestyle. Though criticized by many psychologists, this method does show immediate results. Of course, relapse can be high if the addict is not monitored regularly.

Most popular and effective intervention programs today include counselling. One effective approach to counselling is the client-centered counselling, in which the therapist shows (a) unconditioned positive regard (b) empathy and (c) genuineness to the client to help her solve her own problems.

The psychoanalytic approach to addiction assumes that the main cause of addiction is unconscious need to entertain and to enact various kinds of homosexual and perverse fantasies, while at the same time fearing social rebuttal. Psychoanalysts argue that specific drugs facilitate specific fantasies. Drug use is a better substitute than masturbation to entertain homosexual and perverse fantasies. Though this basic assumption is proved false empirically, the psychoanalytic approach is still popular.

A cognitive model of addiction is forwarded by Aaron Beck in his book 'Cognitive Therapy of Substance Abuse'. This therapy is based on the assumption that there are certain core beliefs that the addict himself may not be aware of. For example, an addict may believe that he is useless, but is not consciously aware of his belief. The core beliefs trigger a system of addictive beliefs. Addictive beliefs are imagined benefits of drug use. For example, if your core belief is that you are useless, addictive beliefs like "drugs are fun", "drugs help me escape the world", "I am not accountable to anyone if I use drugs", etc. are triggered, while the individual is not consciously aware of the core beliefs, he is consciously aware of addictive beliefs. These addictive beliefs increase the craving for drugs. Cognitive therapists try to uncover underlying core beliefs and negative thoughts to solve the problem of substance abuse.

Motivational interviewing is a variation of client-centered therapy, whereby the therapist doesn't confront the client with the problem. Rather, the therapist leads the client to her own conclusion by asking questions that focus on discrepancies between the current state and the individual's ideal self-image. The mechanism is basically that of cognitive dissonance.

It is acknowledged by most psychologists that a supportive peer group helps better cope with withdrawal symptoms. Hence, logically, group therapy is an effective intervention. In group therapy, behaviours are modified through role playing, psychodrama, discussions, etc. Some behavioural techniques are quite effective in treating substance abuse disorder. A popular behavioural technique is aversion therapy in which the drug is paired with an aversive stimulus, such as electric shock. When the client is conditioned, her response (conditioned response, CR) to the drug is similar to that of her unpleasant response to the aversive stimuli. A problem with this therapy is that though successful in laboratory conditions, it doesn't guarantee behavioural change in real life. In other words, the response learnt in laboratory doesn't get transferred to real life situations. A client may reason that now that she is outside the institution, she won't get shock if she tries drugs!

Aftercare and relapse prevention

As studied in the transtheoretical model, there is a high danger of relapse after the client is released for reintegration into society. Whether the individual relapses or not depends on her coping skills. Martlett and Gordon (1985) have forwarded the relapse prevention model. This model is represented in the figure. According to this model, relapse happens in two stages. In a high risk situation, first lapse takes place (single occurrence of drug use) and then relapse (back to the situation before treatment). There are four psychological processes involved in lapse (Martlett and Gordon, 1985).

1. Self-efficacy
2. Outcome efficacy
3. Attribution of causality
4. Decision-making process

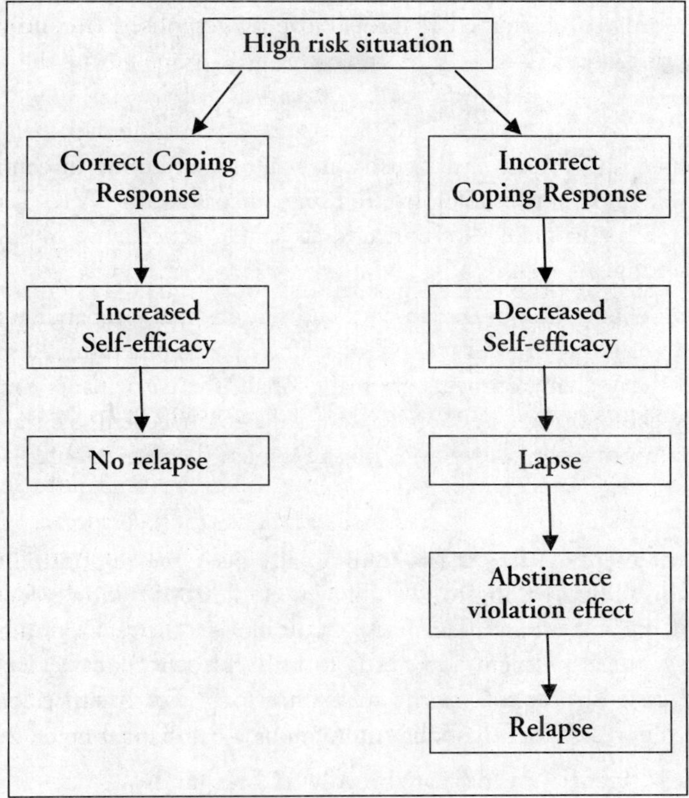

Fig. 3.3 : Relapse mechanism Adapted from Martlett and Gordon (1985)

Suppose I, as a rehabilitated addict, encounter a relapse-provoking situation (for instance, meeting a former addict peer). If I am offered drugs, my efficacy determines whether I can resist it. The outcome expectancy of drugs use also affects my decision. If I take the drug this one time, what rationale do I use to explain my lapse? If I use external attribution ("the peer forced me"), I am confident that this is only one occasion and won't be repeated. But, if I use internal attribution ("It is my fault! I can never quit!"), the chances of relapse increase.

The transition from a single lapse to relapse is explained in terms of abstinence violation effect. After one or two lapses, the individual gets negative thoughts, such as, "I couldn't abstain from using drugs! I can never recover! I can never recover! I cannot quit". This further reduces the self-efficacy to resist the use of drugs. With lowered self-efficacy and rationalisation that one can never be free from drug dependence, relapse becomes inevitable. Abstinence violation effect is but a ***self-fulfilling prophecy*** about one's inability to resist drugs. Every time the prophecy gets fulfilled (by lapses), the belief gets strengthened. Ultimately, the individual relapses.

In the task of rehabilitation, workers help the client deal with such relapse-provoking situations. The individual needs to be trained in proper coping responses. Secondly, regular follow-ups must monitor her situation.

Virtual reality in relapse prevention

How does one deal with relapse-provoking situations? One way is by training in competencies to cope with the situation. These days, psychologists are using Virtual Reality (VR) Technology to provide an environment wherein alcoholics and addicts can practice how to say 'no' to drugs/alcohol in a realistic setting.

Basically, the VR environments consist of certain cues and settings that a rehabilitated person might find challenging, such as a bar with imbibing patrons; a rave party; or a dimly lit room with drugs in a drawer. Provided the VR environments are real enough, the participants' cravings are intensified. So now, the psychologist can develop coping skills in the client by training and retraining. And the client can practice the coping skills till she can use them in real life.

Role of social agencies

In India, the management of drug addicts has traditionally been the responsibility of the family or the social group the addicts belong to (Tamhankar et al., 2005). However, there has been greater appreciation of the role of social agencies of late, due to the realization that drug addiction is a psycho-socio-medical problem and needs to be tackled holistically. In contrast, social agencies have played a significant role in the west since long. For instance, one of the successful social agencies in the west is the Alcoholic Anonymous. (Tamhankar et al., 2005).

The nature of work of social agencies in India are broadly of three kinds:

1. Research on extent of drug abuse in society and collecting epidemiological data
2. Prevention of drug abuse
3. Rehabilitation

Organizations, such as the UN Office on Drugs on Crime (UNODC) and Indian Council of Medical Research (ICMR) are involved in research on the extent and type of substance abuse disorders. Many reports of these agencies are available on the internet.

Then there are agencies (both NGOs and government sponsored agencies) that are involved in primary prevention of substance abuse. They seek to educate targeted groups and improve the self-efficacy of members of their target groups in resisting the temptation of substance abuse. Some agencies are involved in awareness generation about bad effects of drug abuse. Some NGOs even use street plays in innovative ways to sensitize people about the issue.

Still other agencies are involved in rehabilitation. For example, take the case of ARPAN. ARPAN stand for "Association of Recovering Peer Action Network"; the word means 'to present' or 'to offer in dedication' in Sanskrit. ARPAN works on the principle that for any recovering person, motivation and guidance are the two major pre-requisites. Hence, there is need for a peer group to motivate the patient to tolerate the withdrawal symptoms. Basically, drug abuse is the result of incorrect socialization in a deviant peer group. Hence, a solution to this is resocialization in a functional peer group.

A few social agencies have come up that seek to provide a therapeutic community to rehabilitating drug abusers. For example, Kripa Rehabilitation Centre (KRC) offers a non-discriminating supportive community living, helping people to introspect and bring about changes in their lifestyle. KRC's model of therapeutic intervention is based on Yoga and T'aichi (indigenous therapies of the East) and seeks to bring about lifestyle changes and in turn, resolution of substance abuse. (Tamhankar et al.m 2005). The impact of KRC's holistic therapeutic intervention programme for de-addiction has been empirically studied. Aparna Tamhankar and her co-workers (2005) studied the effect of KRC's de-addiction programme on 40 employees of Bharat Petroleum Corporation Limited (BPCL). Of the 40 clients, 18 recovered completely from addiction and 80% remained sober for three months.

Rehabilitation of Criminals

There are many types of criminal behaviours. In most cases of crime, criminal behaviour is propelled by a host of social, economic, political and emotional factors. Most criminals are not born criminals, but have been led into crime due to circumstances.

Most of the convicts who are jailed are first-timers, i.e., they have shown criminal behaviour for the first time and have been jailed for that. "They commit anti-social acts due to negative attitude towards life, humanity and country and that too, in a fit of some negative emotions, like anger, fear, hatred, passion, lust, greed and jealousy. The criminal act… can also be attributed to their inability to tolerate injustice meted out to them or their near and dear ones; frustration of some important psychobiological needs; wrong attitudes towards life and others; wrong upbringing and treatment or unfortunate circumstances of their life. Whatever be the genesis or dynamics of their criminal acts, they are always redeemable. If these youngsters are helped to control and regulate their emotional reactions, rectify their attitudes towards others and their psychophysical needs are taken care of, they can always be mended and brought back into the main stream" (Jain, 2004).

The philosophy behind rehabilitation of criminals is to bring them back into the main stream. Not every criminal is redeemable, but the majority of them are. Most of the criminals who have committed grave offence have done it in a fit of anger, or due to a wrong decision. Indeed, majority of the criminals are first-timers. They are convicted for one time crimes. But, the problem is that once convicted, they become social outcasts. All life, they live with the social stigma of being convicted criminals. Hence, there is the need for rehabilitation.

Problems of convicts

Convicts are the persons who have shown criminal behaviour and have been punished by a court of law with imprisonment of certain duration. There are many types of convicts – rapists, thieves, gang lords, contract killers, murderers, etc. Most of the criminals are criminals by circumstance. Suppose you find that your wife is cheating on you and in a fit of anger, you kill her. You become a murderer, but you aren't a murderer past redemption. You can still live a life of dignity and meaning, in spite of the crime that you have committed.

These are certain problems faced by convicts in living a life of dignity and meaning. Some of these are:

1. After a long period in the jail, when convicts are released, they find it hard to reintegrate to society. One major problem is of finding a job. After staying for five years in a jail, for example, an individual doesn't find his skills enough to get a job. If he has two years of experience in an industry, he doesn't fit the profile of any job. He doesn't have the experience to get a job equivalent to his age. Neither does he get a job equivalent to two years of experience, because younger people are preferred for the job. Secondly, many things must have changed during the period he was in jail. For example, technological changes are fast. A person in jail is not abreast of these changes.

2. There is also the problem of reintegration with community when released. Usually people view an ex-convict with suspicion. There are widespread prejudices and social stigma. It is not even sure if the returned prisoner's family will accept him. A few convicts stay in jail for long periods (10-14 years) for one-time grave offences. 10-14 years is a huge time and society, social norms and values change in that period. These convicts find it very tough to adjust.

3. The jail is like a total institution. It cuts you off from society altogether and new social norms (of the jail convicts community) determine your behaviour. If you stay in such a society for 8-10 years, cut off from mainstream society, it is really tough to adjust to the mainstream society when released from jail.

4. There are certain grave problems faced by convicts when in the jail itself. One major challenge is to find meaning in life. The social stigma attached to crimes is so high that one does not have much hope of leading a life of dignity. This instills a fatalistic attitude and learned helplessness in them. The convicts have very low expectancy from the rest of their life. As a result, they are demotivated from taking any initiative that may help them realize their potential, thereby increasing their subjective well-being.

5. There are many environmental stressors that a convict has to deal with. They have non-existent personal space. Most Indian jails are crowded and various psychological impacts of crowding are relevant in the case of Indian jails. The convicts have a restricted sex life. Owing to this, many turn to homosexuality. Often, newly convicted adolescents are subjected to sexual harassment by senior homosexual convicts. This increases the risk of HIV/AIDS among convicts.

The social life in Indian jail is not conducive to healthy development of the individual. Since many criminals with diverse background and diverse personalities are put together, clash and violent acts are common. Frustration over all the above factors leads to greater aggression. Recreational facilities are limited and are provided to those who have better understanding with the jail staff.

Hence, we can easily see that the stressors in jails are so many and so intense that they can overwhelm the individual convict. The convict faces problems, like depression, anxiety, anger, delusions, etc. Many convicts feel guilty about their acts and suffer from trauma, related to the act of violence.

Interventions

The interventions to rehabilitate criminals, made in the jail setting, are two-fold: one, to help them cope with environmental stressors, help them develop their personality and help them to explore meaningful goals. Two, to help them develop skills that would lead to smooth transition from jail to society. Rehabilitation is an attempt to train and refrain the convicts till they attain maximum functional ability. Both forms of interventions are important in contributing to the goals of rehabilitation.

Various skills are imparted to convicts when they are in jail, so that they find themselves more potent when they leave the jail to join society again. For example, many convicts study through distance education mode and even get degrees. IGNOU has its study centers inside some major central jails of India (It has a study centre in Tihar Jail). Jail authorities try to assess the skills of various convicts and give them suitable employment within the jail. There are many such measures being undertaken in jails.

The role of psychologists in intervention is most profound in attempts to change the convicts' attitude, personality, coping skills and motivational pattern. We have already seen how stressful jail life is. ***Guilt feeling, tensions over family relations, anxiety, aggression, frustration over non-existent sexual life, homosexual negative thoughts, depression, etc.*** are recurring problem that obstruct the rehabilitation of criminals. To tackle with these problems, interventions based on cognitive behavioural therapy have been found to be effective.

In the Indian setting, meditation-based approaches have been hugely successful in dealing with these problems. A most successful intervention programme is that of Vipassana Meditation in Tihar Jail under Kiran Bedi's guidance (she was then the police commissioner of Tihar jail). Namita Ranganathan and her colleagues (2008) at Delhi University have observed that Vipassana helps prison inmates to attain peace of mind, deal with their emotions related to the crime that they have committed and reconstruct their identities. From their study of Vipassana camps in Tihar Jail, they concluded that Vipassana meditation has a number of psychological benefits. This includes:

- Better emotional control
- Better anger management
- Developing a sense of hope for the future
- Confront feelings of remorse and guilt
- Deal more positively with life behind the prison walls.

An interesting trend observed by Ranganathan and Colleagues is that the meditation programme had more committed following in the age group of 20-30 years, particularly by those who had been implicated for serious crimes like rape, murder and dowry-killing. Another study on impact of Vipassana on jail inmates has shown that there is considerable reduction in neurotic predisposition and feelings of hostility and an enhancement in the sense of hope and will-being following Vipassana (Chandramani, Dhar and Verma, 1998).

Other forms of meditation like, transcendental meditation have also been proved to be effective in reforming and ultimately rehabilitating prison inmates. Bunk (1979) has found positive effects of 'Hatha Yoga' and mantra mediation on the psychological health and behaviour of incarcerated men. Preksha meditation, based on Buddhist philosophy, has also been found to give effective solutions for problems faced by jail inmates. In one study, Dr. Swatantra Jain (2004) of Kurukshetra University showed that when Preksha meditation was conducted on 28 adolescent convicts of Borstal Jail (in Hisar, Haryana) for 15 days, the inmates differed on scores of attitudes, values, and personality factors between pre-test and post-test.

Role of social agencies

Social agencies have made their presence felt in recent years in the field of rehabilitation of people with criminal behaviour. For example, SRIJAN is a sister organization of the Art of Living foundation spear-headed by Sri Sri Ravi Shankar himself. SRIJAN tries to solve various problems of jail inmates and the problems of rehabilitation into mainstream society, when the inmate is released from jail.

The India Vision Foundation was started when Dr.Kiran Bedi received the Ramon Magsaysay award. Dr. Bedi, the first lady IPS officer, is also known for converting Tihar Jail into a therapeutic jail. She had initiated many rehabilitation programmes and India Vision Foundation (IVF) seeks to further these programmes.

Rehabilitation of Victims of HIV/AIDS

AIDS stand for Acquired Immune Deficiency Syndrome. It is caused by a virus called Human Immunodeficiency Virus (HIV) that attacks the immune system, specifically the T-cells that are crucial for fighting diseases. The disease spreads through transmission of bodily fluid, like blood, serum, etc. from one individual to another. The prime means of spread of HIV virus is by sexual contact and use of infected syringes. Another means of spread of HIV virus is that of transmission of bodily fluid of a pregnant woman into her fetus, thus infecting the baby in it. There is no cure for AIDS. Till date, the most efficient treatment is Anti-Retroviral Therapy (ART). ART helps to slow down the progress of the disease, but can't cure the individual of the infection. Hence, the primary concern of psychologists in the case of AIDS is prevention. The proverb 'Prevention is better than cure' is most relevant in the case of AIDS.

In this section, we will study various strategies for prevention of HIV/AIDS and once the disease is communicated to an individual, problems faced by victims of AIDS and psychological rehabilitation to solve these problems.

Prevention

In the absence of any cure, the only means of controlling the AIDS epidemic is by changing high-risk behaviours that transmit the virus. Hence, the challenge of AIDS is more of a psychological problem than a medical one. High-risk behaviours include having sex with multiple partners; men having sex with men without using condoms; not practicing safe sex when having sex with more than one partner; using infected syringe; sharing of syringes when injecting drugs into the blood.

Perhaps the most risky behaviour is unsafe sexual behaviour. Two concerns in this regards are:

1. The risk of AIDS can be reduced substantially by the use of condoms, but people seem to be reluctant to use them.
2. Many people indulge in sexual behaviour with multiple partners. In a study in USA (Reinisch et al., 1988), it was found that 37% of husbands and 29% wives had at least one additional sexual partner besides their spouse/partner. Approximately, one-third men had sex with a prostitute.

Prevention programmes target the high-risk groups, as well as provide information to general population. These programmes are mostly of the following types:

1. Education programmes
2. HIV/AIDS awareness programmes
3. Community-based intervention
4. Harm reduction programmes targeted towards drug addicts

1. *AIDS education programmes*

Schools are an ideal venue to promote healthy behaviour because they consist of young people who could be prevented from picking risky habits. School-based interventions are done through sex education in general and education regarding AIDS in particular. AIDS specific educational programmes are based on various theoretical models. For example, the cognitive models emphasize the role of attitudes, beliefs and cognitions in preventing high-risk behaviours. The Social Learning Theory, on the other hand, stresses on modeling and increasing perceived self-efficacy. Flora and Thoresen (1988) have a model AIDS prevention curricula, based on the Social Learning Theory (Kool and Agrawal 2006).

The table below shows some educational approaches their curriculum is composed of:

Table 3.1 : A Comparison to some Educational Approaches for Primary and Secondary Preventions of AIDS among Adolescents†

Theoretical approach	Educational approach	Primary approach	Secondary approach
Cognitive/ emotional	Providing knowledge Self talk	Regarding avoidance of certain behaviours	Regarding safer sex practice

† Source: Flora & Thoresen, 1988.

Theoretical approach	Educational approach	Primary approach	Secondary approach
	Self efficacy	"I don't have to have sex" Perceive ability to resist sex	"It is OK to use condoms" Perceived ability to use condoms
Behavioural	Behavioural outcomes Social Skills	"Avoiding too much alcohol increases my control over sex behaviour" Resisting peer pressure for sex	"I can talk to my partner to use condoms" Negotiating with partner for safe sex
Societal	Socia support systems Incentives Vicarious	Peer encouragement for avoiding sex Getting social rewards for avoiding sex Training older peers to demonstrate avoidance of sex	Peer encouragement for safer sex Increased intimacy permitted if partner agrees to limit sex Modelling of safer sex practices

Though it is easy and more effective to apply AIDS education programmes in the school setting, these education programmes can be introduced in other settings, like adult education organizational training, AIDS awareness camps, etc.

2. *AIDS awareness programmes*

Many risky behaviours are the results of lack of awareness about AIDS. Long ago, I had read in a news article that sex workers in some part of India believed that AIDS can be cured by bathing in Coca Cola. Though you may wonder where the connection for such weird notions arise, the truth is that the awareness level about AIDS is very low. Owing to this, many people still indulge in unsafe sex.

Due to this very reason, the National AIDS Control Organization (NACO) invests heavily in creating awareness about AIDS. The mass media – TV, radio and newspapers, is the main medium of creating awareness regarding AIDS. The question is how effective is mass media based awareness in preventing risky behaviour? In a landmark study over five years in Tanzania, Vaughan and his colleagues (2000) have demonstrated the effect of awareness programmes aired on Radio Tanzania on attitudes and behaviours of people. This study is discussed in greater detail in the chapter on mass media.

Besides mass media, other mediums, like street plays, community event, fairs, etc. can be used to generate awareness about AIDS.

3. *Community-based intervention*

Community-based interventions are made to reduce risky behaviours in a variety of populations, such as, adolescents, homosexuals and urban women. Many intervention programmes have been developed with varying degree of success. Here, we will be discussing two programmes designed by Kelly and his colleagues, that have been found to be quite successful approaches.

The first is the behavioural skills approach developed to target small groups at high risk, like gay people, sex workers, etc. The intervention aims at developing some skills in the target population, so that they can resist the temptation of high-risk behaviour. These skills are developed through:

1. Risk education and sensitization (for e.g., making them recognize the fact that they are vulnerable to HIV).
2. Self-management training (for e.g., keeping condoms in pocket, reducing alcohol consumption and drug use before sexual behaviour. Drug use before sexual behaviour is associated with unsafe sex).
3. Sexual assertion training (for e.g., being assertive about safe sex when negotiating with partner, learning to say 'no' to unsafe sex).
4. Developing social support networks.

Another influential approach developed by Kelly is the Popular Opinion Leader (POL) approach. This intervention approach is based on the philosophy that if a new behaviour is adopted by opinion leaders, they subsequently influence others to adopt the behaviour. For example, visualize your village or your locality. There are certain 'leaders' who are eloquent and have an opinion on every issue. They are often talkative and act as if they know all, from political issues to scientific issues. Other people of the locality attentively listen to these 'opinion leaders' and adopt their behaviour. The POL approach (also called Social Diffusion Model) influences these opinion leaders to change their risky behaviours. Behavioural changes in them spread to other members by social diffusion, i.e., by the influence of opinion leaders, other members of the community also change their behaviours.

In one study, Kelly et al. (1991) conducted a survey among gay men in a city. After this, they introduced POL intervention on 43 popular opinion leaders in gay bars. The opinion leaders were trained in HIV-related risk education and skills to resist risky behaviours. They were asked to endorse behavioural changes to their peers. A post-intervention survey was conducted among gay men in the city on comparing the post-intervention and pre-intervention survey, Kelly and colleagues found that the proportion of men engaged in unprotected and intercourse decreases from 37% to 27%. This demonstrates the efficacy of POL approach to intervention.

4. *Harm reduction programmes*

Harm reduction is a prevention strategy which does not seek to reduce risky behaviour; it rather seeks to reduce the harmful effects of the risky behaviour once the individual shows the same.behaviour For example, HIV/AIDS is transmitted when two people share infected syringes. Many drug addicts share syringes to inject drugs to the blood stream. This is a risky behaviour, and other prevention strategies try to stop this behaviour. But, what if drug addicts continue to show the risky behaviour? You try to reduce the harm. Needle and syringe programmes are aimed at providing new syringes to drug addicts in return for already used syringes. This reduces the harm caused by the risky behaviour (injecting drugs into blood).

Rehabilitation

Till now, we have discussed the efforts to prevent HIV infection. But, what if one gets AIDS? The belief of rehabilitation workers is that there is life after AIDS also. Owing to recent developments in ART, AIDS patients can now live for years after getting AIDS. Hence, there is a huge scope for leading a normal life after AIDS. Yet, it is not that easy. The AIDS victims face some psychological and social problems that prevent them from leading normal lives. Rehabilitation aims at resolving these psychological, social and psychosocial issues. Before looking into rehabilitation measures, let us first discuss these issues.

AIDS-related stressors

AIDS is associated with many stressors that lead to psychological reactions. First, there is the issue of facing the truth. It has been found that when an individual receives a HIV positive test report, she experiences a mixture or shock, denial, guilt and fear, as well as dilemma over whether to disclose the illness to others (Ostrow et al., 1989). This acute psychological response is followed by delayed responses, such as emotional distress, depression and anxiety.

Since there is no cure to the disease, the victim experiences a loss of control. Due to a lack of control over the disease, the victim many experience learned helplessness and powerlessness. Due to learned helplessness, the individual tends not to take medical help or anti-retroviral therapy (ART). This further aggravates the problem of AIDS.

Mandy victims demonstrate a fatalistic attitude. People with fatalistic attitude, we know, have high need for dependence and don't take any initiative. Due to this, the victims lose the motivation to fight AIDS and lead a normal life.

AIDS is also related to many cognitive reactions. Due to the feeling of guild, the victim may develop many negative thoughts and beliefs. These negative thoughts and beliefs, in turn, affect their self-concept. The victims develop inferiority complex and a belief that nothing can happen from now onwards. Indeed, learned helplessness, dependence, etc. are due to false beliefs about sexuality and intimacy. Those tested HIV-positive, feel guilty over their previous sexual behaviour. They start maintaining psychological and social distance from their family members. Due to this, they don't get the much needed social support and caretaking. Secondly, they lose intimate relations at the time of psychological upheaval.

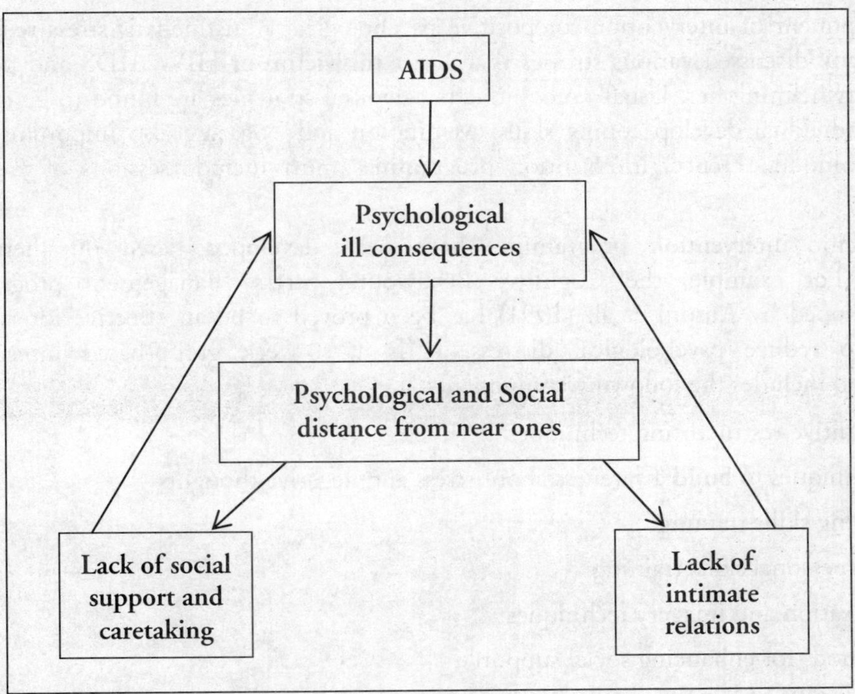

Fig. 3.4 : Dynamics of guilt feeling, relations with closed ones and psychological consequences of AIDS victims.

Psychosocial consequences

Social stigma refers to prejudices against certain abnormalities. HIV/AIDS is associated with social stigmas. These stigmas vary from society to society and affect the individual victims in multiple ways. For example, in many parts of India, it is believed that AIDS spreads through touch and contaminated water. Due to these prejudiced beliefs, AIDS victims face social exclusion. In Ghana, the AIDS stigma is so strong that women are too secretive about it and don't disclose their HIV positive status to anyone. Because they hide this truth, they don't get access to treatment, and to financial and emotional help (Mill, 003; of Kool and Agrawal, 2006).

Social stigma itself is a psychological stressor. A major coping strategy to deal with psychological problems is to talk about it to others and receive social support. But owing to the stigma, victims don't get social support. Non-disclosure of information itself leads to anxiety, lowered self-concept and continued fear of getting 'busted' (as if the victim is a criminal!) by society.

Interventions for rehabilitation

A major component of intervention for positive psychological adjustment is stress reduction. We have already discussed various stresses that affect the victim of HIV/ AIDS and pose the danger of overwhelming her. Usually, cognitive behavioural strategies are found to be effective to help the individual develop coping skills. Meditation and Yoga are also important stress-reduction techniques. Hence, intervention programmes must include sessions of yoga and meditation.

Many specific intervention programmes have been developed based on therapeutic philosophies. For example, the Cognitive Behavioural Stress Management programmes (CBSM) developed by Antoni et al. (1991) has been proved to be an effective intervention programme to reduce psychological distress. It is a 10-week group-based intervention programme and includes the following components:

- Cognitive restructuring techniques
- Techniques to build awareness about stress and negative thoughts
- Coping skills training
- Interpersonal skills training
- Relaxation and imagery techniques
- Methods for enhancing social support

Please note that CBSM is a holistic programme that also addresses cognitive problems of AIDS victims. AIDS victims often have negative thoughts, false beliefs, fatalistic attitude and suffer from learned helplessness. Cognitive restructuring helps the victim to develop a meaning in life and substitute false beliefs with realistic beliefs about a future in spite of AIDS.

Removing AIDS stigma

In order to rehabilitate an AIDS victim, we need to provide her with a job and status in the community. Unfortunately, AIDS victims often lose their jobs and lose their membership of the community (that is, face social exclusion) due to social stigma. Hence, there is a need to remove stigma attached to AIDS. So, how do we remove that stigma? It is a problem of changing people's attitude and behaviours. One way to change the attitudes and beliefs is through popular opinion leaders (POL) on the lines of POL intervention approach discussed earlier. But, its efficacy is doubtful, given the stigma is due to people's fear of contacting the disease. Hence, they would prefer to be on the safe side, rather than change their attitude.

Stigma is a prejudice. Prejudice is an attitude. Prejudice leads to discrimination. AIDS as a social stigma leads to discrimination. To reduce stigma, awareness programmes should be conducted. Awareness about the exact nature of AIDS should be created through mass media. Theatre and roadside drama are also mediums to propagate messages regarding AIDS. A cheap and effective method used in many developing countries, like India, is the use of community theatre specialists (Kool and Agrawal, 2006). From a survey of some researches, Kool and

Agrawal (2006) conclude that awareness programmes are not always beneficial. The benefits of awareness programmes are more when the person can get the information in the privacy of his home, rather than in public places. Hence, internet may be a more effective medium of AIDS awareness programmes.

Role of Social Agencies

The nodal social agency sponsored by the central Government of India to fight the AIDS epidemic is National AIDS Control Organization (NACO). 'NACO envisioned an India where every person living with HIV has access to quality care and is treated with dignity. Effective prevention, care and support for HIV/AIDS is possible in an environment where human rights are respected and where, those infected or affected by HIV/AIDS, live a life without stigma and discrimination' (NACO, 2008).

NACO organizes its own awareness programs and prevention programs and provides facilities for ART and rehabilitation of AIDS victims. At the same time, it cooperates with many NGOs that work in the field of AIDS prevention and rehabilitation. Among the many NGOs working in this field, a few have been discussed here.

The AIDS Awareness Group (AAG) creates awareness about HIV/AIDS/Sexually Transmitted Infections in the jails, red light areas, slums, schools, colleges, etc. AAG has introduced awareness sessions and street plays inside Tihar Jail (note that jail inmates are especially vulnerable to AIDS. Due to long duration of sexual deprivation, many engage in MSM (men having sex with men). Such homosexual behaviour is not socially recognized. Nor are the prison inmates encouraged to use condoms). Another social agency called Action, Service and Hope for Aids (ASHA) was established in 1998 in Bangalore. It provides the following services:

1. The AIDS helpline and telephone counselling service
2. Adolescent sexual health education in India
3. Prevention of mother to child transmission of HIV infection
4. Awareness of urban slums
5. Capacity-building

Further details of these programmes are put up on the website *http://www.ashaf.org/*.

J-volunteers is an unique program, most of whose volunteers are from the IT industry. They are trained in AIDS awareness, after which they reach out to people to spread the awareness through power point presentations, street plays and personal testimonies from HIV positive people.

3.4 Aging and Rehabilitation

A human being faces developmental challenges in every stage of life span. There are challenges that the individual has to face in childhood, in adolescence and in adulthood. No wonder then, that there are challenges to face in old age also. However, the challenges faced in old age are quite different from that of other stages. Many of the challenges in old age are quite disabling in nature and the individual may not be capable of recovering from these all by herself. There are social disabilities, physical disabilities and mental disabilities that accompany the process of aging.

Not every individual needs help in old age. A person who has maintained a healthy lifestyle and exercises regularly, for example, doesn't have many physical problems. Yet, some generalizations can be made regarding problems of aging, as under:

1. *Physical disabilities:* The deterioration of physical health starts from the age of 40 years. In the middle ages, muscles become weaker and less flexible. By the age of 70, bones become more brittle and hardened ligaments make muscular movements slower.

2. *Sexual decline:* There is a decline in both fertility and sexual drive in the old age. in the case of women, fertility starts decreasing right from the middle ages till menopause happens at 50. Male fertility often persists for the life time, but it also starts declining from middle ages. There are many psychological correlates of reduced sexuality. Reduced sexuality causes alarm and anxiety in many people. For some people, it is associated with lowered self-esteem.

3. *Stressful events:* Many people in the old age have experienced high stress events, like the death of loved ones. The death of a spouse is especially worrying, given that husband and wife are said to form a close bond in old age. The bond of spouses also includes companionship. Since most old people are retired, they find it tough to get companions from younger age groups. Death of a spouse means no companion for most part of the day.

4. *Cognitive decline:* Like other body parts, the brain also declines in late adulthood. The aging brain reduces tissues at a very fast rate. In a longitudinal study, Magnetic Resonance Imaging (MRI) was used to measure the loss of brain tissues among participants who were 59 to 85 years old. (Resnick et al, 2003). The study analyzed the brain of participants over a 4-year period. The researchers found that over the 4-year period, the participants lost tissues at the average rate of 5.4% per year. It was also found that the rate of loss of tissues was lower for healthy participants.

   Old age is also marked by a significant reduction in memory abilities. Perceptual speed, measured by reaction time in the laboratory, declines in old age. Owing to this, the recall and recognition ability decreases. In the case of intelligence, it has been observed that while fluid intelligence decreases, crystallized intelligence doesn't change significantly.

5. *Cognitive impairment:* Disorders of the brain, such as dementia, occur with greater frequency in the old age. Dementia refers to abnormal brain deterioration, accompanied by loss of cognitive abilities. Dementia interferes with daily functioning

in the individual. Senile dementia refers to dementia that begins after the age of 65. Dementia occurs mostly because of Alzheimer's disease, but can occur due to other diseases, like Parkinson's disease, Huntington's disease, etc.

Dementia leads to problems like:

- Impaired memory
- Language problems
- Loss of ability to perform familiar tasks
- Poor judgment
- Confusion and distress

Over half of the people diagnosed with senile dementia show a combination of depression, anxiety, disordered thinking and paranoid reactions that resemble symptoms of Schizophrenia (Passer and Smith, 2007, p.432).

6. *Social disability:* People usually retire at the age of 60-65 years. Even if they do not retire, they don't have the ability to perform up to the mark in jobs. Besides, it is not advisable to work in old age. No wonder old people don't have any source of income. A few people save money from an earlier age and hence have financial security. But, most of the old people are financially dependent on their children and significant others. They are also dependent on others for caretaking. The caregiver is usually a family member. Hence, old people are excessively dependent on social support.

   But, what if social support is not available? Many people find it stressful to take care of elderly parents. Still others consider the elderly as a burden. An alternative is institutional living in old age homes. Many studies, like that of Anantharaman (1980) and K.Agarwal and Rastogi (1979), have found that institutionalized subjects perceive more health problems, are less active and have higher alienation scores than those living with their families. This may be because of the deplorable conditions of our old age homes. These old age homes are not well-maintained, don't have adequate recreational facilities and their caretaking staff to old people ratio is very low.

Rehabilitation

Above, we have discussed some problems that an aging individual may face. These problems are stressful and have the potential to overwhelm the individual. Hence, there is a need to rehabilitate the aged. Rehabilitation includes assessment and interventions.

Assessment

When an elderly person shows unusual behaviour or can't perform her daily tasks properly, she is referred to a psychologist. Before making therapeutic interventions, the psychologist needs to know the nature of problems faced by the aged individual. The prevalence of depression in older adults who are chronically ill or physically disabled has been reported to be as high as 59% (Knight and David, 2004). Symptoms of depression must be carefully observed and an assessment of the nature of depression should be made. This is especially important because physicians often can't detect depression in old people.

Secondly, the psychologist also need to know about environmental factors that make the life of the aged more stressful. Has she suffered the death of a near one? What is her relation with her caregivers? What are her interactions with her family members?

Finally, insomnia is a major reason for impaired daily functioning. Sleep disturbances are frequent in older adults. Hence, the psychologist should also check if the older adult suffers from chronic sleep difficulties (Knight and David, 2004).

Interventions

An intervention program has to include a variety of therapies, given that older adults suffer from many different psychological impairments. From an evaluation of literature on psychological treatments, Gatz and colleagues (1998) recommend that efficacious interventions for older adults should include Cognitive Behavioural Therapy (CBT) for sleep disorders and cognitive treatments for clinical depression. CBT has also been found to have good effects on older adults with generalized anxiety disorder (Wetherell et al., 2003). Behavioural interventions and environmental modifications (based on conditioning principles) are quite effective to rehabilitate persons with dementia (Gatz et al., 1998). Cognitive training should also be imparted as it slows down cognitive decline.

Some alternatives to CBT exist. For example, brief psychodynamic psychotherapy (PDP) has as effective results as CBT in treating depression in late life.

Family-based interventions

Some of the most salient issues in psychotherapy with older adults appear within the family context. Older adults often depend on family members for both emotional and instrumental support. In the event that these family relationships become strained, disruption of support can ensure, resulting in distress for older results. Exploration of older adults' family histories and interpersonal techniques can often inform the therapeutic process in such cases. (Knight and David, 2004).

The focus of intervention, here, is on contextual factors that may cause stress to the older adult. An effective intervention in his case is family therapy. Family therapy for older adults is directed towards caregivers and family members. We must understand that caregiving for older adults is also stressful, and caregivers may at times face distress. Hence, psychoeducation and psychotherapy for caregivers is generally effective in reducing burden and depression, increasing subjective well-being and increasing caregiver mastery (Sorensen et al., cf. Knight and David, 2004).

Old Age Homes

Another intervention strategy to change contextual factors is to convert old age homes into therapeutic communities. Old age homes in India today are facing many problems- they are over-crowded, there are not sufficient recreational facilities, caregiving staff strength is low, etc.

Such an environment affects the subjective well-being of residents of such old age homes. The challenge here is to convert the old age home into a therapeutic community, where older adults get rich stimulation and some interesting work to keep them busy. Here, the role of rehabilitation worker is important, but more important is government policy and the motivation of policymakers, to help older adults lead a life of health and happiness.

3.5 Juvenile Delinquency

Legally speaking, discrimination is made between criminal behaviour in adults and minors. Criminal behaviour shown by minors is called juvenile delinquency. The discrimination is made on the basis of the rationale that juveniles are not competent enough to stand trial. They have lower maturity and decision- making skills. Hence, the treatment given to them is rehabilitation, not conviction.

We all know that no one is a born criminal. Most criminals are victims of circumstances. In the case of adults, punishment is necessary because criminal behaviour is the result of a conscious and mature decision. But, children are unable to take such decisions. Further, it is easier to mend the ways of juvenile delinquents than adult delinquents. Hence, there is the need for rehabilitation.

Causal factors in juvenile delinquency

Many causal factors have been identified, that cause juveniles to commit delinquent acts. Many theoretical traditions also exist to explain delinquent behaviour in children. It may be stated that none of the theories can explain all incidences of juvenile delinquency. Indeed, most acts of delinquency involved a multiplicity of factors. Let us discuss some dominant causal factors:

1. *Predisposition:*

   Some of the earlier theories on juvenile delinquency considered it as the result of predispositions, biological or genetic factor, or personality traits that predispose the individual to commit crime. Since it is a predisposition, these individuals show criminal behaviour even in childhood. These theories have largely been discredited today. Some correlation between mental disabilities and criminal behaviour in children have been found, but this is neither a cause in most cases of juvenile delinquency (JD), nor a dominant cause.

2. *Family factors:*

   Most scholars are unanimous about one dominant causal factor in juvenile delinquency, that is, socialization. Two primary mediums of socialization are family and peer group; and both are involved in causing a juvenile to go delinquent.

   Family provides the context that motivates a juvenile to show delinquent behaviour. According to the theory of parent-child relationship, how a child's psyche develops depends on the parents' parenting style. Many studies have given evidence that rejecting attitudes of parents, broken home, lack of cohesion between parents, etc. are responsible for unsatisfactory parent-child relationship and increase the vulnerability of delinquent acts.

3. *Delinquent peer groups:*

   Peer groups always have immense influence in the decisions that an adolescent makes. When an individual is rejected by parents, she feels insecure in the family as a small group. As a result, her attachments to the peer group increases; with increased attachment, influence of the peer group is also high. Many delinquent acts of children, like drug abuse, pick pocketing, alcoholism, etc., are the result of being influenced by a delinquent peer group.

4. *Socio-economics status:*

   An unusually high proportion of juvenile delinquents arise from lower socio-economic status (SES) background. Many psychological reasons interact to create conditions of delinquency in lower SES groups. One reason is that children and adolescents in lower SES groups have higher frustration because of conditions of disadvantage and deprivation. Greater frustration leads to greater aggression and hence, delinquent behaviour. A.K.Tandon and his colleagues (Tandon, Bajpai, Tandon and Shukla, 1978) compared aggressive and non-aggressive delinquent groups in one study. It was found that aggressive delinquents came from low SES families, experienced parental deprivation and showed greater hostility than the non-aggressive group. This study validates frustration-aggression as a causal factor.

   Another factor linking low SES to juvenile delinquency is the delinquent sub-culture. In low SES groups, the cultural values and norms are not the same as the mainstream culture. Rather, these groups develop their own norms and values. Hence, sub-cultures develop. Many sub-cultures develop in slums of various cities. In many sub-cultures, crime and violence are justified, sometimes even glorified. A person who commits a big criminal act is appreciated and made the hero. If you were a member of such delinquent sub-culture, you would be motivated to commit criminal acts, not for material benefits, but to get praise and appreciation in the group. In one study, K.S. Shukla (1977) had observed that a large number of adolescent JDs in his study were slum dwellers. Many came from families with low parental income and impersonal interpersonal relations among family members. These adolescents felt a loss of status in mainstream society and compensated it by achieving a status in delinquent sub-cultures.

   A third factor linking low SES groups to JD is stress. Children from low SES groups have intense stressors- deprivation, hunger, environmental stressors, crowding, health stressors, etc. Some children use delinquency as a coping strategy to cope with these stressors. According to the theory of escapade, the many stressors in the life of a child from deprived groups lead to intense anxiety. Some life situations become emotionally intolerable. To escape from such anxiety, they resort to delinquent behaviour. This theory partly explains the behaviour of children who show compulsive delinquent behaviour. Some children steal because it is a compulsive impulse in them. This compulsive behaviour gets reinforced by the fact that it reduces anxiety.

A fourth factor may be that the parents of low SES group children show different behaviour from the parents of high SES group children. Mukherjee (1979) studied parental reaction to delinquent acts in three groups. Group I and II belonged to families in a slum area, while Group III was from a posh residential area. JDs of all three groups had been apprehended by police for indulging in illegal acts. Mukherjee found that group I delinquents were largely left to fend for themselves, while Group II delinquents threw their children out of homes (if the crime was serious). In Group III, parents made all efforts possible to release their children. An interesting conclusion from this study is that various causal factors, like parenting style, peer group and SES don't act independently, but are interwoven in a complex manner. Low SES affects not only juvenile behaviour, but also parental behaviour. Also, one has greater contact with deviant peer groups in low SES localities.

5. *Psychoanalytic perspectives:*

   Psychoanalysts believe that psychic energy is released from the id. This energy is released from the body by channeling it through various activities. For example, the psychic energy corresponding to sexual instincts (called libido) is channeled and dissipated when an adolescent masturbates. But, when an adolescent has been discouraged from masturbating, he has a guilty feeling when masturbating, sohe doesn't masturbate. As a result, the psychic energy gets build up in him. This makes his behaviour unstable. The psychic energy may be released slowly by small delinquent acts; alternately, if the boy suppresses the energy it bursts in one time and the adolescent shows extreme violent act.

6. *Modelling:*

   According to the Social Learning Theory, we initiate what we see if we are vicariously reinforced by the behaviour of role models. This is true in the case of juvenile delinquents. Many JDs come from families where parents have also shown criminal behaviour, while others model their behaviour in line with their peer group. Media has a deep influence on anti-social behaviour in this regard. The influence of violent behaviours in the media on children is a matter of immense debate and research in psychology. These issues are discussed at great length in the chapter on media psychology.

Prevention

To prevent delinquent behaviour in minors, we first need to identify delinquency prone subjects. Many studies have shown that behavioural problems are the best predicators of JD. Usually parents and teachers ignore these behavioural problems, or punish children for showing such behaviours, misunderstanding the behavioural problems for willful disobedience and arrogance.

Another sign of future delinquency is truancy. Truancy is marked as the beginning of delinquent behaviour. Truants use defence mechanisms of withdrawal, isolation and denial, and their families are characterized by disturbed parent-child relationship (Pandey and Nagar, 1980).

Once identified, what kind of interventions should be introduced for delinquency prone students? Since most of the problems are due to disturbed parent-child relationships, interventions must aim at mending these relations. Schools should introduce parent-teacher meetings, so that parents are included in the academic life of the student. When parents start taking interest in their children's academics, children don't feel that their parents have a rejecting attitude.

Another prevention strategy is to provide counselling services in schools. Many children, especially adolescents, can't cope with extreme emotion. Counselling services provide help to children to cope with extreme stressors. Many a times, counsellors detect behavioural problems and disturbed relationship with family members from their interaction with the student. They may call up the concerned parent and educate the parent about the issue and how a change of child rearing practice can help the child.

Rehabilitation

As already mentioned, delinquent behaviours in children are due to incorrect socialization. So then, what should be the right strategy to rehabilitate them? It is 'resocialization'. Resocialization can happen in family, as well as in peer groups. Hence, psychologists advocate two methods- group therapy and family therapy. In group therapy, groups of juvenile delinquents are brought together and trained in behavioural skills, role taking, discussions, etc. In family therapy, the juvenile is retained in the family and the entire family undergoes therapy.

Usually, after the JD is produced in a juvenile court, she/he is sent to a correctional facility for a definite period. In that period, psychological interventions, in the form of role modelling, role playing, psychodrama, behavioural modifications, client-centered therapy, etc. should be introduced. Unfortunately, the correctional facilities in India are usually not well maintained. Neither are sufficient funds available, nor is the rehabilitation staff that skillful.

Role of Social Agencies

A number of NGOs are involved in prevention of juvenile delinquency and the rehabilitation of delinquents. A few of these agencies and their activities have been discussed here.

NANBAN is a social agency that works among street children of Madurai with the aim of their integration with the mainstream. Butterflies is a Delhi-based NGO that deals with children, who are largely victims of poverty, runaways and those who are destitute and have been abused. The Vatsalya Foundation of Bombay aims at rehabilitation of street children.

An oft mentioned organization in the context of juvenile delinquency is Prayas. Prayas provides correctional guidance to juvenile delinquents in New Delhi. It is known for the effectiveness of its education and therapy programmes.

There are many such other organizations in others parts of India. A Google search and exploration of such organizations and their activities is recommended to the student.

3.6 Victims of Violence

Violent events are high stress events. Though the stress is of short duration, it is unpredictable and intense and the victim has no control over the event. Such traumatic stressful violence includes rape, terror attacks, riots. The victims are usually those present on the site of violence and directly affected by the violent acts. But, this is not necessarily the case. Terror trauma has been noted in people who have just heard a bomb blast. What is important is that while the actual violent event is of very short duration, the traumatic experience is so stressful that there are psychological consequences.

In a longitudinal study by NGO Swanchetan, between 2000-2008 among the victims of rape, it was found that at least 12% victims of sexual assault did not share their trauma with anybody for 10 years or more. About 70% feared that the offender would return to hurt them again. Around 70% pretended to be alright to avoid talking on the subject. About 65% of the victims had different symptoms of PTSD even 6 months after the occurrence. And roughly, the same percentage stated that they had suicidal thoughts intermittently for 2 years. The findings of this study reveal the long-term psychological impacts of violence.

Today, it is generally agreed among psychologists that Post Traumatic Stress Disorder (PTSD) is a natural response to violence. Of course, there are resilient individuals, but the victims of violence are usually common people. Hence, PTSD is a natural psychological reaction to violence. There are other psychological reactions that a victim may suffer from. An immediate response to the act of violence is the shock accompanied by denial of the occurrence of the event. These are acute psychological responses to the acts of violence. But, if the violence persists for long, the victim may jump back to an earlier psychosocial stage (called regression) as a defense mechanism to cope with the stressors. This is called psychological infantilism.

Besides PTSD, shock and denial, there are other possible psychological consequences. Women victims of rape and riots experience a reduction in self-concept and self-esteem. Some victims of terrorist attacks may even go into depression. Generalized anxiety may be the result of intense fear that the vent may occur again.

Assessment

To provide help, we need to first identify victims of violence who suffer from severe psychological problems. As evident from the study by NGO Swanchetan, many rape victims don't disclose their inner trauma even for ten years and more. Similarly, soldiers in the military suffering from PTSD don't usually seek psychological help for themselves, because it is associated with a stigma in their peer group. A solider asking for psychological help is perceived not to be strong-willed and hence, his status in his military peer group reduces. In general, asking for psychological help is a taboo in Indian society. Further, victims of violation of modesty can't ask for psychological help because they have a high need to maintain privacy. They need to maintain privacy because the violation of modesty (including rape) is itself associated with stigma towards the woman.

Yet, there are symptoms of trauma that family members and counsellors can identify. Some of these are:

1. Victims get frightening dreams at night.
2. They develop an intense fear of some places. For example, a victim of rape may develop a fear of travelling alone, or of lonely, dark places. Victims of terrorist attacks develop a fear of crowded places, market places and temples. I was in Delhi when the multiple bomb blast took place in September, 2008. A friend of mine had seen the attack at Connaught Place (CP). He developed fear of open spaces where bombs can be planned! Surprisingly, not only he, but many other people who did not directly experience the terrorist attacks, also developed a fear of crowded places.
3. The violent event is so traumatic that the images seep into memory and become a part of the unconscious. The victim compulsively and automatically recalls these images again and again. As a result, the victim relives the traumatic experience many times over. Family members usually don't detect this symptom because victims try to avoid talking on the subject. But, professional counsellors talk to the client on the subject, showing unconditioned positive regard and genuineness. By this, the victim gets the confidence to talk out about the images that she compulsively visualizes.

   Once the counsellor detects the existence of PTSD or other psychological problems in the victim, the counsellor studies the type and extent of psychological reactions through interviews or paper-and-pencil tests.

Secondary Prevention

The long-term effects of traumatic events can be countered by giving immediate crisis assistance. Immediate crisis assistance given to victims of violence is also called secondary prevention. The prime aim of immediate crisis assistance is to help the victim cope with the shock and traumatic images. For this, debriefing exercises are conducted in the hospital (where the patient is admitted), or even near the site of the violence. If an experienced psychologist is not available for debriefing, the victim can be connected to one through telephone hotline.

Another job of secondary prevention is to prevent the victim from recalling the experience again and again. More the number of times you recall a traumatic event, deeper the images of the event go down. Unfortunately, victims of violence have to give evidence to law enforcement agencies. Owing to this, they have to narrate the whole event again and again to police, to media persons and in court. On an average, a rape victim has to narrate her experience six times. That is why, many feminists demand that the first testimony taken by the police in the hospital should be done in the presence of a magistrate.

A major concern with terrorist attacks in India these days is that attacks are becoming very frequent. Yet, there is no policy to provide secondary prevention to victims of terrorist attacks. Those who are injured are taken to hospitals. All others receive no psychiatric or psychological help.

Rehabilitation

After the counsellors have assessed the extent of psychological reactions in the victim, the next step is rehabilitation. Psychologists agree that the best way to deal with a traumatic event is to talk about it with the family members. Family members should encourage the victims to talk about her emotional reactions, her feelings. Besides this, family members must ensure that the victim doesn't get exposed to events that remind her of the violent event. For example, TV news reporting about terrorist attacks must not be shown to the victim.

The rehabilitation process of victims experiencing extreme psychological and emotional reactions includes certain therapeutic interventions. Yoga and Meditation have been found to be effective in dealing with PTSD. Meditation relaxes the body and proves effective in dealing with emotional reactions.

The counselling process is very important in this case. Counselling is important because the victim usually avoids talking on the subject. The counsellor shows compassion and empathy to establish trust with the client. When the counsellor states (as an expert) that what the client goes through is natural, it increases the confidence of the client. She opens up and pours out her grief in the counselling sessions. This helps in cathartic release.

The worst kind of experience after the violence, is reliving the violent act. Every time the victim re-lives the experience, she experiences similar strong psychological responses. To treat this, psychologists use imagery. The concept is to condition the images of the violent act with relaxation. The victim is asked to visualize moderately traumatic events. Such visualization is accompanied by high arousal and anxiety. The victim is trained to relax her body every time she visualizes the images. One can't be aroused and relaxed at the same time. Hence, the visualization triggers a somatic relaxation response that prevents the psychological response. This process happens in steps, till the time the victim is able to relax while re-living the entire violent incident.

In the assessment, if the psychologist finds that the victim suffer from loss of control, feeling of impotence, negative thoughts, depression, etc., she may recommend cognitive therapy for the client. Cognitive restructuring of false beliefs, like, "I could not help it! I am powerless", "I can't do anything about it", helps the client to make a realistic appraisal of the violent event.

Role of Social Agencies

The role of social agencies is uniquely important for the rehabilitation of victims of violence. The victims of rape and sexual assault can't get regular treatment in public hospitals because of the high need for privacy. PTSD patients usually don't themselves ask for psychological help because of the stigma attached, or because of lack of awareness of help available. In some troubled locations, such as Jammu and Kashmir, the number of patients of terror trauma-led PTSD is so large, that they don't get enough psychiatric help. Hence, the need for social agencies is there.

Social agencies provide counselling to victims of violence in strict privacy. We have already discussed a research finding of NGO Swanchetan. This NGO provides therapeutic assistance to victims of rape and sexual assault in strict privacy. Owing to the privacy clause, many women who have suppressed their trauma for years have come forward to discuss their problems. Another service, popular in USA and now being picked up by some NGOs in India, is to provide an online hotline for sexual assault victims. This is a form of cyber therapy that uses a secure and anonymous instant-messaging type format to establish communication between victims and trained crisis support volunteers.

Of the many organizations involved in rehabilitation of victims of violence, a name that stands out is Médecins Sans Frontières (MSF). This is an international agency with an active presence in India also. MSF provides relief to victims of violent incidences, like terrorist attack, bomb blasts, etc. MSF has a strong presence in Jammu and Kashmir, given that people of the state have been experiencing violent sets of chronic nature for the last 20 years.

■ ■ ■

Psychology Applied to Human Resource Development

4

EDUCATION PSYCHOLOGY

Chapter outline

4.1 Psychological Principles Underlying Effective Teaching-Learning Process

The teaching-learning process aims to bring about major cognitive and behavioural changes in the learner. As such, there are many psychological theories a teacher can borrow from to make the process more effective. The many theories for children's education are subsumed under three orientations used in psychology:

	Orientation	Prototype
1.	Individual Difference Orientation	Stemberg's Theory of Intelligence
2.	Developmental Orientation	Piagetian Theory of Cognitive Development
3.	Social Context Orientation	Vygotsky's Theory
Besides above, educational psychology derives from other fields of psychology, like:		
4.	Motivation	
5.	Memory	
6.	Conditioning	

Piaget's theory and learning process

Piaget's theory states that the human infant develops cognitive skills in four stages. In the first stage called the sensorimotor stage, the infant forms a schemata by assimilation of new information from the surrounding and accommodation (i.e., modifying the already formed impressions in the light of new evidence). These two processes together are called ***equilibration***. The most essential lesson from Piaget's theory is that the child actively interacts with her environment to form mental representations of the outside world. Hence, Piaget's argument was that children need to construct their understanding of the world rather than accept it from others. Both, assimilation and acculturation are active processes and cannot be achieved in a traditional classroom situation where information was delivered didactically. Hence, Piaget makes a strong case for replacing didactic learning by discovery learning. The role of the teacher is to facilitate learning situations in which children can find things for themselves and thereby construct their understanding. By facilitating learning situations, the teacher creates disequilibrium in the cognition. This disequilibrium should motivate the child to discover and learn.

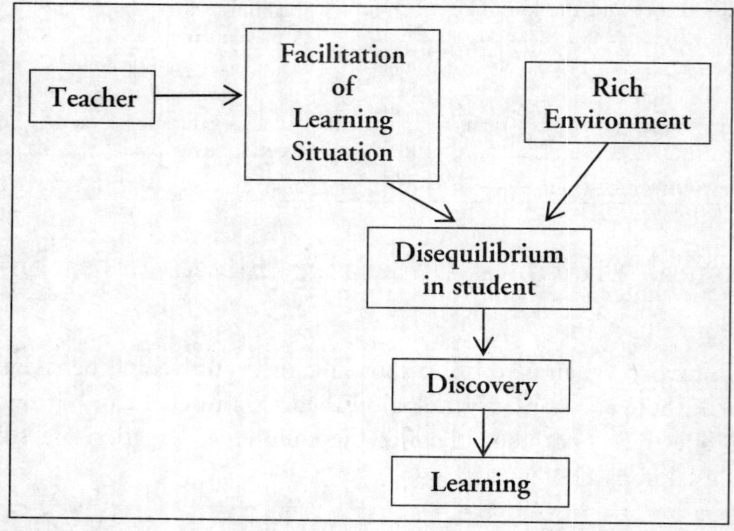

Fig. 4.1 : Illustration of Piaget's Theory

Vygotsky's theory and the learning process

Like Piaget, Vygotsky also saw the child as an active agent of her own learning, but he emphasized on the extent to which learning is mediated by the child's context. Mediation is a key concept of Vygotsky's social construction theory, referring collectively to the ways in which culture interacts with cognitive development. Children absorb knowledge about how to behave in certain situations by observing other people. Through a process called 'internalization', they imagine themselves doing the same and when a similar situation arrives, they can emit the same behaviour.

Vygotsky had argued that competence of a child is the maximum limit that it could perform with help from the context. The difference between its competence and actual present performance is called 'Zone of Proximal Development'.

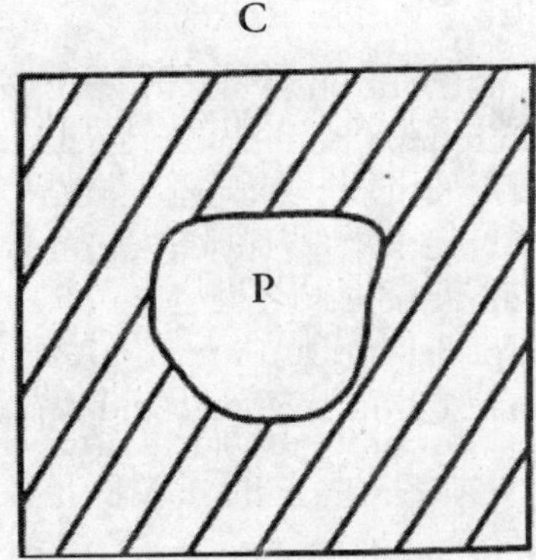

C = Competence P = Present Performance

ZPD = Zone of Proximal Development = C – P

ZPD represents the potential that can be realized in a child by giving appropriate environmental stimulation. Hence, Vygotsky's conceptualization of the teaching-learning process is that of an interaction between the learner and an adult instructor. The difference between what a child can understand on her own and what it can potentially understand through interaction with others is the ZPD. Vygotsky's theory is influential in the sense that it puts the teacher at the center of the teaching-learning process. This theory, no wonder, forms a core component of present researches on teaching-learning effectiveness.

Intelligence and learning

Neural development in a human child is somewhat plastic. The neural connections in which electrical activity is frequent, becomes stronger and larger. These neurons begin to expand, allowing an increasing specialization of functions of these areas. The electrical activity is more frequent in areas which are related to specific kind of environmental interactions. Hence, cognitive skills that are practiced a lot become sharp.

Regarding intelligence, it has been found that intelligence is modular, i.e., there is no single general factor of intelligence; there are multiple centers of intelligence in the brain and there are multiple abilities that together are called intelligence. Further, intelligence includes creativity and pragmatism. The information processing theories of intelligence claim that increasing experience of the world allows more efficient information processing, allowing greater development of intelligence. Hence, intelligence isn't just inherent, but can be developed in every child to an optimal level.

Intelligence theories lend to the field of education the concept of 'Individual Difference' in students. The teacher needs to understand that some students are, to take an example, better in mathematics than others. These students can prepare math better than others. The teacher has to take care of the individual differences in needs of students while teaching.

Motivation

A major goal of the teaching-learning process is to motivate students towards academic achievement. Hence, the teacher has to use various techniques (for instance, goal setting) to keep students motivated. Students also need to be motivated to listen to a lecture- how to make a lecture more interesting? Crack jokes? Give periodic breaks? Or teach through various mediums in order to catch the attention of students' multiple senses? The issue of motivating students is discussed in another section of this chapter. Special measures to motivate students from deprived group background are discussed in the chapter on disadvantage and deprivation.

Conditioning

Educational psychology was dominated by behaviourist principles in its early days. Though greater emphasis is given to Cognitive School of Psychology today, behaviourist principles are no doubt valuable. Conditioning principles are very useful in teaching students with learning disabilities and retardation. Chaining and shaping are especially useful for these students.

Regular feedback and reinforcement of good performance by rewards are some lessons from the Behaviourist School of Psychology. However, there are some cautions. It has been found that extrinsic rewards tend to demotivate intrinsically motivated students, as rewards act as justifications for their effort and decreases their motivation. Some warnings about use of punishment are also sounded out. Punishment to change behaviour is discouraged by behaviourists as punishment doesn't teach what to do. It only tells the students what not to do.

Memory

The rich research conducted by cognitive psychologist has resulted in greater insight into how information is encoded and stored. Many techniques to improve memory have been forwarded by psychologists for the benefit of teachers. For example, information that is encoded in multiple modalities (visual, verbal, etc.) is better memorized. Many such principles are discussed in another section of this chapter.

4.2 Learning Styles

"Styles" describe relatively stable personal preferences on how information processing is undertaken. For example, a mechanic who checks a car for problems has a style of his own, in how he goes about doing his work. Learning styles refer to all the systems of classifying individual differences in learning. There are individual differences in students regarding how they learn; how they prefer to process information given to them. I am very uncomfortable to study from teachers' notes. Back in my days in IIT Kharagpur, I used to frequently go to the library to study from original books. On the other hand, many of my friends used to note my professors' lecture. Some were more comfortable in writing in point form in the exams; others were more graphic and used many diagrams to explain their answers. Hence, there are individual differences in how students learn and express their learnt information. Learning styles include cognitive styles (preferred manner of information processing in any student) and learning strategies.

Literature Survey

From a literature survey, it is evident that there are many conflicting conceptualizations of learning styles without any theoretical framework to connect them. Scholars have proposed a variety of learning styles, many of these are often similar, but different names make them more confusing to use. Let us discuss a few conceptualizations of learning styles.. Kolb (1984) had made an influential early classification of various learning styles into two dimensions:

1. Convergent-Divergent thinkers
2. Assimilators-Accommodators

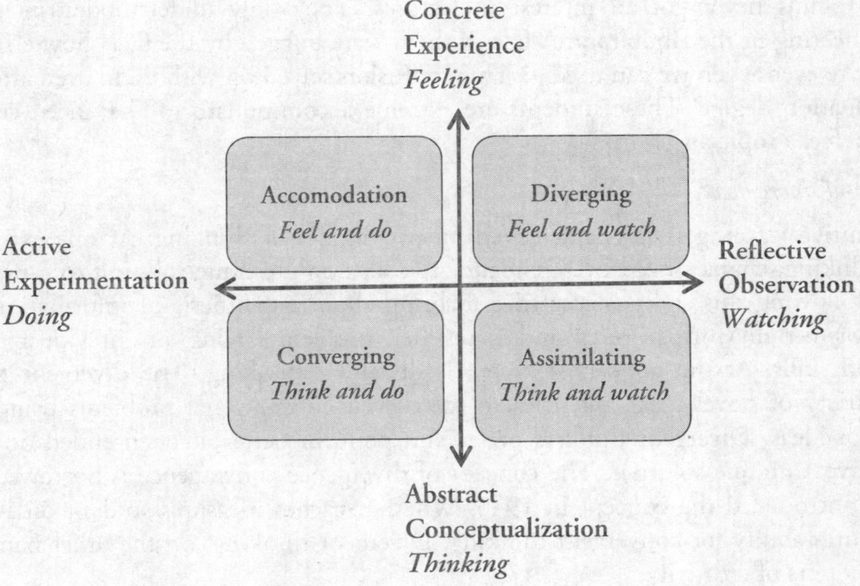

Fig. 4.2 : Kolb's learing Styles

He had reasoned that any student lies on the above two-dimensional space. I will discuss various learning styles, but before that, let me discuss other scholars' conceptualizations on learning styles. Entwistle (2000) has given a distinction between deep processing style and shallow processing style. Going a step forwards, Schmeck (1988) had distinguished between three styles on this dimension- deep, shallow and elaborate. There are many other conceptualizations. In a review of literature, Sternberg (Sternberg and Zheng, 2001) recently observed that the most proposed learning styles deal with one or the other pole of the following dimensions:

1. Analytic-Wholistic
2. Concrete-Abstract
3. Verbal-Visual processing

Let us discuss in detail some of the important dimensions of learning styles:

1. Based on Piagetian theory, this dimension was forwarded by Kolb (1984). According to him, assimilators process information abstractly, while accommodators can perceive information concretely (other dimensions proposed by various scholars, like abstract-concrete and active-reflexive are similar to this). Hence, accommodators process new information by activities, such as discussion and experimentation. Assimilators tend to manipulate information internally rather than externally. Hence, they can make better use of situations, like lectures to learn.

Back in my undergraduate days, I could easily conceptualize how electricity is generated in generators from lectures and books. This was because I was an assimilator. On the other hand, some of my friends never got an interest in lectures. They only understood principles of electrical engineering in the laboratory. A few of them were bugged by the fact- how electricity flows in the wire even when we can't see it? This confusion stayed on with them even after they got their graduation degree! These students are extreme accommodators. They need concrete information to feel a topic and learn it.

2. Convergence-Divergence

This is a cognitive learning style characterized by two modes of thinking. At one extreme is convergent thinking, characterized by a tendency to focus on a unique solution to a problem. The student following this style usually tries to bring about a synthesis of information. The student follows certain formal rules and bases her problem-solving on previously learnt knowledge and skills. At the opposite extreme is divergent thinking. The divergent thinker produces a variety of novel ideas and tries to solve even conventional problems using these divergent set of ideas. Divergent thinkers prefer and perform better at open-ended questions that do not have a unique solution. The concept of divergence-convergence is borrowed from Guilford who introduced the concept in 1946. When a teacher measures student on IQ, she basically measures ability for convergent thinking. Divergent thinking, on the other hand, can be measured by tests of creativity.

3. Reflection-Impulsivity

This dimension was first identified by psychologist Jerome Kagan in 1958. Reflection or reflectivity is the tendency to consider and deliberate over alternate solutions to a problem. The impulsive learner is spontaneous and tends to respond without much deliberation. As a result, the reflective student takes more time, but comes out with correct answers. The impulsive student gives quick reply, but the frequency of errors is high. This dimension is similar to another style called ***Sensory-intuitive style***. Learners at the sensory end of the continuum prefer to rely on evidence of their senses in solving problems, whereas those at the intuitive end rely more on speculation, hunches and imagination.

4. Visual-Verbal learners

Some learners better understand and memorize information received through visual mode; while others do it better with information received through verbal mode. Visual learners tend to understand and remember information better when in the form of diagrams, pictures and films. Verbal learners are more comfortable with lectures and discussions.

5. Deep and shallow learners

This dimension is derived from the levels of processing theory forwarded by Craik and Lockhard in 1972. Entwistle applied the concept to educational psychology. The learning style- shallow or surface learning involves relying on single sources of information and learning key points by rote. Learners adopting a surface strategy limit what they study and learn to the strict requirement of the syllabus. Deep learning, by contrast, is characterized by the motivation to understand the topics as deep level as possible.

At the time when I started preparations for Civil Service Examinations, I found that some students rely almost exclusively on coaching institute notes. These students were appalled on seeing a thick textbook and were against reading anything new. These students are shallow processors and would do better with coaching and tuitions. On the other hand, many others would go to the library and read new books on the topic, irrespective of whether they are that relevant to the syllabus. These are deep processors and can do self-study. Their answers reflect a richness of content and maturity.

Utility of Learning Styles

Psychologists have devised various inventories to measure learning styles and to understand a learner's cognitive styles, strategies and approaches to learning. For example, Schmeck (1988) has devised an inventory to distinguish between deep processing style and elaborate processing style. But, the question is, why do teachers need to understand learning styles? Of what use it is to them?

The teaching-learning environment is a system. In any system, there needs to be a fit between the sub-systems. This system is no exception. So, as to achieve a good fit between the two sub-systems, the teacher should understand the strategies, styles and approaches that the student prefers over alternative styles. This helps the teacher to teach students in their preferred style.

Some implications of the use of learning styles are:

1. Accommodators need to be taught by practical's and experiments. They can't internalize lectures as efficiently as assimilators.
2. A holist (hypothesis-led) strategy may result in smart answers, but may be wrong at times. The Serialist learner (data-led) is meticulous, but slow. The teacher needs to adjust her teaching speed to both.
3. Visual learners can be better taught with the help of graphs, presentations, PPT slides and movies. Verbal learners, on the other hand, should be encouraged through lectures and discussions.
4. Deep learning should be encouraged among all students with the help of appropriate motivators, such as varied source of study and teaching through varied stimuli.

Learning styles have also been linked to motivation. According to Entwistle (2000), learning styles are a combination of intention (or motivation) and processes. The teacher benefits from understanding the student's 'processes' as well as 'motivators'. Students are self-regulated when the material taught conforms to their style.

Retarded Students and their Training

Because of many genetic, biological and environmental influences on intelligence, no two individuals are alike. There are students at both ends of the intelligence distribution with unusual mental abilities. Those at the lower end are the ones labeled as mentally retarded or cognitively retarded. A note of warning at this point is that intelligence itself is a debatable issue among psychologists even after decades of research; hence it is incorrect to call anyone mentally retarded. ***Differently-abled*** is a more accurate term than mentally retarded, because IQ is not a measure of all types of intelligences. Even in the case of severe retardation, many individuals have been found to be exceptionally talented (for example, the idiots savants) in a few abilities.

The focus of the section will be identification, training, and rehabilitation of the mentally handicapped. The concept behind training mentally retarded students is to provide them with a support system that can help them lead a life of dignity and worth. It has been seen that early intervention helps all types of retarded students. Most members of this group are only mildly retarded (IQ: 50-70) and given appropriate social and educational support, are capable of functioning adequately in mainstream society, holding jobs and raising families.

Trainings strategies for retarded students are multi-pronged, multi-dimensional and necessarily tailor-made for the individual. Here, the psychologist needs to be both a scientist and an artist. Training disabled kids is both a science and an art. It is a science because it works within the frame of theoretical developments in psychology. It is an art because training has to depend on the trainer's ability to innovate and be creative in training the student.

Various issues dealt by the trainee are:

1. Identification and assessment of abilities and disabilities
2. Deciding on least restrictive environment
3. Training for disabilities
   (a) Learning disabilities
   (b) Social disabilities
   (c) Behavioural disabilities
4. Rehabilitation

We will discuss these issues in detail. But before doing so, let us look at some theoretical foundations regarding conceptualization of mental retardation.

Theoretical Foundation

Traditional explanations of disabilities were grounded in superstitious belief systems and many retarded individuals were abandoned or exterminated. By the 1800s, these explanations gave way to certain quasi-experimental explanations. The year 1801 was a landmark in the history of training and education of mentally retarded; it is in this year that Itard undertook to train and educate Victor, the wild child of Aveyron. Victor was discovered by three hunters in 1799 in the forests of Aveyron in France. Most likely abandoned at an early age, he grew up isolated from human contact and stayed naked in the wild. At about the age of 12, he was discovered and several medical experts concluded that the boy was mentally deficient. Itard disagreed, noting that it took intelligence to survive in the wild; his contention was that special education and care would enable the child to develop functional skills.

Itard provided sense training to Victor with special emphasis on communication and problem-solving skills. Itard didn't seem to be very successful, but a student of his, Edward Seguin, devoted his entire life to training retarded students. He developed procedures for working with the mentally challenged within an educational framework.

Since these days, the medical model of explaining retardation had been quite popular. The medical model advocated that disabilities originate within the child and are manifestations of underlying biological problems. This faulty view led to incorrect training strategies, such as institutionalization. A major problem with institutionalization was that the retarded couldn't get much needed ***family support***, nor could they develop ***social skills***. These people were often ***labelled*** as retarded, whereas only few of them are severely retarded. The mildly retarded, who constitute a majority, can lead a normal life with some special education. For them, institutionalization worsened the problem.

The good news is, there has been a transition from medical model to socio-cultural and ecological approaches. These contemporary approaches attribute the causality of disability to the transaction between the demands of the environment and the behaviour of the individual. Also, many psychologists today contend that most educational disabilities are primarily social constructions. If suppose, you test some students of a town school on IQ and find that students scoring under 75 have mental retardation; you now take the IQ test to a school in a tribal locality on the periphery of the town. There, you find that most students fare low on IQ. The fact is that there are so many sub-cultures in the same place that an objective IQ measurement is not possible. Many disabilities are social constructions (i.e., how society defines ability).

Identification and Assessment

Psychologists usually label those children as mentally retarded who get following scores on IQ tests:

IQ	Label
50-70	Mild
35-50	Moderate
20-35	Severe
Below 20	Profound

Typically, the process of identification starts with a ***teacher referral***. Before giving the referral, a team of teachers and school administrators make a ***pre-referral intervention,*** in which the student's educational needs are fulfilled by special education in the classroom. Overtime, if the term concludes that the student hasn't made any progress with the intervention, the child is referred formally for special education.

Once identified, the mentally disabled student needs to be provided with specialized training. But before training, the trainer needs to assess the student and find out her strengths and weaknesses. The most popular tool of assessment is the standardized IQ test. A problem with this test is that it just gives the extent of disability, not the nature of disability. There are many who are labelled retarded but are exceptionally good in, say, mathematical ability or musical talent. Also, IQ test scores greatly vary from culture to culture and even between sub-culture. If a school has students from mainstream culture and from various sub-cultural groups (e.g., lower castes), the ones from sub-cultural groups may score low on IQ.

A more appropriate test is the ***criteria-referenced assessment***. It consists of a hierarchy of tests across several domains, including social skills, communication skills, academic skills and maladaptive behaviour. This assessment helps the trainer to assess which intelligences the student can master better.

Least Restrictive Environment

There are many disadvantages of institutionalization, that is, sending retarded children to special schools with residential facility. Some of these are:

1. The child is cut-off from her family. Family support is not available.
2. The child is unable to learn social skills that would help her later when she is rehabilitated. The scope of integration with society is lost.
3. Institutionalization is always attached with social stigma.
4. When mentally retarded students don't get to interact with normal students, normal students don't grow up with sensitivity to the needs of the retarded. Whereas, if they are in the same school, it has been found that normal students are less prejudiced and more ready to help. This, in fact, increases their sense of empathy.

   Institutionalization, in fact, is not necessary for mildly and moderately challenged students; rather, institutionalization harms them by attaching a social stigma. The ideal environment for any student is the one with her non-disabled peers in a normal school. However, there is a trade-off between educational setting and personalized assistance. Hence, based on assessment results, the trainer decides on a Least Restrictive Environment (LRE) in which the student has to be trained. LRE is the educational setting that is closest to the regular educational setting that can still meet the student's individual needs. Hence, the trainer has to choose from a continuum of services depicted in the diagram below:

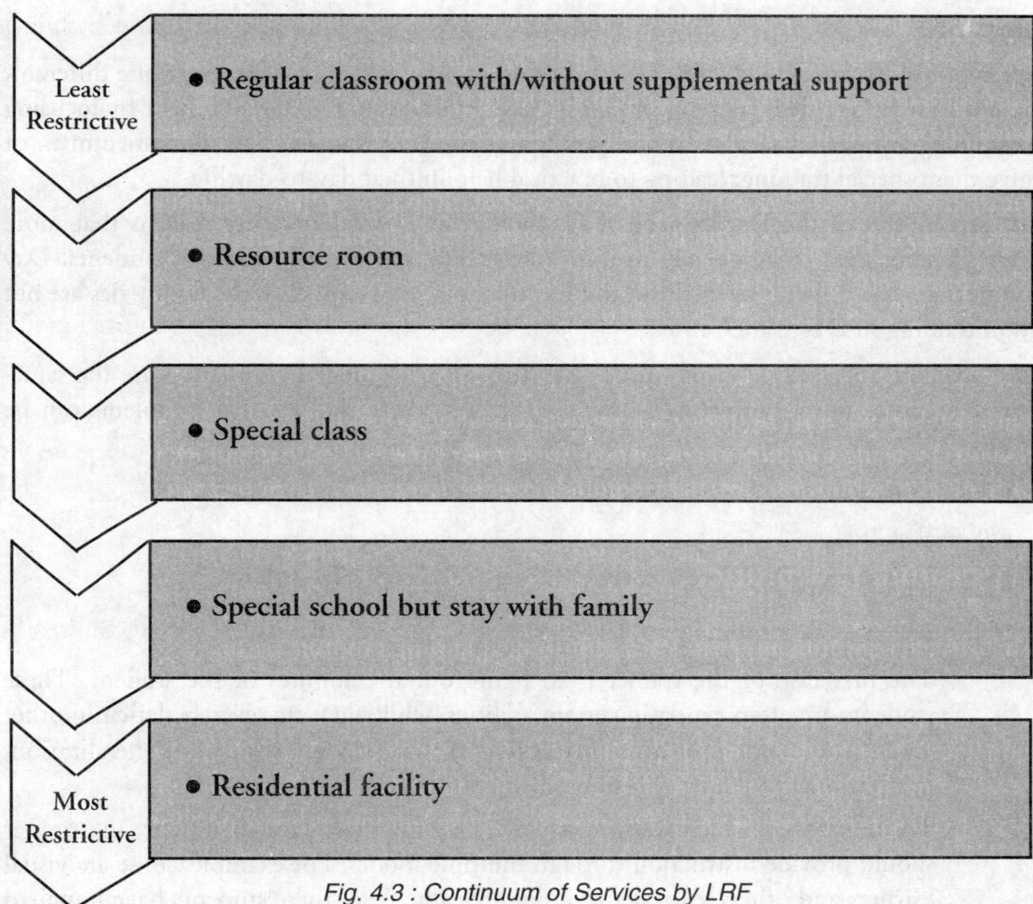

Fig. 4.3 : Continuum of Services by LRF

If the trainer assesses that the student can make it with regular classroom, it is the best environment. This usually is the case with mildly retarded students. Some special assistance or extra classes for the student may be undertaken. This environment is the most inclusive one; hence, training retarded students in the classroom is also called 'inclusion'. If the trainer doesn't find this sufficient, the retard is taken out of regular class and put exclusively in a special class, consisting solely of children with mental retardation. These special classes have smaller student-to-teacher ratio and usually include some paraprofessionals. If the trainer finds that a student's condition is improving, she can put the student back in regular class. This is called 'mainstreaming'.

For the severely retarded, it is very tough to place them in regular schools because of the individualized assessment and training that they require. Special school is recommended, though the trainer tries to let the student stay with her family. But, if the functional retardation is high, the trainer may recommend a residential facility for the child. This is the most restrictive environment and should be an option of the last resort for the benefit of the retarded student.

Training Needs

The needs of mildly, moderately, severely and profoundly retarded students are quite different. For the moderately retarded, training should include functional skills development by focusing on motor integration, language skills and perceptual and motor skills. The ultimate aim must be to give them special training, leading to practical help in their day-to-day life.

Arun Sen (2000) of the Department of Psychology at Delhi University reasons that more Day Care Centers need to be opened to train moderately and severely retarded students. Day Care Centers are less difficult to institute and less costly to maintain; also, the family ties are not severed in training in Day Care Centers.

In the ultimate analysis, the needs of no two students with mental retardation are the same. Every student poses novel problems for the trainer. Yet, these skill-retarded problems can be grouped as:

- Learning skills
- Social skills
- Behavioural skills

(a) *Learning skills training*

The first task of the trainer is to figure out the abilities of the student. These students are often expert in certain abilities, while they are severely deficit in other areas. The major problems in learning are the student's lack of generalization, motivational problems and unusual styles.

To understand which learning style is best for the retarded student, the trainer should provide instruction through multiple modes. For example, some are visual learners and others learn better kinesthetically. Also, these students have impaired short-term memory ability and lower attention span. Teaching them from multiple modes helps to use all their senses to encode information.

Lack of generalization is yet another problem commonly faced. The disabled student may be unable to generalize across settings (e.g., from school to home), stimuli (e.g., verbal instruction to written instruction) or across individuals (e.g., from trainer to parents). Hence, the trainer must teach across settings, stimuli and individuals to ensure that responses learnt under one condition are replicated in other conditions. (Singer-Dudek, 2004).

Motivational problem is the most challenging of all problems. Most retarded students have a low attention span and low motivational drive. Hence, the teacher should maintain an optimal pace of instruction and must ensure that the student has pre-requisite skills to perform the task. Prabhu and Prabhu have emphasized the need for spaced learning and overlearning in an acceptable environment with sympathy, warmth and understanding. Regular feedback and proper reinforcement (both verbal and material) should be provided.

The teacher also can take the help of developments in Information Technology (IT) to teach the differently abled. Deepalaya, an NGO, recently launched an IDU computer center to help cater to children with special needs. Officials at Deepalaya have found that learning computer skills can be stimulating and funny. Those who have been trained by Deepalaya have developed a new sense of self-confidence and their attitude towards life has become increasingly positive. "The audio-visual medium is a great way to reach/teach children as it helps in better understanding and comprehension as well as retention" says Sashwati Banarjee, executive director of Sesame Workshop India. (The Times of India, 21-07-2008).

(b) *Social skills*

When mentally retarded students are placed with their normal peers, they face certain problems in adaptation. Many often have difficulties in understanding the rules of conversation even though they have sufficient communication skills. They also have difficulty in understanding the feelings and emotions of others. Here, the trainer can use techniques, such as, vicarious reinforcement and observational learning to teach appropriate social skills.

(c) *Behavioural Problems*

Behavioural problems are most common among mildly retarded children. The problems are usually not because of the retard per se, but because of incorrect reinforcement by parents and peers. Behavioural deviance ranges from assaultive behaviour to extreme withdrawal. Some retarded children engage in bizarre behaviour, like stereotype (repeating an activity again and again, common in autism), self-talk and self-injurious behaviour.

We know that all behaviours are emitted because of reinforcement. Such behaviours may be emitted because of inability to communicate or attempt to gain attention or escape an aversive task. Stereotype, for instance, is emitted because the behaviour itself is reinforcing (by sensory stimulation). Some other behaviours are reinforced by the attention the behaviour draws.

The challenge for the trainer here is manifold. Parents don't have understanding of behaviourist theories and hence misinterpret the behaviour as willful disobedience. Instead of looking for environmental variables to behaviours, they attribute the behaviour to the child's personality.

The trainer needs to work with parents and teachers to modify these behavioural deviances. Functional behaviour assessment is used to identify the antecedents for unusual behaviour and remove them. The trainer also teaches reinforcement techniques to teach the child appropriate behaviour.

Training for Rehabilitation

The philosophy underlying rehabilitation of mentally retarded children is to help them adapt to the community and lead a life of dignity. Kirk (1962) has given certain guidelines about how to train the mentally retarded for rehabilitation:

1. Social competence should be developed, so that the retarders can get along with other people. This can be done by conditioning them in numerous social experiences.
2. Occupational competence should be developed through vocational guidance and training. This would help them participate in work and earn their own living.
3. Autonomy can be developed in them by teaching them emotional skills.
4. They should develop habits of health and sanitation.

It is very tough to rehabilitate the profoundly retarded individuals (IQ below 25). They have intellectual capacity of a child of 2-4 years' age. Rehabilitation aims to help them look after themselves. Luckily, they constitute only 5% of total population of the mentally retarded. For the moderately and severely retarded children, certain skills have been identified. Sen (2000) argues that they can be trained in simple repetitive jobs under personal supervision. They can be made productive and rehabilitated. Those with mild retardation (IQ: 50-75) are capable of receiving special education and can learn semi-skilled jobs of a routine nature.

4.3 Learning Disabilities

Learning disability refers to a disorder in one or more of the basic psychological processes involved in oral expression, listening comprehension, written expression, basic reading skills, mathematical calculation and mathematical reasoning. However, the disability is not learning disability (LD) if the cause of disorder is mental retardation or emotional disturbance.

All the major disorders that lead to LD can be broadly categorized into two disabilities:

1. Reading disability or Dyslexia
2. Arithmetic disability

Dyslexia involves difficulties in phonological processing. Dyslexic students cannot make out the relation between letters and sound. They have poor decoding abilities, difficulties in spoken language and poor reading comprehension. Students with arithmetic disability usually have problems in visuospatial processing and in short-term and long-term memory. They face immense difficulty in solving even simple mathematical problems.

The specific problems associated with learning disabilities are generally life-long, though many of the problems can be attenuated by instruction and accommodation (Instruction refers to special instruction techniques; accommodation refers to certain adjustment in normal classes to facilitate learning by the LDs). Students with dyslexia can learn to read and can become functional readers. Similarly, those with problems in mathematical reasoning can be given special mentoring to do so. However, early detection and intervention is necessary. As seen in the Hindi movie *Taare Zameen Par,* if students with LD aren't detected at an early stage, parents may misunderstand them and punish them. Punishment often can lead to behavioural problems and depression.

Assessment

Assessment is necessary because it helps to make an estimation of extent of disability and nature of disability. Various popular assessment tests are Standardized Achievement Test, informal reading inventories, and curriculum-based assessment. Since the underlying problems are cognitive, test of reaction time are also found effective in identification of LD. Specifically, the Das-Naglieri Cognitive Assessment System (CAS) based on PASS model can be used to assess students' learning disability.

Selection of Environment

Going by the logic of least restrictive environment, learning disabled students ought to be accommodated in the regular classroom. This is because of the long-term benefits in development of social skills in them. However, special education in the form of evening classes or Sunday classes also help. The point is, accommodation by peers and teachers in schools and special training programmes, like perceptual-motor training, complement each other in mainstreaming of the learning disabled.

Interventions

Interventions for learning disabilities in students include school-based interventions and special education and training facilities. Some of these strategies are:

Special Education and Training

(a) Psycholinguistic training

(b) Perceptual motor training

(c) Behavioural modification

(d) PREP

School-based interventions

(a) Effective instruction by teacher

(b) Direct instruction

(c) Peer tutoring

Special Education and Training

Many popular techniques to train students with LD exist with varying degrees of empirical backing. For example, the perceptual motor training works on the principle that children with learning disability have problem in sensory integration as in difficulty to plan and execute motor acts, disorder in form and space perception, etc. The idea is that direct sensory motor training can mitigate the disorder.

Behavioural modification makes use of principles of behavioural school. A behavioural analysis is made, then the behaviours that are subject to change are defined, modification routine is followed and finally behavioural changes are analyzed. PREP, on the other hand, is a cognitive technique. PREP stands for PASS Reading Enhancement Program and it is based on Das and Neglieri's PASS Model. It is a remedy curriculum designed to improve planning, attention and information processing strategies that underlie reading. A similar curriculum has been developed to help students with arithmetic difficulty.

School-based Interventions

Effective instruction by teachers can go a long way in helping LDs tide over their problems. The teacher should actively interact with students and provide regular feedback. Overlearning can help. Remedial techniques can be introduced to facilitate the learning process of LD students. For example, students with dyslexia can be encouraged to use tape recorders for projects; because of spelling difficulties, consideration should be given to not reducing grades because of spelling errors. Students with arithmetic disability should be allowed to use calculators.

Engelman and Becker, two researchers based in University of Oregon, had developed a technique called Direct Instruction to teach LD students. Basically, they had married behavioural modification techniques with classroom instruction to get very positive results. Programs based on Direct Instruction provide explicit, step-by-step guidance for teachers, strategies for correcting student errors and systematic practice with many different examples.

Peer tutoring has been found to be quite an effective intervention for treating learning disability. In peer tutoring, students work with each other in a one-to-one setting and they alternately take the role of teacher and pupil.

Case Study: The case of Sanjeev

To understand learning disability further, we will now turn to a specific case narrated by Kate Currawala (President of Maharashtra Dyselxia Association) in Education Times (Times of India, 06-10-2008). Is remedial education necessary for students with dyslexia? Dyslexia affects the normal functioning of the sensory-motor circuits in the brain, with an adverse impact on memory, reading, writing, processing of information and motor co-ordination. The fact that the LD child has to struggle with ordinary, daily tasks has devastating impact on her self-esteem and confidence. Currawala argues that a good remedial intervention programme addresses academic, motor and psychological difficulties and establishes adequate coping skills.

Take the case of Sanjeev who took professional help from Kate Currawala as a nine-year old. Although Sanjeev had already repeated a year, he lagged behind his classmates in almost every subject. Underlying his poor reading and writing skills were deficits in the visual and auditory processing '....Sanjeev was quiet and withdrawn, easily stressed out when faced with even a simple task and ready to give up without much effort. His parents were reluctant to try remedial education, because the thrice-a-week regime would leave less time for homework and tuitions'.

But eventually, his parents opted for special education. The special educator gave Sanjeev multi-sensory language instruction to improve his reading and spelling. Through a cognitive enhancement programme, the special education worked on his visual, auditory attention and organization skills. The cognitive enhancement programme included a series of graded puzzles and activities that built the necessary skills, without putting him through stressful academic work. The educator used innovative techniques also; to tackle Sanjeev's impulsivity and low threshold for frustration, he was made to play ludo, snakes and ladders and cared games. Gradually, 'as he began to enjoy the tasks and feel more confident of his skills, the youngster actually began to look forward to his remedial session….. within a few months, his academic skills also noticeably improved'.

Remedial education holds importance because the special educators work on basic skills, which form the foundation for reading and writing.

Conclusion

Learning disabled students have the ability to grow up and become academic achievers, if they are provided the requisite support system at an early stage. This support system consists of not only the school psychologist and special educators, but also teachers and parents of the child.

Gifted Students and their Training

Students who have high general mental abilities or artistic skills are called 'gifted students'. These students are deviants in the sense that they differ from normal students in a classroom and need special guidance. Just like learning disabled and mentally retarded students, gifted students are exceptional. While mentally retarded students are at one extreme of the learning curve, gifted students are at the other extreme.

Defining 'Gifted'

There is not much agreement regarding test instruments and assessment procedures to detect and label a student as gifted. Lewis Terman (1925), the developer of Standford-Binet scale, found from a longitudinal study of twelve years old children, that those with IQs above 135 can be called 'gifted'. Although his views haven't been unanimously accepted, there is some argument that those lying two standard deviations above the mean score of 100 are gifted. In his book, 'The School Wide Enrichment Model', Renzulli has observed that giftedness shouldn't be confused with success. People who have achieved recognition as gifted, possess a well-defined set of three interlocking cluster of traits.

These three clusters of traits are:

1. Mental abilities
2. Ability for creative problem-solving
3. Motivation and dedication

Hence, in contemporary research, stress is not on IQ score (which itself is quite subjective and gives culture-based scores), but on common trails of gifted children. According to Usha Pandit, an educational consultant with MindSpring, some common traits of a gifted child are:

1. Thinking, imagination, learning, leadership
2. Potential to perform in at least the top 5% areas of ability
3. Good at handling abstract and complex ideas
4. Boundless curiosity
5. Sophisticated sense of human
6. Ask interesting, difficult or unexpected questions
7. Skeptical, critical, evaluative and quick to spot inconsistencies

Do They Need Training?

As pointed out by Renzulli, not every gifted child becomes successful, but every gifted child had potential to become successful. Giftedness is related to mental ability, but success is related to many other factors, such as motivation and dedication, contextual stimulation to help them realize their potential and proper guidance.

Terman's research had established as far back as 1925 that early grade advancement acceleration and motivation in childhood helps gifted students to better realize their potential. Hollingworth (1926), among others, has shown that gifted students face motivational and attitudinal problems in regular grade-level classrooms.

In the light of above discussion, I will now turn to the problems faced by gifted children in family and school. This will help us understand what their training needs are. Some major problems faced by gifted children are:

1. *Curiosity:* Gifted children are curious. While this is a plus, it also creates problems. Gifted children often ask many thought provoking questions in the class. As the teacher gets frustrated that she doesn't know the answer to the question, she may also think that the student is showing willful disobedience. Often, the prime focus of the teacher is to complete the syllabus hence, she is not responsive to the intellectual needs of the child. Rather, her discouraging remarks may act as a punishment to the student.
2. *Discipline:* Many schools work on the principle of discipline. Precocious students are quit talkative and imaginative. Discipline doesn't suit them as discipline expects similar behaviour from every child. When they break the discipline, (which they do since they are this way) they are punished. Punishment tells them what behaviour not to emit, but does not tell them what behaviour to emit. This often leaves them frustrated.

   Though I don't claim to be gifted, I used to face immense problems in my schooldays because the teachers couldn't tolerate my curious questions. One teacher had made a rule that I shouldn't open my mouth in her class. And whenever I did (which happened quite spontaneously), I was punished! Most of my traumatic schooldays I have spent standing on the bench or kneeling down outside the class. Think what kind of impact that kind of treatment has on a child's self-esteem! The child never realizes where he went wrong, because his behaviour isn't reinforced; just punished. He has a list of DON'Ts but no Dos. Discipline frustrates the giftedness in him.

3. *Teaching method:* Gifted students demand different teaching methods. Highly gifted student learns not only faster than others, but also differently. Standard teaching methods try to simplify complex subjects; gifted students thrive on complexity. Hence, these students often get frustrated with the teaching method. Some even drop out of the school, because they don't find the school sufficiently stimulating.

   Rote memorization is a standard learning method in school. But gifted students are conceptual driven. If they are expected to do rote mugging, they can't do it. As a result, it is possible that they will be academic underachievers.

4. *Comfort:* Once parents and teachers find out that a child is gifted, their expectations from her are high. They put unusual pressure on the child to perform. This makes the child feel uncomfortable. When I was in fifth grade, I used to write good poems. When my parents realized that I have a talent in composing poems, they pressurized me to write more. I was asked to sing in front of every guest who visited our house. My parents considered me a trophy to be boasted about. Even some teachers patronized me to compose poems for them. Ultimately, I became so frustrated that I stopped writing poems. And you missed the opportunity of living in the times of a great poet! Hence, the comfort level of a gifted child has to be high. Parents and teachers need to understand this before pressurizing her with expectations.

5. *Multiple ages:* A 5-year old may read like a 9-year old, play chess like a 10-year old and talk to toys like a 2-year old. Because the child lives many ages simultaneously, parents and teachers sometimes misunderstand them for being too arrogant, too mature or too childish. They don't understand how to train a child whose various skills attain various degree of maturity.

6. *Social problems:* Gifted children are skeptical, critical, evaluative and quick to spot inconsistencies. Because of their superior skills, sometimes they become arrogant. Most gifted children have problems in adjusting to their social context. They are usually not popular in their peer groups and they don't find their peers in the peer group interesting.

Interventions for Gifted Students

The first step of intervention is assessment. The assessment doesn't simply mean taking an IQ test. This is because, many gifted students are immensely talented in one area of intelligence and quite average in others. Hence, the task of assessment is to evaluate the exact nature of giftedness.

Further, the school psychologist has to select a suitable educational setting for the gifted students' needs. The strategy should be to find the least restrictive environment subject to the condition that the child is intellectually satisfied. The continuum of services for least restrictive environment (LRE) for gifted students is:

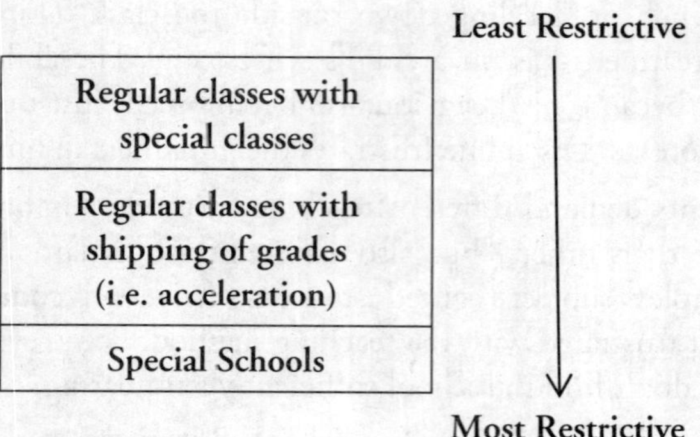

Fig. 4.4 : Services for Gifted Students

Regular classrooms treat all students with the same spirit of egalitarianism. This may bore and demotivate the gifted students. Hence, there is need for special classes to home her intellectual abilities.

The next stage is special skill development. Earlier, a general and homogeneous curriculum was given to all gifted students. Today, specialized programs focus on specific talents. For example, a child with exceptional talent in art can be made to participate in an after-school art class. A student who is precocious in mathematics can be included in a mathematics club. Nowadays, summer camps have become quite popular among parents of gifted children.

Conclusion

The task of training gifted children is as challenging as the task of training mentally retarded children. Our world doesn't accommodate differences that easily; both gifted and retarded face a problem in proper person-environment fit.

4.4 Career Counselling

Counselling is face-to-face interaction performed by individuals with specialized training in the field, to assist people in having a clear understanding of them. Career counselling is based on the philosophy that a satisfying and self-actualizing work life across the lifespan is essential for one to realize her potential and lead a healthy and meaningful life. Career counsellors help clients to:

- Make career choices and adjustments.
- Deal with mid-career crisis and transitions.
- Optimize work life across the life span.

Career Theories

Many psychologists have been involved in theorizing various aspects of career choice made by individuals. Here, we will discuss three important strands of research on careers. These strands aren't contradictory but complementary; they cater to different aspects of career counselling.

Frank Parson's Decision-making Factors

The fundamental notion that has driven career counselling for the last one century has been Frank Parson's contention that there are three broad decision-making factors in making a career choice. Parsons (1909), who is considered the father of career development psychology, was of the view that three factors should be considered by an individual before taking a decision:

1. Clear understanding of oneself, including one's attitudes, abilities, interests and limitations.
2. Understanding the requirements of the job and job profile (often referred to as knowledge of the world of work).
3. Understanding of the relation between the above two factors.

Donald Super's Theory of Vocational Development

Super's influential theory brought to the field of career counselling the idea, that career counselling is a lifelong process. Career itself gets defined and redefined across the lifespan of an individual. Hence, career counselling needs to help the individual in adapting to work life and in undergoing major transitions across the lifespan. Super (1957, 1965) had divided the vocational life cycle into five stages and many sub-stages. Let us discuss the major stages of his vocational development cycle:

1. *Exploration stage* (15-24 years) refers to the time when most adults try to make a transition from study life to work life. Most youths explore various fields to decide upon a preferred career. Even when committed to a career option, the individual is only tentatively committed. If the first experience is not rewarding, the individual may shift to another. After graduation, for example, I had joined Tata Steel and had plans to make a career in electrical engineering. Later, however, I decided to go for Civil Services.
2. *Establishment stage* (25-44 years) starts when vocational exploration ends and the individual is now ready to make career in an occupational area. While the job is stable, the individual is oriented towards learning new skills and garnering a variety of experiences relevant to the work.
3. *Maintenance stage* (45-60 years) begins around the mid-40s age. The opportunities for career advancement are now fewer and the major worry of the individual is to retain her achieved status, rather than to improve it.
4. *Decline stage* begins at the age of 60-65 years. People in this stage prepare to leave the workplace as retirement is closer.

Holland's Theory of Vocational Personality Types

Holland's theory is the most widely used and researched person-environment fit model of career counselling. This theory reasons that people search for environments that best fit their personalities and will derive most satisfaction in finding this fit. He had categorized people's personalities into six types (RISASEC):

R – Realistic
I – Investigative
A – Artistic
S – Social
E – Enterprising
C – Conventional

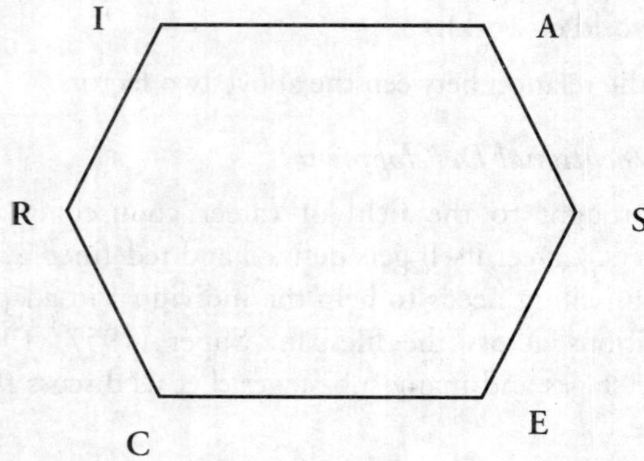

Fig. 4.5 : Concept of RISASEC (Holland's Theory)

He arranged these personality types on a hexagon (Fig. 4.5). Distance on the hexagon gets translated into psychological distance. Hence, R-type is closer to I-type and C-type, but most different from S-type.

Holland's theory has been extremely useful, because it makes the job of career counsellor methodological. The first step is to use some interest inventories and attitude tests to assess the client and find what vocational personality type she is. Secondly, study the world of work and divide various jobs into six categories. Third step is to make a proper person-environment fit, i.e., match the personality type with the job profile where the client will be best fit to work in. This theory has also been checked across cultures; validated in some while falsified in other cultures. Holland's theory has been found valid among participants of a study conducted by Leong and his colleagues (1998) in India.

Table 4.1 : Super's stages of Vocational development.†

Stage	Approximate Ages	Key Events and Transitions
Growth Stage	0-14	A period of general physical and mental growth.
Prevocational substage	0-3	No interest in or concern with vocations.

table contd…

† Adapted from Zaccaria (1970).

Stage	Approximate Ages	Key Events and Transitions
Fantasy substage	4-10	Fantasy is basis for vocational thinking likes and dislikes.
Interest substage	11-12	Ability becomes the basis for vocational thought.
Exploration stage	15-24	General exploration of work.
Tentative substage	15-17	Needs, interests, capacities, value and opportunities become bases for tentative occupational decisions.
Transition substage	18-21	Reality increasingly becomes a basis for vocational thought and action.
Trial substage	22-24	First trial job is entered after the individual has made an initial vocational commitment.
Establishment stage	25-44	The individual seeks to enter a permanent occupation.
Trial substage	25-30	A period of some occupational change due to unsatisfactory choices.
Stabilization substage	31-44	A period of stable work in a given occupational field.
Maintenance stage	45-65	Continuation in one's chosen occupation.
Decline Stage	65+	Adaptation to leaving work force.
Deceleration substage	65-70	Period of declining vocational activity.
Retirement substage	71+	A cessation of vocational activity.

Career Counselling in Practice

Career Counselling is both an arts and a science. The career counsellor has to provide objective information, such as results of interest inventory (so that client can understand herself; this is the first pre-requisite of decision-making according to Parson's theory) and world of work information (so that client understands requirements of the job: this is the second pre-requisite of decision-making according to Parsons). Hence, the counsellor is a scientist. At the same time, she has to help the client make subjective decisions based on above objective information and other subjective information that the counsellor gets while discussing the issue with the client. Hence, she is an artist!

It must be understood that career counsellor is no more than a facilitator, a catalyst. She should not direct the client and let her take her own decision. This is because we are intrinsically motivated to identify and realize our potential. The counsellor's duty is to provide us genuine, sincere vision and objective facts. It is the client who has to find the best career path for herself.

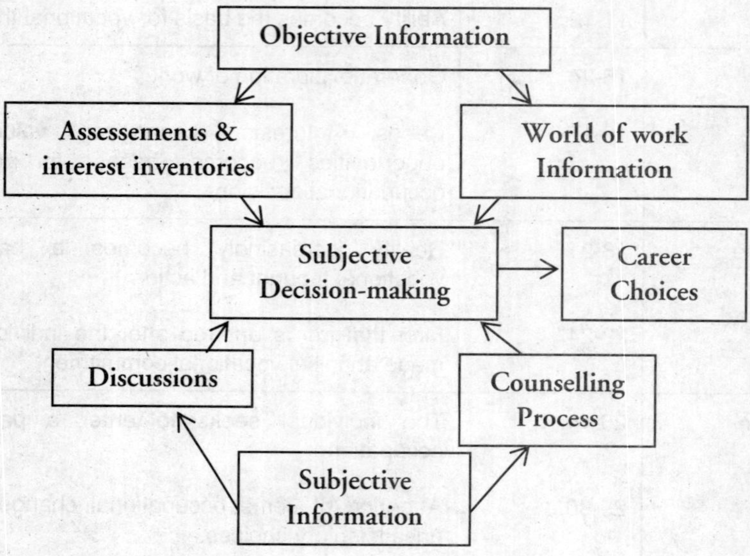

Fig. 4.6 : Various sources of information in career counselling and career decision choice

Let me illustrate this with an example. Suppose I go to a career counsellor to assess my career options. I am interested in civil services, but I am not sure. The counsellor puts me through the following steps:

1. He tests me on Campbell interest inventory and multiple aptitude tests to know my interests and aptitudes.
2. He gets me information regarding the world of work of a civil servant, what it needs to be a civil servant, etc.
3. He finds that I am a generalist, I rank above average on multiple intelligences, but not excellent on any one. He finds my preferences from the results of interest inventories. We talk about how much my abilities match the preferred career option I am interested in. Note that I am the one who takes the decision, he just provides non-directive guidance.

Vocational Guidance

School and college students pursue classes with the hope of getting some job after graduation. They attend classes to enhance their skills in some specialized areas; however, many graduates do not get jobs; of others who do, about two-third are those who got the job by chance or took the only job available to them. As a result, they aren't usually content with their job. The high unemployment and under-employment rate, as well as high drop-out rates in our educational system and job placement suggests that mere academic orientation is not sufficient in education. Vocational guidance is a solution to this problem. Vocational guidance seeks to guide students throughout the student life, in learning skills that are pre-requisite for getting a good job and performing successfully in the job. Basically, it seeks to facilitate the transition from school to work. Still, it is not limited to the final year of graduation. Vocational guidance is provided right from kindergarten.

Vocational Development Theory

This theory is the basis of vocational guidance programmes provided in schools and colleges. This theory states that people's idea about vocation changes in stages from childhood to adolescence. The two stages and six sub-stages that this theory talks about are:

1. Growth stage
    - 1.1 Fantasy sub-stage (0-10 years)
    - 1.2 Interest sub-stage (11-12 years)
    - 1.3 Capacity sub-stage (13-14 years)
2. Exploration stage
    - 2.1 Tentative sub-stage
    - 2.2 Transition sub-stage
    - 2.3 Trial sub-stage

In the growth stage, children only form images of various vocations and try them out by imagination. In the fantasy sub-stage, students use their imagination to take on different career roles. For example, I aspired to be a doctor, an engineer, a scientist and a professor, variously when I was a kid. In the next sub-stage, they consider various areas of interest. Finally, they become aware of career demands in the capacity sub-stage. The identification of alternatives to choose from hasn't yet occurred.

Real exploration of various vocations starts in the exploration stage. When considering various career options, adolescents first choose a tentative career goal in the tentative sub-stage. When the youth works towards aspiring the career goal, she is in transition sub-stage. Once a career goal has been met (by placement or job offer), the youth takes on the job on a trial basis in the trial sub-stage.

Strategies of Vocational Guidance

Vocational guidance programs are generally composed of three levels of assessment. Level-1 assessments are conducted during the elementary school years. The trainers focus on the child's understanding of self, interpersonal skills and decision-making skills. Development of a healthy self-concept and a proper frame of reference are necessary pre-requisites for future skill development. Level 2 guidance is given in high schools. The goal of level 2 is to maintain and encourage career exploration and to assist students in formulating tentative career goals. The guidance team conducts various tests to understand students' interests and abilities.

Level-3 guidance is provided during under-graduation period. A variety of assessment tools are utilized by the counsellor; interviews and observation are also used to understand the student.

Two prime objectives of this level are:

1. Determine the training needed to attain post-graduate education or job placement.
2. Determine the skills an individual needs to make a successful transition from school to work.

Nowadays, many professional courses are offered to undergraduate students in various universities. This is done to increase their skills for placement in appropriate jobs. For example, Delhi University provides courses in computers, animation, journalism, marketing and communication so as to improve students' vocational skills. Yet, this is not sufficient. Vocational guidance should start form primary school.

Career Counselling Versus Vocational Guidance

Career counselling and vocational guidance have similar subject matter, yet are different concepts. In fact, career counsellors are much different from vocational guides in the way they practice and in their strategy and goals. Career counselling believes that for a healthy life and to realize optimal potentialities of self, the individual must have the appropriate career over the life-span.

Vocational guidance on the other hand, is concerned with the transition from student life to job life. So as to smoothen the transition, it seeks to train students in skills that will help the student in properly adjusting to job demands after she joins her job.

The aim of career counselling is to help the individual lead a satisfied career life and gain actualization from her career. It is about making the right choice so as to ascertain a proper person-work fit. The aim of vocational guidance is to reduce underemployment and high dropout rates among freshers in industry.

4.5 Training for Improving Academic Achievement

There is a stark difference between learning and performance. While learning is a relatively permanent change in behaviour and knowledge base, performance is the efficiency in completing a task. Tests of academic achievement (like, CBSE, ICSE exams) measure performance. The teacher's role is to impart learning as well as to motivate the students for academic achievement. Training for academic achievement includes classroom teaching strategies and motivation and training to improve memory.

Classroom Teaching Strategies

There are broadly two teaching styles to choose from- Direction transmission approach and Constructivist training approach. In direct transmission, the teacher decides what needs to be discussed and learnt. She makes the teaching process more interactive by giving feedback to students and by making the teacher-student communication two way. If the teacher decides to follow the direct 'transmission approach', she can use the following strategies to improve academic achievement:

- Achievement depends on the extent to which the teacher structures learning. This can be done through outlines, organization charts and summaries.
- Practice, it is said, makes a man perfect. Practicing newly taught skills regularly improves achievement. Overlearning of some key concepts also helps in better academic performance.
- Teacher quizzing and questioning improves student learning. The teacher should ask clear questions and give the student time to formulate answers. The teacher should also promote divergent thinking and multiple ways of approaching the same question.
- Feedback improves academic achievement. Feedback in the form of praise or assertion helps the students know when they are correct.
- Making students work together cooperatively in class work and homework usually improves achievement.

The direct transmission approach has the teacher as the center of the focus. On the other hand, constructivist training has minimal interference by teachers. The constructivist approach is based on Piaget's ideas. The student is left in environments and situations that are rich in discovery opportunities; students discover concepts for themselves. The role of the teacher is limited to answering questions that may be asked by the students while they attempt a task.

Kohlberg and Mayer (1972) had contrasted direct transmission and constructivist views of instruction. They point out that constructivist approach is superior in learning and academic achievement. However, there are certain shortcomings of this approach:

1. The teachers need to be extremely talented, so as to answer any question asked to them by the students.
2. Discovery learning is a slow process and the student may take any direction to learn. Hence, there is no definite framework or target.
3. Sometimes the students may make incorrect discoveries. For example, discovering a long solution for a problem will induce them to solve similar problem in same way.

To reduce these short-comings, yet to retain the advantage of constructivist approach, another approach called guided discovery is used. In guided discovery, the teacher poses some questions (i.e., guides) when the students start performing a task. The questions are included to direct the students to discover in a specific way. Such guided discovery teaching is also called Scaffolding. Like the scaffolding of a building, the teacher supports when needed; and reduces the scaffolding as the child's mental processes, which are under construction, are increasingly able to handle the task.

Which of these is the best training strategy to improve academic achievement? Most contemporary researchers believe that a combination of instruction learning and discovery learning is the best teaching strategy for higher student achievement.

Motivation for Academic Achievement

Students need to be adequately motivated for learning if their aim is to improve their achievement. Some strategies that can be used to keep students motivated are:

1. *Rewarding achievement:* Behaviourists believe that to get a favorable behaviour, the teacher should reinforce it with a reward. However, it is not that simple! When an intrinsically motivated student is given an explicit reward, the student's future intrinsic motivation decreases. This phenomenon is called over-justification effect, whereby the student justifies her behaviour by extrinsic rewards. For example, suppose a child writes good poems and his poem-writing fetches him various gifts in functions. As long as the gifts keep coming, its fine. But when the gifts stop coming, the child in fact is less motivated to write poems.

   An alternative effective form of reinforcement is praise. Praise works best when (a) the teacher makes clear what was praiseworthy, (b) is sincere and genuine is praising the student, and (c) praises only for desirable student behaviour.

2. *Mastery goal orientation:* As has been discussed in Dweck's theory (see chapter on sports psychology), mastery goal orientation means that the student always compares himself with others in the class. His motivation may be due to a need for success or a fear of failure ("I will study because if I fail, the whole class will laugh at me"). In ego-orientation, the student can't get the most out of himself. He doesn't realize his potential but realize as much as needed to be successful, relative to others. Hence, the teacher should promote mastery goals and the way to do so is by promoting intrinsic motivation to achieve mastery in any skill. To promote intrinsic motivation, the teacher should:

   (a) Give some degree of autonomy to the student in trying any task.

   (b) Improve the perceived competence of the student by increasing her self-efficacy and confidence.

   (c) Show affection, emotional attachment and relatedness to the student.

3. *Encouraging moderate risk taking:* Many students are afraid to take risks because of the fear of failure. Teachers should promote moderate risk-taking behaviour in students as risk-taking is related to achievement. You may ask how? Take the case of a child who refuses to try to write, fearing that because of her bad writing style she would write

miserably. If she doesn't even write, how will she improve her writing skills? I remember, many of my friends in school didn't practice essays, fearing that what they write might be miserable. As a result, they couldn't improve and did poorly in exams.

4. *Pygmalion effect:* In a classic study by Rosenthal and Jacobson (1968), a test was administered in a classroom and the teachers were informed that few students were exceptional, but actually they were not. However, their academic achievement improved dramatically in a later test. The researchers concluded that this was because of teachers' behaviour towards these students. Teachers had increased their expectancy (expectations) from these students. Pygmalion effect throws light on the fact that teachers' expectation can potently be used to improve academic achievement.

   It must be warned at this point that teachers' expectancy is a double-edged sword. Many studies among deprived group children in India have shown that teachers have high expectations from upper caste students and very low expectations from lower caste students. This affected the academic achievement of these students. Hence, removing teacher prejudices and training teachers to be expectant from students is a step towards improving academic achievement of students.

5. *Co-operative learning:* Co-operative learning refers to any instructional process where small groups of children are formed to maximize each student's learning. Also called peer tutoring, this technique has become popular of late because of the strong empirical evidence backing it, as an effective strategy to improve academic performance. Many studies conducted on the lines of Sherif's cave experiment have shown that cooperative learning has positive effects on student performance. A major reason attributed for its success is that both the learner and the teacher are of similar ability and so better appreciate the difficulties faced by each other in learning.

6. *Increasing self-concept and self-efficacy:* A student is high in self-efficacy if he succeeds once in a while. Otherwise, he may not be adequately motivated and worse, may suffer from learned helplessness. Learned helplessness is a situation in which the student has no expectancy, i.e., he believes that whatever his efforts be, he couldn't perform. The student develops a fatalistic attitude towards exams. The lesson for the teacher here is to provide lectures that are challenging but not so much as to overwhelm the student.

   Self-efficacy can also be increased by modelling, i.e., by introducing role models who the students recognize with. For example, the teacher can reason that a student of a senior batch was average in studies, but finally performed very well in board exams because of his hard work. Role models help in vicarious reinforcement and motivate students to strive for academic achievement.

   Locus of control is another major factor in motivating students towards achievement. Students with external locus of control attribute failure to themselves and success to situational factors. Such attribution errors are the result of incorrect self-concept. Jayakanthan, for example, has found a significant positive relationship between self-concept and academic achievement. Hence, self-concept should be developed through personality development programmes. This is especially important when teaching students from deprived group backgrounds.

Training for Improving Memory

Teachers are often concerned about how to present information, so that the information is adequately processed and retrieved by the students. Here, they can borrow from the rich subject-matter of cognitive psychology. In this section, we will discuss various psychological principles underlying good memory, how they can be applied in educational settings and their merits and demerits.

Some important psychological principles underlying memory enhancement are:

1. *Concepts:* Most of the information that is retrieved by the brain is stored in the form of concepts and categories. These concepts are organized hierarchically. Hence, hierarchical organization of new information by the teacher helps in better understanding of new concepts. For example, suppose the students of a Motions Picture school are asked to memorize various movies in which Shahrukh Khan has acted. The teacher can organize all information hierarchically to help in better memorization.

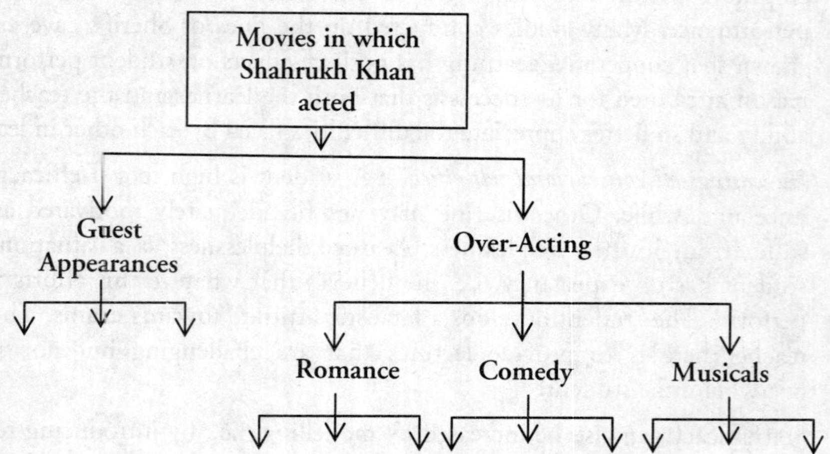

Fig. 4.7 : Organisation of information in hierarchical manner

2. *Imagery:* Information that is received by the short-term memory can be encoded in two forms- visual-spatial form and verbal-symbolic form. Both ways of encoding are inter-related and it is easier to recall information that is stored as both images and concepts. In fact, the dual-code hypothesis states that concrete sentences are more likely to be stored as images, while abstract sentences are coded only verbally.

The lesson for teacher is that to make learning more effective and to improve memory, both verbal lectures and visual presentations (through diagrams, maps, PPT presentations, etc.) are necessary.

3. *Mnemonics:* Mnemonic refers to any technique that can be used to aid memory. Most popular mnemonic strategies can be represented as POLKA.

   POLKA stands for:

   P – Peg words   O – Organization   L – Loci

   K – Keywords   A – Acronym, Acrostic

   In the method of loci, one visualizes to-be-recalled items on familiar landmarks. For example, the students can visualize a list of words by linking the words to landmarks that she encounters when coming to school, such as school bus, school peon, teachers, black board, etc. In Pegword, you are required to associate new words to a list of words you already know. The difference between loci and pegwords is that loci are the association between items and images; the second is association between items and items.

   In the Keyword method, an interactive bridge is formed between the sound of a word and a familiar word. For example, the Hindi word 'Murkh' means '"idiot" and sounds like "molar". This way "molar" can be linked to the word "idiot". In acronym, you use the first letter of a word as a cue to recall. For example, POLKA stands for the mnemonics discussed here. In aerostic, on the other hand, you use the first letters of a phrase as a cue to recall. For example, "Pappu observed Laloo kissing Aunty" is an acrostic that represents the same information that POLA represents.

4. *Method of PQRST:* PQRST technique is a technique to help students in studying their textbooks and remembering better. Developed by Thomas and Robinson, this technique states that retrieval of information read is more when you study a book by following the five stages:

   (a) P – Preview

   (b) Q – Question

   (c) R – Read

   (d) S – Self-recitation

   (e) T – Test

5. *Other techniques:* Many Dos and Donts about improving memory are derived from various psychological theories. For example, proactive interference occurs when information learnt earlier interferes with new learning; hence the student should sleep immediately after studying. Overlearning has been found to be effective on the logic that more you learn an item, stronger is the neutral connection of that item stored in memory and become stronger the neural connections, faster and easier the retrieval.

Drawbacks of memory techniques

Specific memory enhancing techniques, like mnemonics and PQRST techniques ultimately depend on the motivation of the student to use these techniques. Further, no one technique or method applies for all students. Which technique effectively improves memory of a student depends on the student's learning style. A solution to the problem is that the teacher should use multiple techniques at the same time to improve memory. But, this doesn't seem very practical as the focus of teaching may shift to memorizing!

Finally, many of the techniques discussed here are heavily student-centric. The teacher's intervention is limited in how a student reads a textbook. He may or may not use the PQRST technique, for instance, when studying, even after repeated encouragement from the teacher.

Use of Psychological Tests in Educational Institutions

No two students are alike. The fact that individual differences in students exist, necessitates the use of psychological tests for better understanding of the individual child. The idea is to understand the student, her abilities, interests and personality, etc. The many tests that are conducted in schools are oriented towards one of the three central orientations of psychology:

1. Individual differences orientation
2. Developmental orientation
3. Social context orientation

Let us now discuss various psychological instruments that are popular in educational institutions, and their utility. There are tests to measure:

1. Cognitive development
2. Development backwardness
3. Interests and vocational leanings
4. School achievement
5. Students' social environments
6. Child pathology

1. Cognitive development

The oldest test or cognitive development is the Stanford-Binet scale that defines IQ as comparison between a student and what is considered normal at the age. Today, the most popular scales for measuring cognitive development are Wechsler Preschool and Primary Scales of Intelligence (WPPSI) and Wechsler Intelligence Scale for Children (WISC).

There are many alternatives to IQ testing in order to assess cognitive development. In Piagetian task testing, certain phenomena that Piaget attributes to, specific stages of cognitive development are examined, for example, where the child can show cognitive abilities of seriation, conservation, etc. Dynamic testing, on the other hand, is based on Vygotsky's concept of Zone of Proximal Development. The test is conducted in two phases. In the first phase (also called interaction phase), an adult familiarizes the child with a task, gives hints about how the task could be completed and motivates the child. In the second phase, actual testing takes place, in which the child's performance is checked. Basically, dynamic testing tests the competence of students, i.e., their ability to perform with support from teachers.

Some tests measure the reaction time of students. These tests are based on the assumption that being intelligent involves being able to process information quickly. Many studies (for instance, Mohan and Jain, 1983) have shown that speed can be taken as an index of intelligence. Reaction time measures many cognitive faculties, such as, short term memory, iconic memory, etc. Anima Sen and Arun Sen, the most prolific researchers in the area of mental retardation in India, have successfully used tests based on reaction time to assess mental retardation.

2. Development backwardness

Not all students pass through Piaget's stages at the same age. It is necessary to test the students with developmental backwardness, so as to decide on any remedial education for them. Many other tests have been devised to test backwardness in language development, moral development, etc.

3. Interests and vocational learning

Students study with the ultimate expectation of landing a job that would suit their interests and vocational learnings. Career decisions are tough to take and many-a-times the student is not sure what to do. These days, schools take the service of vocational psychologists to help the students understand their interests and preferences. Some major interest inventories used in schools are the Strong Interest Inventory (SII), Kuder Occupational Interest Survey (KOIS), Campbell Interest and Sill Survey (CISS), etc. The Self-Directed Search (SDS) and the UNIACT Interest Inventory are two tests, based on Holland's Six RIASEC dimensions. The utility of these tests have been extensively supported by empirical research. Many studies have confirmed that interest inventories effectively differentiate and predict important career behaviours. These tests are useful to decide which field to specialize in, which elective subjects to take and what vocational skills to develop for job placement.

4. School achievement

To get an admission into higher studies in western countries, one has to give the Student Achievement Test (SAT). SATs are useful in placing children in various educational level. In India, we have entrance examinations for various engineering colleges and medical colleges; these examinations test students less on achievement and more on ability. Ability tests are predictive tests that predict performance in the future. Standard tests to measure ability also exist. For example, the Differential Aptitude Test (DAT) measures a student on nine different abilities.

5. Student's social environments

Students are deeply affected by their peer groups. Students tend to nominate peers with whom they would like to play. Due to this dynamics, there are three types of children in school- popular, unpopular and neglected. School relationship instruments, such as Moes's

Social Climate Scale, try to assess the social status of a student in school peer groups and throw light on peer group influence on the student. For example, if a student is found to be a longer, teacher intervention can be suggested to make him more acceptable in student circles.

More than peer group, the family affects a student's psyche. Hence, several questionnaires have been devised to measure parental styles- authoritative, authoritarian, rejecting or laissez-faire. These questionnaires help the school psychologist understand family factors behind any maladaptive behaviour of the student and give suggestions to parents, if needed. School psychologists also use psychological test to measure the school environment, that is, how the school environment fosters well-being, achievement motivation and confidence in pupils.

6. Child pathology

Childhood pathology can be measured by *Achenbach's* Child Behaviour Checklist (CBCL). Beck's depression scales have been remodeled for children and named Kovacs's questionnaire. It allows us to identify clinical cases of depression in children. The attention Deficit/ Hyperactivity Disorder (ADHD) is a test to measure lack of attention and impulsivity among children in the age group 4-18 years.

4.6 Value Education and Personality Development

Value refers to a mode of conduct (means) or end state that is personally preferable to an alternate mode of conduct. Hence, values affect our behaviour by defining goals (end state) and means to attain the goals. Values form a basic part of our personality structure and hence, develop very early in life. Unlike attitudes, it is very tough to change values; they are much more permanent, once formed. Hence, there is a need to foster proper values in children. Value education refers to train children with proper values at school for healthy personality development.

What are proper values and why is it necessary to foster these in schools? There are three types of values:

1. Universal values
2. Cultural values
3. Personal values

Universal values are highest order values; they relate to sensitivity for humanity, love, brotherhood, compassion and empathy. These need to be developed in children, so that they can grow up to become responsible citizens and humane creature.

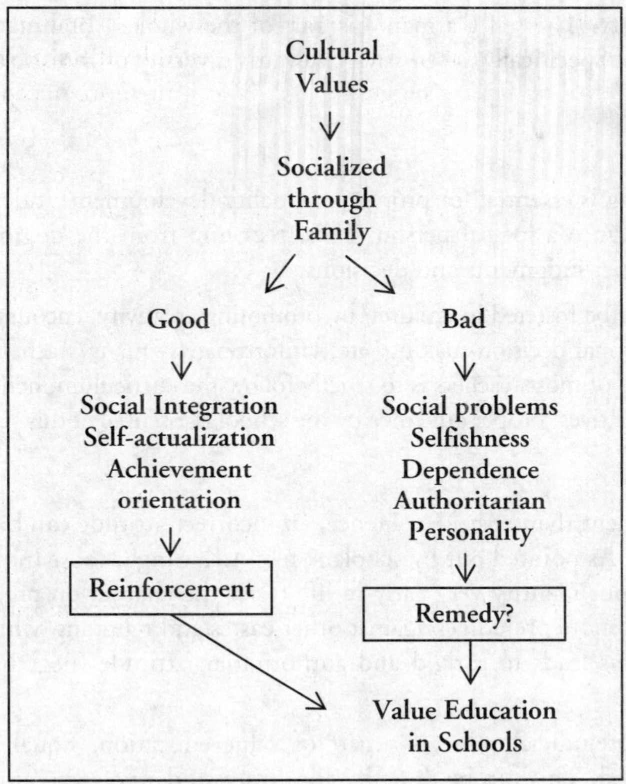

Fig. 4.8 : Values associated with education and personalities

Culture values are the values that are influenced by family and significant others. For example, in Indian society, a caste hierarchy exists. A.K. Singh has found that caste and religious identity become prominent in Indian children at an early stage. Due to this, some cultural values (e.g., "I am superior to Hari because I am Brahmin and he is Vaishya") get socialized into the child's psyche. This is dangerous. Hence, there is a need to teach proper cultural values in schools.

The values that one learns in one's family are specific to his/ her sub-culture (Brahmin sub-culture, Muslim sub-culture, deprived groups sub-culture, etc.). These are not conducive for social integration. Hence, the need for value education in schools.

Personal values are those which affect an individual's motivation and striving for success. Basically, this is the most important category of values for personality development. What is your level of motivation? What motivates you? Entrepreneurship? Fame? Self-actualization? Success? Money? Altruism?

Value education in schools can follow several strategies. A few strategies are:

1. Development of collectivistic values

In western society, the individual is viewed as distinct from the collective. The "self" is clearly differentiated from society. Hence, there is a need for sensitizing the individual towards society. Fortunately, Indians have a collective orientation. Hence, our cultural values promote sensitivity towards society. The self ("atman") is part of the whole ("Brahman"). Schools need to reinforce these values. Specifically, a sensitivity towards diversity of Indian society needs to be instilled in children.

2. Reflexive thinking

Rational, logical thinking is essential for proper personality development. Independent thinking helps the child develop into a logical person. This frees him from the dogmas of society and helps him in taking proper judgments and decisions.

Reflexive thinking can be fostered in children by promoting creativity, encouraging initiatives by children, assisting in rational decision-making, etc. Unfortunately, many teachers don't encourage creativity. The prime aim of most teachers is to strictly follow the curriculum; hence they discourage children from taking initiatives. Proper guidance by the school is essential at this stage.

3. Removal of prejudices

Values are more permanent than attitudes. Hence, an incorrect attitude can be changed, but an incorrect value can't be. As pointed out by scholars, like A.K. Singh, most Indian children get a caste identity and religious identity very early in life (refer the chapter on prejudices and social integration). Parents promote prejudices against other castes and religions, which get embedded in the value system. This leads to a rigid and authoritarian attitude (negative) towards other communities.

Hence, removal of prejudicial value is a part of value education. Equal status contact in schools should be enabled. This can be done by admitting students from various backgrounds. Superordinate goals should be set by clubbing together students form varied social backgrounds in group projects. The jigsaw puzzle is a good example of how values towards diversity can be fostered (see chapter on social integration).

4. Personality development

Personality heavily depends on the parenting style of parents. If parents show a rigid parenting style, characterized by rejection of the child and neglect, the child may develop authoritarian personality. This and other personality problems arising out of child-rearing practices, can be ameliorated in school education. However, it depends heavily on the kind of relationship the teachers develops with a child. If the teacher shows unconditioned positive regard to the child and is warm and affectionate, he/ she can greatly influence the future course of the child's life. Problem here is that, Indian schools have a very high student to teacher ratio, due to which teachers can't give personal attention to each student. Hence, a student counsellor or school psychologist must be appointed to look after the welfare of students who show extremes of behaviour (like withdrawal, depression, etc.)., (The movie "Taare Zameen Par" depicts one such case where interpersonal relation between a teacher and a learning-disabled child helps the child not only overcome his dyslexia problems, but also his lost confidence!)

■ ■ ■

5

WORK AND ORGANISATIONAL PSYCHOLOGY

Chapter outline

5.1 Personnel Selection

Recruitment of personnel is an activity whereby candidates who would best match a task, the team at the workplace and the organisation are selected by the company for employment. In this, the work psychologists and HR personnel use certain selection criteria to predict the future performance of a candidate on the job. Hence, it is a process in which predictive validity of the selection criteria determines to what extent selection has been successful.

Various outcomes of the validity of selection criteria are:

	Rejected	Selected	
Performer	Miss	Correct Selection	Candidate Ability
Non-Performer	Correct Rejection	Wrong Selection	
	Selection Criteria		

Fig. 5.1 : Selection criteria matrix

The aim of a work psychologist is to maximises "correct selection" and minimises "wrong selection" (or "false alarm"). Recruitment typically follows the following steps:

1. Job Analysis

Job analysis is an activity that enables the work psychologist to define the job specifications. It includes a combination of methods – existing employees who work on the particular task can be interviewed. Observation of the job gives insight into behaviors that are expected of the prospective employee; biodata of existing and former employees who have worked on similar jobs can be of help in getting an idea about what should be the background of a candidate for the job. For example, a company has found that students from IIT Kharagpur are much more efficient than that of IIT Kanpur in doing a specific job. It may be because of the excellent laboratory facilities in IIT Kharagpur, but this the HR personnel infer from study of biodata of existing employees.

Also work psychologists study the amount of group activity that the task involves. If the task needs to be performed by a team, the interpersonal skills and emotional intelligence need to be assessed also.

Furnham (1997) believes that a job analysis should provide details of the minimum professional knowledge that would be acceptable for the task, the basic skills needed to perform the task and the ideal personality traits that the prospective candidate must have to fit into the job.

These three items can be referred to as:

1. Knowledge
2. Skills
3. Attitudes

2. Selection of Criteria

There is no absolute method of scan out wrong selection and sero in one the deserving candidates. Based on job analysis, a decision criterion is drawn, the criteria specify what knowledge, skills and attitude should be minimally present in the right candidate.

3. Selection of instrument

After deciding on the cut-off knowledge, skills and attitude, now the task is to measure these three properties in an individual. For this, a variety of instruments, like application blanks, psychometric tests, interview and aptitude test are used. All these are discussed in detail in the next section and the student is suggested to read the tests in the light of a present discussion.

A major challenge in selection of instruments is that some instruments (such as interview) are very subjective. These tests have low validity.

4. Recruitment proper

Candidates are invited to apply for the vacant post through application blanks. The application blanks ask for biodata, a reference and academic grades. Biodata throws light on the skill-set of the candidate; references on her personality and attitude; and academic grades help assess her knowledge.

After an initial screening based on the application blanks, candidates are called and selection instruments are operated on them. Their performance is assessed and final decision is taken before intimating the results to them.

Training and Human Resource Development

Simply stated, human resource development refers to a focus on increasing the skills and resources of humans, in this context, employees. Human Resource Development (HRD) today is an important philosophy of organissations because of the simple reason that in these changing times organisations have to continually upgrade their human resources (skills, knowledge, etc. of employees) to meet challenges of changing times. Intrinsic here is also the philosophy that better human resources mean better resources at the disposal of the organisation.

Pareek (1991) defines HRD as 'a new systematic approach to proactively deal with issues related to individual employees and teams, organisations and a movement to develop organisational capability to manage change and challenge.' HRD includes training of employees, but doesn't exclusively consist of training. Training of employees no doubt contributes to human resource development, but training is a one-time activity (during recruitment and from time to time), but HRD encompasses a vast array of systems that lead to enhancement of human resources.

In this context, it is appropriate to understand HRD as a matrix so as to understand the range of HRD. HRD is a continuous process and it encompasses many human units and systems.

Pareek (1991) has referred to six human units as the foci of HRD:

1. Individual employee
2. Role
3. Dyad
4. Teams
5. Inter-teams
6. Organisation

He has also identified six HRD systems of activities:

1. Appraisal system
2. Career system
3. Training system
4. Work system

5. Cultural system
6. Self-renewal system

These two axes together form a 6 x 6 HRD matrix. In this section, we will discuss training and career systems in detail. Other systems have been covered in other sections of this chapter. For example, appraisal system is discussed when discussing psychological tests for employee appraisal; work system is dealt with in power, leadership and ergonomics chapters.

5.2 HRD in India

Human Resource Development (HRD) is an all-encompassing concept. While it can be narrowly defined as efforts to improve the skill sets of employees, a broader definition includes all efforts to optimise human units and processes. Given the fact that HRD is a concept with such wide connotations, obviously cross-cultural variations would exist in the interpretation of HRD; hence, a need to situate HRD in Indian context. In this section, we will deal with the concept of HRD as understood in India and look into an appraisal of HR development in practice in India. For this purpose, I have referred to an excellent essay, 'HRD in India; Prospect and Retrospect' written by Prof. Udai Pareek back in 1991. I have shamelessly summarised the theorisation of HRD and appraisal of HRD in practice in Indian organisation as discussed by Prof. Pareek in this essay.

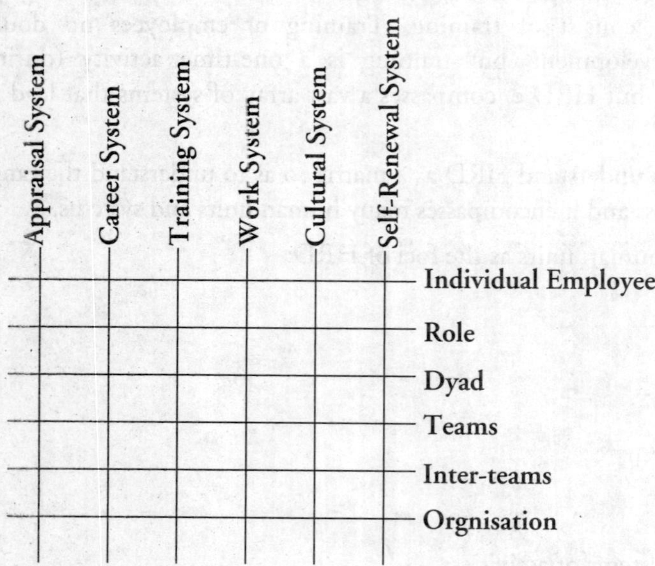

Fig. 5.2 : The HRD Matrix

Prof. Pareek basically adheres to a very broad definition of HRD. The center of his focus is not just employees, but also other human units like teams and dyads. Further, he talks about six systems that influence the human units (also six in number). Hence, he presents a "HRD

Matrix", a 6 × 6 matrix of six human units cut through by six systems. This HRD matrix can be represented as in the figure. The definition presents us with a framework within which we can assess HRD in India.

The Human Units

The human unit as the most basic unit of an organisation is given below in detail:

1. The Individual Employees

The individual employee is the most basic unit of an organisation. No wonder, it also is a key unit of emphasis of HRD. The development of individual employees typically has three important elements- self-management, competence building and advancement. Competence building refers to the development of professional skills in the individual. Self-management refers to the development of skills that would enable the individual to manage her emotions, to set realistic goals, analyse one's own performance, etc. Advancement refers to career prospects of the employee in increasing age and experience, the employee develops new competencies; hence the need for a career plan. This also is the responsibility of the HRD.

2. The Role

Every employee has some status in the company. She has this status with respect to other employees (superiors, colleagues, subordinates, etc.) who interact with her. Every status is accompanied by certain expectations regarding the role the employee has to perform. These role expectancies define the role of the employee. This is an important human unit asthe role is accompanied by high stress and lower performance. Hence, the need to develop roles.

The three main aspects of development of roles with which HRD is concerned are:

- Optimum stress
- Autonomy
- Linkages

We have seen in another section in this chapter that too low stress or too high stress is detrimental for optimal performance. Hence, a need to ensure that roles have optimal job demand and average level of stress. Also, greater autonomy should be provided in role performance to those employees who want to take initiatives. Autonomy should also be attached to those posts, where role demands a creative nature of work. Thirdly, linkages between various roles should be built. This is important because the goals attached to individual roles should converge and the individual employees should understand the role of her job in fulfillment of organisational goals.

3. The Dyad

Prof. Pareek defines a dyadic group as an employee and his supervisor. A dyadic group is the basic building block in an organisational structure; hence, Prof. Pareek stresses that the stronger the dyads, the stronger the organisation will be. The role of HRD in building strong dyads includes three elements:

- o Trust
- o Mutuality
- o Communication

Trust between an employee and her boss is necessary for work to be smooth. At the same time, mutuality (i.e., a helping relationship in both members of a dyad help each other) between the employee and the supervisor strengthens the relationship in the dyad being built.

4. The Teams

Many dyads together form a team. For example, suppose a software company has got a consultancy assignment. The assignment is dealt by a project manager (PM). Under him, there are two senior software workers (SSW) and under each SSW, there are twenty juniors (JW). So, (PM -> SSW), (SSW -> JW) are various dyads. But together, the PM's team works on a common goal. Hence, the dynamics of these groups need to be monitored by HR and healthy team climate needs to be developed.

The criteria that HRD should focus on, according to Prof. Pareek, are cohesion and resource utilisation. Teams should be cohesive and should create synergy. Effective teams are those that are able to best pool together resources at the disposal of individual employees and utilise the same.

5. The Inter-teams

In many organisations, much of the resource is wasted because of lack of coordination between various teams. The marketing team may, for instance, demand goods of a certain quality, but the production team may be more concerned about quantity and may even be ready to compromise with quality. Hence, there is the need to develop cooperation amongst various groups in the organisation. Departments, division and function should be targeted to develop cooperation towards fulfillment of common organisational goals.

6. The Organisation

HRD activity with respect to the organisation as a whole should focus on (a) growth, (b) impact and (c) self-renewal. Growth is the perpetual motivation of any organisation. Any organisation that doesn't grow becomes stagnant and may decay. Hence, a focus on growth is there. But, growth on accepted lines doesn't always proceed smoothly. Owing to fast changes, a need for self-renewal may be felt. The HRD must organise activities to brain storm on the working of the organisation and how to better the standards. HRD also focuses on the impact the organisation has on outside entities, such as other organisations, customers, etc.

HRD Practices in India

Now, that I have discussed the six human units that are catered to by HRD, let us now discuss various HRD practices in India.

Prof. Pareek provides a six-fold system classification of HRD practices in India which are discussed as under:

1. Appraisal System

Appraisal of an employee's performance (or potential) helps the HR to understand the employee better and dole out rewards in the form of bonuses. At the same time, appraisal system provides a feedback to the employee regarding her performance.

There are three main appraisal systems:

(a) Performance appraisal
(b) Potential appraisal
(c) Performance coaching or counselling

Prof. Pareek observes that most Indian organisations have focused only on performance appraisal. However, in the absence of other appraisal systems, performance appraisal has been reduced to just a mechanical exercise. Potential appraisal, which is the appraisal of the employee's potential to do new work and counselling to develop good skills are other systems of appraisals which need to be implemented to complement performance appraisal.

2. Career System

A major component of human resource development is career system. Work career is an important part of adult life. The adult employee passes through several developmental phases within her job life. Hence, the need for a career system to help the employee sail through developmental phases (For more details on developmental phases, refer to Super's theory).

Three broad components of career systems are:

- Experiences
- Opportunities
- Career planning

Experiences are most useful for an employee at an entry point. Experience is necessary for employees to move up in the organisation; hence there is a need for HRD to make concerted efforts to expose the employee to various types of work. These days, many Indian companies are pursuing activities, like on-the-job training and job rotation scheme to expose employees to varied experiences.

But, so that an employee can prove herself, she needs ample opportunities. It is the role fo the HRD to design an organisation structure, so that an employee with ability has opportunities to take more responsibilities as she matures. Career planning is involved in charting special career paths for individual employees.

3. Training System

The training system is one of the most well-defined elements of HRD. Since HRD traditionally focuses on skill development, training is central to HRD. Unfortunately, it is being very inadequately treated in most organisations. Attention to identification of training needs, preparation of a training strategy, development of a training method (pedagogy), curriculum designing (to meet specific needs), evaluation, follow-up and post-training support, are all important components of a good training system. Although training is extensively used for human resource development and large budgets are spent on training, on the whole, training is not taken seriously. (Pareek, 1991).

A career system which is fast gaining popularity in Indian organisations is mentoring. In mentoring, an entry level recruit is anointed to a senior officer who guides the recruit in matters of career and also personal life. When I was in Tata Steel, I had been provided with a mentor who helped me with many issues that I couldn't have confident with others. Prof. Pareek observes that this is based on the Indian guru-shishya relationship. In many other organisations, a buddy system is also used where the mentor isn't much older to the employee. By this, the employee gets someone of her eye group, she can confide to. In National Academy of Direct Taxes (NADT), where I am presently undergoing training, one faculty member is appointed as counsellor to eight trainees. The counsellor is always accessible to the trainees.

4. Work Systems

Work system is not covered by the traditional, narrow definition of HRD.

However, Prof. Pareek strongly believes that HRD must deal with at least four aspects of work systems:

- Task analysis
- Quality of working life
- Productivity
- Role stress

Task analysis refers to an analysis of the psychological and physical traits needed for an employee to perform as specific job. Task analysis is hinged on the logic that maximum efficiency is achieved when a proper person-environment fit (her, employee-work fit) happens. Productivity and role stress are two related topics. While productivity depends on employee motivation (again how to motivate employee is decided by HRD), role stress happens due to a variety of reasons discussed elsewhere in this chapter. Finally, the quality of work life affects both employee motivation and role stress. Prof. Pareek argues that in improving the quality of work life, factors like participative management, workplace democracy, autonomous work groups, etc. have to be introduced. Other new introductions in the field of work systems include stress management, introducing quality circles, etc.

5. Cultural Systems

Prof. Pareek defines organisational culture as 'cumulative ways of thinking and behaving shaped by the values, attitudes, rituals and sanctions in an organisation. Operationally, development of culture would involve developing a strong corporate identity, development of important values, building healthy traditions and developing consistent management practices' (1991). Cultural systems, which cater to the development of appropriate organisational culture, are the most neglected part of HRD.

Many Indian companies have adopted organisational culture practices of Japanese companies and have benefited from it. However, it must be kept in mind that an organisational culture that suits organisations of a country is different from that of culture of organisations elsewhere. There is a need to study in greater depth, the organisational culture that would best suit Indian organisational climate.

Some recommendations for development of culture, mentioned in Prof. Pareek's paper are:

- Development of strong corporate identity.
- Developing important values and ethics.
- Building healthy traditions and practice, such as induction programmes, promotions, exit policy, retirement policy, etc.
- A robust communication system, whereby employees placed variously in the company hierarchy can communicate with each other.

6. Self-Renewal Systems

An organisation should be concerned with both growth and its health. As it faces new challenges with changing times, there is a need to renew the organisational focus. Hence, a major job of HRD professionals is organisational development (OD). The focus of OD is on developing process competency to increase organisational effectiveness. Organisation Development aims at maintaining profiles of organisational health, monitoring organisational health, assisting sick departments, helping interested units and departments in self-renewal, conflict management, creation of strong teams and so on, and establishing processes that build a climate to promote enabling capabilities in the organisations. (Pareek, 1991).

Towards Conclusion

HRD is a very contemporary and vibrant field of activity. The student is recommended to stay up-to-date with research scholarship on this topic in various journals. As of now, the prime debate is whether to evolve HRD according to the Indian culture, or to adopt successful forms of organisational practices from abroad? Most researchers say, from their experience, that elements of our own culture should be explained, but good practices of other cultures should also be promptly experimented with.

5.3 Training

The theoretical skills that a student learns in her university aren't of significant use in the industry. Even if an employee can be directly inducted for skilled job, she may not perform optimally. Hence, the need for post-recruitment training is there. Besides this training, the need for training arises every time a new technology is introduced or when the employee is given new responsibilities. In case some employees rise to managerial positions, their task becomes more of a challenge in managing their subordinates. Hence, the need for managerial training is there. Finally, the HRD philosophy is that HRD is a continuous process and the employee's skills need to be updated from time to time, keeping it in line with changing times.

The role of occupational psychologist is to examine the needs of the employee, of the organisation, and of the task, decide upon the most appropriate training programmes, drawing from the rich psychological knowledge and taking feedback from the employee.

In this context, the system approach to designing a training programme can be studied:

Training Needs Analysis

Conducting training on ad hoc basis or purely for short-term goals in myopic; it needs to be well organised and planned. Hence, the occupational psychologist makes a training need analysis, consisting:

- Organisational analysis
- Task analysis
- Person analysis

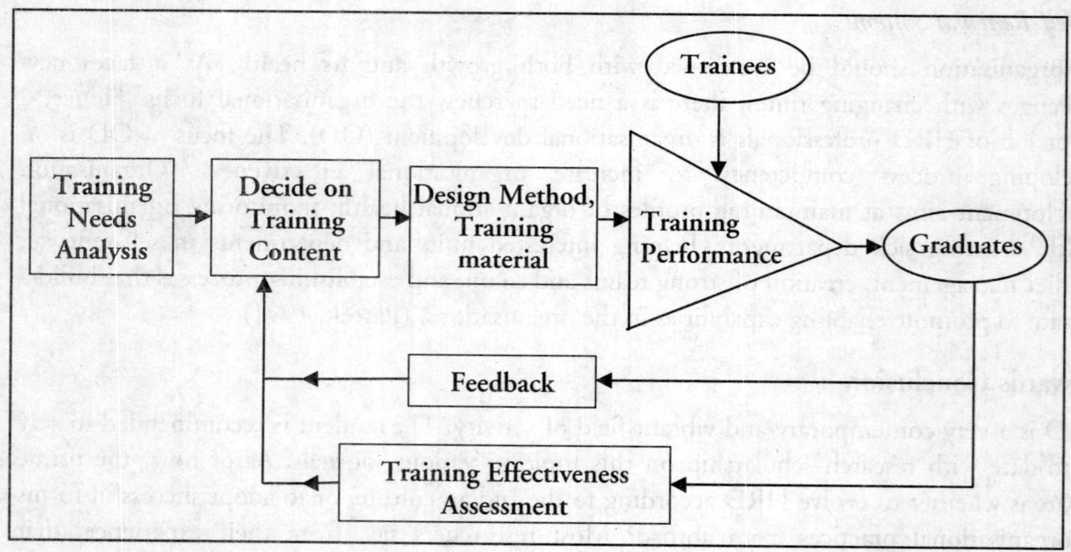

Fig. 5.3 : System Approach to Training Based on Prem Prakash (2004)

There are certain superordinate goals of the organisation, irrespective of the goals of various tasks and departments. First, the training designer needs to examine the organisational goals (present) and its vision (future) and decide upon the best way to achieve the goals and visions. For example, if an organisation plans to computerise all its processes, then what are the needs of the organisation? What kind of skill sets in its employees will help the organisation in meeting its goal? Evidently, the employees have to be made computer-literate.

Then, the training designer needs to prepare a task analysis. Task analysis is a study of skills, materials, knowledge and tools, etc. that employees would need to do the task efficiently. In task analysis, the overview of what the training program is going to consist of is built. Person analysis, on the other hand, refers to matching of skills of individual employees to the needs of the job. If at any time, it is found that her skills are deficient in optimally performing the work, further training is suggested.

Psychological factors in Training

Before we proceed to study various training programs designed by psychologists in industries, it is necessary to understand certain basic psychological principles underlying training:

Actual Practice: For learning to be most effective, trainees must be actively involved in the learning process rather than just passively receive information. For instance, I watch a video of someone operating a truck. I can't put it into practice by driving a truck. The training program needs to provide the trainee with ample opportunities to learn herself. Class lectures, videos and manuals would definitely make you a better learner, but you can't learn as long as you haven't experienced the job first-hand.

Massed and Distributed Practice: Certain tasks are learnt more readily when the trainee is trained on a few relatively long practice sessions (massed learning). Other tasks required a larger number of relatively short practice sessions for better learning (distributed learning). Most studies have shown that the general distributed learning results in better learning. In a meta-analysis of 63 studies, it was found that for jobs demanding relatively simple tasks, distributed practice with short rest period is more effective. But, for more complex tasks, longer rest periods was more effective. In both cases, distributed practice was more effective (Donoran and Radaserich, 1999).

Whole and Part learning: Should a task be learnt by breaking it into parts or should it be learnt as a whole? Research work has concluded that not one of these is the best strategy in all conditions. It is seen that when the task is of high organisation, whole task learning is more efficient. But, when the task involves low organisation, part training method is more efficient. Most work psychologists try to combine both these methods to reach at an optimal learning strategy.

Transfer of Training: This refers to the extent that the skills learnt during training are transferred to the actual job. The transfer of training can be both, positive or negative. In positive transfer, the training helps in improving the performance of the employee at work. On the other hand, negative transfer happens when the skills one learns interfere with her work.

They are many factors on which transfer of training depends. Some of these are:

(a) If there is a close correspondence between the behaviors and attitudes taught in training and the behaviors and attitudes at work, then positive transfer happens.

(b) If there is little similarity between training environment and work environment, then negative transfer takes place.

(c) Negative transfer occurs when older skills conflict with newer skills; if the older skills are conflictual, interference between pro-active memory and retroactive memory takes place. Hence, some strategies to unlearn old skills must be employed before new skills are imparted.

(d) Older workers, particularly those over 50 years of age find it difficult to transfer training. Borteous (1997) opines that older workers have problems adapting to new technology.

Above factors should be kept in mind when designing training. Now-a-days, computer simulation and virtual reality are popular for training. Here, the psychologist tries to simulate real work conditions and behaviors in virtual world. In one study, 58 aviation cadets of Israel's Air Force were required to begin flight training. Some of these were first trained for 10 hours in a computer game that simulated the kind of activities a pilot would perform in the cockpit of an actual fighter plane. It turned out that those who got the simulation training performed better than those who didn't when the real flight training started (Gopher, Well and Barakot, 1994).

Feedback: Feedback, or the "knowledge of results" indicates to the trainees their level of progress. Feedback helps the trainee in correcting and changing any inappropriate behavior that she has learnt during the training otherwise, she would keep practicing the inappropriate behavior. Also, feedback helps maintain the motivation to perform.

Training Methods

(a) On-the job training:

This training takes places on the job where the trainee is supposed to be posted later. It happens under the supervision of an experienced operator who has been operating the machine.

Some advantages of this training method are:

1. It is cheap. No separate training facility or training staff are needed.
2. The transfer of training is positive. The job performance in training situation will carry over to actual work situation because both are the same situations!
3. The motivation to learn is high because the training situation is relevant to the trainee.
4. Feedback is immediate and visible as good performance shows.

However, there are certain concerns regarding on-the-job training, like:

1. Workers and supervisors have to take time out of their regular work to train trainees. This can be expensive in the long run by affecting productivity.
2. On certain jobs, giving an untrained employee access to hasardous machinery may pose a safety risk not only to the trainee but also to other employees.
3. Usually, the trainers are current workers. They may be experts in their job, but not necessarily good trainers. Performing a job and teaching the job to another are different tasks.

(b) Vestibule Training:

As seen, on-the-job training isn't always advantageous and may sometimes hamper normal functioning of other employees. Hence, a simulated workspace can be established at a separate training facility. This is called vestibule training. Vestibule training makes use of equipment's similar to those existing in actual workplace, but relies on skilled instructors to train new workers. Here, trainees are under no pressure to perform; they have the scope to make errors and learn from errors. Yet, vestibule training has certain disadvantages:

1. It is costly to maintain a separate facility with dedicated teaching staff.
2. There are chances of negative transfer of training. Often, obsolete equipments that are retired from the production floor are used in vestibule training. This may lead to negative transfer of training.

(c) Computer Aided Instruction (CAI)

CAI is based on Skinner's concept of programmed learning. The software acts as the instructor and provides the trainee with a task that depends on her performance in the previous task.

CAI has many advantages over traditional training methods:

1. Trainees are actively involved in the learning process.
2. Trainees can work through the software at their own pace.
3. The feedback is immediate.
4. It is just like a private tutor; since the CAI software provides individualised instruction.
5. CAI can be used with any number of employees at any time, without any concern for trainers' availability.

(d) Net-based training

Net-based training is a form of distance education, where training courses are available at a central server on the net. It has all the advantages of CAI; at the same time, it is 20% to 35% lower in cost to traditional classroom instruction (Schults and Schults, 2002).

(e) Behavior Modification:

Positive reinforcement can be used in many situations in the workplace to change behavior. Usually, the work psychologist makes an assessment called 'performance audit' to determine the behaviors that can be modified for more efficient job performance. Then the employee is rewarded for displaying the desired behaviors. Punishment isn't used to modify behavior because it only tells what behavior not to follow. It doesn't speak of the appropriate behaviors to follow.

(f) Business Games

Business games try to simulate a complex organisational situation. The aim of business games is to develop problem-solving and decision-making skills in mangers. Usually, the trainees are divided into two teams. Both teams are given some hypothetical situation and certain problems and they have to compete in better solving the problem. Business games have been found to help management trainees gain experience in decision-making, team play, role taking (one members is made the leader of a team. As the leader, she is the boss), and techniques to better handle stress. I recommend to you a tele-series called "The Apprentice" to have a peep into how business games are played. This series is hosted by the millionaire Donald Trump.

(g) Role Playing

In this training, management trainees are asked to act out a particular role, 'displaying whatever behaviours they believe are appropriate in a given situation, they act out these situations in front of a group of trainees and instructors, who offer comments on their performance'. (Schults and Schults, 2002). Role playing 'enables trainees to understand the views of subordinates and acquaints them with the role they will be expected to play as managers. It provides practical experience as well as feedback from other trainees and instructors'. (Ibid, p.177).

(h) Diversity Training

Ethnic and caste prejudice and sexual discrimination that are prevalent in society often get reflected in interpersonal relations in the organisation. Diversity management, to reduce ethnic prejudices and sexual discrimination, is a prerogative of an organisation. Hence, there is need for diversity training. The aim of diversity training is to make the employee take up the perspective of a minority community individual or of a woman; how they must be feeling on being discriminated against. This is done through lectures, videos, role playing, sensitivity training and confrontational exercises, etc.

Career Development and Planning

Today, organisations recognise that it is their responsibility to provide their employees with opportunities for personal growth and development.

Basically, there are three distinct career stages in the life (between 20 years to 60 years) of an employee:

1. Establishment stage 2. Maintenance stage 3. Decline stage

These stages have been dealt in detail in the section on career counselling in the chapter on Educational Psychology. The growth needs of an employee in all these stages are different and need to be met by the organisation for proper HRD. For example, the establishment stage employee is concerned about learning more and varied skills. Hence, she must get opportunities to train, to attend university workshops and to go study leave for higher studies. The employee in maintenance stage needs to fulfill her self-actualisation need and the company should give her greater job control to do so. In the decline stage, the employee can provide counselling service to the employee to cope with various stressors; put in place a good exit policy, so that retirement process becomes hassle-free.

Sensitivity Training

Whenever we talk about training, the first thing that comes to mind is an exercise to improve professional skills to work on some machine. One needs technical skills to work in a factory; computer software skills (proficiency in software languages, debugging, troubleshooting, etc.) to work for software company, etc. But, as one moves higher up the organisational ladder and takes up managerial posts, there is another skill that becomes more important than software skills- it is the human software skills. Here, I am referring to good interpersonal skills.

Interpersonal skills become necessary for a manager as he/ she has to take on the perspective of others and has to relate with others in a more meaningful way. Hence, the need for training to improve skills in group setting is there. Sensitivity training is one such attempt to provide human software skills. It helps a participant to understand why others do whatever they do.

Sensitivity training is an outgrowth of research efforts of Kurt Lewin and his colleagues. They were concerned about the dangers of autocratic leadership, hence tried to identify the skills needed by a leader to be 'sensitive' to group needs.

Sensitivity training is a process-oriented programme and focusses on certain goals, like:

1. Making participants more aware of the emotion of themselves and others in the group and increase their sensitivity towards others' emotions.
2. The ultimate aim of the training is to have intense experiences leading to life-changing insights.
3. In sensitivity training, participants also attempt to perceive and learn from the consequences of their actions.

The base philosophy of sensitivity training has been ably articulated by Kurt Back: "Sensitivity training started with the discovery that intense, emotional interaction with strangers was possible.

It was looked at, in its early days, as mechanism to help reintegrate the individual man into the whole society through group development. It was caught up in the basic conflict of America at mid-century: the question of extreme freedom, release of human potential or rigid organisation in the techniques developed for large combines". Today, sensitivity training is generally accepted as an effective means to reduce racial discrimination and sexual harassment in the workplace; so also to reduce conflict among managers.

Sensitivity Training Procedure

Sensitivity training consists of 8-10 people. Most of the participants are managers from different organisations. They don't know each other; nor are they formally introduced to each other when they are brought together. There is no agenda and no leader to tell them what to do. The trainer sits with them without revealing her identity. She pretends to be one of them, from some organisation.

In the beginning, there is no formal agenda. The 'ice-breaking' phase starts when people start speaking to each other and try to get to know each other.

The trainer, who is sitting among them, intentionally brings in some topic of a controversial nature for discussion. For instance, topics like, reservation for scheduled castes in private sector, sexual harassment, recruitment of Muslims and discrimination faced by them, etc. A debate starts which turns into a heated argument leading to accusations and misunderstanding. Some participants become uncomfortable and want to leave. This phase is known as 'emotional storming' session.

At this point, the trainer becomes open and expresses her feelings in a minimally evaluative way. This serves to provide feedback to participants. In the next phase, interpersonal relationship develops and members are able to understand the other participants' point of view and accept it. Finally, the participants together explore the relevance of the experience in terms of situations and problems in the organisation.

5.4 Evaluation

Sensitivity training is quite popular in organisational and school setting. However, there are quite a few debates on the utility of sensitivity training. Roy, for instance, has questioned the utility of T-group programmes because these programmes are based on western research and reality. Will they fit into the organisational reality in India?

Some researchers are concerned by reports that individuals who have participated in T-groups have serious emotional breakdown and need psychiatric case. Some others have pointed out that sensitivity groups invade the privacy of an individual; hence are not rightfully within the domain of organisations.

Variations of Sensitivity Training

There are several variations of sensitivity training. Some of the important ones are T-group training and transactional analysis (T.A.). The goal of T-group is to give the trainee an understanding of why she acts towards other people the way she does and why other people act the way they do. This fosters an understanding of others and helps managers to better manage relationships. Further, there are three types of T-groups- stranger groups (participants are strangers and have come to the training from different organisations), family groups (participants belong to the same department and know each other quite well) and cousin groups (where participants belong to different departments of the same organisation).

Transactional analysis is a theory of personality and also a form of psychopathology developed by Canadian psychoanalyst Eric Berne. A form of sensitivity training is based on transactional analysis (T.A.).

The basic philosophy is that three ego states co-exist within the same personality:

1. The child
2. The adult
3. The parent

T.A. through sensitivity training seeks to improve interpersonal relations by adjusting the balance between these ego stages.

Encounter Groups

Many psychologists consider encounter groups as a type of sensitivity-training groups. Yet many others do not because of difference in rationale, goals and methods. In general, encounter groups put a greater emphasis on individual growth than on group interaction. Encounter group training aims at helping participants gain insight into particular social and personal problems and learn to cope with them mere effectively.

The flexibility of encounter groups is more than that of T-groups. Hence, many formats of encounter groups have evolved. One format deserving special mention here is the marathon format. In the marathon format, members meet one weekend and keep discussing without even breaking for sleep. The logic behind using the marathon format is that the "opening up" process (i.e., the expression and exploration of personally meaningful feelings) is hastened by such intense contact. Also, inhibitions are lowered due to fatigue. Finally, since now they are separated from the outside environment for a long period of time, the influence of group experience is the maximum.

The marathon encounter group has been called a "pressure cooker" because of the emotional tensions that gets built up. Also, like a pressure cooker it is capable of compressing the amount of time required for the training to be effective (Coleman, 1969).

Learning in Sensitivity Groups

Till now, we have only been running around the bush, discussing what the objectives of sensitivity training are; what is the procedure used in various formats, etc. But, how does learning happen in sensitivity training? To understand this, we move to the source inspiration Kurt Lewin.

Lewin had stated that any kind of change in the learner moves through three stages:

Unfreesing -> Moving -> Freesing

For the desired new learning to occur, we need to unfreese the individual. This can be done by generating certain amount of tension or anxiety. Anxiety is aroused due to the nature of face-to-face encounter where one's personal feelings get expressed. Also, defense mechanisms get weakened and this creates anxiety. Anxiety is good because it helps the individual get loose from her pre-conceived notions and habitual ways of reaching. This unfreesing helps because only then one can 'move' (i.e., learn new attitudes and feelings). The second stage (moving) occurs because in all forms of sensitivity training, the individual is given feedback about her behavior by other members of the group. At the end of this process, the new learning is 'freesed' and the individual carries over the skills in human relation management outside the training.

Psychological tests in the industry

Psychological tests are used in organisations in every stage of manpower planning. Psychologist tests are expectation of employees, their perceptions, attitudes and values orientation.

These tests can be studied in terms of various industrial functions, as:

1. Recruitment tests
2. Performance appraisal
3. Integrity tests
4. Tests to assess employee attitudes and motivation

Recruitment Test

As already mentioned, recruitment is based on knowledge, skills and attitudes of the candidates.

To measure these, certain instruments used are:

1. *Bio-data:* The concept behind study of bio-data is to list the environmental factors commonly found in successful and unsuccessful candidates. Based on these, weighted application forms are constructed. These forms are filled by candidates and submitted to the HR of the company; based on the application blanks (candidate's background – academic, extra-curricular, etc.) initial screening is done. This assessment can be discriminative at times. For example, a HR manager with casteist attitude may unconsciously screen out the bio-data of a candidate from lower caste background. In another situation, suppose no woman has ever worked in the shop floor of a manufacturing firm. That doesn't mean women mustn't be considered for the job.
2. *Interview:* Interview is an approach to know the candidate first-hand. Interview may take a structured or unstructured form. Unstructured interviews are similar to an informal chat. There is no fixed procedure or aim of the interview. Rather, the candidate is selected by a hit-and-miss approach. The reliability and validity of such interviews are questionable. Herriot (1989) is of the view that unstructured interviews are prone to sex bias as the interviewers are often male and are more likely to engage in comfortable chat with male candidates. Hence, many employers prefer a structured interview, where set of questions are asked to all candidates in a particular order. It is a sort of verbal psychometric test with quite satisfactory validity.
3. *Work Sample Tests:* These are used to measure knowledge and skills. Knowledge can be measured by a simple quiz test. Skills can be measured by asking the candidate to provide a work sample. For example, a web designer may be asked to design a website; a software programmer may be asked to write a program. These are relatively easy to measure and have good face and predictive validity.

   Some aptitude tests are used on fresher, since they are fresh from college and don't have any industrial skill. Aptitude tests try to predict the candidate's aptitude for some specific job. The skills could be developed later by training.
4. *Psychometric testing and assessment:* Intelligence tests are used to assess an individual's underlying ability to solve problems and adapt effectively to their environment.

There are two major types of intelligence tests:

- Group tests, e.g. Block test
- One-to-One test, e.g. WAIS
- In employee selection, usually group tests are preferred because they are cheap and easy to administer vis-a-vis, one-to-one testing. However, group tests have low predictive validity. These tests are also culture specific, i.e., a test specifically designed to test individuals of mainstream cultures isn't sensitive to minority sub-cultures. Also, there is the risk of ***test sophistication*** (the more tests of a particular kind that an individual does, the faster her performance becomes. Many coaching institutes, for example, help students practice for intelligence tests).

Attitude of the candidate is important. In any job, the social skills of an individual affect his and his work group's performance.

Some ways to test attitude are:

1. Reference 2. Group discussion 3. Projective tests

Employers already ask for references, but references can be misleading at times. Group discussion displays an individual's interpersonal skills, so also her emotional intelligence. However, many participants of a group discussion can't participate because of their communication problems or because of other candidates' dominance over the discussion.

Projective tests, such as a Thematic Apperception Test (TAT) are another way to assess attitude. TAT consists of 30 pictures and drawing of two or more individuals in a range of ambiguous social setting. The person being tested is asked to make a story on the pictures. In the story, she projects her attitude. Projective tests are highly subjective and rely heavily on the skills of the tester. This subjectivity leads to problems of reliability. Work psychologists need to be sufficiently trained to use these tests.

Personality tests are used by the employer to get a picture of the candidate's basic traits, so that these can be matched against the demand of the job. Two popular personality tests used in recruitment are- Eysenck Personality Inventory and Cattell's 16-factor test. Eysenck's personality inventory, for example, throws light on whether a candidate is emotionally stable or neurotic. Also, a candidate can be an introvert or extrovert. Extroverts are sociable, outgoing, impulsive, like taking risks and it is difficult to condition them. Introverts are quiet, cautious, have a high level of anxiety and are easy to condition. This helps the employer assess whether the candidate is good for the job or not.

There are many criticisms about personality tests and psychometric tests in general. Eysenck (1998) stated that 'intelligence tests have generated more heat than light', meaning that such tests create more controversy than provide information.

It is often argued that psychometric tests lack validity and reliability because it is easy to cheat. Intelligent candidates can give answers that they feel are appropriate, rather than telling the truth. However, if a test is well-designed and includes a lie scale (i.e., including statements that can't just be true to check test-taker's honesty), many contend that this kind of cheating can be avoided. For example, 'I have never been late in life' is so improbable that it is a lie.

Personality tests have the underlying assumption that personality characteristics are stable. However, certain studies have shown the influence of situational factors. For example, Jessup and Jessup 91971) correlated scores on Eysenck's personality inventory and pilot training in Royal Air Force (RAF) in UK. It was found that pilots with low extraversion score initially showed high extraversion after successful completion of training.

Performance Appraisal

Most organisations carry out formal evaluations of employees' job performance, called performance appraisal.

This appraisal is used to:

- Distribute performance-based bonus
- Decide on promotions
- Decide on termination of employment

For instance, Mckinsey grades every employee on a scale of 5. The employee who scores 2 or less in three consecutive years in asked to leave the company.

There are broadly two types of performance appraisals- Ranking tests and Rating tests.

Ranking tests are used to rank employees according to their performance relative to other employees in the division. Problem with this test taking method is that an employee who performs satisfactorily may be ranked as "poor" in relation to others. Many scholars and management consultants are of the opinion that this testing pattern has potential to lower employee morale.

Rating tests are preferred over ranking tests, as here mangers are asked to rate the employees on a scale rather than relative to others. The most popular method to rate employee performance uses graphic rating scale.

A sample of this scale is:

Q. Which face reminds you of the employee?

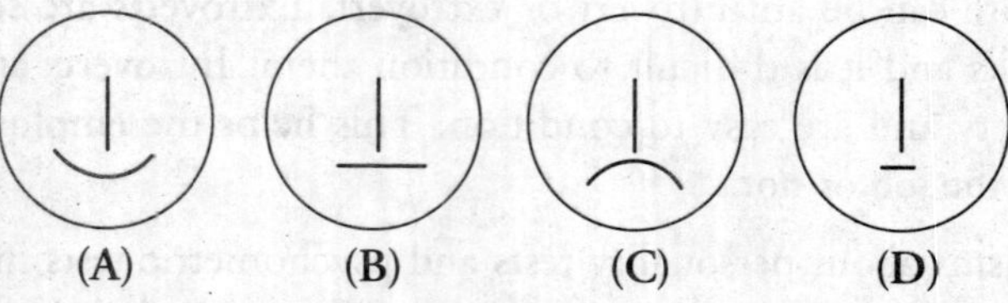

Two other tests are Behaviorally Anchored Rating Scale (BARS) and the Behavioral Checklist. In BARS, 'this rather chooses the voting category by choosing the behavior that is most representative of the employee's performance on that dimension. Research on the BARS method suggests that this scale provides more accurate ratings of employee behavior than to traditionally anchored rating scales' (Mclntire and Miller, 1999, p.541).

As in every psychological test, rating tests also are liable to errors. Leniency error occurs when the rater rates every employee liberally. Severity error occurs when all employees are rated below what they deserve. Central tendency error occurs when the rater tends to give average rating to all employees. A halo effect is one in which the rater's judgement on one dimension (which is usually very high) tends to make the rater judge the employee similarly on other dimensions. These errors occur because raters have to make subjective decisions, while quantifying job performance of the employee.

With increasing job transparency, 360th feedback is being used in rating employees. Here, the employee is rated by her boss, peers, subordinates and customers as well as by herself. This reduces the risk of rating errors.

Integrity Tests

With economic pressure to become more efficient, employers today have become more concerned about issues of employee theft. In recent times, many thefts have come to light in the BPO industry in India. Fitsgerald (2003) notes from a study in Canada, that employee theft is responsible for 33% of theft from retail stores. He contends that integrity of employees must be tested during recruitment and after major thefts. Assessment for integrity tests can be by physiological measures or pencil-and-paper tests.

The polygraph, or the lie detector test, is the most popular physiological measure. The machine generates a number of graphs of skin resistance, heart rate and respiration. It is assumed that if the person taking the test lines, it leads to different responses. Paper and pencil test are based on projective methods. It must be reiterated that both tests have low reliability in detecting lies. Polygraph users may make the "Othello error", i.e., take signs of distress (which are manifested as emotional arousal in the polygraph) as proof of dishonesty. A meta-analysis of integrity tests in 1993 by Ones, Viswesvaran and Schmidt has yielded encouraging results.

Tests to Assess Employee Attitude and Motivation

An employer needs to know employee attitude and perception on a range of issues from time to time. For example, if a Steel Company wants to go for a major restructuring, it must first assess workers' attitude, least they decide to oppose it under trade unions.

Likert's Attitude Scale and Social Distance Scale can be used to assess employee attitude. Fitsgerald believes that psychological tests can shed light on prevalence of sexual harassment and gender discrimination in the workplace. This kind of assessment is, in fact, part of employer's moral duty to manage diversity.

Motivating employees is an important role of HR. To motivate employees to work towards organisational goals, the HR must be aware of employer attitudes and beliefs, their expectation from the organisation, etc. For example, if employees are motivated more by perks and services, like hospital facility, education for children, etc., it will be fruitless to give them more money. Psychologists have devised tests to measure work motivation. For instance, Kanungo has developed a popular test to measure job satisfaction and job involvement.

5.5 Theories of Work Motivation

Behind every goal-directed behavior, there is motivation. More the motivation to achieve certain goals, more are the chances that the individual will show purposive behavior. More the purposive behavior of employees to strive for task goals and organisational vision, better the efficiency and output of the organisation. Employers don't miss this simple and direct link between organisational effectiveness and employee motivation.

The challenge here is to determine what constitutes motivation? How to motivate employees towards organisational goals? Traditionally, it was believed that employee behavior should be controlled by rewards and punishments. This view was behaviorist view and has since been contested by many content theories (Maslow's Hierarchy of Needs and Hersberg's Two Factor Theory) and process theories (like Vroom's Expectancy Model). We will start the discussion of this section with Maslow's Hierarchy of Needs which is a humanistic approach as opposed to be behavioristic approach predominant at the time.

Maslow's Hierarchy of Needs

Maslow's Hierarchy of Needs wasn't specifically designed for work motivation. Rather, it was a general theory that became immensely popular in managerial circles. This theory states that a hierarchy of needs exists. The fulfillment of needs of one stage (lower) in the hierarchy only leads to a concern for the needs of the next stage (higher). Unless the needs of a stage are fulfilled, the employee doesn't strive for the needs of the next stage.

Fig. 5.4 : Maslow's Hierarchy Pyramid

- *Physiological needs, safety needs and social needs*

At the base of the pyramid, lie the physiological needs of hunger, thirst and sex. Non-fulfillment of these needs lead to physiological deprivation and an intense motivation to fulfil these needs. However, once these needs are met, it ceases to be a motivation. If it is not met, the individual ignores other needs but when it is met, the individual's needs move on to the next stage, i.e., safety needs.

Safety needs refer to the need to ensure that one is safe from physical and psychological threats. An environment which is predictable and where the individual perceives some degree of control fulfills this need. It must be noted here that the point at which one becomes content with safety is quite subjective. An adolescent staying in a slum, for instance, has very low safety needs. On the other hand, an old woman living alone has more safety needs.

Once physiological and safety needs are met, social needs of the individual become important. Need for affiliation and need to be rooted in a social group are important motivators. It can be pointed here that Elton Mayo had observed that there are informal social groups in organisations. He found many employees following social group norms rather than managerial incentive. This may be because when earlier needs are fulfilled, social needs become stronger.

These three needs, lower down in the pyramid are deficiency needs. Next, Maslow discussed certain needs that were path-breaking in HR Management of the time.

- *Esteem Needs, Growth Needs and Self-Actualisation Needs*

Esteem needs refer to the desire for personal achievement and recognition for the work done. This is associated with the need for self-respect and status. Esteem needs are not affected by the pay (unless pay is a symbol of status), rather by the degree of autonomy and responsibility that is provided to employees.

Next come the growth needs which need not be essential, but provide opportunities for personal growth and self-actualisation. Growth needs include cognitive needs (the need to know; the curiosity to express the environment) and aesthetic needs (the need to appreciate beauty and art). The implication of these needs is that creative expression can be intrinsically satisfying. Those who are unable to meet these needs at work, try to fulfil these needs in leisure time. The lesson for management here is that by facilitating the fulfillment of growth needs, it can harness the creativity of employees.

Self-actualisation needs, the most controversial of Maslow's needs, is at the top of the pyramid. Humanistic theorists believe that given the chance, human being is intrinsically motivated to realise her full potential, i.e., to actualise herself. Maslow argues that not everyone is fortunate enough to strive for self-actualisation. Only those, whose earlier needs are met, seem to strive for actualisation.

Appraisal of Maslow's theory

Maslow hierarchy had become very popular in business circles ever since Maslow proposed it. However, Maslow didn't back up his theory with any research. Other researches into his hierarchy have shown some lacunae in the theory. Some concerns are:

- The claim that without fulfillment of lower needs, the individual doesn't strive for needs placed higher up in the hierarchy has been proved wrong in many cases. For instance, people have been found to compose poetry in concentration camps!

- The hierarchy projects *needs* as if they are objective. How much of physiological needs are enough? How much safety would satisfy the individual, so as to enable him to move up? It is quite subjective and depends on the perception of the individual. The individual's cognitive processes have been ignored in drawing this theory.
- Though immensely popular, its application value is extremely low. How does one measure self-actualisation? Rather, how do we detect self-actualisation? It is too subjective concept to be used in practice.
- Finally, Maslow's Hierarchy of Needs is culture-biased. It represents the need hierarchy as it exists in individualistic, western cultures. For instance, in collectivistic traditions of the East, social needs are preferably met before safety needs. Also, the concept of actualisation is different in different cultures. In India, the satisfied man strives for spiritual unity of Atman (self) with Brahman (universe). This is actualisation in Indian context.

Herzberg's Two-factor theory

Herzberg had conducted a study on work motivation of 200 accountants and engineers employed in firms in Pennsylvania, USA in 1950. From his study, he found that the factors involved in producing job satisfaction are different from the factors that produce job dissatisfaction.

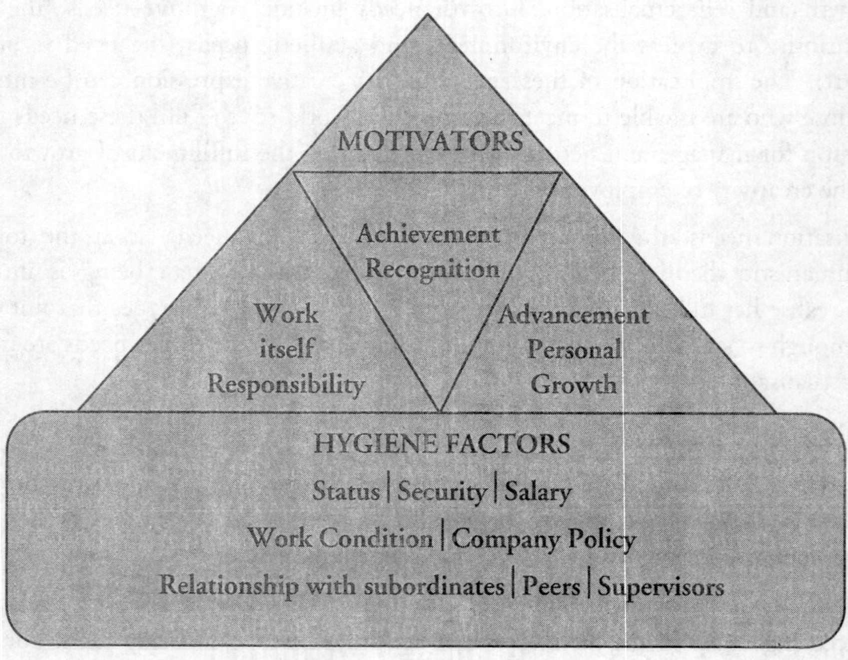

Fig. 5.5 : Herzberg's Two Factor Theory

Maslow made the distinction between higher and lower order needs, that is, growth needs and deficiency needs. Herzberg opines that these needs are not two ends of a continuum. Rather, factors which remove dissatisfaction are called hygiene needs; they don't provide motivation. Hence, he talks about two issues:

1. Satisfaction vs. non-satisfaction
2. Dissatisfaction vs. non-dissatisfaction

Please also note that Herzberg's hygiene needs (i.e., factors affecting job context) are related to extrinsic motivators (pay, job security, working conditions, company policies, etc.), whereas motivator needs are related to intrinsic motivators (curiosity, need for status, need for self-fulfillment, etc.)

Herzberg's theory has deep implications for management. It states that factors like salary don't' motivate employees. Salary is necessary, but not sufficient condition for motivated behavior. Hence, the need for job enrichment; secondly, all dissatisfies need to be removed. Just paying salary won't work. The concept of worker welfare is important here because without basic hygiene factors, the employee stays dissatisfied.

An Appraisal

Herzberg's theory was based on interviews with a sample of 200 male engineers and accountants of firms of Pennsylvania. It is dangerous to generalise the theory to other situations. This theory has been challenged by many scholars, one prominent among being Victor Vroom. Vroom (1984) claimed that the Two-factor theory was only one of the conclusions that could have been reached from the study conducted by Herzberg. It is also possible that Herzberg made the fundamental attribution error when conducting his study, i.e., in his method, Herzberg probably attributed good results to his theory and bad results (that were contradictory to his hypothesis) to situational factors!

Landy (1985) suggests that in the Two Factor theory, Herzberg defines satisfaction and dissatisfaction the way people think about it in western countries. If that is so, it doesn't have cross cultural validity. Satisfaction depends on people's perception, which in turn depends on the culture one belongs to. Swalapurkar has found that for Indian middle class, factors like salary and job security act as motivators.

Kats (1978) has suggested that job satisfaction isn't an objective construct as Herzberg wants us to believe. Rather, it varies throughout work life. Kats interviewed 3,085 employees working in the public sector and private sector in USA. He found a relationship between job satisfaction and length of time in employment and that it changed over time. Indeed, what individuals want out of a job can vary with age, sex, social group and individual expectations.

In spite of these criticisms, it cannot be denied that Herzberg contributed substantially to understand work motivation. He extended Maslow's need-hierarchy and made it more applicable to organisational settings. Also, his concept of job content factors helped managers to go for job enrichment.

Vroom's Expectancy Theory

Expectancy theory marks a departure from the content theories of work motivation. Expectancy theories are cognitive theories in the sense that they focus on the employee's need perception. Secondly, these theories are process-orientated. Two dominant expectancy theories to be discussed here are Vroom's theory and Porter and Lawler's development on Vroom's theory.

Vroom was inspired by the cognitive theories of Lewin and Tolman; and so believed that human behavior is the result of active interaction between individual characteristics (personality traits, needs, attitudes and values) and perceived environment (such as job requirement, role clarity, supervisor's style and work culture).

To use Lewin's famous formula,

B = f (P, E) where B = Work Behavior

P = Employee Characteristics

E = Work situational factors

Vroom, in 1964, forwarded his theory in which he reasoned that motivation is the result of three different kinds of cognitions:

1. *Expectancy:* The belief that one's effort will result in performance.
2. *Instrumentality:* The belief that the performance will be rewarded.
3. *Value:* The perceived value of the rewards to the employee.

This theory can be explained with the help of an example. Suppose Hari is a worker in a power plant. Before doing a task, he thinks whether his efforts will lead to performance. If he doesn't have the skills to perform the role or the organisation doesn't give him sufficient autonomy, his expectancy is low.

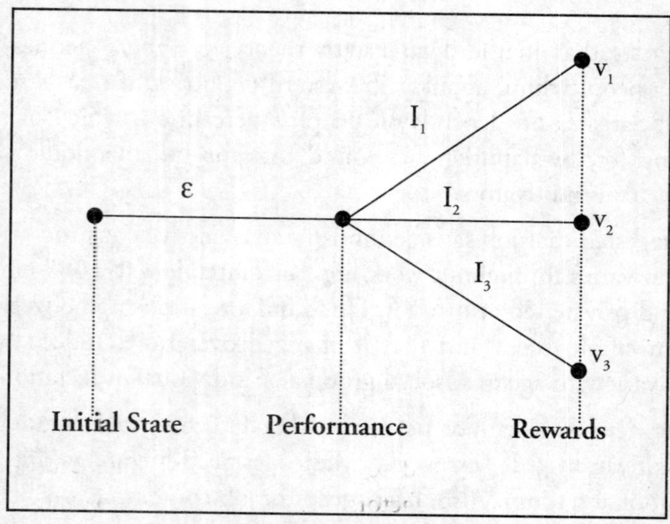

Fig. 5.6 : Vroom's Model

But, if his expectancy is high, he now reasons- Why should I perform? Will I get rewarded? How instrumental is my performance in getting rewards? Suppose for the kind of performance, the company policy states that Hari will get bonus (reward 1), health insurance (rewards 2) and greater work responsibility (reward 3). The instrumentality for each outcome varies from +1 to -1 means that the performance is necessary and sufficient condition for the reward. For example, Hari won't get bonus without performing. Negative instrumentality means that the performance may in fact hamper the attainment of reward. Suppose a worker wants healthy benefits (reward) but will lose it if he gets transferred to another department, the instrumentality is negative.

Also important here is the value that Hari attaches to the rewards. If Hari doesn't value health insurance or already has one, his value (V_2) is low for reward. 2. If he fears that his better performance will increase his work load, the value V_3 (corresponding to reward 3, i.e., greater responsibility) may be negative. Many workers in a steel company I worked in feared that if they did something in front of the manager, they may be called again to do the work!

Hence, Hari's perception that performance (P) will be rewarded (R) is:

$$[P \rightarrow R] = \sum_{K=1}^{3} I_k V_k$$

Hari's belief that an effort will lead to the said performance is E_j. There may be many efforts and many different performances. Hence, this particular performance is called E_j. Hence, Hari's expectancy here is:

$$\text{Expectancy} = E_j \sum_{K=1}^{3} I_k V_k$$

His total expectancy from different work challenged is:

$$\text{Expectancy total} = E_j \times \left(\sum_{k} I_k V_k \right)$$

Vroom's expectancy theory has important implications for the industry.

Some major implications are:

1. Motivation is not directly linked to job performance. The causal link isn't direct. Rather, there are personality factors, skills, abilities and values that affect job performance.

2. The individual needs to be given ample opportunities to carry out the job. She won't put an effort if she lacks ability or if there is no organisational support. Clarity of role also affects the expectancy that an effort will lead to a performance.
3. It is not the instrumentality of the outcome in getting rewards, but the perceived instrumentality that matters. Hence, the company policy needs to be clear and there ought to be transparency in performance appraisal.
4. Before rewarding an employee, the HR must ascertain what value the employee attaches to the reward. The value that one attaches to a reward is based on her personality traits, attitudes and cognitions. Hence, the HR must conduct attitude tests to assess employees' reward preferences before rewarding them.

Porter and Lawler Theory

Porter and Lawler (1968) have expanded and reinterpreted the expectancy theory of Vroom. This model is represented in the diagram below:

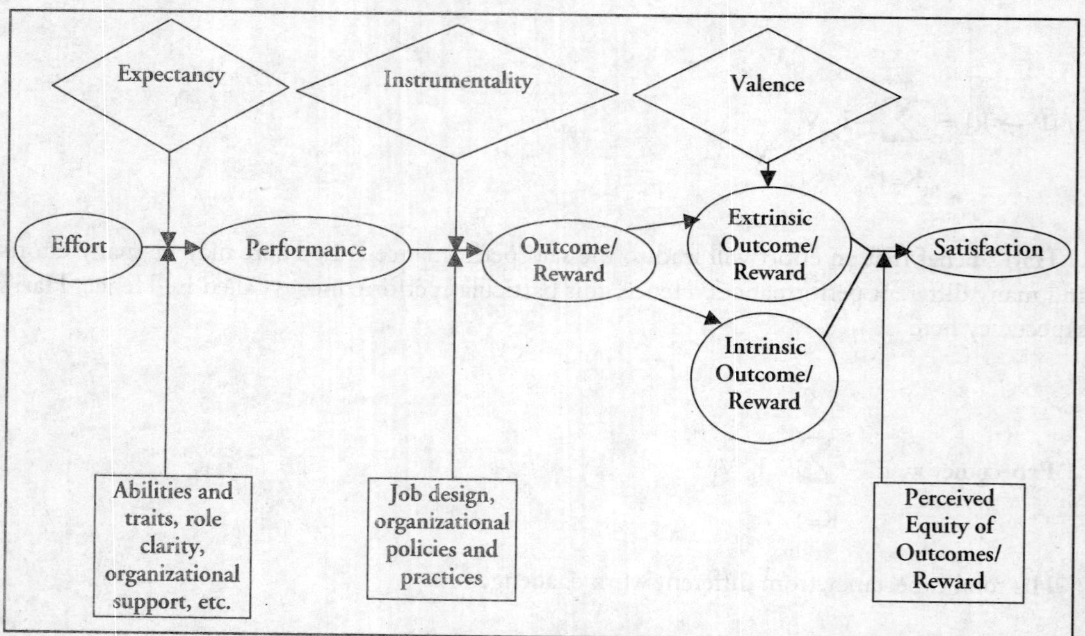

Fig. 5.7 : Porter and Lawler's expanded expectancy model [Adopted from Porter & Lawler (1968)]

Porter and Lawler have made some important additions to the Expectancy Theory, as seen in the diagram. Some of these are:

- The fact that performance depends on abilities, traits, role perceptions and organisational support has been made expect. Role perceptions refer to the clarity of job description and the extent to which employees know how to direct their efforts towards effective performance. Many-a-times, due to ambiguous role descriptions many employees don't realise where their efforts would lead to best performance.

- This model argues that performance leads to both extrinsic and intrinsic outcomes. While extrinsic rewards depend on other factors, like valence (i.e., value of the reward to the employee) and equity perception, the relation between performance and intrinsic rewards is direct.
- This theory also tries to incorporate Adam's (1965) Equity Model. It states that the extent to which extrinsic rewards will lead to satisfaction depends upon the perceived equity of rewards, i.e., the extent to which the output to effort ration of the employee is equal to that of others.

An Appraisal

The cognitive nature of Expectancy Theory 'does a good job of capturing the essence of energy expenditure. A manager can understand and apply the principles embodied in each of the components of the model. Instrumentalities make sense. The manager can use this principle to lay out clearly for subordinates the relationships among outcomes (e.g., promotions yield salary increases, four unexcused absences result in a suspension of one day). Similarly, the manager can increase reward probabilities by systematically rewarding good performance'. (Landy, 1985, P.336-337) Vroom's theory has provided many insights into work behavior, as discussed earlier.

However, the Expectancy Model has some lacunae, like:

- Expectancy theories of Vroom and of Porter and Lawler, are normative models. These models assume that people use rational cognitive processes, carefully calculating expectancy, valence and instrumentalities. Many people aren't this rational and don't measure their outputs and inputs to make perceptions.
- The theory pays little attention to explaining why an individual values or doesn't value a particular reward. These models don't borrow from the concept of need to determine what rewards are valued and why. The theory has concentrated on the process to such an extent that it ignores the content, i.e., the needs of employees.

Adam's Equity Theory

Adam's Equity Theory is based on the Social Comparison Theory. Equity theory argues that people tend to compare their contribution to work and benefits with others in the organisation. Basically, the employee selects some referents to whom she compares her output to input ratio. The person is motivated by the perceived fairness of benefits received for certain amount of work.

The state of equity is reached when:

$$\frac{\textbf{Person's outcomes}}{\textbf{Person's inputs}} = \frac{\textbf{Other's outcomes}}{\textbf{Other's inputs}}$$

Please note that the outcomes and inputs mentioned above are perceived outcomes and inputs, not objective ones. Inequity happens when either of the following conditions occur:

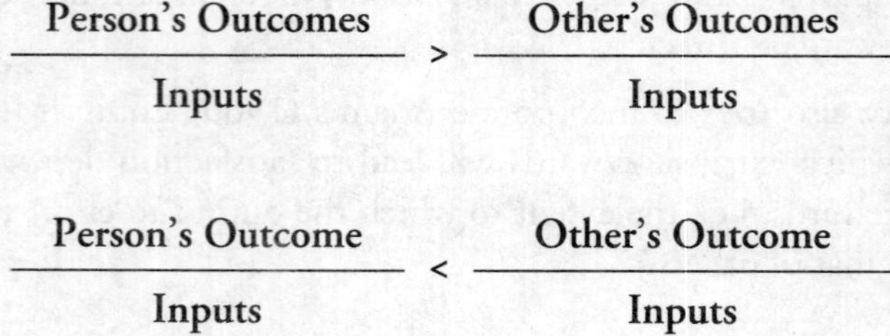

$$\frac{\text{Person's Outcomes}}{\text{Inputs}} > \frac{\text{Other's Outcomes}}{\text{Inputs}}$$

$$\frac{\text{Person's Outcome}}{\text{Inputs}} < \frac{\text{Other's Outcome}}{\text{Inputs}}$$

This feeling of inequity leads to tension, that in turn, leads to motivation to bring about equity.

To reduce inequity, the individual is motivated to perform the following behaviors:

1. Change the inputs
2. Change the outputs
3. Change perceptions about self's outcome-to-input ratio and also other's.
4. Change the referent and in the worst case
5. Leave the organisation

For example, if an individual perceives that her outcome-to-input ratio is more than others, she feels that she receives more reward than she deserves. Hence, to reduce the inequity she may work harder (increase input) or changes her perception ("I deserve the money I get because I am smarter than other employees"). On the other hand, if her reward-to-input ratio is perceived to be less than others, she may try to improve her output, reduce her input ("Hari gets the same bonus for working only four hours why should I work for six hours?") or change perceptions ("Hari does smart work. Hence, he is more efficient"). If still unsatisfied, the employee may leave the organisation for another.

An Appraisal

Equity theory beautifully combines the notion of cognitive dissonance with social exchange to forward a guideline to managers about doing distributive justice to employees. Another implication is that procedural justice is also important. It is not equitable distribution of rewards in ratio of inputs that affects employee motivation, but the perception of it. Hence, the procedure arrived at when making an appraisal has to be transparent. The subordinates must be aware of the rules you use in calculating rewards for their work.

While the theory makes strong intuitive sense, research on the theory has revealed mixed results. Indian researchers have found that Adam's theory has cross-cultural validity, but needs to be suitably modified. Socio-cultural factors determine the extent to which equity principle can explain employee satisfaction.

For instance, Murphy-Berman and his colleagues (1989) found that Indians preferred reward disbursement more on the basis of employee need than on the basis of merit. This is a trend opposite to that of Western countries. It might be because of our collectivistic values of protecting the weak and the needy; or may be because the workers who were studied adhered to socialistic ideology of rewarding to each according to his needs.

5.6 Leadership

Leadership is the ability to influence the activities of a person or a group of persons towards the attainment of certain goal or goals. In the organisational context, it is sometimes used interchangeably with management, though significant differences exist.

In the section on power and politics, we have discussed that there are three types of influence processes:

1. Compliance 2. Internalisation 3. Identification

Manager is an employee who has been given formal authority of the organisation. Hence, he can influence his subordinates by compliance,whereas, a leader influences by internalisation and identification also. Hence, a manger may or may not be a leader. For example, when I used to work in a steel plant, I was given the post "Manager, Electrical Maintenance". I had influence on the workers in the sense that if I order, they are bound to do my work. But was I a leader then? I was new to the place, young and had no practical experience. The experienced foremen couldn't internalise the fact that I could handle my job, let alone identify with me. Hence, a manager may or may not be a good leader. Alternatively, an outside consultant who doesn't have any formal authority may become a leader because the employees have internalised the fact that the consultant is an expert in steel processing.

What is leadership? What is the most effective form of leadership? We shall now discuss various models proposed to explain leadership and then move on to a typology of various leadership styles.

Models of Leadership

The different models of leadership have been discussed below:

Trait Models

Some of the earliest researchers of leaderships believed that leadership is a disposition, i.e., there are certain personality traits and personal characteristics of leaders. These researchers tried to uncover some traits and abilities that could determine how good a leader one can become. However, their studies haven't been able to give any conclusive results, and they have been largely discredited. Today, it is generally recognised that no one is a born leader.

Behavioral Models

When researchers became discouraged by the trait models, they started focusing their attention on what leaders do in their job. The main concern of behavioral models was to identify dimensions of leadership behavior. One dominant model was forwarded by researchers at Ohio state university.

These researchers managed to isolate two major dimensions:

1. Consideration
2. Initiating structure

Consideration (i.e., relationship-oriented) behaviors reflect the extent to which a leader is concerned for subordinates' well-being. A leader high on consideration is friendly and approachable; he has a good rapport and two-way communication with his subordinates. Initiating structure (i.e., task-oriented) behaviors reflect the leader's concern in getting jobs done and making the organisational structure work at optimal efficiency.

The two dimensions are independent of each other, i.e., a leader high on consideration can also be high on initiating structure.

Any leader's behavior lies in the following grid:

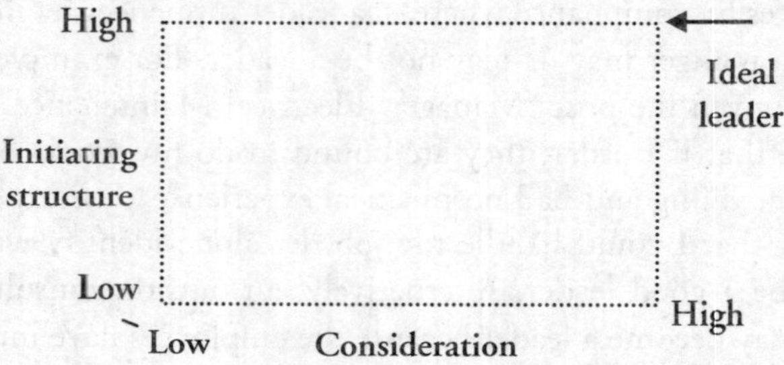

Fig. 5.8 : Behavioural traits of leaders

Even though both trait and behavioral models focus on personal attributes of the leader, they are different. Trait models propose that leadership is a predisposition whereas behavioral models show that leadership can be cultivated.

Situational Models

Both the models discussed above are universalistic approaches, i.e., attempts to find leadership attributes that are valid across situations. Starting from the 1960s, situational models became popular. Also called the Contingency Models, these state that the most appropriate style of leadership depends on the situation in which the leader works. As the situation varies, leadership requirements also vary.

The Least Preferred Co-Worker (LPC) Contingency Model introduced by Fiedler (1967) argues that when selecting leaders, a person's leadership style should be matched with the situations.

There are three situations variables one should consider before matching:

1. Leader-member relationship.
2. Task structure, i.e., the extent to which procedures have been established for performing the task.
3. Position power, i.e., control of resources such as money or information.

Hersey and Blanchard (1988) had proposed the now popular Life Cycle Model in which they identified four leadership styles – telling, selling, participating and delegating. The model reasoned that 'maturity' of the followers is the key factor on which the appropriate leadership style for the situation will depend. Hence, new employees with low maturity will be best suited for telling style (which means high on task-orientation and low on relationship orientation), whereas for most mature employees, delegating style is the best.

	Task-orientation Low	Task-orientation High	
Low	**Delegating style**	**Telling style**	**Relationship orientation**
High	**Selling style**	**Participatory style**	

Fig. 5.9 : Leadership styles as per Life Cycle Model

Another popular model is the Path Goal Model developed by House (1971). It is based on the concept of self-fulfilling prophecy. It states that employees will tend to live up to the expectations that leaders have of them. That is why, the more effective leaders are those who set up the work environment in such a way that employees can attain goals set by the leader and find the experience satisfying.

The Normative Decision Model forwarded by Vroom and Yelton (1973) states that there are three decision making styles:

1. Autocratic
2. Consultative, in which leader takes decisions but consults followers.
3. Group decision is the decision taken by consensus.

There is no right or wrong approach and which approach to take depends on:

1. Quality of decision required, and
2. Extent to which it is important for other members of group to accept the decision taken. Of the recent situational models of leadership, I consider the Tri-dimensional Leadership theory relevant here. Yuki (2003) who forwarded this theory opines that leadership behavior can be described in three broad categories:
    1. **Task oriented** where the leader is primarily oriented towards efficiency and reliability.
    2. **Relations oriented** where the leader is most effective in managing human resources.
    3. Change-oriented, where the leader is most effective in innovation and adaptation to the environment.

This theory reasons that effective leaders integrate above behavior in a way that is consistent with the situation.

Leadership Styles

There have been many conceptualisations of leadership styles, most of these concentrating on two axes with autocratic and democratic styles on extreme ends of first axis and permissive style and directive style on other ends of the second axis.

These can be represented as under:

	Permissive	Directive
Democrats	Participating decision making Autonomy in task implementation	Participating decision making Leader control over task implementation
Autocrats	Leader makes decision High autonomy to members in task implementation	Leader makes decision Low autonomy to members in task implementation

Fig. 5.10 : Types of leadership

As seen in the situational models discussed earlier, none of the styles mentioned in the two dimensions is the appropriate style. The best style of the above depends on the organisational context and nature of followers.

Let us discuss the above four styles, along with few others:

5. Laisses faire style
6. Transformational leadership

1. Directive autocrats

These leaders take their own decisions. Communication is downward and directive, hence employee has less freedom in task implementation. The leader and followers are psychologically distant. This style is best suited when the followers are unskilled. For example, a contractor can be directive autocrat when dealing with his laborers. Ganguli is of the opinion that Indian workers prefer to be directed and work better with autocratic styled leaders.

2. Permissive autocrats

The leader makes decisions, but gives considerable autonomy to followers in carrying out tasks. This style of leadership is quit suited for the military; leaders take decisions but cadets have considerable autonomy in execution.

3. Directive Democrats

The leader consults his followers in taking decisions; however he takes an active interest in work implementation. This is quite suitable when followers are technically sound and highly skilled. Participatory management is conceptually an offshoot of this style.

4. Permissive Democrats

Not only decision-making is participatory, employees have considerable autonomy. This is the case in organisations with matrix structure, rather than in bureaucratic organisations. This is most suited when employees are quite mature and self-motivated. An extreme version of this is Laisses faire.

Transformational Leadership

Transformational leaders exert considerable influence over the followers by proposing an inspiring vision. They describe in clear, emotion-provoking manner, an image of what the group can become. Not only a vision, they also provide a route for attaining the vision. They have high confidence level, high degree of concern for followers and good communication skills. While "transactional leaders" are those skilled in day-to-day transactions in the workplace, transformational leaders help the organisation through change. Indeed, transformational leaders often come to prominence in times of intense change and lead the organisation during transformations.

The reason why transformational leadership is at the center of focus is that such leaders are visionaries, innovative and can help revitalise any organisation in tune with changing time. Take, for example, the case of Steve Jobs. He himself isn't much of an innovator, but his motivations of vision has helped Apple Inc to revitalise its position in world marked by coming with new cutting edge products, like iMac, iPad and iPhone.

Also, Conger and Kanungo (1998) have argued that transformational leadership in essence is proactive, entrepreneurial and change-oriented; hence it is best suited to meet the needs of change in a developing country like India. Hence, the importance of transformational leadership is evident.

Let us now discuss some major characteristics of transformational leadership, as noted by Bass (1985):

1. Vision
2. Charisma
3. Consideration of emotional needs of employees
4. Intellectual stimulation

1. Vision

As the name suggests, transformational leaders seek to transform the organisation in the face of competition, new technologies and other external challenges. To be able to transform, a leader needs vision. Vision is the ability to be sensitive to changes in organisation's environment, the ability to perceive a future advantageous position to which the organisation must move to progress. A transformational leader should not only be able to provide a vision, but must also show a path to attain the visionary goals and must be able to articulate the vision to her followers. Hence, she has an ideology that she uses to articulate his vision.

2. Charisma

Charismatic leadership was first recognised by Max Weber as a concept explaining how certain leaders can influence followers by emotional attachment. Charismatic leaders, by virtue of their personalities and interpersonal skills, are capable of exerting an extraordinary influence on followers without resorting to format authority. House (1977), who had constructed an ideal-type of charisma, believes that subordinates try to identify with a charismatic leader and internalise her values.

3. Consideration

The Behavioural Model discussed in last section talks about two dimensions of behavioural orientations of leaders- consideration and initiating structure. Transformational leaders are high on both dimensions. They are high on consideration because they act as mentors to their followers, give preference to two-way, face-to-face communication and give due regard to training and human resource development. They are high on initiating structure because they are skilled at getting jobs done and in making the organisation work at optimal efficiency.

4. Intellectual Stimulation

Since transformational leaders seek to transform the organisation, they are potent enough to show subordinates new ways of looking at old problems; they emphasise on rationality and nurture an organisational climate of intellectual stimulation. For example, Ganesh and Joshi (1985) analysed scientist Vikram Sarabhai's transformational leadership style in institution-building. They found that Sarabhai had used multiple strategies, like networking, trusting and caring in institution-building at Indian Space Research Organisation (ISRO).

Leadership style in India

A major area of interest of organisational psychologists in India is- What is the optimal leadership style suited to Indian situations? From the situational models, we know that the appropriate leadership style varies from situation to situation. Hence, we need to understand both- work situation and follower qualities before concluding on the leadership style most suited to Indian conditions.

At this stage, a small literature survey can be done. Pestonjee (1973) reported greater satisfaction among Indian workers under democratic supervision. Many other studies have verified this. Problem is, many other studies have found contradictory trends. Many studies have found that autocratic style is best suited for Indian workers. Ganguli for example, has observed that many Indians like to be directed and work best under autocratic leaders. Why this anomaly in research findings? What conclusion can you draw from these findings?

Prof. J.B.P.Sinha concluded that the contradictory research findings reflect the way leadership styles were defined by various researchers. He argues that Indian researchers saw autocratic and democratic styles as dichotomies rather than two ends of a continuum. He has postulated that somewhere on the continuum lies a leadership style most suitable to Indian conditions.

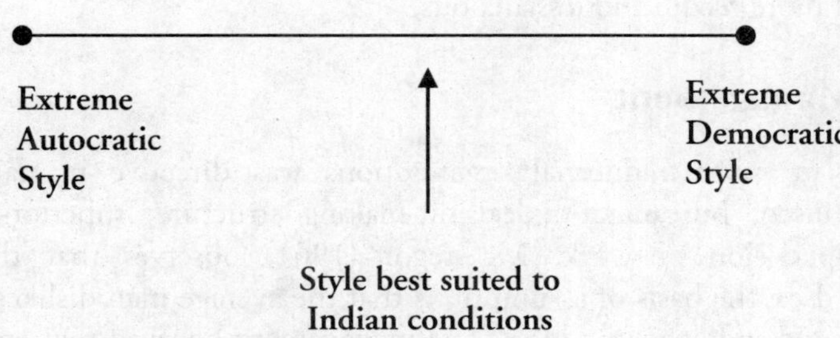

Fig. 5.11 : Continuum of leadership styles

The Nurturant-task Leadership Style

Based on the Indian situation and nature of workers in India, J.B.P. Sinha has proposed the Nurturant-task leadership style (NTL style).

But, before getting into defining it, let us learn some salient points about work situation in India:

- Work is not intrinsically valued in India and there exists a culture of 'aaram', i.e., rest and relaxation without any scope for hard work. Indians perform work as a favour to others. The logic stated for this is that work is believed to exhaust the individual by draining out her energy which she believes to be precious and limited. Hence, she prefers to expend it only in return for some favour.
- Indians have a high sense of insecurity. Due to this sense of insecurity, they work for accumulation of more money, position and status. Hence, Indians have a high need for power.
- We Indians have lived within the ethos of caste system for a long time. The superior-subordinate kind of relationship of the caste system has had a pervasive effect on our collective unconscious. Hence, we can't be autonomous. We don't' have the maturity for self-motivated behavior. That is why, we prefer bureaucratic hierarchies over other forms of organisations.
- Indians are collectivistic and search for personalised relationships.

Prof. J.B.P. Sinha concluded from the above factors that Indian workers have high dependency. Hence, the leader has to be directive and set definite tasks (i.e., be task-oriented). At the same time, Indian workers have high need for personalised relationships. Hence, the leader must be nurturing.

A few characteristics of the task-nurturant style proposed by him for Indian conditions are:

1. It is more task-oriented than employee-oriented. The leader should maintain strict discipline and should have structured expectations from subordinates.
2. The leader prefers a two-way communication to address Indian ethos and cultural values that promote dependency. The leader should nurture the employees, so as to make them feel more secure and less anxious.

5.7 Participatory Management

The management style in most traditional organisations was directive in nature. These organisations had centralised, bureaucratic decision-making structure, superior-subordinate hierarchy and strict supervision of work. McGregor (1961) observes that this kind of management was followed on the basis of assumptions that the average man dislikes and avoids work and is passive, lazy and indolent in nature. The management believed that employees are solely motivated by extrinsic rewards and need to be controlled by management using a carrot-and –stick policy. Hence, there was strict supervision of work.

McGregor goes on to argue that work is as satisfying and natural for people as play. However, play is internally controlled by the individual, while work in directive managerial firms is externally controlled by the manager. As a result, the work which should come naturally to people becomes unnatural.

Participative management is based on the philosophy that workers are of various degrees of expertise and maturity. Mature workers are self-directed and creative at work, if they are given greater control over their work. Argyris, for instance, has argued that as individuals mature from infant end of personality continuum to adult end, they desire more freedom and participation. By letting them mature, we can improve their performance but if we keep strict controls, we tend to resist their maturity. Hence, there is need for participatory management.

Participatory management is a managerial style that seeks to provide two-way communication and involvement of sub-ordinates in decision-making process. It is one among many managerial styles and is not necessarily the best in all situations. However, in certain situations, it is the most efficient form of management. So, when is participatory management the most efficient form of management? It has been observed that an optimal level of participation is good for a company depending on its organisational climate and employee profile. For instance, workers in India have high dependence needs, wants to be directed and lack team orientation. For them, participatory management may not be the appropriate style. However, in case of BPO companies and silicon companies, like Infosys, Wipro and Google, employees are well-educated and experts in their work. If a conducive work environment prevails, participatory management can be introduced in these companies.

A few pre-requisites for participatory management are:

1. The participant should have the ability, intelligence and knowledge to participate (of course, autocratic style is more preferable for unskilled labourers!).

2. Participation is most suitable for companies where many emerging decision situations arise.
3. Potential benefits of participation should be more than the cost (in terms of time).
4. The subject of participation must be relevant to the employee; otherwise she perceives it as another work load!

Advantages of Participatory Management

If the pre-requisites are fulfilled, it is strongly recommended to go for participatory management.

This is because of the following advantages of participation of workers in management:

1. Fulfillment of needs

Participatory management fulfils many essential needs of the employee. For example, better two-way communication provides a sense of security to the employee. Participation leads to greater job control which, in turn, fulfils their self-esteem needs. Freedom at work place motivates employees to fulfil their potential for self-actualisation. All this leads to higher job satisfaction and lower attrition. Employees' creative contribution helps the organisation to innovate and come out with new and more efficient work routines.

2. Employee Health

According to The Job Control – Job Decision Model of Karesek (discussed in the section on stress), stressful jobs are those, where job demand is high but job control is low. On the other hand, if job control is high, the job isn't as stressful. Stress is a dangerous psychological and physiological condition that not only affects employee health, but also their performance at the work-place. Participation is an effective way to increase the resources at the disposal of the employee to help her cope with work-related stressors.

3. Ego Involvement

Participation implies mental and emotional involvement rather than mere muscular activity. It is due to this reason that employees start contributing extra in terms of creative work and better performance. For example, employees at Google India are encouraged to participate in product design strategy related decisions. Many of its products are creative output of its employees.

4. Acceptance of Responsibility

Participation encourages people to accept responsibility in their group's activities. Participation is a social process by which people become self-involved in the organisation. They become responsible employees, rather than machine-like performers. As an employee begins to accept responsibility for group activities, she becomes more receptive to team work, because she sees in it a means to fulfil group goals.

This responsibility that workers can take up is helpful to the organisation in times of emergency. For example, managers in many manufacturing companies (take, for example, Tata Steel where I worked) are recent graduates. Their knowledge of shop-floor activity is limited; their theoretical know-how often doesn't match with practicality. Involvement of junior employees in decision-making process helps in better management of the concern. It leads to better performance, lesser breakdowns and faster trouble-shooting.

5. Other Benefits of Participatory Management

Participatory management makes any decision to change easier. In many industries, the decisions taken are top-down. Workers feel that their interests haven't been amply considered before making any major change. Often they resort to strikes, trade union militants and in worse situation vandalism. Participation of skilled workers in taking decisions goes a long way in better acceptance of change.

Secondly, organisational power increases with participative management. Contrary to common perceptions, power in organisations is not a zero sum game. The autocratic view of management is that power is a fixed quantity, so someone must lose what another gains. The view of participatory management is that power can be increased without taking it from someone else. In participatory management, the employee's power increases without taking it from someone else. In participatory management, the employee's power increases because she gets to influence the decision-making process. At the same time, the manager's power over the employee increases because now the employee is personally responsible for execution of the decision!

Beside above, there are other benefits, like better communication (due to cooperation and consultation through the organisational hierarchy).

Managerial Effectiveness

Just like there are numerous theories to understand who makes a successful leader, there is also significant research on what makes a manager more effective. In any organisation, the manager is in charge of significant resources, and has to make many critical decisions regarding both material and human resources. Hence, it becomes necessary to understand what constitutes managerial effectiveness in order to have an efficient organisation. Managerial effectiveness can be defined as 'something a manger produces from a situation by managing it appropriately, producing the results or meeting the targets in every sphere of the activities of organisation'. (Rastogi & Dave, 2004).

Broadly, there are three approaches that psychologist have used to study managerial effectiveness:

1. *Traditional approach:* This emphasises the ability to set and achieve goals, where it is implicitly assumed that managerial effectiveness leads to organisational effectiveness.
2. *Organisational level competency-based approach:* There are numerous long-term and short-term challenges from both internal and external sources for an organisation. In its effort to meet its strategic goals, the organisation tries to create an efficient system and environment for this whatever skills and characteristics a manager needs is studied in this approach.
3. *Individual level competency-based approach:* This approach focuses on the individual rather than the organisation. 'The purpose of this approach is to develop transferable (generic) managerial skills that are applicable across different circumstances both nationally and internationally.' (Rastogi & Dave, 2004)

Characteristics of effective managers

Research on managerial effectiveness seeks to find out variables (persons and environmental) that have links to effective managerial behavior. However, let me warn you that no definite trait or characteristic applies to effectiveness across situations. The desired characteristics in an effective manager vary as per the context. Yet, there have been attempts to distinguish broad characteristics of successful leaders. For example, managerial effectiveness has been linked to role behaviors (Mintsberg, 1973), coping with pressure and adversity, integrity (Kaplan, 1997) and knowledge of the job (Kotter, 1988). These days, significant research energies are being directed towards managerial effectiveness is global settings.

For example, Gregson, Morrison & Black (1998) have identified five characteristics of successful global leaders:

1. Context specific knowledge and skills
2. Inquisitiveness
3. Personal character, including integrity
4. Duality, i.e., the ability to manage both uncertainty and tension, and
5. Savvy (how business savvy and organisational savvy the manger is)

We will use a model developed by Leslie, Dalton, Ernst and Deal (2002) to study the characteristics of effective managers.

This model is presented in the figure:

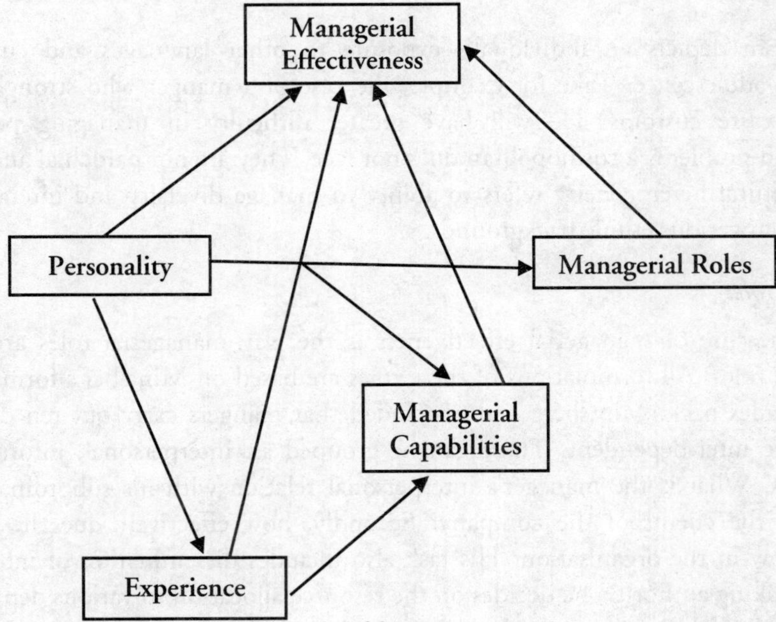

Fig. 5.12: A model to study managerial effectiveness

As is evident from the model, the variables in effectiveness are interdependent and affect each other. Also, there are numerous variables within these broad categories.

Let us study these variables in greater detail:

1. Personality

At one time it was believed that certain traits are more favourable in effective managers. This line of thought has since been discredited; however, traits help explain what kind of experiences and situations a manager is more drawn towards. Studies conducted on personality traits (using the NEO-PI as base) have found that conscientiousness, extraversion (Barrick & Mount, 1991), agreeableness and neuroticism have positive correlates with job proficiency in Western countries. Efforts are underway to find consistent cross-cultural conclusions though.

2. Experience

Of course experience maters in how a manger executes his work. The role of experience is especially critical in global settings. Leslie et al (2002) have found three major variables of experience that influence a manger's effectiveness. These are especially important in global settings:

- Cosmopolitanism
- Cultural heterogeneity
- Organisational cohort homogeneity

Cosmopolitanism depicts an individual's exposure to other languages and cultures in his childhood and adolescence. Take for example, the case of a manger who strongly believes in religious and caste customs. He will have greater difficulty in managing people in the workplace. Such problems a cosmopolitan does not face. They are not parochial and are open to new ideas. Cultural heterogeneity refers to ability to manage diversity and interact effectively with people from various ethnic backgrounds.

3. Managerial roles

An essential measure of managerial effectiveness is the way managerial roles are performed. What are these roles? All formulations of these roles are based on Mintsber's formulation more than three decades back. Mintsberg had concluded that mangers carry out ten different roles which are quite inter-dependent. These can be grouped as: interpersonal, informational and decisional roles. What is the manager's interpersonal relation with his subordinates; with his boss and with the clients of the company? Secondly, how effectively does he monitor the information flow in the organisation? His task also includes dissemination of information. As the decision-making authority, he decides on the resource allocation to various departments and tasks, and represents the organisation during negotiations.

4. Managerial capabilities

This refers to the skills that a manger has developed. There are three major categories of capabilities:

- Learning behaviors
- Resilience
- Business knowledge

Learning behaviours include the motivation and skill to work and learn across cultural differences, the willingness to take the perspective of others and the capacity to learn from workplace experiences. Resilience refers to the ability to manage time and stress, factors that might be more salient when the management task is global in scope. The third skill groups business knowledge, represents knowledge of the business and business practices. (Leslie et all, 2002, p.3).

5.8 Stress and its Management

Stress refers to a psycho-physiological state that results when certain features of an individual's environment attack or impinge on that person; these features create an actual or perceived imbalance between demand and capability to adjust stress is dealt in detail in the chapter on health psychology.

In this section, we will deal with certain issues related to stress in the workplace. Organisational stress is not necessarily negative. Indeed, stress has both positive conse-quences (eustress) and negative consequences (strain). Relation between stress and perfor-mance is curvilinear. Hence, for any individual, the effect of stress can be represented as:

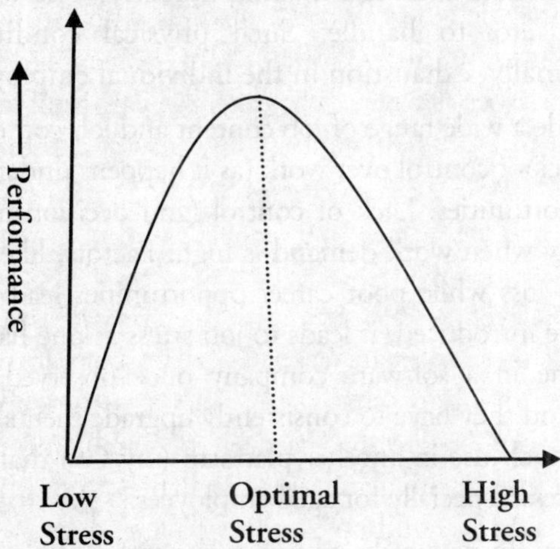

Fig. 5.13 : Impact of stress on performance

The exact nature of stress on an individual and its impact on her depends on many mediating factors. But before that, let us discuss the causes of job stress, i.e., stressors at the job site.

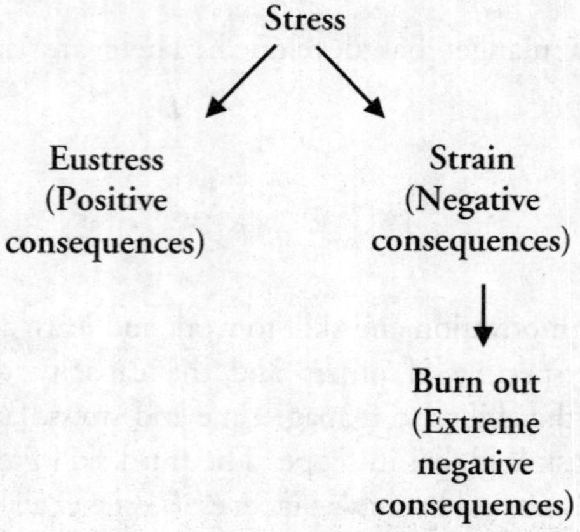

Fig. 5.14 : Types of stressors

Causes of Job Stress

Job stress may be due to demands within the work environment or by non-work demands. The four major categories of job stressors I seek to discuss here are:

1. Physical stressors
2. Task stressors
3. Role stressors
4. Interpersonal stressors

1. **Physical stressors** refer to aversive physical working conditions, or strenuous work environments. This includes poor ergonomics in the workplace. The condition is even worse in, say industrial construction and steel making industry. There is high noise, heat, dirty working climate, etc. to handle. Such physical conditions lead to chronically aroused state and finally, exhaustion in the individual employee.

2. **Task-related job stressors** include a wide range of job content and job context factors, like work overload, time pressure, lack of control over work (as it happens under directive style of leader) and poor career opportunities. Lack of control (and decision-making power) leads to extreme stress, especially when work demand is high. Factors, like job insecurity create anxiety about future job loss while poor career opportunities lead to frustration. Even when new technologies are introduced, it leads to job stress as one has to learn new skills. An acquaintance of mine in a software company once observed that software technologies change every year and they have to consistently upgrade their skills. If you are an expert in Java, if is of not much use in another platform (say C#) that has just been developed. This poses greater stress, especially for aged employees.

3. Role stressors in the workplace are primarily of two types: (a) Role conflict and (b) Role ambiguity.

   Role conflict emerges in the organisation due to the dynamics of role expectations from the employee and her ability at role performance. Inter-role conflict occurs when the expectation of different roles (e.g., the role of an employee and mother) are in conflict.

Intra-role conflict occurs when the role expectations of different people (for example, of the boss and of a colleague) are in conflict with each other and other person-role conflict happens when one's personal beliefs and values are in conflict with the role that she is expected to perform (for example, if a sales manager believes that client shouldn't be cheated, but his organisation asks him to use some devious tactics to increase sales).

A.K. Srivastava (1985) conducted a study using standardised psychometric tools on a group of 400 first-line supervisors (technical). He assessed the supervisors' role stress, need achievement and job anxiety. From ANOVA, he found that role conflict and role ambiguity have a significant effect on anxiety pertaining to job life.

4. Interpersonal stressors pertain to stress due to leadership styles, organisational politics, discrimination at the workplace, sexual harassment and abrasive personalities. The two most stressful leadership styles for people at work are rigid, autocratic leadership behaviors and laisses-faire, or very passive leadership behaviors. Abrasive personalities can be the source of intense interpersonal stress and emotional pain on the job. Organisational politics is a source of job stress, with some research showing that it has a great adverse impact on women than men. Poor diversity management leads to job stress for the minority worker who feels there are unequal workplace barriers to success. Sexual harassment is a major job stressor, most often for women' (Encyclopedia of Applied Psychology, Vol. 2, 2004, P.468).

   Non-work stressors, like marital and family problems can also lead to stress at the job place.

Models of Job Stress

Broadly, there are three kinds of models of job stress: 1. Interactional model, 2. Moderator models 3. Transactional models.

Early models of job stress were interactional models, i.e., were focused on the cause of job stress (stimulus) and its impact (response). Most of these models postulated that the more demanding the stressor, the greater the chance that it would lead to strain. Later, researchers realised that stressor- strain relationship may be moderated by other factors, like age, gender and individual differences. Both the models had their limitations. Though both tried to explain the relation between stressors and their consequences (strain), both ignored the stress process.

Transactional models were then developed to understand the stress process, i.e., how stress develops and proceeds, rather than just the consequences. These models often used the idea of fit. Stress happens due to failure of a proper person-environment fit. Due to misfit between environmental demands and individual's perceived capacity to meet these, stress response develops. This concept of fit helped these researchers explain job stress as a process.

Now, let us look at some specific theories that will be of use to us in understanding this chapter in depth.

- The Person-Environment Fit theory (P-E fit theory) assumes that stress occurs because of incongruity between person and her environment. This incongruity can be between demands of the environment and the abilities and competencies of the individual, or between the needs of the person and supplies from the environment.

- The job demand-job control model states that there are two basic dimensions of work place factors – job demand and job control. Job demands are the workload demands put on the individual, while job decision latitude refers to the employer's ability to take decisions and hence be in control of the work. Karasek (1979) combined the two dimensions to arrive at a 2-by-2 matrix, that can be represented as:

	Job control		
Job Demand	**High-strain jobs**	**Active jobs**	**High**
	Passive jobs	**Low strain jobs**	**Low**
	Low	**High**	

Fig. 5.15 : The Job Demand – Job Control Model of Karasek

This theory proposes that stressors' impact is most severe when job control is low and job demand is high.

- The Vitamin model was proposed by Warr (1987) to specify the relationship between stressors and employee health and well-being (Fig. 5.16). Drawing an analogy with vitamins, he assumes that there are two types of work characteristics.

  Some features of work have linear effect up to a level, after which the effect becomes constant; just like the effect of Vitamin-C on body. For example, salary, safety, etc. are such factors. Some other work features have a curvilinear relationship on employee well-being, just like Vitamin D (Excess of vitamin D may cause skin cancer). Examples are job autonomy, social support and skill utilisation.

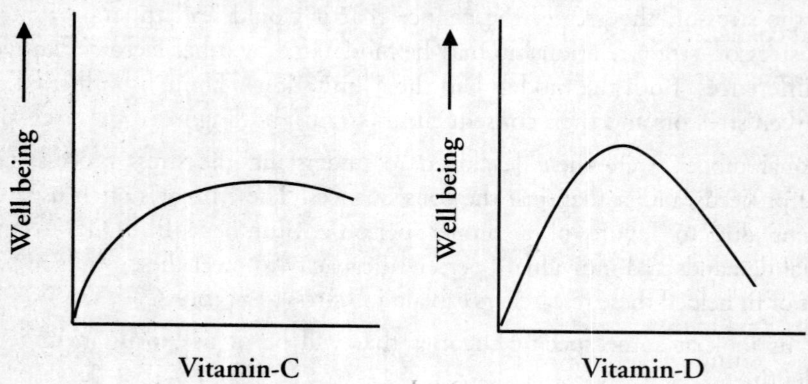

Fig. 5.16 : Vitamin Model of Warr

Consequences of Job Stress

Job stress can lead to both, positive consequences (eustress) or negative consequences (strain). An extreme form of negative consequence is burnout. The exact nature of stress depends on many mediating factors (to be discussed next) and the intensity of stressors. Eustress or healthy stress leads to better performance and even health benefits, like cardiovascular efficiency that one gets from aerobic fitness.

Strain, on the other hand, leads to both psychological and physical ill-health. It leads to greater absenteeism and lower performance output. Burnout is a special form of strain. Maslah (1982) has used a three-dimensional model to define burnout.

The three primary elements of burnout, according to him are:

1. Emotional exhaustion
2. Depersonalisation
3. Lack of personal accomplishment

The employee suffering burnout is emotionally exhausted and doesn't have any emotional energy to manage a stressful encounter. Then the individual starts seeing herself as an object and beats herself in a detached way. This is de-personification. Finally, there is a lack of personal accomplishments, i.e., a tendency to devalue performance in negative ways.

Mediating Factors

As already pointed out, stress doesn't always lead to strain and when it does, there are many mediating factors that decide on the effect of stress. These mediating factors are alternately called resources. Resources refer to the condition within the workplace and to individual characteristics that can be used by the individual to cope with stress.

Some important mediating factors are:

Work conditions

1. Control at work
2. Social support and work group factors

Individual characteristics

1. Coping styles
2. Self-esteem and self-efficacy

1. *Control at work:* Control at work refers to an employee's opportunity to influence one's work behavior in relation to work goals. Many studies have been conducted within the framework of Karasek's (1979) job demand-job control model. It has been found that individual in high strain jobs often suffer from cardiovascular illness (high strain jobs are those in which job demand is high but control is low). In a qualitative review of empirical studies on Job Demand Job Control Model, it was found that individuals in high-strain jobs show the lowest scores in psychological well-being (Van Der Doef and Maes, 1999).
2. *Social Support and Work Group Factors:* House (1981) has reasoned that social support is the resource provided by others (peers) in terms of emotional, informational and

instrumental support. Support enhances needs directly by satiating needs for *affiliation, approval* and *security*. It also enhances *self-esteem* needs of the individual employees. Secondly, social support reduces inter-personal tensions. One of the major stressors at work place is social stressors that can be reduced by a conducive social environment. A recent meta-analysis by Viswesvaran and his colleagues (1999) has shown that social support is negatively related to strain.

Work group factors, like group cohesion and team climate also play a significant role in reducing the effects of stress. Small groups provide psychological safety and collective efficacy that buffer the negative effects of stressors. Indeed, strong evidence exists that those individuals who work in teams experience better well-being than those who work alone (Carter and West, 1999).

3. *Coping styles:* When facing stressful demands form environment, individuals make certain cognitive and behavioral efforts to manage them. These efforts are called coping strategies. According to Lasarus and Folkman (1994), coping refers to the 'constantly changing cognitive and behavioral efforts to manage specific external and/ or internal demands that are appraised as taxing or exceeding the resources of the person (p.141).

   Important styles are:

   (a) Problem-focused coping

   (b) Emotion-focused coping

   (c) Avoidance coping

   Empirical studies have concluded that problem-focused coping leads to better health, while avoidance and emotion-focused styles lead to poorer well-being. Sharma and Acharya (1991) studied role stress and coping behavior among electrical engineers. They conclusively found that engineers who utilised avoidance coping compared to those who used approach coping (i.e. a style in which one directly approaches the problem) had higher job anxiety.

   Self-efficacy and Locus of Control: Self-efficacy has been found to mediate between stress and its consequences. Self-efficacy is the individual's belief that she is competent enough to face a challenging work.

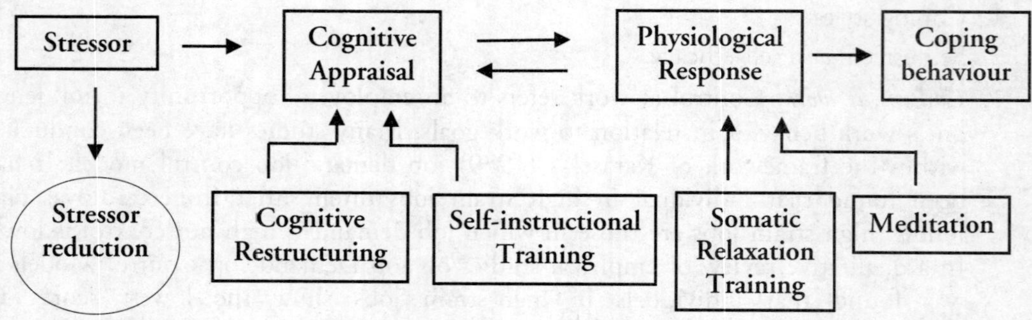

Fig. 5.17 : An overview of stress management programs and the stress-mechanism they target. [*Based on Passer and Smith (2007, P. 505)*]

Self-efficacy increases one's confidence and she makes a more positive cognitive appraisal of a stressful situation than another person who is low on self-efficacy.

A similar concept is that of locus of control. Individuals with internal locus of control see themselves as able to control their lives. When one feels that she is in control of her life, she tends to exert more direct action against stressors. Daniels and Gupy (1990) had conducted a longitudinal study in which they found a positive effect of an internal locus of control on well-being of workers.

4. *Personality factors:* An individual's personality has significant influence on her ability to withstand stress. Introverts tend to withdraw from interpersonal relations that produce stress (i.e., show avoidance coping style) and by avoiding communication make interaction and problem solving more difficult. Personality of an individual affects the way she appraises a specific situation as stressful and also her response to the perceived stressor. Considerable research has been conducted on the differences of type A personality and type B personality in their coping response. Type A people are characterised by impatience, competitive spirit, restlessness and aggression. The dominant hypothesis is that type-A personality has negative effect on stress coping. However, the relation between personality type and strain is still debatable. Michael Frese observes that while type-A behavior shows enhanced stress in one study, it shows attenuated stress in another. Other research results also have been inconclusive.

Stress Management

In view of the negative impacts of stress on employees and the organisation at large, it becomes necessary to take some stress intervention measures, both at the organisational and individual level. Best way to reduce stress is the removal of stressors. But, that isn't always practicable. Hence, psychologists have devised therapies to help the client manage cognitive appraisals and physiological responses.

To attack stress, we need to attack at every mechanism involved in stress. These are represented in the figure. Also, we need to discuss various changes that can be brought about at the organisational and individual levels to increase resources and reduce stressors.

1. Stress Management Programs

Some stress management program I intend to analyse here are:

- Cognitive Appraisal Management

  Example: Cognitive restructuring using RET

  Self-instructional training of Meichenbaum
- Physiological response management

  Example: Somatic relaxation training

  Mediating and Yoga

Cognitive appraisal plays a central role in determining how we perceive stress. This is the reasons why leading cognitive theorists, like Ellis and Lazarus believe that controlling cognitions is the most powerful means to control stress.

Ellis 91962) believes that a relatively small number of irrational core belief lies at the root of maladaptive negative emotions. Due to these core beliefs, we become more vulnerable, emotionally, to stressors than otherwise. Cognitive restructuring is a technique to systematically detect, challenge and replace these core irrational beliefs. Ellis' RET is an important and popular therapy under cognitive restructuring techniques.

An alternate approach is self-instructional training. Mandelbaum (1965) reasoned that if people can learn to talk to themselves, they can change their cognitions in order to perceive stressors differently. This would help them to better cope with stress. In self-instructional training (SIT), the therapist prepares different self-instructions for the client to use at four critical stages of the stressful episode:

1. Preparing for the stressor.
2. Confronting the stressor.
3. Dealing with the feeling of being overwhelmed.
4. Appraising coping efforts after the stressful situation (i.e., evaluation for future feedback).

Let us take the example of the software engineer who has to submit a project in two days. She can 'prepare for the stressor' by reasoning that if she remains focused, she can complete it. "Worrying won't help… rather it will decrease my performance".

"I will do my best and not worry".

Confronting the stressor entails a different set of instructions like: "As long as I am cool, I am in control of the situation".

When coping with the feeling of being overwhelmed, she may instruct herself: "Take a deep breath. Relax and Slow things down"; "Focus!"

In the last stage, the software engineer would appraise the situation and how she coped with it. It helps her to get feedback for better coping next time.

Stress management training also includes training people to control their physiological responses in stressful situations.

Two popular techniques are:

1. Somatic relaxation training
2. Cognitive relaxation via meditation, yoga, etc.

Somatic relaxation training works on the principle that a person can't be aroused and relaxed at the same time. In this training, people pair tension release with a trigger word by classical conditioning.

Step1: Tense various muscles of the body.

Step2: Mentally say the trigger word (ex. "Relax") and relax your muscles.

After this conditioning exercise, whenever the person feels stressed out, he can mentally say the trigger word ("Relax"). Due to conditioning, physiological relaxation will take place.

Meditation and Yoga are approaches to relax the mind rather than the body only. Evidence exists that meditation also leads to physiological changes in blood pressure and heart beat. There are many techniques of meditation.... In one, the person sits quietly in a comfortable position with eyes closed and mentally concentrates on the word "Om" with each exhalation.

The Stress Reduction and Relaxation Programme (SRRP) was designed by Dr. Cabot Sinn of University of Massachussets, on the lines of Hatha Yoga. It is a popular programme in organisations in managing stress. Yoga has also been found to show therapeutic value in dealing with PTSD. Recently, a professor of Psychiatry at New York Medical College, Dr. Gerberg, demonstrated the effect of yoga on PTSD suffering tsunami sufferers of Tamil Nadu. She found that yoga has superior effect than counselling in reducing stress.

The scientific basis of meditating and yoga comes from the fact that these techniques consciously control alpha waves in brain. These waves are related to feeling of tranquility and hence prevent chronic stress and tension.

Both somatic relaxation training and cognitive relaxation (yoga etc.) are potent tools to manage stress. While somatic relaxation is more potent in managing an unpredictable stressor, mediation is more potent in controlling chronic stressors.

2. Stressor Reduction

A major goal of stress management programmes is to educate employees and employers about various sources of stressors. Once individuals know about a source of stress, they can try to use problem solving techniques to alleviate it. For example, once aware that large noise is causing negative affect and physiological arousal, the employees can wear ear plugs when in factory. Ergonomics can be used to reduce stressors. For example, what is the optimal assembly line speed to match the worker's ability? Finding it out and using ergonomics can reduce physical stressors.

3. Increase in resources

Resources at the disposal of the individual employee, like job control, can be increased so as to reduce stressors. Participation in decision-making and training, to impart skills and increase competence are appropriate resource addition steps. Training reduces strain because it helps the employee work smarter, not harder. Training increases the Person-Environment (P-E) fit by increasing competence of employees to deal with work environment.

Increasing two-way communication is an important resource increase step. This is because even if employees aren't given significant job control, better two-way communication helps employees voice their problems. This is better as it helps the employees and management both to directly approach (i.e. problem-focused coping) the stressors. An additional resource, according to Frese (1999), is social support. Social support can be increased by forming small groups for team work and management training.

4. Lifestyle changes

Changes in lifestyle of employees (healthy diet, low alcohol and tobacco consumption, physical exercise and playing sports, etc.) help in enhancing well-being and reducing stress. Unfortunately, the modern lifestyle is haphaard and doesn't follow any disciplined routine. A diary study by Sonnentag has revealed that work-related activities performed in leisure time have a negative impact on a person's well-being. Other studies have also confirmed that a proper work-leisure balance is part of a healthy lifestyle. Taking note of this, many Indian companies have started building gyms near work-place. Infosys Bangalore, for example, has a state-of-the-art gym in its work campus. In many companies the staircase is made salient so that employees take the stair case (rather than lift) to work. Such relatively small amounts of daily physical exercise (such as, walking to work and walking stairs) have an enormously positive effect on handling stress.

5.9 Power and Politics in Organisations

Power refers to a psychological force at the disposal of one person that can influence the behavior of another. Politics in an organisational context refers to activities of an individual or group to obtain, enlarge and use power. It must be understood that in interpersonal relations, power is not a static quantity. It is dynamic.

Various processes that are involved in power in organisations can be studied as:

1. Power dynamics
2. Bases of power
3. Sources of power
4. Politics and political tactics

Power Dynamics

Power leads to change in behavior, but what are the psychological processes underlying the change of behavior?

Power is the ability to influence the behavior of others. Hence, power is a potential while influence is the actual application of power. How power is applied by leaders over followers is an area of concern of social psychologists. According to Kelman (1958), there are three types of powers:

1. Compliance
2. Internalisation
3. Identification

Compliance is a surface change in behavior, owing to coercion ("Carrots and stick"). It is based on legitimate power. Compliance, however, doesn't lead to any change in the target individual's attitude. Owing to this, the influence persists only when the behavior is under surveillance.

Internalisation on the other hand, means subjective acceptance of leader's power by a follower. As a result of this, the followers' attitude changes. While compliance lasts only as long as the employee is under surveillance, an internalised follower continues the behavior even without surveillance.

Identification is based on the actor's charisma. The followers imitate her behavior and attitudes to gain her approval. Identification happens when employees' need for acceptance and self-esteem are fulfilled by leader's close rapport with followers.

Psychological Process	Behaviour
Compliance	**Temporary**
Internalization	**Permanent**
Identification	**Motivated**

Fig. 5.18 : Types of power and their effect on human behaviour

Bases and sources of Power

To understand the bases of power, we will discuss the taxonomy forwarded by French and Raven (1959):

1. Reward
2. Coercion
3. Legitimacy
4. Reference
5. Expertise
6. Information

Reward and Coercion are based on behaviorist notions of reinforcement and punishment to influence behavior. These two bases only lead to behavioral changes without any change in the underlying attitudes and values. Even the behavioral change is subject to continued surveillance. An individual possesses legitimate power when she derives the power from the charter of the company. Compliance, internalisation and identification – all three are involved in legitimate power. The director of a firm can use power on subordinates by compliance or internalisation ("The director has asked as to do it!"). Also, employees identify with her.

Referent power is based on followers' identification with the agent. If my boss is my role model, I will try to imitate him and do what she asks me to do.

Expert power is the ability of an individual to perform a task no one else can. For example, design engineers have more power than software engineers in a company because design engineers are few and have domain expertise. If a person is an expert on an issue, followers internalise the fact that she is an expert and follow her suggestions.

Information power leads to cognitive changes in the subject (on whom power is applied), leading to internalisation.

The source of power can be broadly grouped as:

1. Position power 2. Personal power

Position power is based on formal position in the organisation, while personal power on the inter-personal rapport between agent and subject. Various influence processes, bases of power and sources of power and their relation can be represented as under:

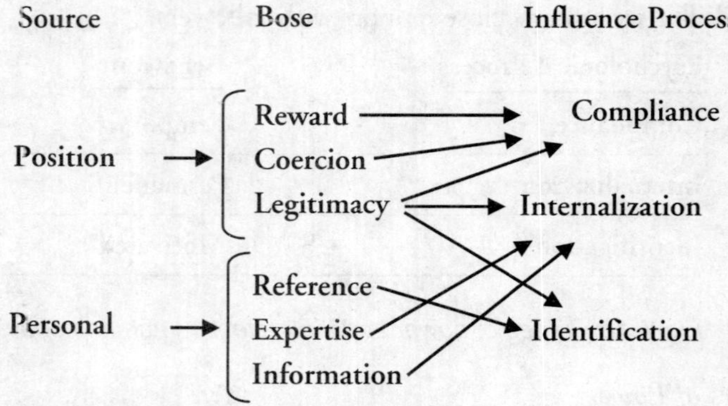

Fig. 5.19 : Illustration of Source of Power

Politics

Organisational power enables an employee to influence the decision-making process. Hence, every employee yearns for more power. Politics refers to all activities undertaken by the employee to gain power.

A few strategies for playing politics are discussed below:

1. Increasing indispensability

Power comes from indispensability. One of the prime tactics is to increase indispensability. This can be done by increasing centrality or increasing expert knowledge. An individual can increase her centrality by deliberately accepting responsibilities that bring her into contact with many functions or with many mangers. She then can increase the dependence of others on her.

Specialised organisational skills that are indispensable for the organisation can lend immense power. When I was working in a steel company as a new recruit, certain employees never disclosed their technical skills to me, lest I understand how things work and trouble-shoot during problems. This way, they take all credit for troubleshooting work.

2. Mentoring

By developing good rapport with a powerful manager, it is possible to rise up the organisational ladder with him. This is beneficial to the top managers also. Top managers often act as mentors to aspiring lower level mangers as planning for succession is an important political tactic. The protégé gains power by attaching to the top manager as protégé. The top manager consolidates his power by grooming him for succession.

3. Coalitions

This is a common political tactic in many organisations. Coalitions are often built around a trade-off. I support you on an issue of interest of yours; in return you support me on an issue of interest of mine. Coalitions can be both internal and external. Coalitions can be built at various levels in the organisation, so also with external entities, like customers and officers of financial institutions from which the company gets its capital.

Coalitions are dynamic in nature as they are made and broken easily, depending on environmental conditions. Hence, there is a need for coalition management. Co-option is an important strategy for coalition management. It allows on sub-unit to overcome the opposition of a second sub-unit by involving it in decision making.

For example, giving an opponent an important managerial role makes him a part of the coalition.

4. Manipulating the decision-making process

Politics refers to all activities motivated towards gaining power. Power is the ability to influence organisational decisions. One of the political tactics is to control the decision making process itself. This can be done by controlling the agenda or bringing in an outside expert. Typically, managers and coalitions try to control various business committees. By this, they can control the agenda that has to be tabled in a meeting on a given day. Alternatively, the manager can bring in an outside expert who subscribes to his view.

The outside expert is supposed to be neutral and an expert on the issue. This lends a legitimacy to the manager's position. In many cases, the outside expert is not neutral at all and has due knowledge of the coalition's views.

5. Devious Tactics

Devious political tactics are those that are morally difficult to defend. A few devious tactics often used in organisations are:

- Divide and rule
- Backstabbing
- Preventing the opposing faction from attending the key meetings or gatherings

Divide and rule is practiced by playing two rival factions against each other. To do this, the manager/ coalition spreads rumours or encourages completion between the two factions. As opponent stay divided and weak, the coalition consolidates its power. Backstabbing happens when an employee X attends to have a pleasant relation with employee Y, all this time planning Y's demise.

Costs and Benefits of Organisational Politics

Organisational politics is an integral and inevitable part of the organisation. Due to a hierarchy with few people at the top, the control of scarce resources like promotions and budgets becomes inevitable. It does not mean that politics is evil.

Politics has the following positive functions towards organisational effectiveness:

1. It can improve the choices and decisions that an organisation makes.
2. An organisation that confers power on those who help it the most can take advantage of political process to improve managerial effectiveness.

However, excess of politics can turn out to be dysfunctional. Politics can promote conflict; excessive politics will mean more time spent on fighting over resources allocation and making decisions, rather than implementing decisions.

An organisation reaps the benefits of politics based on the assumption that power flows to those who can contribute to the organisation most. Suppose that the top management becomes entrenched and is able to defend its power and property against its opponents. Even if the performance suffers, the top management has institutionalised power by occupying all important roles in decision-making committees. In such a case, flow of power to the deserving will be choked.

Hence, politics in organisations has both positives and negatives. To reap the benefits accruing from the political process, the organisation must maintain a balance of power between various coalitions and stakeholders. Whether power and politics benefit or harm an organisation is a function of the balance of power between organisational groups.

Power and Politics in Indian Organisations

As in other aspects of organisational culture, cross-cultural variations exist in power relations and politics in organisations. Hence, we should investigate into the nature of power play in Indian context. Luckily a detailed study has been made by Sinha.

Sinha has also drawn upon many other research studies to come to the following tentative conclusions about power relationships in Indian organisations (discussed in Dwivedi, 1995):

1. Unwarranted power conflict is widespread in Indian organisations. Many managers have false apprehensions that others are conspiring against them. Such premature impressions lead to reactive application of power. Many employees are suspicious that other employee may be up to some mischief, such as back stabbing, reporting negatively to higher authority etc. Mutual suspicions develop ultimately leading to power conflicts.
2. Personal linkages of caste and kind groups make the power relations very complex. A manager, who has 'contacts' in the government or politics, can draw upon these external agents to play politics in the organisation. It is very rampant in public sector units. Even a peon or an attendant can play politics if she is from a caste many local ministers are from; or if she has a relative in a strong position in the bureaucracy. Even in the private sector, many people try to be in the good books of IRS officers, so that they could use their contacts to enhance their status inside the organisation!
3. Authority system is the preferred form of distributions of power and privileges in Indian organisations. Indian workers and executives prefer a hierarchical order of power. This may be because, reasons Sinha, the Indian social structure (based on the hierarchy of castes) creates a tendency to prefer hierarchy. In most organisations in

India, a bureaucratic set up in place, where an employee looks up to her supervisors for guidance and patronage, and provides the same to her subordinates.

4. An accommodative-manipulative game of politics is widely prevalent in several Indian organisations. In this game, the strategy of a player (i.e., an employee) is to enhance her own power base and erode the power base of those employees who are a threat to her influence in the organisation. However, all this manipulation is accommodative, that is, employees indulge in this game without resorting to any open conflict.
5. The lesser the power differential (difference, between perceived power) between two employees, the greater is the politics they play to dominate each other, at times leading to open conflict.

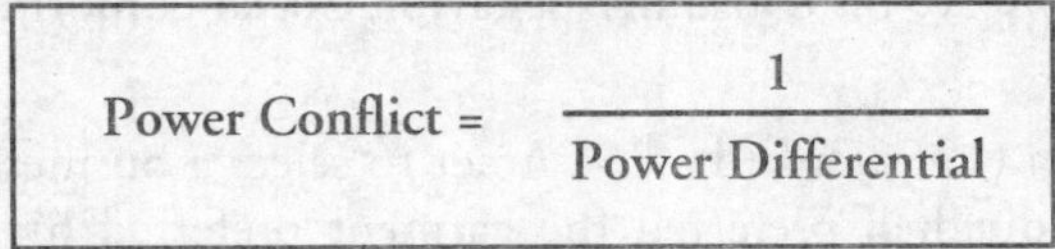

$$\text{Power Conflict} = \frac{1}{\text{Power Differential}}$$

Fig. 20 : Formula for power conflict

5.10 Consumer Psychology

Consumer Psychology is the study of psychological processes underlying the acquisition, consumption and disposition of goods, services and ideas. In this section, I seek to introduce you to consumer psychology. One way to do this is to discuss the consumer buying process. Five major areas of study in consumer psychology are environmental factors, information reception memory systems, personal factors and decision- making. These can be represented as a model shown below. Each of the factors are discussed next.

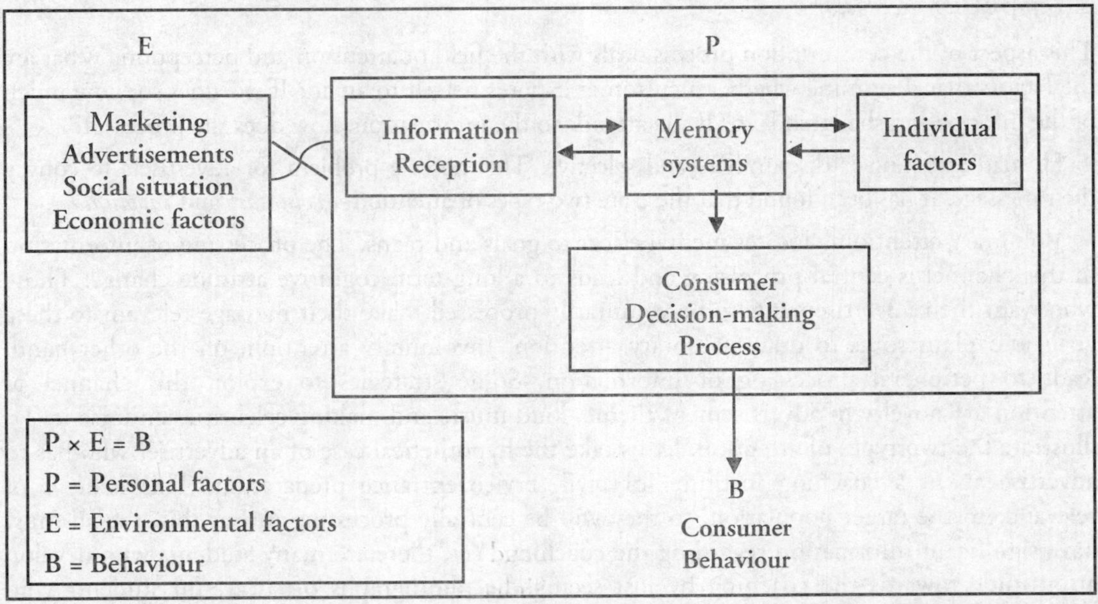

Fig. 5.21 : A model of Consumer behaviour. Based on Mowen (1989)

1. Environmental factors

There are many external stimuli that intent to influence consumer behavior. Some of these are marketing appeals, economic factors and feedback of the outcomes of previous purchases. Marketing appeals include various advertisements, product packaging and sales messages Indeed, marketers are involved in a great deal of research to find out customer preferences and also, what internal factors of the customer may induce her to buy a product.

On a different note, the consumer situation in which consumer takes her decision also makes a difference. If you frequently visit shopping malls, you already know that the ambience and appearance has an impact on behavior. You can easily get a cold drink at Rs.10/- but still many prefer to take their cold drink in big restaurants after paying a hundred bucks for it! The social situation also has a major impact on consumer behavior. Social conformity in buying behavior has been observed.

In one study, Venkatesan (1966) asked a consumer to select a business suit. Even though all suits were identical, the individual preferred the garment preferred by other members of his groups. This study was modelled on the lines of the Asch (1956) conformity study. Once, I had purchased a pink T-shirt even though I knew pink isn't the colour of guys. This was because all my friends told me that it looked good on me!

The ultimate goal of the consumer also determines her behavior. For example, if I want to purchase a product to gift it, my behavior is much different than that if I purchase a product for myself. People who are self-conscious about their looks are quite concerned about the brand of clothes they purchase. I often purchase shoes from the neighborhood shoe vendor. But a friend of mine always gets Nike stuff (he has a girlfriend!).

2. Information Reception

This aspect of the consumption process deals with the field of attention and perception. What are the factors that determine whether a customer exposes herself to an ad? If she does so, how much of the information she attends to? If she attends to the information, how does she process it?

Human attention is discriminate and selective. This poses a problem for advertisers to convey their message. It has been found that there are two types of attention – *voluntary* and *involuntary*.

Voluntary attention allocates mental effort to goals and plans. The processing of information in this channel is central processing and leads to a long-term cognitive attitude change. Those who want their advertisements to be voluntarily processed make their message relevant to these goals and plans so as to draw voluntary attention. Involuntary attention, on the other hand, leads to peripheral processing of information. Some strategies to exploit this channel of attention are novelty in advertisement theme, loud music and making celebrities endorse it. To illustrate the two types of attention, let us take the hypothetical case of an advertiser who has to advertise about a coaching institute for civil service entrance preparation. This issue is of relevance to the target population, so they will be centrally processing it. For this, the ad must have significant information regarding the coaching. Yet, there are many students who develop an attitude towards the coaching by just seeing the photographs of successful students who endorse the coaching institute. These students basically do peripheral processing.

Both, voluntary and involuntary attention, are active cognitive processes. However, it has been found that the consumer can learn without active information processing, by a process called low-involvement learning.

Krugman (1965) observes that consumer defenses are lowered when messages are learnt by low-involvement. Hence, messages are received relatively uncritically and the consumer may later be prompted to buy products without any well-thought reason. This concept is called subliminal perception when the message received is too weak to be consciously perceived.

Consumer psychologists have also contributed in developing tools for assessment of information reception. For example, tools have been developed to measure pupil dilation and eye movements to estimate attention that the consumer pays to a message. These tools have multiple usages in developing ads. For example, if I want to place an ad in a newspaper, which part of the ad will the consumer focus on? Consumer psychologists have developed elaborate eye-tracking devices to identify the features of an ad that capture a consumer's attention.

3. Memory System

The consumer is bombarded with hundreds of messages every day, most of which reach short-term memory and vanish. Only a few reach the long-term memory. Consumer psychologists are particularly interested in learning how consumers place information received about a product into long-term memory. The consumer is bombarded with hundreds of messages everyday about products. Some of the messages are attended to and then stored, while others are ignored and never placed into long-term memory. Consumer psychologists have come out with some interesting findings. For instance, Sawyer (1974) has found that repeated messages have a greater likelihood of being encoded. Other studies have shown that context acts as a cue in retrieval of information; hence changes in context affect the ability of people to retrieve information. Hence, advertisers should try to use *trademark logo* and *brand names* as reduced cues to remind the consumer of the whole product. Finally, images have been found to have better storage. Hence, images should preferably be used in advertisements and are superior to text advertisements.

4. Individual Person Factors

When taking decisions about which product to purchase, the consumer often refers to her long-term memory. She tries to make rational cost-benefit analysis before making a choice. However, man is an irrational creature. Hence, the final judgment that is taken is subjective. In the subjective judgement, many other factors matter, like the consumer's personality, beliefs, motives, and attitudes. For example, I won't attend to a banner on costly clothes if I don't' have the attitude towards that, i.e., if I believe unbranded clothes that come cheap will satisfy my needs.

Similarly, there are many motivating factors that seek to motivate the consumer. Do you have these motivators on your ad? Some major social motives are need for achievement, for affiliation and for power. Take the hypothetical case of a cold-drink maker who wants to motivate the youth to purchase it. What should his ad be like? Most commercials of cold-drinks show groups of individuals having fun; this is because their target market (the youth) are most motivated by the need for affiliation.

At one time, Freud's Psychoanalytic Theory was very popular with consumer psychologists. There was an attempt to embed various symbols appealing to consumers' unconscious motives in TV and print ads. Today, it has fallen into disrepute. Today, a popular activity among personality researchers is trying to predict liking and preferences for certain products. This is called psychographics. The philosophy behind psychographics is that self-concept often translates into a person's lifestyle. Understanding lifestyle preferences help in better targeting products towards consumers.

'An example of psychographics may be found in a study by Sadalla and Burroughs (1981). These researchers investigated the eating preferences of individuals and how these preferences related to their opinions, interests, and activities. They classified food into five categories – vegetarian, gourmet, health, fast and synthetic. (Synthetic foods are high-technology items, like processed becon, instant eggs, instant breakfast drinks, and highly processed cheese snacks). They then identified individuals whose food preferences could be classified as falling into one of the five categories. These same individuals then rated themselves on a variety of characteristics. In addition, another group of subjects described what they thought vegetarians, gourmets, high teachers and so on would like. The results were surprising. The way people rated themselves was in close agreement with the way others rated them. Vegetarians were seen as non-competitive, sexual and liking crafts and fold dancing. Gourments were perceived as using drugs, living alone and liberal. Their hobbies were glamour sports and gambling.(Mowen, 1989).

Psychographic information can be extremely useful for marketers to design their ad. Suppose I want to design an ad for vegetarian food consumers, now I know what their values and lifestyle preferences are. I could easily use these in deciding on the theme of my advertisement.

5. Consumer Decision-making

This is the final step underlying any consumer behavior. The process that consumer decision making takes can be represented as shown in the figure:

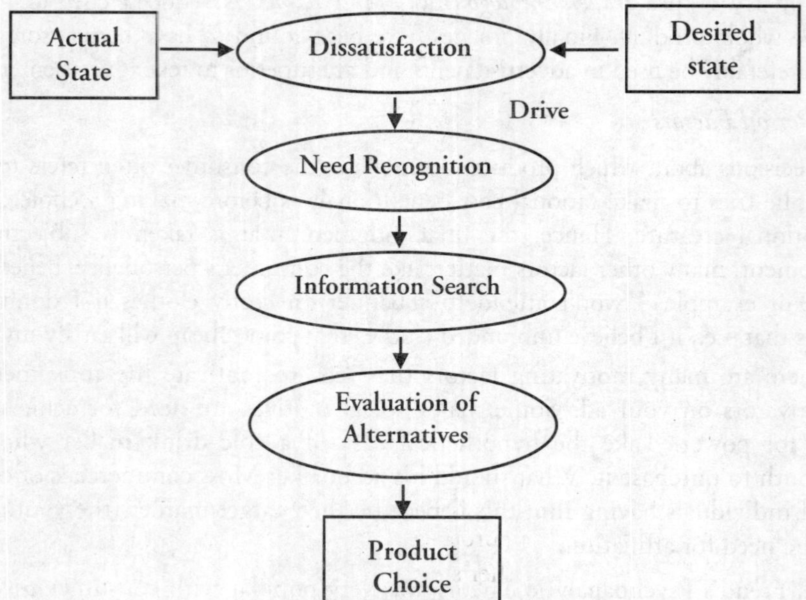

Fig. 5.22 : Consumer Decision Making process

A dis-satisfaction occurs when the consumer's actual state and desired state are not the same. This dissatisfaction can in fact be created by repeatedly persuading to the consumer that the actual state lacks something. Indeed, some companies create demand for their products! For instance, if I get a cathartic fixation on a cell-phone, I visualise myself in a desired state, where I have the ultra hi-tech phone. Comparison of the two states leads to dis-satisfaction (tension) which drives me to need recognition. Once I recognise my need, I search for information.

There are two types of search processes- internal search, in which I search my long-term memory for products that may solve my problem. I may try to recall advertisements, or the mobiles of friends that I have handled earlier. External search involved looking in newspaper classifieds, talking to friends and visiting the showroom. I may check for the phone on the internet or take referral opinions of my friends. After I have some alternatives to choose from (say iPhone, Nokia, Motorola, Samsung, etc.), I will evaluate them based on subjective probability and weightages. I give to various attributes. Here, my personal attitude and preferences determine the weight I give to any specific feature.

Suppose, I want a mobile with very good sound and music quality, then the weightage I give to the second row in the above box will be high. Suppose now, that the quality of sound of mobile-2 is high; so W_{22} will be highest.

After the evaluation, I calculate the sum of weightages for all three mobiles and purchase one with largest weight. It must be reiterated now that we often do not do such rational calculations, rather use heuristics to decide upon a choice.

	Mobile-1	**Mobile-2**	**Mobile-3**
Camera	W_{11}	W_{12}	W_{13}
Music	W_{21}	W_{22}	W_{23}
Touch-screen	W_{31}	W_{32}	W_{33}

Fig. 5.23 : An illustration of weightages given to choices

At times, we don't even make a choice. If you have gone shopping with your mother, you must have seen that she suddenly finds a product that she likes so much that she immediately purchases it without comparing it with other such products. Even when one is loyal to a brand, she doesn't make rational calculations before purchasing that specific brand.

Black box model

The black box model is briefly discussed as an alternative to Mowen's (1989) model. This model talks about the interaction of stimuli, individual differences, decision process and consumer responses (Sandhusen, 2000, p.218). The focus here is not on the processes inside a consumer, rather the relation between the stimuli and consumer response. 'Environmental factors' consists of the marketing stimuli that are planned by companies (the 4Ps), whereas 'environmental stimulus' refers to the social factors, mediated by economic, political and cultural circumstances of a society. A drawback of this model is that it considers the consumer a rational person who takes decisions after thorough calculations. In reality, human consumers are not this rational and often make use of heuristics and gut feeling to take decision.

ENVIRONMENTAL FACTORS		BUYER'S BLACK BOX		BUYER'S RESPONSE
Marketing stimuli	Environmental Stimuli	Buyer Characteristics	Decision Process	
Product Price Place Promotion	Economic Technological Political Cultural	Attitudes Motivation Perceptions Personality	Problem recognition Information search Alternative evaluation Purchase decision	Product choice Brand choice Dealer choice Purchase timing

5.11 Ergonomics

Ergonomics is the branch of organisational psychology concerned with fitting jobs to people, rather than people to jobs. The basic principle behind ergonomics is that both operator and machines are sub-systems of one single system. Since both operator and machine work towards a single goal (i.e., getting the job done) and they have to do it in co-ordination, they constitute a single system.

With rising complication of computing technology and machine design, it is seen that machines become unfriendly for operators to handle. This may lead to reduced performance, stress, errors in operation and accidents.

The scope of Ergonomics

Ergonomists design jobs, work places and equipment's to maximise performance and to minimise accidents, fatigue and energy expenditure. As such, the scope of ergonomics is very vast. If you make certain changes in your study table to make it more convenient for you to study, it is ergonomics. At the same time, if a manufacturer designs car, the steps she takes to ensure driver's comfort are part of ergonomics. Human factor engineering is a part of ergonomics, but not necessarily all of ergonomics. Human Factor Engineering (HFE) is based on the man-machine system. But ergonomics is also concerned with comfort of the employee in the workplace, and of all employees.

Focusing on the organisation, the scope of ergonomics includes:

1. Product design
2. Workspace design
3. Workplace design
4. Research

Product design is the crucial stage of developing a product and selling it to the consumer. Ergonomists are involved in design of nay product (from a mere sewing machine to sophisticated racing cars) that demands expert help to make machines user-friendly.

Workspace is the organisation of a workstation for an individual worker. When the workspaces of an entire group or organisation are combined, it is called workplace. Workspace design looks into issues prevailing in making the workstation of an employee more comfortable.

Workplace design, on the other hand, looks into issues of all employees' interactions. For example, when organisations try to reduce their bureaucratic structure, they desire to have a workplace where communication and approachability are easier. Ergonomists recommend to them open offices. Open offices means to eliminate private chambers. Groups of desks in one large area, divided by temporary participations make an open office. Each employee's space in the open office is called a cubicle. Her comfort inside the cubicle is determined by workspace design.

Ergonomics is not based on any general principle. Ergonomists borrow from basic principles of psychology and certain engineering disciplines, but as such ergonomic design varies from situation to situation. Due to this, ergonomists require large amount of data. Many psychologists involved in ergonomic research provide these data through manuals and journal articles.

Psychological Principles underlying Ergonomics

Ergonomists see the work environment as a single man-machine system consisting of two information-processing sub-systems-man and machine. Ergonomists focus their attention on making the man-machine interface more user-friendly.

This system can be represented as under:

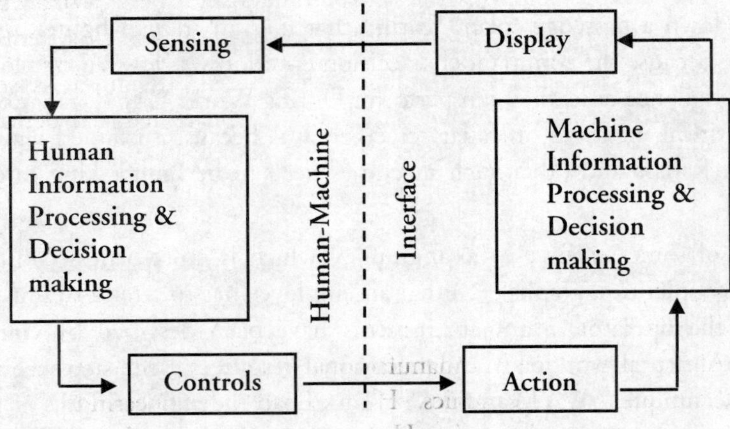

Fig. 5.24 : Man-machine system

A variety of psychological principles are used to engineer user-friendly machines. What needs to be understood here is that application varies from one case to another. Let us, however, discuss certain general principles.

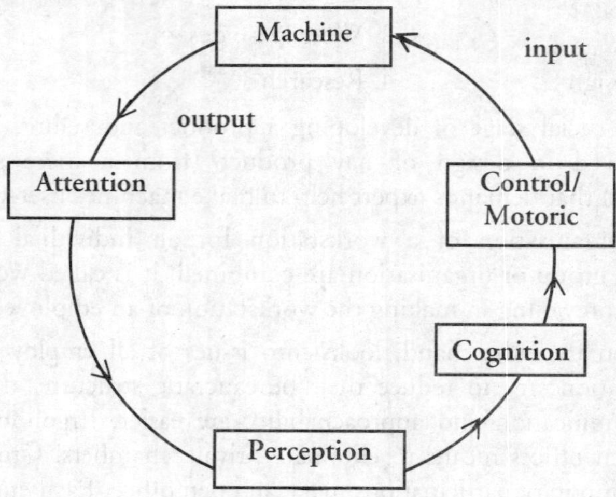

Fig. 5.25 : Psychological variables in ergonomics

1. Attention

Various attention principles that must be kept while designing an ergonomic task are psychophysics, attention resource limits and processing. Attention refers to human ability to focus information processing on selective events over a specific period of time. Psychophysics tells us about the stimuli that fall between the absolute thresholds of human sensation. This principle is useful in ergonomics. For example, it is very difficult to detect changes in a plane travelling through fog (for the pilot). The concept of difference threshold is used to design sensors that amplify signals by certain ratio.

Signal detection theory tells us that attention is affected by both external and internal factors. USS Vincennes struck down a passenger plane fearing that it is an Iranian fighter aircraft. It committed such mistake because the commander's decision criterion was low. Also, people have a limit on the nature of vigilance tasks they can perform. During World War II, radar operators missed some rare but critical messages on radar screen. It was because sustained vigilance by humans has limitations. Radars and other such machines need to be built taking care of this limitation.

Attention makes use of some resources, the amount of which is more or less constant and limited. The stimuli (data, pictures, graphs etc.) that an employee has to attend to mustn't lead to mental overload of the operator. Many instruments have been designed by engineering psychologists to measure mental workloads and attentional resources, such as the Subjective Workload Assessment Technique (SWAT) and NASA Task Load Index (Nasa TLI).

Attention can be both automatic and controlled. Automatic processing doesn't involve any effort, nor does it eat up much attention resources. Certain task can be performed by automatic processing after training. Training helps in automating and routinising some functions- this is taken into consideration when designing machines.

2. Perception

It is understood that both external stimuli and prior experience are used by perceptual schema to interpret the world. Illusions and hallucinations also occur because of top-down processing of information. This human limitation (a strength otherwise) poses a big challenge in designing displays. During World War II, for example many planes crashed because the altimeters were faulty and planes flying at low attitude couldn't make out figure-ground relations properly.

3. Cognitions

A group of ergonomists study how the operator can be aided in decision-making. This becomes essential because today the amount of information available in real-time is huge. For example, an operator sitting in the control room of a power plant has to go through numerous data. These data come in real-time and he has to refer to present and past data to make out the problem and decide a corrective step. Due to limitations of working memory capacity, he may fail or use biased heuristics.

Two popular support aids provided by ergonomists to help the operator deal with this problem are:

- Knowledge-based supporting aid
- Decision support system

A knowledge-based supporting aid is a technical entity for information-processing that gives certain conclusions to the user. For instance, if I am mechanical engineer and I went to trouble school problems in boiler of a power plant, I can feed data of past three days to the supporting aid and gets various graphs and analysis.

Decision Support System (DSS) contains decision procedures for managers. There are thirty seven variables in a power-plan automation system. Decision to be taken depends on all these variables. This makes the number of possibilities to decide from more than a thousand. DSS provides guidelines to operators about what might have gone wrong. Without DSS, the operator has to base his decision on heuristics (based on past experiences) and memory recall.

4. Control/ Motoric

Compatibility is one of the most important factors to be considered in system design. This is especially significant in stressful conditions where learned habits breakdown and cause errors in action. Technological development is continuously challenging the user friendliness of control. For example, lever is giving way to switch, switch to keyboard, keyboard to mouse and mouse to touch-screen. Ergonomists are involved in cutting-edge research in speech and automated image processing input.

Another major challenge for ergonomists is the modelling of sensory motoric regulation of operators in flight and driving tasks. Tracking experiments are a class of research conducted in this direction.

5. Anthropometrics and Population Stereotypes

The study of man's physical configuration is called anthropometrics. Body dimensions are important since the operator must fit the workspace in such a manner that he will be comfortable and will be able to utilise all the displays and control on-the-job. Take, for example, the construction of a seat in a heavy truck.

To make the driver comfortable, various factors have to be optimal:

- Body measurement
- Reaction time
- Noise factor

But then, there is a problem here. We can't design trucks individually for drivers of all sise. Hence, manufacturers use population stereotypes. Population stereotypes are a particular option chosen by a large proportion of a given population,that is statistically predominant. It can also mean any way of behaving that is predominant in the population. Ergonomists use these preferences of the majority to design their products. For example, to design the driver seat, I would first take data on height of various drivers, draw up a stereotype (i.e., height range in which majority of drivers fall) and design seat that will be optimal to them.

■ ■ ■

6

Sport Psychology

Chapter outline

6.1 Sport Psychology

Sport Psychology refers to the scientific study of human behaviour and experience in sport. Sport psychology has two sub-units- it includes the researcher who studies sportsmen and their behaviours; and the sport psychologist who uses the knowledge base of researchers, to make psychological interventions in improving the performance of sportsmen.

What is the need for a sports psychologist? Coaches and trainers focus almost exclusively on left brain activities including game plans, strategy and technique, speed, agility, etc. Right brain activities include balance, emotions, music and visualization, all of which can enhance performance, but these are often neglected by athletes. The job of a sport psychologist at the individual level is to develop and enhance skills based on right brain activities. At the group level, the psychologist examines various psychological factors operating at group level to assist in enhancing performance of sportsmen in team games.

6.2 Psychological Interventions

A variety of psychological interventions are recommended to enhance the performance of sportspersons in both individual and team games. First, we would look at certain interventions common to most games, then go on to discuss certain psychological factors that specifically affect team games and how these can be remedied.

1. Arousal

The ***Yerkes-Dodson law*** states that an inverted U relation exists between arousal and performance, i.e., an over-aroused or under aroused individual can't perform her optimal best. Oxendine (1970) has verified this law in the case of many sports. Sports coaches aren't adapt at explaining what the optimal level of arousal is. An over-aroused sportsperson has lower concentration and inferior focus. Over-arousal also can lead to anger and aggression while playing. So, how to ensure optimal level of arousal?

Oxendine (1979) observes that the amount of arousal necessary for optimal arousal is dependent on the nature of the skill involved in the game. Games which need complex skills need a lower level of arousal, because arousal interferes with cognitive activities, such as concentration, fine muscle movement and coordination. For example, playing golf needs great amount of concentration and calculation. Hence, it is not good for a person playing golf to be over-aroused. Similarly, in the case of shooting, sharp perceptual skills and attention are necessary. On the other hand, higher level of arousal benefits games that require less complex skills, but more strength and endurance.

The sport psychologist usually first determines what level of arousal is good for a particular sports. Then the psychologist trains the sportsperson to maintain that level of arousal. Usually, a relaxation technique is learnt by the sportsperson. The psychologist conditions (by classical conditioning) a trigger word to the relaxation. Whenever the sportsperson thinks about the trigger word, she becomes relaxed. In the real sports, if she gets over-aroused at any time, she says the trigger word to herself and immediately, she becomes relaxed. Her state of extreme arousal is moderated.

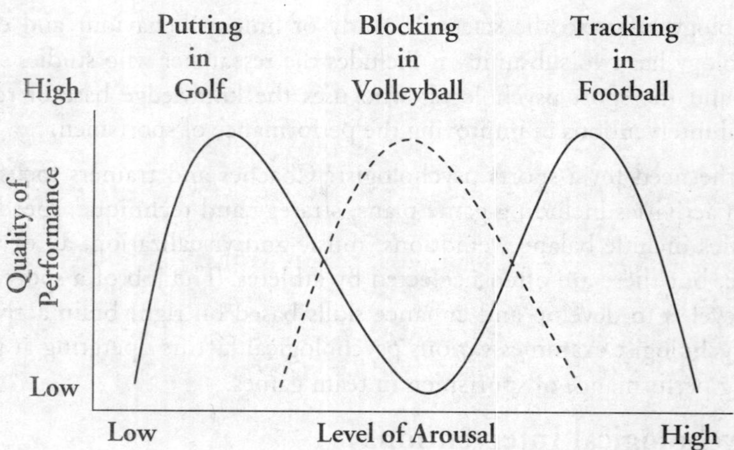

Fig. 6.1 : Graph depicting arousal and performance

In a study by Maman Paul and Kanupriya Garg (2012), biofeedback was taken from basketball players by reading their heart rate variability (HRV) as they played under pressure. They found that self-efficacy and performance of the players increased after training on coping with anxiety.

2. Imagery

William Arthur Ward had once opined, “If you can imagine it, you can achieve it. If you can dream it, you can become it.” He was basically stating how powerful a tool imagery is. Imagery is a cognitive process in which one uses her mind to **create an experience** that is similar to a physical event. **Karlene Sugarman**, author of the book, ‘Winning the Mental Way’ observes that the body cannot distinguish between something that is really happening, and something that an individual visualizes. Hence, the mind can be used to:

- Recall past performance that were good and practice them in the mind.
- Correct technical errors committed previously.
- Put one-self in various situations and visualize how to tackle the situation.

Mental practice, it has been found, is quite helpful. When you practice executing a skill in your head, it becomes a conditioned response. When a skill becomes a conditioned response, it comes to you instinctively when you are in the field.

The sport psychologist teaches the sportsperson how to use all her senses in imagery. First, the sportsperson is trained in external imagery, by showing videos of past events. The sportsperson is made to spot her errors and visualize the correct response in that condition. Then, the sport psychologist trains her in internal imagery, by asking her to visualize certain situations and what her response would be to such situations.

3. The 4C

Concentration, Confidence, Control and Commitment are the 4C's that psychologists consider the main mental qualities important for successful performance in most sports.

Concentration is the mental ability to maintain focus. If the sportsperson is distracted, her energy can't be channelized in the right direction and hence, reduced performance. Hence, psychologists train sportspersons in concentration. Different sports require different kind of concentration. Some require sustained concentration (e.g., cycling, tennis, and squash), others require short bursts of concentration (e.g., cricket, shooting and golf), while still other games, like sprinting and skiing require intense concentration.

The psychologist identifies what kind of concentration is needed in a particular sport. Then she identifies common distractions, like anxiety, mistakes, negative thoughts, fatigue and weather. The sportsperson is then trained on controlling and handling these stressors.

Confidence is the result of a comparison that a sportsperson makes between her ability and the goal. Self-confidence results when the individual thinks that she has the ability to achieve the goal. Under-confidence results when she thinks she can't do it. Over-confidence results when the individual is complacent and isn't putting the extra effort to win. While under-confidence and over-confidence are both harmful, self-confidence should be inculcated in the sportsperson. To improve self-confidence, the sports psychologists often use mental imagery to help the sportsperson visualize previous good performances, imagine various scenarios and how one could cope with them.

Control in the 4C refers to emotional control. Two emotions that the athlete feels tough to tackle are anger and anxiety. When a sportsperson becomes angry, the cause of anger often becomes the focus of attention. The concentration shifts from the task to the cause of anger and performance deteriorates. Due to decreased performance, confidence on self is reduced which leads to more anger! Anger becomes a vicious cycle which over-arouses the player and makes her lose her concentration.

Another such emotion that hampers concentration and confidence is anxiety. Anxiety can be physical anxiety (sweating, nausea, etc.) of mental (worry, negative thoughts, etc.) or both. To tackle anxiety, sports psychologists train the sportspersons in relaxation. For anger, certain anger management techniques are used. Self-instructional therapy is quite popular among sports psychologist as a means for anger management.

Commitment refers to how focused and motivated the sportsperson is towards her ultimate goal. There are many hassles that a sportsperson has to face in day-to-day life. In the face of this, keeping up one's morale and commitment is a challenger. To enhance and sustain the sportsperson's commitment level, the psychologists usually use goal-setting techniques which will be discussed next.

4. Motivation

Motivation drives behaviour towards a goal. Here, the goal is to win the game and / or to excel in performance. Before discussing various techniques used by sports psychologists, let us understand first the nature of motivation of athletes. According to the Achievement Goal Theory of Dweck (1986), there are broadly two orientations of the individual playing a game-mastery orientation and ego orientation. In mastery orientation, the focus is on personnel; giving maximum effort to realize the individual's full potential. Those with mastery orientation are intrinsically motivated. They don't compete with others, but with themselves. They always strive to get their best from their potential. Ego orientation, on the other hand, implies that the athlete seeks to perform better than others. She compares herself with others when setting her target. In the ego-approach style, there is competitive orientation. One wants to be better than others. In the ego-avoidance style, there is a fear of failure. One fears that she may be negatively evaluated by the audience if she doesn't perform up to the mark and this motivates her to perform.

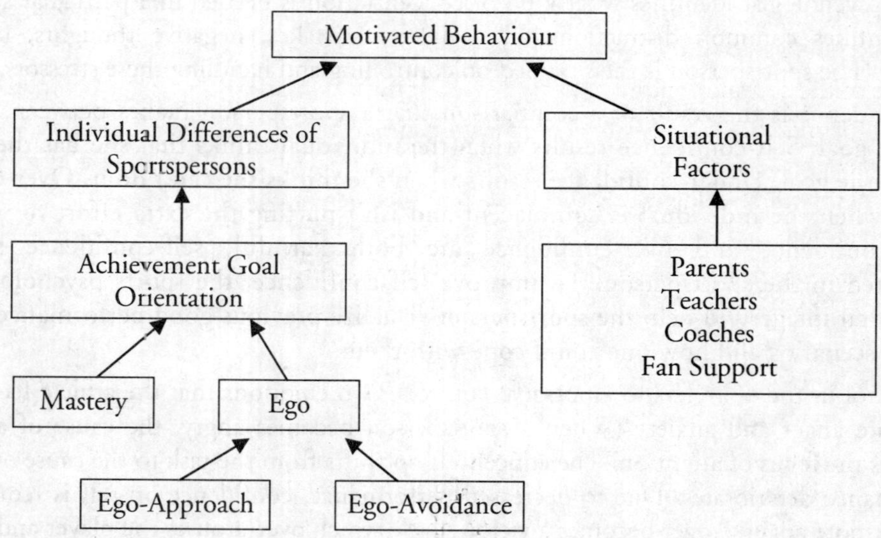

Fig. 6.2 : Basis of Achievement Goal Theory

So, which of these styles is the best? Obviously, the ego avoidance style is not good. It leads to a fear of failure. When fear of failure motivates one to perform, she can't give her best. Rather, the sportsperson suffers from anxiety and lack of focus.

Mastery goals are better than ego-approach goals. This is because when one is motivated by mastery goals, she enjoys doing her work. This keeps up her motivation and commitment. She strives for mastery, without bothering for what is the performance of others. In the ego-approach style, the goal is to be better than others and stay there. If you don't face any more challenges, you don't try to realize your full potential. Sports psychologists recommend that while training off-field, one must be motivated by mastery goals; but once you are in the real game, you should be motivated by ego-approach goal. Ego-avoidance goals are dangerous and should be avoided.

Many psychologists have observed that goal-setting improves performance. The sports psychologist helps the sportsperson to set SMART goals.

SMART stand for:

S – Specific
M – Measurable
A – Action-oriented
R – Realistic
T – Time-bound

The goal should be specific and realistic. It ought to be challenging, but not that challenging as to overwhelm the sports trainee. The goals should be measurable and continued feedback should be provided by the coach and sports psychologist. Often, chaining and shaping techniques are used to teach trainee sportspersons complex motor skills.

Goal-setting is easier said than done. There are many pitfalls in setting goals, which the sports psychologist should analyze and remove.

Some of the common mistakes in goal-setting are as under:

(a) *Setting too many goals:* Too many goals at one time confuse the brain and diffuse energy. As a result, athletes and coaches end up accomplishing none of them. Instead, athletes should pick the goal that is most important and master it first. Then, the athlete can move on to the next goal.

(b) *Failing to set process goals:* Some coaches make the mistake of setting outcome goals, while ignoring process goals. A football coach may set a goal for the team to win the state championship tournament in next winter. This is fine as an outcome goal. But, the coach also needs to set process goals and meet some performance benchmark in time-bound manner.

(c) *Setting unspecific goals:* Goals should be specific. For example, if a coach wants to increase the stamina of a player, she should not set 'increase stamina' as a goal. The coach should find out the means of increasing stamina and give clear goals- 'run 2 miles in 12 minutes'.

(d) *Focusing too much on ego goals and not enough on mastery:* Ego goals are outcome goals and invariably mean winning in sports. Some coaches and players tend to focus too much on outcome goals, while neglecting mastery goals. Mastery goals are about improving skill and performance, regardless of outcome. Concentrating on mastery goals improves you incrementally over time. Even if you are not winning, you are getting better at the game.

5. Confidence-building

Psychological interventions are required to build confidence in a player. Confidence plays a big role in competitiveness of a player. Lay audience usually believe that a player should believe in herself in order to be confident. A belief in self's ability is enough to garner confidence. But, that is not so. Confidence develops by a complex psychological process. Secondly, coaches at times confuse cockiness with confidence. If you feel good about yourself, you are confident; if you do not feel good, but pretend that you feel good, that's cockiness. A confident person is strong, but a cocky person is insecure. A cocky person pretends that he is confident; but truly he is affected by lack of confidence.

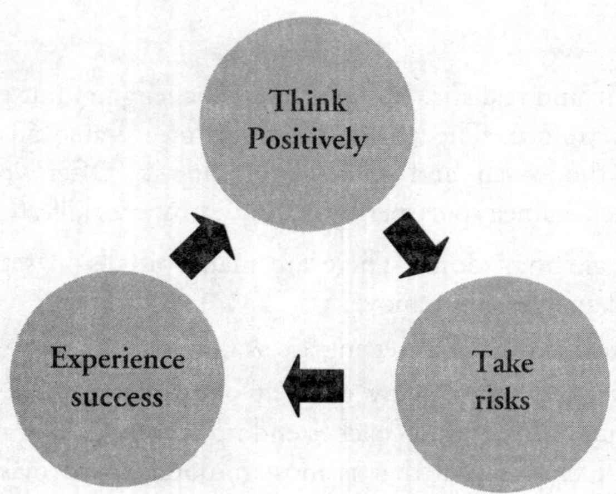

Fig. 6.3. : The virtuous cycle of building confidence

Psychologists have found from analysis of sportsmen that confidence develops in three stages that form a virtuous cycle, namely (a) think positively, (b) take risk, and (c) experience success. Experiencing success gives a positive reinforcement and increases positive thinking. Confidence-building process should include these three components in day-to-day training. More the reinforcement, more the confidence. The coach should be careful to challenge the player with achievable risks, so that the player does not get demotivated. Consistently experiencing failure gives a negative feedback and can break the virtuous cycle.

6. Focus

Successful athletes are masters of focus. Optimal focus helps an athlete in consistent and smooth execution. It improves performance,whereas faulty focus leads to inconsistent execution and deteriorates performance. Hence, focus is important.

Distractions are of two types- **internal** (such as, negative thoughts) or **external** (such as, reaction of the audience). Training for focus helps the athlete in managing both kinds of distractions and in focusing on the goal at hand. Empirical studies have shown that faulty focus leads to higher than optimal arousal and leads to bad performance. Hence, training for focus is an integral part of sports coaching.

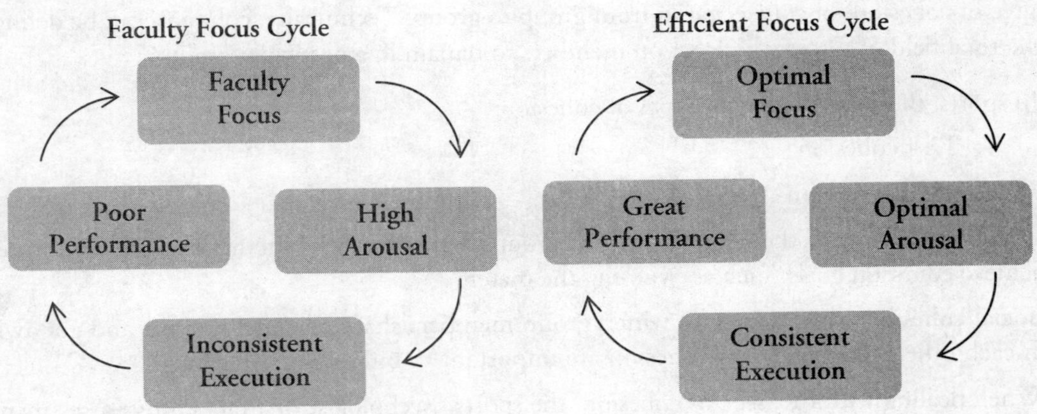

Fig. 6.4 : The focus cycle

Strategies to improve focus include:

(i) Training to focus on the process rather than the outcome.

(ii) Deep breathing practice.

(iii) Focus on what the athlete can control (this leads to an *internal locus of control* feeling, and stabilizes the arousal level).

6.3 Psychological Interventions in Team Sports

There are, broadly, two types of sports- interactive and co-active. In interactive sports, like football and hockey, overall performance depends on interpersonal dynamics of the sportsmen. In co-active sports, like swimming and golf, individual performance doesn't depend on other's performance. Cricket is a hybrid wherein the batsman's behaviour is coactive, but the fielding team's behaviour is interactive. There are many psychological factors involved in interactive sports and demand psychological interventions to enhance group performance. Some of these are:

1. Social loafing
2. Group cohesion
3. Co-ordination factors

Steiner (1972) observes that a good team is more than a group of skilled players. If members don't work together, in coordination, then:

Actual Productivity = Potential productivity – Losses due to faulty group processes.

'Social loafing' refers to a phenomenon wherein individual performance decreases when the individual finds herself in a group. According to Woods (1998), social loafing is essentially the result of decrease in motivation. This may happen due to reduction in the sense of responsibility. Woods, therefore, believes that sports coaches and psychologists should monitor and give feedback on performance to each individual and to the group, rather than only to the group.

Cohesion is the psychological process that transforms a collection of individuals into a group. Degree of cohesion, of course, varies from group to group. Technically, cohesion can be defined as the total field of forces which act on members to remain in a particular group.

In sports, there are two major types of cohesion:

1. Task cohesion
2. Social cohesion

Task cohesion refers to the degree to which group members work together and are committed to achieve common goals, such as, winning the match.

Social cohesion is the degree to which group members share personal rapport and goodwill with each other. Both forms of cohesion are important to build effective teams.

When dealing with the issue of cohesion, the sports psychologist first takes direct assessment, as given by the players, to determine the amount of cohesiveness in the team. Then she takes certain steps as below:

- Conduct periodic team meetings.
- Build mutual respect among members and try to remove any prejudice or misunderstanding among the members.
- Develop effective two-ways communication between players.

Coordination factors refer to the degree to which each player's skills are meshed together with the skill of others in the team. This has to be a central feature in sports training in interactive sports. Hence, training time should include practicing, for example, passing a football among players, timing and pattern of player's movements when scoring a goal or when taking a penalty corner (Gross, 2005).

Rehabilitation of Injured Athletics

A major challenge for the sports psychologist is to rehabilitate injured athletes. It has been found that injured athletes commonly experience tension, depression, anger and other forms of emotional distress (Leddy et al, 1994). Hence, a lot of research is now being done on the rehabilitation of injured athletes.

Many models have been established to explain psychological responses to sport injury. Initially, stage models were very popular. According to *Kübler-Ross* (1969) Stage Model, inured athletes with terminal illness go through five stages:

1. Denial
2. Anger
3. Bargaining
4. Depression
5. Acceptance

Another Stage Model, presented by Hardy (1990), states that emotional reaction after injury has two phases:

1. A reactive phase
2. An adaptive phase

The reactive phase includes shock and negative emotions, such as depression, anger and denial. The adaptive phase includes positive emotions, such as confidence and hope.

A major shortcoming of stage models was that they failed to account for individual differences in response to athletic injury. Hence, many researchers started building models based on cognitive appraisal of injury. According to one such model (Proposed by Brewer, 1994), injured athletes' personal factors and situational factors influence their responses to injury.

Psychological interventions in the case of injured sportspersons are varied and various techniques are suitable for various conditions. Some techniques found to be effective are:

- Counseling which includes active listening, exploring coping strategies and challenging negative beliefs, etc.
- Cognitive interventions, including positive-self-thought, rational reasoning, etc.
- Cognitive-behavioural interventions, such as self-monitoring of distress, self-talk to manage pain and anxiety, etc.

Relaxation therapy, including stress reduction, training yoga and meditation (Naoi and Ostrow, 2008).

■ ■ ■

7

MILITARY PSYCHOLOGY

Chapter outline

7.1 Mental Health Isues of Soldiers

One major job of military psychologists is to promote psychological well-being among the soldiers and other employees in the military. This is increasingly becoming a challenge given that cases of suicide, fratricidal murder and depression are on the rise. Also, the job description of the military has broadened, owing to the fact that they are asked to do any kind of job, including building bridges after Tsunami and keeping peace when riots erupt. Their job description today is not restricted to just protecting the border.

The military environment is 'characterized by jobs with high stress, low autonomy, little personal control over workplace, long working hours and / or deployment in combat-related or in internal security duties, in insurgency-affected areas that entails chronic exposure to potentially traumatic events (Sharma & Sharma, 2008).

The psychological effects of such stressors are multi-dimensional. The role of military psychologist here is to recognize the psychological vital signs in military domain, using various psychological assessment tools; design and implement various intervention programmes; provide counselling to soldiers who are in need of it; and to rehabilitate retired and handicapped soldiers, who usually show strong signs of depression and anxiety.

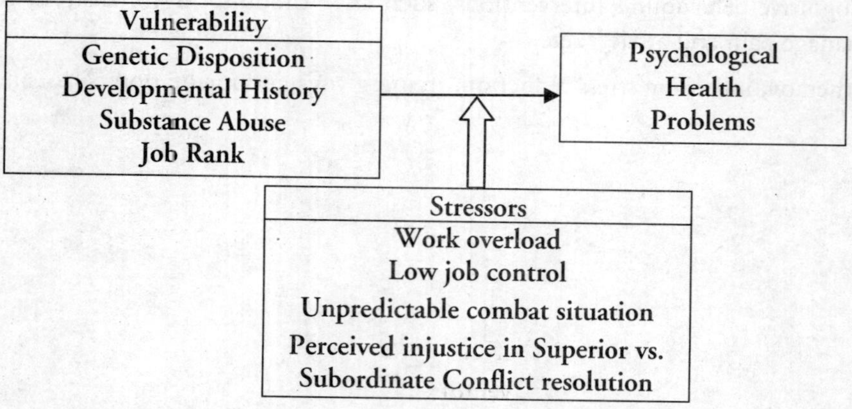

Fig. 7.1 : Factors affecting Psychological Health in Military

Mental Health Problems

The effect of stress depends on two factors- the environment and the person. Environmental stresses are no doubt, intense, unpredictable, chronic and uncontrollable for military personnel. But, individual vulnerability to stressors also determines who gets mental health problems and who doesn't. Qualities, like resilience and military hardiness in individuals help them to better cope with stress.

But, once stress affects an individual's well-being, how does it get manifested? Sagar Sharma and Monica Sharma (2008) argue that there are three stress-induced vital signs critical to an individual's well-being. These are:

1. Anxiety
2. Anger
3. Depression

Individuals high on these key indicators suffer from many mental health problems, like Generalized Anxiety Disorder (GAD), Panic Disorders, Post Traumatic Stress Disorder (PTSD) and Depression.

Military personnel are more vulnerable to anxiety related disorders than civilians, owing to the greater probability of encountering traumatic and life-threatening events. Military personnel are most vulnerable to PTSD. Anxiety and depression, in general, lead to impaired quality of life and put immense psychological burden on those affected.

Anger is another vital sign that is of concern to the psychologist. When an individual directs his anger towards himself, he may try to commit suicide. When he directs his anger towards persons perceived by him as unfair and unjust, it may lead to violence and fratricidal murder. The number of cases of suicide and fratricidal murder (killing one's colleague or superior) in the army is on the rise. A major reason for this is intense anger, coupled with anxiety and depression.

7.2 Psychological Interventions for Positive Health

Assessment

Now, that we know that anxiety, anger and depression are three symptoms of underlying psychological ill-health, the next job is to assess and monitor these signs in soldiers. Sagar Sharma and Monica Sharma (2008) argue that the way physicians routinely measure pulse rate, blood pressure and body temperature; the same way military psychologists should measure anxiety, anger and depression in soldiers regularly. Hence, their emphasis is more on early detection, so that remedial counselling and intervention strategies can be used to mitigate the mental problems.

The most widely used psychological tests to assess and monitor these three vital signs are:

1. State – Trait Anxiety Inventors (STAI)
2. State – Trait Anger Expression Inventory (STAXI)
3. State – Trait Depression Scale (STDS)

The STAI measures State Anxiety (S-Anxiety) and Trait-Anxiety (T-Anxiety). T-Anxiety refers to 'relatively stable individual differences between people in the tendency to perceive stressful situations as more or less dangerous or threatening', while S-Anxiety refers to 'psychophysiological emotional state, that consists of subjective feelings of tension, apprehension, nervousness and worry and activation (arousal) of the autonomic nervous system' (Sharma & Sharma 2008).

To put it simply, T-Anxiety measures to what extent an individual is generally anxious. S-Anxiety on the other hand, measures the level of anxiety at the present time.

In responding to the S-Anxiety items, subjects respond to how they feel at the very moment the test is conducted. T-Anxiety items check to what extent the subject is generally anxious. A representative sample is (Sagar & Sagar, 2008):

S-Anxiety present: I feel tensed; I am worried.

S-Anxiety absent: I feel relaxed; I feel secure.

T-Anxiety present: I worry too much over something that doesn't matter; I feel nervous and restless.

T-Anxiety absent: I am content; I am pleased.

The State-Trait Anger Expression Inventory (STAXI) measures state – anger (S-Anger) and trait-anger (T-Anger). S-Anger is an emotional state marked by subjective feelings of anger, varying in intensity from mild annoyance to intense fury. T-Anger refers to individual difference in the disposition to experience anger. You must have observed that some people in your college are quite short-tempered, while others are as cool as ice, even when provoked. This difference in disposition is measured by T-Anger.

In the S-Anger scale, items are like the one given below:

"How do you feel now?"

(a) I feel angry (b) I am furious

(c) I feel irritated (d) I am cool

On the other hand, the items of T-Anger are like:

"How frequently do you feel angry?"

(a) Almost never (b) Sometimes

(c) Often (d) Almost always

Similarly, the State-Trait Depression Scale (STDS) measures predisposition to depression (Trait-depression or T-Dep) and actual depression at the moment (State-depression or S-Dep). A representative sample has been provided by Sharma & Sharma (2008):

S-Dep present : Feel miserable, sad, gloomy

S-Dep absent : Feel safe, enthusiastic, peaceful

T-Dep present : Feeling low and hopeless

T-Dep absent: Generally feeling strong, hopeful about future

These three-inventories (STAI, STAXI and STDS) have been found to have good reliability in assessing and monitoring the prevalence of anger, anxiety and depression in the military. Following Spiel Berger and Sharma (1976), the cross-cultural adaptations of these tests have been done by many scholars. Many translated versions of these tests are now used in various countries.

Intervention

What should be the approach to treat those who are assessed high on anger, anxiety and depression on the various scales discussed above? You may state that counselling is a possible route, or psychotherapy. However, Sagar Sharma and Monica Sharma reason that working with people on an individual basis should be an exemption. This approach carries the risk of stigmatization. Hence, they have suggested some other measures:

- *Post-trauma rehabilitation:* Once a soldier is assessed to have PTSD or any other anxiety disorder or depression, he should be removed from combat duty and put in 'rest and recoup' camps. They should be put at good physical comfort and their families should join them in these non-conflict transfer assignment.
- *Trauma Event Management (TEM):* TEM is an alternative to complete medicalization and hospitalization. Here, a team of trained medical officers and behavioural health professionals provide therapeutic and medical assistance.
- *Buddy debriefing:* It has been found that talk is the best and most effective remedy of trauma. Psychologists recommend talking to peers about the traumatic event as an effective way of dealing with trauma.
- *Self-care strategies:* The concept behind self-care is to empower soldiers to themselves cope with stressors and emotional distress. Usually, a team of professionals prepare a self-care guide for mental health in simple language and includes guidance regarding relaxation exercises, yoga, meditation, healthy lifestyles and social networking, etc.

Besides above direct intervention strategies, military psychologists also recommend certain preventive intervention strategies. These strategies often aim at reducing the stressors that soldiers experience. Hence, these strategies investigate the sources of stressors that could be handled by intervention and better organizational practices.

Some of the strategies recommended by Sharma & Sharma (2008) are:

- Military training must include more psychological training programmes, like hardiness training.
- Mental problems are the result of person-environment misfit. One strategy is to restructure the organizational work environment.

  Military Command and the Specialists can sit together to discuss about various ways in which to restructure the rigid, disciplinary hierarchy of the military, to better meet the demands of soldiers and officers.

- A job in defence is a job with low job control and high job demand. According toKarasek's Model (see the section on stress), this itself creates high stress. The leadership style of officers in the military is predominantly autocratic with low freedom for subordinates. A clear set of guidelines must be given to officers regarding how they could deal with their subordinates; deterrents and sections must be aimed at officers who seek to harass cadets.
- Finally, certain measures, like a ***feedback*** system, a prompt ***grievance redressal*** system, team building, fair ***conflict resolution, clear*** and ***accessible communication*** channels, enforcement of a ***buddy system*** in each battalion or company and sound performance appraisal system, etc. help in stress reduction in the military.

Comprehensive Soldier Fitness

The common approach in dealing with psychological problems by armies across the world is to provide more training and conduct more tests to detect symptoms of disorder. This is a reactive approach to deal with psychological problems in the military. Psychological studies have, however, concluded that this is not the most efficient strategy to maintain positive health in soldiers. Studies have concluded that a long-term preventive health strategy should be implemented to strengthen soldiers, their families and army civilians. Soldiers should be kept ready for longitudinal assessment and training all through their service tenure. Soldiers should be tested and assessed in frequent intervals. Educational programs and training should be carried out for improving mental health, not therapeutic programs (soldiers are often reluctant to participate in therapeutic programs because of the stigma attached to therapy and their own denial of psychological problems).

This new approach has been adapted by the US Army in 2008, when it established the Directorate of Comprehensive Soldier Fitness.

Key aspects of this approach are as under:

(a) Readiness of soldiers for continued assessment and training should be enhanced.

(b) Soldiers should be tested and assessed in frequent intervals, irrespective of whether any physical or psychological problem is detected or not.

(c) Educational programs and training should be carried out for improving mental health, not therapeutic programs (soldiers are often reluctant to participate in therapeutic programs because of the stigma attached to the therapy and their own denial of psychological problems).

Psychological Tests in Military

The job profile of defence personnel is substantially different from that of normal jobs. These are high-risk jobs making substantial demand on the physiological and psychological resources of the personnel. Hence, an important preoccupation of psychologists in defence is to evaluate the psychological fitness of present and prospective defence personnel. Psychologists devise psychological test for use in selection, training and counselling. Also, tests are devised to be used in recruitment to specialized operations, such as Border Security Force (BSF), Black Cat Commandoes, Special Protection Force, Sub-marine staff and even in policing in Jammu and Kashmir and in states of the North-East.

The job of defence personnel today is so vast and diversified, that specialized tests have to be designed to select personnel for specific tasks. Let us now study in greater detail, how psychological tests are devised and used in military.

Selection

Psychological tests are used in the recruitment of soldiers and officers, as well as in selection of soldiers for special purpose missions. All these have different criteria for selection and the psychological attributes demanded of a candidate vary. Yet, there are certain basic psychological attributes that are desired of all personnel.

In the recruitment process, there are two stages (Swedfeld and Steel, 2000):

1. Screening – out, and
2. Screening – in

In the screening-out stage, the central concern is the assessment of psychological and emotional stability. Is the candidate free from psychopathology? Even if he is, what are the chances that he will develop these is future? What is his vulnerability for various mental problems? The screening out stage can effectively make use of standard psychological tools such as MMPI-2, pencil and paper test and intelligence tests. This stage's main purpose is to decrease the risk of "false alarm" (i.e., decrease the risk of selecting a candidate with psychological vulnerability that would make him unsuitable for the job).

For the screening-in-stage, specialized tests are designed. In India, these tests are developed by Defence Institute of Psychological Research (DIPR).

The design follows the following steps:

1. Job analysis
2. Validation
3. Criteria selection
4. Instrument selection
5. Development of classification batteries

The **job analysis** varies when selection is for specialized posts. But, for simple recruitment at entry level, there are certain common features of the job. A military job is one 'with high stress, low autonomy, little personal control over workplace, long working hours, and / or deployment in combat-related or in internal security duties in insurgency wrecked areas that entail chronic exposure to potentially traumatizing events' (Sharma & Sharma, 2008).

The job analysis so developed has to be **validated** by military psychologists against training performance or attrition. If the job analysis criteria selects 'false positives' who cannot cope with training, then the job analysis needs to be relooked and changed.

After job analysis, the next task is to design a **selection criterion**. On what criteria should candidates be selected? Put in another way, what are the attributes that a prospective soldier should have? A group of psychologists in U.S.A have examined a wide array of attributes and identified 30 individual attributes that predict effective on-the-job performance of soldiers in U.S. Army Special Forces. These can be broadly grouped into four categories:

1. Cognitive attributes include judgement and decision-making, planning, adaptability, creativity and specific cognitive skills, such as auditory, mechanical, spatial, math and perceptual speed and accuracy.
2. Communication attributes include reading and writing ability, language ability and verbal and non-verbal communication abilities.
3. Interpersonal, motivational and character attributes include diplomacy, cultural adaptability, maturity or emotional stability, autonomy, team playership, dependability, initiative, perseverance, moral courage, motivating others, and supervising.
4. Physical attributes include swimming, flexibility and balance, strength and endurance. (Kilcullum et al., 1999).

The next step is selection of an **instrument** or a range of instruments to measure candidates for these criteria. Sometimes new tests are designed, while at other times standard tests can be used. For instance, McDonald et al. (1990) had studied US Naval Special Force using a standard test that measures the five traits of the Big Five Personality Factors. They found that successful candidates are more sociable (i.e., high on extraversion), emotionally stable, likeable (i.e., high on agreeableness) than unsuccessful candidates. Hence, standard tests also can be used to assess certain criteria.

For selection into high-risk and specialized work groups, specific psychological tests are needed. For example, the Special Protection Force (SPF) is a group that provides security to Very Important Persons (VIPs), including the President of India, the Prime Minister, etc., where vigilance is required. The members of SPF need to have exceptional vigilance, more than that required in normal defense. Hence, soldiers are tested on these attributes before assigning them to such specialized jobs. Concepts of Signal Detection Theory (SDT), psychophysics and ROC – curves are used to design test to select personnel for such specialized tasks.

Above steps are used to design selection tests for a specific aptitude or mental ability. However, given the large number and variety of military jobs, these steps cannot be carried on for each new job. Hence, **classification batteries** are developed to match particular aptitudes with particular job requirements. Given the large number of military jobs, determining the best combination of jobs for each test is also a challenge. This challenge is tackled by the concept of clustering. Jobs that are found to have similar requirements are bunched together and linked to the same set of tests.

Non-cognitive tests

Non-cognitive tests are conducted to profile candidates on the basis of their temperament, personality, ethics, or interests. These tests are usually self-reported tests, in which a candidate is given few choices, or a situational question to answer. A major challenge with non-cognitive tests is that since they are self-reported, there is a change of faking. An individual candidate would present herself in the most positive light possible, rather than in terms which will reflect her characteristics more accurately.

However, psychologists have conducted research to safeguard non-cognitive tests against faking. As a result, they have come out with tests that have a *forced-choice measure*. A forced-choice measure presents options in such a way that the most desirable option is not obvious. The candidate is 'forced' to choose between two desirable and two undesirable options. This will prevent the candidate from looking for the most desirable option and she will select the option that best describes her personality.

Such tests are also being used in the *Ethics* paper of the Civil Service Mains Examination. Situational questions with multiple possible answers are posed. Some candidates try to use jargon from philosophy to strike a middle ground. Naturally they don't get good marks. Other candidates apply their personal ethical standards in giving answers. Those with genuinely high ethics will naturally fare better. Hence, the best way to tackle such non-cognitive tests is to take training to develop right value system, rather than to take coaching and parrot synthetic answers.

Selection for high risk operations

The selection process for high-risk military operations is more detailed and meticulous than the selection for enlistment into the defence services. High risk military operations include cross-border reconnaissance, cross-border surgical strikes, undercover intelligence gathering, spying, etc. This kind of job requires superior physical and psychological prowess. It requires high degree of adaptability. Commando forces, the MARCOS (Marine Commando Force), the Special Forces, etc., recruit the best of officers from among defence officers for high risk missions.

Picano and his colleagues (2006) conducted a detailed job analysis and concluded that the special characteristics needed for a wide variety of high-risk operations, from running Special Forces to working as an intelligence operative, are six in number.

These are:

(i) Emotional stability

(ii) Adaptability

(iii) Teamwork abilities

(iv) Physical stamina and fitness

(v) Sound judgment and decision-making

(vi) Intrinsic motivation

These characteristics are similar to the seven characteristics identified by the Office of Strategic Services (OSS) of America to select clandestine intelligence operatives during the World War II. The OSS had selected seven characteristics, which are as under:

(i) Motivation for the assignment

(ii) Energy and initiative

(iii) Effective intelligence

(iv) Emotional stability

(v) Social relations

(vi) Leadership

(vii) Security

Training

Psychological tests are used in training of cadets also. Usually, these are ability tests and achievement tests. In a typical training programme, a test is conducted before the training begins (Pre-test) and another after the completion of training (Post-test). The difference between the two test results show the skill improvement of the soldier. This becomes very important in defence because the equipments are very costly to operate. Hence, cadets are trained on simulators or in inferior-quality equipment. Tests help assess the transfer of training that is supposed to happen between training and real conditions. There are also other utilities of tests in training:

1. If the difference between pre-test and post-test is low generally for soldiers, it may mean that the training programme needs to be updated.
2. The effectiveness of simulation games and virtual reality in improving various cognitive skills for real-life situations can be assessed.
3. Sometimes, training simulates real-life combat conditions. Tests help assess the psychological response of soldiers in such conditions.

Counselling

The defence personnel face high-stress and hence are especially vulnerable to various mental problems, like PTSD, personality disorders, depression, etc. (discussed earlier in detail). The challenge to the defence psychologist is to detect the incidence of these disorders and provide immediate counselling before the condition aggravates. The need for counselling among personnel is assessed by a variety of inventories, some of which are discussed in an earlier section in this chapter.

7.3 Human Factor Engineering in Defence

Many complicated machines are used in defence. There are hi-tech tanks, planes, fighter planes, radars, submarines, etc. These machines have very high degree of sophistication and are supposed to perform critical tasks. However, these machines aren't supposed to perform, but the human-machine system needs to be optimized. We need to understand that human cognitive and motors abilities have limitations. The best man-machine system is one, where human factors are considered before designing the machine.

Human factor engineering is a branch of study that seeks to establish a man-machine fit by including the constraints of human factors when engineering the machine (i.e., when designing). The need for human factor engineering (HFE) in defence arouse for the first time during World War II. Prior to the war, many sophisticated machines were developed by engineers; engineers lacked any knowledge of how human factors (cognitive response, emotional response, perceptual skills, etc.) vary in combat situations. Hence, they didn't consider these factors in designing machines. As a result, many accidents occurred during the World War II. During the war, a pilot was required to take split – second readings of instruments, make rapid decisions and then react fast to control the machine. Indeed, the engineers never cared to measure the operator's reaction time. They did not understand that the operator was a human and there were limits on his/ her cognitive and motor abilities.

Some of the basic principles of HFE have been discussed under 'Ergonomics" in the chapter on Organizational Psychology. However, the challenges of HFE in defence are different from that of normal organizational or work settings.

Some of these challenges are:

1. H.F. Engineer has to take special care of combat environment. The human response (emotional and psychological) in real combat situation is different from that in normal situations. For instance, it may be very comfortable to use a complex gun. But, how does a man – rifle system perform in the tension of combat? How do psychological and physiological changes in the soldier affect the performance? Is the rifle well-designed to accommodate such changes in the man? If a rifle needs lot of force to pull the trigger, it may be tough to use the rifle in face-to-face action at the border.
2. Modern military equipments are very complex and costly. Inappropriate man-machine integration could lead to death. Even small errors could be fatal. Also, in modern warfare, the scope of errors should be low, as the enemy machines are pretty hi-tech and operator friendly! Hence, the H.F. Engineer has to walk a tight rope.
3. Conducting research and getting data for HFE is tougher in case of military than otherwise. Usually, these data are considered confidential; hence countries don't share their research findings. Researchers at Defence Institute of Psychological Research (DIFR) are "Indian" researchers and prefer not to share their findings with other countries. Same is the case with other countries. Secondly, the research to be conducted to know various cognitive and motor responses to a specific design can't be approved in the design of another machine. The data collected are very specific data.

While the challenges are more, the advantages of HFE in defence are many too.

Some of these are following:

1. Makes equipments easier to operate.
2. Increases reliability and reduces errors.
3. Reduces possibility of accidents.
4. Reduces amount of training required.
5. Reduces the stress on operators and contributes to their well-being.

Reduces the number of personnel to do the job; also, those with lower aptitude could be employed to operate machines.

■ ■ ■

Psychology Applied to Socio-Economic Problems

8

APPLICATION OF PSYCHOLOGY TO DISADVANTAGED GROUPS

Chapter outline

8.1 Disadvantage and Deprivation

A (wo)man is the product of his (her) 'nature' and 'nurture'. The nature-nurture controversy, on the extent of influence of each in a (wo)man's development, is a continuing one in psychological literature. Yet, all agree that:

Genes * Environment = Human Development

Genes usually set the 'limit' to development. Environment determines the actual development within this limit. For example, try as much as he does, a dog cannot fly. No amount of practice or rich environmental stimulus can make a dog fly because flying is not genetically encoded in its genes. Yet, environment determines a large part of development, i.e. a deprived environment can lead to non-optimal development.

The resources at the disposal of human society are limited, but the number of individuals and their needs are not. Some are placed at an advantage to appropriate the resources; others less fortunate, are at a disadvantage. Disadvantage leads to deprivation.

The disadvantaged need not always be deprived of all resources. A daughter of a conservative, rich man is disadvantaged in education if her father doesn't let her study. She is relatively deprived with respect to her brother. Yet, she is not absolutely deprived.

Hence, disadvantage is the result of unequal access to resources – physical, cultural and educational, among others. Deprivation is a condition or a state of being that the disadvantaged faces.

Relative and Absolute deprivation

Relative deprivation is a subjective concept; it implies that an individual or a group perceives himself (themselves) relatively deprived in relation to another individual (group).

It was political scientists, like Runcimann and Gurr who found that when we perceive a deprived state, we don't perceive objective deprivation. Rather, it is our expectations that we use as an indicator. *Egoistic relative deprivation* is that felt by an individual within a group, while fraternalistic relative deprivation is felt by a group with respect to another.

Absolute deprivation, on the other hand, is an objective construct. As a result of disadvantage, if an individual, a family or a group is bereft of basic necessities for healthy living – food, rich natural surroundings, proper housing, nutrition, health facilities, etc., the resultant deprivation is absolute deprivation.

The differences between relative deprivation and absolute deprivation are:

1. Former is subjective experience while later is an objective condition.
2. Absolute deprivation is the result of disadvantage. The same may or may not be the case with relative deprivation. A Hindu group may be relatively deprived if reservations for Muslims are introduced; while, in fact, according to the Sachhar Commission, the Muslim community as a whole is at a disadvantage (is facing social exclusion) and hence, is absolutely deprived of jobs and modern education.
3. Logical consequences of the two are vastly different. Relative deprivation leads to prejudices and in extreme cases, conflict and violence. Absolute deprivation leads to conditions discussed in this chapter.
4. Relative deprivation may or may not be the fallout of absolute deprivation. For example, factory workers don't feel relatively deprived of managers because they believe that mangers deserve the pay they get on the basis of merit. Yet, many workers feel relatively deprived, form unions or resort to working class militants. Relative deprivation, its occurrence and its prevalence is a much more complex phenomena, than absolute deprivation which can be gauged by objective economic criteria.

Prolonged Deprivation

'Prolonged deprivation' refers to absolute deprivation for a prolonged period of time. It may refer to absolute deprivation of nutrition, of health support, a rich and stimulating environment or deprivation of parental support or many of these factors working together. Prolonged deprivation is a significant concept in psychology because prolonged deprivation in childhood can lead to numerous psychological impairments. The way prolonged deprivation of vitamins C can lead to Scurvy, or that of vitamin K can lead to Kwashiorkor (which is common in children from poor families), the same way prolonged deprivation of stimuli can lead to psychological consequences.

Development = Environment * Genes

Many studies have shown the effect of prolonged deprivation of a rich environment on the development of an individual. For instance, Blackmore and Cooper (1970) conducted an experiment in which some kittens were exposed to only stimuli that leads to perception of horizontal objects; and some other kittens were exposed to stimuli that lead to perception of vertical objects only. After sometime, they found that the kittens that were exposed only to horizontal images couldn't detect vertical edges and vice-versa. This experiment demonstrates that perception is plastic.

In a way, not just perception but the whole brain is plastic. The human infant has a very small brain in comparison to other animals. This is because otherwise the infant brain couldn't fit into the mother's womb. Even though the infant's brain is small, it has nearly all the neurons that an adult brain has. It only doesn't have the neural connections, i.e., links between various neurons. As the child actively experiences the world, various stimulations cause links to develop in neurons related to those stimulations. For example, there are some neural cells in the brain that specifically work in mathematical problems solving. If the child does many rich mathematical problems, the connections of these cells become stronger. On the other hand, if the child is deprived of a stimulating environment, connections don't develop and the brain's functionality related to these cells is low. This plasticity of the brain is not life-long. After some years, the brain becomes rigid and even a rich environment can't help develop these skills. Prolonged deprivation leads to such an effect.

Take the case of Genie. Genie was deprived of language skills, among other stimuli, for 11 years before she was discovered. She could never learn proper language because her brain had ceased to be plastic. Now, compare yourself with a child from a slum. It is evident that the child has lived in a deprived environment for a long time, while in your case, you have been fed with a golden spoon. At every stage of cognitive development, you have had teachers and parents to provide you with a rich, stimulating environment. When this wasn't sufficient, you joined some coaching classes to further hone your mathematics skills. No wonder, the part of the brain related to mathematical skills, for instance, is well-developed in you. But, what about the slum kid who didn't even get a pollution-free environment?

Genie: A case study

Genie (born 1957) is the pseudonym of an American feral child who was a victim of severe abuse, neglect and social isolation. Her circumstances are prominently recorded in the annals of linguistics and abnormal child psychology. When she was a baby, her father concluded that she had a severe intellectual disability, a view which intensified as she got older. This caused him to dislike her and withhold care and attention. At approximately the time she reached the age of 20 months, he decided to keep her as socially isolated as possible; so he kept her locked alone in a room from that time until she reached the age of 13 years and 7 months. During this time, he almost always kept her strapped to a child's toilet or bound her in a crib with her arms and legs completely immobilized, forbade anyone from interacting with her, provided her with almost no stimulation of any kind, and left her severely malnourished.

The extent of her isolation prevented her from being exposed to any significant amount of speech, and she did not acquire language during her childhood as a result. Los Angeles child welfare authorities discovered her on November 4, 1970. Scientists studied Genie for a long period after she was found, to see how prolonged deprivation in her childhood affected her. She made substantial advances in her overall mental and psychological development after being discovered. Within months, Genie had developed exceptional non-verbal communication skills and gradually learned some basic social skills, but even by the end of the case study by psychologists, she still exhibited many behavioral traits, characteristic of an unsocialised person. She also continued to learn and use new language skills throughout the time they tested her, but ultimately remained unable to fully acquire a first language.

Genie's is one of the best-known case studies of language acquisition in a child with delayed linguistic development outside of studies on deaf children. Susan Curtiss argued that even if humans possess the innate ability to acquire language, Genie demonstrated the necessity of early language stimulation in the left hemisphere of the brain to start. Since Genie never fully acquired grammar, Curtiss claimed that Genie provided evidence for a weaker variation of the *critical period hypothesis*. Genie's non-verbal skills were exceptionally good, which demonstrated that even non-verbal communication was fundamentally different from language. Because Genie's language acquisition occurred in the right hemisphere of her brain, its course also aided linguists in refining existing hypotheses on the capacity for right-hemisphere language acquisition in people after the critical period.

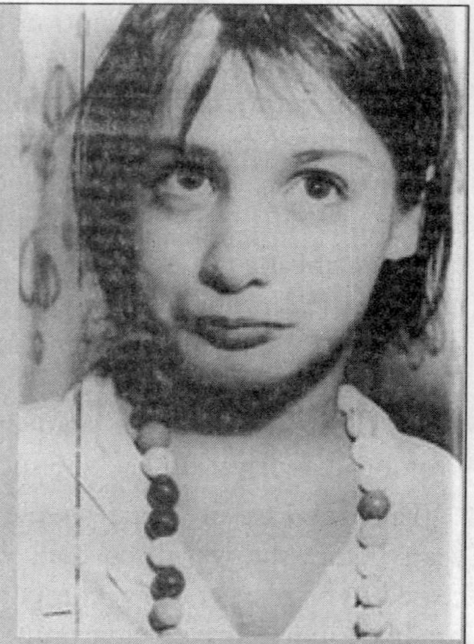

'Genie' – Wikipedia

In one landmark study, A. Agarwal and K.K. Tripathi of Gorakhpur University selected 200 adolescents and young adults from Uttar Pradesh in India and Nepal (150 from India and 50 from Nepal) and applied a Prolonged Deprivation Scale (PDS) to segregate them between those with High Prolonged Deprivation (HPD) and others with Low Prolonged Deprivation (LPD). The PDS scale consisted of fifteen measures of deprivation, that included physio-economic deprivation and experiential deprivation. They then studied the future orientation (FO) of the two groups – HPD and LPD.

'Future Orientation' is the extent to which an individual thinks about the future, anticipates future consequences and plans ahead before acting. FO is the key indicator of goal-setting, ambition and achievement motivation. FO drives young adults towards careers and work goals. Individuals with high FO will have higher chance of getting a successful career. Individuals with low FO will have lower chances of getting a successful career. The study by Agarwal and Tripathi (1984) found that HPD group had lower FO than the LPD group. This was true for both cultural groups – Indian group and Nepalese group. LPD subjects, having suffered deprivation to a lesser extent, contemplated more about those events which could occur in the coming stages of their life, as opposed to high deprived subjects who envisaged fewer goals in future. This study established a clear linkage of prolonged deprivation in socially disadvantaged groups with goal setting and achievement motivation.

Prolonged deprivation and its effects – cognitive, perceptual, intelligence-related, motivational and personality-related, are the focus of psychological studies that are discussed in this chapter.

8.2 Disadvantage and Deprivation: In perspective

If a student from Dalit background (erstwhile untouchables, who still have to do menial jobs and stay at the bottom of social hierarchy) is unable to compete with the son of a middle-class individual, in competitive exams, like IAS and IIT JEE, is it because he has inferior ability or because of some disadvantage? His low performance is due to a combination of disadvantage and deprivation. The fact that he can't get proper guidance or can't afford coaching puts him at a disadvantage. Even the fact that his peers discourages him to prepare for IIT JEE ("You can't make it. Rather than, wasting time, join my Mechanic Shop!") is a disadvantage for him.

Secondly, his birth and upbringing has been mostly in deprived environments (slums in cities and shanty settlements away from the village in rural areas).

He hasn't been exposed to rich environment (pre-school education, healthy play life, nutritious food, training in intelligence behavior, etc.) during "critical period" of his growth. This impairs his cognitive faculties and puts limits on optimal development of abilities. Many-a-times, slum children are exposed to child sexual abuse, violence and drugs at an early stage. Their language development is slow and stunted. No doubt, the slum kid can't compete with others in competitive exams. So, my friend, if you have got admission into an IIT or AIIMS or any other prestigious institute, it is not because you deserve it; rather because you are lucky to be treated well by your parents (Genie was born in an affluent family, yet was deprived of basic stimulants till she was 13, because of a mentally sick father!).

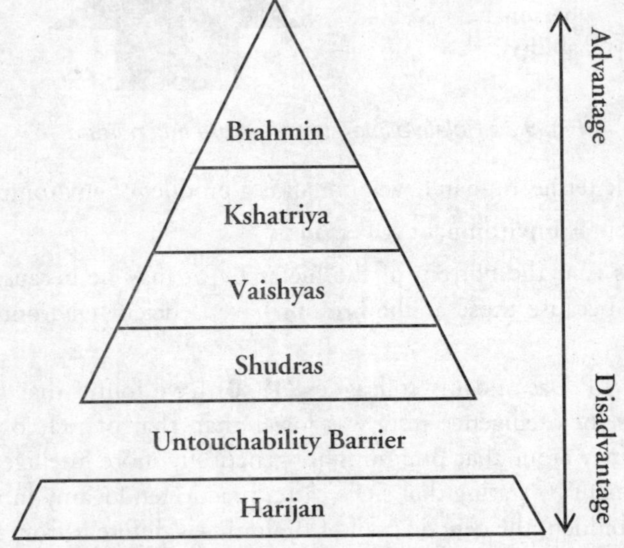

Fig. 8.1 : Social Hierarchy of India and related disadvantage

Now the question is, why intervention? Intervention is needed to teach the deprived group children because they are part of the human resource of the country. Their deprivation and disadvantage is not only harmful to them, but also to the nation- the country cannot harness the best potential in its citizens! The issue has become even more pressing with policymakers emphasising that India's huge population is an asset, a demographic dividend. But, if these students are not taught and motivated to achieve, the demographic dividend will turn into "demographic disaster". A demographic disaster will increase ratio of dependents (including those youth with high dependence motivation) to that of working population.

8.3 Deprivation: Nature or Nurture

A major issue that psychologists have looked into is whether deprivation is due to deficiency in environment or difference between the deprived groups and non-deprived groups. The *deficit argument* is a nurture argument that states that, for instance, scheduled castes have deficient environmental stimuli; hence show lower performance and are at the bottom of hierarchy. The *difference argument* states that the classes at the top and bottom of the hierarchy are genetically different in abilities.

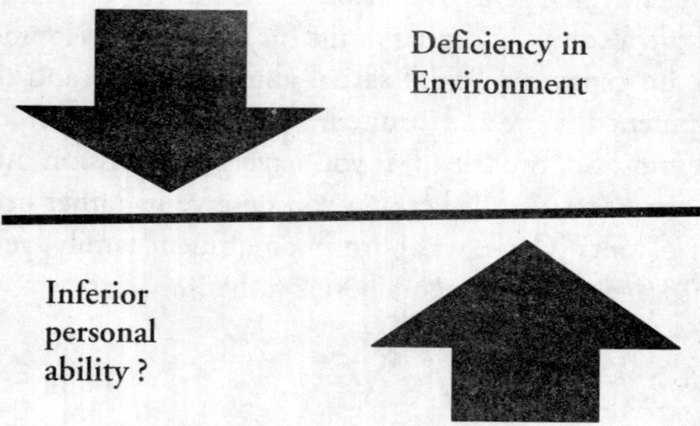

Fig. 8.2 : Relative interplay of nature and nurture

To put it in very simple terms, human development is a product of environment and person.

Human Development = Environment X Person

If a class of citizens is at the bottom of the hierarchy, it may be because of genetic factors (different abilities) or because those at the bottom have deficient environment due to which they stay at the bottom.

For example, Prof. J.P.Das and his colleagues (1970) have found that the performance of poor Harijan students in intelligence tests was lower than that of rich Brahmin students. A value-biased observer may argue that Brahmins are genetically more intelligent than Dalits. She may support her argument by stating that since castes practice endogamy in marriage and inter-caste marriages are forbidden, the genetic pool of Brahmins is different from that of Dalits. This argument is similar to the arguments made in the west in relation to race, that whites have better intelligence than blacks.

The white-black 'difference' has today been largely discredited in scholarly circles. Same is with the genetic hypothesis of castes. Many studies have proved that Dalit children brought up in advantaged situations perform as good as Brahmin children. G. Misra and B. Tripathi (1980), for instance, found that high and low caste groups with similar experiential background (i.e., similar environments) demonstrated almost similar levels of performance on cognitive and intellectual tasks. Om Prakash (1982) compared scores on Raven's Progressive Matrices for different caste groups and found that low caste children of literate parents actually scored higher than the children of high caste literate parents.

Hence, it can be said that difference in experiential background, rather than genetic difference, leads to derivational effect. Even here, there are some anomalies. You must have heard that diamonds are found in coal mines and that lily breeds in polluted water. These phrases mean that certain individuals from deprived groups rise and perform exceptionally good. If nature doesn't matter and only 'nurture' (i.e., experiential background) matters, how can we explain this phenomena? How can one individual who has been deprived of environmental stimulation at an early age rise so high and no other can get out of the vicious circle?

To explain this phenomenon, Prof. J.P.Das (1973) has proposed a modified threshold hypothesis. This hypothesis states that if we recognise a threshold for intellectual ability, children above this threshold are hardly affected by disadvantageous conditions; children below this threshold are, however, strongly affected. This hypothesis reconciles nature with nurture. It basically states that ability and deprivation interact and jointly influence performance.

Consequences of Disadvantage and Deprivation

Any society can be visualised as a system with various sub-systemic elements inter-linked. Disadvantage and deprivation create a situation in which various physical, social, cultural, economic and psychological dimensions are affected. Further, these systems affect each other also.

There are two types of consequences of deprivation- visible and invisible. Visible consequences include physical, social, cultural and economic consequences; invisible consequences include psychological consequences. Visible consequences are visible, but cannot be explained without understanding invisible consequences. This is because all sub-system interacts dynamically. Invisible consequences are causes for visible consequences as well as the effect of visible consequences.

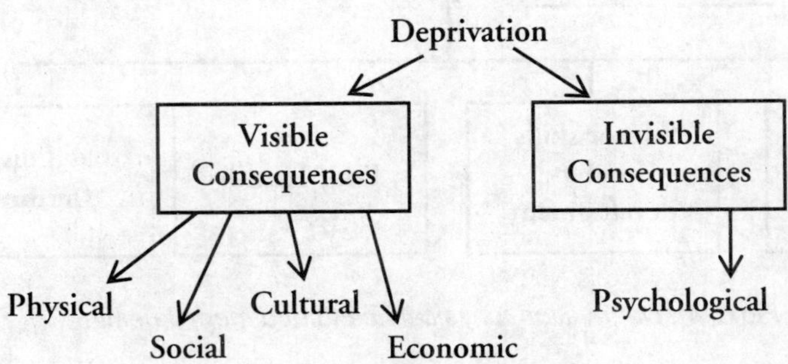

Fig. 8.3 : Consequences of deprivation

Hence, various physical, social, cultural and economic consequences can be studied best by psychologists. Visible consequences and psychological variables of deprived groups have figured ground relation, i.e., these consequences stand on psychological variables.

Various visible consequences of disadvantage and deprivation can be dealt under the following headings:

1. Physical and mental health
2. Socio-cultural consequences
3. Social mobility issues
4. Economic consequences

1. Physical and mental health

Disadvantage leads to deprivation from good quality and appropriate quantity of nutritional intake. This leads to malnutrition. Malnutrition leads to stunted growth and also other consequences. Malnutrition adversely affects cognitive functioning and basic cognitive processes and increases the chances of poor health (Misra & Mohanty, 2000).

Many studies have shown that nutritional intake is a function of Socio-Economic Status (SES) and malnutrition results in cognitive and health impairment. For example, Gupta et al. (1985) have reported lower growth standard for slum children. Dutta Banik (1982) has found from a longitudinal study of children's growth from birth to 14 years of age that height and weight measures are related to SES. Also, nutritional status is positively correlated with general development of cognitive and motor functions. For instance, Agarwal et al. (1987) have found from a large-scale study on 6-8-year old rural children in Varanasi that severity of malnutrition is proportional to impairment of intelligence, verbal reasoning, short-term memory, perceptual and spatial skills, fine motor coordination and scholastic achievement.

This mechanism can be represented as:

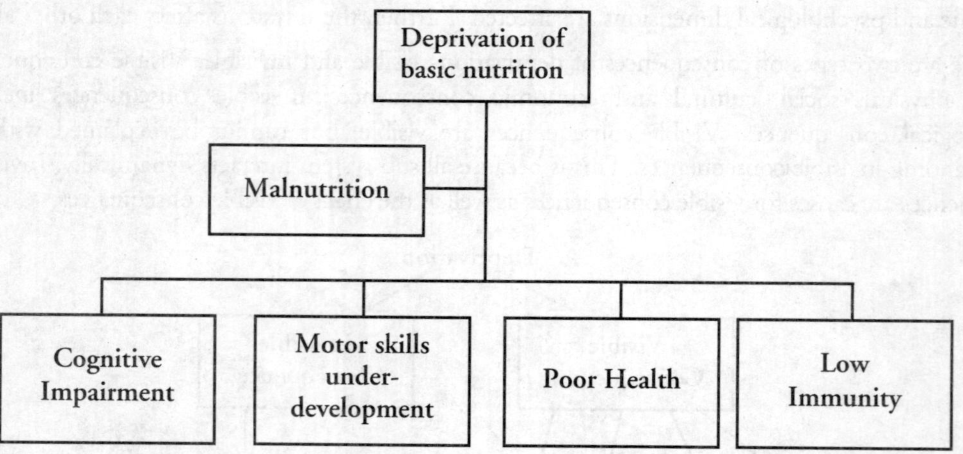

Fig. 8.4 : Deprivation, physical health and mental health

Apart from physical health, deprivation also impairs mental health. Prof. Giriswar Misra and Prof. Ajit K. Mohanty (2000) reason that incidence of psychiatric disorders among the poor and the disadvantaged groups is much higher than advantaged groups. Mental health problems are much more frequent among lower social classes in the class hierarchy. This is perhaps because "the experience of growing up in different social classes are related to individual differences in coping styles, stress tolerance and access to supportive social relationship. Experiences in lower social class leads to low self-esteem, intellectual rigidity, sense of fatalism and greater susceptibility to stress", which increases the vulnerability of mental health problems (ibid, p.125).

As per the Stress-vulnerability model of mental health—

Psychopathology = Stress X Vulnerability

Vulnerability is high because of intellectual rigidity, sense of fatalism and incorrect stress-coping style. Stress is high because social support is low, environmental stresses are high (for example, water and air pollution are high in slums; crowding is high, due to which personal space is low) and stress is chronic. The nature of functional adaptation to socio-cultural change also affects rate of psychopathology. For instance, Sharma and his colleagues (Sharma, Michael, Reddy and Gehlot, 1985) found that psychiatric morbidity among slum dwellers of Jaipur was higher for distant migrants than for those who migrated from nearby. Evidently, adaptation stress was higher for distant migrants.

In another study (Misra et al, 1996) the health status of two tribes from the Chota Nagpur plateau were studied:

1. Birhors, a nomadic tribe
2. Oraons, a sedentary tribe

It was found that Birhors had greater physical, psychological and psycho-physiological problems than Oraons. Birhors are nomads and hence have to adapt to changing conditions often. Hence, functional adaptation is a mediating factor between low SES and mental health problems.

Greater ***emotional disturbance*** and ***neurotic traits of restlessness*** have been observed among children from lower SES. Bhatia and his colleagues (1989) had conducted a survey in which they found that nail-biting was prevalent in a relatively younger age (2-5 years) among high SES children than among lower SES children. Nail-biting is prevalent among lower SES children even at the age of 9-12 years.

Attributions of prejudice

A side-effect of social disadvantage is the negative stereotypes attached to socially disadvantaged groups (SDGs). Social disadvantage is a triple whammy. Social disadvantage puts the group at a disadvantage in the social structure. Secondly, it leads to deprivation. Thirdly, disadvantage and deprivation lead to certain stereotypes about the socially disadvantaged group. The stereotypes adversely affect the mental health of members of the SDG. For example, Schmitt & Branscombe (2011) have found that for members of SDGs, attributions to prejudice are likely to be internal, stable, uncontrollable and convey widespread exclusion and devaluation of one's group. For members of Socially Privileged Groups (SPGs), the attributions to prejudice are usually localized.

Dimensions	Attributions of SDGs to prejudices and stereotypes	Attributions of SPGs to prejudice and stereotypes
Causal locus	Internal	External
Stability	Stable	Unstable
Controllability	Uncontrollable	Controllable

Causal locus indicates what causes an individual attributes an event of discrimination to. It has been seen from various studies that when an individual from a SDG is discriminated against (because of prejudices of the perpetrator), she attributes the discrimination to her own faults (i.e., she has high internal causal locus). The attributions that she makes remain stable over time, and do not easily change. This shows that her response to discrimination affects her psyche in the long run. Empirical research has also shown that such individuals perceive the attributes to be out of their control.

These psychological mechanisms are quite critical in understanding and effect called the *self-fulfilling prophecy*. When others develop negative stereotypes about an individual from a SDG, her response to such stereotype is usually mired by internal causal locus and high stability. This leads to internalisation of such stereotypes. Because she perceives such stereotypes to be out of her control, she does question the stereotypes. As a result, she behaves exactly the way the others had branded her with the stereotype. As a result, the stereotypes get reinforced and it turns into a vicious psychological cycle.

Schmitt & Branscombe (2011) have conducted studies which consider women as a socially disadvantaged group. They found results in line with above. But, same concepts can be applied to other socially disadvantaged groups (such as ethnic groups, racial groups, castes, tribes, etc., that are lowly placed in the social hierarchy).

The **Rejection-Identification Model** of attributions to prejudice was forwarded by Branscombe and his associates (1999). They suggested that negative stereotypes about a SDG harm psychological well-being. But, negative stereotypes also tend to increase identification with the in-group, which in turn, leads to positive psychological well-being. This model is very useful in understanding reinforcement of disadvantage in SDGs. A student having a disadvantaged socio-economic status (SES) is adversely affected when teachers and fellow students develop negative prejudices about them. This harms her psychological well-being. To cope with it, she identifies herself with the group strongly. Since most members of the group are in low-paying jobs or are unemployed, she develops Low Future Orientation (FO), low goals, low ambitions in life.

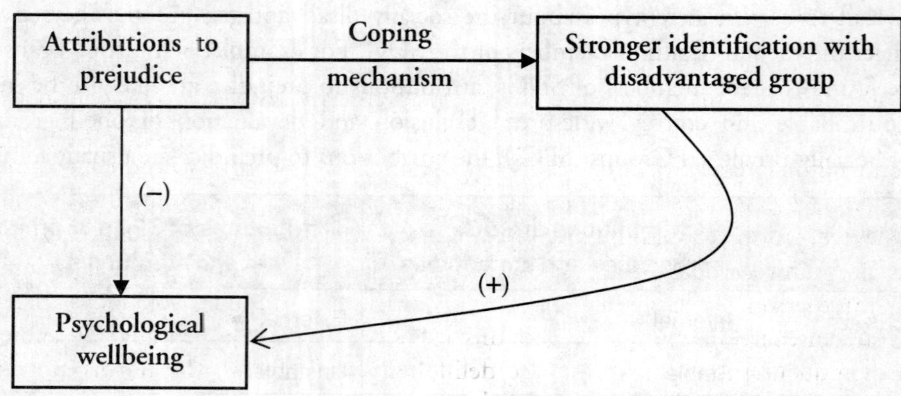

Fig. 8.5 : The Rejection Identification Model of coping with discrimination

2. Socio-cultural Consequences

The social norms, values, social climate and the built environment of a slum is not the same as that of a middle-class residential area. This is because disadvantage and deprivation lead to a fatalistic attitude and high need for dependence. Owing to this, the need for achievement is low and hence social mobility is low. Without social mobility, members of a low SES group cannot get better pay and standard of living.

This reinforces the conditions of disadvantage. For example, if a dalit labourer's son studies hard and becomes an IAS officer, he can rise above the conditions of disadvantage. However, if by socialisation, he internalises the belief that he cannot become an IAS officer, his expectancy is low and hence he doesn't study. This is often referred to as *self-fulfilling prophecy.*

In one study, Saraswati and Dutta (1990) analysed the children and adolescent girls growing up in rural poverty and urban slums. They found that children are socialised to non-competitive coping styles, narrow goals and acceptance of destiny.

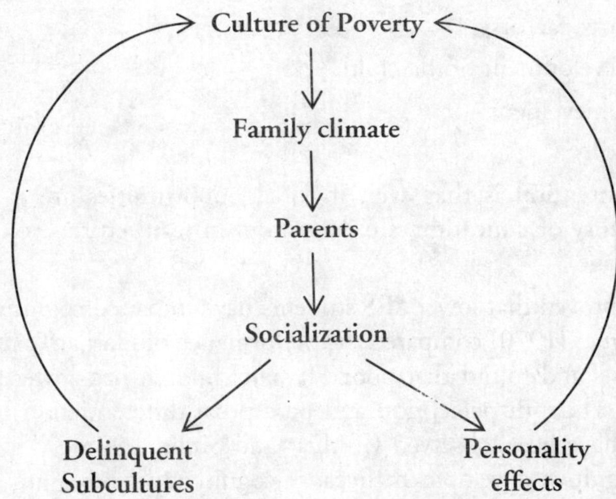

Fig. 8.6 : Dynamics of socio-cultural consequences of deprivation

As a result of the above vicious circle, a culture of poverty develops. Frustration due to perpetual low SES condition makes many youths deviant. These youths form peer groups with delinquent sub-cultures. A.K. Tandon and his associates (1978) have tried to classify delinquents into aggressive and non-aggressive delinquents. They found that aggressive delinquents came from low income families, experienced parental deprivation and showed greater hostility as compared to non-aggressive group. K.S. Shukla (1977) has observed that a large number of juvenile delinquents are slum dwellers. These come from families with low parental income and impersonal interpersonal relation among family members. Shukla concludes that these delinquents are insecure in the family and this loss of status is compensated by achieving a status in a delinquent sub-culture. In these delinquent sub-cultures, the norms are different from (often antagonistic from) the norms of the mainstream society. An individual member is appreciated for pick-pocketing or snatching and respected in the group.

On an individual level, this culture of poverty affects children's personality also. Mohan and her colleagues (1990) have found that deprived children are high on neuroticism and low on extraversion. Disadvantage has also been causally related to ***alienation***, withdrawal, autism and other ***anti-social and anti-psychotic traits*** (Helode and Kapai, 1986). Such personality traits reinforce the culture of poverty and are resistant to change.

3. Social Mobility

Social mobility refers to the movement of individuals and groups between different positions in a system of social stratification. In the present context, my concern is- how many individuals from low SES achieve higher income and higher social status in a generation? Not many, why? It is known that in spite of culture of poverty, equal access to education can lead to social mobility. Education is the most potent tool of mobility. So much so that, some believe universal education will lead to an egalitarian society. However, the link between education and social mobility is not direct.

It is mediated by three factors:

1. Cognitive development of the child
2. Academic achievement
3. Linguistic skills

The psychological contention is that even if equal opportunities are available for education (including similar quality of education, similar school infrastructure, etc.) students from lower SES are at a disadvantage.

Many studies have proved that lower SES students have impaired cognitive development. Prof. J.P.Das and his colleagues (1970) compared the performance of Harijan and Brahmin children on certain intelligence tests and found that poor Harijan children had lower scores. Differences in perceptual skills, such as depth perception and perceptual differentiation between deprived and non-deprived groups have been observed (J.P.Das and Sinha, 1975). Why is this so? Deprived groups have lower cognitive development because cognitive processes are experientially shaped, and therefore, lower stimulation in a child's experiential world would interfere with her cognitive development. In fact, it has been found that (Misra & Tripathi, 1980)

$$CC \propto \frac{1}{D}$$

i.e., Cognitive Competence (CC) is inversely proportional to degree of deprivation.

Second factor influencing social mobility is academic achievement. It has been found that disadvantaged students prefer ***dependent and non-participatory learning style,*** while advantaged students prefer independent and participatory learning style (B.P.Verma and Sheikh, 1992). Besides learning styles, poor school achievement of deprived students is also related to cognitive readiness, home environment and social climate. Hence, Misra and Mohanty observe that "poor or slow cognitive development affects general task performance, as well as academic achievement and motivation which are associated with prospects of economic and social mobility".

Another area of concern is linguistic skills of the disadvantaged. I have studied in an English medium school right from childhood. Hence, I had a mastery in the language. Now, take the hypothetical case of Hari, a student from a Bhudaneswar slum. He talks in Oriya in his house and goes to an Oriya school. After schooling, when he joins graduation, he finds that there is an absolute hegemony of English. A.K.Mohanty and M.Mohanty (1985) have seen that the duality of official language (English) and home language (Oriya) leads to linguistic handicaps for low social classes. Other studies have found similar results from other linguistic regions.

The above dynamics can be represented as:

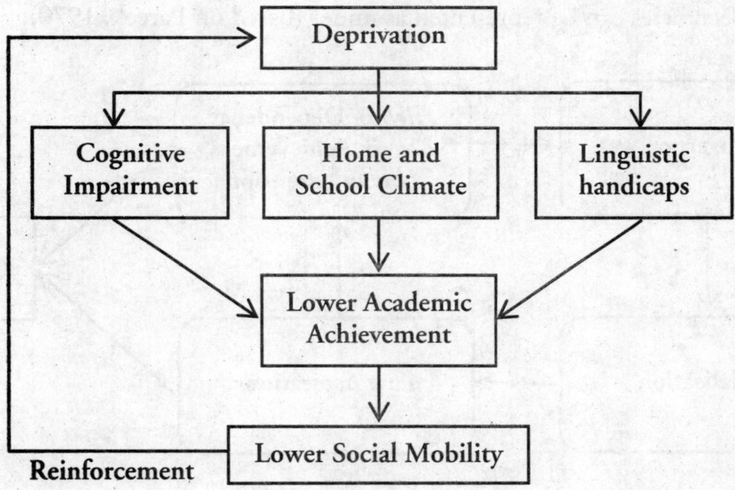

Fig. 8.7 : Vicious circle of deprivation and lower social mobility

4. Economic Consequences:

Economic disadvantage leads to poverty. Poverty leads to deprivation and deprivation breeds poverty by a vicious circle popularly called 'culture of poverty'. Economic factors are the cause and the effect of poverty. Lower economic status leads to disadvantage. But, how does disadvantage and deprivation lead to poverty as an economic consequence?

Pareek (1970) presents a model wherein there are two mediating factors:

1. Expectancy
2. Motivation

This model has been discussed in the chapter on Community Psychology. Basically, Pareek states that economic development depends on three factors—

D = AM × EM – DM

Poverty gets reinforced because of the unique motivational pattern among the deprived groups. Deprived groups are high on the need for dependence (DM) and low on achievement motivation (AM) and extension motivation (EM). Prof. J.B.P.Sinha has found that in scarce resource conditions deprived groups show hoarding behavior rather than sharing behavior. This shows that they have lower EM. Giriswar Misra 91982) has observed that deprived groups are lower on AM than non-deprived groups. No wonder, the economic development among deprived groups is lower.

It has also been seen that deprived groups have lower expectancies. Prof. Durganand Sinha (1969) found that villagers from less developed villages showed wither unrealistic aspirations, or very low levels of achievement. Rath, A.S. Dash and U.N.Dash (1979) have also found that the occupational aspirations of scheduled castes and scheduled tribe children are low.

The nexus between economic consequences of deprivation (poverty) and motivational patterns and expectancies can be represented as under (based on Pareek, 1970):

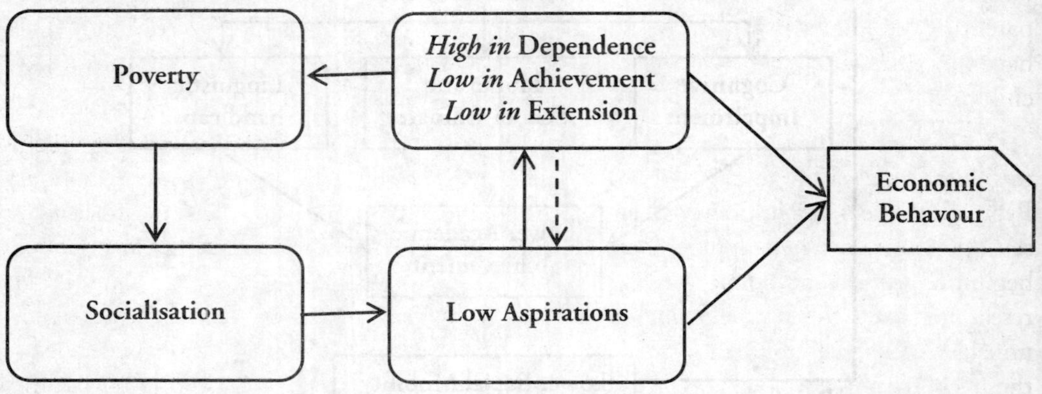

Fig. 8.8 : Deprivation and Motivation (based on Pareek, 1970)

A.K. Singh (1983) aptly observes that the culture of social disadvantage inculcates the ***psychology of a puppet*** characterised by helplessness, self-pity, apathy, pessimism and fatalism.

8.4 Educating and Motivating the disadvantaged

The most potent instrument for developing the conditions of the disadvantaged is by social mobility, and social mobility can best be possible through academic achievement and entrepreneurship. Motivating the disadvantaged towards entrepreneurial development has been separately covered in the chapter on Economic Psychology. In this section, the focus is on early interventions to educate and motivate disadvantaged children for academic achievement. Why early intervention? Because "psychological intervention, are rooted in the assumption that human development is critically shaped by the experiential base received by a person. The interventions generally aim at strengthening and equipping individuals from disadvantaged and deprived backgrounds with skills and competencies necessary for effective functioning in the society". But, before discussion on interventions to educate and motivate the disadvantaged, it is necessary for us to understand the problems faced by the disadvantaged.

Educational problems of disadvantaged children

Many studies have focused the impact of socio-economic disadvantage on academic achievement. The academic achievement of deprived group children are generally lower than that of children from advantaged groups, due to a variety of reasons including home environment, parental support, school climate, teacher expectancy and self-efficacy, etc.

Some of the research findings on this issue are:

Home environment: Parental support directly affects academic interest and academic achievement. In a series of studies, A.K.Singh and his colleagues (A.K.Singh, 1983; A.K.Singh and Jaiswal, 1981) have shown that parental support compensates for the adverse effects of low SES. Ironically, the home factors are usually strong in low SES families. Many come from families with parental psychopathology, family conflict, broken homes, harsh and inconsistent parenting, etc. Parents usually do not stress on academic achievement because they themselves have low expectancies; they are high on need for dependence and pass on this attitude to their children.

Teacher expectations: Pygmalion effect refers to a self-fulfilling prophecy, whereby people tend to behave the way others expect them to behave. The first major experiment demonstrating Pygmalion effect in children was by Rosenthal and Jacobson (1968), and it was in the school setting. The researchers applied a standard Ice test to children in an elementary school at the beginning of the academic year; 20% of the children were selected at random and the researchers told the teachers that these 20% have scored high on Ice tests and hence, have unusual intellectual abilities. When the children were retested at the end of the academic year, these children showed massive gains in Ice test, relative to other children. Rosenthal and Jacobson concluded that this was because of subtle effects of the teachers' expectations. As in this study, unfavorable teacher expectations can lead to lowered academic achievement.

This is exactly what happens in the case of deprived group children. For instance, Rath, A.S.Dash and U.N.Dash (1979) found that maximum number of Brahmin students and minimum number of scheduled caste students were labelled by teachers as good in studies. Teacher expectations, further, exactly reflected in school achievements of Brahmin and scheduled caste students. Problem is, social class and caste significantly influence teacher expectations about student success. This may be because of deep-ingrained stereotypes or prejudices of the teacher. Even in the face of information which prove teachers wrong, such as success of low caste students whom teachers expected to perform poorly, teacher expectations are maintained (R. Sharma, 1985). This is because teachers attribute the success not to the child, but to a chance or faulty tests. Low caste students internalise these patterns of attribution of teachers and develop an ***external locus of control.***

Learning Deficiencies: As has already been discussed, disadvantage and deprivation are accompanied by lower cognitive and intellectual development. For example, children suffering from prolonged deprivation are found to suffer from deficiencies in cognitive abilities (Misra, 1987), higher mental tasks requiring languages skills (D.Sinha, 1982) and in general levels of intelligence, perceptual abilities and spatial skills. This is manifested in learning disabilities.

An interesting trend seen is that differences in cognitive factors between students belonging to the socially advantaged and socially disadvantaged sections is not large in lower grades. This may be because prolonged deprivation shows effects in later grades. Researcher results confirm that the differences between the two groups become progressively larger with each grade in the school. For instance, A.K.Singh (1983) drew the academic achievement curves of the socially disadvantaged and advantaged groups and found that they were in the form of a broom-stick. They were narrow at lower grades, but became wider in favour of advantaged students in later grates.

This can be represented as:

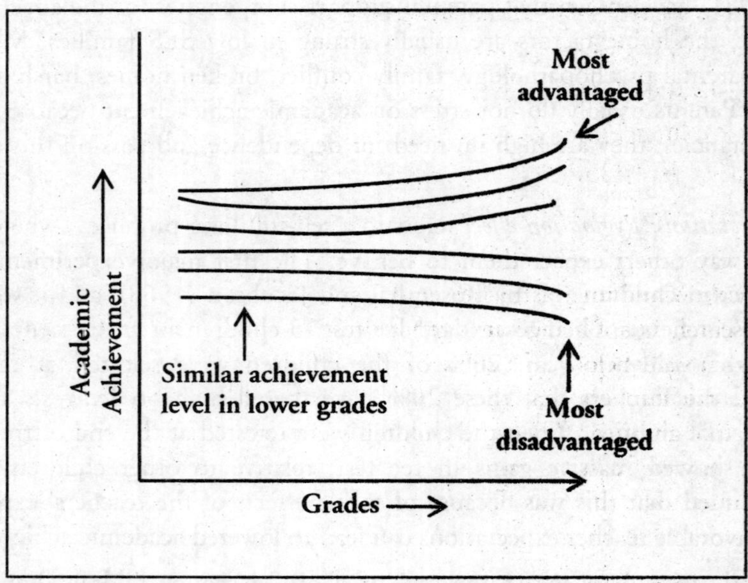

Fig. 8.9 : Academic achievement curves across socio-economic backgrounds

School climate: School climate has a direct influence on the academic achievement of students. Rath (1976) has noted that hostile climate of the school compels socially disadvantaged children to drop out of school. On the other hand, supportive school climate is conducive for the low degree of fear of failure (Pandey & R.C. Tripathi, 1982).

The peer group is a singularly important factor affecting academic achievement. Pandey (1980), for instance, found that lack of peer support is responsible for the irregular attendance of scheduled caste students in school. Another issue is the role of peer groups in schools with mixed groups of students. It has been found that clubbing together deprived and privileged children in the same school leads to lower academic success for deprived children than if they study in ordinary schools with all peers from similar background (D. Sinha, 1982). This may be because they are probably discriminated for their deficiency which further retards their learning process (J.B.P.Sinha, 1990). Further, having homogeneous peer groups is better as it lends the student security and warmth; the negative effects of self-fulfilling prophecies are also low.

Language: Annamalai (1987) has observed that many of the educational problems of lower-class children may be due to differences between home language dialect and school language. A K. Mohanty and M. Mohanty (1985) studied students from disadvantaged groups of Orissa and found that the duality of school language (English) and home language (Oriya) leads to linguistic handicaps. This problem is especially acute in the case of tribal students; tribes have their own dialect distinct from English as well as regional languages (Oriya, Hindi, Tamil, etc.). When they are made to attend English medium or Oriya medium or Hindi medium schools, they start off with a disadvantage!

Now, that we are aware of the various problems faced by disadvantaged groups in education, we can move on to strategies to educate and motivate the disadvantaged.

These can be dealt under the following headings:

1. Psychologists' suggestions for structure change
2. Psychological interventions
3. Community – based intervention
4. Strategies to motivate children in school

1. *Structural changes:* Structural changes in the school climate include changes in curriculum, training of teachers and appointment of teachers from similar background, counseling, etc. Change in curriculum is essential because children from deprived groups usually belong to a culture much different to the culture of mainstream societies. The curriculum should reflect their cultural outlook and world view. More emphasis should be given to teaching subjects that have functional significance for them. Support in the form of counselling and guidance are important. Liddo and Khan (1990) have demonstrated that counselling of bright underachievers from rural background leads to self-understanding, self-acceptance and enhanced academic performance.

   Going a step further, A.K.Singh (1983) argues that since the deprived children lack parental competence and parental support relevant to their schooling, the school should function as a substitute for family and friends. He, therefore, advocates "Ashram type" schools. Perhaps, residential schools with good infrastructure may salvage the deprived group students from the unfavorable conditions of their families.

   Pre-school education has been strongly recommended for deprived group students. The logic is that when joining schools, the deprived group students are already at a disadvantage with respect to advantaged group students. This is because of the rich experiential base that students from advantaged groups get. In a study in Orissa, Jachirck and Chatterjee (1989) have reported that pre-school education has significant effect on cognitive abilities of children.

2. *Psychological interventions:* Psychological interventions are based on the assumption that human development is critically dependent on the experiential base of the person. Hence, major psychological interventions have looked into compensatory mechanisms for lack of experimental base of deprived group students.

Few major interventions are:

(a) Family interventions

(b) School-based interventions

(c) Cognitive interventions

Family-based interventions aim at increasing the expectancies of parents and motivate them to develop attitude, conducive to child education. Anand Lakshmy (1990) has observed that an intervention programme is most likely to succeed if mother is involved in the programme. Thus, intervention programmes should aim at educating mothers on the importance of stimulating play activities. Mothers should also be trained in skills that would enable them to offer a stimulating environment for their children.

Similarly, interventions in the school setting should focus on creating a rich experiential base for students. Sandeep and Pushpa (1981) propose that efforts for developing curriculum, teacher training, modification of school organisation and innovations in teaching methods for disadvantaged students must be coordinated by school psychologists.

Many studies have shown the efficacy of cognitive interventions in developing the cognitive skills of the disadvantaged. Rath (1982) argues that though there are manifest learning disabilities, the children from the deprived groups are not deficient in basic neurocognitive functions, hence manifest learning disabilities disappear after a short training course.

Rath has suggested that learning deficiencies can be overcome using intervention programs based on:

1. Perceptual training
2. Behaviour modification
3. Form-discrimination, and
4. Reinforcement processes

A few other techniques recommended by various scholars are:

5. Verbal self-instructional training
6. Operant manipulation of response and reward
7. Self-efficacy treatment
8. Brainstorming
9. Hypothetical problem-solving

Rath (1952) had studied the effect of verbal self-instructional training and operant manipulation of response and reward on children from low SES tribal families and daily laborers in Orissa. He found that both kinds of training were effective in remediation of impulsive tempo in children.

Singh (1983) reported that high self-efficacy treatment also improves the intellectual abilities of disadvantaged group children. Lastly, Verma & Verma (1994) used techniques, like brainstorming, generation of alternatives and hypothetical problems-solving for a period of 16 weeks to successfully increase the problem-solving performance of deprived children.

The classroom as a Social Tension System

Garcia & Cohen (2011) from the Stanford University have proposed that the classroom should be viewed as a social tension system in order to prepare intervention programmes. Tension systems consist of forces in a dynamic state of interaction that remains relatively stable over time. When a psychologist views the school as a tension system, he accepts that there are a number of forces that can help or hinder academic performance. Further, because of the interactive nature of these forces, they feed off the effects of other forces. For instance, teachers tend to place low-achieving students in low-expectation tracks, which makes the peers lower their expectation from such students. As a result, they are viewed as less worthy of attention. They perform poorly, which reinforces the teachers' and peers' belief.

Hence, interventions should:

(a) Identify the different forces at play in the school environment.

(b) Understand the dynamics of such forces, whether such forces have positive or negative impact on academic performance of students.

(c) Prepare intervention strategies.

Garcia & Cohen (2011) further go on to identify key psychological processes in an individual from a socially disadvantaged group (SDG) that are affected by the school tension system:

I. *Stereotype threat:* Members of SDGs worry that their poor performance could confirm the negative stereotypes in the eyes of others. This is called stereotype threat and can cause stress that undermines performance. Changing the psychological environment will thus, improve performance. In a study in the US, it was found that Whites performed better than Blacks in academics. Blacks were told that the GRE exam does not test academic performance and then made to give the GRE. Their performance improved. This, and many other studies, have lent empirical evidence to stereotype threat.

II. *Collective threat:* Racial prejudices in the classroom may lead to group solidarity among the students from a SDG. To cope with the stereotypes, they develop a sense of solidarity and strong in-group identification. Students from a SDG may, thus, develop a chronic concern that fellow group members may be judged in the light of a negative stereotype.

Hence, racial and ethnic minorities who are subject to negative stereotypes face two kinds of stressors- a threat to their individual self-worth and a threat to the image of the group they value a lot.

Interventions at the school should identify the forces at work, and how the forces create stereotype threat and collective threat. These forces have to be, then, removed from the school environment.

The movie 'Hichki' is an apt representation of psychological intervention at the school-level. The movie portrays students from low-SES admitted into a school on the basis of quota. All these students have been bunched together in F-section. Teachers perceive them as unruly and underachievers. The movie shows some initial attempts made by some members of F-section to gel with other students. But, other students also shun them on the basis of general stereotypes developed by the teachers.

The actress Rani Mukherjee portrays the role of a new teacher trying to motivate these students towards academic success. She starts with the premise that the *academic gap* between other sections and F-section is due to long-held prejudices. She faces lot of resistance from the students due to both stereotype threat and collective threat. The students are chronically worried about the image of their group. When one member of the group is caught cheating, all members stand up to support him. Understanding these psychological processes will improve effectiveness of any intervention process.

3. *Community-based Interventions:* Community-based interventions are based on the philosophy that community participation is the most effective way to provide alternative educational and vocational training opportunities to the disadvantaged. In recent years, many NGOs and social agencies have got involved in educating and motivating the disadvantaged towards development.

A few notable organisations are (Misra & Mohanty)—

1. Alripu, New Delhi
2. Eklavya, Bhopal
3. Gyan-Prabodhini, Maharashtra
4. NANBAN, Madurai
5. Butterflies, Delhi
6. BOSCO, Cochin
7. PRACHITI, Pune

Alripu is an education provider that adopts a non-pedagogic approach by allowing learners to program at their own pace. Eklavya, on the other hand, works in association with the formal education system. Its attempt is to bring about changes in formal school education. Gyan-Prabodhini extends opportunities for all-round development of youth from deprived groups. It promotes leadership qualities, motivation and vocational training among the youth.

NANBAN, BOSCO and Butterflies are organisations involved in rehabilitation of street children, destitute and working children. In their effort to integrate these children to the mainstream, they undertake vocational training and practical education for these children. PRACHITI trains youth from slum background for social work.

4. *Strategies to motivate the disadvantaged in school:* Before investigating various strategies to motivate the disadvantaged to join schools, it is necessary for us to understand the needs of the student. Indian schools are marked by large absentees, drop-outs and lack of interest in studies. Hence, an exercise in building a need hierarchy may be undertaken.

I propose the following hierarchy:

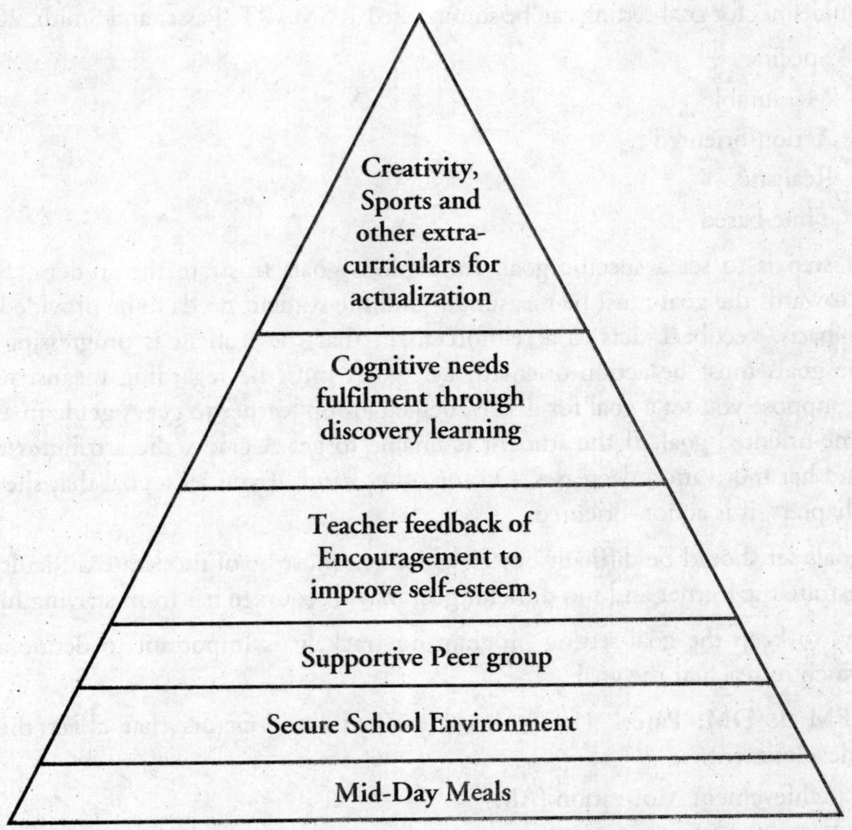

Fig. 8.10 : A needs hierarchy to motivate students from lower SES background

Some general strategies to motivate students towards academic achievement are mentioned in the chapter on Education Psychology. Specific strategies to motivate the disadvantaged group children are essential because the needs and orientations of these students are quite different.

Certain specific strategies are:

Increasing Self-efficacy: Most students from deprived groups show a pattern of attribution in which they attribute success to external factors and failure to themselves (Sinha). This motivational pattern can be changed only by increasing their self-efficacy. To increase self-efficacy, role models can be introduced for vicarious reinforcement. An individual similar to the children who have achieved much in life can act as role model. Sometimes, local leaders and teachers themselves can act as role models. **Verbal Persuasion** also is a potent method to increase self-efficacy. The messages that we get from others affirm our abilities and strengthen our efficacy beliefs.

Systematic Goal-setting: Setting challenging yet achievable goals increases the motivation towards academic success. The children from deprived groups aren't motivated by long-term rewards, rather by instant gratification. Goal-setting in a systematic manner increases competence.

Five guidelines for goal-setting can be summarised as SMART (Passer and Smith, 2007).

S – Specific
M – Measurable
A – Action-oriented
R – Realistic
T – Time-based

The first step is to set a specific goal. Ambiguous goals frustrate the student. Secondly, the progress towards the goal must be measurable and the student needs to be provided feedback on a regular basis. Feedback acts as a reinforcement that the student is progressing towards the goal. The goals must be action-oriented, i.e., goals must be regarding means, not ends. For instance, suppose you set a goal for disadvantaged group learner to get A grade in any subject, it is outcome-oriented goal. If the student is unable to get A-grade, she attributes the failure to herself and her motivation decreases. On the other hand, if you set a goal that she should learn certain chapters, it is action-oriented.

The goals set should be difficult but realistic, i.e., must be of moderate difficulty. Easy goals made frustrate the learner and too difficult goal may discourage her from striving for it.

Finally, to keep the goal-setting program on track, it is important to define a time frame within which to reach at the goal.

AM, EM & DM: Pareek (1970) has identified three factors that affect the motivation towards development:

- Achievement Motivation (AM)
- Extension Motivation (EM)
- Dependence Motivation (DM)

He states that economic development is a function of these motivations (=AM × EM – DM). He identifies these as three factors behind the poverty of deprived groups. Hence, we should inculcate AM and EM and discourage DM in schools. AM can be increased on the lines of the Kakinada Study (McClelland & Winter, 1969). P. Mehta (1976) has developed an intervention program in the educational setting on the lines of the Kakinada setting. This can be used to improve AM among disadvantaged children. EM refers to extension motivation, i.e., motivation to co-operate with others in a social setting towards a goal. EM can be increased by devising programs on the lines of Robbers' Cave Experiment of Sherif (Pareek, 1970). The jigsaw technique developed by Aronson and his co-workers (1978) and other cooperative learning programs can be used to increase EM. Johnson (2000) observes that these programs lead to an increase in self-esteem and academic achievement and decrease in prejudices.

High need for dependence (DM) develops in children during the socialisation period when the hopelessness, powerlessness, fatalistic attitudes and fear of failure of family members are internalised. Dependence motivation can best be countered by education during which fear of failure and lack of initiative can be replaced by realistic aspirations. Prof. Pareek (1970) suggests that dependence motivation can be decreased effectively by use of ***sensitivity training***, wherein children experiment with new patterns of behavior and develop inter-dependence in place of dependence.

■ ■ ■

9

PSYCHOLOGY OF SOCIAL INTEGRATION AND PREJUDICE

Chapter outline

9.1 Psychological Problems of Social Integration

Social Integration: The Concept

Indian society is a multi-cultural, multi-ethnic one in which people are divided on the basis of religion, caste, creed, tribe, ethnicity, race and other myriad parochial lines. In such societies, not all groups have equal access to resources. This leads to a conflict of interest. However, this conflict of interest is not just economic in nature. There are social, structural and psychological variables involved in such inter-group tensions.

Social integration refers to an attempt made to reduce social tensions and create a common identity among members of a society about being part of the society. If you seek to create a common identity among members of a nation, it is known as 'national integration'.

Why social integration? Because social tensions, prejudices and conflicts are social problems. They are dysfunctional to the society and dangerous to the people and society at large. How social integration? By creating a common consciousness, a common 'we-feeling' among members of the community- what our Constitution calls fraternity.

How can this common identity and common consciousness lead to social integration? Basically an individual has many identities at the same time. I am on Oriya by language, an Aryan by race, an agnostic by religion, a Hindu by culture, a Khandayat by caste, a Kshatriya by Varna and male by gender. I have numerous identities, but not all my identities are active in social interaction. There is only one manifest identity at one time. For example, when the Assamese people mobilised against Bengali people in Assam, one group (the Assamese group) was formed on the basis of linguistic identity against another group (the Bengali group). But later, when the Assamese people agitated against illegal Bangladeshi migrants to Assam, their manifest identity was 'Indian' versus 'alien'.

The aim of social integration is to make a common manifest identity among diverse sections of the population. You may be Oriya, Tamil, Bengali, Hindi, Gujarati, Hindu, Muslim, Christian, Munda, Ahir, Bramin, Meena, etc., but if in a 'WHO AM I?" test (basically this test has a list of twenty blanks)you have to write how you define yourself in the order of importance of your various identities, and you put "Indian" before other identities, it is an indication of social integration.

For example, suppose one writes:

1. I am Smarak Swain
2. I am son of Mayadhar Swain
3. I am a bureaucrat tax collector
4. I am an Indian
5. I am an Oriya
6. I am a resident of Bhubaneswar
7. I am a Hindu
8. I am ……..

In this, we see that the individual's "Indian" identity is stronger than his "Oriya" identity. If a majority of people of a nation have their nationality ("Indian" here) as their manifest identity a 'we feeling' develops. While boundaries of language, caste, race, religion, etc., still exist, they don't' create social tensions.

Group Formation, Favoritism and Fanaticism

The concept of social integration can't be appreciated properly without understanding what happens when social integration fails. As I have already marked, an individual's group is based on her manifest identity. What if the manifest identity of a small group of people is being "Oriya" rather than being "Indian"? A small group of Oriya chauvinists develop. Each member has favourable attitude towards other Oriyas, but not to other non-Oriya Indians. This group looks at others as an out-group.

As group favoritism develops (due to psychological factors discussed later in this chapter), contact with out-group decreases. Prejudices about out-groups become strong. This small group influences other Oriya people, so that the group becomes strong and looks at other communities with disdain. Rumours and false attributions like "Bihari immigrants are spoiling our economy", "Marwaris are dominating our business", "Bengalis are selfish and mean", become deeply ingrained beliefs.

The next step of inter-group tension, if not controlled, is escalation to conflict and violence. Poor Bihari immigrants or Marwari businessmen may be targeted in this hypothetical case. Once conflict breaks out, the manifest identity becomes stronger. For example, the Sikh community always seemed to be a group within the larger Hindu community. The events of 1970s and 1980s led to a strong identity among Sikhs about being a separate religion.

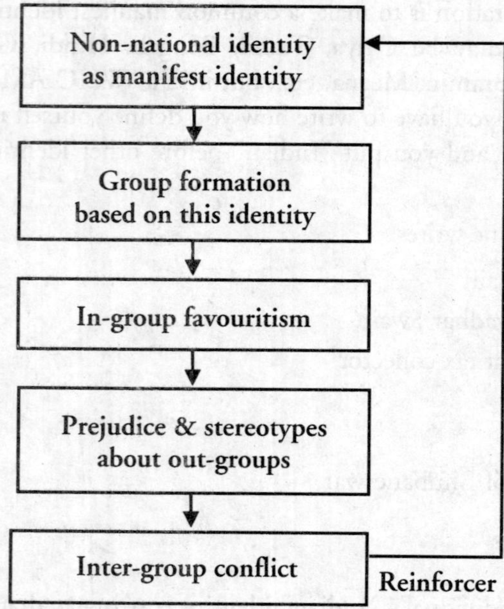

Fig. 9.1 : Reinforcement of inter-group conflicts

9.2 Nature and manifestation of Prejudice

'Prejudice is an attitude (usually negative) towards the members of some group, based solely on their membership in that group…..' —Baron and Bryne (1991)

An attitude is a consistent manner of thinking and feeling about people, groups, objects and events. An attitude 'towards a socially significant material is called a social attitude. Social attitudes are individual attitudes directed towards social objects'. (Venkatasubrahmanyan, 1973, p.6) Prejudices are negative social attitudes. But mind it, just as attitude, prejudice is an individual level phenomenon. Then how does prejudice manifest in groups? Venakatasubrahmanayan (1973) explains that when individual attitudes become strongly inter-conditioned by collective contacts they become highly standardized and uniform within the group. They become collective attitudes. Collective attitudes, i.e., similar predispositions of disfavor in many people, turn out to be "group prejudices" that usually affect one or the other aspect of intergroup relations in a society. The social psychological problem of group prejudices arises when many people have similar predispositions regarding an out-group. (ibid, p.2)

Nature of Prejudices

Prejudice is a type of attitude. Hence, it has all the three components of attitudes:

- The cognitive component of prejudice is stereotype. Stereotypes are exaggerated beliefs about a group based on irrational attributions. Basically, we humans continuously make pre-judgments in the light of insufficient evidence. Suppose, you stay in a hostel and find that the Bengali students in that hostel stay untidy, you make a judgment that "all Bengalis are untidy". Basically, you generalise few instances without sufficient evidence. This leads to stereotypes.

- The affective component refers to a deep feeling of hostility towards a group. This includes racism, casteism and sexism. This component is strong in an individual if such emotional hostility has been imbibed from parents and family. The cognitive component can be changed relatively easily by showing that members of a group don't conform to stereotypes, but it is tough to change affective components.
- Behavioural component of prejudice is prejudice in action. Emotional hostility (effective component) provides motivation to act against a group. Stereotypes function to justify negative emotions towards the out-group. Finally, the action (behavioural component) towards a group determines the manifestation of prejudices. Allport (1954) proposes that the manifestation of prejudices in behavior towards an out-group varies from minor to major forms.

He has talked about five stages in the continuum from minor behavioural discrimination to major ones:

1. *Anti-locution*: This refers to hostile talk, verbal denigration, jokes, etc. Anti-locution was widely practiced among upper castes in relation to lower castes in traditional India.
2. *Avoidance*: Keeping a distance from members of groups, but not actively inflicting harm. This was widely practiced against the untouchable castes in India. Indeed, that form of avoidance was institutionalised. It was believed that untouchables are 'polluted' and should be stayed away from. Another instance I can give from personal experience. I frequent a locality for good food. This locality has a majority of Muslim residents. Surprisingly, many of my friends invited there have been uncomfortable about going there. They just want to avoid the localities!
3. *Discrimination*: This refers to actively and explicitly expressing one's attitude in conduct towards a group. Many Punjabi landlords of Rajinder Nagar in Delhi have severe prejudice against Biharis. When Bihari students come to Rajinder Nagar to prepare for civil services, they find it tough to get rooms on rent because of discrimination! (It is also possible that I am prejudiced that Punjabi landlords are prejudiced against students from Bihar. This example is not based on empirical evidences).
4. *Physical attack:* This includes all types of communal riots, violence against Dalits, nativism, etc. Take the case of anti-North Indian violence in Mumbai. Of course, it is politically motivated, but many participants actually have negative feelings against north Indians.
5. *Extermination:* This means to drive a group of people out of the country or kingdom due to prejudices and hostility. Thankfully, this case is not applicable to India owing to a rule of law enforced on the basis of the Constitution.

The nature and manifestation of prejudices between in-group and out-groups will be made clearer in subsequent sections, when we study various theories of prejudices and social conflicts.

Causal Factors of Social Conflicts and Prejudices

Social conflicts are a product of multiple causes. These causes are also varied as there are political, social, economic and psychological causes. In this section, we will investigate certain causal factors of social conflicts from a socio-psychological perspective. You must bear in mind, all through, the difference between conflict and prejudice. Prejudice is both the cause and effect of conflict. Yet, prejudice is neither necessary nor sufficient condition for conflict. In this section, we will concentrate on theories and perspectives behind both social prejudice and social conflict.

Broadly, these theories are of two types- theories that search for causality in the individual personality and those that search for the causes in group dynamics. The first set of theories is dominated by psychoanalysts, like Adorno, Kakkar and Dollard. However, these theories have increasingly come under criticism.

Personality factors

Social phenomena, like riots, caste conflicts and tribal agitation are inter-group in nature. But, is it possible that there are some basic traits that pre-dispose the members of these groups to indulge in some acts?

Adorno and his colleagues set out to find an answer to this question in Nazi Germany in the 1940s. They used techniques like interviews (to find out political views and childhood experiences) and projective tests, like the Thematic Apperception Test (TAT) designed to reveal unconscious attitudes about the minority Jewish group. Adorno and his colleagues (1950) concluded that some children are subjected to harsh and authoritarian parenting style in childhood. While these children consciously have very high opinion of their father, they are hostile towards their fathers unconsciously. Unable to resolve the conscious adulation and unconscious hostility, they project their hostility onto minority groups. Hence, the authoritarian personality refers to people who are rigid and inflexible, and are intolerant to ambiguity. They submit to authority (a result of conscious adulation to father authority right from childhood) and are hostile to people of lower status.

Sudhir Kakkar (1990) has proposed another dimension of the psychoanalytic tradition. While considering ethnic violence in India, he observed that group identities fulfil some psychological functions. Basically, the human psyche has both a "good self" and a "bad self". A psychologically healthy person successfully integrates her good and bad selves. (If you are one of those people who introspects, are aware of your shortcomings and are ready to accept that you are wrong when reasoned to logically, it means you have a well-integrated self). If one is not able to integrate her good and bad selves, she feels anxiety whenever her bad self surfaces.

Kakkar states that to increase her feeling of well-being, the narcissistic personality suppresses the bad self into the unconscious. She is good and her group is good. She places her group at the center of the universe and projects the bad self on others. The object of projection can be a caste, ethnic or religious community.

Why does a person become narcissistic? Kakkar explains that in the process of socialisation, often parents nurture narcissism in children. You tell me, have your parents ever told you that partition of India in 1947 happened because of communal politics? No. They say Jinnah was solely responsible for partition. Have your parents ever told you Hindus have killed members of minority community in riots and that it was bad? Most parents are either neutral or sympathetic to rightist terror organisations that kill innocent women and children in the name of Hindutva. This reinforces the perception in Hindu children that "Hindus are good". While the fact that Hindu rioters have done dastardly acts (like, rape pregnant women, burn children to death) is not focused on, we and our significant others highlights the fact that innocent people died in terrorist attacks (and we attribute the terrorists to a "bad group": Muslims of India).

My point her is, both Hindu group and Muslim group (and for that matter other groups) have "good" and "bad" characters. In every group there are people with extremist views and extreme ideologies, so also people with rational, modern attitudes. But, during socialisation, we are taught that ours is a good group. Hence, we project the bad characteristics onto other groups. Not only parents, group myths also nurture narcissism. For example, the political struggle between Rana Pratap and Emperor Akbar was a political struggle after all, between the greed of political elites. But, when any one narrates the story myths are narrated- not the political struggle but the struggle between a "Hindu Rana" and an "imperial Muslim ruler" is narrated to children.

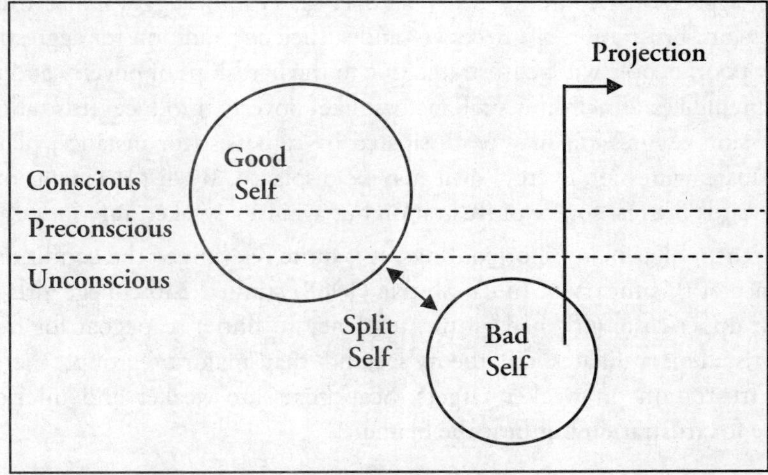

Fig. 9.2 : Psychic Characteristics of a Narcissistic Personality

Kakkar reasons that, "Hindus are regularly possessed by Muslim Bhutas and these Muslim Bhutas are considered the strongest, vilest, most alien, demonic projections of the unconscious Hindu mind. The Muslim demon is the traditional container of Hindu conflicts over aggressive impulses. While under its influence, a Hindu may well transgress deeply held taboos regarding violence. (See Hutnik, 2004). Basically, the bad self that is suppressed into the unconscious is a 'demon' that threatens to come to the conscious. Not able to accept a demon within himself, the Hindu uses defense mechanisms to make it a Muslim demon, a 'Muslim bhuta'.

Shortcomings of these theories

Today, the Psycho-analystic School doesn't find many adherents. Its most objectionable proposition is that it considers the individual as the cause of group prejudices. During conflicts, even the most rational persons show group favouritism. Does it mean that all the members of that group have gone through harsh and authoritarian parenting style? No!

Further, the authoritarian personality explains aggression by a majority group member towards a minority group member; not the other way round. For instance, take the case of Sikh terrorism. The Hindu-Sikh tension first arose in 1970s. Before that, there was not much hostility between Hindus and Sikhs. Does it mean in this specific generation majority of Sikh youth had harsh and incorrect child rearing? Why did the minority Sikh group develop hostility towards the majority Hindus?

According to Nimmi Hutnik (2004), group dynamics is much more important than personality in explaining ethnocentrism and prejudices. Still, it was important for us to study these theories because they explain individual differences in prejudice and conflict within a group. Now, we will turn our attention to the Frustration-Aggression Theory that finds causality in environmental factors (rather than the person or group), yet follows the psychoanalytic school in explaining its theory.

Frustration-Aggression Theory

The frustration-aggression hypothesis of Dollard et al. (1939) suggests that frustration always produces aggression. Frustration is a necessary and sufficient condition for aggression. If a society is economically poor, people will be frustrated due to the hardships of poverty and there will be an escalation of prejudices. Environmental factors like poverty produce frustration. Frustration produces aggression. Aggression may be dissipated by catharsis (for instance, playing sports is a channel to dissipate aggression energy) or it may be displaced. By displacement, the frustration is directed not towards the real source of frustration but against a weaker, inferior target.

Though the theory has many shortcomings, it is quite relevant to the conditions in India. To test the relevance of this theory in India, Shukla (1988) studied 240 college girls of Bodh Gaya. She found that upper-caste girls had greater tendency to find a scapegoat for frustrations than lower caste girls. This validates the theory's stand that majority groups (here upper caste) displace their frustration on weaker targets. Scapegoats are weaker and inferior people who aren't the cause for frustration but bear the blame.

9.3 Theory of Relative Deprivation

Political scientists, like Gurr (1970) and Runciman (1966) have found that when we per-ceive a deprived state, we don't' perceive objective deprivation. Rather, it is our expectation that we use as indicator. Hence, they conclude that the sense of deprivation is subjective. This relative deprivation may be a result of prejudice and also a cause for prejudice.

There are two types of relative deprivations:

1. Egoistic relative deprivation, based on comparison of self with other individuals.
2. Fraternalistic relative deprivation based on comparison of in-group with other groups.

Fraternalistic relative deprivation explains various caste and religious tension in India. The pro-reservation and anti-reservation agitations by various caste groups are because of relative deprivation. High caste people are much more prosperous than OBC/ SC/ ST groups statistically.

Yet they feel relatively deprived when greater reservations are given to other groups. When the government introduced 33% reservation for OBCs in educational institutions in 2004-05, there were widespread protests. This was in spite of Dr. Manmohan Singh's assurance that the number of seats for general category won't be reduced; only extra seats will be added. During the agitation, many ideological and emotionally toned articles and speeches had created feelings of hostility (affective component of prejudice) between general and reserved category students.

This theory also explains conflicts and social tensions in Hindu-Muslim, Hindu-Sikh, ethnic majority-tribal and linguistic relations. Tripathi and Srivastava (1981), for example, found that among Muslims feelings of relative deprivations in term of political freedom, job opportunities etc. are associated with more hostile attitudes towards Hindus. Those Muslims who were low on relative deprivation showed lessor hostile attitudes.

Realistic Group Conflict Theory

People have their own group as the center of their lives and rate other groups with reference to their groups. This tendency of individuals is called ethnocentrism. Hence, there is a need to study the dynamics of inter-group relations. A landmark in the study of inter-group relations is the realistic Group Conflict Theory.

In the now famous Robber's Cave Experiment, Sherif and his co-workers (1961) took 22 white, middle-aged protestant children to a summer camp. They were divided into two groups-the Eagles and the Rattlers. In the first stage, each group had to work on some task that needed cooperation within the group. Sherif observed that very soon, a group identity developed in both groups. In the second stage, the two groups were exposed to each other. A sports tournament was organised between the two groups. This led to considerable inter-group tension. Rattlers stereotyped all Rattlers as brave, tough and friendly and all Eagles as sneaky and stinker. Reverse was true for Eagles. The tension precipitated into open conflict even before the tournament started and the Rattlers' flag was burned. A fight ensued and the camp counsellors had to intervene to stop the fight.

Sherif concluded that inter-group conflict arises as a result of a conflict of interests. Competition is a sufficient condition for hostility or conflict. Sherif's study has been validated by many other studies. Many sociological studies in India have found that riots take place in those cities, where Muslims are relatively prosperous. In general, we can state that the relation between two groups vary from cooperation to competition on a continuum. More the competition, more is the inter-group tension and more is the prejudice against the out-group.

This theory was a landmark in studies of prejudice when it was proposed- it stressed that the causality of prejudice and conflict lies in inter-group relations, not interpersonal relations. However, this theory has also been challenged by many later scholars.

Social Identity and categorisation

In reaction to Sherif's contention that competition leads to inter-group conflict and prejudice, many scholars, notably Tajfel (1981) argued that group favouritism comes naturally to groups. Tajfel found that mere categorisation of subjects into two groups is sufficient to produce group favouritism. Tajfel used random toss of a coin to separate some participants into two groups. He found in-group preferences even in these groups.

He explains that an individual always tries to maintain a positive self-image. This self-image has two components:

1. Personal identity
2. Group identity

To have a better self-image, people try to maintain a better group identity. For a better group identity, we are motivated to view our group as positively as possible. Hence, we highlight its differences for other groups and undermine the similarities.

The social identity theory essentially implies that the stereotypes that one holds about one's own group should be significantly more favourable than those of the outgroup. Indian researches have validates this point. For instance, Hussain (1984) found that both Hindus and Muslims evaluated the ingroup significantly higher on affiliation and the outgroup was evaluated higher on aggression. Khan (1988) found that Hindus have negative, derogatory images of Muslims regarding their physical appearance. Muslims, on the other hand, perceived Hindus as money spinners who charged high interest rates, and were dishonest, jealous and unreliable.

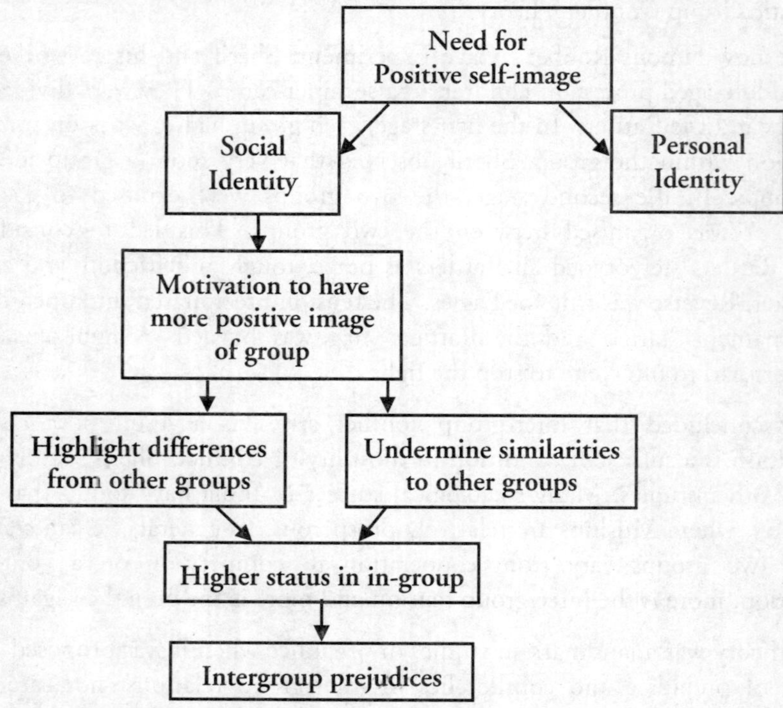

Fig. 9.3 : Social identity dynamics

Norm Violation Theory

We hear much news about how a trivial event like killing of a cow by a Muslim leads to riots; playing music near a mosque leads to violence, etc. How can such large-scale conflict result from something so trivial?

De Ridder and Tripathi (1992) have forwarded a Norm Violation Theory (NVT) to explain this. What happens when a member of one group (say Muslims) violates the norms of another group (say Hindus)? According to this theory, violation of norms of group B by group A results in group B attributing malevolent intent to group A's behavior. This, in turn, provokes a negative reaction from group B towards group A. This negative reaction of group B violates the norms of group A. Group A believes that group B did it internationally, with malevolence. When the situation escalates, violent group behavior results.

This theory is important because it helps us understand that conflict happens in stages. Intergroup conflicts usually start with very trivial issues (like a fight between two students, or a small argument etc.) and escalate to large-scale violence. This theory provides a causal factor behind escalation of conflict.

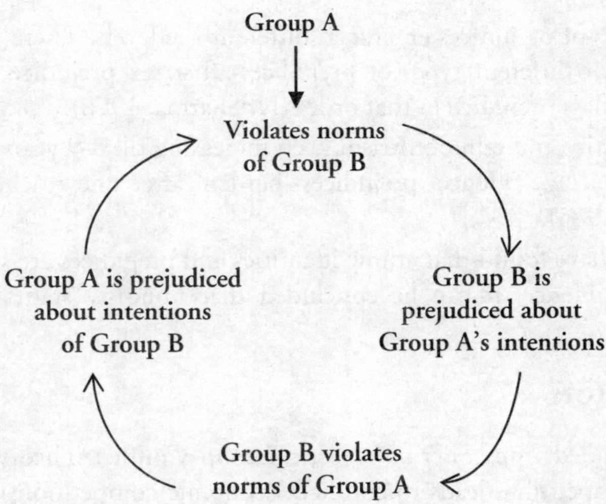

Fig. 9.4 : Norm Violatiion mechanism

9.4 Role of child rearing

Psychologists widely acknowledge the fact that ethnic identities are a major cause for prejudices and that ethnic identities develop during the process of socialisation. Major factors that play crucial role during socialisation are parenting style, attitudes and prejudices of parents, community one belongs to, etc.

For instance, Hassan (1983) had divided parents into four categories and compared the development of prejudice in children of these four groups of parents.

The four categories are:

(a) Prejudiced parents
(b) Prejudiced father and unprejudiced mother
(c) Prejudiced mother and unprejudiced father
(d) Unprejudiced parents

Hassan found that children of prejudiced parents showed the highest degree of prejudice, while those of the fourth category showed least. A.K.Singh (1985) has found that religious identity (i.e., ethnocentrism) develops very early in childhood. He compared four religious groups (Hindu, Muslims, Sikhs and Christians) and found that majority of children from all these religions learn to show a preference for one's own religion as early as 4-5 years of age.

Some general findings with regard to development of ethnocentrism and prejudices in children are:

(a) Prejudice increases with age (Vyas, 1973)
(b) Religious identity and prejudice are inter-related and religious identity develops earlier.
(c) Different types of prejudices emerge at different age levels. There is a sequence in the development of different types of prejudices- first sex prejudice, followed by caste, religious and class prejudice in that order (N. Sharma, 1978).
(d) Religious identity and ethnocentrism keep increasing till 8-9 years of age and become stable after that age. Hence, prejudices 'harden' after one reaches 8-9 years of age (A.K. Singh, 1985).
(e) Many studies have found that ethnic identities and prejudices are stronger in minority communities. Hence, it can be concluded that minority status strengthens ethnic identity.

9.5 Economic Factors

We have already concluded from Sherif's realistic Group Conflict Theory that competition, including economic competition, leads to conflict. Economic competition is a strong factor in communal riots in India.

For instance, Engineer (1984) suggests that some features common to riots are:

- A section of Muslims is economically well-off and appear to be potential economic competitors of Hindus.
- Core issues are economic or political, ignited by some trivial incidence.
- Riots are pre-planned rather than spontaneous. Hence, economic motives rather than emotionality is the major reason behind riots.

Increasingly, the riots taking place in recent times are characterised by loot, plunder and destruction of property. These indicate the economic motive behind the conflicts. A.K.Singh (1988) makes an interesting observation that the jealousy that leads to conflict is itself irrational. A few members of the Muslim community or Dalit community become prosperous, and they are perceived as the symbols of the community. In objective terms, the community as a whole may be economically backward, but the envious perceive all members as equally prosperous.

9.6 Leadership as a factor

Many sociologists and political scientists have highlighted the role of political elites in the instigation and spread of riots. They argue that political elites themselves are pretty secular, but mobilise people on narrow parochial lines to meet their narrow political interests.

Psychologist explain this as, 'At moments of societal crisis otherwise mature and psychologically healthy individuals may temporarily come to feel overwhelmed and in need of a strong and self-assured leader' (Post, 2004, P.196). Post calls these leaders as "hate mongering" leaders who fulfil their personal ambitions by harnessing the need for followers to follow a leader. The follower tries to identify the leader with a father-figure who will relieve her of all dilemma and keep off crisis. Especially in the case of India, where a huge proportion of people suffer from poverty and hardship, people are highly vulnerable to the influence of such leaders.

9.7 Dimensions of Social Conflict and Prejudice

Of the many social conflicts that plague Indian society, there are four particularly salient dimensions- caste conflict, religious conflict, linguistic conflict and class conflict. Basically, caste, religion and language form strong units of identity of Indians. Hence, groups are often formed on the basis of these. Class conflicts is not based on membership of any parochial group; rather it is an expression of tension between various economic classes in an industrial economy. With the growth of industries in India, a sizeable working class and many trade unions have been formed. Prejudice and conflict in the context of class is also of our interest, given the fact that good class relation is crucial for peace in an industrialised society.

Caste

In a way, caste has been the most persistent form of social relations in India for centuries. Many changes have occurred in India, but caste is able to resist any attempt to eliminate it. Even today, caste forms an important ethnic identity for any Indian. On the other hand, though caste hasn't gone extinct (as predicated by many scholars), it has changed its character with changing times. If we need to study conflict and prejudices in caste, we should study it in three phases- caste in traditional India, caste in British India and caste in free India.

1. Caste in Traditional India

In traditional India, various castes (jatis) were arranged in the form of a hierarchy. The hierarchy was exploitative in the sense that there was a strict division of labour between various caste. Member of one caste cannot perform the job sanctioned to other caste. For example, a member of washer man caste was prohibited from becoming blacksmith, which only a member of blacksmith caste could become. No prizes to guess which castes performed the neat and valuable jobs. The Brahmin castes and Kshatriya castes were sanctioned to perform various tasks that were considered desirable. The upper castes also had greater control over land, production and capital.

Was there caste conflict in traditional India? Many instances of conflict between Brahmin castes and Kshatriya castes for supremacy are known. But, what about the conflict between upper castes and lower castes? Secondly, was there any caste prejudice in traditional society? Surprisingly, many scholars used to believe that there was none. This is not true. Caste system has always been an exploitative system where lower castes have been discriminated against. Especially the untouchable castes were subject to many discriminations- they couldn't touch anything used by upper castes, they couldn't use any public amenities (like ponds, schools, etc.), couldn't own property, etc. Now, how can there be discrimination without prejudice? Discrimination is the behavioral component of prejudice.

Yes, there was prejudice in traditional society, but it was institutionalised prejudice. There was a widespread belief that various Varnas (there are four varnas into which all jatis can be categorised- Brahmin, Kshatriya, Vaishya, Shudra) have come out of various parts of Brahma's body. Brahmins have come out of brahma's brain, so are the purest and most supreme. Shudra castes have originated from Brahma's feet, so are least pure. In addition, the untouchable castes are polluted. This notion of purity and pollution on which the whole caste system was based in traditional Indian society is itself a prejudice. If you think that you are pure or that some other person is polluted, you are simply prejudiced.

The caste system is a classic case of how prejudices are institutionalised into general values; are passed from one generation to another by socialisation, and lead to widespread inter-group discrimination. If there was so much prejudice and discrimination, next question is why did it not lead to caste conflict? Many sociologists have explained that inter-caste relations were mired by cooperation and conflict. Caste tensions always existed, but didn't escalate into revolt by lower castes? Why? This is because of co-operation. If you remember Sherif's realistic Groups Conflict Theory, you know that conflict is the result of competition. Competition and co-operation are at either ends of a continuum. Conflict among upper and lower castes was low because of co-operation between these castes.

The Jajmani System is a system of economic exchange which existed in traditional society between various castes. In this system, Kulin castes (lower castes) used to work for Jajman castes (land owning castes) in return for an assured income. Jajmani system fostered inter-dependence and co-operation. The landlord couldn't till his land without agricultural labourers. The labourers couldn't earn a livelihood without working for landlords. Not just as labourers, the washermen, barber, artisans, temple priests, etc., worked for the landlord with the assurance of a share of the produce. The Jajmani system provided a job security to all Kulin castes; hence cooperation, not competition.

2. Caste in British India

In colonial period, the co-operation of castes slowly changed into completion. First, the Britishers introduced private property and capitalist form of farming. In capitalist farming, landlord hired and fired free labour at will. This led to breakdown of jajmani system. The special relation shared by Jajmans and Kulins broke.

Secondly, British rule opened up new opportunities. Many non-traditional job opportunities came in the way of caste people- jobs in army, in modern industries and modern legal profession were opened to all castes. Though upper castes benefited most from these occupations, many lower caste members also benefited and became prosperous. These, economically prosperous lower caste members desired for a higher status in society.

From the above two points, we can make two conclusions:

(1) Co-operation of jajmani system was turning into competition- competition for modern jobs and competition for agricultural land.

(2) Economically prosperous sections of lower castes wanted higher caste status. To get higher caste status, many of these lower castes started emulating the customs of upper castes and demanded higher caste status.

For example, suppose the Noniya caste (belonging to Shudra varna) want to get Kshatriya status. It starts emulating the customs, rituals and manners of various Kshatriya castes. The Noniya caste also justifies that it is a Kshatriya caste using some mythology to explain why it is so. This phenomenon is called Sanskritisation. Sanskritisation was first discovered by eminent sociologist M.N.Srinivas.

Why is Sanskritisation significant for us in a psychological study of conflict? Because, it shows that lower castes considered the upper castes as a *reference group*. If you emulate Shahrukh Khan, evidently Shahrukh Khan is your role model. You want to gain all the popularity and fan base of Shahrukh Khan. It is because you consider the identity of a superstar as more positive than yours. Exactly the same was the situation of lower castes which were sanskritising. They were emulating the upper castes and claiming to be upper castes as they considered the upper caste identity more favourable and positive than their own identity. This is validated by many research findings. For example, Paranjpe (1970) found that Harijans had a negative self-image while Brahmins had the most positive self-image. Similarly, Majeed and Ghosh (1981) found that the scheduled castes displayed a strong negative social identity in relation to upper castes.

What was the nature of caste conflict in colonial period? Many sociologists have reported that attempts of lower castes to sanskritise were met with resistance by upper castes. This period also saw many peasant movements (by lower caste groups) against upper caste landlords. Many of these movements were violent. Political conflict between upper castes and lower castes also became prominent. In Tamil Nadu, a strong anti-Brahmin movement emerged under the leadership of Periyar. This movement was instrumental in creating strong feelings of hostility against Brahmins. In Periyar's ideology, the Brahmins were 'alien Aryans' who were exploiting the Dravidian non-Brahmins. This also created deep-rooted prejudices against Brahmins.

Outside Tamil Nadu, the most vociferous political activist was B.R. Ambedkar. He was instrumental in formation of a 'Dalit identity'. However, he was not that successful in mobilising Dalits for political action.

3. Caste in Contemporary India

While discussing Sanskritisation, I mentioned how lower castes had a negative self-image during colonial period. This has changed remarkably in post-independence era. Thanks to various social and political movements (prominent being Dalit Panther Movement, Bahujan Samaj

Party), caste awareness has increased in Dalit castes. Today, the Dalits assert their Dalit identify. They no longer see the upper castes as a reference group; nor do they try to sanskritise. Rather, today there is a horizontal solidarity in most caste groups.

Today, the prejudices based on religion (that some castes are purer because they came out of some parts of Brahma) are becoming irrelevant. But, castes are not dying. Rather, caste identity is becoming stronger. There is competition among various castes during election to grab political power. This competition has made caste a pressure group.

Besides competition for political power, there is also competition for economic resources. Caste conflict between upper and lower castes are more frequent in villages where some lower caste members have become prosperous.

Now, let us look into certain patterns in inter-caste prejudice observed in contemporary India:

1. Though caste conflicts have always been between the top and bottom strata, there have been increasingly greater number of conflicts between middle castes (OBCs) and Harijans (M.P. Singh, 1979).
2. The earlier ambivalence of identity among lower castes, reflected in Sanskritisation and religious conversion has been replaced by an aggressive assertion of Dalit identity (M.P.Singh, 1979).
3. Caste identity and prejudices develop in children by 4-6 years of age. For instance, Tiwari and Misra (1980) investigated some primary school students in Faridabad city. The students were quizzed about their caste name, their knowledge of different castes, the caste of their best friends and the caste of students they find unpleasant. It was found that 75% of children between 4-6 years of age were able to give their own caste names. Also, majority of students sought friendship within their own castes and avoided making friends from other castes.
4. Studies have found that upper castes are more prejudiced than lower castes, while other studies have found that lower caste members are more prejudiced. I believe that generalisation is dangerous. Inter-caste prejudice varies from place to place depending on historical events, persistent conflicts, feeling of being discriminated against, etc.

Religion

The problem of prejudice and conflict is not as severe in any other case as it is in the case of religion. One of the major challenges to social integration in India is the challenge of communalism and fundamentalism. Of the many factors behind communal riots, one that is especially prominent is prejudice and mutual suspicion between two major religious groups of India- Hindus and Muslims.

The widespread prejudice between Hindus and Muslims in India has been empirically tested and well documented. For example, Mohsin (1984) studied ethnocentricity and ethnic prejudice among Hindu and Muslim undergraduate and postgraduate students of Patna and

Utkal universities. He found strong ethnic prejudices in both Hindus and Muslims. He also makes an interesting observation that the prejudiced attitudes of Hindus and Muslims towards each other have become a part of the social norms as these prejudices are shared by most members of respective communities.

Prejudices between the two communities have practically become so widespread in respective communities that one wonders how could such prejudice develop and get reinforced!

Let us look at a few psychologically relevant causal factors:

1. History

False beliefs are an important cognitive component of prejudice. And false beliefs are picked up by an individual from false readings in history. Communal writers of history often give a communal colour to political battles in history. The battles between Akbar and Rana Pratap, or between Aurangazeb and Shivaji are shown as battles between Hindus and Muslims. Hero-myths are created by projecting Rana Pratap, Shivaji and Guru Govind Singh as saviours of Hinduism and likes of Akbar and Aurangzeb as villains. While it's true that Aurangzeb was a religious fanatic, Akbar was one of the greatest secular rulers. It is never pointed out that Muslims fought for Rana Pratap and Shivaji, while Hindus fought for Akbar and Aurangzeb. Ultimately, these were political struggles. These hero-myths help ideologues to justify their ideology (A.K.Singh, 1988). False beliefs about history create strong hostility towards the out-group.

2. Fear Psychosis

One important factor that generates and reinforces prejudice is fear. Muslims fear of being assimilated by Hinduism, like Buddhism and Jainism. Their minority status itself creates fear in their minds. Frequent riots further reinforce the fear. Fear is nothing but an emotion. Such negative emotions further strengthen prejudices.

Hindus, on the other hand, fear that they may become a minority in India. This fear is fueled by statistics that Muslim population increases at a greater rate than Hindu population. The true explanation for this is that Muslims are relatively poorer economically than Hindus. Hence, fertility rate among Muslims is higher. Yet, the rate is not as high as to turn Hindus into a minority anytime in future. The fear is, at best, irrational.

3. Relative deprivation

As discussed in an earlier section in this chapter, you feel relatively deprived when you compare yourself with a reference group and perceive the reference groups as economically better off than you. Muslims often compare their present status with (a) their past history as rulers, (b) Muslims in Islamic nations, and (c) with the Hindu community. Empirical studies have also demonstrated that Muslims who feel highly relatively deprived in relation to other groups have more negative out-groups attitudes than Muslims who do not (Tripathi and Srivastava, 1980).

4. Memories of Past injustices

It is a fact that partition was overwhelmingly supported by Muslims and memory of the partition of India still lingers in the collective unconscious of Hindu psyche. The partition is perceived as an injustice. Similarly, the images of Babri Masjid being demolished has seeped into the collective unconscious of the Muslims psyche. When provided appropriate cues, such images surface in the consciousness and severely affect the judgments of people.

5. Economic Motives

Many scholars have identified underlying economic motives behind the ideological posturing of various parties involved in a riot.

It is argued that when a few Muslims become prosperous, it triggers irrational jealousy and envy among Hindus. This jealousy fuels prejudice. Based on a number of case studies, Engineer (1984) has identified certain common characteristic features of riots, like:

(a) Riots occur in towns where the proportion of Muslims is more than 30%.

(b) A section of Muslims is economically well-off and appear to compete with Hindus.

(c) Core issues are economic or political, triggered by some trivial incident.

(d) Riots are pre-planned rather than spontaneous.

From these conclusions, we may deduce that while prejudice plays a role in religious conflict, human motives also play a significant role.

Now, we turn our attention to some trends in prejudice seen in Indian research.

Some conclusions drawn from various studies of intergroup prejudice in India are:

1. Muslims are more prejudiced than Christians, who in turn are more prejudiced than Hindus. (Enayatullah, 1984). It seems that minority status strengthens group identity and ethnocentrism.
2. Prejudice is negatively correlated to religious information (Hassan, 1981). Lesser the religious information, more is the prejudice.
3. Personality variables, like authoritarianism are more powerful correlates of prejudice than religious affiliation, caste status or rural-urban origin (Hassan, 1981).
4. Religious prejudice is related to socialisation within one's group. Both, religious identity and prejudice develop early in childhood because parents and significant others pass on their prejudice to the child. This problem is cyclic because religious prejudices have become a social norm. False beliefs about out-group get inherited by the child.

Language

Social interaction between various linguistic groups are marred by stereotypes like, "Bengalis are clannish", "Marwaris are avaricious", "Andhras are crude" and "Tamils are cunning" (Venkatasubrahmanyan, 1973). In my graduation days (I used to study in a college in Kharagpur,

West Bengal), we used to have very negative feelings about Bengalis. Most students in campus believed that Bengalis are narcissists; saw their culture as the best and themselves, the center of the world. Non-Bengali students surprisingly tend to generalise such stereotypes to all Bengalis, irrespective of individual differences.

Linguistic prejudices won't be a social problem, however, if only such stereotypes are held about people following a language. They become a social problem when language becomes the basis of discriminatory treatment. The root cause of conflictual inter-group relations based on language lies in historical events. Hence, we need to discuss these in short.

In the course of preparation of the Indian Constitution, it was envisioned that Hindi should become the Lingua Indica in the course of time. This implied that southern states (following Telugu, Tamil, Kannada, etc.) had to learn an alien language. This was not acceptable and southern states vociferously opposed the imposition of Hindi on them.

Though Hindi wasn't imposed and English remained the official language, there was widespread suspicion and fear among Tamils regarding Hindi. Such prejudice has led to *anti-locution* and avoidance of Hindi-speaking population in towns of Tamil Nadu. In the 1960s and early 1970s, the prejudice about Hindu domination was so high that names written in Hindi in public places, railway stations and post offices were erased in Tamil Nadu. In mid 1960s, there was even a clamour for secession.

Empirical studies have also validated this supposed antipathy towards Hindi among non-Hindi speaking population. For example, Sharma (1964) studied Tamil-speaking and Telugu-speaking students in some colleges in Madras city by using a variant of Bogardus Social Distance Scale. The researcher's aim was to find out the social distance an individual would maintain with various linguistic groups. Sharma found that Hindi-speaking group was put at the bottom of the preferential order (i.e., students wanted to maintain maximum social distance from them). Tamil students placed the Hindi-group at 9th spot, while Telugu students placed them at the 10th (last) spot. This type of prejudice exists not just between southerners and Hindi, but between any two groups based on language. For example, Rath and Das (1957) studied the attitudes of caste Hindu Oriyas towards Bengalis, Biharis, Andhras, Punjabis, Adivasis and Harijanas. It was found that the subjects chose favourable traits for Oriyas, while choosing a large number of derogatory attributes for out-groups.

Why do prejudices develop based on language? Since the formation of linguistic states in 1950s, group identity of people following various languages have strengthened. Using Tajfel's *Social Identity Theory*, it can be stated that when group identity is strong, group favouritism develops. Since all of us keep making pre-judgments in the face of incomplete evidence, we develop stereotypes about linguistic out-groups.

Another major reason is political. Language is often intrinsically related to one's unique culture and people easily become sentimental about their language. This is harnessed by political leaders to create prejudices about other languages. For example, the Shiv Sena movement and later Maharashtra Navnirman Sena have used the "Marathi Manoos" as a tool for political mobilisation. Discrimination and violence against Hindi-speaking immigrants have been lately observed owing to mobilisation by political leaders.

9.8 Psychological Strategies for Handling Conflict and Prejudice

Society in India is a multi-cultural, multi-ethnic one in which people are divided on the basis of religion, caste, creed, tribe, ethnicity, race and many other factors. Realistically speaking, it is not possible to obliterate the lines of caste, tribe or religion. Comparing with the American society, we can observe that there is a "melting pot" where a single language (English) and a single culture (Pop culture) are followed throughout a large country. That can't be the case with India.

However, a sensitisation can be brought among citizens about being part of a society. The aim here is to reduce prejudice and conflicts by better understanding of members of out-groups in an individual.

What do the theories of prejudice and conflict tell us? Before discussing the psychological theories, first let us discuss the economic and political ones. Many economists believe that reduction of poverty and equal access over resources can reduce prejudice. This looks easy theoretically, but practically not immediately possible. Besides, it is not objective deprivation of resources but subjective expectations that lead to competition and conflict. Political approach advocates the obliteration of boundaries. Conflict develops on the basis of language, so it imposes a single homogeneous religion/ language on the whole country. This can happen in a totalitarian from of government. For example, the Chinese government is contemplating a policy to give name to babies so that their ethnic identity is not evident from their names. Such a policy can't be implemented in liberal democratic countries like India. Besides, the Chinese government hasn't been very successful. The forced assimilation of ethnic minorities into the majority Hun is facing violent resistance from Tibetans and Muslim minorities.

Psychological theories have an advantage in that they provide insights into inter-group and interpersonal relations that can be used to develop interventions at school, organisation and community levels to reduce prejudice and conflict. Let us evaluate various psychological theories in the light of present discussion. The Psychoanalytic School puts excess emphasis on child rearing practices (CRP). Prejudice can be reduced by following appropriate CRP. But, how far is it practical. We can't force parents to show a definite parenting style. However, theories like the realistic Group Conflict Theory provide good directions for interventions. The theory makes it very clear that removing competition and replacing it with superordinate goals and cooperation reduces hostility. We all remember how the Kargil conflict in 1998 between India and Pakistan united all Indians into a 'we group'. At that time, defense of India was our superordinate goal.

The social identity theory of Tejfel states that group favouritism is natural and inevitable. However, if boundaries between groups can be made more blurred or flexible, then group membership is no longer a central part of social identity.

Psychologists have drawn inspiration from the Game Theory in devising strategies to reduce conflict. In the prisoners' dilemma experiment, various parties tried to find out a possible win-win approach. Conflicts are based on the logic of win-lose. One party has to win and the other has to lose. But, psychologists assert that by negotiation, a possible solution to conflict can be found out which is a win-win solution.

Now, let us move on to specific intervention strategies to prevent, reduce and resolve prejudices and conflicts.

Interventions

Before going into the question of 'how' in intervention, we need to tackle 'who'. It is not possible to introduce interventions for whole societies. Interventions can be produced in an organisation (for example, diversity training), or in the local community (for example, use of pranchayats, gram sabha or other civil society groups to introduce interventions). However, the best target groups for short-term and small-scale interventions are young children. Their socialisation process in underway and they still haven't formed rigid attitudes. Following A.K. Singh (1985), we know that children form a complete ethnocentric identity by 4-5 years of age and their prejudices become rigid 8-9 years of age. Hence, intervention should work best in primary schools.

A few major intervention strategies are:

1. Contact

Contact has been advocated by Allport (1954) as a means to reduce stereotypes. The logic is that contact helps in reality testing. As a result, our negative attitudes, stereotypes and false beliefs get falsified.

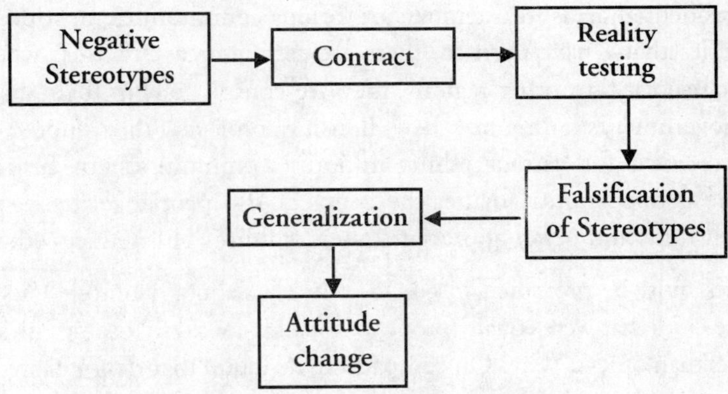

Fig. 9.5 : Role of contact in reducing negative stereotype

Numerous studies have demonstrated the effectiveness of contact in preventing prejudices. However, contact as an intervention strategy can fail if some conditions are not there. For example, the upper castes and lower castes have been in contact from time immemorial (except the untouchable castes). Then, why couldn't a Brahmin realise that there was nothing special in him which is absent in other castes? Hence is the need to fulfil the conditions for contact to succeed.

These are:

1. Contact should be equal status contact.
2. No competition, but co-operation and pursuit of common (superordinate) goals.

3. Intervention should monitor and increase the frequency, duration and meaningfulness of interaction between members of various groups.
4. Institutional support from government employers and teachers is necessary.
5. Contact fails if these agents are not enthusiastic.

The contact between higher castes and lower castes for generations failed because the contact wasn't equal status contact. Upper castes believed that they originated from some superior part of Brahma's body and so had higher status. Their higher status affected their interaction. Another major factor is the frequency, duration and meaningfulness of contact. I have observed that many students from North-East India come to study in Delhi University. But they stay in their groups and their interaction with others is minimal and limited to academics. This doesn't reduce prejudice, rather may increase prejudices.

Strategies based on the above philosophies are:

- Diversity should be promoted in schools and colleges. Teachers should be trained to give tasks that encourage co-operation among students. Greater premium must be given to members of minority community, lower caste students, children of single parents, children from different regions, etc. during admission to nursery classes.
- Common residential areas for members of various communities must be encouraged. In all the cities that I have been to, there are certain areas (ghettos) where Muslims live in great majority. In other regions, they are conspicuous in their absence. When the state governments announce new housing projects, they should keep some percentage reserved for various ethnic minority communities. In a single housing society, there is opportunity for healthy contact. Also people get to see each other's habits and customs and better appreciate others' culture. This reduces ethnocentrism.
- Civil societies must be promoted in cities. Political scientist Ashutosh Varshney (2003) studied some cities that were equally prone to riots. He found that some cities experienced far more riots than others. Why? On comparison, he found that riots are low in cities with strong civil society groups because they act as contacts between various communities. Here, institutional support from government to promote civil society is essential.

2. Superordinate Goals

Setting of superordinate goals has shown positive results as an intervention strategy in schools. Aronson and his co-workers' (1992) 'jigsaw method' is an example. They provided some problems for children in schools to work on. However, to solve the problems, special skills of each student of the group needs to be applied. A student may be good at reading, but not good at writing precise. Another may be good at summarising. So, give them a task where each one uses her special skill towards fulfilment of superordinate goals. When the students participating in the activity are from diverse background; prejudices reduce.

In organisations, diversity management strategies should include business games that create superordinate goals. Similarly, panchayats should be composed of women members and members from SC and ST background. Community activities should include these members. Co-operation fosters understanding.

3. Categorisation techniques

Group conflict and group prejudices develop because of categorisation of people into groups. Hence, a logical strategy is to restructure mental representations regarding categorisation.

There are three main strategies to tackle categorisation:

1. Re-categorisation
2. De-categorisation
3. Cross-categorisation

Re-categorisation seeks to develop a common identity (for example, "Indian"), rather than many distinct identities. The existence of a shared identity decreases the salience of differences between two groups and highlights the commonalities. In de-categorisation, interventions try to eliminate group categorisations. Group prejudices develop when we start believing that all members of a group are similar. So, train the students to understand that individual differences exist. This is called individuation. Train people to perceive an individual as a unique person, rather than member of a group.

Problem with re-categorisation in India is that ethnic differences are significant and salient. Factors, like caste and religion are important parts of the self-concept of a person. De-categorisation can be effective in Indian context, but needs lot of training resources. A strategy which has been found to be especially fruitful in the Indian context is cross-categorisation.

'Crossed categorisation refers to the crossing of one dichotomous categorisation (A/B), by a second one (X/Y). This means that some people who belong to a group according to one categorisation, simultaneously belong to another group according to a second categorisation'. (Hutnik, 2004). For example, groups are formed by categorisation. So, an Oriya may categorise all people into two categories – Oriya and non-Oriya. This is a dichotomous categorisation. In crossed categorisation, you create another dichotomous categorisation, say, Indian and non-Indian. Now, the individual doesn't form two groups, but four; they are:

- Oriya, Indian
- Oriya, non-Indian
- Non-Oriya, Indian
- Non-Oriya, non-Indian

Earlier, a categorisation into Oriya and non-Oriya made all non-Oriyas as out-group. After crossed-categorisation, non-Oriya Indian aren't an out-group! Hence, the negative stereotypes against non-Oriya Indians, if any, aren't strong enough.

The effectiveness of cross-categorisation has been demonstrated empirically in Indian conditions. Indeed, one of the earliest studies on this was done in India. Sridhara (1984) studied the attitudes of monolingual (Kannada only) and bilingual (Kannada and Tamil) children between the ages of 8 and 10 years. He found that bilingual children perceived fewer differences between Kannada and Tamil people. In another study, Ghosh and Huq (1985) studied prejudices of Bengali Hindu and Benali Muslim subjects in India and Bangladesh. This study is significant because here language was crossed with religion. The conclusions were also encouraging. Inter-group differentiation was found to be low.

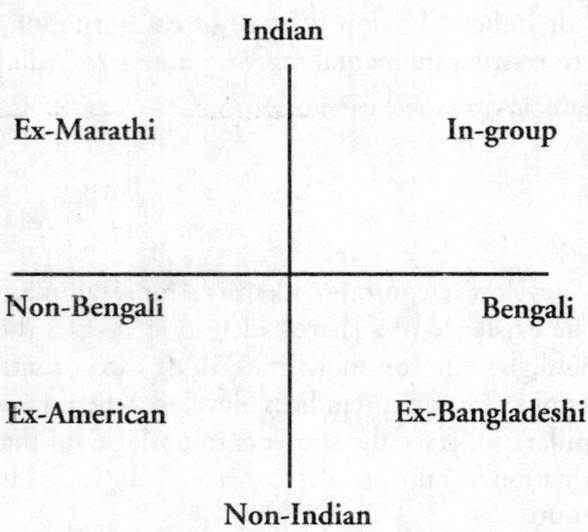

Fig. 9.6 : Mental Representation of Crossed-categorizations

4. *Propaganda*

Hassan (1981) observes that when a person faces with a dilemma of choosing one of her several dilemmas, she chooses the identity which has greater social respectability. Indians have plural identities and in interpersonal and inter-group relations, people can 'switch' identities. Naturally, making the 'Indian identity' the strongest identity helps. This can be done by propaganda and by value education in schools. 'Unity in diversity' was a motto I learnt in school and it has strongly influenced my psyche. I respect the pluralities in Indian society, even while being proud of being an Oriya agnostic! School curriculum should be drawn keeping this in mind that plural identities must be respected, but Indian identity must be strengthened.

5. *Self-counterconditioning*

Many attitudes form by conditioning. Especially, prejudices are conditioned by parents and peer groups during socialisation. A technique to handle such conditioning is self-counterconditioning, which primarily involved role-play.

Some suggestions to teachers to use role-play to reduce prejudice have been given by Venkatasubrahmanyan (1973):

(a) Ask students to collect information that highlights merits of people against whom students have developed prejudices. For example, if a Hindu student believes that all Muslims are violent, ask her to collect information about sayings of Prophet

Mohammad on peace, on the discourses of Sufi saints, etc. The teacher's praise acts as an operant counter condition to reduce prejudices.

Similarly, the student may be asked to do a project on the merits she has observed in an out-group. Often, we are prejudiced against tribal groups because we don't understand their culture. A study of their culture for a project work or presentation helps her to better understand the culture of out-groups.

(b) Students can be made to play the role of an out-group member in a psycho-drama depicting the out-group members favourably. For example, a Brahmin prejudiced against a Dalit may be asked to play the role of a Dalit who has been discriminated against. Such exercises help a student to take on the perspective of others.

(c) Books and literature highlighting the merits of the out-group should be made available in the library and should be incorporated in school curriculum.

(d) Students can be made to participate in group discussions and competitions, where they indirectly do role-play by arguing in favour of an out-group. For example, why do you think tribal people lead a happier life than more civilised ones? How is their dormitory culture better than ours? What about their egalitarianism and honesty?

6. Modeling Influence

One often tries to imitate the actions and feelings of a role model. 'Gandhians' are a group of people who follow the ideals of Gandhi. Such is the power of modeling. No wonder, it is considered an effective strategy to reduce prejudice and conflicts.

Venkatasubrahmanyan (1973) has suggested certain strategies to be used by teachers in schools to reduce prejudice:

(a) Some students are very popular and influential in school. Such students often become house leaders or captains in certain activities. They are role models for other students. The teacher can make such popular student leaders play the role of an out-group member in a favourable light. When the student leader is rewarded for playing such roles or doing good deeds (by symbolic rewards like praise or medals), other students get vicarious reinforcement.

(b) Punishment of role models is also a strategy. If a prejudiced role model is rebuked and ashamed for her prejudiced views, students get discouraged from expressing their anti-feelings.

(c) Teachers are themselves role models for students and their behaviours and views affect students. Hence, the teachers should be trained to express favourable attitudes towards out-groups.

7. Personal Value Confrontation Technique

Psychological theorists, we have seen, stress on personality factors in prejudice and conflict. We need to account for individual differences in developing prejudice. The authoritarian personality is more vulnerable to join right wing extremist organisations, like Bajrang Dal and Students' Islamic Movement of India (SIMI), than others. Some interventions can target youths who are influenced by right-wing ideologies. One strategy of targeted intervention that has received good support is the personal value confrontation technique.

In this technique, cognitive dissonance is brought about by showing the discrepancy between their attitudes. For example, a radical individual who considers himself a nationalist and is prejudiced against minorities, can be reasoned that a nationalist stand for his nation. The spirit of the nation is the Constitution of India. The Constitution stands for equality, freedom and human rights. Then how can he commit human rights violation against the minorities? When the attention of authoritarians is drawn towards the incongruity between their personal values, their attitudes tend to improve.

Measures to Achieve Social Integration

Psychologists have conducted empirical studies and have used the results to guide us with strategies for handling conflict and prejudice. But, these strategies will remain bookish strategies unless made a part of public policy. Social integration is an important objective of the government. Hence, public policies have to be devised to achieve social integration. Based on the strategies for reducing prejudice and conflict, what measures can policymakers take to achieve social integration?

We will discuss some measures that have been taken in India and internationally, with examples:

(a) Integration of ethnic minorities

In any society, there is a majority group (Hindu people/ Hindi speaking people/ caste Hindus) and many ethnic minorities (Muslims/ Tamils/ Tribal groups). What should be the right policy towards minorities?

Broadly, there are four styles to cope with minority status:

1. Assimilation: Assimilatory style refers to completely accepting the majority culture (A) while giving up one's original culture, i.e., A+B=A.
2. Integration: It refers to a style wherein positive qualities of both cultures are sought. The two cultures (majority and minority) interact to produce a composite culture.
3. Separation: Here, the two cultures co-exist in a society, but do not interact. The interaction is only superficial.
4. Marginalisation: In this situation, the minority community doesn't interact with the majority. At the same time, it is marginalised from access to resources to such an extent that it cannot maintain its own culture.

Let me give some examples to explain the four concepts above. You must have met some people who say that Hindi is the national language and must be enforced throughout the country. They are assimilationists. They want to impose their culture (language is a part of culture) on non-Hindi speaking population.

Separation is widely visible in Indian cities between Hindus and Muslims. Due to mutual suspicion and prejudice, Hindus stay in Hindu localities and Muslims stay in Muslim localities. Their contact and interaction is superficial. It is said that the rich language Urdu was formed when Persian met Sanskritic languages. There have been great many cultural interactions between Hindus and Muslims in history. But, today owing to prejudices and fear of riots, they remain separated.

Marginalisation is a problem faced by many tribal groups. Whenever a new heavy industry is set up in tribal areas, they are displaced. Further, the influx of non-tribal persons to work in the industries leads to cultural distortion of tribal cultures (which have evolved in isolation). Hence, the tribes stand marginalized.

I explained these terms because you need to understand social integration in the right context. The best strategy to bring about social integration is to respect diversity and cherish commonalities between various groups. The Sri Lankan Government did not respect diversity and imposed Lankan dialect on Tamils. This snowballed into a civil war! India, on the other hand, respected its linguistic diversity. States were formed on linguistic lines and Hindi was made only a nominal national language. This led to integration!

Hence, important principles of social integration are:

- Respect diversity. Do not try to assimilate minorities. Rather, stress unity in diversity. Respect the plural identities, but make the Indian identity the strongest of all identities.
- Encourage cultural interaction and understanding.
- Respect the political and economic rights of minorities, such as tribes. Ascertain equity and fairness in resource allocation to various communities. Establishing industries by displacing tribes gives job benefits to engineers and technicians who will work in those industries, not the tribes. On another note, the extremely low representation of Muslims in government jobs needs to be looked into.

(b) De-segregation in schools

Students should not be segregated on the basis of their ethnicity. Psychology tells us that the government should make de-segregation as a pre-condition for funding and support. Government should promote a healthy ethnic mix in schools in order to promote 'contact' between children of different ethnic backgrounds. Towards this goal, the government should enforce affirmative action and reservation for ethnic minorities and lower castes. However, mere reservation will not work. Governments need to ensure that each classroom should have a healthy ethnic mix and schools should celebrate festivals and customs of all ethnicities.

That de-segregation in schools promotes social integration and reduces prejudice has been acknowledged by the US Supreme Court. There were separate public schools for 'coloured' students in the USA few decades back. In what is now considered an important reform in the USA, psychologist Kenneth Clark rallied his colleagues working in social psychology to agitate for common public schools for White and Coloured people. Some of the greatest social psychologists of America testified as expert witness in the US Supreme Court. The Supreme Court concluded that segregation of White and Coloured people in the USA had detrimental effect on Coloured people and ordered the government to desegregate public schools.

Cue from such public policy cases is that government should ensure that government-funded schools and colleges, even if run as minority institutions, should have a healthy mix of ethnicities.

(c) Training and propaganda

Propaganda goes a long way in promoting amity between ethnic groups. Government can run propaganda through its PR wing, through its television programmes and through the school curriculum. Another strategy is to train students in associating positive characteristics with out-groups and vocally dissociating negative traits associated with out-groups. One oft-cited success story of training leading to social integration is that of the US Army. There was significant animosity between White and Coloured soldiers in the US Army up until the late 1970s. In the 1980s, the US Army consciously implemented training programs to increase co-operation between White and Coloured soldiers.

One effective strategy applied by the US Army was the level playing field. All soldiers were treated similarly right from probation. Training was equally rigorous for White and Coloured soldiers. The training academy had a no-discrimination policy and punished any expression of racist sentiment with unfavourable rating and even termination of military career.

The National Academy of Direct Taxes (NADT) at Nagpur requires its trainees to conduct cultural evenings on certain occasions. Every cultural evening has a 5-minute programme on national integration. It may be in the form of cultural parade or a fusion of folk dances from around the country. Such cultural programmes helps trainees appreciate cultural diversity. It also improves co-operation and co-ordination.

(d) Second language learning

Bilingualism increases multiculturalism. When a child learns a new language over and above her mother-tongue, she develops the ability to interact with children from other cultures. This improves *cultural contact*, and thus multiculturalism. This theory suggests that rather than imposing a single language across the country (English or Hindi), students should be encouraged to gain proficiency in at least one language, other than the mother-tongue. Schools in UP and Bihar should offer Tamil and Oriya as second language, while schools in Tamil Nadu and Orissa should offer Hindi and Gujarati as the second language.

■ ■ ■

10

PSYCHOLOGY OF TERRORISM

Chapter outline

10.1 Psychology of Terrorism

Terrorism has been a subject of intense study in the file of psychology. Yet, there is no consensus about what constitutes terrorism. Terrorism, simply put, is any act of violence against innocent, unarmed civilians. Hence, it can include:

- State sponsored terrorism (e.g., Nazi terror)
- Majority terrorism (e.g., Riots)
- Minority terrorism (e.g., Bomb blasts, suicide attacks)
- Terrorism supported by external agencies

The focus of psychological study is the terrorist organisation, its members and its group dynamics. But before we get into it, we should differentiate between terrorism and secessionism. Please not that my focus here is the kind of terrorism in India sponsored by external agencies, like Naxalite terror, separatist movements of North-East, Punjab issue, Huji and LeT, among other organisations. In this perspective, terrorism refers to "the use or threat of violence, by small groups against non-combatants of large groups, for avowed political goals" (Kallen, 1979, p.9). Hence, while secessionism is a goal, terrorism is a means to a goal.

In this chapter, we will look into certain misconceptions in psychological literature regarding the terrorists and go on to study the real nature of terrorist organisations and various group and individual factors involved therein.

10.2 Terror Profiling and its Criticism

In the beginning, psychological studies of terrorism tried to draw up a "psychological profile" of terrorists, i.e., a common personality disposition that explains all terrorist acts. Psychologists reasoned that if a person can commit such ghastly acts (killing women and children) without any moral bearing, then he must be mentally ill. Further, it was reasoned that terrorists are poor, illiterate and brain-washed; that they come from narcissistic families. However, various terrorist attacks have consistently revealed that many terrorists come from normal families, have stable jobs and a happy, married life. Mumbai Police have caught some terrorists who used to work in high-profile software companies and hard six-figure pay!

The mental illness explanation has been discredited today. Most modern day terrorists are highly literate and are mentally healthy. That is the reason why they easily get mixed up in crowds. Hence, Nimmi Hutnik (2004) reasons that the search for a "terrorist personality" has been somewhat useless. This is because, she argues, 'terrorism is essentially a group phenomenon. Terrorist organisations are not just aggregates of separate individuals; they are groups that exact stringent conformity, hold a common set of norms and values, offer lucrative rewards and mete out heavy punishments'. It can be confidently concluded, that terrorists represent a psychologically heterogeneous population. Various factors, including psychopathology, are responsible for terrorism; but not only a single factor is necessary or sufficient for terrorism.

Terrorists are ordinary people. How can ordinary people perform such deeds?

If terrorists are ordinary people, a second question is- how can ordinary people do such acts? It is tough for us to believe when we read news reports that software engineers or students might have conducted acts of violence. Many find it so unbelievable that they accuse the police of fabricating innocents as terrorists!

That ordinary people can perform evil deeds under the right circumstances has been validated by two classic studies of social psychology- Milgram (1974) and Zimbardo (1972).

These two studies show that even if an individual views an activity as morally wrong, he may indulge in it. Stanley Milgram (1974), a Yale university psychologist, showed that obedience to authority relieves many people of moral responsibility, thus making them more likely to behave cruelly towards others. Milgram recruited subjects through advertisements in a local newspaper for a "Study in Memory". He instructed the participants to quiz an individual (his accomplice) on a task of memory. If the individual gives wrong answers, the participant should give him/her electronic shocks. The shocks were not real, but the accomplice acted as if he suffered from shock. Milgram found that many participants easily applied high shocks for minor errors in memory recall!

'Milgram's study clearly demonstrates that, under certain circumstances, the tendency to obey an authority figure is very strong, even when causing harm to an innocent person. This may explain why terrorists who sacrifice themselves through suicide bombs are vulnerable to the command of those perceived as authority figures in a terrorist cell. The masterminds of terror operations may have significantly social authority and influence over their followers and often a simple request is all that is necessary for a terrorist act' (Zillmer, 2006).

In another experiment, Philip Zimbardo (1972) asked a group of ordinary college students to spend time in a simulated prison. Some were randomly given the duty of guards and were given uniforms. They were instructed to enforce certain rules. The remainder became prisoners, were locked in cells and were asked to wear humiliating outfits. Zimbardo observed that after some time, the simulation became very real, as guards became cruel and devised degrading routines. From this study, we know that once someone is assimilated into a terror cell, it becomes easy to take on the role of a terrorist.

How does one become a terrorist?

A previous notion about why anyone becomes a terrorist was that some psycho-social disorders or inherent disposition impel a person to become a terrorist. But, this has long been debunked, since terrorism is a group phenomenon. However, social psychologists could not explain for long as to why a person would decide to become a terrorist. Borum (2004) draws on recent research to conclude that a person who becomes a terrorist rarely makes a conscious decision to become a terrorist. Most involvement in terrorism happens by gradual exposure and socialisation. According to Borum, two key psychological factors are involved in it.. These are *motives* and *vulnerability*. Motive is a need, while vulnerability is susceptibility to succumb to persuasion or temptation. Motive is a push factor, while vulnerability is a pull factor.

There are four categories of motivation among persons who become terrorists. These are:

(a) The opportunity for action

(b) The need to belong

(c) The desire for social status

(d) The acquisition of material reward

There are three categories of vulnerability among persons who become terrorists. These are:

(a) Perceived injustice

(b) Strong identity with the in-group

(c) Belonging with the in-group

When motivation, vulnerability and opportunity are there, a person gets exposed and socialized into a life of terroristic violence in steps. Frederick Hacker (1983) developed a model that shows progression into terrorist violence in three phases. These are:

(a) *Phase 1:* Awareness of oppression

(b) *Phase 2:* Recognition that the oppression was 'social' and therefore not unavoidable

(c) *Phase 3:* Realisation, that it is possible to act against the oppression

(d) *Initiation as a terrorist:* At the end of the third phase, the individual concludes that working within the system to reform will not work; and starts believing that self-help by violence is the only effective means of change.

Based on an analysis of multiple militant groups, Borum (2004) has arrived at four phases in which an individual becomes a terrorist. We shall try to demonstrate these phases with examples in Kashmir. These are:

(a) *Its not right:* Socialisation for terroristic violence begins with a grievance or some perceived wrong in the person's social environment. Taking the case of Kashmir, separatists have been active in Kashmir since a long time. Separatists were tolerated as India is a democracy and thus, tolerates all kind of ideologies. Terrorism grew in Kashmir only since early 1990s. Terrorism in initial years were sponsored from cross-border. But, the phenomenon in recent years is home-grown terror. Why has terrorism grown in Kashmir in recent years? As per armed force veterans, it is because Wahabi priests are dominating the mosques of Kashmir valley. They have replaced the peace-loving Sufi priests. Wahabi priests develop a perception of wrong-doing on part of the establishment in prayer meetings, community gatherings and in madarasas. This is the first step of socialization.

(b) *Its not fair:* A perceived wrong or deprivation promotes grievance, but not resentment. Resentment happens when the deprivation is a relative deprivation; that is, when the individual feels that the wrong-doing is unjust. In Kashmir, many supporters of Burhan Wani (the Hizbul Mujahideen terrorist who was gunned down in 2016) consider the encounter an injustice on their fellow citizen. Many individuals developed resentment against the offensive action of the security personnel.

(c) *Its your fault:* In the third phase of socialisation, the individual is made to believe that although bad things may happen in life, injustices happen due to some cause. When an individual starts believing that he or his in-group has been a victim of injustice, then he presumes that someone else is in fault for the condition. In Kashmir, the youth have attributed blame with the Indian State.

(d) *You are evil:* Up until now, there was only resentment. But, resentment does not induce a person to engage in terroristic violence. For him to shed his inhibitions to aggressive behaviour and engage in violence, he needs a justification. This is usually done by dehumanizing the victims, by casting them as evil. Terrorists in Kashmir attack and kill innocent civilians because they have branded the civilians as evil.

10.3 The Terrorist Organisation

The research literature regarding psychology of terrorism is small in quantity. This may be because of the fact that terrorists are elusive figures. Psychologists don't usually have access to terror organisations. Yet, some studies on imprisoned terrorists have helped us to understand some basics regarding the terror groups. Here, I seek to focus on the terrorist organisation than the terrorist, because as contended earlier, terrorism is a group phenomenon.

The dynamics of these organisations can be studied as under:

1. Recruitment
2. Group dynamics
3. Motivational processes
4. Decision-making

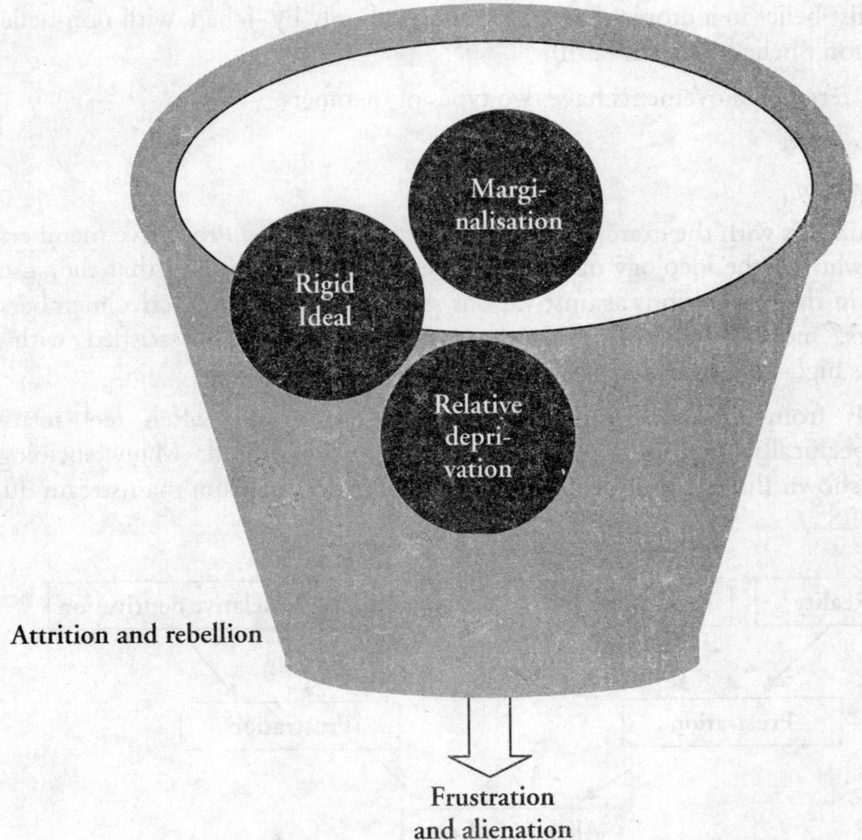

Fig. 10.1 : Psychological factors behind frustration and alienation

1. Recruitment

Although terror recruits come from a psychologically heterogeneous background, there are a few conditions that motivate an individual to join a terrorist group. Zillmer (2006) argues that there are some pre-requisites that lead an individual towards terrorism.

Many studies conducted on terrorists in Jails of Israel and USA have revealed that terrorists are frustrated and disillusioned with society. There may be many reasons for disillusionment. Many well-educated, intellectual studies resort to terrorism. Zillmer explains that these students have a rigid ideal. When faced with reality, they get frustrated. For example, who join Naxalite movements? Many members of Naxalite forces are rural peasants and tribal, but many city-based educated students participated in it. These students have a rigid view of the world; they rigidly follow an ideology based on some interpretation of Marxism. Finding that reality is more imperfect than the 'communists utopia' promised by Marx, many of these students join the Naxalite movements. Same is the case with many radicalised Islamic students. They have a fundamentalist belief in a utopia that can be achieved only by 'Jehad' with non-believers (those who don't believe in their faith).

Typically, terrorist movements have two types of members:

1. Pro-active
2. Reactive

Let me explain this with the example of the Naxalite movement. Pro-active members are the leaders, who set the ideology of the movement; it has been found that they use hi-tech laptops in their operations against various state police forces! Reactive members are the followers, mostly drawn from lower castes and tribals, dissatisfied with the government's high-handedness.

Individuals from low socio-economic status (SES) groups often feel relatively deprived. Specifically, the unemployed youth feel marginalised. Many sociological studies have shown that minority youth in India feel frustrated from mainstream due to their lower SES.

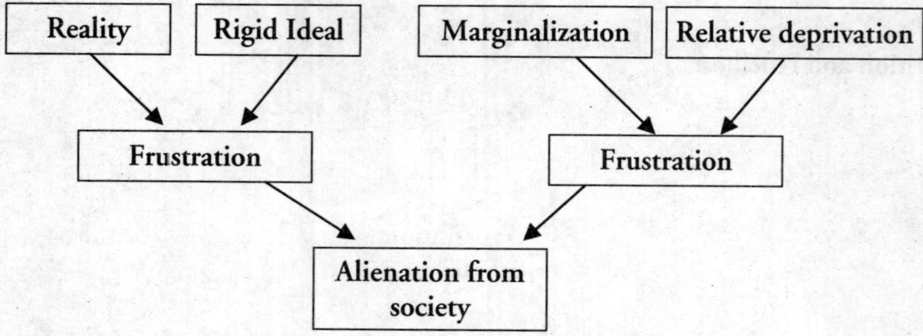

Fig. 10.2 : Factors that prompt individuals to join a terrorist group

Now, why would these frustrated individuals join a terrorist group? These frustrated youths are alienated from society. They don't have a strong status in mainstream groups. For them, the terrorist organisation becomes a peer group. In the group, their social esteem is high. In India, many peer groups of unemployed youths from ethnic minority communities feel alienated from mainstream due to various socio-economic reasons. These groups are picked by terror cells of external agencies, like ISI and Harkat-e-Mujahideen (HeM) that give their life a so-called meaning.

2. Group Dynamics

The terror network of an organisation may be vast, but various terror cells are small groups, where intense, face-to-face interaction happens. This results in strong group solidarity. Due to group solidarity, group identity becomes more important than self-identity. The individual's personal attitudes become irrelevant; he is ready for self-sacrifice for group cause. This partly explains suicide bombings.

3. Motivational Processes

The terrorist organisation fulfills various needs of the individual. Group goal provides a meaning to the life of individuals alienated from society. In a literature survey, Hutnik (2004) has observed that beyond material rewards (terrorism is a major employer in Pakistan!), there are emotional, social and cognitive rewards also, as:

- Common hatred of a common enemy is a strongly shared emotional need.
- The group acts as a substitute for family and fulfills the need for love and affection.
- The individual's sense of self-righteousness fulfills cognitive needs and enhances self-esteem.
- Media attention serves as an important reinforcement for the need for power.

4. Decision-making

In terrorist organisations, members move towards greater extremes of behavior and ideology. Why does this happen? This tendency is called **risky shift phenomenon**. This happens due to group thinking. In group thinking, individuals in a group tend to think similarly. As a result, all tend to veer towards supporting extreme ideas. Group thinking takes place due to various reasons represented in the following diagram:

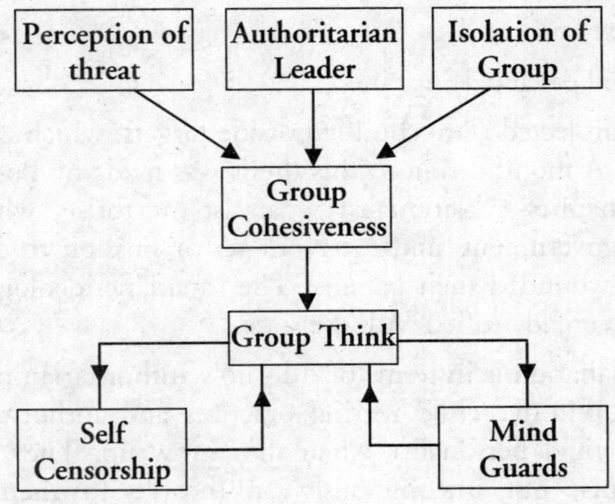

Fig. 10.3 : Reasons for group thinking

All the above factors are satisfied by a terror group. The leader is often radical and authoritarian; the group operates covertly and is often isolated. Further, group cohesiveness ensures that members self-censor any opposition they have, to the decisions taken. Due to this, decision taken tends to be extremist in nature. Even a non-terrorist group with common anti-national ideology may become terrorist group because of risky shift.

5. Attrition and Rebellion

The terrorist organisation is one which doesn't have an exit policy for its employees! There are strong group norms against any form of rebellion. Post (2007) argues that if anyone leaves, it is upsetting to others. Also, defection can set a trend. Hence, those who leave the organisation are pursued by their former companions. This makes the effort of the government to induce them to surrender and rehabilitate more challenging.

Personality Dynamics

Today there is a consensus among scholars that terrorism can be best understood by group factors rather than individual factors. Yet, the ***personality pathology*** thesis is still adhered to by few scholars. Presently, the most fashionable versions of this thesis are Neo-Freudian theories, specifically the contributions of Post (1984).

Though this thesis may not be completely correct, it may be able to answer a few questions. Who are more vulnerable to becoming terrorists? Take the hypothetical condition of two individuals in same situation. One joins a terror organisation and another doesn't. Why? This thesis suitably explains the differences.

The essence of Neo-Freudian explanations is that narcissistic wounds at an early age split the self into two parts:

(a) A grandiose "me" and

(b) A hated and devalued "not me"

The second self is projected onto specific outside targets, which are blamed and hence, become scapegoats. A modification to this thesis was made by Post. Post identified two types of inner dynamics- "Nationalist-Separatist" terrorists who are loyal to their parents, reject the government, and carry out terror mission to take revenge from the government which wounded their parents. The "anarchic-ideologues" who are disloyal to their parents, and are identified with the state.

An alternate explanation is in terms of Adorno's authoritarian personality (Adorno et al., 1950). Due to punitive child rearing practices and authoritarian parenting style, children develop a rigid personality when they grow up. They consciously love and respect their parents, but unconsciously are hostile to them. They project the unconscious hostility as hatred towards weaker sections. Hence, they are intolerant to ambiguity and show excessive conformity and submission.

10.4 Solution to the Problem of Terrorism

There are three major kinds of terrorism affecting the Indian nation- majority terrorism, minority terrorism and externally-sponsored terrorism. Majority terrorism includes ethnic and communal conflicts; these are mostly political problems and can be resolved by political will. What about minority terrorism? Few active minority terrorist groups are SIMI, Indian Mujahideen, Nationalist Socialist Council of Nagaland (NSCN), United Liberation Front of Assam (ULFA), etc. Right wing political forces are extremely critical of these groups; they advocate ban on these organisations and also repressive laws, like Prevention of Terrorism Act (POTA). How far are these effective? From a psychological perspective, repressive laws can aggravate terrorism, rather than reducing it.

Tough terror laws work on the principle of theory of deterrence. This theory presupposes that the perpetrator will carry out a rational cost benefit analysis before engaging in the terror act- if the costs (severe punishments) outweigh the benefits (gain from crime), the terrorist will resist. This is based on ***normative models*** of decision-making. This deterrence model, however, fails to stop terrorist acts, because these are crimes of passion or ideology. "Suicide bombers", or Jehadis do not make any rational calculations before carrying out attacks. The theory of deterrence simply fails to understand human irrationality.

Confrontation *vs.* Negotiation

Applying the Norm-Violation Theory of deRidder and Tripathi (1997), it can be said that if Group A (Police) break the norms of Group B (terrorist organisation) by repression and brutality, Group B would be hurt and further be motivated to break the norms of Group A, by causing law and order problems (For the theory in detail, see the chapter on prejudices and social integration). Hence, confrontation is not a long-term solution. Terrorists would keep bouncing back; worse, they would use more innovative means to attack and create terror if repression is used. Hence, POTA is a noted solution. So, what are the strategies that can be used to remove terrorism?

1. Negotiation:

Negotiation is the best tool to increase understanding between two groups (here, the state and terrorist groups). Negotiations have been effectively used in co-option of many terrorist groups. For instance, many terror groups in North-East India that demanded freedom and a separate state have given up their terrorist methods after negotiations. The Bodo Autonomous Council as a solution to the Bodoland problem is an illustration. Negotiation with terror source countries, like Pakistan and Bangladesh, are also yielding slow but positive results.

Why does negotiation succeed? It succeeds because it helps reduce the prejudices of two sides and subsequently fosters understanding. The hatred of terrorist organisations and the activities of terror funding countries are a result of prejudices about the Indian state. For example, many neighboring countries perceive India as a huge country that can be a security threat anytime in the future.

2. Controlling Majority Terrorism

A major reason for minority terrorism in India is majority terrorism in the form of riots. Majority terrorism acts create a fear psychosis, that is, insecurity and hopelessness among minority groups. Some individuals from these groups have psychic wounds, which they project on the Indian state. In line with the Norm Violation Theory, it can be said that it is tough to suppress minority terrorism, but majority terrorism is often politically motivated and can be stopped by police reforms and appropriate delivery of justice system.

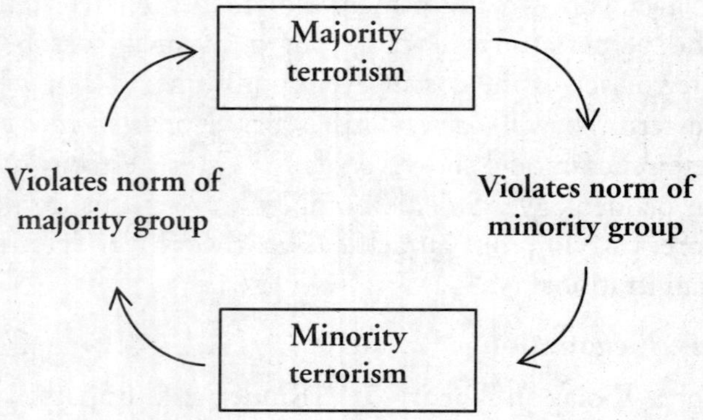

Fig. 10.4 : Inter-relationship between terrorism by majority and minority groups

3. Value Education:

A very effective intervention is school education of **peace** and non-violence and inculcation of a sense of nationhood. National integration can be best achieved by inculcating values regarding useful citizenship and tolerance.

It has been that of late, many terrorists caught are young, college-going students. They are basically fished young by ideologues and brain-washed. Hence, training in ***reflexive thinking*** and ***sensitization to community*** are useful means to combat terrorism.

Intervention strategy in high schools and colleges must concentrate on inculcating realistic ideals. Many terror recruits are disillusioned youths. These educated youth usually have unrealistic and rigid ideologies, as a result of which, they feel disillusioned when faced with reality. For instance, main leaders of the Naxalite terror attacks are educated students who hold the Marxian vision of a 'utopia', however impractical it may be. Their acceptance of Marxist ideology is rigid and their goals are unrealistic. Setting of realistic ideals and pragmatic world-view by teachers of social sciences is necessary.

4. Targeted interventions:

All members of a terrorist group don't have similar personality; there is no "terrorist personality". However, terrorists can be broadly divided as:

(a) Pro-active

(b) Reactive

Pro-active terrorists are those who have a misplaced sense of righteousness and rigid ideologies. They become leaders, mobilizing people on the lines of their ideology. Reactive terrorists, on the other hand, turn to terrorism to avenge for some perceived harm done by society. They are usually the followers and commit the ground-zero terror acts. For the proactive terrorists, a preventive step is not to let them become terrorists. Usually, these ideologues first become members of some ideological organisation before moving over to terrorism. When they are members of such ideological organisations (such as SIMI, RSS, VHP, CPI youth wings, etc.), they can be targeted by showing the ***discrepancy between their basic belief in compassion and humanity and their prejudiced attitude*** towards the state or society.

For the reactive terrorists, a preventive step is that, those individuals who have been orphaned by riots, or have suffered due to some violent acts can be targets for rehabilitation. The aim here is to heal the past wounds and to reintegrate them to mainstream society. Inability on our part to do this marginalizes them and they find solace in being part of a terror group and targeting their psychic wounds towards the government.

5. GRIT:

Osgood's (1962) Theory of Graduated and Reciprocated Initiatives in Tension Reduction (GRIT) states that if a nation makes some unambiguous peaceful gestures, the adversary is likely to reciprocate. This is the logic behind goodwill gestures, like unilateral ceasefire by Indian army in Kashmir valley every year during Ramzan. A problem with this approach is that the adversary in modern Islamic terrorism is faceless; how can one negotiate GRIT with them?

6. Psycho analytic methods:

Psycho analysts believe that the cause for terrorist activities can be attributed to the individual terrorist's personality. This makes it nearly impossible to apply this method to remove terrorism. Insight therapy can be done on a captured terrorist to rehabilitate him, but not on an individual prone to join a terrorist group.

Celebrated psycho analyst Sudhir Kakkar, however, gives some suggestions (Times of India, 02-10-2008). He states that violence is justified by our community and hence, internalized by us. He states that two qualities that we encourage in our children also encourage violence, they are—

1. Moral idealism
2. High self-esteem

Idealism is dangerous because 'it is inevitably accompanied by the belief that the end justifies the means. If you are fighting for God, for the oppressed or for your religious community, then what matters is the outcome, not the process'. Hence, you don't hesitate to take to terrorism.

Kakkar forwards a long-term strategy to deal with violence. In the long term, 'we need to focus our educational efforts on emphasising the value of compassion, of which fairness and tolerance are important constituents ...... compassion is as national as violence. We now know from experiments using brain imaging that watching the suffering of someone who appears to be a victim of violence, activates a similar "pain network" in our brains. Hence, educational institutions should focus on means rather than ends in giving moral education. From Kakar, we learn that morality can be harmful as it justifies ends. Further, moral idealism leads to a rigidity of opinion that legitimises any means (including terror) to reach at goals.

7. Rehabilitation:

Many recruits of terrorist organisations happen to be juveniles who are the product of broken homes or deprived environments. Juveniles with broken homes or with no home at all seek for a small group and strongly identify with their small group. According to Tajfel's Social Identity Theory (see chapter on prejudices), it is natural to boost the positives of one's own small group. If this small group (i.e., peer group) is picked up by a terror network, the individual naturally accepts terrorism and finds some justification. Hence, there is a need to rehabilitate juveniles facing social problems in childhood.

10.5 Victims of Terror

(Source: "Terror Anxiety cases up by 50%: Psychiatrist" in Times of India, 07-10-2008).

Terror attacks are unpredictable events that lead to acute stress. The victim, whether injured or not, has low control over the event and experiences low self-efficacy. The victim relives the experience again and again in her head even after the blast. Even if a victim has just heard the blast, it can lead to Post-Traumatic Stress Disorder (PTSD). Old persons and children are especially the victims for whom psychological problems are high. The very thought of another attack creates a sense of uncertainty and helplessness. Nightmares, fear of market places, loss of appetite and reclusive behavior are some symptoms that the individual suffers from terror trauma.

Some of the symptoms can be systematically presented as:

- Bad dreams
- Hearing blasts even when there is no blast
- Loss of appetite
- Disturbed sleep
- Reclusive behavior
- Conflict with family and friends

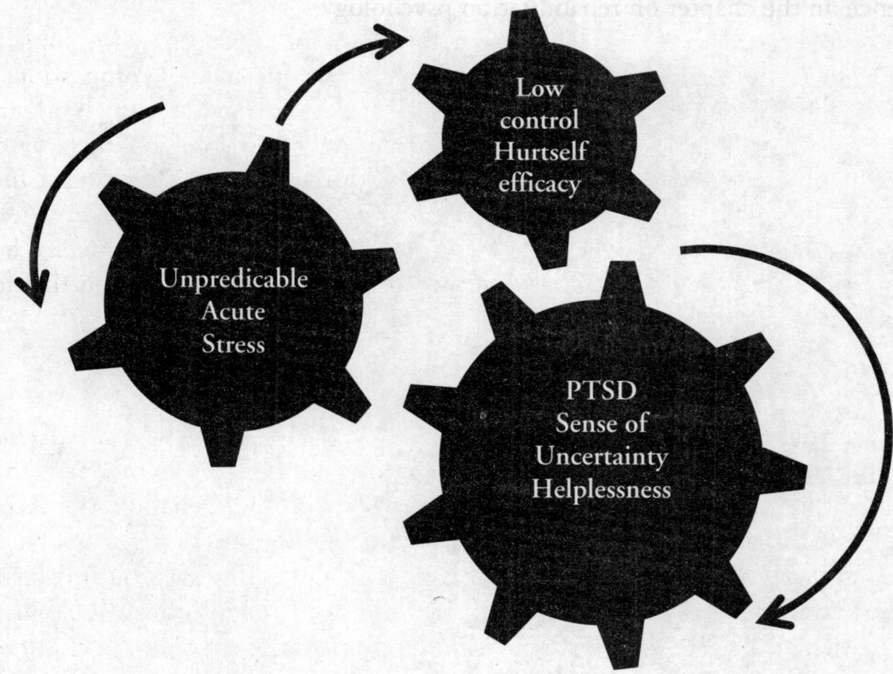

Fig. 10.5 : Psychological effect on victims of terror

To cope with terror trauma, the following five steps are suggested:

1. Talk. Voicing fears and listening to other's fears helps in release of internal panic.
2. Be vigilant of surroundings. This helps control the sense of helplessness.
3. Maintain routine, especially with children and adults.
4. Limit exposure to repeated news and discussions of violence.
5. Consult a psychologist, but only if symptoms persist or aggravate.

Experts reason that in terror trauma, family support is more important than professional help. Professional help must be sought only if the trauma persists or aggravates. Family members must ensure that the individual is not overwhelmed by the environment and must be made to feel secure.

Generalised Anxiety

Till a few years ago, trauma was limited to the affected. But now, the impact of terror images has seeped into the general public's subconscious, reasons Dr. Avdesh Sharma. For instance, in a recent event, many died because of stampede in a temple. The stampede happened because of a rumor that bombs were planted in the temple, leading to panic in the crowd. This shows the generalised fear psychosis that people are going through due to terrorist attacks.

Note: More angles are discussed under the heading 'rehabilitation of victims of violence' in the chapter on rehabilitation psychology.

■ ■ ■

11

PSYCHOLOGY OF GENDER

Chapter outline

11.1 Issues of Discrimination

Prejudice is an extreme attitude, often negative. Discrimination is the behavioral component of prejudice, the cognitive component being stereotype and the affective component manifesting itself in sexism. Allport (1954) proposed that the behavioral component of prejudice varies from minor to major forms of discrimination. He has talked about five stages in the continuum from minor behavioral discrimination to major ones:

1. Antilocution: Hostile talk, verbal denigration, sexist jokes, etc.
2. Avoidance: Keeping a distance, but not actively inflicting harm.
3. Discrimination: Exclusion from education and work, etc.
4. Physical attack: Violence against women.
5. Extermination: Not applicable in case of gender discrimination.

The issues of gender discrimination are multi-dimensional. Though Allport's classification provides a guideline, it is not enough to explain the whole gamut of discrimination against the female gender. Ruth E. Fassinger (2008) argues that there are three dimensions of discrimination, which together can be represented as given in the figure:

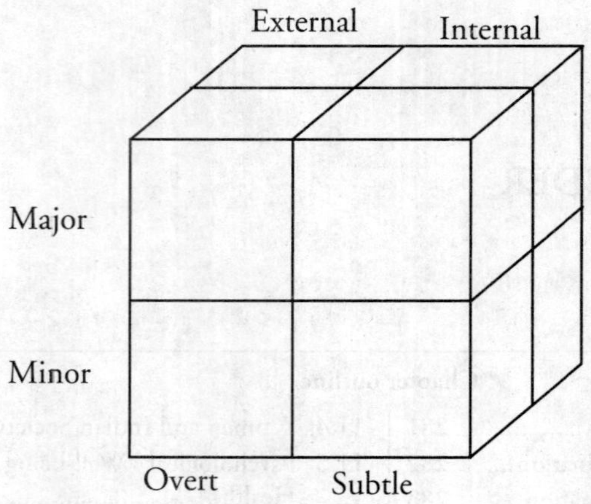

Fig. 11.1 : Dimensions of gender discrimination

I will discuss issues of discrimination in terms of above three axes.

Overt and Subtle Discrimination

Sexist events exist on a continuum that range from subtle to blatant. Blatant, or over sex discrimination has been defined by Benokraitis (1997) as unequal and harmful behavior towards women that is international, unambiguous and visible. It includes a range of behaviors, like job discrimination, differential salary, sexual harassment and physical violence. For instance, it has been found that there is a 'gap' in average pay of male and female employees doing the same job. Even jobs are categorised according to gender and are based upon society's stereotypes about who should become a manger and who should become a nurse. Unfortunately, the jobs that carry a female stereotype (like secretary, nurse, etc.) are low-paying, than those that are associated with male stereotypes (Shop floor engineers, managers, etc.).

Sexual harassment is another form of overt discrimination with grave implications. Asking for sexual favors, touching and playing with women's sexual organs are certain forms that this discrimination can take. It is not only unethical, but also may lead to demoralization and decreased self-esteem in women.

On the other end are subtle sexist behaviors. Subtle sexism includes behaviors like sexist jokes that denigrate women. It is often believed that such remarks and jokes are harmless, but research has shown that women are negatively affected by sexist humour (La France and Woodzicka, 1998). Benokraitis (1997) reasons that sexist jokes put women in a difficult situation where they have to choose between whether to laugh, so as not to offend colleagues and superiors, or not to laugh and be seen as humorless. Another example of subtle sexism is gender discrimination in the classroom.

External-Internal discrimination

External discrimination refers to external barriers and discriminatory behaviors. Internal discrimination, on the other hand, refers to discriminatory attitudes that have been internalised by women. For instance, take the case of Sati death of Roopa Kanwar in the 1980s. Sati was dignified by society to such an extent that she internalized the belief and voluntarily decided to burn with her husband's body. Similarly, you must have observed that many Bollywood songs contain the word "baby" for women. In general, women are typified as "item", "hot" and to use the local word, "maal". This is basically objectification of women's body. Women internalise this objectification, form an objectified body consciousness and accordingly, are obliged to look good. In some offices, sexual harassment in the form of indecent touch is internalized by women. Though their self-concept is hurt and self-esteem takes a beating, women suffer all this without complaint.

The worst form of internalisation is the internalisation of cultural devaluation of women. This often happens during socialisation. Parents use reinforcements and punishments to reinforce sex role stereotypes; at the same time the cultural devaluation of girls, widely prevalent in patriarchal societies like India, is also internalised. The major problem with internalisation of discrimination is that women can't even resist the discriminatory treatment. They see the discrimination as legitimate.

Major and Minor Discrimination

Let us take two organisations. In one, no training facilities are available to women, nor are they put in responsible posts. In another, all this is theoretically available but the women aren't encouraged to take advantage of training facilities. The discrimination in the first case is a major one, while in the second case it is a minor one. Both forms of discrimination have effect on women. Indeed, the effect on women can be quite similar. For example, if girls in a village aren't allowed to study in schools, it is a major form of discrimination. On the other hand, if they are allowed to attend school but there is no encouragement to excel, effectively their self-efficacy and expectation are low. As a result they don't' perform well. This is a minor form of discrimination, with similar effects as the major form.

Glass-ceiling Effect

In most modern organisations, the company policy advocates gender equity in recruitment and promotions. Theoretically, any woman employee can get to the top. This is also good for the organisation, because the most deserving of employees should rise to the top; this improves productivity. However, the situation, it seems, is different in practice. Only about 15% of the corporate officers of Fortune 500 companies are women and only six are CEOs. Why the discrepancy?

There are two possible explanations to this; one that women are less capable to be at the top and lead and thesecond possibility is that there exists an invisible barrier that prevents them from moving up. The first possibility has been proved wrong. Yes, women differ in terms of leadership styles. Eagly and Johnson (1990) reason that men and women can lead equally effectively; they only differ in terms of how they lead. Women managers are more interpersonally oriented, less autocratic and more participative. Yet, they are no less effective in leading.

Hence, the only explanation for low representation of women at the top is the existence of an invisible barrier, a glass ceiling above which women couldn't rise. It is a glass ceiling because the reasons for the barrier aren't visible, but psychological (invisible). Psychologists have found various factors in organisation that restrict the rise of deserving women to the top.

These can be studied as:

1. Stereotypes about women
2. Sex discrimination in the workplace
3. Informal networks
4. Women's personal constraints

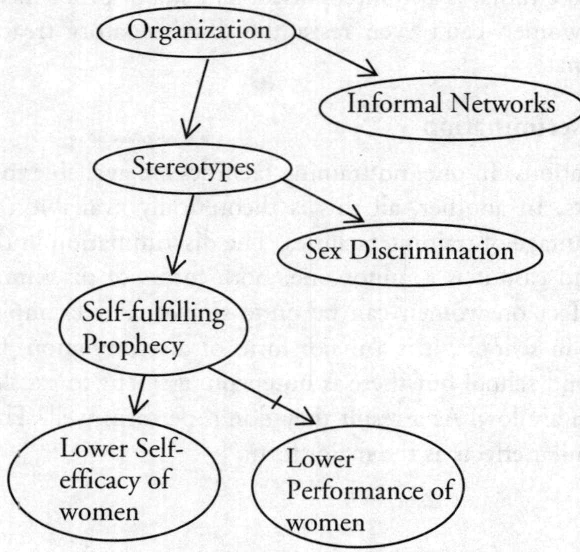

Fig. 11.2 : Elements of workplace that build up the glass ceiling

Sex role stereotypes are formed because of cultural factors. Many stereotypes are internalised by individuals at the time of socialisation. Media also plays a role in creating stereotypes of women mostly as mothers and wives. Someday, check the advertisements on television. You will find that most women represented in the ads are mothers or wives. Occasionally, a doctor or a personal secretary may be a woman. Women professionals are under-represented in the media. These stereotypes have a huge impact on how women are treated in the workplace.

For example, Eagly et al (2002) have found from a meta-analysis that women who exhibit a more masculine style are perceived as less effective, than women who use a feminine style. Also, women who use a feminine style are seen as less effective, than men who exhibit a masculine style! In a leaderless group consisting of both men and women, a man tends to emerge as the leader.

These stereotypes discourage women from rising in two ways:

1. Success in job performance of women is attributed to luck instead of ability (Ragins and Sundstrom, 1989).
2. Self-fulfilling prophecy that women can't perform a job efficiently makes women feel low on self-efficacy. This leads to decreased performance and reinforces the prophecy and prejudices.

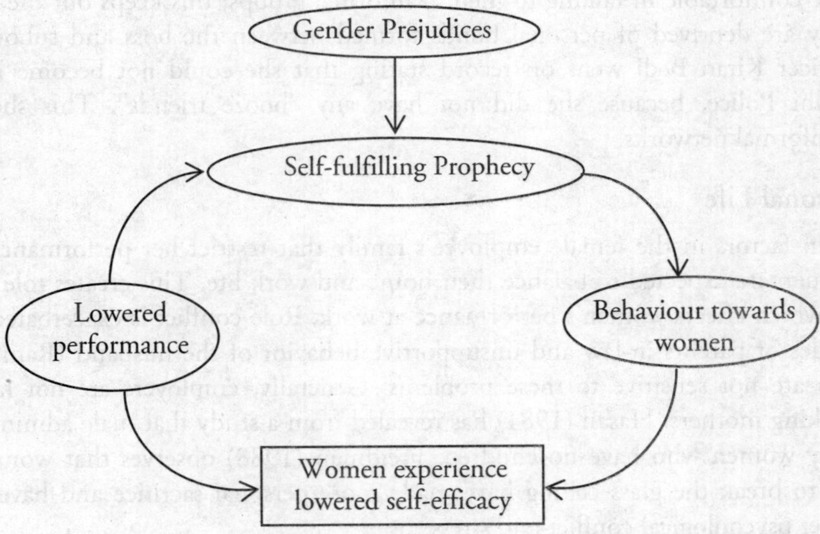

Fig. 11.3 : Dynamics of Self-fulfilling prophecy against women

Stereotypes also lead to sexual discrimination in the workplace. Many-a-times, managers don't realise that they are discriminating as the discrimination is subtle in form. For example, during job recruitment, the interviewers make a perception about the candidate from his/her biodata. In the face of limited information, biodata of women are screened out. Herriot (1989) reasons that unstructured interviews are prone to sex bias, as the interviewers are often male and are most likely to engage in a comfortable chat with male candidates. Training is an integral part of resource development. Even here, male employees are preferred. As a result, many female employees can't get exposure to managerial skills. Horgan (1989) opines that two underlying reasons explain why women continue to be largely unsuccessful in s organisations- it is much more difficult for women to gain managerial expertise; and most women's managerial experience has to be evaluated for sex appropriateness.

Ambiguous role expectations from women also reduce their performance at work. For instance, Morrison et al. (1987) reported from their research that contradictory expectations from women often derail their career. They are expected to be tough but not "macho"; to be ambitious, but no to expect equal treatment!

Verma and Stroh (2001) make an interesting observation that male supervisors tend to rate their male subordinates higher than their female sub-ordinates, while female supervisors tend to rate female sub-ordinates higher. Given that most managers at the top are male, only males are recruited to the top. This becomes a self-sustaining and self-reinforcing system.

11.2 Informal Networks

Many personal bonds are formed in the informal office networks. These are usually male-only groups. Men are comfortable in talking to men in informal groups; this keeps out the women. As a result, they are deprived of personal bonds formed between the boss and subordinates. Former IPS officer Kiran Bedi went on record stating that she could not become Director General of Delhi Police, because she did not have any "booze friends". This shows the importance of informal networks.

Women's Personal Life

There are certain factors in the female employee's family that restrict her performance in the workplace. Women are expected to balance their home and work life. This creates role conflict and high stress which affects women's performance at work. Role conflict is exacerbated by the inflexible attitudes of parents-in-law and unsupportive behavior of the husband (Rani, 1976). Even employers are not sensitive to these problems. Generally, employers are not favorably disposed to working mothers. Hasan (1981) has revealed from a study that male administrators prefer to employ women who have no children. Freidman (1988) observes that women who have succeeded to break the glass ceiling have made more personal sacrifice and have had to experience greater psychological conflict and stress.

11.3 Diversity Management

Diversity management is a managerial concept that believes that the sorganisation can take certain pro-active steps to break the glass ceiling and reduce discrimination against women and minority ethnic communities. In this section, we will concentrate on gender issues only.

The biggest challenge in shattering the glass ceiling and bringing about gender equity is that companies don't usually realise that the glass-ceiling exists. Since most of the discrimination is subtle and owing to psychological factors, these are not easily recognised. Once recognised, the best way to deal with them is to directly address the issues of discrimination.

Some of the initiatives that corporations have successfully taken are:

1. *Recruitment:* Unstructured interviews are quite subjective in nature and often tend to show sexist biases (Herriot, 1989). So, a better alternative is to take structured interview.

2. *Work culture:* To make the work environment more conducive to women, it needs to be changed. Work culture can be effectively changed by undertaking socialisation training programmes, like diversity-awareness training and harassment training. Diversity training programs teach people to 'confront personal prejudices that could lead to discriminating beahviours. Through lectures, videos, role playing and confrontational exercises, employees are learning, in a way, how it might feel to be a female worker being sexually harassed by a male boss. Trainees are forced to deal with their own sexist and racist attitudes and to learn to be more sensitive to the concerns and viewpoints of others' (Schults and Schults, 2002), P. 180).
3. *Glass ceiling:* This is best dealt with when it is recognised and directly attacked. Hence, steps, like tracking of progress and appraisal by managers should be taken. Wirth (2001) is of the opinion that career tracking identifies women with high potential and helps them gain visibility and experience. These high potential women are exposed to special leadership development jobs and training to facilitate their rise to the top. Parikha and Shah (1994) have studied 500 women in the management sector. They found that the attitude of the top management and the visibility of senior women professionals as role models were crucial for the growth of women employees.
4. *Women's Network*: Women's network in the workplace must be encouraged. Assignment of mentor is a significant step in enhancing women's position in the workplace. The availability of mentors has been directly linked to higher pay and greater career growth (Karen, 1985). s Organisation must, hence, try to formalise women's networks and mentorship programmes.
5. *Reducing role-conflict:* Substantial research has shown that an effective way to break the glass ceiling is by helping female employees better balance work and family responsibilities. Maternity leave, flexible work arrangements, telecommuting and flexi time are some measures the sorganisation can take to reduce role-conflict in women.

Gender stereotypes and self-fulfilling prophecy

A 'self-fulfilling prophecy' is a prediction that causes it to become true due to positive feedback between belief and behavior. The term was coined by sociologist Robert Merton. He described self-fulfilling prophecy as, 'The self-fulfilling prophecy is, in the beginning, a false definition of the situation evoking a new behavior which makes the original false conception come true. This specious validity of the self-fulfilling prophecy perpetuates a reign of error. For the prophet will cite the actual course of events as proof, that he was right from the very beginning.'

A simple example of self-fulfilling prophecy is when you see teachers discouraging a student. When teachers call a student an idiot and a simpleton, the student starts thinking that he is a simpleton and does not have the aptitude to study. So, she loses interest in studies. As a result, she gets low marks. This proves the teacher correct and reinforces the teacher's notions about the child.

Stereotypes often lead to self-fulfilling prophecy. Stereotypes are generalised view or pre-conception about attributes or characteristics that are or ought to be possessed by members of a particular social group. Yet, when a stereotype is used for a person, the person starts feeling that it is true. As a result, her behaviour changes and she acts in ways that conform the stereotype.

Stereotypes are pervasive in the interaction of a society with the female gender. These stereotypes creep in when the girl is a child and take deep roots in the girl child's mind. As per the United Nations Human Rights (UNHR), a **gender stereotype** is a generalised view or preconception about attributes, or characteristics that ought to be possessed by women and men or the roles that should be performed by men and women. Gender stereotypes can be both positive and negative, for example, "women are nurturing" or "women are weak".

Some common gender stereotypes associated with men and women are as under:

Men	Women
Men are tough and powerful. Men are unfeeling and insensitive. Men are logical, sensible and rational. Men are afraid to commit in a relationship and form an attachment. Men are primarily interested in their careers or vocations. Men do not have a primary interest in marriage and parenthood.	Women are helpless and childish. Women are sensitive and intuitive. Women are scatterbrained, unstable and irrational. Women can easily form deep emotional attachments. Women do not have a primary interest in their careers or vocations. Women are primarily interested in a long-term relationship and parenthood.

These gender stereotypes deeply affect the psyche of women when they are children and young adults. Innocuous acts, such as jokes on wives, asking the daughter to make a cup of tea, not allowing daughters to go out of house after dark, create gender stereotypes. Girls internalise such stereotypes and act according to it. These stereotypes have been created by society. Girls and women conform with the stereotypes because they have internalised them. The society sees women conform to stereotypes, which proves the stereotypes right. This reinforces the society's faith in stereotypes. It works like a vicious cycle of belief and confirmation.

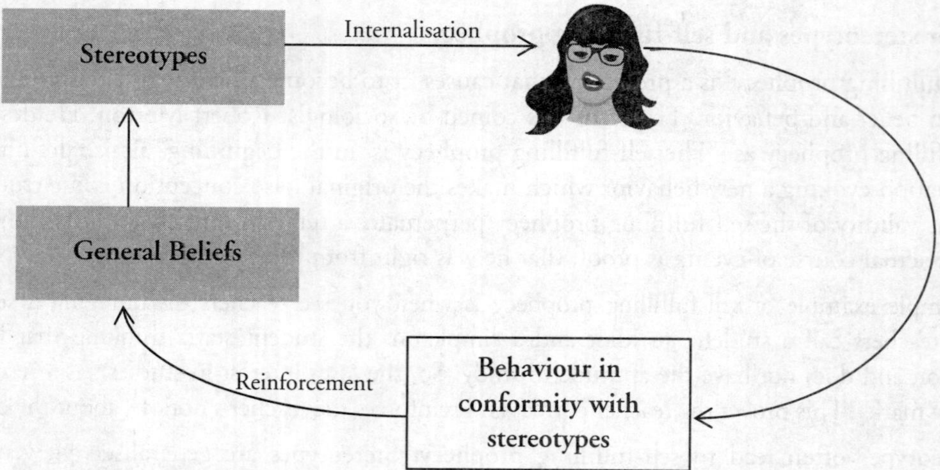

Fig. 11.4 : Vicious circle of stereotypes created by self-fulfilling prophecies

Clinical studies have shown how sex-role stereotypes are internalised by men and women. Oakhill and his associates (2005) asked participants to read word pairs in which 'engineer' or 'secretary' word (men are stereotyped in engineer roles and women are stereotyped in secretary role) was followed by a kinship term, brother or sister. Some word pairs were congruent, such as engineer – brother and secretary-sister; and other word pairs were incongruent (such as engineer – sister or secretary-brother). The participants were asked to decide for each pair whether they could be used to refer to the same person. They were explicitly instructed to suppress their gender stereotypes. Participants responded more rapidly to congruent than incongruent word pairs.

Many other studies have confirmed the widespread prevalence of gender-role stereotypes. Hill and Flom (2007) used a preferential looking paradigm in which children watched male and female actors performing masculine and feminine stereotypical activities, to see if children also internalise stereotypes. They found sensitivity to gender stereotypes at 24 months of age, but not at 18 months. Poulin-Dubois and his associates (2002) used a generalised imitation paradigm in which children selected a male and a female doll to imitate masculine and feminine stereotypical activities. They found that 24-month-old girls, but not boys, were sensitive to the violation of gender stereotypical activities.

After this book's first and second editions were published, many readers emailed the author asking why persons mentioned in the book in third person are referred to as 'she' and 'her' instead of 'he' and 'his'. The question itself is an example of internalising of stereotypes.

Self-fulfilling prophecies work in self-reinforcing cycles;especially in the case of gender stereotypes, they work in vicious cycles. To stop the vicious cycle and replace it by virtuous cycles, schools and the media need to play a positive role. Schools and media need to show women and men in various stereotype-busting roles. Women who have blasted stereotypes should be projected as role models.

11.4 Women and Indian Society

The cultural construction of Indian womanhood

Sex is only biological difference between men and women. Gender, on the other hand, is cultural difference; gender differences are cultivated and propagated by the culture and need not reflect actual, objective difference between men and women. No wonder, the social construction of women varies from society to society. This section discusses various social constructions of gender in Indian society. We will discuss about the feminine identity, psychological well-being and mental health in women, sex role stereotypes, work life of women and then move on to understand discrimination against women in Indian society, all through the developmental life span.

The dominant Hindu culture in India is polytheistic and believes in a plurality of Gods and Goddesses. Unlike the monotheistic religions of Christianity and Judaism, the cultural construction of Hindu culture includes the construction of strong, powerful goddesses, like Durga, Kali, Laxmi and Shakti. If such females are the objects of worship and veneration of a cultural community, 'it is logical to expect that women in general would benefit by sharing that elevated status. It may even be assumed that the widespread acceptance and valorisation of positive constructions of feminist in goddess figures serve as enabling models for women and for men in their treatment of women in real life. It may also be assumed that the autonomous constructions of female divinity, such as Kali, Durga and their many spin offs representative of Stri-Shakti (woman power), may supplement or challenge the equally widely prevalent modelsof female meekness, subordination and obedience' (U. Vindhya, 2005) that are characteristics of the Pativrata ideal.

But no, this is not the case. While a duality in construction of Goddesses exist (between Shakti, Kali and Durga on one hand and Sita, Savitri and Anasuya on the other), this is not reflected in the construction of feminine identity. The construction of the Indian woman lies solely on the concept of Pativrata, with Sita as the ego ideal (Kakar, 1981). Also, the cultural burden of morality (purity, virtue, chastity, self-sacrifice, etc.) on women is more severe for women than men. The woman's sexuality in India is considered something to be kept under control. This is the reason why girls are supposed to be married away before they reach puberty; and widows were, at one time, concerned to commit Sati by jumping into their husband's burning pyre.

The Feminine Identity in India

To analyse the female identity in India, we shall borrow from Jungian concepts. Carl Jung (1954) had reasoned that every individual has a collective unconscious that he/ she inherit from his/her ancestors. The collective unconscious is expressed in the form of archetypal symbols, like fear of darkness, good and bad, mother, etc. (these symbols automatically develop in our unconscious because we have inherited these). Jung reasons that there is a collective female aspect in every male's unconscious, called anima and a collective male aspect in every female's unconscious called animus. Hence, the identity of any woman consists of her feminine self and her masculine self (animus). A healthy, unified self develops when both masculine and feminine self are integrated. In an ideal socialisation process, the daughter is given the freedom to show both feminine and masculine behavior. But what happens in India?

In Indian culture, women are supposed to rigorously follow the Pativarta ideal, due to which their feminine self is promoted and their masculine self is suppressed. You must have observed that in your class, there are certain girls who behave like boys. They are discouraged to do so. As a result, they are unable to integrate their selves into a unified one. For a girl with a strong feminity and weak masculine nature, this doesn't pose much health problems. But, for girls with strong masculine tendencies, this leads to a fragmental psyche and mental health problems.

Sex Stereotypes and Sex Roles

Many studies have tried to picture various sex stereotypes pre1valent in Indian society. For instance, Sethi and Allen (1988) have compared sex stereotypes in USA and India using a psychological test called Bem Sex-Role Inventory. They found that in Indian society, instrumental traits, such as aggression and competitiveness were preferred in men and expressive traits, like warmth and affection were preferred in women. However, they found certain traits which were gender specific in USA, but were desired of both genders in India. These include family-related traits, like being obliged to the elderly and showing loyalty to family and assertive traits. The findings that assertive traits were desired in both men and women was counter-intuitive; Sethi and Allen reason that this implies the subtle strength of Indian women who can be quite assertive when dealing with men.

While Sethi and Allen had used the BSRI, others like Sripat (1989) and Bharat (1994) studied sex-role stereotypes by asking open-ended questions to the respondents; "What are the qualities you desire/ or do not desire in an Indian woman?" Sripat wanted to find out if there have been any change in sex-role stereotypes owing to urbanisation, industrialisation and constitutional changes. He found that though more progressive (modern) values were desired in Indian women, yet the traditional ones continued to be valued. I believe this is more harmful to women. If they are expected to fulfil traditional roles and modern roles, that is, (to take a hypothetical case), the role of a housewife and that of a professional, this will lead to greater role conflict. Also, if they have to conform to both traditional stereotypes and modern stereotypes, conflicts between various stereotypes will further create anxiety among women. Even in the study of Shalini Bharat (1994), it was found that husbands of career women (doctors, engineers and management executives) perceived the Indian woman as intelligent, career-oriented and outgoing; but they also valued women's traditional qualities, like being nurturant, loving, supportive and patient. Many respondents clearly emphasised that working women need to balance between work and home. Surprisingly, even women (including career women) perceived themselves in these dual terms. Bharat argues that such duality of sex-role stereotypes creates tension and conflict and explains mental health problem of working women.

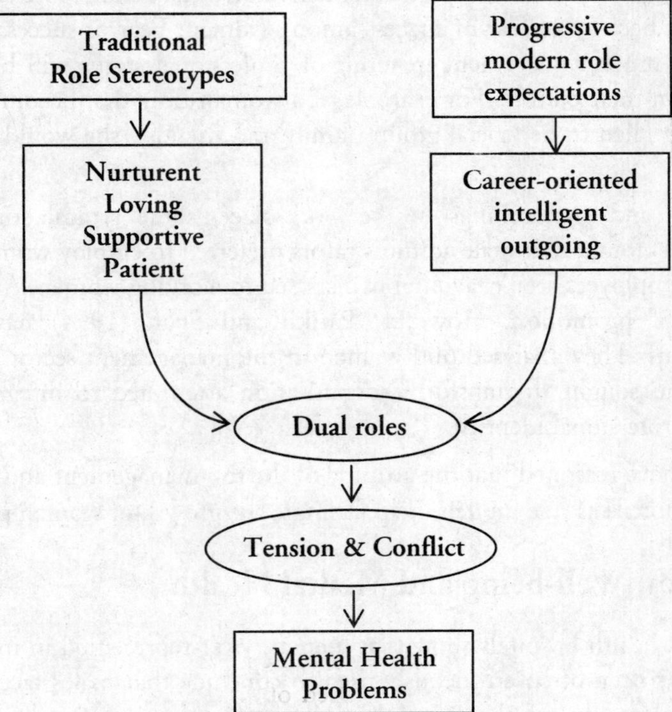

Fig. 11.5 : Role conflicts in women

Women and Work in India

Men's role as provider of the family is both socially accepted and valued; hence men in India don't face any psychological problems. However, the woman who works out is kind of a deviant; she faces problems in:

(a) Performing her role in the household
(b) Exploring professional excellence, and
(c) Dealing with workplace sexual discrimination

This results in three kinds of problems:

1. Role conflict
2. Fear of success
3. Discrimination

Role conflict will be discussed under a different head on mental problems. Now, let us check out certain work-related issues. Tarabadkar and Ghadially (1985) examined achievement motivation and job satisfaction among 50 professional and 50 non-professional men and women, using the Thematic Apperception Test (TAT) and a job description method, respectively. They found that men, in general, were more achievement-oriented than women. Even professional women were lower on achievement motivation than professional men. The authors believe this is because of fear of success among women. Fear of success happens when women fear that too much achievement in terms of professional status will be conflictual to their traditional role in their culture. For example, if a woman fears that becoming a managing director will make her alien to her social group (family and friends), she would show low need for achievement.

Regarding barriers and glass-ceilings in the work-place, some typical studies exist. For instance, Hasan (1981) found that male administrators preferred to employ women who had no children. Generally, employees aren't favourably disposed to working women. Another problem is that of barriers of promotion. However, Parikh and Shah (1994) have made some encouraging revelations. They analysed 600 women in the management sector and found that women managers who sought to transform sorganisation attempted to integrate their other identities with their professional identity.

Parikha and Shah have reasoned that the attitude of the top management and the visibility of senior women professionals as role models, help facilitate the growth of women professionals.

11.5 Psychological Well-being and Mental Health

Statistics from mental health hospitals show that men are over-represented in mental hospitals. This statistical fact has been often erroneously used to conclude that males face larger number of mental health problems due to the stressful burden on men to run families. Davar (1999) argues that such a conclusion is misleading; truth is that more women suffer from mental problems than men. The hospital statistics only reveal the exclusion faced by women. Most women patients don't get hospitalisation facility.

There are numerous reasons why women face a greater incidence of mental problems, some primary ones being:

1. Deprivation and malnutrition
2. Fragmentation of psyche
3. Role-conflict

Women in India are more malnourished than men. The girl child is discriminated against by parents in providing food and health facilities. Malnutrition is positively linked to mental problems. The fragmentation of psyche refers to the duality of feminine self and masculine self, that doesn't get easily resolved in Indian culture.

Shweta Rajwade has discussed an interesting case where the masculine self and feminine self don't get integrated due to parental attitudes. This case was studied by Wright (Lemma-Wright, 1995). The girl having mental problems was a young Muslim girl, called Aysha. She found it hard to meet people, to go out alone and to have intimate relationship with men. She had dreams of being a man and showing off her penis to an audience who applauded her. Aysha always tried to look masculine, by wearing short hair and clothes which would make her body shapeless. She expressed disgust at her own body and her sexual experience was conflictual.

A background study helped Wright to find out that Aysha was the fourth child of a strict Muslim family. Her father had expected her to be born a boy. Aysha felt that she had disappointed her parents by being born a girl. Rajwade (2005) reasons that Aysha has been possessed by her animus (her masculine self) and had set aside her own feminine nature. She had internalised the beliefs of the male dominated Indian society and had strongly *internalised the devaluation of the feminine.* This case represents a unique case that problems of a fragmented psyche can take. In a healthy person, the masculine and feminine selves are suitably integrated. In Indian women, this is not the case so.

While the fragmented psyche results due to incorrect socialisation, another major reason for mental health problems is role conflict among working women. For instance, Tarabadhar & Ghadially (1985) noted that work-family conflict was expressed in 63% of the TAT stories that working women wrote. Men's stories didn't reflect any such conflict. Bharat (1994) had, in a study, analysed the sex-role stereotypes of husbands of working women. She found that most husbands clearly emphasised that working women need to balance their home and work life. Even women perceived themselves in these dual roles. Bharat concludes that the tensions and conflicts inherent in dual roles explain mental health problems in working women. Other factors, like parental status, also affect mental health. Shukla and Verma (1986) have found that the presence of children in the age group 6-12 years and above 12 years are strongly associated with poor mental health. On the other hand, women with "empty nest" (i.e., where children have left home for studies or job) and those without any children enjoyed good health.

Women Across Developmental life-span

Discrimination against the girl child, in the form of male preference, starts even before birth in India. Vedic verses pray that sons be followed by still more sons, never by daughters. A newly-wed bride is blessed: "May you be the mother of a thousand sons". Feticide behavior, in which a female fetus is detected and killed before birth, has gained moral legitimacy from these scriptures. Further, the expectancy from a girl child is low. A son is needed to participate in religious rituals and to earn and feed the parents in their old-age.

The male child is adulted by one and all in the family; whereas, the female child faces the spectra of cultural devaluation of girls. Sudhir Kakkar (1978) argues that this may lead to a heightened female hostility and envy in the girl towards males. However, there isn't that kind of strain between the sexes. Kakkar argues that this may be because the girls and women turn the aggression against them and thus, transform the cultural devaluation into feelings of inferiority and hopelessness.

The girl child is trained to become a 'good woman', with Sita as ego ideal. This training starts in late childhood as the girls have to be married off early. She is married off preferably after her first menstrual cycle as it is feared that if she isn't married for some time after the menstrual cycle begins, she may make wrong use of her sexuality. Hence, in most early marriage cases, the adolescent period is suppressed in the girl. Upon marriage, 'an Indian woman must direct her erotic tenderness exclusively towards a man who is a complete stranger to her until their wedding night; and she must resolve the critical issues of feminine identity in unfamiliar surroundings without the love and support of her family members (Kakkar, 1978, p.23).

The bride comes to her in-laws' house not as a wife, but as a daughter-in-law. In the social hierarchy of this new family, she occupies one of the lowest rungs. Obedience and compliance with the wishes of elder women of the family is expected of her. She has to perform some of the heaviest household chores. Basically, she has many roles to play, but no status. She gets a status only when she becomes the mother of a son. Her identity rests primarily on the mother-son relationship.

The husband-wife bond at marriage is weak. The husband's mother often is quite apprehensive of the wife's sexuality and the control her sexuality can have over the husband; hence, she tries to keep them separate. Real intimacy between husband and wife develops later in married life.

Ironically, when this same woman becomes a mother-in-law, she treats her daughter-in-law in the same way her mother-in-law treated her. Smarak Swain (2009) calls this cycle the 'saas-bahu-nanad' cycle, in which a woman interacts in certain specific ways with other women, when she is in three phases of her life corresponding to the statuses nanad (sister of a man), bahu (wife of a man) and saas (mother of a man). Hence, this exploitation of women in patriarchal system of India has been institutionalised.

11.6 Violence against Women in India

Acts of violence against women include dowry deaths, wife battering, sexual violence and trafficking in girls. Female feticide and female infanticide are also forms of violence. The focus of Indian gender psychologists has been domestic violence. They have tried to investigate into reasons for domestic violence of the masculine identity of the husband, social norms, women's acceptance, etc.

Some of the causal factors unearthed by psychologists are:

Misplaced masculine identity

U. Vindhya (2007) observes that the masculine identity in India is socially constructed and is equated with aggression, hostility towards women, dominance and rigid gender role expectations. These pathological qualities are part of how our culture defines the masculine identity. On top of that, this misplaced sense of masculine identity is strong in those who have had an incorrect socialisation. Dhawan and colleagues (1999) observe that attitude, such as acceptance of physical chastisement of women and notions of male entitlement are strongly associated with parenting styles of mothers. Often the preference of male child over the female child creates a notion in the male's psyche that he is special and the female is an organism of inferior status. Such attitudes are cultural norms that are variously internalised by males during socialisation. These males who internalise such attitudes of male superiority to a greater extent, are more prone to resort to violent behaviors.

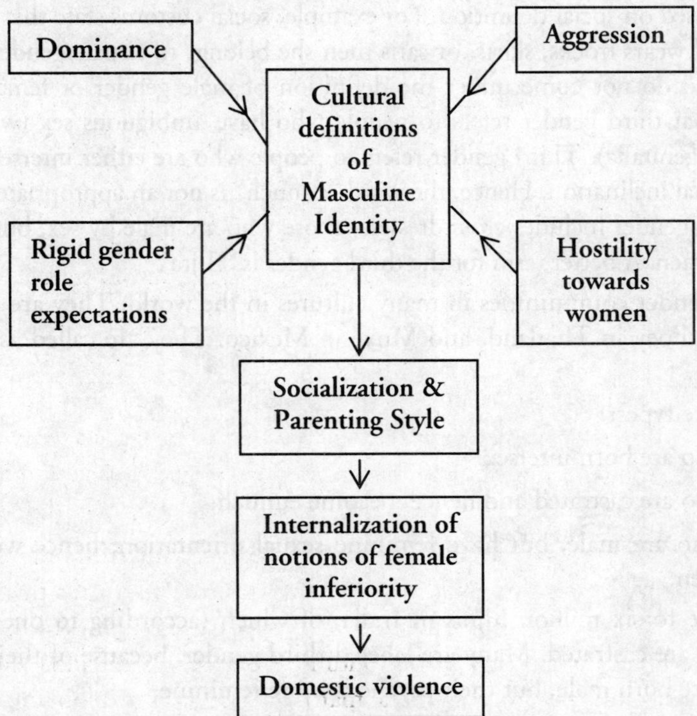

Fig. 11.6 : Machanism of internalization of Masculine stereotypes by a male individual

Traits of the perpetrators

While cultural norms create notions of female inferiority and legitimise violence against women, individual characteristics ultimately matter when it comes to the real act of violence. Vindhya (2007) reasons from a literature survey that suspicion, negativism, masked dependency and low self-esteem of the perpetrator make him more vulnerable to violence against women. Mitra (2002) had studied men who were accused of domestic violence and found that they had constricted cognitive processes, poor impulse control, negativism and suspicion and poor social skills. Those who inflicted only psychological abuse had impaired reality orientation compared to those who inflicted both physical and psychological abuse.

It has also been noticed that husbands who physically and sexually abuse their wives also tend to be sexually active outside marriage and have multiple partners (Martin et al, 1999). Mitra (2002) argues that those husbands with illicit relations usually attribute their extra-marital relations to the alleged failure of the wife in fulfilling the expectations of a 'good wife'. I think this may be a form of projection or some others defense mechanism used by men to rationalise their extra-marital relationship and comfortably display outrage and violence against women accusing them of not conforming to womanly and wifely behavior.

11.7 Discrimination Issues of the third gender†

Sex is the biological difference between man and woman. Gender refers to differences between man and woman based on social definition. For example, social customs state that if an individual is female by sex and wears frocks, skirts, or saris then she belongs to female gender. Third gender refers to people who do not come under the definition of male gender or female gender. It is wrongly believed that third gender refers to people who have ambiguous sex (who are intersex, that is, have mixed genitalia). Third gender refers to people who are either intersex or are socially deviant in their sexual inclination. Hence, the word "eunuch" is not an appropriate word to define the third sex. Third gender includes cross dressers- those who are male by sex, but prefer to dress like and act like women. A better term for the third gender is 'Hijra'.

There are transgender communities in many cultures in the world. They are called baklas in the Philippines, Kathoey in Thailand, and Muxe in Mexico. They are called as Hijra in India and Pakistan.

Hijras are of three types:

- Those who are born intersex.
- Those who are castrated and hence, become eunuch.
- Those who are male, but have feminine sexual orientation; hence wear and behave like women.

There are some five to six million hijras in India, of which (according to one estimate) only about eight percent are castrated. Many are labeled third gender, because of their psychological orientation. They are born male, but their psyche is more feminine.

† Source: Swain (2009, p. 57-59).

Initiation

Becoming a hijra is a process of socialisation into a "hijra family" through a relationship characterised as ***chella*** "student" to ***guru*** "teacher", leading to a gradual assumption of femininity. Typically, each guru lives with at least five ***chelas***; her ***chelas*** assume her surname and are considered part of her lineage. Chelas are expected to give their income to their guru, who manages the household. Hijra families are close-knit communities and often have their own houses. Often the children initiated into a Hijra family are abandoned or sold by their family.

As already reiterated, not every Hijra is castrated, but if castrated, there is a process to it. Hijra tradition is deep-rooted in Hinduism; hence the process is actually a ritual by which emasculation takes place. Emasculation is the total removal of penis, tests and scrotum. In this ritual, boys are taken into a jungle and their testes and scrotum are cut with a knife without applying anesthesia. This process is called ***nirvana,*** which means rebirth. The priest then folds back a strip of flesh and creates an artificial vagina.

Problems

Hijras are social groups that exist on the margins of society. No wonder, they face extreme forms of social exclusion. The word 'hijra' itself is considered a derogatory word.

Some serious problems of Hijras are:

1. *Lack of employment opportunities:* There are few opportunities available to Hijras. Most of them make a living by begging, performing in ceremonies and in prostitution. Owing to negative prejudices towards them, they are not employed in industry or offices.
2. *Prostitution:* There are about 2000 eunuchs in prostitution in the Eunuch Lane of Bombay. They face atrocities similar to that of women in prostitution. In addition, they have higher chance of getting infected in HIV/ AIDS. This is because their social status is even lower than female prostitutes. So, they are generally more available for high-risk sex. It has been observed that for many Hijras, 'sex work is the only option, because no one is willing to employ them because of their gender identity. Even as commercial sex workers, hijras are the most vulnerable group as they are placed right at the bottom of the hierarchy of sex workers. This results in their having little bargaining power and being unable to ensure that their customers practice safe sex. They are also at risk of violence both from customers and the police.
3. *Education:* Hijras become so after they are adopted by "hijra families". These families stay on the margins of society. Their social status is low. Hence, they do not get any formal education. Wherever there is a possibility, schools also deny providing them education with normal students.
4. *Violence:* Violence against Hijras, especially Hijra sex workers, is common and brutal. Violence against hijras starts with prejudices and negative attitudes. Prejudice is 'translated into violence, often of a brutal nature, in public spaces, police stations,

prisons and even in their homes. The main factor behind the violence is that society is not able to come to terms with the fact that hijras do not conform to the accepted gender divisions. In addition to this, most hijras have a lower middle-class background, which makes them susceptible to harassment by the police. The discrimination based on their class and gender makes the hijra community one of the most disempowered groups in the Indian society".

5. *Discrimination:* Due to their social exclusion, it is but natural, that they face discrimination in getting permission to stay in residential complexes and health facilities. Some people are of the opinion that the law is also discriminatory. Owing to Section 377 of Indian Penal Code, they are not recognised. When a bureaucracy cannot place them into male or female gender categories, the same bureaucracy also can't deliver welfare services to them.
6. *Political rights:* At many places, hijras are not given the right to vote. Eunuchs were granted voting rights only in 1994. Even in any official document, you usually find only two categories- male and female.

■ ■ ■

12

Application of Psychology to Environment and Related Fields

Chapter outline

12.1 Environment Psychology

Environment psychology is a field or psychological study that investigates the relationship between human beings and the environment, in order to enhance human well-being and improve human- environment fit. Environment psychology has a broad and multi-disciplinary focus- it borrows from various theoretical traditions of psychology and uses this knowledge base to study the impact of human behavior on the environment and that of the environment on human behavior. Further, the field is involved in promoting pro-environmental behavior and conservation behavior.

Some of the recurrent issues in research literature of environmental psychology are:

- What is the impact of environmental stressors, like noise, pollution and crowding on human behavior?
- How do we cope with these stressors?
- What is the impact of human behavior on environment? Why do people use environment degrading technology and how do these affect environment?
- How to motivate people towards showing conservation behavior? How can awareness about environmental issues be increased?
- How can psychological principles be used in architecture, in designing houses, schools and public places? Ergonomics that looks in to person-environment fit in the work place is also a part of environmental psychology.

The basic concept behind environmental psychology is that changes in environment lead to two inter-related experiences for an individual- **stressor** and **stress response**. A **stressor** is a stimulus that forces an organism to adjust its behaviour to deal with it. Stressors can be short-term stressors or long-term stressors. Events, like an accident or a terrorist attack are short-term stressors. Stimuli, like noise, air pollution, water pollution, traffic in Bangalore city, crowding, congested human settlements (such as the ones we find in slums) etc., are long-term stressors. Environment-related stressors are usually long-term stressors.

Stress response happens in three stages. First stage is the **alarm reaction** stage, in which the body mobilises resources as an initial reaction to a threatening event. Physiologically, the arousal level (level of adrenaline in the body) rises rapidly. The stage abruptly ends if the stress subsides. But, if the stress continues, stress response enters the second stage, the **resistance** stage. In this stage, the body tries to revert to normal functioning while coping with the effects of the additional adrenaline in the body. Arousal level is lower than the arousal level in first stage, but higher than normal.

If the stress situation continues, the individual enters the third stage, i.e., **the exhaustion stage**. The body's energy reserves get depleted and this lowers resistance of the body. Body's immune system becomes weak. This increases chances of continued high pressure, heart attacks, strokes, and other ailments.

Environmental psychology studies the response of an individual to long-term stressors, like noise, crowding, air pollution, crowded habitat, urban settlements, etc. Psychologists have established that prolonged stress can have adverse impact on physical and mental health. The impact of prolonged stress on an individual's health is referred to as the **General Adaptation Syndrome (GAS)**. GAS is central to the study of environmental psychology.

A significant body of empirical evidence has proved that prolonged stressors lead to GAS. One well-known example is the study of 'executive monkeys' by Brady (1958). In this study, pairs of monkeys were confined in a compartment and each had an electrode attached to one of its feet. Both monkeys received an electric shock every 20 seconds unless one of the two monkeys (called the 'executive monkey') prevented it by pressing a lever that was located in front of it. The experiment was continued for six hours at a time, twice a day. The executive monkey learnt that pressing the lever prevented shocks. It managed to prevent future shocks by pressing the lever. However, the executive monkeys were found to develop ulcers, while the passive monkeys did not. The study has been used to explain the role of prolonged stressors on employees in an organisation. Nevertheless, the result is similar for the common man living in an ultra-loud and ultra-polluted environment.

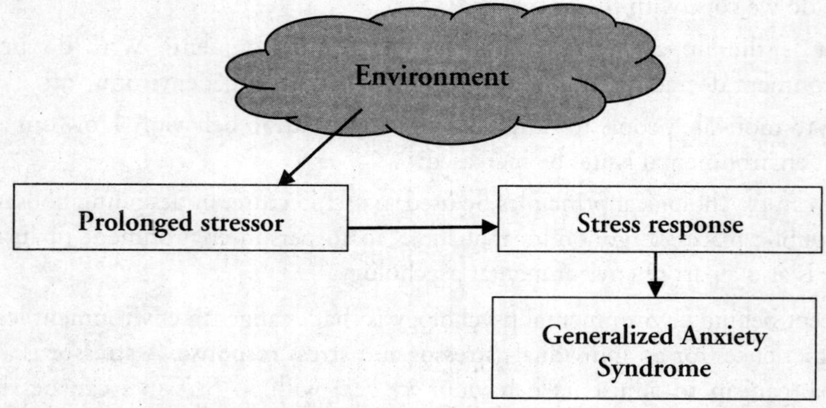

Fig. 12.1 : Pollution as stressor

Environmental psychology also tries to understand the effect of environmental stressors on performance of a person. The **Yerkes-Dodson theory** states that performance does not vary linearly with arousal level. Performance increases with arousal up to a point and then decreases. Hence, low arousal is as bad for individual performance as high arousal is. Crudely speaking, a student staying in an AC room with cozy bed and lounge has too much of luxury and hence, low arousal level. Her performance will be low. Another student living in a shanty establishment in a slum area besides a noisy railway line has to cope with too many stressors. Her arousal level will be too high. Both students' performance will suffer.

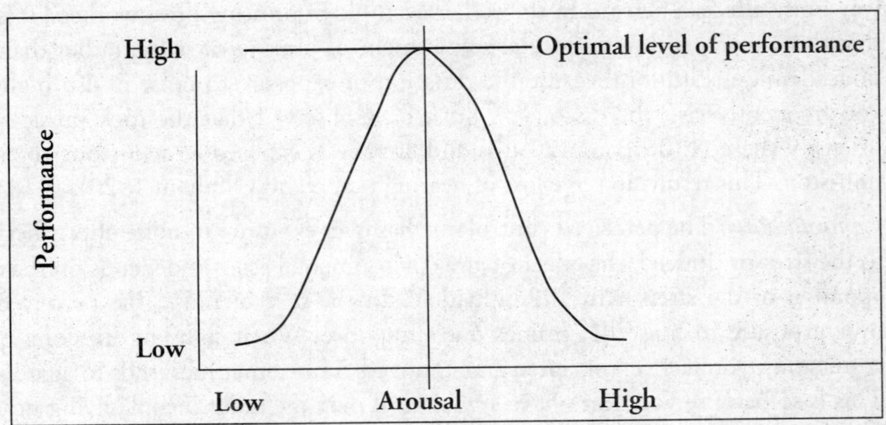

Fig.12.2 : Impact of stress on performance

Noise

Noise is an unwanted sound. As a sound, it is stimuli also. Sound waves in noise have certain characteristics that affect the sensory processes in the ear associated with hearing. Further, they are a burden on attentional processes. Yet, this is not the whole story. Researchers have found wide and far ranging effects of noise on the human psychological functioning. From a psychological perspective, noise is defined as an environmental stressor that affects human functioning.

The effect that noise has on a person is mediated by many factors, like nature of noise and human perception of the noise. Five factors that affect the nature of stressors, that is, predictability, intensity, duration, controllability and chronicity, also hold the same for noise.

The relative influence of the five factors can be discussed as under:

1. *Predictability:* Any sudden and unpredictable event in the surrounding automatically draws our attention towards it. The sudden blast of a cracker, or abrupt noise created by factory always draws our attention. Not only this, unpredictable stimuli lead to automatic arousal. When you see a snake (unpredictable stimuli), you become alarmed. Such psychological response is also produced due to unpredictable noise.
2. *Intensity:* Intensity of noise has been correlated with hearing difficulties in many studies. For example, Raja and Ganguli (1993) have found that the hearing capacity

of workers in a printing press were adversely affected by noise as compared to a group of employees in an academic institute. They note that the noise the printing press workers were exposed to was 110 dB. Not only hearing ability, researchers have found that exposure to high intensity noise (more than 90 dB) increases blood pressure, heart rate, skin conductance and catecholamine's (Cohen and Weinstein, 1982). Other studies have concluded that exposure to high level of noise is related to cardiovascular disorders, digestive disorders and allergic reactions.

3. *Duration:* The duration on any given day that one is exposed to noise also affects the way noise affects a person. In the earlier example of printing press workers, it is possible that those workers showed greater impairment of hearing capacity, rather than workers of academic institution because the duration of exposure to noise is also high there. If you frequently visit the disco, you must have observed that the rock music is of high intensity there (110 dB to 120 dB) and anyone is exposed to it for one to two hours non-stop. This results in serve loss of hearing (Labo and Oliphant,1928).

4. *Controllability:* The perceived control one has over exposure to noise affects her response to the stressor. Indeed, the effect of any environmental stressor depends on the cognitive appraisal of the stressor by the individual. In the case of noise, the perceived control over exposure to noise determines one's response. When standing in along queue for admissions, you feel very irritated and annoyed. This sometimes leads to aggression also. This is so because you don't have any control over the noise. People living near railway tracks become irritated because their perceived control over the stressor is low. On the other hand, if you are attending a noisy party, you don't get irritated by the noise, because you could control your exposure to the noise by leaving the party.

   In the experiment, people were given the opportunity to control noise (by, for instance, having the option to switch off a loud speaker). They tolerated the noise easier than a group of people without control over noise, without even using the control device (Glass and Singer, 1972).

5. *Chronicity:* Seyle's General Adaptation Syndrome hypotheses forwards that when an individual is exposed to a stressor for a persistent period of time, her bodily resistance becomes active. But after sometime, exhaustion happens and the individual copying strength decreases. The response to chronic noise also happens to be exhaustion. The body stays at an over-aroused state for a long time, till its resources are exhausted. Then a number of physiological and psychological problems result. This is the reason why urban residents are advised to stay in residential colonies, away from market noise or the noise of airports and railway tracks. Yet, many urban settlements are exposed to chronic noise, that leads to negative effect.

Effects of noise pollution

In the above discussion, we have already noted some effects of noise. Now, let us systematically study the multi-dimensional effects of noise pollution:

1. Performance

The effect of noise on performance has been researched the maximum in Indian psychological literature on noise pollution. The general conclusion is that motor and manual performance increases with noise intensity up to a level, after which performance starts decreasing. For example, performance has been found to increase less than 100 dB noise, relative to quiet condition (Bhattacharya et al, 1978) and decrease beyond 110 dB conditions.

From a literature survey, Uday Jain and M.N. Palsana (2004) observe that cognitive task performance can be explained by using the arousal model. From the Yerkes-Dodson law, we know that performance has an Inverted-U relation with the level of arousal. Indian researchers have shown that similar relation holds between cognitive task performance and noise level for complex tasks. Noise being a stressor, increased noise level is associated with higher arousal; hence this relation. However, performance did not seem to deteriorate for simple tasks.

Specific cognitive functions, like vigilance and attention span also seem to be adversely affected by noise (Rastogi and Das, 1993, see Jain and Palsana, 2004). Reduced vigilance and attention span obviously affect the job performance of many workers and security guards.

Besides the effect of noise on work performance, another area of concern is the effect of noise on student's performance in schools. In one study, the effect of noise on school children's perceived was tested (Bronzaft and McCatrhy, 1975). The school building had two sides. One side was close to a railway track and hence exposed to noise from trains. The other side was free from such noise. The researchers compared the student's performance on reading assignment. It we found that the reading skills of student on the quiet side was much superior to that of students of the noisy side.

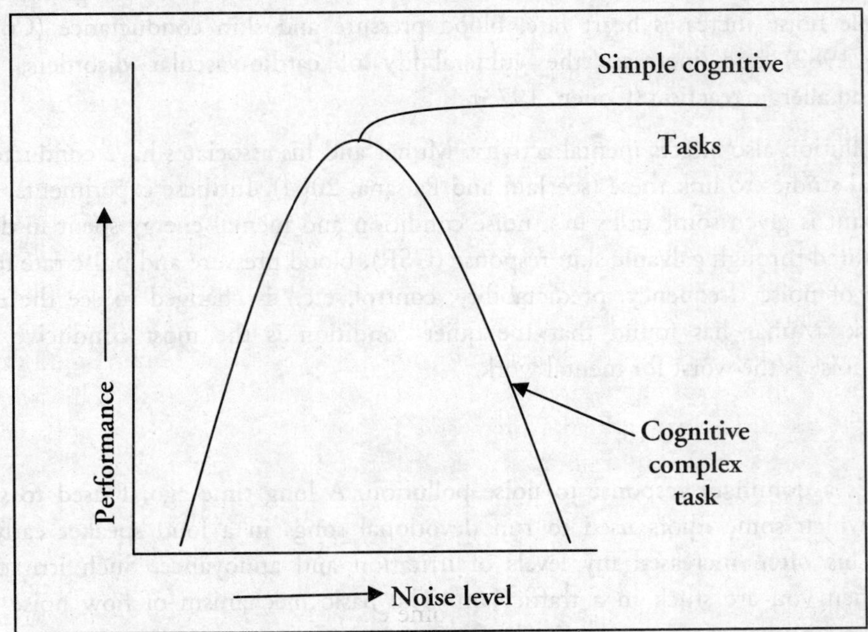

Fig. 12.3 : Effect of noise on performance

2. Hearing Capacity

Two factors seem to hold the key to the effect of noise on hearing capacity: **intensity and chronicity.** Many studies conducted on workers working in noisy environments have demonstrated the effect of noise on hearing. The Raja and Ganguli study discussed earlier showed how hearing capacity of printing press workers to 110 dB noise daily was lower than other workers.

Why does this happen? Basically, the human ear has three parts- outer ear (that receives sound stimuli), middle ear and inner ear.

Some components of the middle ear and inner ear vibrate in response to sound. The sound has an amplitude and frequency. The sound frequency determines the frequency of vibration of eardrum. Every time sound waves strike the eardrum, the eardrum vibrates at a corresponding frequency. This is communicated to the brain by a complex mechanism. **Loud sounds** have high amplitude and effect the strength of vibration. Now, guess what happens when you are exposed to abnormal levels of noise for a long time. The ear drum losses its plasticity, that is, sensitivity. It is unable to pick up sounds of lower frequency and amplitude.

3. Mental and Physical health

Noise is associated with stress and arousal. Both, stress and arousal demand many psychological resources. Due to this, noise becomes associated with ill-health. Exposure to high intensity and unpredictable noise increases heart rate, blood pressure and skin conductance (Cohen and Weinstein, 1982) and increases the vulnerability of cardio-vascular disorders, digestive disorders, and allergic reaction (Cohen, 1973).

Noise pollution also affects mental activity. Muhar and his associates have conducted many experimental studies to link these (see Jain and Palsana, 2004). In these experiments, typically the participant is given some tasks in a noise condition and mental energy spent in doing the task is measured through galvanic skin response (GSR), blood pressure and pulse rate measures. The nature of noise (frequency, predictability, control, etc.) is changed to see the effect on mental work. Muhar has found that the quiet condition is the most conducive and the unperiodic noise is the worst for mental work.

4. Aggression

Aggression is a dominant response to noise pollution. A long time ago, I used to stay in a locality in which some idiots used to run devotional songs in a loud speaker early in the morning. This often increased my levels of irritation and annoyance. Such irritation also increases when you are stuck in a traffic jam. The basic mechanism of how noise leads to aggression can be represented as given in the figure.

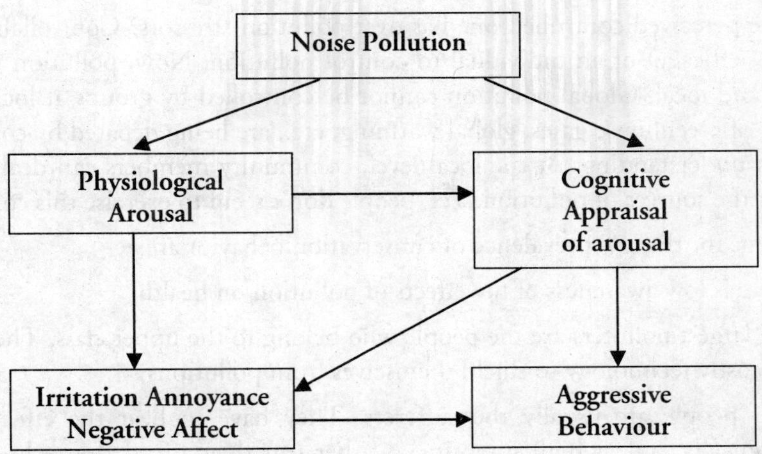

Fig. 12.4 : Effect of Noise Pollution on Aggressive Behaviour

The effect of noise pollution on aggressive behavior is mediated by two sets of factors. First is the cognitive appraisal. If you are watching rock concert (which is more noise and less music!) and you are enjoying it, you don't get annoyed by the noise. On the other hand, if you are in the middle of traffic, you don't enjoy the noise. If any small incident happens (say a small argument with a stranger), you become irritated and annoyed. High arousal and irritation are second set of factors. Together, the two sets of factors lead to anger as an emotional response that leads to aggressive behavior.

You must have read newspaper reports about road rages in the big cities. These road rages start with small arguments over. Someone not able to park his vehicle, or some small accident;people turn aggressive and violent, many-a-times leading to death!

12.2 Pollution

The issue of pollution- air pollution, water pollution, soil pollution is one of the persisting problems in third world countries, like India. The health effects of pollution on people are significant. In fact, some toxic pollutants even mutate our genes, leading to defective gene structure.

Talking of pollution as a stressor, let us understand how serious the problem is in terms of predictability, intensity, controllability and chronicity. As regards intensity, pollution as a stressor is very intense in urban areas, especially in metropolitan cities with huge population, high vehicular emissions, sewage wastes, high amount of non-biodegradable products and usage of inefficient energy. The exposer to pollution, however, varies across social classes. The upper class is the greater polluter (in terms of energy consumption); yet upper class members can afford to adopt to climatic changes and avoid pollution stressors by staying in clean buildings with air conditioned climate. They also have the best supply of clean water. On the other hand are the lower class members, who stay in slums and other shanty locality. For them, pollution stressors are **chronic.** They are especially affected by air pollution. They are chronically exposed to an extremely polluted built environment.

What is the perceived controlled one has over pollution stressors? Controllability here refers to ability (i.e., efficacy) of an individual to control pollution. Now, pollution happens at two levels- global and local. Global pollution cannot be controlled by groups at local levels. Issues, like emissions of greenhouse gases, global warming, etc., are being debated by countries in order to reach at an understanding. At the local level, community members can deal with pollution by controlling the sources of pollution. Yet, people don't seem to exercise this control. Why?

A few reasons for the low prevalence of conservation behavior are:

1. There is low awareness of the effects of pollution on health.
2. The largest polluters are the people who belong to the upper class. They can afford to use costly technology to shield themselves from pollutions.
3. Poor people are usually the sufferers. They have to bear the effects of pollution chronically and at high intensity. Neither can they afford the technology to shield from pollution, nor are they aware of the effects of pollutions. No wonder, they don't show conservation behavior.

The effects of pollution on physical health are well-documented. There are also many serious effects of pollution on mental health and psychological well-being.

Some of these are:

1. Mental ability

Various toxic wastes in polluted air and water have been reported to affect mental ability. Some toxic substances, like lead and asbestos have the ability to retard proper development of the brain. In one study, S. P. Sinha and Vibha (1994) tried to correlate lead pollution with IQ level. They formed two groups of participants, one from high traffic density area and the other from low traffic density area. Hair samples were collected and tested for lead. IQ level was also assessed using Wechsler Intelligence Scale for children. As obvious, the children from high traffic density area had more lead in their hair (because vehicular emission has high concentration of lead). However, Sinha and Vibha also found that this group had lower level of IQ!

May be one of the reasons why children from disadvantages groups, who stay in slums, show low cognitive development (see chapter 8) is exposure to pollution.

2. Performance

Pollution affects work performance. People working in highly polluted areas have to use up lots of resources in coping. They face lung problems and have breathing difficulties. Poor vigilance performance and eye complaints have been observed in traffic policemen exposed to vehicular pollution in comparison to general policemen. (Gupta & Rastogi, 1991).

Various types of pollution seem to affect attention, perception, memory, intelligence, respiratory system, etc. For example, organic solvents have been found to reduce memory, digit span and dexterity (Saxena, 1992).

3. Heat and aggression

Now, we turn our attention to psychological consequences of pollution at the global level, that is, global warming. While global warming has generally benefitted the countries at higher latitudes (by way of increased crop productivity, milder climates, etc.), the effects on countries of tropical areas are quite negative. One area of concern is hot weather. Psychologists have found that high temperatures lead to negative feelings and aggression. For example, drivers of automobiles without air-conditioning were studied by Kenrick and Mac Farlane (1986). They found that in a traffic jam, the horn-honking of drivers increased in ambience temperature. This shows that impatience and annoyance of drivers increase with rise in heat.

Crowding

Crowding is defined, in a psychological sense, as a psychological state emanating from the felt lack of spaces (Stokols, 1979). Hence, crowding is not a construct; rather a subjective experience. Density refers to objective crowding; it is a physical measure of the number of persons in a given space. The subjective experience of crowding, on the other hand, is a psychological state, and hence, is mediated by many human factors.

Human Factors in Crowding

Uday Jain and Girishwar Misra (1990) reason that 'density in itself as no effect on mood and behaviour. It is the experience of crowding which is responsible for negative effects. The distinction between objective crowding (density) and the feeling of crowding (subjective experience) led researchers to identify the variables mediating the feeling of crowding' (Misra, 1990, P.267). Hence, if I am enjoying myself in a high density disco, I am not experiencing crowding, nor is the disco crowded. On the other hand, a local train with the same density may seem crowded to me.

The mediating factors responsible for crowding are of special interest to psychologists. These mediating factors refer to individual differences, that is, differences in human factors, like attention, cognitions, emotional response, gender, age, etc. Let us study some of the mediators in the experience of crowding.

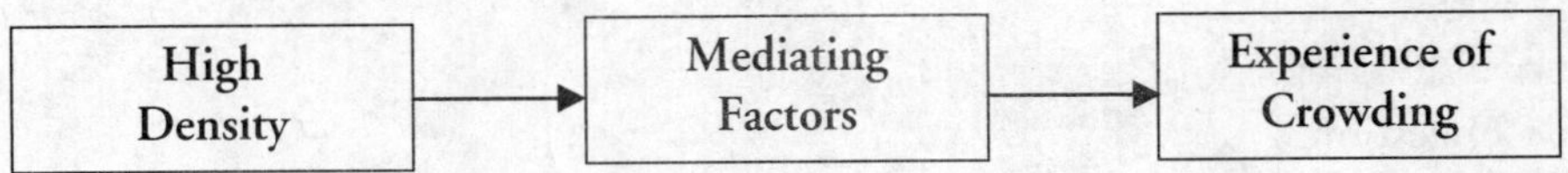

Fig. 12.5 : Conceptual link between density and crowding

1. *Stimulus overload:* The Overload Model explains crowding in terms of excessive stimulation. We know that the attentional resources at our disposal have limited capacity. Through the process of attention, information is processed. In high density conditions if information is received at a high rate from different sources, it strains the attentional resources and leads to negative affect (Sacgart, 1978). Does this explain why we don't feel crowded in discos, but do feel crowded in local trains with same density? In discos, our

attention is more towards the DJ's music, we are almost oblivious of other sounds. On the other hand, 'noise' reaches us from many sources in local trains.

2. Behavioral constraints: The degree of behavioral freedom one has in high density conditions is low. If the person is okay with it, she doesn't experience crowding, but if she minds the reduced freedom of movement, she experiences negative affect.

3. Arousal and Attribution: The Two-factor Theory of Emotion states that any emotional response is the result of psychological arousal and the factors one blames for the arousal (i.e., cognition of factors one attributes the arousal to). High density leads to over stimulation of sympathetic nerves that leads to arousal (Evans, 1972). Now, if the individual attributes the cause of her stress to the density, she experiences crowding. In a disco, you are over-aroused. But, since you are a little high on vodka and are on the dance floor, you attribute the arousal to 'fun'. In a local train, you don't have any other factor to attribute your arousal to. So, you experience crowding. I had once taken an extremely introverted girl to a disco (seriously, I am not exaggerating!). She neither danced, nor enjoyed the music. Her response to my question on the disco was that it was crowded.

4. The perceived scarcity of resources may be an important factor in crowding. According to the ecological model (Wicher and Kirmeyer, 1977), perceived scarcity of resources leads to negative affect. In crowded local trains, you often don't find a seat, or a place to stand and you curse the railway ministry. This scarcity of resources leads to a feeling of crowding. A person who daily commutes in the local train and is comfortable standing on others feet doesn't experience crowding.

Content of the experience of Crowding

Now, that we know the factors that lead to crowding (high density, followed by many mediating factors), let us turn our attention to the experience itself. What is crowding? What feelings (or emotional and cognitive responses) do you refer to as crowding?

Uday Jain (1991), the first Indian psychologist to study crowding, has proposed four types of experience in crowding:

1. Negative affect
2. Loss of control
3. Congestion
4. Disturbance

If you feel crowded, it may be because you experience all or any of the above feelings. Negative affects refer to mood disturbances, irritability and annoy. Loss of control refers to the feeling of helplessness. It is associated with limited freedom and limited movement. Congestion is the feeling of lack of space. Every individual has a perceived personal space (which keeps varying) and she desires for that much space. Anything less than that, leads to congestion. Disturbance is the feeling of being disturbed. In high density situation, disturbance generally occurs due to noise, invasion of privacy and harassment (Jain and Palsana, 2004).

Effects of crowding

Jain and G. Misra (1986) have forwarded a theoretical model of the behavioural consequences of crowding. This model 'posits that crowding is a psychological state experienced on the basis of high population density as mediated by physical resources and coping mechanisms. Depending upon the moderating effects of these variables, people may experience different degrees of crowding in similar or identical environments, having the same degree of density' (Jain and G.Misra, 1990).

The above logic can be represented as:

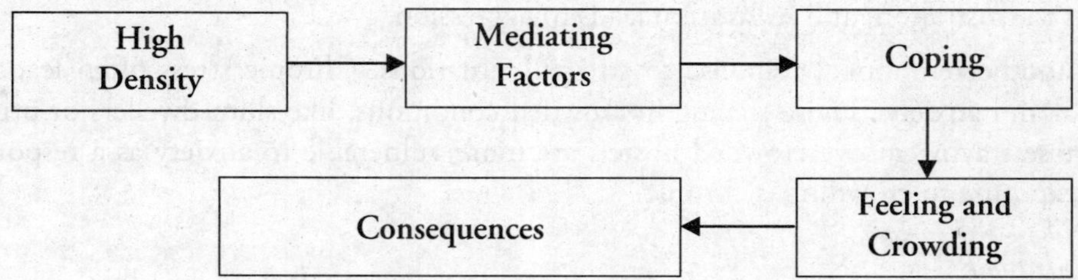

Fig. 12.6 : Essence of Jain and Mishra Model

The consequences of crowding are manifested at three levels: individual, interpersonal and societal. The model of Uday Jain and Giriswar Misra also specifies some of the consequences.

These consequences are represented in the box below:

Table 12.1 : Consequences of crowding

Personal	Interpersonal	Societal
Stresses Health Status Aggression Anxiety Withdrawal	Competition Interpersonal Attraction Helping	Participation in social activities

Let us discuss some of the above consequences:

1. Health Status

As a stressor, crowding elicits over arousal of sympathetic nerves of the automatic nervous system. Hence, it has effects on health similar to that of other stressors. Crowding may cause physiological changes, like increased blood pressure and changes in the cardio-vascular system. In one study, Evans (1975) put five males and five females in a small room for three and half hours and measured the subjects' heart rate and blood pressure. Then the subjects were put in a larger room (lower density) and these measures were again taken. The conclusions validated that in high density conditions, heart rate and blood pressure become abnormal.

2. Aggression and Anxiety

High density and overcrowding have been correlated with aggression. However, there is a debate on what causes aggression. One reason may be that crowding induces negative feelings in the individual, which may manifest in the form of aggression. High physiological arousal compounded with negative feelings lead to aggression. Jain and G.Misra observe that negative feelings induced by crowding make people more and more susceptible to repulsion rather than attraction, social tension than harmony, aggression is competition. Competition over rare resources leads to frustration; and frustration leads to aggression.

Anxiety is another emotional response to stressful situations. Chronic stress often leads to chronic arousal and anxiety. Those staying in crowded conditions, like slum-dwellers or prison inmates, or those staying in overcrowded hostels are more vulnerable to anxiety as a response, because their exposure to crowding is chronic.

3. Social Withdrawal

Social withdrawal is a coping strategy to escape the stressors of crowding. If one uses this as a strategy, it itself becomes an ill-effect of crowding. Basically, those who share a small house with many family members may experience crowding chronically. To cope with the chronic stressors, some people loosen social bonds and withdraw from social support (Evans et al. 1989). Ironically, social support is an important moderator of stress. In the section of stress (see chapter 2), I have discussed how social support reduces the impact of stressors. By social withdrawal, the individual makes use of an incorrect style to cope with stress.

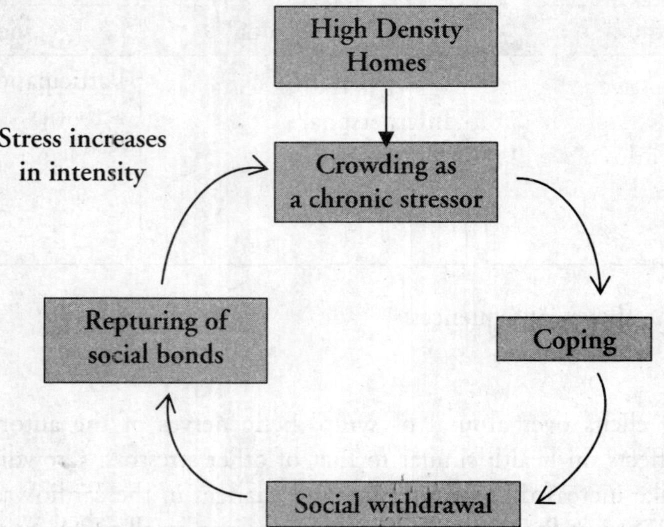

Fig. 12.7 : Vicious Cycle of Crowding and Social Withdrawal

4. Task Performance

Many empirical studies conducted in recent times have demonstrated that crowding impedes task performance and inhibits the realization of optimum potential of the individual. For example, Nagar and Pandey (1987) have found that crowding leads to a deterioration in performance on cognitively complex tasks. The effect of crowding on simpler tasks (that don't require high cognitive resources) is not substantial. Crowding also affects performance on memory tasks. Hence, the academic performance of a student in a crowded classroom or a crowded exam center may be adversely affected due to lower memory recall ability.

5. Competition

A direct fall out of high population is that the amount of resources available to each individual is less. In one study, Uday Jain (1987) manipulated high-low social density and adequate and scarce resources. The 'feeling of crowding' and 'preferred interpersonal distance' of subjects were measured. It was found that subjects experienced greater crowding under scarce resource condition than adequate resource condition.

Competition itself leads to other undesirable consequences, like frustration, anxiety, etc. On the other hand, competition tolerance moderates the effects of high density stress.

6. Helping behavior

A very peculiar effect of high crowding situation is bystander apathy. Suppose a person is injured in an accident in the middle of the road. Many people gather around, but none seems to help the person. This is because of a diffusion of responsibility in crowd. Every person thinks that he/ she is less responsible to help the person because of the presence of so many others.

Other than this effect, general helping tendency also may decrease in crowded environments.

7. De-individuation

De-individuation is a psychological state that people may experience in crowds. De-individuation individuals lose their individuality and uncritically follow group norms that may emerge in crowds. The individuals in a crowd do not know each other; this anonymity perhaps reduces restraint and the individual may lose her individuality once this happens; she follows the norms that may evolve in the crowd.

When an individual loses her individuality and becomes disinhibited, she may indulge in many anti-social actions, like participate in a mob; vandalise public property without any reason, etc.

8. Interpersonal attraction

Long-term density confinement has been correlated with low attraction. For example, Baror and Bell (1976) conducted an experiment in a hostel where three students were accommodating in double rooms. The researchers compared these students with other students who lived two each in double rooms. They found that former students were less satisfied with their room-mates and were less cooperative than the latter group of students.

This finding holds immense significance in Indian context, given that our prisons, hostels and even homes are overly crowded.

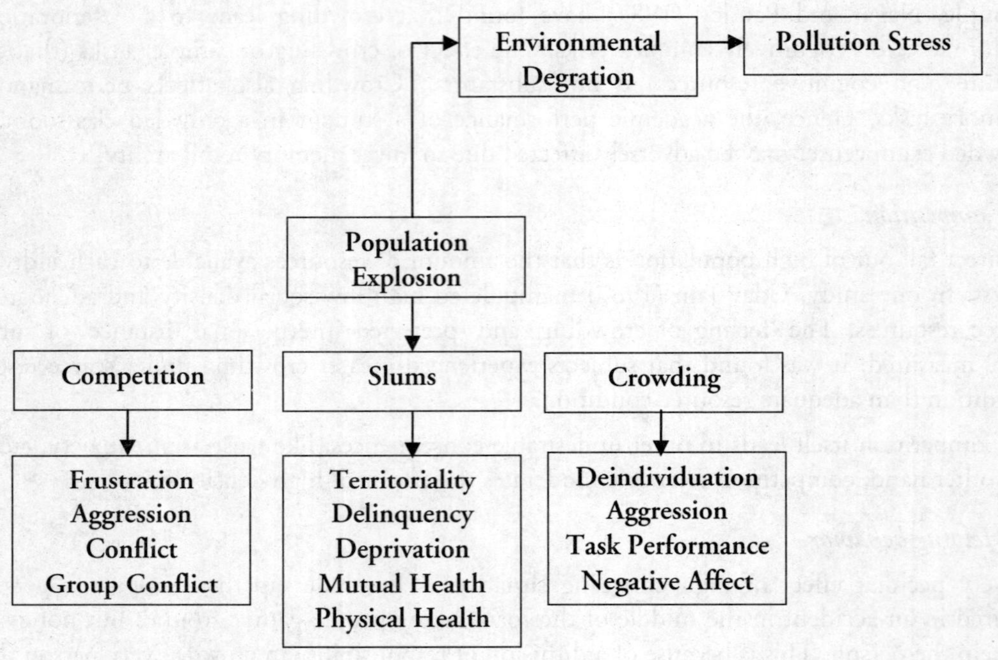

Fig. 12.8 : Effects of Population Explosion

12.3 Psychological consequences of Population Explosion

Population explosion is one of the pressing problems faced by India and many developing countries. Two direct consequences of population explosion are high population density and excessive pressure on limited resources. Excessive pressure on limited resources leads to unsustainable exploitation of resources, which also leads to pollution. The situation is especially acute in urban environments. Here, the population density is unusually high. Natural environment is polluted due to excess emission of pollutants by a huge population. The build environment in urban places mostly consists of unplanned localities, high density and low personal space in neighborhoods and slum settlements. In this section, we will explore some important psychological consequences of population explosion and high population density.

For this, we shall follow the model given in figure:

1. Competition

Competition over limited resource is a direct fallout of high population. If population is high, the per capita resources available is low. Jobs available are limited along with economic opportunities and food produce.. Competition leads to undesirable consequences, like frustration and anxiety (Jain and G. Misra, 1990). On top of that, competition can give way to violence and conflict. In the face of limited opportunities, one group is bound to become more prosperous than another. Differential prosperity fuels feelings of relative deprivation. While the core reason is economic, the conflict that ensures is psychological. The feelings of relative deprivation get directed as feelings of hostility towards a more prosperous outgroup.

Many studies conducted in India have concluded that riots and caste conflicts are a result of economic prosperity of certain sections of minority groups (See page 206). Sherif's Realistic Goal Conflict Theory also argues that intergroup competition leads to prejudice and group conflicts. All these are potential consequences of competition by a large population on a small resource base.

2. Slums and Urban environments

The worst effects of population explosion are on urban environments. Urban areas usually have more opportunities than rural areas. Due to high in-migration, urban areas become much more densely populated than the average population density of the country or state. Due to high population in very small urban areas, there is pressure of land, of good housing and basic amenities, like clean drinking water. 'Unable to meet the staggering demands for basic amenities, cities of India are characterized by teaming hovels of dirt and garbage, overcrowded and noisy lanes and a proliferation of slums. The proportion of urban populations living in slums varies from 20 to 30%. It is estimated that 1,080 slum clusters dot the sprawling megalopolis that Delhi has become. These settlements are deprived of the basic amenities of water supply, sewage and drainage systems and waste disposal facilities. This creates unhealthy living conditions' (Siddiqui and Pandey, 2003).

The people who stay in slums are disadvantaged people. They are deprived of a rich environment. Deprived of stimulations, they face many problems of physical health (for example, malnutrition) and mental health. Many studies have confirmed that they have inferior cognitive development and maladaptive personality traits. Their motivation pattern is dominated by high need for dependence and powerlessness (for details, refer the chapter on deprived groups).

3. Deviance and Delinquency

When population is high, competition to meet common goals (in terms of jobs, resources, etc.) is also high. However, the poor don't get enough opportunities to realise these goals. They are at an obvious disadvantage in realising these goals. For example, an English educated child of a rich father who can afford coaching has better advantage than a student from a slum. Non-attainment of goals leads to frustration. These people get induced to engage in crime and other deviant acts.

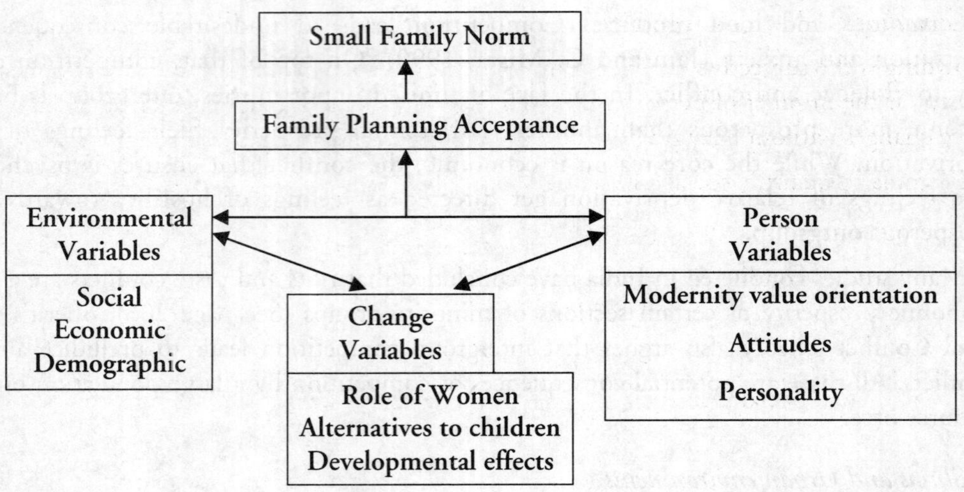

Fig.12.9 : Factors affecting the acceptance of family planning

Often, a sub-culture develops in lower socio-economic status (SES) localities. It is the sub-culture of delinquency that values crime, breaking laws and making easy money. Many children are recruited to these delinquent groups at a young age.

The crime rate in cities and nearby areas is higher than normal because of the phenomena of deviance and delinquency. With more population pressure, the incentives to show deviant behavior will also increase.

4. Spatial Behavior and Population Explosion

Two spatial concepts relevant to psychological studies are territoriality and personal space. Territoriality is the visible space occupied by a person. It is the territory that the person 'owns' in the sense that she can regulate the entry of others in this space. For example, I have a separate room in my house. I can regulate the entry of others into the room. Hence, it is my territory. On the other hand, in many slums five to six people stay in the same room. The territory of each may be negligible or absent.

Personal space is an invisible boundary one maintains while interacting with others. This is a very subjective concept. Personal space keeps varying depending on the individual's mood, time of the day, situation, the person she is interacting with, etc. For example, I would be very close and intimate with my girlfriend (at-least I will try to be. It also depends on her personal space). In the case of a close friend, my personal space will be less; with an obnoxious acquaintance my personal space becomes more. I will prefer to maintain some distance from strangers.

Many studies have focused on the psychological variables involved in territoriality and personal space. Jain (1987) raises concern that in high population density condition, the personal space is encroached upon. Indeed, many people staying in high density cities don't have any territoriality.

5. Crowding:

Crowding is the subjective experience of population density. There are broadly two meanings of density, if the number of persons in a given space are changed, the social density changes; if the space changes without changing the number of people, it is called spatial density.

Formula to quantify social and spatial density has been given below:

$$\textbf{Density} = \frac{\textbf{Number of people}}{\textbf{Space occupied}}$$

$$\textbf{Social Density} = \frac{\textbf{Number of people}}{k_1}$$

$$\textbf{Spatial Density} = \frac{\textbf{Number of people}}{k_2}$$

Where k_1, k_2 = Constants

Many psychological studies (for example, Jain, 1987) have shown that the feeling of crowding is associated with both spatial and social density. Various effects of crowding and high density are separately discussed in another section in this chapter.

Motivating for small Family Norms

Planners and scholars of India had realised the pressing problem of population explosion even before independence. Hence, a family planning programme was incorporated in the First Five Year Plan itself. The family planning programme has been a priority issue in all Five Year Plans since then. Yet, the impact of these programmes at central level, or in various states has not been impressive. Majority of Indian families don't follow the small family norm.

There are a host of social, economic and demographic factors involved in fertility behavior. These factors are, however, mediated by psychological factors, like attitude, values and personality of the husband and wife, the communication between the couple, etc. To motivate people towards small family norm, we should attack at the base factors (demographic, social and economic) as well as mediating psychological factors.

12.4 Fertility Behavior of Indians

Overall, there are three categories various people can be divided into:

1. Those who don't have knowledge of family planning and so don't follow small family norm.
2. Those who have knowledge of family planning, but their attitude towards small family norm is negative.

3. Those who have positive attitude towards small family norm, but do not show corresponding behavior.
4. Those who have positive attitude towards small family norm and show corresponding fertility behavior, such as having safe sex during risk period of menstrual cycle, using contraceptives, etc.

The fourth category is the desired category that every family planning worker wants people to be in. From a psychological perspective, the third category is most challenging. Why do these people have positive attitude towards small family norm, yet don't do family planning? Ravi Kumar Verma (1990) observes that a 'highly favourable attitude towards family planning followed by a very low practice has posed serious problems to researchers and planners alike'. And worryingly, a significant chunk of people belongs to this category. For instance, N.L. Srivastava (1975) found that nearly three-fourths of newly married males he surveyed in different parts of Patna city said that they were not in favour of large families. Nevertheless, 50% of all the pregnancies reported were unplanned.

Awareness of family planning and its advantages lead to a positive attitude towards small family. This attitude is necessary, but not a sufficient condition for fertility behavior that leads to small family norm. At this point, it may be right to discuss some individual variables affecting fertility behavior.

Based on a literature survey, R.C. Tripathi (1989) points out some factors that affect fertility behavior:

1. Lower social class urban men prefer a large family size than their wives.
2. Rural men and women desire a large family size.
3. Higher the education level and status of women, the lower is the desired family size.
4. Traditionalism is associated with a higher family size norm.

Some characteristics of those who adopt small family norm in comparison to those who don't are:

1. Value orientation

Value of free will, activism, individualism, modernism, secularism and adventure are positively correlated with the desire for small family (Katiya, 1976). On the other hand, traditional value orientation seems to promote large families. In an intensive study of family planning among Muslims in Kanpur, Khan (1979) observes that negative attitudes towards family planning are due to religious fatalism, fear of complications, husband's authority and lack of communication. Many other studies have found that fertility behavior is similar for Hindus also. So, it can generally be said that traditional value orientations, like patriarchal authority (resulting in subordination of wife's views), religious taboos, etc., hinder adoption of small family norm.

Another factor that affects fertility behavior is a strong value preference for sons. Son preference is a dominant value of our social system and finds explicit mention in our ancient scriptures. Son preference is closely associate with adoption of small family norm. The chance of getting a son till date, the probability of getting one is now higher. Hence, if a couple don't get a son in their n^{th} attempt, they get motivated to try for a $(n+1)^{th}$ time for son. I know a person who had nine daughters before having a son. Every time he guessed that now that he has so many daughters, the probability of having a son is more in the next attempt (though logically it is only 50%).

2. Attitude

Attitude is closely related to value orientation. However, those people with open attitude are more prone to accept family planning programmes, than those with authoritarian attitudes.

3. Personality

Many studies have established that acceptors of small family norm are more prone to change, possess rational thinking and have high subjective efficacy (Khan and Prasad, 1980). In a study comparing the personality traits of adopters and non-adopters, it was found that an adopter woman tends to be less anxious and more intelligent (Kumar and Gairola, 1981).

4. Motives

Many studies have found that the primary motive of having many children is old age security. Paliwal (1979), for instance, analysed the motives for desiring a third child in a village near Lucknow. The dominant motive was to have greater old age security.

Social Norm *vs.* Small Family norms

According to Fishbein and Azfen's Theory of Reasoned Action (TRA), two factors (attitude and subjective norms of the group) influence behavior. Perhaps this explains why positive attitude towards small family is not followed by corresponding behavior. Many traditional and religious norms oppose family planning measures, like use of contraceptives, abortion, etc. Catholic Christians are staunchly against abortion because they believe the fetus is a living child of God. Similarly, some Hindu and Muslim cults are against surgical contraception methods, like vasectomy.

In a classic study, Gore (1973), showed how the issue of family planning is still a taboo among tribal groups. Approximately 17% of the total tribal respondents in his study simply refused to answer questions pertaining to attitudes towards family planning. About 70% of the respondents evaded questions about the actual use of contraceptives. If such is the taboo about family planning, adherence to small family norms will obviously be low, even if the attitude is positive.

Motivating for Small Family Norms

Till now, we have just discussed factors that are conducive to or resistive to fertility behavior. This was necessary in order to make you feel the enormity of the challenge of motivating for small family norm.

Most of the government policies are based on following strategies:

1. Awareness generation through advertisements, social messages, etc. These strategies help to change attitudes, which are necessary, but not sufficient to motivate people for small family norm.
2. Rewards and punishments for showing fertility behavior. Many incentives are given to people in order to induce them to go for small families. At some stages, punishments were also meted out for having large families. Fortunately, these have been done away now.
3. At some point, especially during the emergency period, compulsory sterilisation was practiced. Not only was it unpopular, compulsory sterilisation didn't have any long term impact. Indeed, it did harm the family planning programme. People became alienated from family planning and started looking at these programmes suspiciously. All the good work done to create positive attitude towards family planning was lost.

How good a motivator is reward?

This has been the subject of much intellectual discussion. Behaviorist scholars would naturally state that rewarding behavior for small family increases the probability of it. But, this is not that simple. In the Hawthorne studies, Elton Mayo observed that employees' behavior was more motivated by group norms than rewards (bonus, pay, etc.) given by mangers. On similar lines, it can be stated that rewards aren't as potent as social norms in determining fertility behavior. In fact, they aren't good motivators at all. This was demonstrated by Khan and Prasad (1980). They studied the role of monetary incentives, when used as independent variables, explained less than 1% variance.

Now let us turn our attention to some interventions suggested by psychologists to motivate people towards small family norms:

1. Sex Education

Schools have been the favourite target of psychologists for interventions, because of the fact that values and attitudes can be best fostered here. Sex education (and health education, in general) should be made a part of curriculum of schools. Sex education is necessary because many people don't have the requisite knowledge about controlling family size. Tell me, if you don't know which period of menstrual cycle is risky, if you don't know the use of condoms, if you don't know what contraceptive pills are, or if you don't know that pregnancy can be aborted, can you follow a small family norm? Surprisingly, many people don't even know! I know, only because I am quite curious about these things. But, many don't have access to these sources of information. For them, sex education is schools is necessary.

In one study, 500 mothers of newborns were interviewed in maternity wards (M.L.Sinha, 1976). Approximately 31% of the women were not aware of family planning techniques. How do I motivate people towards small family norms, if 31% are simply beyond my range of influence! Hence, the need for sex education. S.R. Desai and N.R. Mehta (1976) have found that groups which received health education about contraceptive methods practice it more in comparison to those that do not.

2. School Education

School education as a strategy for family planning must not be restricted to sex education. Rather, the curriculum must be made more broad-based to make the students' attitudes and personality more modern and progressive. 'Modernity value orientations, such as, entrepreneurship, openness to change and subjective efficacy may be inculcated at the stage when young boys and girls are fantasising about their future. The advantages of delaying marriages should be conveyed to young boys and girls that would enable them to move around for various career alternatives.' (R.K.Verma, 1990).

3. Changing Social norms and values

Social norms appear to me as the biggest resistance to adopting small family norms. Hence, motivation strategies should include strategies to change social norms. In the chapter on Community Psychology, we have seen how social norms can be changed by concerted action of the community. The value preference for sons should be made specific focus of attack by panchayats and community leaders.

4. Awareness Creation Sensitive to social norms

Not all social norms can be changed. Religious norms are too resistant to changes. Further, various sub-cultures have their own values and folk stories. Awareness programmes can be more successful when they incorporate these folklores and religious symbols. For instance, you can design messages that say Pandu had five sons, but Dhritarashtra had 100 sons. In the battle of Kurukshetra, Pandavas won because Pandu could take better care of 5 sons. There are so many religious scriptures in Hindu literature, that in some of them you will surely find phrases that promote small family norms.

Gulati and Moni (1975) believe that motivational methods should be consistent with the sub-cultures in which they are used, because every society has its own system of communication. There are, for example, many tribal communities in which pregnancy is considered a blessing of God. These people will obviously find messages to prevent pregnancy as sacrilegious. So, you need to innovatively present your message.

5. Role Models

Role models are a very potent source of motivation. People vicariously experience the success of role models and this motivates them to follow the behavior of role models. Female role models can be highlighted to show to people that girls can also make it big in life. For those people who go for large families to get sons, showing female role models increases their expectancy from daughters.

Those members of the community who have had less number of children and have succeeded in life can also be used as role models. This increases the subjective efficacy of people. If one sees role models who have restricted family size to two children, have amply provided for the children and the children have succeeded in life, he/she is motivated to allow small family norm.

12.5 Impact of Rapid Scientific and Technological Growth

What may the impact of science and technology be on environmental degradation? Technology has no impact on environment. It is the ***application of technology by humans*** that leads to environmental degradation. Hence, the impact of scientific and technological growth on environment is mediated by ***human factors***. If the technological progress were judiciously used, it wouldn't lead to environmental degradation. Science is a body of knowledge. Technology is the application of science. Technology empowers the human to exploit his/ her natural environment. In this section, we will study human behavior in relation to the ability that technology empowers the humans with.

In the primitive period, technology that humans had at their disposal was primitive. There was axe, there was the wheel and some weapons of war. Hence, the extent to which humans could exploit the environment was limited. Technology kept changing with time and a landmark change happened during the Industrial Revolution in Europe. Since then, technological growth has been rapid and man is all-enthusiastic to adopt new technologies to be in greater control of nature. If rapid technological growth is that harmful for our natural environment, why do we use it?

A host of factors are involved in this; some of which are:

1. Diffusion of responsibility

You see the impact, still you engage in environment-degrading behavior. A major reason for this is that an individual weighs the advantages of not using the technology with the advantages of using the technology. The advantage of not using technology is a collective one, but the advantage of using the technology is a perianal one. For example, you are prompted to conserve energy by switching off light when not in use. The advantage of conserving energy is collective, but the advantage of consuming energy is personal. This leads to a social dilemma- whether to conserve energy or enjoy that energy extravagantly. In case of collective responsibility, a diffusion of responsibility happens. An individual may reason that if she uses technology incessantly, she benefits personally; and since others are showing conservation behavior, she also benefits from the collective benefit of less pollution. Problem is, when all individuals start thinking this way, the personal benefit of each is less than the collective loss in term of environmental degradation.

2. Risk Society

Sociologist Ulrich Beck had forwarded the concept of risk society to explain the dominant attitude of modern society.

We use technology and are aware that:

(i) Given the rate at which we are exploiting nature, it is not sustainable in the long term, and

(ii) The side effect of many technologies is pollution.

Still we use these technologies. We take the risk of using these technologies. People hope that new technology will be invented that will better exploit the environment in the future and be less polluting.

For instance, we are incessantly using petrol as a source of energy. We have developed technologies to harness oil from land and from sea-bed. We have technologies to drive vehicles using oil. As the oil resources get depleted from earth, we don't stop using it. Rather, funding for alternate sources of energy has increased. We have developed nuclear power plants to replace oil sometime in the future. Now that we know the uranium reserves are limited, we are researching on finding technology for fusion power plants that will use hydrogen to get very high energy.

In every step, we humans are taking risk. Nuclear power plants are more risky than thermal power plants. A small security failure in nuclear plant can lead to large-scale disasters. The waste products of nuclear power are toxic and non-biodegradable. Mere exposure to these waste products leads to genetic changes in a human. Their disposal is a bigger challenge than the waste products of thermal power plants (pollutants, like carbon monoxide, carbon dioxide, etc.)

3. Habit

Behaviorist psychologist Hull had stated that motivation to show a behavior is the product of habit strength and drive. If a behavior is habitually elicited, the habit strength for that behavior is high.

Now consider yourself. You have been born and brought up in a society, where technology is used in every step. In urban places, you have always travelled in buses, cars and bikes. Your lifestyle is a product of technology. You can't do without air-conditioning in summers. Now-a-days, you can't even manage without a mobile phone (which is toxic and non-biodegradable once you stop using it and move on to your next phone). These are some habits we can't give up. Our grandparents could happily commute using bullock carts. But, we can't do without using motor vehicles. We don't have the patience to do so. We live in a world with different levels of perception regarding lifestyle. Technology that you have grown up with affects your perception. The need of the hour is conservation behavior; sustainable development can only happen if simple living is practiced. But, our habits make us dependent on environment unfriendly technology for living.

Now, let us turn our attention to some impacts of man-made interventions in environment.

Some of these are:

1. Pollution
2. Disasters
3. Depletion of resources
4. Depletion of forests

What is important from a psychological sense is that all these impacts directly affect human life. Man-made disasters, like the Bhopal gas tragedy severely affect the life of people. Not only this, disasters have been found to lead to anxiety, Post-traumatic Stress Disorder (PTSD) and depression, etc.

12.6 Conservation Behavior

By now, I guess you have an overview of the psychological effects of environmental stressors on human behavior and effects of human behavior on the environment. Put simply, this is E – B – E pattern, that is, environment (E) affects human behavior (B), which in turn affects the environment and the process goes on. The area of concern for us is that humans show behavior that is environment degrading behavior; we extravagantly consume energy, water and other natural resources and we use technologies that pollute the environment. For a healthy person-environment relation there is a need to promote conservation behavior among people.

Why do we need to promote conservation behavior among people? Why doesn't it come naturally to people? This is because, when people contribute to a social cause, they do not get immediate rewards. For instance, the incandescent bulb consumes much more energy than compressed fluorescent lamps (CFL). But, CFL is costly and an individual may not see any direct benefit of using CFL. Platt's (1973) Theory of Social Trap states that when immediate rewards overpower us, we may even indulge in self-destructive behaviours.

Some possibilities of behavior with respect to the environment, according to me, are:

1. Conservation behavior as part of social and religious norms. For example, in some tribal societies of India, felling of trees is considered a religious offence. Tress are considered sacred.
2. Conservation behavior due to morality. Some people feel morally responsible to show conservation behavior.
3. Environment degrading behavior because of lack of awareness of environmental degradation.
4. Even when aware of the problem, one may not show conservation behavior as she may not be able to relate conservation to her personal needs. For instance, the air pollution in your city may bother you, still you use an inefficient, old scooter to drive.
5. You may be facing a social dilemma.

Let us discuss social dilemma, in detail, in the context of conservation behavior. We know that before acting out a behavior, people take decisions based on many subjective judgements and calculations about the benefits of the behavior. Social dilemma is a dilemma you face in taking decision between acting for personal interests and acting for long-term community interests. Take the example of taxation. If you don't pay tax, your personal benefit is that you save the money. The tax collected is used for community services like health, police, etc. If many people evade tax the way you do, these services won't be available and even if available, won't be of necessary quality. By this, you may be worse off.

Very similar is the social dilemma in case of environmental behavior. Before performing a behavior (say buy CFL), you wonder if the benefits are greater. If you think that the collective benefit is more than personal benefits of not buying CFL (save money), then you decide to buy CFL (which is a conservation behavior). If you find the personal benefits of not buying CFL more; you keep using environment degrading fluorescent lamps.

Interventions

Some psychological suggestions to promote conservation behavior are:

1. Awareness generation
2. Increase rewards for conservation behavior
3. Penalty for anti-environment behavior should be prompt and the delay between behavior and penalty should be low (Platt, 1973).

Ecological awareness is, according to Uday Jain and M.N.Palsana (2004), the first step for any action against environmental degradation. Awareness of environmental problems foster positive attitude towards conservation. For instance, higher levels of awareness to vehicular pollution has been found to be associated with an extremely favorable attitude towards reducing pollution (mathur and Vohra, 1991).

School-based awareness creation is a potent strategy to increase the level of awareness. This is because the level of awareness depends on personal values. Prakash and Singh (1991) have found that values such as humanism, materialism, orientation, outcome and work orientation have a strong relationship with ecological awareness. Such values should be promoted in schools, while including environment-related issues in the curriculum.

■ ■ ■

Psychology Applied to Socio-Economic Development

13

COMMUNITY PSYCHOLOGY

Chapter outline

13.1 Concepts of Community Psychology

'Community' refers to a set of social relationships based on something which the participants have in common- usually a sense of identity. It is used to refer to rural and semi-rural regions and homogenous neighbourhoods in urban areas, where social solidarity among members is high. Community psychology is a branch of applied psychology that involves working at a community level.

Hence, community psychology encompasses many fields of psychology related to the role of the community. Historically, the concept originated in reaction to the hospitalisation model of treating mental health problems. It was found that in many cases of mental health problems, hospitalisation and medication, in fact was detrimental to their health. Hence, a strong movement evolved for treating mental disorders in community-based support systems. From this beginning, community psychologists started conducting interventions in communities for solving other social problems.

There are three major sub-fields within the field of community psychology, namely (a) Empowerment, (b) Liberation Psychology and (c) Social Justice as a core Value (Orford, 2008).

The practice of community psychology is different in different societies. For instance, community psychology in the Latin America is concentrated heavily on Liberation Psychology; while community psychology in the USA and Canada has developed in the field of social justice (diversity, racial harmony, political psychology, etc.). Empowerment has been the focus area of community psychologists in India.

We shall be describing these three concepts as under:

(a) *Empowerment*

Zimmerman (1995) had floated the concept of *psychological empowerment.* He had argued that confidence and self-esteem of an individual cannot be divorced from the context in which a person feels empowered. When members of a community come together and develop a shared confidence (a common internal locus-of-control), they develop a feeling that together they can agitate to meet common goals of the community. Such shared feeling leads to social movements. Such shared feeling influences a community to proactively tackle social problems.

Each member of a weak community is known to have low self-esteem and a fatalistic attitude. The individual feels overwhelmed when confronted with a social problem. She knows that she cannot tackle the problem. But, if the community comes together and develops a shared narrative, the members of the community develop a different form of confidence. Community psychologists study the social energy that rises out of such group mobilisation and how it can be effectively used against social evils. Community psychologists devise strategies to develop a sense of empowerment in communities, where individual psychological empowerment is not possible (due to feelings of fatalism and external locus of control).

Most of the studies in community psychology in India are in the field of empowerment. We shall be discussing these concepts under subsequent sections.

(b) *Liberation Psychology*

Liberation psychology deals with mechanics of political mobilisation. Members of the poor and deprived classes usually develop feelings of fatalism, passivity and conformity. The community, as a whole, is seized by an oppressor. The community members have resigned to their fate and conform to the directions of the oppressor. For instance, Martin-Baro (1994) found that the 'popular classes' in Mexico were mired by fatalism and passivity. The challenge of a community psychologist, as per him, was to recover historical memory, expand horizons from a limited and fatalistic focus on how to survive in the present, towards visualising a different future.

There have not been much studies on liberation psychology in India. Liberation psychology focuses inordinately on revolts and rebellion, which may be more relevant in a pre-colonial India than in a post-colonial India. One can see parallels between Martin-Baro's ideas and that of freedom fighter Bal Gangadhar Tilak. Tilak realised a great problem in mobilising Indians for revolting against the British. Indians had a fatalistic attitude and a reverence towards the 'white skinned' British. They had forgotten their common historical identity. So, Tilak started Ganapati festival and Shivaji festival to instil a sense of pride in the community's own identity. He tried to shift the focus of his community from short-term survival to an alternative future of *swaraj*. His methods were later followed by Mahatma Gandhi too.

Although this author could not find any noteworthy study on liberation psychology in India in recent times, liberation psychology is nevertheless important in an Indian context. Liberation psychology can help psychologists in India understand the caste system. Community psychologists can use concepts of liberation psychology to portray the *Zamindar* or landlord as an oppressor. Secondly, they can retell history to highlight the contribution of lower castes to society and country. They can also use role models of successful persons from the community to motivate members of lower caste communities.

Liberation psychology can also be used to fuel feminism and instil a sense of confidence among women. Patriarchy is an oppressive system that puts barriers in the form of marriage laws, imagery of ideal women and social norms. Collective action of women would help them agitate against the patriarchal system.

(c) *Social Justice as a core Value*

A key target of community psychology is to instil social justice as a core value. Orford (2008) says that community psychologists have taken inspiration from the writings of economist Amartya Sen. Sen's book Development as Freedom (1999) has stated that national goals of development focus on GDP rather than individual well-being. The argument given by policymakers is that economic development would benefit everyone in the long run (basically the 'Trickle Down Theory'). But, Sen has stated that economic development should not be at the cost of short-term universal human services, such as education, health and social security.

Sen was interested in five types of instrumental freedoms:

(i) Economic facilities

(ii) Political freedom

(iii) Social opportunities

(iv) Transparency guarantees

(v) Protective security

Fondacaro and Weinberg (2002) have traced the ways in which social justice has been fostered in community psychology work. Community psychologists have emphasised, among small groups and community leaders, the importance of voice and participation in decision-making, decentralisation and local control by people in their indigenous communities. If members of a community are involved in local decision-making, they can agitate against social injustice. If their voice gets heard, they can participate actively in the political process. They can raise demands for transparency in functioning of the government.

Community psychology in Indian context

In Indian context, a major focus of community psychology has been social change and development. At independence, an ambitious programme called Community Development Programme (CDP) was designed by the state. The programme was designed by economists and touted to be a programme to mobilise the villages which were seen as the prime forces of India's development. It failed miserably. Since then, many psychologists have been involved in providing research conclusions with regards to what the right path of development is.

The first ever psychologist to attend to the challenge of social change was Prof. Durgananda Sinha. Prof. Sinha, father of India's Community Psychology Movement, made a classic analysis of the CDP in his book "Indian Villages in Transition" (1969). He reasoned that the Indian economists who had designed CDP had used an overtly top-down approach and had ignored the human factors in social change. Sinha, in fact, even drew a need-structure of villagers by using various measures for assessing needs and inspirations of villagers (1966).

Professor Durganand Sinha (1922-1998) is the most well-known psychologist of the Indian sub-continent. He is internationally renowned for contributions to the advancement of cross-cultural psychology. Prof. Sinha 'founded the Department of Psychology at Allahabad University, which is now a Centre for Advanced Study in Psychology. He related psychology to social change through analysis of value orientation across generations and emphasised indigenisation and development of a problem-oriented psychology.' (Bhatia & Sethi, 2007).

In recent times, many psychologists have taken an active interest in community-based approaches to social problems and social change.

At this point, it is apt to discuss certain points relevant to community psychology:

1. *The Challenge for Community Psychology in India*

   Different societies have different needs from community psychologists. For instance, Tokyo is the loneliest city in the world. The city also sees the largest number of suicides in the world. The challenge for community psychologists in Japan may be to develop social support mechanism. But, in India, the individual is deeply engrained in a large network of family, kin, class and neighbourhood. Social support is not as big an issue in India as issues like immunisation, birth control, education of the girl child, etc.

   In India, the key challenge for community psychologists is to make community-level interventions to effect social change. Empirical studies have revealed that people in India have a high belief in the theory of *karma*, due to which they *uncritically accept* misery and inequality. Owing to this, people do not come together to work towards removing social problems. Communities are social systems that serve to meet human needs. A vibrant community exists in India (unlike in individualistic societies). But, the communities are not aware of the efforts required to meet needs of their members. Communities in India fail to mobilise to address social problems because of the *uncritical acceptance* of poverty and social ills.

   This is the largest challenge of community psychology in India. To address this, psychologists in India make interventions at the community level, in coordination with social workers. Interventions are at two levels: meso-level (community representatives), and macro-level (residents of the community). Interventions are not made at the micro-level (specific individuals). Therapists, and not community psychologists, intervene at the micro-level.

Bhatia & Sethi (2007) opine that interventions at both meso-level and macro-level are important. Practitioners generally contact the 'panchayat' as first part of the intervention. The Panchayat consists of five members of a village community who are selected by its members to resolve disputes. Any interaction with a community is most effective when routed through the Panchayat. For instance, if a community worker wants to promote education of the girl child, she should present the justification to the Panchayat and other elders of the community. People of the community are open to change, when the rationale for a scheme is presented to them by the Panchayat. Therefore, to target a program to shed age old beliefs in a community, community workers should involve the local community leaders.

2. *Community and Mental Health*

Behaviour is a product of interaction between person and environment. Hence, maladaptive behaviour is the result of improper person-environment fit.

$B = f(P, E)$

Clinical psychologists often concentrate on the Person factor (P-factor) to correct maladaptive behaviour. The inherent flaw in the attitude of clinical psychologists is that individual differences exist. Some people are more deviant than others and hence, wide variations in p-factor exist. Rather than correct the p-factors by hospitalisation, the environmental factors (E-factors) can be made more accommodating. Indeed, many mental problems happen because of rigid environmental conditions. For example, mental problems are more prevalent among lower socio-economic status (SES) people because of the deprived environment they live in. Rigid expectations by family and community often result in maladaptive behaviour.

Community psychology uses a philosophy different from that of clinical psychology. It believes that proper person-environment fit needs to be achieved to treat mental disorders. While clinical psychologists try to 'treat' the person, community psychologists try to make the environment (community and family) more flexible, accommodative and sensitive. Hence, instead of hospitalisation, community psychology prefers community support centres to treat mental problems.

Many field studies have proved that community-based interventions are more effective than traditional medical model.

This is primarily because of the following reasons (Kool and Agarwal), 2006):

(i) Patients and their families are able to override the stigmatising effects of institutionalisation.

(ii) Allowing patients to stay in the community keeps intact the social support system which are important for the maintenance of sound mental health. Institutionalisation breaks the linkages with family and friends.

(iii) Community-based treatment is much cheaper than institution-based therapy.

(iv) The penetration of mental services would also increase because many people who do not seek professional help for fear of stigma can get treatment. Specifically, in the case of women, it has been seen that they have greater mental problems in India but get fewer opportunities for treatment. This method can increase the reach for such women.

Community Mental Health Programme aims at the 5 A's – availability, accessibility, affordability, acceptability and assessment. (WHO, 2001).

2. *Social Change and Development*

Development means *planned* social change. It is a value-biased concept used by economists because economists believe that by economic planning, progressive social change is possible. It is value-biased because the social change is not planned by members of the society/ community, but by external agents, such as policy-makers and economists. The ideology of development refers to a belief about what should be the action plan for social change. It is not determined by people, but by policy-makers. In short, the ones whom we seek to modernise by social change aren't consulted when determining what is good for them!

3. *Concept of Social Energy*

Social energy is the key to understand social action. Fossil energy drives a car. Motivational energy drives individual behaviour. But then, what about collective behaviour like social movements? These collective behaviours (i.e., social action) are driven by social energy.

There are three steps to the creation of social energy (J.B.P. Sinha, 1990):

(a) Experience of extreme social deficit.

(b) Outcome efficacy, i.e., belief that it is remediable.

(c) Social efficacy, i.e., disposition of social groups to take initiative.

Prof. Jai B.P. Sinha argues that Indians are of collectivistic orientations and hence are embedded in groups and collectivities. Social energy easily develops in such groups. How then can Indians be called fatalistic and dependence prone? Social arousal (i.e., social energy) is more oriented towards traditional action (such as, engaging in rituals, following one's ancestral occupation, etc.) than modern social action. Groups in India can be aptly mobilised on the lines of religion, customs and traditional social action rather than modern social action. Think, how effectively can social problems, like drug abuse, alcoholism, fertility behaviour and environmental degradation be solved if people are mobilised to collectively act towards removing these problems from their community!

So, what is the solution? Prof. Sinha believes that social energy needs to be *redirected*, i.e., channelled towards progressive social action. They do this by mobilising people using traditional symbols and cultures towards solving social problems for development. Take, for instance, the case of Mahatma Gandhi. No leader before him could become a mass leader. No leader could mobilise the rural population of India the way he could, for the National Movement. The National Movement was modern, social action aimed at formation of a free democratic society. Yet, Gandhi used many traditional symbols and Hindu rituals to mobilise people. He claimed that he wanted to establish a "Ram Rajya" and frequently quoted from the Gita.

Hence, the potential for social action is there in Indian collectivities. The social energy is, however, traditionally oriented. The local leaders and community psychologist need to *channelise* to local traditions and customs.

Such interventions, when conducted through local leaders, are more effective. P. Mehta (1983) has narrated a case of tribals of a village who were mobilised by local leadership to implement development sciences for the village. Co-operatives and Panchayts work successively in many parts of India (P.Mehta, 1978) primarily because members of these institutions and local citizens know each other personally; panchayat leaders are revered tradition.

4. *Community as a social system*

If you seek to find ways to remove social problems and make developmental designs for a community, you need to understand various institutions and individual factors that stabilise the society. By analysing the community as a social system, we can know the sub-systemic factors that reinforce and sustain this system. One such system has been proposed by Prof. Udai Pareek (1970). Prof. Pareek claims that behaviour (B) is a result of motivation (M) and value (V), which in turn are caused by the social system (SS) in which the individual lives.

The paradigm is represented as:

(SS) → (M<V) → (B)

These values and motivational patterns are proposed by social system and in turn, help maintain the social system. Hence, the social system attains stability.

This system has been represented by Pareek as:

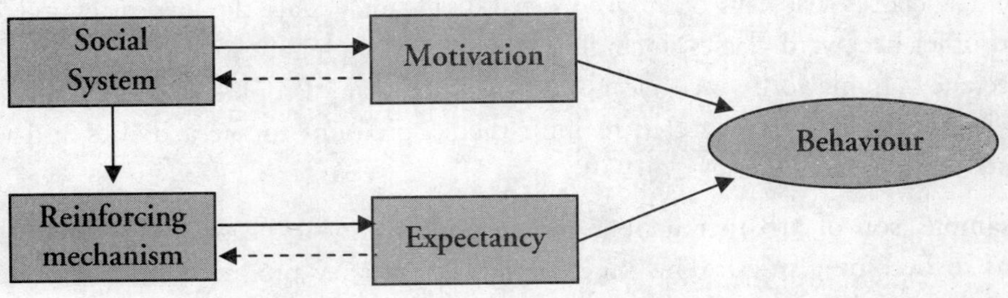

Fig. 13.1 : Pareek's model of Social System

Reinforcing mechanism is central in this model. These mechanisms reinforce not only the social system, but also the level of expectancy and motivational patterns. These mechanisms include child rearing practices, the school system and other institutions of socialisation. By socialisation, expectancy is passed from one generation to another. By this, expectancies of motivational patterns are institutionalised and routinised.

Conceptualising the community as a system, helps us in understanding the factor that resists change. Also, the model proposed by Prof. Pareek links the *social system* to *individual processes,* like motivation and expectancy and ultimately to individual behaviour. This model can be used in studying individual behaviour in systems that are change-resistant, like 'culture of poverty', impediments to development and economic growth and institutionalised gender differences in society. This model has been applied in various chapters relating to the above issues.

13.2 Social Change

Society can be viewed as a system, with various reinforcing mechanisms that sustain the system. The primary reinforcing mechanism is socialisation that helps the individual internalise social values regarding expectancies. Take the case of an Indian village that is basically a feudal system, divided into various castes. By the process of socialisation, a belief in *karma* and *bhagya* are internalised by an individual, due to which he develops a fatalistic attitude. Renowned social scientists **Max Weber** (1958) had observed that the belief in *karma* and *bhagya* is a major reason for India's under-development. *Karma* is a philosophical construct that states- *do your work without expecting any reinforcement.* This value system discourages expectancy and thereby motivation.

Another feature of the village community of India is the caste system. Though sociologists have shown that it is a dynamic entity, the caste system with its rigidity and exploitative hierarchy has sustained in India from time immemorial. How it has been able to do so, will be an important lesson for any social change analyst.

Prof. Pareek observes that 'as in any traditional society, a section of people in India are underprivileged and discriminated against by those who have enjoyed power for several centuries. The classes that have been faced social disadvantages are the low castes and low caste tribes and other backward classes, including women. In the highly structured society of India, the expectancy framework was clear and well-defined. People who belonged to the underprivileged classes were expected to limit their aspirations to the activities and vocations appropriate to their particular class' (1970).

For example, son of a barber neither got an opportunity to become a priest nor had the aspirations to become a priest. This kind of rigid expectancy produced behaviour that made social change among these people almost impossible" (Pareek, 1970).

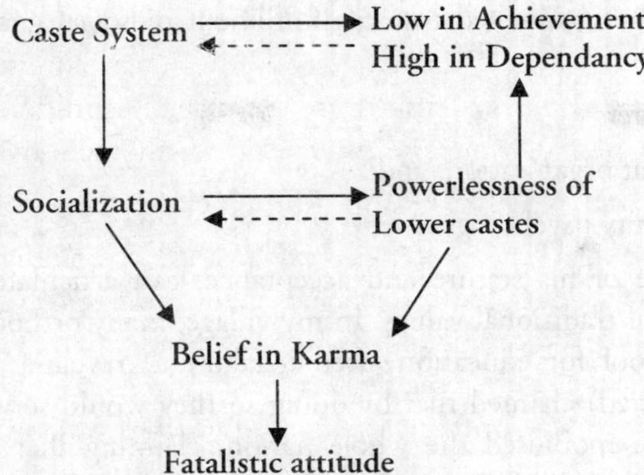

Fig. 13.2 : Resistance to change by caste-based society

Effective strategies for Social Change

Development economists and community psychologists differ widely in the strategies that they advocate for social change. The fallacy in strategies adopted by economists was exposed in Community Development Programme (CDP) and other such programmes for planned social change. Basically, these strategies always ignored human factors in social change. Rather than focussing on changes in attitudes, motivations and social norms of human factors, their focus was on introducing modern technology and infrastructure. As Woytinsky (1975) rightly observed, the main source of India's weakness lies not in lack of innate abilities or technical skills of the people, but 'a lack of initiative, of interest in improving their economic status'. If we transplant overnight 'all the factories of Michigan, Ohio and Pennsylvania to India without changing the economic attitudes of her people, then decades later, the country would be as poor as it is now. On the other hand, if by some magic, the psychology of 150 million employees, self- employed persons and employees who constitute India's labour force were overnight transformed; India would be covered two decades later with modern mills, power stations, and speed highways and her per capita income would have increased many times despite scarcity of domestic capital' (Woytinsky, 1957).

In the light of the above arguments, psychologists have reasoned that the only way to effect social change is to **mobilise** people for social action and social change. No one can change me if I don't want to change! The Community Development Programme (CDP) failed because it was a top -down intervention that aimed to change society by rewards and punishments. The spirit of social change was not internalised by the people.

In the light of these facts, psychologists recommend certain alternate strategies for social change:

1. *Channelling of Social Energy:*

   As seen in page 258, the potential for generation of social energy is there in Indian collectivities. Social energy 'innately' develops in collectivistic societies, like India. However, channelling that towards fulfilling social goals is a challenge.

The energy can be channelled towards fulfilment of social goals primarily by three kinds of agents:

(a) The local leaders

(b) The panchayat organisation, and

(c) The community psychologists

A leader, because of his stature and acceptance, can articulate the need for social change in terms of traditional values. In my village, many orthodox parents sent their daughters to school for education after a 'fakir' (a travelling mendicant who was immensely respected) claimed that by doing so they would serve Goddess Saraswati! Similarly, Gandhi mobilised the whole nation, claiming that by overthrowing the British, he would establish "Ram Rajya". Village councils, like Panchayat provide institutional support; these councils are composed of individuals who are part of the community and hence, have better rapport with the locals. A crucial agent here is the community psychologist, or the trained para-professional in her absence. Community psychologists, due to their strong background of theoretical research, can study the need structure of the community and identify various needs of the community. They provide the leader with a rich research- based knowledge and facilitate the process of social change.

2. *Changing Motivational Pattern:*

The self-sustaining social system (SS) affects individual behaviour (B) through motivation (M) and value (V)

$(SS) \rightarrow (M, V) \rightarrow (B)$

Hence, to break the vicious cycle, an appropriate strategy is to change motivation of the individuals. According to Pareek, there are three factors responsible for development (i.e., social change) (1970). This he represents by the formula:

$$D = AM \times EM - DM$$

Where, D = Development

AM = Achievement Motivation

EM = Extension Motivation

DM = Dependence Motivation

It has been seen that as in other traditional societies, Indian communities are characterised by high levels of DM and individuals have low AM ad EM. While achievement motivation has been popularised by McClelland's theory (see chapter 11), EM and DM are also important concepts to be looked into. High dependence motivation leads to fatalistic attitude, lack of initiative, fear of failure and low risk taking. Extension motivation refers to motives that orient the individual towards cooperative relation with others. In a country like India, one individual can't possibly progress all by herself. Rather, cooperative development of all members of the community is an effective strategy for social change. Hence, the need to increase extension motivation.

Many training schedules have been devised on improving achievement motivation, inspired by McClelland's Kakinada experiment. Dependency needs can be decreased effectively by making use of sensitivity training, wherein people experiment with new patterns of behaviour and develop inter-dependence in place of dependence (Pareek, 1970). Prof. Pareek observes that extension needs can be increased by training on the lines of Sherif's Robbers Care Experiment (see chapter 9) and setting super-ordinate goals.

3. *Small Groups:*

   Small groups are effective means for weak individuals to come together and improve their social efficacy. Many factors underline the importance of small groups as an effective strategy for social change. These have been detailed in another section of this chapter.

4. *Institutional Support:*

   After failure of large-scale developmental programmes, like Community Development Programme (CDP), many scholars have asked that what is the role of government? Well, government has a large role to play as a support system. Rather than top-down approach, government needs to decentralise policy-making and make community members participants of social change. In one village, the villagers took decision and the outcome of the initiative was positive. In another, a NGO took decision. The initiative failed. This emphasises the superiority of bottom-up approach.

   Also, appropriate sensitivity towards the socio-cultural milieu is necessary. S.C. Dube had observed that many programmes are rejected not because the people are traditionally minded, conservative, or 'primitive', but because the innovations, in all their ramifications, do not fit into the total cultural setting of the community'. (1958)

5. *Role of Women:*

   Women are essential agents to change, yet they are often neglected in the change process. Sonalkar (1975) has cited the case of some Adivasi women who had acted to banish alcoholism from their village. Similarly, a field study by Focus on Children Under Six (FOCUS) found that Infant and Child Development Scheme (ICDS) is more successful in Tamil Nadu than other states. Economist Jean Dreze, associated with FOCUS, believes that it was because of women's participation in ICDS in Tamil Nadu.

The importance of women in social change is being increasingly felt; many women-based small groups are being constituted for various social goals. For example, the renewed Sarva Shiksha Abhiyan (SSA) talks of Mother – Teacher Association (MTA) and about entrusting the responsibility of mid-day meals to mothers!

Human Factors in Social Change

The focus of development programmes since Independence has been on social change in the village community. The strategy adopted in these planned social change interventions was to provide technological and infrastructural support to rural folks (farmers, entrepreneurs, small groups, etc.) with the hope that these modern technologies will bring about rapid rural change. The flaw in this thought was that the government couldn't understand that there are two factors involved in economic growth and social change: *technology* and *humanology*. All these programs (such as Community Development Programme, Integrated Rural Development Programme) failed because of the prime reason that the individual farmers in the village were not ready to accept change.

A pre-requisite before undertaking social change is to understand the members of the community (i.e., the human factors) you seek to change. We will not make the same mistake that successive economists in charge of various five-year plans made. Hence, in this section, I seek to provide a sketch of the rural man; the rural farmer and the village entrepreneur; their motivational features and attitudes.

Durgananda Sinha, arguably the foremost researchers on Community Psychology in India, reports that the vast majority of rural people lack the urge for growth and are lethargic and indifferent to material progress (1984). The perceived basic needs are primarily food, clothing and shelter (Muthayya, 1982). The humans in various villages of India are more motivated by instant gratification than delayed gratification. In the midst of such a situation, researchers have found that most farmers are resistant to change. Only a few are change-prone farmers. What are the characteristics of change resistant and change-prone farmers?

Change-resistant People

Change-resistant farmers are those farmers who are unwilling to change their traditional occupations. They are the ones who don't adopt innovations. They don't accept new technologies and hence, can't benefit from various development programs. Some characteristics of such farmers are:

1. Their **aspirations** are limited to the *satisfaction of basic needs.* Their expectancies are limited. Hence, even if a new technology or a new employment opportunity provides better remuneration, they don't get motivated to change over from their traditional occupations.
2. They have **high fear of failure.** Adopting a new technology, for example, is always risky. Although the government provides soft loans to buy new machinery and HYV seeds, these change-resistant farmers don't take the risk. This is because they have a very high fear of failure.
3. These farmers' **belief system** is dominated by *traditional beliefs and attitudes.* They often lack empirical knowledge on their subjects of interest (Alexander, 1982).
4. They have a very *low awareness* of community problems. Indeed, these people don't consider the village society as a community. Rather, they are resistant to any change that demand a partnership of all castes in solving the problems of the village community.

Change-prone people

Many psychological studies have tried to sketch the profile of people who have a positive attitude towards change. They are not status quasits.

In comparison to the change-resistant people, they have some typical psychological characteristics:

1. They have a *realistic level of aspiration* (Hundal and S. Singh, 1980).
2. They are high on *adoption behaviour,* i.e., they are more likely to adopt new innovations. For example, a change-prone individual would send his daughter to school if this facility is available. A change-prone farmer would accept new technologies in his farm.
3. They are better educated, intelligent, show more manual dexterity and less emotionality than change-resistant people. (Rai, 1977).
4. Farmers who are *young in age* are found to be more change prone. Further, graduate farmers have greater economic motivation, risk preference and innovativeness compared to non-graduate farmers. Indeed, illiterate farmers are more fatalistic than literate ones (Hiriyanmaiah and M.K.S.Rao, 1963).
5. Significant positive relationship has been observed between change proneness and need for achievement, risk-taking and aspiration score (P.S.N. Tiwari, 1980).

The above profile of change-resistant members of a community and change-prone members helps us get an insight into the human factors involved in social change. There are many other factors, such as technology, governmental interventions, infrastructure, knowledge of these new technologies, availability of capital, etc. that affects social change. However, all these factors can't lead to change (or development) unless the human factors accept it. Any attempt at changing a community needs to necessarily consider the members of the community and human factors, like attitude, motivation, beliefs, values, etc. A majority of people are change-resistant. They are steeped in tradition and ritualistic behaviour (such as superstitions, sacrifice to God for better rain, etc.). These people can be cajoled to adopt change only if they find the agents of change congruent to their traditional benefits.

13.3 Small groups in Social Action

Small groups are informal, face-to-face, primary groups. Small groups were discovered for the first time in the **Hawthorne studies**. Though small groups are as old as human society (even older), they were 'discovered' in the sense that the role of small groups in social and organisational action was empirically seen for the first time in the Hawthorne studies.

In India, many studies have proved that small groups are potent tools for making community-level interventions. For instance, Moni Nag (2002) has documented how small groups were successfully used in Sonagachi area of Kolkata (which houses a red-light district) as catalyst for social change. Sex workers in Sonagachi had an *external locus of control* and a fatalistic attitude towards life. As a result, they did not make any effort to use protection against sexually transmitted diseases, like HIV/AIDS. Social workers selected few sex workers who showed initiative and trained them. The training instilled a sense of pride and self-confidence in them. Sex workers participating in the training developed a positive attitude towards life and got convinced that they need to protect their health in order to have a good future. They mobilised other sex workers and formed an association. The association enforced safe sex and sex education among its members.

Small groups can be formed automatically or they can be intentionally formed. Research conducted by community psychologists and organisational psychologists in last few decades have brought to the fore the fact that small groups can be formed and used for effective social action and to effect social change.

Some of the features that make the small group a potent tool for social action are:

(i) Generation of social energy

(ii) Advantages of group decision-making

(iii) Role of group norms in social change

(iv) Risk-taking behaviour

(v) Higher extension motivation

1. Generation of social energy:

For any social action to take place, there is a need for social energy. Social energy is best generated in small groups. Because of the informal nature of group interaction,

(a) Problems are better identified and articulated.

(b) Social efficacy about their ability to mitigate the problem develops early.

(c) Expectancy of a better future exists.

The above steps are the preliminary steps of any collective action. Hence, social motivation for action is best developed in small groups.

2. Advantages of group decision-making:

There can be no social action without a collective decision taken towards fulfilment of certain social goals using specific means. Because of the face-to face relation in small groups, decisions are collectively taken. Such group decisions are more effective than decisions taken by a government functionary or an NGO or a social change activist, as every member takes individual responsibility for implementation of the decision. As the individual is part of decision-making process, she can't oppose the decision at a later stage. In one study (Om Prakash, 1984), two villages, wherein development initiatives were being taken were studied. In one, developmental activities were initiated by the locals collectively through small groups. In another, decisions were taken by a voluntary organisation. The former was found to be much more successful than latter.

3. Role of group norms in social change:

It is said that social norms are very hard to change because these are internalised by the individual during socialisation. The most persistent way to bring about social action towards a favourable social goal is to change social norms. But, it is not that easy to change social norms of a community. For example, paying dowry during a marriage is a social norm. It is not easily challenged because if any parent challenges the norm, he faces social boycott and stigma. He is looked down as a deviant. Also, being an age-old practice, it is widely considered legitimate.

From the Hawthorne studies, Mayo had found that small groups develop their own norms. This fact has multiple implications:

(a) Group norms can spread to society and change social norms.

(b) Group norms can control and discipline individual members in ways that even legal authorities cannot.

Individual behaviour is motivated more by group norms than simple reward and punishment. This is the reason why the Hawthorne studies workers weren't motivated by monetary rewards; their performance was contingent upon group norms.

4. Moderate Risk-taking behaviour:

A major factor that impedes social change and economic development in our traditional society is the very low level of achievement motivation. Basically, individuals are more dependence-prone, lack initiative and have high fear of failure. As a result, they show very low risk-taking behaviour. Small groups help in increasing the risk-taking potential of individuals. But how?

We know from theoretical research that **polarizing effect** happens in groups due to which decisions taken in groups are riskier than the decisions of individuals. Groups are prone to take riskier decisions due to diffusion of responsibility. Hence, in groups, the low risk-taking behaviour gets converted into moderate risk-taking behaviour.

In groups, there is a diffusion of responsibility and decisions become less conservative because responsibility for negative consequences will be shared. Fear of failure decreases and this prompts members to approve of bold decision for social action.

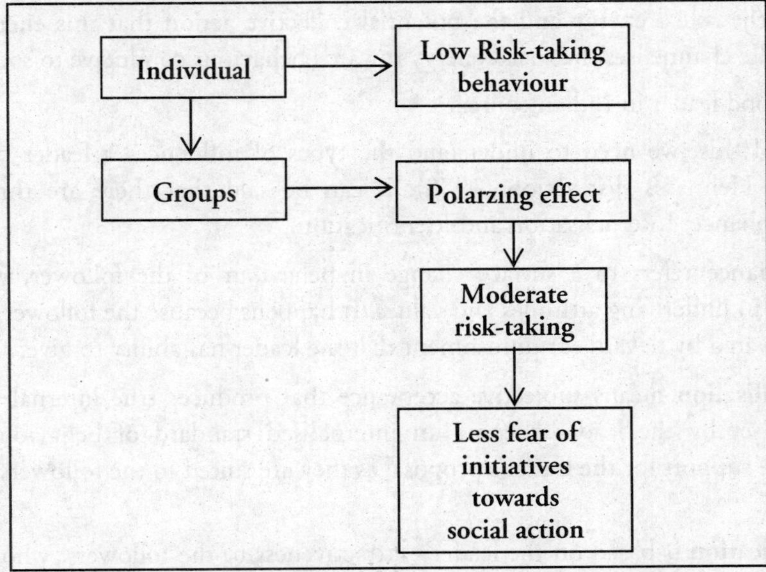

Fig. 13.3 : Dynamics of group decision-making

5. Economic Behaviour:

Small groups have been found to be especially effective for economic development. As seen above, moderate risk-taking behaviour develops that promotes achievement orientation.

Also, D = AM × EM – DM and small groups increase extension motivation of a group. Extension motivation bring the motivation for developing with consideration for compatriots. EM increases in small groups. Since member of small groups cooperate towards fulfilment of a common goal, extension motivation is high in these groups.

Situating Small Groups

Small groups have become popular because of their ability to effect social change. Small groups are being used in social action to bring about economic development, to better the condition of poor, to rid society of social ills and to change age-old norms. For example, self-employed women's association (SEWA) forms small groups of women for entrepreneurial ventures. Small groups have more efficiency to take moderate risks than individuals.

13.4 Leadership and Group Decision–Making

In any social interaction, some people have more power than others. Here, power refers to the ability to influence others. In a village community, the role of local leaders is paramount to effect social change. These leaders have the ability to influence the community members for collective social action. Prof. J.B.P. Sinha argues that since Indians are collectivists, groups in India are quite conducive to generate social energy (discussed earlier in this chapter). The leader, because of the influence and respect he has, can give a direction to his social energy. The leader identifies the social energy and the potential collective action that this energy that can lead to. Further, he channelises the social energy towards behaviour conducive to social change.

So, who is a good leader in Indian context?

To understand this, we need to understand the types of influences a leader can have on followers. Using Helman's distinction (1958), it can be said that there are three types of influences- Compliance, Internalisation and Identification.

- **Compliance** refers to a surface change in behaviour of the follower, without any change in underlying attitudes and values. It happens because the follower's behaviour is motivated by rewards or punishment that the leader has ability to give.
- **Internalisation** means subjective acceptance that produces true internal change; the norms set by the leader become an internalised standard of behaviour. There is genuine support for the leader's proposal as they are suited to the followers' values and beliefs.
- **Identification** is based on the leader's attractiveness to the followers, who imitate the leader's behaviour and attitudes to gain her approval.

Coming to a community setting, there are three major types of leaders affecting the community:

1. Officials of bureaucracy
2. Traditional leadership
3. Charismatic leaders

Officials refers to those leaders who have been appointed by the state. These officials derive their authority from a rational legal constitution. The District Magistrate (DM) and Tehsildar are examples of this kind of leaders. Problem here is that they use *only compliance* as a tool to influence the community. They use only reward and punishment to change the behaviour of community members. Rather than lead to social change, this may in fact increase dependence and lead to a *saviour's syndrome,* where an individual takes no initiative and prefers to be directed. The point is that there is no change in the underlying attitude of people.

Traditional leaders are those who are respected by tradition. *Fakirs*, temple priest, *tantriks* (experts in black magic), the local school teacher and panchayat members are examples of these leaders. They influence by way of both compliance and internalisation. Panchayat is a local leadership which is traditional and has been bestowed with legal power by the Constitution.

It has been seen that traditional leaders are more effective than officials.

This is because of numerous reasons:

1. In India, the government is modern and rational, but the village community is steeped in feudal mentality. Hence, a leader with traditional authority is best suited to influence people.
2. Traditional leaders influence followers by internalisation. Hence, there is a change in attitude of followers.
3. Traditional leaders are part of the community and hence, better understand the needs and abilities of the community. While officials use a top-down approach to social action, traditional leaders use a *bottom-up approach.*
4. Indians are rooted in traditional values and norms. Any attempt to mobilise them needs to make use of these traditional beliefs and values. Traditional leaders do it better than District Magistrates and Tehsildars as these officials aren't from the community.

Using the above argument, it can be pointed out that many early developmental programmes (such as CDP) failed because the officials were vested with power to provide aid and assistance. These officials use rewards to influence behaviours. Hence, the fabled *'fatalistic attitude'* of locals wasn't changed! *The change in behaviour wasn't permanent; people ceased to show the behaviour when state aid was discontinued.* Hence, today a strong case is being made for decentralisation and devolution of power to panchayats.

Charismatic leaders are superior to both bureaucratic officials and panchayats because they influence followers by identification. When followers identify with the leader, they try to imitate actions and opinions of the leader. An appropriate example of charismatic leadership is

Mahatma Gandhi. The man was able to mobilise the masses in Indian villages (who were stereotyped as fatalistic and high on dependence) for the National Movement. Even the most popular national leader before him, Lokamanya Tilak, was unable to mobilise the villages.

Types of leaders	Influence of leaders over people	Examples
Officials of bureaucracy	Coercion	District Magistrate and Tehsildar
Traditional	Coercion and internalisation	Panchayats and other village councils
Charismatic	Identification	Gandhi, J.P.Narayan, Lalu Prasad Yadav

Group Decision-making

Though the leader has an influence over community members, she should include them in the decision-making process concerning social action. Group decision-making has many advantages over an autocratic style of decision-making. Group decisions are *more effective* than individual decisions, as every member takes individual responsibility for implementation of the decision. As the individual is part of decision-making process, he can't oppose the decision at a large stage.

Another advantage of group decision-making is that it leads to *moderate risk-taking behaviour.* Villagers in India have low risk taking potential and have high fear of failure. In group decision, a 'polarizing effect' takes place, i.e., decisions become less conservative. As a result, decisions taken are of moderate risks. And moderate-risk actions are optimal; they are better than low risk or high-risk tasks.

When to go for group decision-making? The leader need not always consult the group as the process is cumbersome, time-taking, and not suitable when quick decisions have to be taken. It depends on (a) situational factors and (b) followers. The leader has to perceive which decisions demand consensus. For example, if a form of action requires cohesion and dissent is dangerous at a later stage, the leader consults the community members before taking decisions.

Arousing Community Consciousness

The causes of social problems are social in nature. Hence, these problems can best be solved by efforts from within the society. External forces, like government policies, have been found to be incapable in solving problems, like AIDS, drug addiction and alcoholism because they are deeply rooted in the society. It is increasingly being realised that community is the best agent for ameliorating social problems. It is, however, found that communities often lack proper awareness about social problems; then how can they collectively act to remove these problems? Community consciousness about social problems is low; hence the need to arose community consciousness for handling social problems.

The above can be illustrated with a few examples. Often, parents of adolescents involved in drug abuse aren't able to identify the symptoms of drug abuse in their children. AIDS is associated with many social stigmas, due to which many AIDS patients find it tough to live a life a dignity after AIDS. They are discriminated against on the perception that AIDS is a contagious disease. Further, the health awareness of community members isn't high; as a result, they don't follow lifestyle conducive for healthy life. Sometimes, community's prejudices even aggravate a problem. For instance, it is generally believed that schizophrenics' children are also prone to mental problems. This belief reflects discriminative behaviour, which may turn healthy offspring of a mental patient into schizophrenia by self-fulfilling prophecy!

Role of mass media

Mass media touted as a potent tool to create community consciousness about social problems. For instance, the government of India invests heavily in communicating messages on small family norms to the people through mass media. Have they been successful? Psychologists believe that not all messages are successful in creating community consciousness.

For instance, the target population may selectively attend to information that confirms their original attitude. Once a message is attended to, we selectively evaluate messages; we are prone to look favourably upon information that suggests our attitudes.

Some psychological aspects need to be taken care of while designing messages to arouse community consciousness by mass media. Individual and group differences need to be considered. Those people for whom the subject has personal relevance, do *central processing* of the message; for them, the message must have rich content. Others process the message peripherally. For them, advertisement with *peripheral cues* should be designed. For example, if one has to design AIDS awareness ads, she faces two target groups. Parents of teenagers find the issue personally relevant and are knowledgeable about AIDS. They would seek high quality messages that are rich in information and logical. On the other hand, the teenagers know less about AIDS and do not find it personally relevant. For them, peripheral processing of ads is better and should be designed accordingly.

Fear has been found to be an effective tool to arouse the community's awareness about social issues. However, according to Mc Guire (1968),t minimal or extreme fear is not effective. At low levels of fear, the individual's id not sufficiently aroused. At moderate fear level, attention and arousal increases as fear increases. When fear is too high, attention decreases again, but this time because defences are used to deal with extreme fear. The message may be *denied or repressed*. Hence, the message must have moderate fear element.

The above relationship can be explained by an Inverted-U relation:

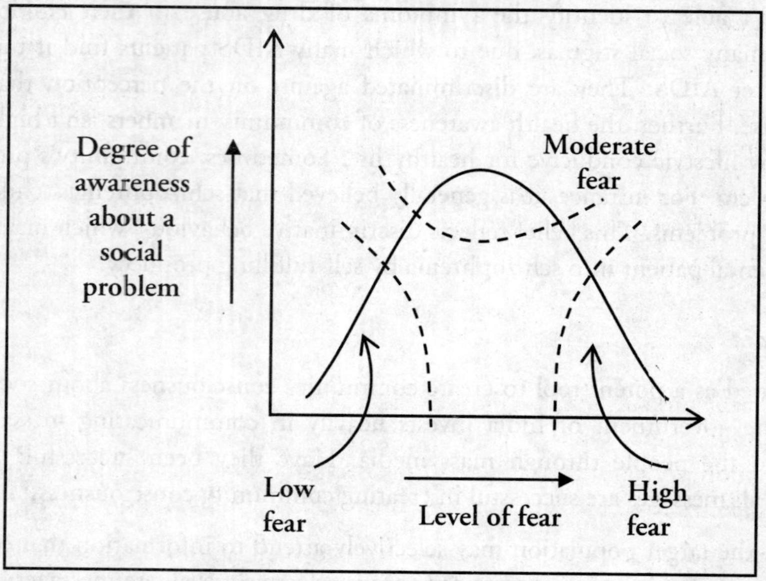

Fig. 13.4: Relation between fear and awareness (based on Mcguire)

A Study as example

(Source: Passer and smith (2007), p. 227)

In the 1990s, Tanzania in Africa faced a growing AIDS crisis that was fuelled by risky sexual practices and widespread misinformation about HIV transmission at the community and individual level. Many believed that HIV was spread by mosquitoes; still others believed that the lubricants on condom cause AIDS. Some believed that AIDS could be cured by sex with a virgin. Unsafe sexual contact between truck drivers and prostitutes further spread HIV.

To combat this crisis, the Tanzanian government produced and aired 208 episodes of radio soap, operate over several years.

The soap operated featured three types of role models:

1. Positive role models were knowledgeable about HIV/AIDS, minimised risky behaviour and ultimately attained favourable social outcomes.
2. Transitional role models began by acting irresponsibly, but eventually adopted safer heterosexual behaviour.
3. Negative role model engaged in risky sex that led to punishing outcomes. For example, a character named Mkwaju engaged in unsafe sex, had unprotected sex with many girlfriends and ignored warnings about AIDS. Later, Mkwaju contracts HIV and eventually dies.

The programs content was designed with three purposes:

1. Create awareness that risk of contracting HIV/AIDS is high.
2. Increase the listener's self-efficacy by showing them how to control the risk.
3. Change behaviour of listeners by inducing them to have less number of sexual partners and use condom when having sex.

In the five-year period in which the programme was aired, the effects were studied by Peter Vavughan and his colleagues (2000) in what is now considered a good longitudinal study. They found that 80% of the listeners found the program useful in increasing their awareness about HIV/AIDS.

Role of Education

Education is a means to socialise a child. As such, it has an important role to play in arousing community consciousness. Consciousness of children towards social problems is increased through information provided about these problems. For example, providing information about drug and alcohol helps in sensitizing students towards these problems.

Not only child education, adult education can also focus on awareness about social problems. Community centres can be used to disseminate information regarding social problems.

Innovative Methods of awareness Generation

Many other means can be used to create awareness about social problems. Distributing informative papers, writing slogans and street plays on social problems are also effective in rousing community consciousness. For example, take the case of Society for Theatre in Education programme (STEP) in New Delhi. It uses street performances to entertain people between 13-25 years of age, while teaching them ways to say no to drugs. This program has been chosen as an example to follow by United Nations International Drug Control Programme (UNDCP) for other NGOs in India.

■■■

14

Psychology and Economic Development

Chapter outline

14.1 Achievement Motivation and Economic Development

Achievement Motivation (AM) refers to striving for success with some standard of excellence. It is a social motive, that is, the motive force varies from society to society. American psychologists David McClelland had reasoned in his books, Achieving Society (1961) and Motivating Economic Achievement (1965) that a positive relationship exists between need for achievement among various societies and economic development of these societies.

In presenting his thesis, McClelland took intellectual inspiration from two people- Winter bottom (1953) and Max Webber. Winter bottom had discovered close association between child-rearing practice (CRP) and the need for achievement in children. Her interference was that mothers of high achievement groups expected their sons to be independent and self-reliant. On the other hand, mothers of low achievement groups place ample restriction upon their sons. McClelland was inspired by that fact that child rearing practice determines achievement motivation. He reasoned that CRP in any society is affected by the value system in that society. Hence, the need for achievement inculcated in CRPs must be manifested in folk tales that are an expression of the value system. Here, he tries to draw a relation between society and achievement motivation (AM). Based on this, he drew up a hypothesis that AM varies from society. To improve this hypothesis, he conducted a study in 30 different societies; he measured children on TAT scores and studied the folk tales of these countries. He tries to correlate the AM in TAT stories to the society.

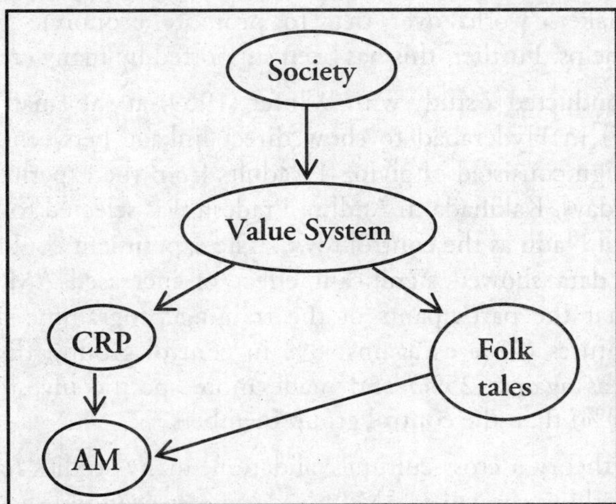

Fig. 14.1 : Effect of social values and beliefs on achievement motivation

Next, McClelland proceeded to study Max Webber's thesis of *Protestant Ethics and the Spirit of Capitalism.* This thesis argues that modern capitalism developed only in protestant society because of the protestant ethic. The protestant ethic is set of values that promote work as a service to God. Hence, protestant capitalists worked hard to earn profits. However, they were not motivated by profits. Rather, they reploughed the profits to back into their business. Webber had reasoned that the protestant ethic had caused this kind of entrepreneurial behavior (thrift + profit making + reploughing profits into the business), whereby profits were not an end in itself, but success in business venture was. But, McClelland argued that there were certain *mediating factors* between protestant ethic and modern capitalism. McClelland found that protestant parents stressed earlier independence and self – reliance in their children (McClelland, Rindlishbacher and Dechorms, 1955). Protestant parents expected their sons to do well in school, and show other competencies at the age of 61/2, while Irish parents made same expectation at the age of 71/2 and Italian parents at the age of about 81/2.

So, McClelland reasoned that protestant ethic had an effect on CRP, which, in turn, led to rise of an Achievement level, which in turns led to the rise of modern capitalism.

From a study of 30 countries, he found that, whenever TAT stories and folklores reflected high AM, the economic growth of that country was also high.

In short, his thesis is based on validation of following arguments:

1. Child-rearing practices affect AM in children.
2. CRPs vary from society.
3. Societies where children have higher AM (as measured from TAT stories and folklores) have higher economic growth.

Evidence

One of the greatest attraction of McClelland's theory was that McClelland believed that AM can be inculcated by training. Since higher AM is related to higher economic growth, it became a mandate for policy-makers world over that to promote economic growth, training in achievement motivation helps. Further, this has been supported by many cross-cultural studies.

McClelland himself conducted a study with Winter (1969) at the small Industry Extension Training Institute (SIET) in Hyderabad to show direct linkage between AM and economic activity. The research design consisted of giving 15 adults from the experimental town training of improving AM for 10 days. Kakinada in Andhra Pradesh was selected to be the experimental town and Vellore in Tamil Nadu as the control town. The experiment couldn't be completed as per the design, but the data showed significant effect of increased AM on entrepreneurial activity. It was found that the participants of the training programme made more definite attempt to start new ventures (22% as against 8% in control group), displayed more active business behavior (51% as against 25%) and made more specific investment in productive capital (74% as against 40%) than the control group members.

To give McClelland's theory a cross-cultural validation, many studies have been conducted in various places of the world to show that AM indeed increase economic activity.

14.2 McClelland's Theory: An Evaluation

McClelland's theory was part of a triangle of modernisation theory, with economist Rostow and sociologists Talcott Persons and McClelland representing the three corners of the theory. Modernization theory believed that developing countries can develop the same way that developed countries did. Hence, McClelland advocated that individualistic AM should be promoted in people. The modernization theory of Parsons and Rostow has largely been discredited today, because of their ideological bias. Then, what about McClelland theory?

McClelland's theory has immense research support from many developed and developing countries of the world. So, how can we discredit the theory? D. Sinha (1984) argues that there has been a tendency among Indian psychologists, as among the psychologists of many other counties to uncritically accept the theory. He calls it the "duplication tendency". He believes that psychologists from India as well as from other developing counties are victims of it.

In the ultimate analysis, the conditions in developed countries are far different from those in developing countries. McClelland's major error was that he thought there is a single type or AM. The nature and manifestation of AM varies from society to society. But McClelland assesses and compares a single manifestation of AM in different countries. From a literature survey, Rekha Singhal and Giriswar Misra (1990) observe that various research findings in India critically evaluating AM are 'particularly encouraging, because they support differences in achievement rather than deprivations of achievement. Theoretically, [these] findings challenge the traditional fixed, trait-based, unidimensional concept of achievements.'

Has McClelland's theory failed in India? Yes, it has. Because the conditions (social, economic, cultural, population condition, etc.) are starkly different here than in the west.

Some major points of argument in this regard are:

1. Resource Availability:

America is the 'new world' with immense resource availability and a stable population. In contrast, developing countries, like India have huge populations and low resource availability. J.P.B Sinha (1968) has found that competitive, individualistic orientation is of limited use when resource is scarce. Competitive orientation is most conducive to development when resources are abundant, whereas connection is better under conditions of limited resources.

Now let's evaluate McClelland's theory in the light of this. He believed that AM, which is an individualistic motivation for excellence, is useful in competitive economic activity. When resources are abundant, such competitive economic activity can lead to fast development. But, when resources are limited and people are so many, such individualistic motivations can lead to conflict among individuals and groups.

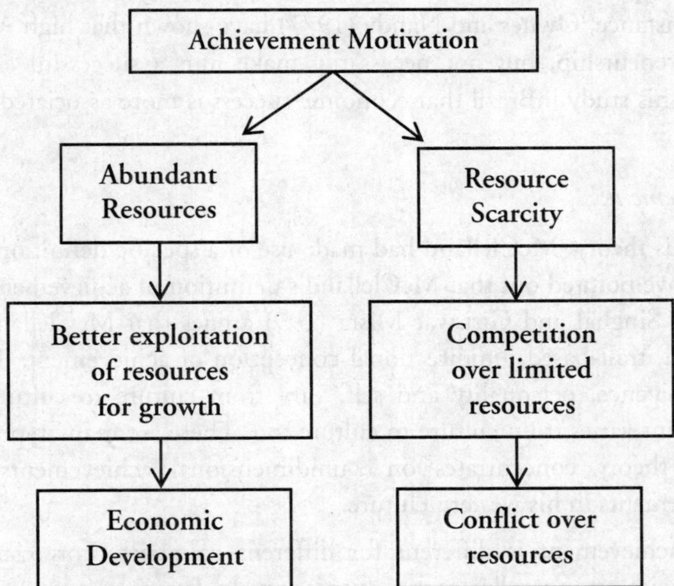

Fig. 14.2 : AM and resources as mediating factor

Hence, AM can in fact be harmful in developing countries.

2. Extension Motivation:

A critical analysis of the generality of McClelland's theory was undertaken by Pareek (1968). He argues that AM alone is not sufficient to promote social development in India. Rather, he believes two other motives (Extension Motivation or EM, Dependence Motivation or DM) must also be taken into consideration. EM is the concern for other people and the society. Pareek defines EM as 'a need to extend the self or the ego and to relate to a larger group and goals.' (Pareek, 1968, p. 18-19). DM plays a negative role in development (D).

Hence,

$$D= AM*EM-DM$$

Here, we see that Pareek also stresses on cooperation rather than being individualistic. AM is, no wonder good, but uncritically we can't say that AM always leads to development. In Indian society, a concern for other people (i.e., extension motivation) is as important as AM. Individualistic achievement orientation without a concern for others won't lead to collective development.

3. Entrepreneurial Success:

McClelland had opined that greater AM leads to greater economist activity. He has assumed that greater economist activity in the form of entrepreneurship leads to economic growth. Here, he is making an assumption that greater entrepreneurship means greater economic activity. But, this is not so. For instance, Ownes and Nandy (1977) have shown that high AM may initiate a person into entrepreneurship, but not necessarily make him a successful entrepreneur. Ray (1983) argues from his study inBrazil that economic success is more associated with dominance over resources.

4. Notion of Achievement:

When forwarding his theory, McClelland had made use of a specific definition of achievement. Many researchers have pointed out that McClelland's definition of achievement motivation was itself flawed! Rekha Singhal and Giriswar Misra (199) argues that McClelland's definition of achievement is fixed, trait-based, unidirectional conception of achievement. The definition of concepts, like intelligence, personality and self, vary from culture to culture. Similarly, the notion of achievement varies from culture to culture too. There are many types of achievement and McClelland's theory concentrates on unidimensional achievements, based on the definition of achievements in his western culture.

The notion of achievement is different for different countries. For instance, Japan is a developed country with strong collectivistic orientation. In Japan, striving for success is more motivated by a concern for the reaction of others or by loyalty to one's group, rather than by satisfaction of personal needs (Devos, 1968). Salili (1975) found in Iran that there is greater emphasis on intentions rather than outcomes in the culture of Iranian society. McClelland perhaps did not realise that AM is, after all, a social motive of striving for success and success is differently defined in different cultures!

14.3 Theory of Achievement Motivation

Achievement motivation is the tendency to strive for success in the light for some standard of excellence against which one's performance is evaluated. Following McClelland's revelation that achievement motivation is related to risk-taking behavior (McClelland, 1962), Atkinson (1957) forwarded an '*interaction model*' of achievement motivation. This model seeks to present a formula stating the need for success and fear of failure involved in doing any task. Based on the sum-total of success motive and fear of failure, the individual takes a final decision on whether to venture for a new enterprise.

There are six variables involved in the Atkinson model:

1. The subjective probability (i.e., expectancy) of success: P_s
2. The subjective probability of failure: P_f
3. The incentive value or success: I_s
4. The negative incentive value of failure: I_f
5. The achievement motive: M_s
6. The motive to avoid failure: M_{AF}

Let's say you want to open a book store in Old Rajinder Nagar Market, New Delhi. Will it work? You have some expectancy of success (P_s). At the same time, you also evaluate the probability of failure (P_f). Both P_s and P_f are subjective quantities because they are your expectancies, not objective probabilities. Similarly, what is the incentive of success (L_s)? What may be the fallout of failure (L_f)? Finally, there is always a fear of failure. What if your venture fails? You will be denounced as incompetent, or a loser. Hence, there is a motivation to avoid failure (M_{AF}). If this motivation is very high, one has a tendency to avoid work, fearing that negative outcome of the work will lead to negative comments from others.

The overall motivation in Atkinson's model has two components- the *tendency to achieve success* and the *tendency to avoid failure.*

The tendency to achieve success

The tendency to achieve success is represented by the formula:

$$T_s = M_s * P_s * I_s$$

M_s is a relatively stable characteristics of the person. P_s and I_s are the person's perceptions about the particular venture.

Escalona (1940) and Festinger (1942) had observed that accomplishment of a tough task is always more attractive to a person than the accomplishment of an easy task. Based on this rationale, Atkinson argued that Is = 1 – P_s. As a result, the formula becomes $T_s = M_s * P_s*(1 - Ps)$.

Two implications of this formula are:

1. The tendency to achieve success (T_s) is strong when a task appears to be of intermediate difficulty. This is because the product $P_s * (1 - P_s)$ is maximum (0.25) when P_s is 0.5. If the difficulty is very high or very low, T_s is low. For example:

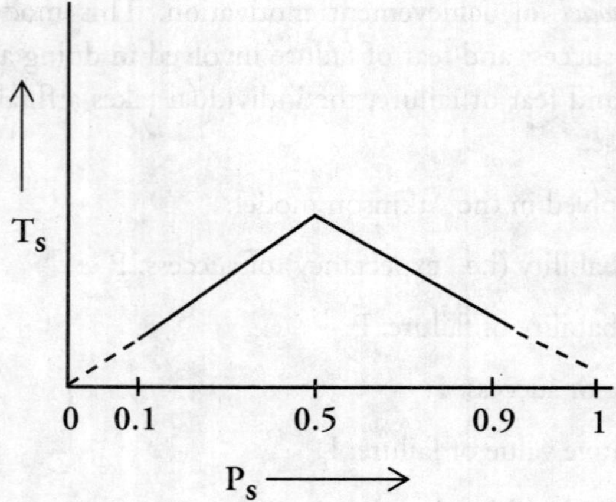

Fig. 14.3 : Tendency to achieve success for different levels of perceived difficulty

(very tough task), $T_s = 0.1 * 0.9, M_s = 0.09 M_s$. similarly if $P_s = 0.9$ (very easy task), $T_s = 0.9 * 0.1 * M_s = 0.09 M_s$.

2. When the task difficulty P_s is held constant, the tendency to achieve success is directly proportional to achievement motivation M_s.

An implication of the formula is that people high on achievement motivation will prefer to go for tasks of intermediate risk. They don't approve of easy task and consider tough tasks unrealistic.

The tendency to avoid Failure:

In contrast to the tendency to achieve success, this is the capacity to react with shame and embarrassment when the outcome of task performance is failure. This is represented by the equation:

$$T_f = M_{AF} * P_f * I_f$$

Atkinson argues that the expectancy of failure (P_f) is strong when the expectancy of success (P_s) is weak, and vice-versa. Hence,

$$P_f = 1 - P_s$$

Also, another hypothesis by Escalona and Festinger states that shame and embarrassment of failure is greater when the task failed in appears easy. On the other hand, if you fail in a very difficult task, the shame and embarrassment is low. From this hypothesis, Atkinson argues that the repulsiveness of failure (I_f) is related to the difficulty of a task (P_s). Hence, he assumes that $I_f = -P_s$.

In other words, if a task is very easy, the probability of success is high (say $P_s = 0.9$). The shame of failure (I_f) is – 0.9 (very high, since the task was very easy).

Hence, $T_f = M_{AF} * (1 - P_s) * (- P_s)$.

Overall, the achievement related behavior, or the tendency to do a task is equal to :

$T = T_s + T_f$

$= M_s * P_S * (1 - P_s) + M_{AF} * (1 - P_s)$

$= (M_s - M_{AF}) P_s (1 - P_s)$

Hence, entrepreneurial behavior is seen more often in people who:

1. Are high on need for achievement.
2. Are low on fear of failure.
3. Take moderate risks and prefer moderately difficult tasks.

14.4 Characteristics of Entrepreneurial Behavior

Entrepreneurship refers to the creative and innovative response to the environment. Such responses can take place in any field of endeavor: business, agriculture, social work, industry or education. Thus, doing new things or doing the same thing in a new way in a simple definition of entrepreneurship. (Rao and Pareek, 1978).

Why do some individuals decide to venture into entrepreneurship while others don't? This individual difference in entrepreneurial behaviour has motivated psychologists to search for some 'entrepreneurial traits'. But as Amar Bhide (1991) puts it, 'there is no ideal profile. Entrepreneurs can be gregarious or taciturn, analytical or intuitive, cautious or daring'. However, this does not mean that no trend in the characteristics of entrepreneurial behaviour can be observed. Rather, interviews with entrepreneurs show some general trends. For example, in the National Knowledge Commission (NKC) on entrepreneurship report, some entrepreneurs were interviewed (NKC, 2007). Some reasons that they stated were:

- Entrepreneurship offers the opportunity to create something of one's own.
- Entrepreneurship is about the sheer joy of an idea and making it work that is, it is intrinsic motivation.
- Entrepreneurship provides a constant learning experience and a continuous process of growth.
- 'Entrepreneurship laws possibilities for constant self-actualization', that is, it is about striving for growth and once in her and potential.
- Entrepreneurship allows people to think outside the box and make thoughts work that is it fulfills need for creativity.

In this Section, I will endeavour some general characteristics that make an individual more vulnerable to entrepreneur's real behavior than others, i.e., characteristic that predisposes some to show your behavior. But, before that, let me make clear, the distinction between entrepreneurship and starting the venture. Suppose I prepare for civil services for years, don't succeed and don't get a job, and don't have the call to go for an alternate employment. If I start a business out of sheer desperation, it is not entrepreneur behavior I am showing. It is because

I am starting a business with the sole motive of getting an income. Entrepreneur behavior is about doing something different with multiple motives, both intrinsic and extrinsic.

Before discussing various characteristics of an entrepreneur, let us check some research results in entrepreneur real behavior.

Characteristics of entrepreneurs: Literature survey

- Rao (1978) found entrepreneurs as aggressive, mentally hyper-active, opportunists, courageous, exploiting in nature and processing a pleasant personality.
- Gaikwad and Tripathi (1970) studied small entrepreneurs of the Tanku region of west Godavari district in Andhra Pradesh and found some pre-requisites of successful entrepreneurship- initiative, drive and hard work.
- Bhattacharjee and Akhouri (1975) empirically state the entrepreneur characteristics of small industry entrepreneurs. They found that the most significant characteristics of successful entrepreneurship are-need for achievement, power and independence, personality modernity, propensity to take risk, business experience, leadership and symbolic or actual rejection by father.
- Meredith and colleagues (1982) identify the six important personality traits of good entrepreneur:

  1. Self-confidence
  2. Risk-taking ability
  3. Flexibility
  4. Need for achievement
  5. Internal locus of control
  6. A strong desire to be independent
- Venkatapathy (1986) has compared the characteristic of first generation entrepreneurs and second generation entrepreneurs. Second generation are those who hail from business families (often marwadi, bania, parsi, etc.) and decide to start their own venture. Venkatapathi found that first generation entrepreneurs are more enterprising, more social and less conventional, do innovative practices and have more positive self- concept then second generation entrepreneurs.
- Pathak (1978) found that a strong desire for independence was one of the personality dimensions of entrepreneurs.
- Satvir Singh (1991) found that fast progressive entrepreneurs are emotionally stable and have high level of self-esteem.
- Sen and Seth (1992) found that entrepreneurs work imaginative, cheerful, self-assertive, decisive, ambitious, socially conscious, mature, integrated and self-confident.

Characteristics of female entrepreneurs

- Shah (1987) had divided women entrepreneurs into three categories to make their characteristics across social classes:

I. Women entrepreneurs of middle and high middle income groups.

II. Women entrepreneur coming from middle and lower middle income group and having science and technology background.

III. Women entrepreneurs of low income group coming from the lower strata of society.

Shah found some common features of women entrepreneurs that were found in entrepreneurs of all the three categories, like need for achievement, initiative, problem solving skills and risk-taking nature. The degree reported utilisation of experience and education as a motive. The low income group was motivated by economic needs.

- Dhillon (1993) studied 40 women entrepreneurs in and around Delhi. The findings show that the most dominant motives were fulfillment of ambition and pursuit of own interest. The findings further reflect that women entrepreneurs have a high need for achievement, independence orientation and ability for decision-making. On the whole, Dhillon found that the typical women entrepreneurs like the independence associated with entrepreneurship and is a dreamer with high hopes, has a positive orientation towards competition and is confident of her ability to do deal with problems.
- KP Singh (1993) studied women entrepreneurs in a major city of India and found that the need for Independence was the most predominant motive for 46% of the respondents. She observes that women entrepreneurs desired to be their own bosses and wanted to maintain their own individual identity. 'A strong desire to prove oneself was the main motive with 21 percent of the respondents... Earning money was the main motive with only 15 percent of the respondents, most of the widows and divorcees had to feed themselves and their families.'
- The dominant elements of entrepreneur motivation in K. P. Singh's study are:

Motives	**Percentage**
To become independent	46.5%
To prove oneself	21%
To earn money	15.5%
Job satisfaction	8.5%
Competition	4.5%
To gain status	4%

The NKC study has revealed that for female entrepreneurs, the independence derived from entrepreneurship and identification of a marketable idea are the two most important motivators. Comparing women entrepreneurs with male entrepreneurs, the study states that more entrepreneurs are more significantly influenced by family background.

The comparison between the two types is given under:

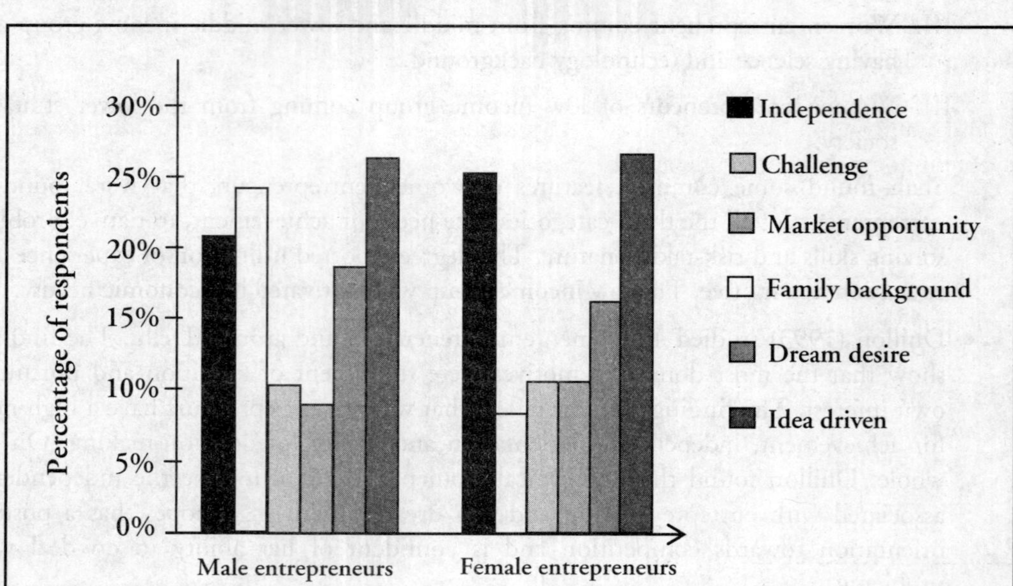

Source : NKC, 2007, p. 12

Fig. 14.4 : Comparison between male and female entrepreneurs

Entrepreneurs: A profile

As seen from the rich literature on entrepreneurial characteristics, there are many features that are found among entrepreneurs. Of course, differences exist on the basis of gender, family background (whether belonging to business families or middle-class or lower-class families), age and levels of work experiences.

But, some persistent traits can be taken and discussed as under:

1. Need for Achievement

As seen in earlier discussion, high need for achievement is positively correlated with entrepreneurial behavior. Many studies have confirmed this. For instance, Andrews (1967) studied two companies (Say A and P) in Mexico City. Company-A had been growing at a very rapid rate for the past 3-4 years, while Company-P had been growing much slower. He found that the top executives of Company A (who were in entrepreneurial position) were high on need for achievement while similar positions in Company P were filled by those managers who were low on achievement motivation. In another study, small line entrepreneurs of a rural village in Orissa were studied (Fraser, 1961). A number of mechanics were assessed on nAchievement. After this, a training to improve nAchievement showed more entrepreneurial spirit and less involvement in traditional agricultural activities that those with low nAchivement.

Many studies have shown the relation between the need for achievement and innovations. Many studies on rural India confirmed that farmers who are high on nAchievement are change-prone and readily adopt new technology. Many studies discussed earlier also show high need for achievement as a persistent characteristic of entrepreneurs.

2. Low Profit Motive

Many economists used to believe that entrepreneurship is driven by profit motive. However, psychologists have proved this to be wrong. Several studies conducted in field and laboratories have shown that entrepreneurs who are high on need for achievement are interested in excellence rather than for monetary rewards. These entrepreneurs are even ready to work in groups and for group goals rather than for themselves or for ego goals.

When National Knowledge Commission (NKC) asked entrepreneurs- 'where do you see your five years from now?', it was discovered that most entrepreneur envision the future of the business in terms of the quality of work and nature of business, rather than only terms of turnover and profits (NKC, 2007). In fact, NKC found that there are many motivators behind entrepreneurial behavior; the share of these factors in the study is represented in the figure 14.5:

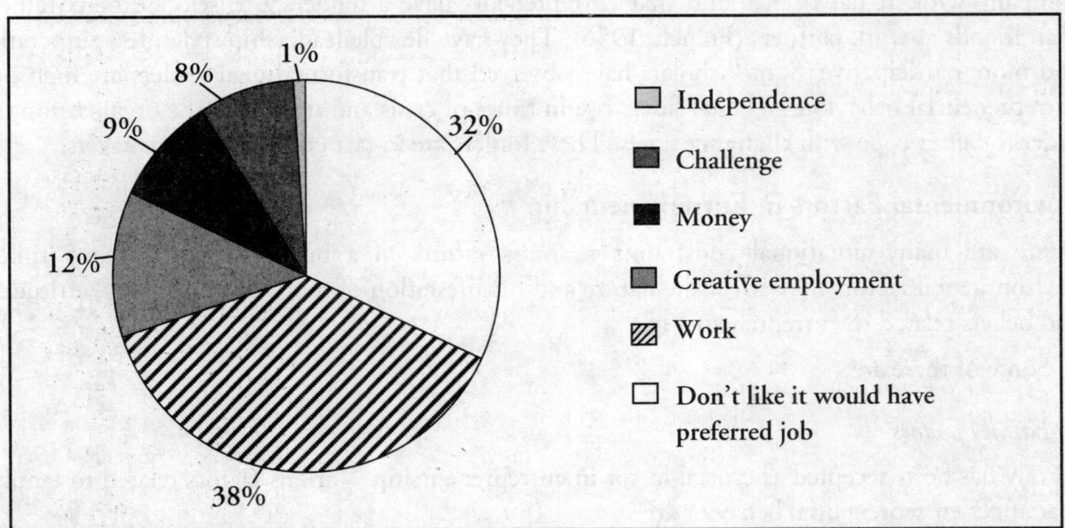

Source : NKC, 2007, P. 17

Fig 14.5 : Drives of entrepreneurial motive

Note that money is the dominant motivator in only 12% of the cases studied.

3. Decision Choices

Entrepreneurial behavior is associated with moderate risk-taking and low gambling behavior. The moderate risk-taking behavior is evident from Atkinson's formula; it has also been demonstrated in many studies.

The gambling behavior of entrepreneurs is of specific interest here, Littig (1959) found that entrepreneurs prefer the bet with shortest odds in gambling. On the other hand, those low on nAchivement like to take greater risk in gambling, expecting greater rewards. Littig explains this by stating that entrepreneurs prefer to venture for tasks over which they have control. They are high on confidence and will take moderate, calculated risks. But, gambling is pure luck, so they prefer the safest bet in gambling.

4. Personality Variables

Some common personality traits have been observed in entrepreneurs. They are high on internal locus of control, show competitive aggressiveness and have a marked preference for autonomy in the job. Hundal and S.Singh (1980) have found that entrepreneurial farmers are high on emotional stability and intelligence and have realistic aspirations in comparison to traditional framers.

5. Inter-personal Relations

This pertains to the leadership orientation of entrepreneurs and the people they prefer to keep company with. It has been found that entrepreneurs have a tendency to select experts rather than friends as work partners (French, 1956). They have flexible leadership styles, less autocratic and more participative. Some scholars have observed that transformational leaders are high on entrepreneurial behaviour. These leaders rise in times of crisis and transform the organisation in order to better cope with changing times. These leaders are in fact entrepreneur managers.

Environmental Factors in Entrepreneurship

There are many situational constraints to one's efforts in a business. At the same time, environmental factors may affect the nature and manifestation of motives, personality, attitudes and beliefs related to entrepreneurship.

Some of these are:

1. Family factors

Family has been accepted as crucial factor in entrepreneurship. Various factors related to family that affect entrepreneurial behavior are:

- Birth order
- Family structure
- Father
- Family support

Some studies have found that first-born children tend to have higher need for achievement and hence are more enterprising, because their parents set high standards for them. This hypothesis, however, has been proved wrong in case of India. McClelland (1961) suggests from study of samples of Indian students from Madras that the younger children may have higher nArch in India.

Family structure also plays a major role. For example, it is said that joint family system of India reduces incentive for hard work, promotes idleness and increases need for dependency among children. Also, when a child stays in a mother- child household (which may result due to divorce or separation or because the mother is unmarried), the need for achievement is lower (McClelland, 1961).

Psychoanalysts stress that a father has an important role to play in the psychic development of the child. Identification with the parent of the same sex is the first and essential step to resolve the conflicts of the phallic stage. No wonder, father has an overbearing influence on development of entrepreneurial traits. Bhattacharjee and Aghouri (1975) have found that symbolic of actual rejection by father is related to entrepreneurial behaviour. Mehta (1966) found a curvilinear relation between boy's nAch and their father's education. When fathers had higher education or lower education, the nArch of boy was higher than that, if the father has secondary school education.

That family support is important not only to start a business, but also for success of the same is evident from a study by Deivasenalathy (1996) on 45 entrepreneurs from sick units and 53 entrepreneurs from successful units. It was found that family support influences success. The NKC study (2007) also found that of the successful entrepreneurs studied, as many as 74% were supported by family.

2. Socio-economic status:

The relation between socio-economic status (SES) and motivation for entrepreneurship is curvilinear. Businessmen in many countries tend to have higher need for achievement if they come from middle class families than if they come from upper or working class background (McClwlland, 1961). Basically, there is a class sub-culture corresponding to each class consisting of certain values. This sub-culture affects attitude towards entrepreneurship.

A major factor impeding entrepreneurship is the social group called 'caste'. Caste system usually puts normative restrictions on the kind of occupation an individual can do. A son of a Brahmin can't expect to do manual labour and a Teli can't expect art schools. Hence, the caste system severely affected the expectancy and aspirations of people. This impedes entrepreneur behaviour.

Kapp (1963) observe that 'caste frustrates the creative powers and lowers the aspirations of large number of people, thereby causing a serious waste of individual capacities and labour resources. Premium on traditional occupations by preventing the development of personal initiative; it works against the emergence of a relationship between individual aptitude performance and earnings'.

Logically, upper castes have greater degree of freedom then lower castes with respect to entrepreneurs. This is also confirmed by Nafzigar (1975) from a study of entrepreneurs from small-scale manufacturing enterprises in Visakhapatnam. He found that a highly disproportionate number of entrepreneurs work from higher castes.

3. Education:

Education is an indispensable tool for skill development and hence, is an important factor in entrepreneurship. Not that education is essential to start a small enterprise, but it does help when an entrepreneur goes for a task which needs specific skills or when the entrepreneurs expand operations beyond local level. McClelland (1966) has observed that countries which invested heavily on education on the average developed more rapidly after a number of years when the educated population have reached working age. Sinha (1968) has also reported positive relationship between education and aspiration in developed countries.

4. Entrepreneurial ecosystem:

Entrepreneurial ecosystem refers to the whole gamut of social attitudes, cultural norms and values and state support to entrepreneurship. These factors immensely contribute to perception about entrepreneurship. For example, if in a society business is looked at as an occupation of lower status, people will be discouraged to be a businessman. The Vaishya castes in India are placed below Brahmin and Kshatriya castes. This places all over esteem on business occupations and discourage other castes from taking up such occupations.

Similarly, if negative attitude towards failure of a business venture is large, the fear of failure in an individual will be high even before she starts her venture. And indeed, the stigma attached with failures is high in many cultures. Hence, many sociologists and psychologists are of the opinion that entrepreneurship should be celebrated, irrespective of its outcomes. The culture is not the only factor that makes up the entrepreneurial ecosystem. There are other factors that can facilitate an entrepreneurial culture or hinder it.

Some are:

- Industrial climate
- Mentoring and networking
- Financial support and extension facilities made available by government

14.5 Government policies for promotion of entrepreneurship

The entrepreneurial ecosystem can become a conductive environment promoting entrepreneurship or a hindrance to the development of it. And a singularly critical component of entrepreneurial ecosystem is the government. Government plays an important part in motivating or demotivating entrepreneurs. For example, during 1960s and 1970s, it was very tough for someone to open a company. It was even difficult to sustain it because Income Tax was as high as 97.5%. That was a time when government was influenced by socialistic ideals and centralised, government controlled Public Sector Units (PSU) can drive economic growth. No wonder, even the most entrepreneurial individual got appalled and couldn't start ventures. For those who still wanted to start the business, decided to do so outside India. For example, Aditya Birla raised an empire based on industries in Malaysia and other South-east Asian countries. While Indians contributed a lot to the development of many other countries, policies of the Government of India slowly became more progressive. Post-1992, the policies now are promoting entrepreneurship in a big way.

The role of the government in promoting entrepreneurship is evident from a study of inter-state patterns of entrepreneurial performance (Sharma, 1976). In this study, the variations in industrial climate in the state of Punjab and Uttar Pradesh related to variations in entrepreneurial performance, and it was found that better the industrial climate, more the entrepreneurial behavior.

Let us study the policies and programmes of the government to promote entrepreneurship in India.

1. Credit and Finance

The source credit flow to weaker sections of the society, so that they can get self-employed, the government has constituted programmes, like SwarnaJayanti Gram Swarojgar Yojana (SGSY), Swarna Jayanti Shahari Rozgar Yojana (SJSRY) and Prime Minister Rozgar Yojana (PMRY) among other such programs. SGSY is a scheme aimed at establishing a large number of micro enterprises in the rural areas. Do it provide credit to rural poor, it is more Holistic in the sense that it covers other aspects, such as organising the poor self- help groups, training, technology, infrastructure and marketing? SJSRY provides bank credit to urban poor and it has two important sub schemes- Urban Self-employment Programme (USEP) and the Development of Women and Children in Urban Areas (DWCUA).

These days, an important concept doing the rounds is 'financial inclusion'. For financial inclusion, the main instrument that the Finance Ministry seeks to utilise is microfinance to self-help groups. Self-help groups have been found to be quite conductive for entrepreneurial development, given the fact that the increased group efficacy and self-confidence of entrepreneurs. Further, the fear to failure in self-help groups is low due to a conclusion of risk and responsibility. In contrast, the individual poor has high need for independency, low self-efficacy and low achievement motivation (for more characteristics of the poor that prevent development of entrepreneurship behavior, see the chapter on Community Psychology).

2. Training

Training has been one of the grey areas of government efforts to promote entrepreneurs. But of late, the Centre and various state governments are looking into the issue of training and skill development in a big way. For instance, the National Knowledge Commission (NKC), 2007) has recommended that vocational education training (VET) should be a priority sector in education. Many of the school students who don't make it to universities don't find the education helpful for self-employment. VET can help develop necessary skills, so that one can venture forth in a business area that demands some basic skill sets. Entrepreneur Development Programmes (EDP) are also conducted to cultivate the skill in unemployed youth for setting up micro and small enterprises. Another set of programmes, called Management Development Programmes (MDP) seeks to provide training to existing entrepreneurs on various areas to develop management skills and to improve their decision-making capabilities. This programme aims to increase productivity and profitability of entrepreneurial ventures.

There are certain specific programmes that aim to help and train certain target groups for entrepreneurship. For example, training of Rural Youth for Self-employment (TRYSEM), Development of Women and Children in Rural Areas (DWCRA), Supply of Improved Toolkits to Rural Artisans (SISTRA), etc.

A new concept in the world of entrepreneurship is technopreneurship, for highly skilled entrepreneurs (mostly graduates) who seek to venture in the fields of electronics, computer software, finance, e-commerce, etc. For them, the government supports various activities in colleges and universities. For example, there are today entrepreneurship cells in various IITs and IIMs to train and guide start-up companies throughout the process of entrepreneurship. The Ministry of Human Resource Development (HRD) actively supports these.

Plan vision for training

The Eleventh Plan aims to launch National Skill Development Mission (NSDM) and proposes to allocate INR 31200 crores for same. During the plan period of five years, the mission is expected to increase the number of trained persons from 2.5 million to 10 million. The government also seeks to involve the private sector through the public private partnership (PPP) in training programs. The NSDM also has action plan to set-up 600 new RUDSETIs (rural development and self-employment training institutes). These RUDSETIs are expected to focus on developing entrepreneurship in collaboration with the entrepreneurship development institute (EDI). EDI, an autonomous organisation was set-up to promote entrepreneurship through educationand training. (Refer www. ediindia. or for details)

3. Extension facilities

Suppose, you take some rural farmers and train them on the merits of horticulture and use of latest technology to productivity, or you train some individuals in achievement motivation, but he/she doesn't have any guidance with respect to the business area he/ she seeks to venture into. This acts as a motivator. Hence, the need for extension service. For example, agricultural extension aims at improving technology dissemination for farmers.

That the government is serious about extension is evident from the fact that in the 2008-09 budget, the Finance Minister proposed the establishment of many new extension centers. To augment agriculture extension, broadcast through radio channels are provided. Kisan Call Centers are now being operated throughout the country to provide expert advice to farmers.

Similar measures to provide extension services are also being provided to entrepreneurs in the rural non-farm sector and in medium small and micro Enterprises (MSME) sectors.

4. Business incubation for entrepreneurship (BTE)

Business Incubation for Entrepreneurs (BIE) is a critical support mechanism for fledging entrepreneurs at the initial stage (NKC, 2007). A typical business incubation program provides the following services to a budding entrepreneur:

- Physical infrastructure
- Administrative support
- Management guidance and monitoring

- Technical support
- Facilitating access to finance

All the above are situational constraints that an entrepreneur faces when he begins his business. Any help in tackling these constraints is akin to motivating the entrepreneurs. The Government at the Centre and those in various states realise this logic and hence, have provided many facilities for incubation. For instance, in order to develop technopreneurship, the Ministry of Science and Technology (MoST) initiated the Science and Technological Entrepreneurship Park (STEP) program. STEP has endeavored to Foster linkages between academic industry and R & D institutions in inculcating an entrepreneurial culture. Another initiative worth mention is the technology incubation for development of entrepreneurs (TIDE). TIDE seeks to set a fund worth INR 25 crores, of which, selected start-ups will receive a funding INR 25 lakhs to INR 50 lakh for a period of two years. This initiative will also be promoted through premier institutions, like IITs, IIMs and IISc.

Government policies for the promotion of women entrepreneurs

The route driver of government policies in India are the Five Years Plans. Schemes for women development in various plans till the Sixth Plan were conspicuous in their absence. The employment policy of the Sixth Plan (1980- 85) had two major goals - reducing under-employment and lowering the age of retirement. The plan provided a 'new deal' for self-employment by providing services, like training, credit, marketing and general guidance for those who wanted to launch their own entrepreneurial ventures. Special attention in the new deal was paid to women entrepreneurs by way of financial and technical assistance. (Chakraborty, 2001).

A definite shift of focus was made in the 7th Plan from the welfare concept to development concept in planning for women. The Plan's main suggestions were to diversify vocational training facilities for women to suit their varied needs, provide marketing assistance at the state level and to increase women's participation in decision-making.

During the last few years, considerable progress has been made in the country to develop new women entrepreneurs through training, and at present many states are involved in WED (Women Entrepreneurship Development) programming and SEP/IGP (Self-employment and income generation programme). Supporting facilities, like infrastructure financing and training have been made quite favorable. There are a number of schemes of the government Prime Minister's Rozgar Yojana (PMRY), a scheme for urban micro entrepreneurs; Development of Women and Children in Rural Areas (DWCRA) and Indira Rojgar Yojana (I.R.Y) for encouraging women to become successful entrepreneurs (Chakroborty, 2001, P.85).

Addition to such specific programs, the government realises that to create a conductive environment, it needs to provide credit, finance and extension assistance. A number of organisations or involved in creating a congenial environment for women entrepreneurs, like:

- National Small Industries Corporation (NSIC)
- Small Industrial Development Organisation (SIDO)
- National Research Development Corporation (NRDC)

- Khadi and village Industries Commission (KVIC)
- National Institute for Entrepreneurship and Small Business Development (NIESBUD)
- Scheme of Interest Subsidy for Women Entrepreneurs (SISWE)
- Small Industries Development Bank of India (SIDBI)
- National Alliance for Young Entrepreneurs (NAYE)
- State Bank of India (SBI)
- Industrial Financial Corporation of India (IFCI)

Nationalised banks, like SBI and various financial institutions play a vital role in encouraging small women entrepreneurs through various credit schemes.

Now, let us look into some current programs, meant for women entrepreneurs, by the government of India:

1. *STEP:* Support to Training and Employment Programme for Women (STEP) was launched by the Central government in 1987. Its various activities for women in traditional sectors include mobilising them in viable groups, arranging for marketing linkages, support services and access to credit. It has immensely benefited women entrepreneurs in the fields of animal husbandry, dairying, handloom, handicrafts and sericulture.
2. *Swayamsiddha:* It is an integrated scheme for economic empowerment of women. It seeks to establish Self-help Groups (SHG) and create confidence and awareness among members of SHGs regarding health, nutrition, education, legal rights, etc. The scheme covers 650 blocks in 335 districts in the country. Each block consists of 100 SHGs under this programme. These SHGs are made mostly through the ICDS (Integrated Child Development Scheme) machinery, but certain states, like Uttar Pradesh, Bihar, Uttarakhand, etc. also take the help of NGOs to implement the programme.

14.6 Motivating and Training People for Entrepreneurship

Given the fact that entrepreneurship drives economic development, strategies to motivate and train people for entrepreneurship have been a prime focus of policy-makers and social psychologists alike. To motivate people, we need to promote an entrepreneurial culture and provide all requisite support for starting a business. Environmental factors can be motivators or demotivators. These factors together constitute the entrepreneurial ecosystem. Strategies to motivate people for entrepreneurship should look into making the ecosystem more conducive and progressive to entrepreneurs. Training refers to planned interventions to inculcate some learning and qualities that promote entrepreneurial behavior. These interventions can be to enhance an individual's skills (so as to make her more competent and confident about the work; this promotes self-efficacy and greater risk-taking behavior) or change her attitudes, values and motives. For instance, a fatalistic attitude coupled with high need for dependence and low need for achievement leads to lower entrepreneurial behavior. This has to be changed through training.

14.7 The Entrepreneurial Ecosystem

Entrepreneurial ecosystem is the sum-total of environmental factors that promote or hinder entrepreneurship. The ecosystem is the prime external force that can act as a motivator or demotivator for entrepreneurship. For instance, when I was an undergraduate student in IIT Kharagpur, I had an idea that could have been converted into a viable business opportunity. But, a business plan (B-plan) doesn't automatically lead to a venture. I needed finance, mentoring, networking with people in the software sector (my plan was related to the software sector), and above all, family support. While my parents discouraged me at every step, I was unable to get any finance or mentors to help me with my plan. Ultimately, I got demotivated and dejected and dropped my plan.

Luckily, today IIT Kharagpur has its own entrepreneurship development body that promotes students and their ideas. This is one among many factors that can motivate the individual to go for entrepreneurship.

In fact, the entrepreneurial ecosystem can be represented as under:

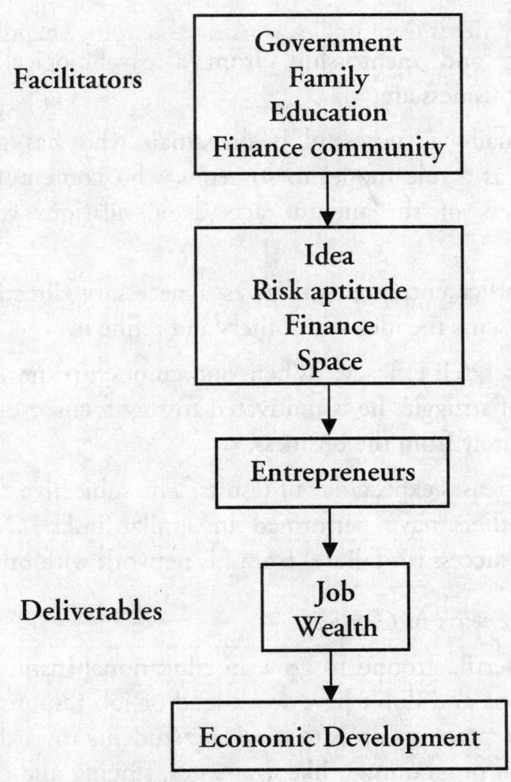

Fig. 14.6 : The Entrepreneurial Ecosystem. [Adopted from NKC (2007)]

The facilitators, namely government, family, education, finance community and non-governmental organisations, all have important roles to play in motivating people for entrepreneurship.

Let us study some measures that can be taken to motivate people towards entrepreneurship:

1. Mentoring and Networking:

A few entrepreneurs decide to start their ventures after many years of job experience. But, many entrepreneurs are young people. They are always in the need for mentors to guide them in the ventures. Also, all entrepreneurs need to have a strong network. Networking helps them a lot in the way they get to communicate with other businessmen and entrepreneurs and learn from their mistakes.

Many interesting initiatives have been taken to provide mentorship and networking facilities to entrepreneurs. For instance, the Bhartiya Yuva Shakti Trust (BYST, also called 'Business and Youth Starting Together') provides key support in networking and in finding an experienced mentor who can help the enterprising youth in meeting various challenges related to the job. Other such organisations are the National Entrepreneurship Network (NEN) and The Indus Entrepreneurs (TIE).

Advantage of networking and mentorship, from a psychological perspective, for an individual's motive to start a business are:

(a) The mentor is usually a successful businessman who has gone through similar situations. He acts as a role model to someone who contemplates to start his own venture. The success of the mentor acts as a vicarious reinforcement for the individual.

(b) Networking with other entrepreneurs gives a necessary direction to one's business plan. One gets to discuss the idea with others and refine it.

(c) Networking increases self-efficacy. When one comes to know about other success stories and stories of struggle, he is motivated to stay focused on his venture and not to back out prematurely from the business.

(d) Networking also increases expectancy of results. The subjective expectancy of results is affected by how others have performed in similar tasks. One gets to learn the strategies to lead to success (or failure) from his network with other entrepreneurs.

2. Encourage Student Entrepreneurs in Campus

Entrepreneurial ability finds fertile ground to grow in educational institutions, where students have great ideas and aspirations and don't have work-load or job responsibility. Hence, a very good strategy to promote entrepreneurship is to motivate students towards entrepreneurship in education institution. Cultural programmes, like dramatics, singing and dancing are promoted in school and colleges; so are sports programmes. In a similar way, entrepreneurial behavior can be promoted. Examples can be cited from the few initiatives taken by certain educational institutions. IIT Kharagpur organises an annual tech-fest 'Kshitij' where B-plan contests are held. Otherwise also, many IITs and IIMs have opened entrepreneurship cells that create awareness about entrepreneurship, accept ideas and refine ideas with the help of experts, allocate mentors to students who contemplate to start their own ventures and provide seed fund wherever necessary.

An 'idea' remains an idea till the time someone shows the route to channelise it. Without the route, the idea dies out. The route is a motivator because it provides specific, measurable goals. A student can never be sure if an idea can become a viable business. If he is not provided with support, he may be mired by self-doubt and ultimately get demotivated. One can't pursue an abstract goal for long. Help of educational institutions to students basically converts abstract goals into specific ones and provide a direction to the students.

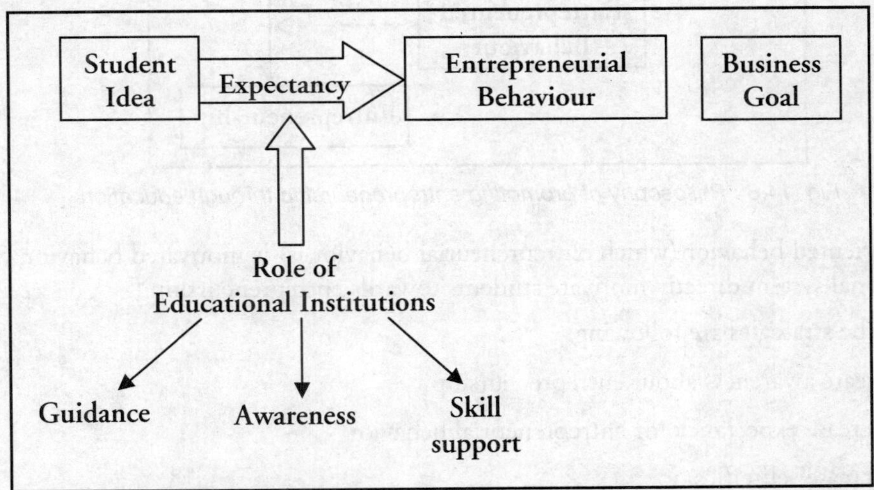

Fig. 14.7 : Motivating students for entrepreneurship

3. Role of Government

It takes around a year to start a company in India. There are many legal and bureaucratic hassles in the process of just starting a company, let alone running it. These hassles are a major demotivator to any person who wants to turn entrepreneur.

Some steps that the government can take to motivate people towards entrepreneurship are:

- Constitute an efficient Single Window System to get clearances.
- Develop proper infrastructure to support entrepreneurs.
- Provide financial assistance.
- Recognise entrepreneurial talent by rewarding and recognising entrepreneurs.
- Explore the possibility of social security for entrepreneurs to encourage risk-taking ability among people.

4. Education

Any educational system that encourages critical and lateral thinking also promotes innovation. Innovation refers to creative ideas that can be converted into a business venture by entrepreneurial behavior. Hence, education promoting reflexive thinking should be imparted in schools and colleges. Agreed this role played by educational system, but ideas don't themselves lead to entrepreneurship. Behavior leads to it.

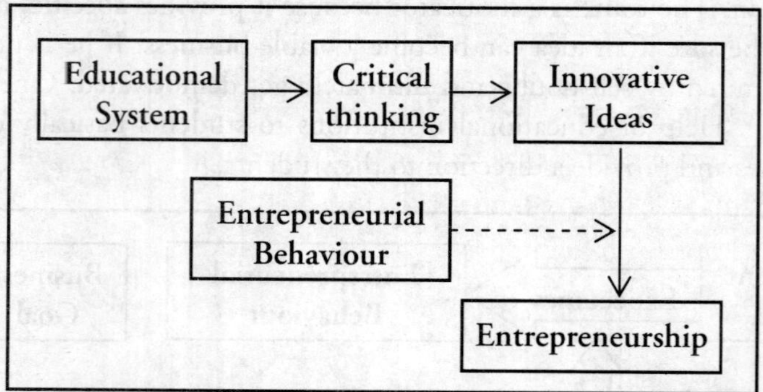

Fig. 14.8 : Philosophy of promoting entrepreneurship through education

An action-oriented behavior (which entrepreneurial behavior is) is motivated behavior. So, how can educational system directly motivate students towards entrepreneurship?

Some of the strategies are following:

- Create awareness about entrepreneurship
- Increase expectancy for entrepreneurial behavior
- Increase self-efficacy

Awareness regarding entrepreneurship can be created by including courses on entrepreneurship in the school curriculum. Today, there are hardly any schools or colleges (other than Management colleges) that give courses in entrepreneurship. Including courses on entrepreneurship increases awareness about various opportunities and hence motivates the individual. Further, case studies of successful entrepreneurs increases expectancy and self-efficacy. IIT Kharagpur's recent proposal to start a school of entrepreneurship is a welcome step and needs to be followed up by other institutes in under-graduate and post-graduate levels.

5. De-stigmatising failure

Failure of an entrepreneurial ventures is associate with considerable social stigma. In contrast, entrepreneurs are appreciated in western societies for their past ventures, successful or failed. The social stigma attached to failure increases the fear of failure in people who want to start their business. Higher fear of failure means lower motivation to show entrepreneurial behavior. Risk-taking ability becomes low. Hence, the government, the Chambers of Commerce (FICCI, ASSOCHAM, CII, etc.), educational institutions and entrepreneurial networks should try to destigmatise failure. One's experience gained from failed ventures should be respected and appreciated. This will go a long way in changing the role of culture from being a demotivator to motivator. The fact that an entrepreneur is gusty and a visionary, irrespective of whether he succeeds or fails can be made a social value by the institutions mentioned above.

Training People for Entrepreneurship

Training interventions are basically of two types- training to increase skills necessary to perform in a new business venture and training to inculcate right attitudes and motivations conducive for entrepreneurship.

Here, we shall discuss the following important interventions:

1. Vocational Education training (VET) and Management Skill Training (MST)
2. Training to improve achievement motivation
3. Training to improve Extension Motives (EM) and reduce Dependence Motivation (DM).

14.8 VET & MET

The irony of our education system is that we are taught to 'mug' passive study materials, whose only utility is as a pre-requisite for university education. But, not every student goes to the university. In fact, most don't! For them, Vocational Educational Training (VET) has been proposed to be quite useful. In VET, necessary skills are taught, the student finds these skills quite useful when he joins a job, and especially useful if he opts for self-employment. Many specialised training institutes have been opened in the country to train entrepreneurs in the Medium, Small and Micro Enterprise (MSME) sector. Ideally, the training should be provided in VET.

Management Skill Training (MST) is necessary to train an entrepreneur. While VET is used to train an individual to become an entrepreneur, MST is used to train an entrepreneur to improve the performance of her business organisation.

Training to improve Achievement Motivation

'The achievement motivated person is a hard-working person who seeks personal responsibility, who sets realistic, but challenging personal goals and who seeks feedback about the effects of his efforts. As such, he tends to do particularly well in those situations which allow for personal control and innovation, particularly entrepreneurial business situation. Historical studies have shown that the level of achievement motivation in a nation's cultural values may be related to the rise and fall of the nations' economy.Hence, there is the need to inculcate who have received achievement motivation training and have shown significant improvements in their business performance, as compared to businessmen who were not trained (Schwitzgebel and Kolb, 1974, P.159).

Achievement motivation causes entrepreneurial behavior. Entrepreneurship causes economic development. Hence, devising of training programmes to train in achievement motivation becomes important. Here, we shall discuss the training philosophy developed by David McClelland, a pioneer in the study of nAchievement.

The importance of McClelland's contribution lies not only in his revelation that nAchievement and economic development are related, but also in the fact that he believed achievement motivation can be inculcated by training. He designed a training course to improve achievement motivation and many empirical studies have demonstrated the efficacy of this course.

In designing the training course, McClelland didn't rely on any single theory of behavior change, rather he borrowed from training techniques of a wide variety of psychological theories-learning theory, theories of attitude change, motivation theory, psychotherapy and mass media research. Based on these theoretical strands, he forwarded twelve propositions to describe how the course should be designed and run (McClelland, 1965). These propositions can be discussed under the following four headings-goal-setting, motive syndrome, cognitive supports and group supports (Schwitzgebel and Kolb, 1974).

1. Goal-Setting

The Achievement Motivation Training programme (AMT) focuses on inducing confidence, commitment and the measurement of achievement in the attainment of goals. To induce confidence and commitment, a change in the belief and attitude of the individual is needed. The logic here is that, if you believe that motivated behavior can lead to entrepreneurial success, your motivation will be high. Belief in the possibility and desirability of change is a pre-requisite for high achievement motivation. Hence, the AMT tries to create this belief in participants by presenting research findings on the relationship between need for achievement and entrepreneurial success.

The more an individual commit herself to achieving specific goals, more is the motive to achieve the goals. Hence, the participants are made to make a public commitment to seek specific achievement goals. Both, confidence and commitment depend on feedback, or the knowledge of results. Feedback helps keep a record of progress towards the ultimate goal. In the AMT, participants are trained in methods of measuring how well they are performing at a given time.

2. Motivate Syndrome

A motive is a schema of goal-directed thoughts. Motive syndrome refers to the integration of such thoughts with actions and real life context. There are three propositions under motive syndrome. First, an individual acquires the motives which she can clearly conceptualise. Hence, in the AMT, participants are given the Thematic Apperception Test (TAT) and are taught to score their own stories. This way, they evaluate for themselves what nAchievement is and how much of it they have upon entering the course. This exercise helps the participants to streamline their thought processes and helps them in clearly conceptualising their nAchievement in terms of their thought processes.

Secondly, the motives need to be linked to actions. Thirdly, the more the motives are applied to events in real life, the more likely the motive will be increased. Keeping these two propositions in mind, the AMT makes participants learn action strategies of people with high nAchievement through illustrative games (often business games), analysis and discuss of case studies and discussion on how these action strategies can be applied to everyday life situations.

3. Cognitive Supports

Cognitive theorists believe that thoughts and actions can be affected through rational dialogue. Hence, first cognitive support that needs to be provided is to explore rationality, that is, how the motive is consistent with demands of reality. Secondly, how a particular action will improve a person's self-image and third, how it is consistent with the individual's cultural values.

The motive will be increased if it is consistent with:

(a) Demands of reality

(b) A stronger self-image

(c) Cultural values

In AMT, these objectives are met through individual counselling and group discussions of nAchievement in relation to folklore, religious books and cultural values. For example, suppose that you have to train people from rural Indian background towards achievement. You explain to them that nAchievement is consistent with religious beliefs. A challenge here is that the concept of *Karma* asks you to work without expecting any reward. So, you re-interpret the concept stating that Krishna wanted us to do our *Dharma,* and our *Dharma* is to work hard and achieve success – material or spiritual, that doesn't matter. You tell them that entrepreneurial goals are consistent to our cultural values.

In our cultural values, entrepreneurship is associated with Baniya and Marwari families who come lower down in the caste hierarchy. So, you stress that in history, many great men and Gods have does manual work. Lord Krishna was a cowherd after all. So, why can't you start a small business of your own? It won't degrade your status. Also, the participants' cognitions can be restructured by rational dialogue- the Marwari and Baniya communities are the most prosperous today because of their orientation towards hard work and because they don't consider any job inferior.

The good news is that there are many religious texts in Hinduism and most of these texts make contradictory statements. Secondly, the meaning of these texts is subject to our interpretation. Hence, we can easily mold religious beliefs to make them consistent to achievement origination. If the Bhagavat Gita talks about *dharma* and *karma* (do your duty without expecting any reward), there are a myriad other religious texts that advocate that striving for achievement and expecting results is your duty.

4. Emotional support

McClelland recognises the role of affective factors in increasing motivation towards achievement. Hence, he states that the AMT trainer should assume a warm, non-directive and accepting role. The role of trainers in AMT is to support open exploration by course members, rather than direct the whole programme. This idea of McClelland is perhaps influenced by Roger's Client Centered Therapy.

Secondly, participants are made to work in groups. Group activities provide emotional support that increases the risk-taking tendency.

12 Propositions of McClelland's Training Course

1. More the reasons the person has in advance about the possibility and desirability of change, more the likelihood of change.

   Application: Increase the belief in possibility and desirability of change by presenting research findings on the relationship between achievement motivation and entrepreneurial success.

2. If you rationally explore how a motive is consistent with demands of reality, that motive increases.

   Application: Individual counselling and dialogue in which the participant rationally explores consistencies with the help of counsellor/ trainer.

3. The more a person clearly conceptualises the motive to be acquired, the more likely it is that he/ she will employ that motive.

   Application: Participants are given TAT and taught to score their own stories.

4. The more an individual can link the motive to related actions, more is the likelihood that the motive will be acquired.

5. The more an individual can transfer and apply the newly conceptualised motive to events of daily life, more is the motivation (i.e., the motive increases).

   Application (of 4 and 5): The emphasis here is on linking thought processes to actions. Hence, participants are made to play business games, analyse case studies and discuss how various ideas can be applied in everyday life.

6. If a motive improves a persons' self-image, the motive strength increases.

   Application: Using methods of cognitive restructuring, the trainer explains how entrepreneurial success brings prestige and happiness.

7. If the motive is consistent with the dominant cultural values, the motive is more likely to be acquired.

   Application: Group discussions on how nAchievement is consistent with folklore, religious books and cultural values.

8. If an individual commits herself to achieving specific goals related to the motive, there is an increased likelihood of the motive affecting her thoughts and actions in future.

   Application: Participants have to make a public commitment to seek specific achievement goals after a period of training.

9. Motive change is more likely to occur if the person gets regular feedback on the progress made towards the goal.

   Application: Participants are trained in methods of measuring how well they are doing at any time.

10. The course trainers should assume a warm, non-directive and accepting role. The trainer should lead discussions and present information, but should let participants explore concepts for themselves.
11. Affective factors are important in increasing motivation. Emotional confrontation helps an individual to clear her thought processes.

    Application: Participants are given the course in retreat settings. By this, emotional and personal confrontation is encouraged and helps the individual in introspection.
12. Emotional group supports enhance motivations.

    Application: Emotional group supports are fostered by encouraging the participants to participate in group activities. Role of self-help groups in entrepreneurial activities is emphasised.

Assessment

Training courses based on McClelland's training design have been run in various developing countries, like Japan, Italy, Mexico, Spain and India. The Indian training course was studied and evaluated by McClelland and Winter (1989). 76 businessmen running small business in the towns of Kakinanda (near Hyderabad) and Vellore were chosen. The group from Kakinada was given a ten-day achievement motivation training, while the group from Vellore became the control group. In a follow-up two years later, it was found that the trained businessmen showed substantial and significant increase in entrepreneurial activity, while the control groups members remained near their initial levels. In other studies, scholars have proved the efficacy of this training. A leading scholar in this area is Prayag Mehta, who has designed interventions for training businessmen and school students towards achievement (1968, 1962, 1972, 1978).

Training to increase EM and decrease DM

Pareek (1970) believes that just achievement motivation is not sufficient to motivate people towards self-employment. Especially in the case of rural folks of India, it has been found that people have high need for dependence, a fatalistic attitude, powerlessness and unrealistic expectations. These traits are contradictory to entrepreneurial behavior and economic development. Hence, Pareek proposes that people should be trained in extension motivation (EM) and should be provided training to reduce their high need for dependency (DM). For this, his proposed training programmes are discussed in detail in the chapter on Community Psychology.

14.9 Consumer Rights and Consumer Courts

Fairness is a pre-requisite for economic development. Market economics tells us that free market increases economic efficiency. More efficiency means more development. But, a free market is not possible without fairness. That is why free markets need to be regulated. Here comes the role of law and regulatory bodies. For instance, the SEBI Act, 1992 is a law passed by the parliament to preserve fairness in stock markets. Any act of fraud or unfair practice is penalised by the SEBI Act, 1992.

This is also the reason why law and public policy try to interfere in a free market transaction between a supplier and a consumer. Policy-makers try to formulate laws that protect the supplier as well as the consumer against possible wrongdoings. There are two schools of thought, with polar views, on what kind of laws to ensure fairness in the market- consumer behaviourists and neo formalists. A policy-maker has to balance between the merits of these two schools of thought so as to make effective laws.

The consumer behaviourists

Consumer behaviourists believe that consumers are limited in their cognitive capacity to calculate and maximise their expected utilities (Silber, 1990).

A typical consumer decision-making process has the following steps:

A. Need recognition and problem perception

B. Deliberation stage

   (a) Choice criteria

   (b) Information search

   (c) Information processing

C. Evaluation of alternatives

D. Purchase

E. Post-purchase evaluation

Consumer behaviourists argue that consumers do not have the cognitive capacity to make objective calculation at the stage of 'information processing', 'information search' and 'evaluation of alternatives'. The evaluation of alternatives usually happens by mere heuristics or subjective evaluation. Hence, the consumers are prone to make mistakes. When a seller uses inducements or marketing gimmicks (discussed later) to sell its products, the consumer may make an irrational decision, even if she is able to calculate the probabilities accurately. Hence, 'reasonable consumers' cannot consistently maximise their rational best interests. Hence, consumer behaviourists argue, policymakers should make special laws to protect the interest of consumers. Policy-makers need to set certain basic standards and quality controls, so that consumers are not duped.

The neo formalists

Neo formalists feel that consumer behaviourists rely too much on psychological concepts. To them, a *sale* is a contract between a seller and a consumer. Once the consumer has decided to purchase a good, she has no right to legal recourse. Consumer assent to contract terms should be strictly interpreted and enforced. They say that 'psychologically sensitive legal standards reduce the moral clarity and precision of contract and tort law' (Silber, 1990).

We will explain the above two viewpoints with two examples. Say, an alcoholic by the name of Antonio has struck a deal with Shylock that he would give a pound of his flesh in return for a bottle of scotch whisky. Shylock can then drag Antonio to court for his pound of flesh. But,

Antonio was not thinking right when he promised a pound of his flesh. What laws should lawmakers promulgate to protect the interest of Antonio and Shylock? Neo-formalists say that the deal was a fair deal. It should be looked at objectively and Antonio should pay a pound of his flesh. But, consumer behaviourists whine that Antonio did not make an 'informed decision'. His subjective urge to drink overpowered his rationality and he made an irrational decision.

Second example is that of beauty creams. Say, a famous beauty cream markets itself as herbal and good for the skin. It induces customers to buy the creams with a hope to bag a good date. But, the cream has a side effect – it leads to skin cancer in the long run. Should the consumer not have any right? If so, what rights does the consumer have? Neo-formalists would say that the company has given a disclaimer on the cover of beauty creams that the cream may have some long-term impact on skin (in extremely small letters). So the consumer is to blame if she gets rashes. Consumer behaviourists, on the other hand, would claim that consumers do not have the capacity to make an 'information search' and 'information processing' properly. Consumers usually do not understand what chemicals are used in beauty creams. Nor are the consumers expert in understanding the impact of paraffin, various acids and compounds. So, naturally the consumer was mistaken. The consumer was duped, because the disclaimer on the cream packet is a general disclaimer. So, the consumer should be suitably compensated.

Who should the policy-maker side with? Neither; and both.

The basic rule of policymaking is to make policies backed by empirical evidence. Different schools may have different opinions. But, law on the basis of opinion is always bad law. Law should always be driven by field evidence and data. So, the policy-maker should collect empirical evidence from psychologists to understand how gullible consumers can be. In certain sectors, such as health products, pharmaceuticals, etc., more stringent consumer protection laws need to be made than other sectors, like dress and toys.

Some weaknesses of the 'reasonable consumer' have been found from clinical as well as field studies over the period of time. These findings have helped the policy makers in strengthening tort laws and consumer protection laws.

Some of these are detailed as under:

(a) *Framing effects and puffery*

In some situations, consumers exhibit a marked preference for one of two choices, not on the basis of objective criteria, but based on how the two choices are presented.

This can be explained with an example.

Situation 1: You buy a movie ticket worth INR 200 and go to the theatre. Upon reaching the theatre, you find that you have lost the ticket. Would you buy another ticket?

Situation 2: You go to the theatre without a ticket. You lose INR 200 in cash on you way. Would you buy a ticket on reaching the theatre? Most people presented with these two situations say that they are more likely to buy a ticket if they have lost money. Even though the two situations are *objectively* similar, there is a default preference among consumers for one situation over the other.

Individuals are inherently more reluctant toward placing at risk a prospective gain, than they are towards potentially worsening an anticipated loss. This leads to framing effect. Neo formalists assume that the way choices are framed has no effect on consumer decision. But, behaviourists have shown, with evidence, that framing effect leads to subjective bias among consumers. If courts arbitrating over a damage suit enquire into framing effect, they may find that the customers have been induced to purchase the product by deceptively framed alternatives. This can help the court in determining more liability of the product seller.

Puffery is an advertisement tactic in which an advertiser makes unsupported subjective opinions and exaggerations. Courts usually do not consider such tactics as deceptive. However, research suggests that consumers get duped by puffed claims too. For instance, if a detergent powder company says that mud is good and shows that mud can be washed off with just a spoonful of its detergent, we usually know that it's a puffed claim. But some housewives actually think that the detergent is much superior to other types of detergent.

(b) *Disinclination to maximise expected utility*

If a consumer were to behave rationally, she would make an information search and then take a decision. But 'reasonable consumers' are not inclined to perform due diligence before making a purchase. An apt example is the act of purchasing a house. In one study of two high-income Connecticut communities, it was found that one-third of homebuyers sought information from just less than 6 homes before buying a house. Almost half of the home buyers did not shop for a loan and merely went to the bank recommended to them (Silber, 1990).

One theory to explain this is that greater the stress and perceived risk in the decision, the less effective is the decision-making process. This brings in irrationality in the process. This is where the neo-formalists claim that consumers are rational fails.

(c) *Inaccurate probability estimates*

Neo formalists also assume that consumers are able to accurately calculate the probabilities of each consequence and thereby value their contracts. Research, however, shows that consumers err even in simple calculations. Most consumers, not even mathematicians, make an estimate of the probabilities of each eventuality. Nor do they calculate the value of benefits or losses from such consequences. When I wanted to buy a car, I did not think how much the car's worth is, how much will be the road tax, the maintenance costs, the petrol costs, viz-a-viz the costs incurred on my bike. I also did not quantify the safety features in a car and how much safer the car is in comparison to the bike. I wanted a car and I brought it.

Some psychologists give the example of first-time consumers of cigarette. When they start smoking, they do so under influence of their peer group or under media depictions of cigarette. They do not calculate the costs on getting lung cancer. But, once they start smoking, they rationalise themselves by attaching small costs to lung cancer.

(d) *Information overload*

Neo formalists say that consumers who have entered into a contract should be held responsible for each and every clause of the contract. Now, say, you purchase a medical insurance. The insurance company makes you sign on six pages of longish conditions written in small font. Do you read all that is written? Do you understand all that is written? Behaviourists have found that consumers' ability to understand contracts is significantly influenced by the quantity and complexity of the information presented to them. When policy-makers or courts ask behaviourists to give their opinion on a suit, they try to see how much of information needs to be processed by the consumer and whether it was just to expect a consumer to process so much of information before taking a decision?

Consumer Awareness for Consumer Protection

The other day, I was eating a burger at a popular eating joint when I found a dead lizard in the burger. The burger was priced at INR 50 and the manager of the joint pleaded to replace me the burger or refund the INR 50. But, is it about the price of the burger? What amount should be refunded? What is the extent of loss to me owing to finding the lizard in the burger? First, there is the issue of health and sanitation. Then, there is the issue of psychological impact of the incident on me. I may get an aversive taste conditioning towards burgers in general. The traumatic experience of having found a lizard in the burger itself is quite traumatic an experience! So, now what should be done? I won't do a thing if I don't have the awareness about consumer rights. But, who shall decide the extent of damage that the burger has done to me? The Judge, of course. But, the judge is not an expert. Hence, he will take the advice of a consumer psychologist.

When a consumer buys a product, there are certain expectancies attached to the product relating to quality and quantity. However, the sellers may use fraudulent methods (in the desire of higher profits) to cheat the consumer. Consumer rights are basic rights guaranteed to the consumer by the doctrine of fairness. To enforce consumer rights, consumer groups resort to legislative control; to claim compensation against violation of consumer rights, they often go to consumer courts. Psychologists best understand consumer behavior from an individual perspective.

The involvement of psychologists here is at multiple levels:

1. Consumer awareness
2. Consumer protection
3. Compensation and consumer court litigations
4. Fraudulent marketing strategies

1. Consumer Awareness

Psychologists have played an important role in education and awareness generation among consumers regarding their rights. The layman consumer is often not aware of the quality of product that she is purchasing. Nor does she minutely scrutinise the product she is purchasing. Even if she finds an anomaly, she is often not aware of her rights in relation to producers; hence can't claim compensation. For instance, consumers have a right to information regarding marked price ingredients used in the product, unit price, etc. If these informations are printed very illegibly on the packet, and the consumer can't read it, it violates the consumer's right to information. Some psychologists have investigated a shoppers' ability to identify ingredients printed on food packages, at a purely perceptual level and have reported how size and clarity of print affects right to information of consumers. There is an increasing trend among consumer psychologists to research into abuse of consumer trust by sellers and producers.

2. Consumer Protection

The 'Consumer Protection Movement' refers to collective action by consumer groups to pressurise the government for better regulations of products. Consumer psychologists have helped the movement by discovering how various product and marketing appeals used to sell products are perceived by consumers. Psychologists try to determine the gap between consumer perception of a product and what the product actually delivers.

(Consumer Perception of Product – What the product actually delivers) = Gap

The gap between consumer perception and product quality is used as evidence for lobbying for legislations to restrict the fraud caused by the producer. Many consumer psychologists are active in studying the ergonomics of products. If a car is marketed as a safe and comfortable one, whereas the producer hasn't taken care of human factors, it may lead to negative impact on the consumer. It may lead to accidents and, in cases, death. The consumer has a right to demand compensation from producer for faulty human factor engineering in the car.

3. Consumer Court Litigation

What if consumer rights are violated by a seller? The consumer goes to the court for compensation. Since the extent of damage to the consumer is qualitative, what should the compensation be? The judge takes the help of the consumer psychologist to determine this. Advocates often take help from psychologists' study to argue their points in the court and bargain for appropriate compensations.

4. Fraudulent marketing Strategies

To maximise profits, some producers use fraudulent strategies. But, to understand how these strategies are made, we need to understand consumer decision-making process. Consumer decision-making goes through the steps shown in figure 14.9:

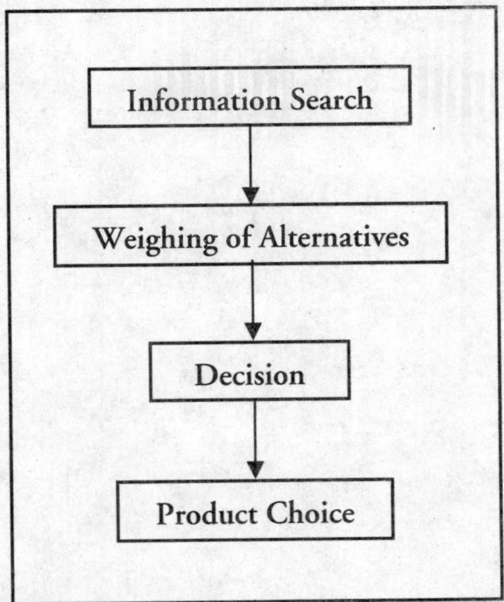

Fig. 14.9: Steps involved in Consumer Decision Making

A basic consumer right is informal decision-making. If first two steps are skipped due to fraudulent marketing strategies, it is unethical. For example, suppose the price written on a label or nutritional content mentioned on the cover of a product is too small to be perceived, 'information search' fails. Such means are used by the producer to cheat consumers. Unethical use of mass media is also prevalent for selling products. For example, subliminal perception strategies were used in 1950s in USA to advertise products. Such strategies affect consumer decision-making without the consumer's awareness. Basically in subliminal perception, the consumer can't consciously perceive the message, but the message makes unconscious suggestions that affect consumer decision. In the 1950s, many marketing strategists used subliminal advertisements in theatres to boost sales of cold drinks and pop corns. Movies in theatres were subliminally superimposed with advertisements, like 'Hungry! Eat Popcorn'. These movies were altered with movies without subliminal messages. It was found that sales of popcorns rose by around 50% for movies with subliminal messages.

Such news is frightening! It means, certain fraudulent marketing and persuasion strategies exist that can influence our decision as consumers! Psychologists conduct research to find out more about these fraudulent strategies and how they affect the consumer. Using this rich research base, consumers can assert their rights.

■ ■ ■

Psychology Applied to Technology Related Issues

15

PSYCHOLOGY OF IT AND MASS MEDIA

Chapter outline

15.1 Developments in Media Psychology

Internet and its related technologies will change almost every aspect of our life – private, social, cultural, economic and political, because (they) deal with the very essence of human society; communication between people. Earlier technologies, from printing to the telegraph, have brought big changes over time. But, the social changes over the coming decades are likely to be much more extensive and to happen much faster than any in the past, because the technologies driving them are continuing to develop at break-neck pace. More importantly, they look as if together they will be as pervasive and ubiquitous as electricity.'

—Manasian (2003, p.4)

15.2 The present scenario in IT and Mass Media

The rapid development of media technology is perhaps the biggest technological revolution of the 20th century. Communication technology, mass media and finally information technology have revolutionised the way people communicate. With increased communication piercing geographical barriers, the world is soon becoming a 'Global Village'. Traditionally, society and culture used to change from village to village. Today, owing to mass media, common cultural characteristics are found on national and even global level.

The boom in mass media and information technology (IT) has opened up numerous avenues for living a different life. With a boom in social networks, netizens have become both consumers and creators of content on social media. Events, such as the Arab Spring, have shown that internet media can be used for influencing user attitude and behavior in a massive way. Terrorist organisations, such as the Islamic State (IS) have managed to recruit soldiers and volunteers from all around the world; thanks to the proliferation of interactive social media. Online groups are revolutionary in the sense that they can be used to influence attitudes, values, and behaviours without the need for physical presence. The relation (and possible addiction) of a person with her mobile phone has become of interest to psychologists. A handy mobile phone is one's window to a huge network of people, places and information.

In the field of cyber psychology, some technologies that are of interest are- Web 2.0 technology and virtual reality. Web 2.0 technology is a modern tool to make websites, browsers, blogs and wikis more interactive. The attempt here is to make the web-human interaction as good as human-human interaction. **Virtual reality** is an attempt to make the web world as 'real' as the real world. It makes use of complex 3-dimensional graphics and artificial intelligence to construct an environment that simulates the real world. Many games have been devised which try to simulate real life action scenes. You can sit here in New Delhi and can play a game of Counter Strike with people from Pakistan, America, Canada, Vietnam or China. You also have the preference of becoming the terrorist and counter-terrorist in the game. You can be an expert in Kung Fu or in jungle warfare by just clicking on options in these games. Hence, this environment is more flexible than the real environment.

Beyond games, virtual reality is now being used to build new worlds altogether. In the game 'second life', you can enroll with a username, then get citizenship of a new country on its virtual world, study, work, buy property, marry, have sex with your wife, cheat on your wife, and get a divorce. You get a chance to live an entirely different life and may even get satisfaction, happiness and well-being in this world, if not in the real world.

Developments in mass media also pose a challenge to psychological studies. TV media is a one-way communication via which the program communicator influences the viewer. All new fashion trends start from TV and movies. New and old ideologies are propagated through TV. Violence, love, hatred, and other emotions are 'learnt' by the viewer through media. Media fosters stereotypes. News media disseminates all types of news – both true and false news. Hence, psychological study of mass media is necessary.

Next, let us investigate some psychological consequences of recent developments in IT and mass media.

Conceptual underpinnings of media psychology

Media psychology applies two key concepts of basic psychology to understand the effect of media on human beings: (a) *perception* and (b) *mediation of reality.*

Media acts as an intermediary between perception of an individual and the reality. This is where the nuances of media arise. As an intermediary, it can show an individual the reality that he wants to see. It can (a) be used by an individual to conform her biases, (b) be used by a user to influence the attitude of an individual, and (c) can be used by an individual to spread her ideas through social networks and 'viral' messages.

There are four major approaches that psychologists use to study mass media and its impact on human behavior. They are as under:

(a) ***Effects approach:*** This is the oldest approach used by psychologists to understand the effects of mass media on behaviour. Under this approach, psychologists tried to study response of persons to media stimuli. Earliest studies involved laboratory studies of radio advertisements and propaganda and what impact they had on individuals. This approach drew heavily on behaviourist theory of Bandura. However, this approach has now moved away from pure behaviourism by applying some cognitive theories as well. Major limitation of this approach is that it tries to measure only the negative effects of mass media on users. It has also been criticized for individualizing study of media influence and ignoring wider social and cultural contexts.

(b) ***Cultivation approach***: Cultivation approach subscribes to the view that exposure to media over time, subtly "cultivates" viewers' perceptions of reality. Cultivists say that psychology should study *media influences* rather than *media effects*. They believe that in this new world where media is an integral part of life, it helps shape our understanding of the world. Hence, media is a key element of socialization process.

Two key ideas in cultivation studies are- *mainstreaming* and *resonance*. *Mainstreaming theory* states that different cultural backgrounds and values gradually converge as a result of international TV culture. Mainstreaming leads to cultural globalization and cultural homogenization. We can see this in action in the form of TV channels and platforms, like Netflix and Amazon Prime. Many young people in India are fans of American crime shows and sitcoms. Most qualified youngsters have watched popular western sitcoms, like *Friends* and *How I met your mother*. Yet, other youngsters in India are fans of Korean drama and romance series on Netflix. Yet, others like to watch Chinese action movies. Such acts lead to acculturation across the board.

Resonance theory states that media simply acts to reinforce people's real life experiences.

(c) ***Gratification approach:*** Uses and Gratification studies ('U&G') study individual differences among viewers, like the effects approach. However, they draw inspiration from Maslow's Humanism School rather than Behavioural School. U&G researchers believe that the media user is in control of what she views. So, rather than studying the user as a passive recipient of effects, we should study the *motives* for using media and the *needs* that media use gratifies.

Gratification approach is based on five assumptions or beliefs, namely:

Sl	Assumption	Illustration
(i)	The user is in control.	I will watch a movie on Netflix only if it interests me.
(ii)	Media use is goal directed and purposive.	I want to follow a web portal because it informs me about electronic gadgets. I also want to follow *The Big Bang Theory* because it lightens me.
(iii)	Media is used to gratify wants and needs.	Media fulfils my entertainment needs, my curiosity needs, etc.
(iv)	Effects of media should be studied in the context of individual differences and contextual factors.	Political propaganda through *Whatsapp* does not enthuses me, as I like to read politics in good old TV channels.

Table contd...

Sl	Assumption	Illustration
(v)	There is competition between media use and other forms of communication.	Shall I watch the new *Marvel* movie or shall I go to the pub for a drink?

(d) ***Active audience approach:*** Although the U&G approach has helped shift the attention of psychological studies from seeing users as active rather than passive, the approach has been criticized for focusing only on the individual and ignoring the social and cultural context of media use. This approach is based on an idea that media users are social groups that are strongly influenced by media.

We will understand this with an illustration. Hypothetically, say, you receive a message on Whatsapp stating that all Hindus will be wiped off from India unless Hindus support the Cow Protection Movement. How will you react? How you will interpret the message depends on your own attitude and worldview.

There are three possibilities:

(i) **The *dominant* code:** You accept the message sent to you and fume over the fact that Hindus are becoming extinct in India.

(ii) **The *negotiated* code:** Audiences modify the message on the basis of their personal experiences. You may take the message with a pinch of salt. This may become true, but then there are so many Hindus around you.

(iii) **The *oppositional* code:** You treat the message with deep suspicion. You may label it as a 'fake news' or a biased propaganda.

There are many theories to explain individual and group behaviours in response to media. These theories are mostly based on either of the above approaches. The *Direct Imitation Theory* states that a viewer imitates whatever she sees on television. This theory derives heavily from the Behaviourist School. The *Affective Disposition Theory (ADT)* states that media and entertainment users make moral judgments about characters in a media narrative. The moral judgments made by characters, in turn, affects their enjoyment of the narrative.

The *media dependency theory* states that in a media saturated world, people have come to depend heavily on media platforms for information about all kinds of topic. DeFleur and Ball-Rokeach (1989) have outlined three key modes in which individuals develop dependencies on the media.

They are:

(a) Media provides information that helps users *understand* the world around them.

(b) Users may depend on media for *orientation,* either in terms of action (deciding to vote in an election, or go to the salon to look good), or interaction (googling for ways to propose your girlfriend).

(c) Users depend on the media for *play* (either for playing a video game or for going to the multiplex for a movie).

The *expectancy value theory* states that we watch TV shows that we expect will fulfill our needs (such as entertainment) and also ones that we value highly (I want to watch all Christopher Nolan movies, because I consider him fundoo).

Psychological consequences

Talking of technological changes, sociologist Ogburn had observed that changes in non-material cultures often follow changes in material cultures (technology for example), but with a lag. This lag is called the 'culture lag'. Changes in technology lead to a lag not only in non-material culture (like norms, values, etc.), but also by human personality. The revolution in information technology has had definite impacts on human psyche. In fact, such has been the speed of impact that it is feared in future, the changes will be too much to adapt to and may lead to a future shock. (Toffler, 1970).

To the credit of IT, it can't be denied that it has many beneficial effects on the individual, the organization and the society at large. No agent of change is devoid of short-comings. IT being no exception, it has its ill-impact on individual humans and groups.

Let us discuss the impacts of IT from a psychological point of view:

1. Impact of internet on learning and creativity

Many psychologists have opined that Internet use reduces the deep thinking that leads to true creativity. For example, Carr (2010) claims that internet has the following impacts on cognition:

- When the brain is bombarded with hyperlinks and overstimulation, it has to give most of its attention to short-term decisions.
- The vast availability of information on the World Wide Web overwhelms the brain and hurts long-term memory.
- The availability of stimuli leads to a very large cognitive load, which makes it difficult to remember anything.

Medical studies have tentatively concluded that the current explosion of digital technology is not only changing the way we live and communicate, it is also altering our brains. In one study, psychiatrist Gary Small studied brain activity in experienced web surfers versus casual web surfers using MRI scans. The study showed that when browsing the internet, brain activity of experienced Internet users was far more extensive than that of novices, particularly in areas of the brain associated with problem-solving and decision-making. However, the two groups had no significant differences in brain activity when reading blocks of text. Gary Small concluded from the evidence that the distinctive neural pathways of experienced Web users had developed because of their Web use.

2. Impact on attention span

Many psychologists have opined that people's ability to focus is being undermined by bursts of information on the internet. Krishnan & Sitaraman (2012) conducted a large-scale study involving millions of users watching videos on the internet, to find their behavior. They have concluded that Internet users are impatient and are likely to get more impatient with time. Users start to abandon online videos if they do not start playing within two seconds. Users with faster Internet connections abandoned videos at a faster rate than users with slower Internet connections. These results show that as Internet services become faster, they provide instant gratification. As a result, users become less patient and are less able to delay gratification to work towards longer-term rewards.

Internet usage statistics also show the impact of internet on attention span. Statistics from 53,573 page views taken from various users showed that 17% of the views lasted less than 4 seconds, while only 4% lasted more than 10 minutes.

3. Disorder of Addiction

A major apprehension voiced by psychologists about increasing influence of computers in human life is that it hampers in the socialization process. Some kids prefer web friends and e-chatting over real friends and real dating. Some people spend an unusually large part of their daily routine on the internet. This may be because they enjoy games or because they are involved in sex chats, or in networking in social network sites, like orkut.com. But when the duration spent on the internet becomes 'abnormal', some psychologists claim that these people may be suffering from Internet Addiction Disorder (IAD).

As of now, IAD is a vague concept and hasn't yet been properly conceptualized. When do you say that a person suffers from IAD? If she spends ten hours a day on the internet? Or if she spends 15 hours a day on the internet? Problem is, people seemed to be addicted to telephones and computers before the advent of internet. Of course, some extreme cases exist, that can be called pathological addiction. If you lose your job, or flunk out of college, or are divorced by your spouse, because you cannot resist devoting all your time to the World Wide Web, you are pathologically addicted. But, if you don't belong to such extreme cases, it is tough to say whether you are showing abnormal behaviour or not.

The latest edition of Diagnostic and Statistical Manual of Mental Disorders (DSM-IV) doesn't have any specific category for internet addiction disorder. However, the research interest on IAD as a mental disorder is on the rise. For instance, Prof. Kimberly Young, a leading researcher in the field of cyber psychology, has started the Centre for On-line Addiction (COLA) to study IAD. After watching internet users for a long time, she has developed a criterion for assessing one's dependence on the internet. According to Prof. Young (1996), you are dependent on internet if you meet four of the following criteria over the last one year:

- Felt pre-occupied with the internet; felt a need to use the internet with increasing amount of time in order to achieve satisfaction; had an inability to control your internet use.
- Felt restless or irritable when attempting to cut or stop internet use.
- Used the internet as a way of escaping from problems or of relieving poor mood.

- Lied to family members or friends to conceal the extent of involvement with the internet.
- Jeopardized or risked the loss of a significant relation, job, educational or career opportunity because of the internet.
- Kept returning even after spending an excessive amount of money for online fees.
- Went through withdrawal when offline.
- Stayed online longer than originally intended.[1]

Besides IAD, there are other disorders associated with cyberspace. For example, cyber neurosis is depression due to breaking of online relations. Many workers in the IT industry who have to work a great deal on the computer and internet, have reported depression and changes in lifestyle. The boom in IT in India is mostly due to BPO industries, where young men and women have to work in odd times. This severely disturbs their lifestyle.

4. Interpersonal Relationships

Interpersonal relation is based on interaction between people. The nature of interaction depends on the mode of communication. Since internet and mass media technology have profoundly changed the way we communicate, they have significant impact on interpersonal relations. As per the "filter model" of Sproull & Kiesler (1985), computer-mediated communication (CMC) is an improvised communication experience, wherein many social cues available in face-to-face communication are filtered out. Hence, if an individual relies excessively on CMC for social communication, she experiences a greater sense of anonymity. This experience leaves a de-individuating effect on the individual, making his behaviour more self-centered and less socially regulated than usual.

The effects of internet use on existing relationships is a topic of intense scholarly interest. The most popular study on this issue was the HomeNet project by Kraut and her colleagues (1998). In this project, the researchers studied some families in Pittsburgh who didn't have computers at home. The researchers gave computers and internet access to these families and did a follow-up study after 2 years. They found that depression and loneliness increased as a function of amount of internet use. Some other scholars also pointed out that owing to long hours spent on the internet, users had less time for interaction with friends and family.

However, both arguments above have shortcomings. Kraut and her colleagues did a follow-up on the same sample after two more years (Kraut et al., 2002) and found that the negative effects they had attributed to internet use had disappeared. It has also been found that heavy internet use does affect the time spent on other activities, but the real decrease is in watching television and reading newspapers, not in social interaction with friends and family.

Relationship formation on the internet is another major issue of interest. These days, finding friends and dates on the internet is in vogue. Indeed, one study found that many internet users

1. Pg 27 of Young (1996).

form close relationship over the net (McKenna et al., 2002). The study found that more than 50% of participants had moved from internet-based relationships to real life one. About 22% participants stated that they were either married, engaged or living in with the partners they originally met over the internet. Moreover, these relationships are as stable as traditional relationships.

Why has internet become so popular as a means for forming relations? Bargh & McKenna (2004) explain that (a) people are better able to express their true selves (those self-aspects they feel are important, but they are not able to express in public) to their partner over the internet than in face-to-face, and (b) when internet partners like each other, they tend to project qualities of their ideal friends onto each other. Kang (2000) rightly observes that cyberspace makes talking with strangers easier. The fundamental point of many cyber-realms, such as chat rooms, is to make new acquaintances. By contract, in most urban settings, few environments encourage us to walk up to strangers and start chatting in many cities, doing so would amount to physical threat.[2]. Next time you see a beautiful girl on the road and feel dejected, that is absurd to walk down and start a conversation; at least try to get her email id or her name, so that you can search her up on orkut.com. Who knows, you may get e-lucky!

Internet Paradox Hypothesis

- The paradox is how a 'social technology' (internet) primarily used for interpersonal interaction could increase social isolation and decrease psychological wellbeing among its users.
- Studies in cyber – psychology have not come out with any decisive conclusion on the issue.
- Some scholars have warned of the harmful effects of e-relations, blaming online technology for disrupting real world networks and creating a "lonely crowd" in cyberspace. Yet, others attest to the fact that internet increases social contract across geographical locations (se LaRose et al., 2001)

Fig. 15.1: Internet Paradox Hypothesis

2. Page 1161 of Kang (2000).

5. IT and Human Needs

IT provides immense opportunities for individuals to fulfil their needs across the need structure – both intrinsic drives and social needs. These needs can, in fact, be represented as a pyramidal structure;

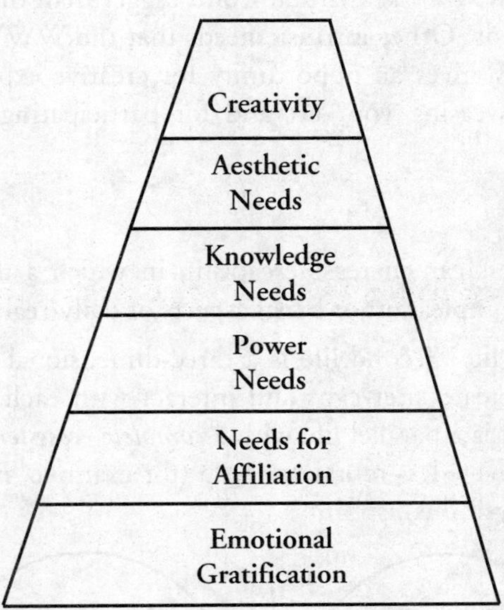

Fig. 15.2 : Pyramid showing human needs IT can fulfil.

emotional gratification is obtained from IT because it is a channel for cathartic release. According to the Psychoanalytic School, cathartic release happens when an individual has an 'outlet' to channelize her psychic energy. When you express your opinions, vent your anger and frustration or express your hatred towards somebody or something on the net, you express your emotions. You may open a blog under anonymous name and express all your feelings. Therapists often believe that expressing oneself is one of the best ways to control anxiety ('Talk', they say!). In a way, blog and discussion forums are therapeutic in nature.

One gets to make many new contacts and friends through social networking sites and apps, such as Tinder and facebook.com. The need for affiliation is also fulfilled through these sites. These days, many love affairs start on Facebook.com. Some sites give the opportunity to chat online, which is also an avenue to meet one's need for affiliation. Sex chat is an avenue for fulfilment of sexual desires, but the exact effect of sex chat on an individual is debatable.

Mind you, social networking sites aren't that good. Many people are maligned on these sites, many hate messages are freely circulated, imposters exist on these networking sites posing as real women and many rumours are spread here. Guess what the psychological trauma would be on a lady who is maligned or is defamed by an imposter on these sites! Sometimes, social network sites also lead to frustration owing to non-fulfilment of needs. After hearing some success stories of people finding partners on Orkut, even I tried my luck. But to no avail! And it really frustrated me.

We must appreciate the power of anonymity on the World Wide Web. Your religion, your caste, creed, race etc., hold no significance on web space. You are an equal citizen and your status depends on your abilities and intellectual vigour. Anonymity mitigates your inferiority complexes and fulfils your power needs; thus boosting your self-esteem.

The World Wide Web (WWW) is a virtual world bigger than the real world. It can virtually fulfill all our knowledge needs. Other intrinsic needs that the WWW fulfils are aesthetic needs and cognitive needs. WWW gives an opportunity for creative expression (through blogs and literary web sites)- for showcasing your art and for participating in contests cutting across geographical boundaries.

6. Escapism

Uninterrupted internet access can increase escapism, in which a user uses the Internet as an "escape" from the perceived unpleasant or banal aspects of daily/real life.

Take the case of Second life. Second life is a three-dimensional (3D) internet-based virtual world that allows users to create alter egos and interact with each other. Second life is not a fantasy tour or voyeurism; it is a parallel life with a *complete ecosystem.* Here, people enjoy more control and more freedom, have less moral hang-up (for example, no moral bindings on extra-marital relations) and no physical constraints.

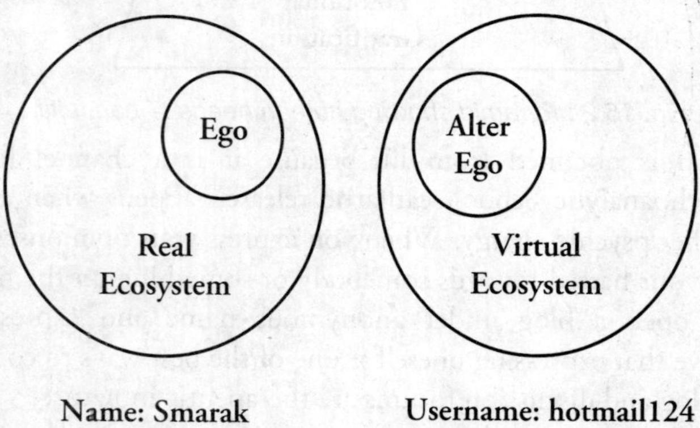

Fig. 15.3 : Comparison of real world and life in 'Second life'

In a virtual world, you can pick a name, a country, a job, buy and sell property, marry, have virtual sex, divorce and remarry. The person you grow intimate to or have sex with is also a real person, but you don't know him/her, you just know his/her identity on 'second life'. What are the ramifications of this? A person gets a new life and hence a new life concept. She now has to 'self' both completely different. Undoubtedly, she finds her new self more desirable. The 'self' in this virtual world has no moral liability, less inhibitions and is not restricted by superego. The virtual ego doesn't face many anxieties the way the real ego does. This may prompt the individual to 'live' on in the virtual world. Many people, who we call addicted to computer games and the internet, stick there because of the new identity they get.

This is not good. Let me point out that Schizophrenia and other disorders are due to split minds; due to a multiplicity of self-concepts. When faced with a problem in real life, the individual must face it or resolve the problem. Instead, if she withdraws to the virtual world, she doesn't resolve her real problems. And, we know that problem focused coping is better than social withdrawal coping style.

7. IT and Organization

IT has had structural impact on organizational communication and work life. Long before internet came, Karl Marx had observed that automation and machines are a source of alienation of the worker from his work. Similar has been the effect of IT. In organisations, most of the communication is done through informal groups and informal means of communication. Kraut and co-workers (1990), for instance, found from a study of an R&D organization that 85% of the interactions are informal and unplanned. The biggest advantage of informal communication is that it fosters an informal social group in the work place.

However, IT tools like Management Information System (MIS) make it easier to communicate via local intranet network. The face-to-face communication in organisations decrease and when this happens, the informal group breaks. When there is no social group in the work place, the individual feels alienated. Wonder what your situation will be if you work in an office for 8-10 hours and you don't know anyone in that office! Many of my friends in software company feel frustrated in working in software companies because of this kind of alienation. The *impersonal nature* of work has especially affected clerical jobs; the kind of jobs many software engineers do at the beginning of their career.

Greater use of IT has the potential to even change the organisation structure. Due to facilitation of communication, senior managers can now communicate to junior officers directly. As a result, the organisational power and utility of middle managers decreases.

8. Digital Divide

Digital divide is the line separating those who have access to internet from those who don't. In the social world, we have many lines separating "haves" and "have-nots". There are literate-illiterates, rich-poor, rural-urban and developed-backward differentiations in society. All of these differences are associated with social exclusion. The digital divide is also associated with exclusion.

Suppose Hari is an expert in psychology and better at it than Shyam. In this hypothetical case, if Shyam is computer literate and knows how to use the internet, he is better off than Hari. He can access the internet for better ideas for his research projects; he can search for research papers and use the vast resources available on the net. Hari faces a disability in this case, even though being internet savvy has nothing to do with being good in psychology. He faces exclusion from a huge resource. The point is, poor people who get sub-standard education are at a disadvantage in studies and employment, if they haven't got training in computers and the internet.

The good news is that the government understands the problem of digital divide as a social psychological one. The 11th five year plan specifically mentions digital divide as a challenge of inclusive growth. Some initiatives in the local and state level have also been taken. For example, Anand is a cooperative body that has a computerized milk collection system; Bhoomi is an initiative of Karnataka government to maintain computerized land records.

Many effects of mass media are covered separately in the chapter on pro-social and anti-social effects of mass media.

Tele-conferencing

Two revolutionary effects of IT on organisations have been tele-conferencing and tele-commuting. Tele-conferencing or video-conferencing has made the world a smaller place to live in. Two executives sitting in their respective offices in, say, Bangalore and Boston can communicate to each other. These days, video-conferencing is a popular tool being used in interviews, in meetings and even in e-governance; but the concern of psychologists is the psychological difference between face-to-face communication (what is informal communication) and video-conferencing. An informal communication eliminates hierarchy, promotes feedback, and interaction. Is video conferencing a good substitute for face-to-face (f2f) communication? This question was empirically investigated by Kraut and co-workers (1990). They gave participants the option of face-to-face and video-conferencing communication. The result was that compared to face-to-face conversations, video conferencing conversations were substantially fewer. Kraut observed that communicators maintained a psychological distance with each other in video conferencing communication, even when the videos had life-sized images.

Why is this so? Some probable reasons why video-conferencing is not a good substitute for informal communication are:

(a) In face-to-face interaction, the *context* of the conversation includes people, objects and the setting of the place. A tele-conferencing situation, on the other hand, is virtual. The social context and physical context of a conversation are important inputs for informal communication. These get missed out when two individuals communicate through video-conferencing.

(b) A communication consists of both verbal and non-verbal *cues*. Though certain non-verbal cues are transmitted through interactive technology, many of the cues don't get transferred. For example, eye gaze, gesture and clothing are some social information that video images do not display as vividly as face-to-face communication does (Kool and Agarwal 2006).

(c) Feedback is an important element of conversational interactions. In a face-to-face conversation situation, eye gaze and facial expressions of the audience (or other members of the communication) provide valuable feedback to the communicator. V.K Kool and Rita Agarwal (2006) observe that when people in the audience of a talk show make expressions, such as head nods or looks of puzzlement, it enriches the communication process. They are skeptical about video-conferencing being able to capture this information using existing technology.

Tele-commuting

Tele-commuting is a concept that has the potential to revolutionise work life on individual, organisational and societal level. It refers to working from locations outside the office, using information technology. The concept is revolutionary, in the sense that it is not mandatory for a tele-commuting employee to come to the office building physically; she can work from her home, or any place she is comfortable to work from. Some advantages of tele-commuting, according to Harpaz (2002) are:

1. The individual works from home and so has increased flexibility (note that this has potential to reduce the role-conflict in working mothers who also have to take care of troublesome kids).
2. The human resource capacity of the organisation increases and it saves in direct expenditure.
3. Since the employee doesn't commute to office in her personal vehicle, there is a reduction in environmental pollution. Tele-commuting is also solution for people with special needs; this way it is beneficial to society at large.

Concerns about telecommuting remain. We have already discussed the importance of informal communication and informal work groups. Harpaz believes that in telecommuting, there is a possible sense of isolation for the individual from her work culture. In spite of this drawback, the prospects of telecommuting are encouraging. For instance, IBM had sponsored a study to compare how three work venues (1.traditional office 2.virual office 3.home office) influence various dimensions of work life and personal life of employees. The results showed that the home office has positive impact on both- work life and personal life of employees, in comparison to the other two work venues (Hill, Ferris and Martinson, 2003).

15.3 Role of Psychologists in IT and Mass Media Boom

Given the many psychological consequences of the boom in IT and mass media, many psychologists (called cyber psychologists) are involved in research on the effects of this boom on the individual human being. Besides research, cyber psychologists are also engaged in developing techniques to maximize the use of IT for people and make the human-internet interface more user-friendly. The role of psychology is not limited to the works of cyber psychology; rather psychologists have benefited in general from the revolution in communication technology. The recent developments in IT and mass media have thrown many challenges for psychologists in general. Let us discuss some of the major challenges faced by psychologists and what role they play in this digital era.

Online Therapy

The internet is a challenge and an opportunity for therapists. Internet opens up new modes of communication for psychologists to deal with clients. At the same time, there are certain concerns regarding the difference between cyber therapy and traditional therapy. Barak (2004) has listed ten differences between online counselling and traditional counselling. These are as under:

I. *Alternative communication channels:* Traditional counselling is face-to-face counselling. It does not give much option to the counsellor and her clients. But, internet counselling can use any mode (individual or group communication) or means of communication (such as typed text, video communication, audio communication, etc.). This provides wide range of options to the clients.

II. *Internet counselling as a supplement:* Online therapy can be practiced as a complementary, adjacent, or adjudicative process to face-to-face therapy. Alternatively, internet counselling can be an independent process of therapy too.

III. *Text-based communication:* Although many means of communication exists online, the pre-dominant method is text-based communication. Writing can often be healing. Many people are more comfortable in sharing their intimate thoughts and deepest feelings when alone, than in the presence of a therapist.

IV. *Effective mode for any approach:* Any theoretical therapeutic approach, method, or technique, can be implemented over the internet for providing counselling to clients.

V. *Record of proceedings:* Since most communication happens through texts, it is easy to maintain a record of the interaction between client and therapist. The counselling dialogue gets saved and the client can revisit the dialogues to introspect and get an insight.

VI. *Program flexibility:* Online therapy may be provided for either long-term interventions or short-term interventions, as well as for single consultations.

VII. *Option of non-human interventions*: Internet can provide interventions through psychoeducational websites, as well as through interactive software. Artificial Intelligence (AI) bots can be used to provide instantaneous interventions. Advanced software communicates with users to assess and provide tailored interventions to deal with specific problems.

VIII. *Free counselling:* Free internet counselling, including supply of information and advice and support, have flourished. There is a clear scope of misuse of this by non-professionals or even criminals. Yet, internet has provided information to a user who could not use any of the standard ways of counselling.

IX. *Pre-therapy and post-therapy guidance:* Internet counselling can be made a part of more traditional therapies as well. The therapy would typically consist of three phases- pre-therapy stages through the internet, face-to-face therapy and taking feedback in post-therapy stage.

X. *Internet counselling can include online assessment:* Internet counselling portals can easily include online psychological assessment procedures. It must be noted here that online psychological tests have often been criticized and do not necessarily give reliable results.

Key advantages of internet counselling are as under:

1. *Anonymity:* Anonymity has positive impact on a client undergoing therapy. Anonymity makes them feel less vulnerable about participating in a group therapy.

That is the reason why in Alcoholic Anonymous (AA), a participant has the option of disclosing her name and personal details. Internet is the ultimate tool of anonymity. Here, you divulge only that much about yourself as you desire. Davison and colleagues (2000) studied the nature of patients seeking social support online and found that people used internet social support groups particularly for embarrassing and stigmatized illnesses such as AIDS.

2. ***Online dis-inhibition effect:*** In the cyberspace, people tend to say things that they normally wouldn't in face-to-face (f2f) situations. Because of anonymity and invisibility, people become bold, uninhibited and disclose such personal emotions, fears and wishes that they normally wouldn't. This makes the task of the therapist easier. She can discover the conscious and unconscious emotions, cognitions and feeling of the client in fewer sessions.

3. ***Flexibility:*** There is greater flexibility in online therapy than traditional therapy. For synchronous communication-based therapy like chat, you still need to take an appointment because the therapist and client chat in real time. Still, the appointment can be scheduled with greater flexibility. If the therapist and client are unable to fix a date and time for the chat, the therapy can continue via asynchronous communication means, such as an e-mail. In e-mail therapy, both parties don't have to be online at the same time.

In spite of these advantages, psychologists treat online therapy with caution. First and foremost reason is that the therapeutic climate of traditional therapies can't be replicated in internet communications. Most of the therapeutic methods were developed keeping in mind the face-to-face environment. We can't just replicate those methods in online therapy. New methods need to be devised; new methods that are more effective for online therapy.

A second concern is about working with sensitive clients in shaky situations. For example, take the hypothetical case of a suicide-vulnerable client. The traditional therapist studies her behaviors to conclude that the client is vulnerable. Accordingly, the therapist can take remedial measures. But, in online therapy, the non-verbal cues aren't transmitted. It is not always advisable to make conclusions based on text messages.

A third concern is that many counsellors without requisite skills manage to fool clients because of lack of regulations. An educational qualification is not sufficient to become a therapist or a counsellor on the net. You need some training to work in the field of IT. There is no regulator to certify psychologists who work online. This makes it easy for those without necessary skills to fool clients.

Psychological Testing

An important role of psychologists is taking psychological test and making assessments. The nature of this service is bound to change with the boom in IT. Many tests are now being administered through the internet. There are certain definite advantages of administering psychological tests online. Some of these, according to Barak (1999), are:

1. Internet-based psychological testing enables fast, simple, convenient and highly accessible testing.
2. Tests are ready for scoring as soon as respondent has taken the test, as the whole process is electronic.
3. Electronic scoring is practically error-free.
4. Updates of test items, scoring techniques, instructions and norms are made at a central server and are active immediately.
5. Tests may be taken at any time and any place convenient to the test user.
6. One capability of internet-based testing that is impossible in standard testing is the use of three dimensional (3D) graphical interface. For instance, in tests of perception, 3D is necessary, and internet can provide the 3D effect.

In spite of the numerous advantages of internet-based testing, there are certain concerns regarding it. Some of the important concerns that need to be addressed by psychologists in order to play the role of test-administrators on internet are (Barak, 1999):

1. Many of the test questionnaires published on the internet are inaccurate. These haven't been developed according to accepted testing standards. As a result, the results of these tests are invalid. Test-takers have no way to determine the validity and reliability of these tests. The results may harm the confidence of test-takers or provide them wrong assessment, based on which, test users are prone to take wrong decisions. For example, suppose I take an unreliable test which predicts that my ability lies in the medical profession, when in fact it lies in engineering, I may be prone to make an incorrect career decision that would change my life!
2. As all communication takes place electronically, the test-taker doesn't know the people who run the testing website. They may have to give highly sensitive information to people they don't know. Hence, there is a problem of privacy here.
3. In order to bypass copyright violations, many tests published online are variations of the original tests. This compromises the quality of the test. Original tests are constructed after meticulous work on validity, reliability, standardisation, etc. Even minor changes affect the quality of test.
4. The test-taker has the right to guidance in every step of test administration. She needs guidance in understanding the instructions, in taking the test and in interpreting the results. These services are not provided by the test user in internet-based testing. If you take an IQ test on the internet, you just get a figure as result. If you aren't a psychologist, what inference about yourself do you derive from "An IQ of 120"? You are simply clueless as a layman.
5. A basic concern is about the extent to which a paper-and-pencil test preserves its psychometric quality when administered online. A few tests are originally constructed for use on internet. But, most are rip-offs of paper-and-pencil tests.

These concerns do not show the shortcoming of psychological tests online; rather, they are deficiencies to work upon, so that psychological test administration through IT can be improved.

Providing Self-Help Guides

Self-help guides are not a new psychological means of intervention, but the way self-help guides are assessed by people at large has changed, owing to the internet. Self-help guides are psychological interventions that guide the individual to help herself in matters of assessment of a problem, evaluate the severity of the problem, understand the scope for positive changes etc. Self-help guides have been found to be extremely useful in helping people with issues, like eating disorders, alcohol dependence, assertiveness, relationship difficulties, shyness, etc.

Before the boom in IT, people who wanted self-help had to purchase relevant material or consult a library. Now, the scope of self-help guides has increased. People can easily access self-help guides if psychologists put them up on the internet. Making self-help guides for the internet throws new challenges for psychologists also. Unlike traditional guides that were in book format, the new guides can be more interactive. The psychologists can include graphics and video images to motivate the client.

Another benefit of developing self-help material over the internet is that people can access these in times of crisis. For instance, many adolescents face sexual problems (or have doubts regarding sex) which they can't discuss with others. Self-help guides provide relief from the trauma by helping them make sense of the problem. Similarly, when faced with crisis situations, these guides provide immediate crisis interventions. The internet user can access help on any subject on the click of a mouse. For instance, Firm and Lavitt have shown that self-help guides for women who experienced sexual abuse and other such trauma experience are of great help. In another self-help intervention, Kovalski and Horan (1998) designed a website that identified maladaptive career beliefs of girls and offered cognitive restructuring intervention to change these beliefs. They found that the website guide had positive effects on many participants.

Human Factor Engineering

There are two major considerations that need to be made when designing a website- the software codes and interactivity of the website. Software codes are developed by software engineers, using languages like HTML, XML, Java Script, ASP, PHP, etc. These codes are useful in storing the web information in a central server and presenting the information to the web users when demanded. Interactivity refers to the web-human interface. How good a person-environment fit does the website provide? This issue is dealt by human factor engineers and psychologists have a key role to play here.

Interactivity is the biggest challenge of all major developments in web technology lately. The Web 2.0 technology is all about giving the users a better experience of the virtual world. When designing a good website, the personal preferences of target viewers have to be kept in mind. For instance, if you are designing a website for farmers who are less computer-educated, you must make the website simple and clear, make greater use of graphics and visuals, etc. On the other hand, a website designed for engineering colleges can have complicated java applets and PHP features.

This work of psychologists finds applications in upcoming fields, like e-commerce and web advertising also. Psychologists provide crucial insight into consumer behavior on the internet. For example, Kargaonkar and his colleagues (2005) have found that the attention people give to web advertisements depend on their beliefs, attitudes and demographic factors. An advertisement should be devised incorporating these human factors for maximum success.

Other Roles

The roles played by psychologists in the recent boom in IT are many-fold. The prime factor in this is that psychological services are essential human services and IT makes it easier for the psychologists to provide their services to the people. The challenge here is to modify the services, so as to effectively present them through internet and mobile phone media. Another major role of psychologists is to research into effects of IT on the individual, organisations and society at large and provide solutions and interventions to mitigate the dysfunctional effects of IT.

Training Psychology Professionals to work in the field of IT and Mass Media

As reiterated earlier, the nature of psychological services changes drastically when provided through IT and mass media. Most psychology professionals involved in providing services through traditional face-to-face communication can't replicate their professional skills on the internet. For instance, a professional therapist trained to provide therapy in face-to-face interaction can't just replicate her skills on the internet. The communication over internet is through text messages, or at max video conferencing. Similarly, career counsellors who practice in face-to-face (f2f) situations can't work with clients on the internet or over mobile phones. The new means of communication needs special training. Some of the important training modules that a professional has to undergo to work in the field of IT and mass media are discussed in this section.

Training in Computers and Internet

The first and basic requirement of working on the internet is to have pre-requisite knowledge about the computer and internet. The psychologist needs to be trained in how to troubleshoot any problem in her computer. If a client is in need of emergency help, she should be able to provide it, even if her computer malfunctions. Secondly, various forms of communication on the internet and their psychometric properties need to be understood. Broadly, there are four forms of communication varying across two dimensions- synchronous-asynchronous and individual-group communications.

	Synchronous	Asynchronous
Individual (1-to-1)	Personal chat	E-mail
Group	Chat room	Forums and E-mail lists

The professional should be skilled in using all these modes of communication. The client may choose any of these modes for communication, as per her convenience. The professional also needs to be trained in the type of therapy or counselling that best suits a form of communication. For example, asynchronous communication doesn't happen online. The therapist/ counsellor can reply to the client after a few hours, days, or even months, so that she can formulate her reply at length. But, in case of synchronous communication like chatting, the therapist has to give immediate reply. It is like face-to-face communication, but not the same. In face-to-face communication, some visual and non-verbal cues are available that are absent in synchronous internet communication. Also, some cues of face-to-face therapy, like empathy (it is an important element of client-centered therapy) are tough to present through internet. Hence, the professional needs to be appropriately trained.

A third major skill that the professional needs to learn is that of internet-based money transaction. A professional should always charge money for her services. This is so as to ascertain that the client doesn't take the interaction for granted and takes the sessions seriously. In order to change a client, the professional should be skilled in dealing with credit card transactions. Much personal information is passed on when credit card transaction of capital takes place. The professional should not only maintain ethics, but also ascertain that the client's credit card number is not being leaked to any hacker. For this, she should have training in network security. I have been to the websites of many self-help guides on the internet. I find security system of these websites very novice. If, for example, you are providing a self-help guide on sports psychology for a nominal fee of four dollars, but your network security is so weak that any hacker can back the client's credit card number, you are causing great monetary harm to your client.

Training in Virtual Reality

What is the use of working on IT platforms, if you can't harness its special features! A major attraction of internet is that of graphics, 3D environment and virtual reality. Graphics and 3D are being used by educational psychologists to motivate students to learn through e-learning. This requires special training. The professionals should be trained in using and manipulating various image files, in creating various perceptions using graphics, etc.

Virtual reality has immense applications in psychological research and applications. Virtual reality is being used in therapy, rehabilitation of drug addicts and in simulation of real-life events. The professional needs to be trained in virtual reality. She should know how to simulate real world in the world of graphics and animation.

Training in Web Designing

The focus of web designing these days is shifting from software coding to human factor engineering. The goal is to make websites more and more interactive and to tailor the website to the needs of the web user. Even small details, like color of the website, the way information is presented, the tables, the fonts, the letter size, etc. should depend on the type of web user. It has been found that user beliefs, attitudes, personality and motivational pattern affect how a certain web design is accepted/ rejected by the user.

The human factor engineer should be trained in techno-graphics, online consumer research, web designing and some basics of software coding, necessary for designing websites.

Training for Mass Media

Many psychology professionals are invited on TV and radio stations to give guidance on various issues, like family matters, husband-wife relations, parent-child relations, etc. They are also invited to give solutions to various problems in newspapers. Some psychologists have regular columns in the Sunday special editions of various newspapers. It is a matter of concern that these professionals are not trained specifically for appearing in mass media. Obviously, only those professionals with good communication skills appear in the media. For those, who don't have good communication skills, training in communication skills is necessary.

Psychology professionals are experts in their field, but when they appear in radio and TV, the situation is different. Viewers and listeners pose certain personal problems to the professionals. In their regular services, psychologists study the detailed history of clients. But here they can't do so. Hence, when answering questions of viewers and listeners, they should not be directive. Special skills are required to provide solutions to problems posed in mass media. For instance, once I had heard a radio programme, in which a caller stated that her boyfriend doesn't want to have sex with her. The guest psychologist stated that her boyfriend may be gay. There may be other reasons, according to me. The boyfriend may be shy, or under confident, or too conforming to Indian values, or wants to go slow. Such judgmental answers by experts are harmful as the girl is bound to take the expert's advice at face value. Hence, the need for training.

15.4 The Internet as a psychological space

'With the advance of computers and online networks, especially the internet – a new dimension of human experience is rapidly opening up. The term "cyberspace" has been mentioned so often that it may at this point seem overly commercialized. However, the experience created by computers and computer networks can in many ways be understood as a psychological "space".....[While interacting with the internet people] are entering a "place" or "space", that is filled with a wide array of meanings and purposes' (Suler, 1995-2008).

This is how Prof. Suler starts his online book on cyber psychology. Basically, he stresses on the fact that when we start "Microsoft Windows" on our computer, we basically open a window to another techno culture realm. According to Prof. Suler, one experiences the cyberspace as an extension of her mind and personalities – a "space" that reflects her interests, tastes and attitudes.

Hence, it is necessary to understand the cyber-experience. How is this virtual world different from reality? To what extent does virtual reality conform to psychology of the real world? Certain basic psychological features of the cyberspace (Suler) are:

1. Reduced Sensations

When interacting with a person over IT, we severely restrict the verbal and non-verbal communications cues. It is mostly through texting that we communicate. Video conferencing scales to reduce this gap in verbal communication, yet it can't let the user communicate non-verbal cues. Anyways, video conferencing is not that popular; Gtalk and Skype that help users talk are increasingly getting popular, yet are severely constrained in communicating facial expressions and body language.

2. Identity flexibility:

The lack of face-to-face (f2f) has an interesting impact on how people present themselves in the net. While chatting or while texting in a forum, you can give yourself any name or even stay anonymous. You can disclose only part of your identity or be someone else when on the net. This is the reason why many fake profiles can be found in social networking sites, like orkut.com. Even if the profile is not false, one doesn't usually disclose all that she/ he is. This again leads to a disinhibition effect. The inhibitions in talking face-to-face are absent. So, you could either open up to anyone; or use this anonymity in the negative way to abuse other people.

3. Equalized status:

The internet is an egalitarian cultural space. Due to flexibility of identity, everyone has an equal opportunity to voice himself. Hence, it is often referred to as the "net democracy". Of course, your writing skills, your persuasive ideas and your technical expertise may make you a first-rate citizen on the net (as the hackers are! as the bloggers are!), but there is no distinction on the basis of caste, creed, gender and race.

4. Altered Perceptions:

Meditation is often called as the fourth state of consciousness after awake, sleeping and hypnotic states. Prof. Suler argues that the cyber space provides an altered and dream-like state of consciousness. I would call it the fifth state of consciousness; here, multimedia and especially 3D animations have altered the laws of gravity and of existence! It is an imaginary world where you can exist as an individual. For instance, while playing the game counter strike, with others connected on the internet, you live the life of the terrorist or counter-terrorist you play in the game. The counter strike arena is fictitious, so are the guns; hence, altered perception.

5. Temporal Flexibility:

In face-to-face (f2f) meetings, you usually don't get much time when responding to the other person. However, in IT-based communications, you get a significantly longer delay. This provides some time for reflection. Over the internet, there are two types of communications- synchronous communication, i.e., communication in real time, like chat and IM; and asynchronous communication, like e-mail communication and posting in forums. In both cases, one has sufficient time to reflect before communicating back.

15.5 Entrepreneurship through E-Commerce

Electronic commerce, or simple e-commerce, has opened up a large door of opportunity for the enterprising individuals. Basically, the internet as a media provides an altogether new channel, where an entrepreneur can start off and reach a huge consumer base, cutting through geographical barriers.

The risk involved in e-commerce is still high; hence, the entrepreneur needs to be aware of basic psychological processes of the consumer. Only by an understanding of the consumer, her psyche and what she desires, an e-commerce venture can be successful. For example, a customer may buy an i-pod from a shopping mall. There, she gets a shopping experience. How do I, as an entrepreneur, induce her to rather buy my product over internet? In every stage of starting an e-commerce business, the entrepreneur needs to apply psychological principles. These stages are:

1. Understanding consumer behavior on IT
2. Task analysis
3. Strategy
4. Web designing: software engineering or human factor engineering?

1. Understanding consumer behavior on IT

The consumer who uses the internet can't be sketched as a single stereotype. The tastes of consumers are as varied as their lifestyle, attitude towards technology and IT and online skills. For example, it is foolish for an entrepreneur to sell fertilizers to small farmers on the internet as these farmers don't have a positive attitude towards technology. Yet, youths attached to farming families can be targeted as they have a positive attitude towards IT.

Scholars have found that various e-shopping personalities can be represented by a continuum with goal-oriented personality and experiential personality at the two ends. For our analysis, we will take these as types, rather than points on a continuum.

Consumers with goal-oriented personality have an internal locus of control; prefer convenience and low sociability and if proper information is available, would prefer shopping online rather than go to a shopping mall.

Experiential shoppers, on the other hand, shop to 'experience' shopping – shopping is fun for them. If you regularly visit the mall on one pretext or the other, you have an experiential personality. My mother has an experiential personality – she would rush off to the market every evening and try out new products! Experiential shoppers prefer to physically examine products and are less likely to buy online (Novak, Hoffman and Yung, 2000).

Suppose you are an entrepreneur about to start your own e-commerce business. How do you attract the customers of above two personality types? It is less challenging to attract the goal-oriented shopper. You just have to provide genuine information and give him the option to choose from a wide range of products. With 'choice' and 'information', these shoppers, with an internal locus of control, would prefer e-shopping. However, care must be taken to present the information coherently and not to overload the consumer with information.

For an experiential shopper, experience makes the difference. She browses largely to be entertained. She mainly browses for auctions, bargains (experiential shoppers are bargain hunters) and for hobby-type activities. Hence, auction sites, like eBay have greater "stickiness" than other e-commerce sites for these shoppers.

A skilled entrepreneur can cater to the needs of all personalities of consumers. For example, rediff.com is a site that provides immensely useful information, has a variety of products you can choose from; at the same time has many bargain offers, discounts and auction facilities.

2. Task Analysis

Suppose I want to start an e-commerce business to sell books to Indian readers. The problem I face here is, I don't' know anything about fiction lovers of India. Here, I need to hire a psychologist as consultant. The psychologist does task analysis to identify the user- her background, knowledge base, expectancies, values, tastes, etc. Secondly, what kind of interaction does every user desire with the website? Does she need to read reviews before purchasing a book? Does she want to know the comments of other customers? Does she want to discuss the book with others? Based on the users and their interaction needs, the psychologist guides the web designer in making the web-site.

Thirdly, targeting online consumers is also a challenge. To do this, one must know about the consumer and where she can be found on the web!

Forrester's techno-graphics segments consumers into ten segments based on:

1. Attitude towards technology
2. Income
3. Motivation to use technology

For specific e-commerce business, like selling rock music videos, one needs to find more about the tastes of target consumer.

3. Strategy

Any e-commerce business makes strategies on three primary factors:

(a) Reach
(b) Affiliation
(c) Richness

Reach refers to (a) how many customers can a firm reach to and (b) how many products or services can be provided to the customer. E-commerce here has an edge over traditional commerce in that it has larger reach. Yet, how do you induce the customer to visit your site? How do you build a loyalty? Here, affiliation is a must. Strategies to develop loyalty must be developed. Richness refers to the type of information and amount of information provided to the customer.

Some recent researches have revealed that traditional concepts in consumer psychology can't be suitably applied in strategizing reach, affiliation and richness over the internet. The internet is a novel psychological space and its orientations are different. Unfortunately, not much research has been done regarding it.

4. Web designing

A website is an interface between the entrepreneur and his clients. Website development is the most important step in development of an e-commerce business. So, who should design the website? Is it the entrepreneur himself? Or a professional software engineer? Or a human factor engineer?

A software engineer is extremely skilled in various web languages, like HTML, XML, Java script and AJAX. As a result, she can give the website extreme flexibility. Unfortunately, she doesn't know anything about the user who would use the web site. Today, not only has the population of users in the internet expanded, but the variety of users also has expanded. Every user desires an interaction with the website specific to the user. The software engineer is not aware of these individual differences. Hence, a system designed without consideration of the user will not be successful.

For instance, a website for university professors can afford to be complex with cutting edge features. However, a blog for the average housewife has to be user-friendly and easy to use. Hence, the need for human factor engineer (HFE). The role of software and human factor engineers are not contradictory, but complementary. HFEs have conducted considerable research to apply psychological knowledge to different aspects of web designing. Research has been conducted to identify problems associated with website navigation, search effectiveness on Google and other search engines, browser compatibility, etc.

For example, Lynch and his colleagues (2001) have found that site quality, trust and positive affect are critical in explaining purchase intention of a user.

The steps that a HFE follow to design a website are:

Psychographics

↓

User characteristics and Preferences study

↓

Compatible website design

↓

Information organisation

For instance, suppose you want to make an art website. Psychographics helps you know the user characteristics and preferences. You can use this information to design a compatible website that would suit the tastes of art lovers. Then you organize information, so that the user doesn't experience information overload and finds it easy to perceive the contents, i.e., can easily navigate and access the webpages.

Multi-level Marketing

Traditional marketing involves selling a product to the consumer. It includes marketing research to find out consumer behavior, tastes and attitudes, advertising and taking feedback from the consumer. The marketing that has become popular on internet is of a much different type called 'affiliate marketing'; here marketing involves multiple levels of marketers.

To illustrate, let us take the case of "Google AdSense", the leading affiliate marketer. An e-commerce business owner's first objective is to get visitors to his website. How to get visitors? One way is the visitors search in Google and reach to the website. But then, here are many such websites! So, the owner wants to market the products/ services posted on his website. To do this, he gives (say) Rs.10 to "Google AdSense" per visitor. He can't directly market his product to end-users as these are many and located at different placed geographically. Google AdSense makes an advertisement banner of the product. Then AdSense asks other website publishers to host these ads on their sites. For instance, a blogger (level 3) can put the ads on Google AdSense. Any visitor to the blogger sees the ad. If he clicks on the ad, he is directly taken to the e-commerce website. For the click, the blogger is paid Rs.7, AdSense keeps a commission of Rs.3. (this is just for illustration). Multi-level marketing can be illustrated as in the following flowchart:

E-commerce owner

↓

Affiliate marketer

↓

Affiliate web publisher

↓

Visitor

Multi-level marketing involves many challenges regarding consumer behavior, though of a different kind than traditional marketing. The concern of an affiliate publisher (here a blogger) is where should I put an advertisement on my website, so as to induce my visitors to click on it and visit the link? The affiliate marketer (here Google AdSense) is concerned- how should I design the advertisement, so as to induce the visitor to click on it? Should I put information text or images? What should be the size of the ad for right perception?

Many cyber psychologists have conducted research on above issues. For example, the concern of an affiliate publisher is to increase the click-through rate. It is the ratio between the number of visitors who click on an advertisement and the total number of visitors to the publisher's website. (here, publisher means web publisher, usually those who have their own websites).

Korgonkar and his colleagues (2001) recommend from their research that factors, such as attention people pay to web advertising and the frequency of clicks depend on web user's beliefs, attitude and demographic factors. Eye tracking experiments have demonstrated that internet users tend to avoid seeing ads when they become more experienced with the internet. These research findings help the affiliate publisher to design the website and in placing the ad at appropriate place.

The affiliate marketer is concerned primarily with form factors, i.e., form of the advertisement. To optimize his revenue, it seeks to understand the effect of size, of animation, image, text and background colour. For example, it has been found that users get irritated with flashy and animate ads, especially the banner size ones (Chandon and Chtourou).

The e-commerce entrepreneur is also helped by psychological research in many ways. While the seller (of products and services through e-commerce) has outsourced a part of the marketing to the affiliate marketer, for long-term benefits he has to build a brand image. To build a brand image, he has to use a communication strategy that increases brand recall and attitude towards the brand. Even if a customer doesn't click on the ad, if the ad is successful in affecting the cognitive and emotional modalities of the customer's psyche, the customer may later visit the website by herself. For example, a few days back I saw an interesting advertisement of www.simplymarry.com. It had an interesting punch line about conducting Swayamvara for the metropolitan bachelors. I, being busy in another work, couldn't click on it and check the site. But later, I myself went to the site. This change in my behavior was because of the persuasive nature of the ad: it had affected both my cognition (a new matrimonial site for city residents!) and emotion (yes, I am a metropolitan bachelor!). Psychologists are also employed to understand ad effectiveness, i.e., how effective is an ad in changing the three components of attitude- cognitive, affective and conative.

15.6 Distance Learning through IT and Mass Media

Traditionally, distance education used to take place in a very restricted manner- a student enrolls, receives curriculum materials in the mail, works on these materials and submits assignments through post. Hence, the nature of learning was slow and ineffective. The advent of IT and mass media has brought about a revolution in distance learning. Now, scholars see the possibility of distance education being as effective as school education. This has potential of revolutionary consequences. However, for distance education to substitute school education, the use of technology (IT and mass media) has to be made more effective from a psychological perspective. There are numerous challenges in successfully affecting this.

Basics of Learning

Before going into the details of distance education through IT and mass media, we need to understand the basic principles of learning. This help us appreciate the challenges of e-learning better. Basically, there are three approaches to learning:

1. Behaviourist approach
2. Cognitivist approach
3. Constructivist approach

Behaviourist Approach

The behaviourist approach to learning is based on the belief that the instructor's role is to transmit information to the student in small chunks and provide immediate feedback to the student's responses. Hence, the implications for e-learning are easy to implement. Two popular behaviourist strategies that can be communicated via mass media are - programmed instruction and directed instruction.

Programmed instruction was pioneered by none other than B.E. Skinner (1968). Here, the content is broken down into learning units and arranged into frames presented with increasing difficulty. The feedback is prompt, as assessment is done every time the student moves from one frame to another. Also, learners have the ability to move at their own pace. Learners cannot jump frames; they can cross over to another frame only after gaining mastery in one frame.

In directed instruction, the instructor 'articulates learning objectives, then breaks them into their component tasks and works students through them in a hierarchical fashion, leading students incrementally from the "bottom up". Recognizing and mastering key concepts is made easier for students by isolating each component, allowing learners to master one component before learning the next and providing students with explicit, teacher-directed instruction and practice' (Lowerison et. al., 2008).

Cognitivist Approach

Cognitivist goes a step further from the behaviourist, by addressing issues relating to how learners cognitively process learning material. Just like the behaviourists, cognitivists design e-learning wherein knowledge is transmitted. But, unlike the behaviourists, they are concerned with the active processing of information, and how knowledge is organized in the brain (Lowerison, et. al., 2008).

An e-learning model based on cognitivist approach in e-learning is Merrill's Instructional Transaction Theory (ITT). ITT emphasizes on development of simulations and graphics for more effective learner guidance. It also attempts to mold instruction to adapt it to individual learners in real time.

Constructivist Approach

The subject of learning in most modern educational organisations today is shifting from behaviourism towards constructivism. The constructivist approach is based on the belief that knowledge is constructed by the learner and the job of the teacher is to provide environments that would help the learner explore and construct knowledge. Hence, the role of the instructor is to provide tools and resources to the learner to build their own knowledge.

It is in constructivist learning that the job of e-learning becomes much more challenging. The goal is not just to provide information, or to aid in information processing, but to provide a rich experiential environment within which the learner can work. According to Clark 92006), many implementations of constructivist learning environments in distance learning fail to fully realize what constructivist learning is.

A popular model based on constructivist approach is problem-based learning (PBL). In PBL, a problem is presented and learning is driven by the experiences of the learner while finding a solution.

Distance Education through IT: A SWOT Analysis

The issue that is bothering psychologist at this moment is that while e-learning has many advantages to traditional classroom learning, there are certain advantages of face-to-face instruction that it cannot replicate. In this section, we will investigate some of the strengths and weakness of e-learning.

A few strengths of e-learning are:

1. The access to information becomes easier.
2. There is a greater flexibility of learning environments. The learner can study using a software/ platform that she is comfortable with.
3. Education can reach many inaccessible parts of India.
4. Instruction is personalized.
5. Learner's control over the learning process increases. She can proceed at her own pace.

Major challenges to e-learning are:

1. How do you sustain learner's motivation in e-learning? In classes, the teacher sustains motivation of student by various techniques discussed in the chapter on educational psychology. For example, the teacher may praise the student in from of other students which enhances the student's motivation. But, what about e-learning?
2. There are certain domains of learning, such as psychomotor learning and attitudinal learning, which can best be done by face-to-face interaction. For example, if you want to change a student's attitude towards corruption, you need to provide her with a role model she can identify with.
3. A major function of the classroom is to help the socialization of a child. By interaction with other students and peers, the student gains social skills. This is absent in e-learning.
4. Very frequent use of internet may lead to tendinitis. Tendinitis is an abnormal expansion of fingers due to overuse (working on keyboards and mouse). Also, there is danger of Internet Addiction Disorder and over-reliance on the internet.

From the above discussion, certain general conclusions regarding distance education can be made, such as:

1. E-learning as a stand-alone learning device is not effective. It has to be supplemented with classroom learning. For example, IGNOU courses are mostly imparted through e-learning. However, IGNOU has study centers in most towns of India, where face-to-face interaction with tutor is available on Sundays. E-learning is a very effective mode of teaching managers and technical staff in organisations. Training in organisations can heavily rely on distance education via IT.
2. The best e-learning tools are adaptive hypermedia. These are softwares that adapt to the learning styles (refer chapter on education psychology and cognitive abilities of various students).

E-learning is, at times, more effective than traditional learning for students with mental retardation. For example, Justine Cassell of North-western University has found in 2008 that children with autism can develop advanced social skills by interacting with 'virtual children' and 'virtual teacher' which might not be possible by hanging out with real children or teachers.

Researchers have developed software that present 3-D animated tutors who talk to students with retardation, learning disabilities and other such problems and develop language skills in them. Such software has also been found to be effective in second language learning. So if you are interested in learning a foreign language, you can sign up for a good distance education program on the internet.

Motivation Models for Distance Learning through Internet

It has been found that a general drawback of distance education is that the learning interactivity is very trivial. E-learning and learning through other modern means of mass media do try to plug the shortcoming, but still there are issues of keeping the students motivated. The drop-out rates in e-learning tend to be higher than in face-to-face settings; as learners often feel isolated (Moore and Kearsley, 1996). Hence, many psychologists have focused on developing models that would help keep up the motivational levels of learners in e-learning. Two popular models are the ARCS Model and the Time Continuum model.

ARCS Model

The ARCS model (Keller, 1987) is a method for systematically designing motivational strategies into e-learning materials. This model presents:

1. Four categories of human motivation.
2. Strategies for enhancing motivation within the above four categories, and
3. A four step design process to incorporate above strategies into instructional material. The four categories of human motivation according to ARCS model are Attention, Relevance, Confidence and Satisfaction (hence the name ARCS).

Let us discuss these in greater detail:

(a) Attention

The first step to any instructional learning is attention. The learner's continued and sustained attention is essential. For this, the learner's curiosity should be aroused. Regular study material presented in conventional fashion often tends to lead to boredom. The level of curiosity can be sustained and increased by the use of graphics or animation. Use of mystery, puzzles, unresolved problems, variability, etc., are other important tactics of grabbing attention.

Carmen Taran (2005) suggests the following techniques for grabbing attention:

1. Manding stimuli
2. Anticipation
3. Incongruity
4. Variability
5. Humour
6. Inquiry
7. Participation
8. Story-telling

Mands are statements associated with highly probable behavioural consequences. For instance, your attention is automatically focused to a source of stimuli that yells "watch out!". Some good examples of manding stimuli are "note that", "please remember that", "it is important to realize that", etc. (Taran, 2005). Incongruity is a conflict between what learners expect to see and what occurs. It increases sensory stimulation and thereby attention. If you can induce the student to ask "how come?", then it means you have succeeded to draw her attention.

Variability is an obvious means of grabbing attention. Variability can be maintained in e-learning by constantly changing the manner of presentation and instructional material. Further, participation enhances attention. Hence, Taran suggests learning activities, such as practice exercises, games or simulations that increase participation and interaction enhance attention.

(b) Relevance

Attention is a necessary, but no sufficient condition for motivation. The learners need to perceive the learning material as consistent with their goals and compatible with their learning styles (Keller and Suzuki, 2004). To increase relevance, it is suggested that a choice in methods of accomplishing course goals can be made. Also, guest lectures can be arranged, where those, who have successfully finished the course explain how it has been relevant and useful to them in their professional and personal life.

Also, it has been noted that goal-oriented behavior can be due to intrinsic motivation or extrinsic motivation (Deci an Ryan, 1985). For extrinsically motivated students, a clear link between the content of e-learning and future career prospects can be by making the instructional material rich and diverse.

(c) Confidence

A basic consideration for learning, whether classroom learning or distance learning, is self-efficacy. Self-efficacy establishes positive expectancies for success, and hence motivates the student. On the other hand, if an instructional material is tough to understand, the learner's confidence is low and she may even give up. A major reason for high drop-out cases in education is lack of confidence on self.

Confidence can be increased by a range of strategies, such as:

- Clearly starting learning goals
- Setting realistic goals
- Organizing material in increasing order of difficulty
- Attributing success to the learner's effort and ability

(d) Satisfaction

Satisfaction is an important motivator in the sense that it fosters positive feelings about the learning experience. Certain strategies to foster satisfaction are:

- Verbal reinforcement
- Rewards

- Feedback
- Personal attention
- Deliberate avoidance of negative influence such as threats, external performance evaluations and overt surveillance (Hodges, 2004).

Now, let us turn to the design process recommended by ARCS Model. This process has four steps:

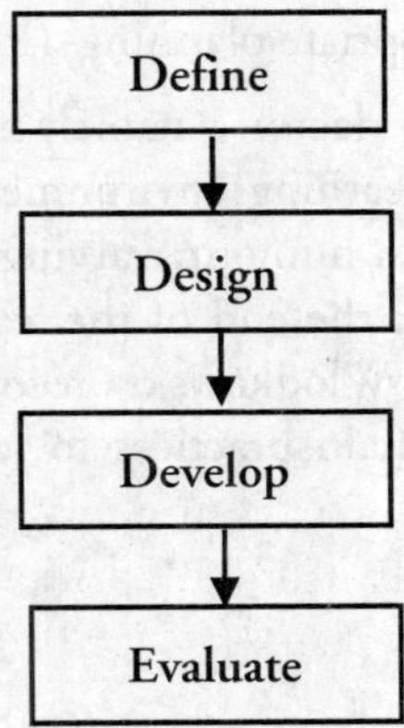

Fig. 15.4 : Design steps of ARCS Model

These steps can be summarized as:

1. **Define:** Define the motivational problem involved in the instructional material. Then analyze the learners and prepare motivational objectives.
2. **Design:** Design the strategies based on the motivational objectives. For example, if the objective is to increase relevance by intrinsic motivation, the strategy designed may be to provide diverse and extensive study material. If it is to increase relevance by extrinsic motivation, then the strategy may be to link the learner's career objectives to the course material.
3. **Develop:** After defining the motivational objectives and designing the strategies, next comes the development of the instructional material. This is the execution process.
4. **Evaluate:** This is the feedback step which gives information about the extent of success of the above three exercises.

The Time Continuum Model

The time continuum model of Wlodknowski (1985) identifies three critical periods in the learning process where motivational strategies should be introduced.

These periods are at the:

- Beginning of the learning process
- During the learning process
- At the end of the learning process

"The factors to be considered at the beginning of the learning process are attitudes and needs. When planning the beginning of a learning experience, the designer should consider how the instruction will best meet the needs of the learners and how a positive learner attitude can be developed. WlodKowski (1985) provides many strategies to address learner attitude. The strategies are centered on easing into the course with icebreaker activities, stating clear objectives for the course and various strategies to help the learners develop a clear understanding of what will be required to be successful in the course. A needs assessment should be performed prior to developing the instruction to aid in appropriate planning' (Hodges, 2004).

During the learning experience, two factors, namely stimulation and affect, are to be considered. To maintain a stimulating learning environment, learner participation has to be enhanced. This can be done via questions, humour, varying presentation style and the issue of different modes of instruction. Finally, at the end of the learning experience, competence and reinforcement are to be considered. Wlodkowski recommends frequent feedback and communicating learner progress as the main practices to foster motivation at the end of the learning experience.

■ ■ ■

16

MEDIA INFLUENCES ON PRO AND ANTI-SOCIAL BEHAVIOUR

Chapter outline

The S-O-R revolution in learning brought to the fore the concept that behaviour is learnt by observation also. Bandura's classic experiment on modelling (1985), now famous as the "Bobo dolls experiment", for the first time, showed that viewing television may have a bearing on attitude and behaviour.

In this experiment, three groups of children were shown a film in which a model acts aggressively towards a "Bobo doll". The first group showed the model being rewarded with praise; the second group saw the model being reprimanded for aggression and a third group saw no consequences for the model. After the viewing, each child was placed in a room with many toys, including a Bobo doll. It was found that children who saw the model being punished showed greater aggressive actions towards the Bobo doll than others. Ever since this experiment, many other experiments have been conducted on the effects of media on behaviour. The effects, as seen from the Bobo doll experiment, are both positive and negative, i.e., media depictions can lead to both anti-social and pro-social behaviour. The effect is anti-social when viewers watch an excess of violence or pornography regularly or play violent videogames. The effect is pro-social when media leads to awareness and sensitization about social problems, empathy, altruism and sharing. This chapter deals with all these issues, so also with issues relating to research findings. On critical analysis, it can be found that the effect of mass media on behaviour is quite ambiguous in research literature. In deeper appraisal of various research findings, it can be seen that most research findings don't reveal a cause-effect relationship. These issues are discussed later in this chapter.

16.1 Violence and Aggression: Depiction in Media

A clear causal linkage between violence in media and violent media has been established by research. Jowett & O'Donnell (1992) have found that people who watch a lot of TV are likely to overestimate the amount of violence and crime that occurs in the world. This makes them anticipate more violence in their own lives. Anderson, Carnagey and Eubanks (2003) conducted a series of studies on the effect of violent lyrics on attitudes and feelings of listeners, and found that college students who listened to a violent song felt more hostile and reported an increase in aggressive thoughts compared to another group that heard a similar, but non-violent song. Rubin and his colleagues (Rubin, West, & Mitchell, 2001) reported that college students who preferred heavy metal and rap music expressed more hostile attitudes.

Psychodynamic theorists believe that watching violence has a cathartic effect on the viewer, enabling her to discharge her "thanados" instinctive energy by acting out vicariously through identification with fictional aggressors. Media is an outlet for these innate impulses, developed by modern society. Other media psychologists don't usually subscribe to this view, specifically owing to many research findings, showing that media violence does lead to certain negative effects on the individual. Some of the major effects of television violence are (Donnerstein, Slaby and Eron, 1994):

1. *Aggressor effect,* i.e., increased meanness, aggression and violence towards others.
2. *Victim effect,* i.e., increased mistrust, fearfulness or what is called the mean-world syndrome.
3. *Appetite effect,* i.e., increase in self-initiated behaviour to further watch violent material.
4. *Bystander effect,* i.e., increased desensitization callousness and apathy towards other victims of violence.[1]

In addition to the above, media affects attitude and behaviour of young people towards sex. Stories and depictions in mass media always portray more liberal cultural mores than are existent in a culture, thus influencing the attitude of young people. For instance, Wells and Twenge (2005) mined data from 530 studies and inferred that sexual attitudes and behaviour have undergone enormous changes in America from 1943 to 1999. Both young men and women became more sexually active over time, as indicated by a younger age of first intercourse, which was lowered from 19 to 15 years among young women. They found the wide access of mass media in this period majorly responsible for the change. Stories and depictions in mass media also lessened feelings of sexual guilt for both men and women.

Why does media violence lead to these effects? Many theories have been forwarded to explain this and multiple psychological factors may be involved in this.

16.2 Factors involved in reflection of media violence in anti-social behaviour

Some of the factors involved in reflection of media violence in anti-social behaviour are:

1. Imitation

The Bobo dolls experiments explained earlier have been used by Bandura to explain that media violence is reflected in behaviour by role modelling. However, the Bobo doll studies have been severely criticized also. These studies had low external validity. The laboratory conditions were artificial and not representative of real life conditions. Secondly, the experiments showed only immediate after-effects of media, if at all. Between a child viewing a TV program and his acting, there may be days, even months gap. The laboratory experiments studied the children immediately

1. Pg 240 of Donnerstein, Slaby and Eron (1994).

after showing them the films. Lastly, the video footage that was shown was that of some models hitting at Bobo dolls. This doesn't bear any resemblance with violence that is depicted in media. Rather, the model hitting at Bobo dolls may have led the children believe that the experiments want them to hit at Bobo dolls!

Today, the Bobo doll experiments cannot be replicated due to ethical considerations regarding its effect on children. Hence, most researchers use naturalistic forms of enquiry, like surveys and self-report measures.

It agreed that initiation is indeed a factor in media influence. However, personality variables of the viewer, the attractiveness of and the degree of identification with aggressive models enhances the effects of media violence. (Donnerstain and Smith, 1997). Indeed, some people complain that media violence glamourizes aggression and makes it an attractive behavioural choice.

2. Excitation

Another explanation for violent behaviour influenced by media is the excitation transfer theory of Dolf Zillman (1971). This explanation is based on Schachter and Singer's (1962) Two-factor Theory of Emotion. The theory states that when any stimulus leads to physiological arousal, we assign a cognitive label to the arousal depending on various situational and personal factors. In the context of media, an example can be cited. Suppose, I watch a violent movie and get very excited (aroused). While coming back from the multiplex, I may get into a trivial argument with the taxi driver; misinterpreting my arousal, I am more prone to behave more aggressively with the driver than otherwise. The mechanism is as follows:

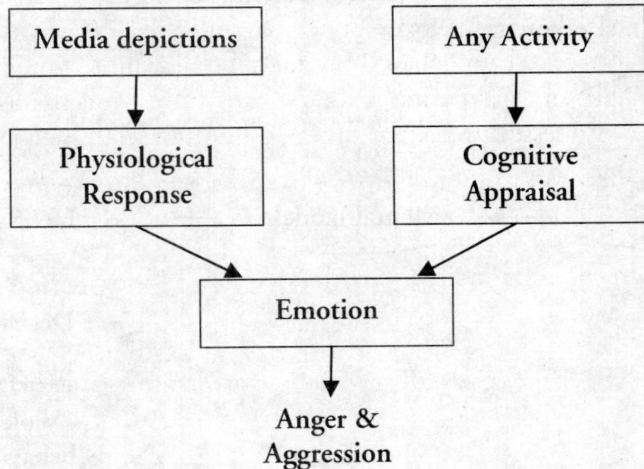

Fig. 16.1 : Two-Factor Theory of Emotion

Problem with this explanation is that it explains only the immediate after-effects of violent movies. The physiological arousal after seeing the movie remains only for a short time after the movie. Besides, such arousal is possible even after seeing children's movies, like Harry Potter and Spiderman, let alone violent movies!

3. Cognitive Factors

Numerous cognitive factors may act together to lead to violent behaviour. Many theories have been forwarded to explain these factors. A look at these theories at this stage is appropriate:

(a) *Exemplification theory:* This theory states that media images and information act as exemplars. Exemplars are instances that together lead to formation of concepts and ultimately mental models. Hence, pro-social information or anti-social information depicted in media influence mental models, which in turn influence decision-making. Decisions made in real life situations affect behaviour.

(b) *Priming theory*: Priming is a process in which one stimulus is linked to another. For example, if terrorism is primed to archetypes of minority communities in news channels, this leads to strong causal attribution of minority community to terrorist behaviour.

(c) *Cultivation theory*: It states that world views are 'cultivated' by media over many years. Due to this perpetual cultivation, some permanent schemas develop in individuals which take them away from reality. For example, more violence is depicted in T.V than normality. This is continuously depicted in media day after the other. Ultimately, it gets cultivated into a permanent schema and the viewer starts believing that violence is too frequent.

These theories aren't contradictory, but complementary. They provide different mechanisms linking media violence with decision-making in real life. For example, exemplars are cultivated due to media. Further, unconscious memories of violent scenes are reactivated if appropriate cues are found in stimuli. (Berkowitz, 1984)

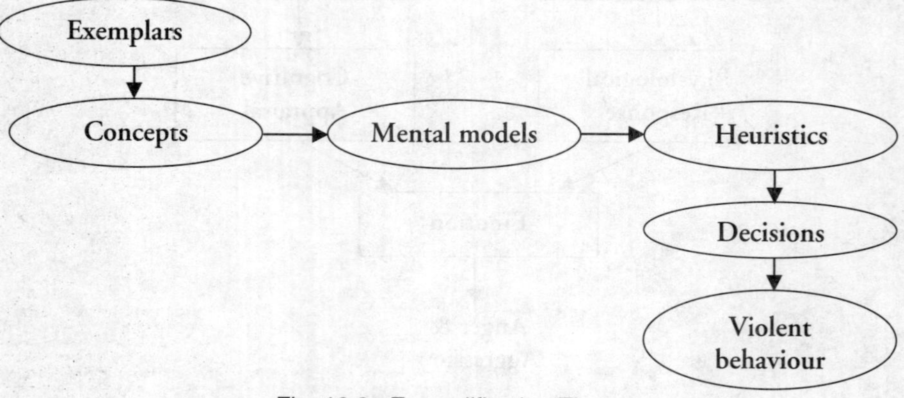

Fig. 16.2 : Exemplification Theory

Pornography

Questions have been raised about how pornography affects a man's sexual attitudes and how it leads to sexual violence and rape. It has been found that many pornographic material model rape myths, suggesting that men are entitled to sex, women enjoy rough sex and only bad girls get raped. Russell (1984) considers rape myths as a factor affecting men's attitude towards rape.

For instance, one study (see Zillman & Bryant, 1989) has found that after five days of viewing pornography, participants gave shorter prison sentences to rapists in a mock trial. This confirms Russell's argument that pornography predisposes men to consider rape as an acceptable behaviour.

Another major effect of pornography is desensitization. Viewing explicit material for a long period of time instills an appetite for even-more extreme material. In an experiment, Zillman and Bryant (1982) showed pornography once a week for six weeks to an experimental group. Later, when left alone with an array or pornographic videos, participants of experimental groups chose significantly more XXX material than control group members. In another study, they found that both males and females reported lower sexual satisfaction with their partners after viewing six weeks of pornographic material.

Thirdly, regular viewing of pornography also increases the incidence of violence against women. In one study (Malamuth et al, 2000), a causal link between violent pornography and violence against women was established. In this study, three groups of male college students were taken. These groups were randomly assigned to watch three kinds of pornographic material:

1. Neutral videos
2. Sexually explicit but non-violent videos
3. Sexually aggressive videos

Later, the participants were required to interact with a female. They were asked to quiz the woman with questions related to general knowledge and to punish her with electric shocks for errors, the intensity of shock varying. Malamuth and her colleagues found that strongest experimental effects (i.e., high shock for wrong answers) emerged when participants viewed violent pornography.

Internet Pornography

There are many ways in which internet pornography is different from video-based pornography. Some of these are:

- *Consumption*: The triple A engine model (Cooper et al., 1999) states that Access, Affordability and Anonymity increases the attraction of internet for sexual pursuits. Similarly, the ACE model of Young (2002) contends that Anonymity, Convenience and Escape create a climate of permissiveness that actually serve to encourage sexually deviant behaviour.
- *Production and dissemination:* Reduced costs of production and simplified distribution have led to democratization of pornography.
- *Violence:* Internet porn depicts more violence than offline pornography (Barron & Kimmell, 2000).

Rape Myth

Burt (1980) brought the notion of "rape myth" to scholarly and public consciousness. The term rape myth involves an individual believing that the victim of a sexual crime, typically a woman, is somehow responsible for her victimization. Rape myth acceptance also includes an individual's feeling that little or no responsibility for the sexual aggression lies with the perpetrator, who is typically a man.

Source: Emmers-Sommer and Burns (2005)

Theories of Pornography

- *Feminist perspectives:* Feminist argument is that all forms of pornography are intended to increase sexual arousal and promote sexist ideology. Pornography portrays women as sex objects and promotes beliefs of social inferiority of women and male supremacy.
- *Social learning theory:* This theory states that 'an individual consuming pornography, vicariously receives positive reinforcement on a variety of levels. At the simplest, operant learning level, observing a nude still may bring about pleasurable arousal, which can influence the individual to consume such material repeatedly because of the reinforcement the experience brings. However, from a social learning perspective, observing a model display herself sexually may connote a behavioural sequence and that symbolic process, associated with the observer's pleasure, may constitute a social learning process…the consumer might observe the male actor receiving pleasure from his actions and often, an initially resistant female target of the action succumbing and being pleasured as well. Even in the most sexually violent material for which the woman is clearly not enjoying the encounter, the man is typically receiving pleasure from his actions'. This way modelling occurs. This kind of learning also leads to perception of women as submissive and their commodification.
- *Aggression models:* These models are similar to Social Learning Theory in some respects. However, they differ from social learning theory as they argue that only violent pornography leads to harmful effects. As per this view, erotica or consensual sexual behaviour in porn should not affect the consumer's beliefs negatively.

Source: Emmers_Sommer & Burns (2005)

Violent Video Games

Do violent video games breed aggression? Yes, argues Davis Grossman (1996). According to Grossman, humans have a natural inhibition against killing. Violent video games weaken players' inhibition against aggression towards others. In one study (Gentile et al, 2004), it was found that young adolescents exposed to more violent video games, also scored higher on psychological tests of hostility.

In another experiment where exposure to violent video games was directly varied (Irwin and Gross, 1995), two different groups of 7-8 year old boys were asked to play two different games- Double Dragon (a violent game) and Excite Bike, where the player raced a motor cycle against the clock (but, there was no violence). After playing the games, each participant engaged in a 102 minute 'free play' with another boy. It was observed that compared to the players of Excite Bike game, the players of Double Dragon exhibited more physical and verbal aggression.

Consumerism

Mass media has facilitated the access of marketers to the consumer's psyche through advertisements. Needs are being created by anchoring role models in advertisements and by changing life goals, interests and attitudes of consumers. Consumerism leads to a consumerist culture where people keep consuming (without limits) without any increase in the level of satisfaction or happiness. This 'conspicuous consumption' may lead to increased exploitation of natural resources. Increased consumption (of let's say petrol) also leads to increased pollution and environmental degradation.

Hence, we see that a psyche of consumerism is embedded in an individual by priming of advertisements, which as grave consequences.

Research into the influence of media on aggression and violence: A critical evaluation

Many research results have firmly established the fact that media violence is a causal factor in aggression and violence in viewers. Or have they? There are certain inherent problems in psychological research, due to which the various findings aren't beyond doubt. Broadly, there are three kinds of researches conducted on media influence:

1. Experimental studies
2. Correlational studies
3. Field studies

The major problem with experimental studies is their artificiality. These studies are conducted in laboratories. Here, one can't measure the effect of media violence on people in the long term (say one year). The immediate impact is what is observed. Secondly, the situations created to observe violence aren't representative of real life situations.

Correlational studies are studies in which a relationship between media violence and violent behaviour is established. For example, in one study (Maintyre and Teenan, 1972), the subjects watched certain videos and a violence rating was assigned to each of these videos. The participants were also rated on their deviant behaviour. A significant positive correlation was found between viewing of television violence and aggressive behaviour.

A major drawback of correlational studies is that they don't tell us about the cause-effect relationship between the two variables. It is possible that a third variable has caused both the two variables. Many researchers have tried to minimize this deficiency by controlling the impact of a third variable. Still, another deficiency remains. If variable X is correlated with variable Y, has X caused Y or Y caused X? Owing to these deficiencies, it is difficult to make a proper causal linkage between two events. For instance, Chaffee and McLeod (1971) have created two hypotheses. Correlational studies can falsify (or prove true) both the hypotheses, but cannot decide which is the correct one between the two.

Hypothesis 1: Television violence increases aggressive behaviour.

Hypothesis 2: Aggressive people watch violent TV programs.

Similarly, field studies have some inherent limitations. They can't be replicated and there is a long list of mediating variables that can confound the relation between media violence and viewer aggression.

The exact effects of the influence of television violence can't be easily determined because the stimulation provided by videos and television programs can interact with several other extraneous variables. Specially in the case of longitudinal studies (that are ideal in establishing a relationship between the two variables), there are too many intervening factors. Hence, research findings point towards a positive correlation between media violence and individual aggression, but the results should be taken with a pinch of salt.

16.3 Media Influences on Pro-social Behaviour

Pro-social behaviour refers to a variety of behaviours; there are diverse behaviours that come under the umbrella of pro-social behaviour. Behaviours, like altruism, empathy and sharing are examples of pro-social behaviour. Awareness about social problems and action towards solution of these problems also form part of pro-social behaviours.

Many research findings have shown a positive correlation between pro-social media and pro-social behaviour.

These can be discussed under the following heads:

1. Media and children

Psychological literature on children and media agree to the fact that educational media are hugely beneficial for children. Greenfield (1984), for example, has shown that screen presentation of educational material can be highly successful, if used as supplement with printed texts.

In one experiment, investigators tried to study the effect of a TV model on six year olds (Sparfkin, Liebert and Poulous, 1975). One group of children viewed an episode of Lassie in which there was a rescue scene; a second group viewed the same show without such a scene and a third group watched numerous episodes of Brady Bunch. After seeing the shows, the children participated in a game in which winner could receive a prize. In the midst of the game, they came in contact with a group of puppies who were whining unhappily. The first group spent more time in trying to comfort the puppies than other groups, in spite of the fact that stopping to help the puppies would interfere with their goal (to win the race).

There are, however, certain mediating factors in relationship between pro-social media and pro-social behaviour. The moral development of children is one such factor. In one study, Zillman and Bryant (1975) examined the empathetic response of two groups of children who were in two different stages of moral development to a fairy tale program. In the fairy tale, a good prince is cheated and banished from his empire by a bad prince. He subsequently returned and had revenge. Three different climaxes were shown:

1. The revenge was mild and forgiving.
2. Revenge matched the wrong done by the initial wrong.
3. Revenge is unnecessarily brutal.

It was found that older children displayed highest facial joy for the second ending. They favored neither mild revenge or extreme revenge. But, same was not the case with younger children. This shows that empathy is strongly determined by character judgments.

2. Sensitization to Social Problems

Media plays an essential role in sensitizing viewers towards social problem. TV viewership increases the awareness of people towards various problems, like HIV-AIDS, drug abuse and alcoholism, etc. However, the type of media one is exposed to, makes a difference in the level of awareness.

In one study, Ananga Lavalekar (2000) of the Jnana Prabodhini's Institute of Psychology in Pune examined the degree of awareness pertaining to social problems among high school students in relation to media. It was observed that the choice of media and children's awareness of social problems were positively related. The students with larger exposure to "masala" movies had significantly less information about the social problems as compared to those who had less exposure to films. Also, students who preferred to read mostly the sports and movie supplements of newspaper, had significantly less information about social problems as compared to those who prefer science supplement.

Lavalekar argues that if media is used properly and methodically according to the needs of different age groups, it can work wonders.

3. Health Awareness

Media is an invaluable means of communicating information. Media has played an important role in promoting desirable behaviour, like road safety and handling electric equipments. Media has also played an important role in communicating health messages, like those of HIV/AIDS, smoking, drug abuse, etc.

How effective are these campaigns? In a field experiment in Tanzania, Vaughan and his colleagues (2000) studied the effect of a soap opera transmitting a program about HIV on Radio Tanzania. The program had three kinds of role models- positive models who had lesser sexual partners and practiced safe sex; transitional models, who initially practiced unsafe sex, but changed their behaviour later in fear of AIDS and negative models who had many sexual partners and practiced unsafe sex. The negative models ultimately die. In this five-year longitudinal study, Vaughan and his colleagues studied the effects of the radio program on listener's attitudes and sexual practice; they found a reduction in prevalence of unsafe sex among those who listened to the soap opera.

Mass media also is useful to the community psychologist who is involved in community-based interventions. In a village-based study in North India, A. Agarwal (1995) identified many issues in the use of mass media for prevention of diseases, recognition of symptoms and health promotion. This study showed that impact of mass media is substantial when it is used in conjunction with factors, such as social participation in community, interpersonal communication and anticipating changes in life chances. However, A. Agarwal cautions that an excessive reliance on mass media without coordinated support of formal and informal systems in the community, is not suitable for health promoting behaviour in rural areas.

4. Public Opinion

Public opinion is mediated by the flow of information from mass media. Hence, the mass media plays a crucial role in political dynamics of the country. Media representation of various social and political issues makes citizens aware of their rights, various problems and their solutions.

5. Education through entertainment

Information about social issues can be embedded in soap operas and movies. For example, movies like Swadesh, Taare Zameen Par and Range De Basanti sensitize people towards certain social issues, while providing wholesome entertainment. In India, the issues in soaps are explicitly pro-social, ranging from local issues (e.g., dowry death) to health issues (e.g., alcoholism discouraged to global issues (like, environmentalism).

It must be kept in mind that such health messages can backfire, because viewers are often not as sophisticated as producers consider them to be. Brown and Cody (1991) had for instance, studied the effects of the popular series "Hum Log" broadcast during 1980s with the aim of advancing the status of women. Although the program was immensely successful, many female viewers identified more with the traditional matriarchal female character rather than be independent daughters.

6. Altruism through media programming and video games

Studies have shown that different types of media programming may evoke altruism in children. Wilson (2008) found from a study that channels aimed at younger viewers, such as Nickelodeon and Disney Channel, had significantly more acts of altruism than the general-audience channels, like A&E and TNT. Wilson examined the programming of 18 different channels, including more than 2,000 entertainment shows, during a randomly selected week on television. The study revealed that 73% of programs contained at least one act of altruism and on an average, viewers saw around three acts of altruism an hour. Around one-third of those behaviours were explicitly rewarded in the plot, potentially sending the message that these acts of pro-social behaviour can come with positive consequences.

Ostrov, Gentile and Crick (2003) studied children for two years for the purpose of investigating the role of media exposure on pro-social behaviour for young boys and girls. The study concluded that media exposure could possibly predict outcomes related to pro-social behaviour.

Some experiments have suggested that pro-social video games may increase pro-social behaviour in players. However, the validity of such experiments and reliability of their results, have been suspicious. Critics argue that these experiments falsely dichotomize video games into 'pro-social' and 'violent' categories despite significant overlap. For instance, a study by Ferguson and Garza (2011) concluded that exposure to violent video games was associated with increased pro-social behaviour, both on-line as well as volunteering in the real world. The researchers speculated this may be due to the pro-social themes common in many violent games, as well as team-oriented play in many games.

Appendix

Chapter 17. Measurement of Individual Differences

17

MEASUREMENT OF INDIVIDUAL DIFFERENCES

Chapter outline

17.1 Nature of Individual Differences

The fingerprints of no two individuals are the same. But, this is not where individual differences begin or end. An individual has a unique identity. Individuals differ on their beliefs, attitudes, perceptions, thinking, intelligence, aptitude, motivations, emotions, etc. Indeed, there is a long list of psychological variables about which individuals differ.

The challenge in front of psychologists is to assess these individual differences. To do so, they use psychological tests. Psychological tests try to establish a norm about the general population and assess as individual with respect to the norm. Also, it should be noted that any psychological test measures only one or a limited number of aspects of individual differences. The sum total of individual differences is so vast and wide spread, that it is not possible for a psychological test to measure all these aspects.

Another significant aspect of individual differences is that when measured on a scale, differences of a normal population can be mapped into a graph, to look like a normal distribution. A normal distribution looks as given in the diagram shown:

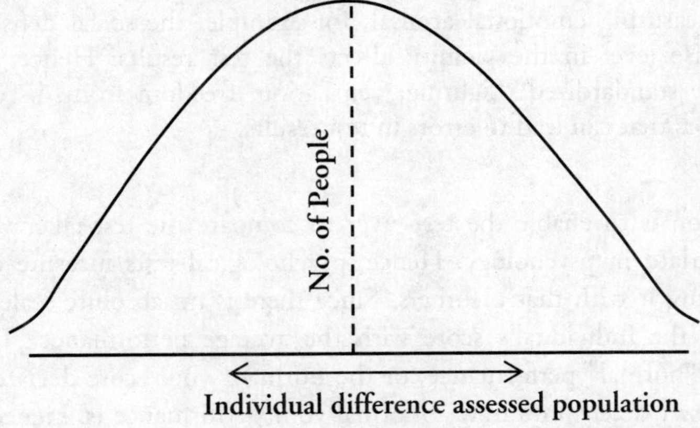

Fig. 17.1 : Differences of a normal population

In the above normal distribution, we see that a majority of people in the population lie within one standard deviation on both sides of the central line. For example, in an IQ test, the number of people with IQ of 100 (Central Tendency) is maximum. The number of extremely retarded or extremely talented students is equally low.

17.2 Characteristics of Psychological Tests

A psychological test is a standardized and objective measure of a sample of behaviour (Anastasi, 1954). Psychological tests are just like tests in any other scientific discipline, trying to assess an individual based on observation of a carefully chosen sample of behaviour. In view of this, the principal characteristics of psychological tests are that they:

1. Measure individual differences
2. Are standardized and established norms
3. Are of average difficulty
4. Are theoretically objective and always aim towards the goal of objectivity

Standardization

Standardization means that there is a uniformity of procedure in administering and scoring the test. Various conditions in the testing process must be controlled (i.e., standardized) in order to make the scores of different individuals comparable. For instance, suppose a teacher teaches a topic in more detail in one section of a class and in lesser detail in another section, and both sections are given the same academic tests; the scores of the former section will be higher than normal and that of the latter section lower than normal. Owing to this, the scores won't be comparable. The scores won't also be comparable if the two sections have different teachers. This difference in condition holds immense significance in psychological tests, because unlike school tests, there is a need to be as objective and error-free as possible.

To secure uniform testing conditions, the test constructor has to provide detailed instructions about how to administer each newly developed test. Normally, standardization includes such factors as the *materials employed, time limits, ways of handling queries from test takers, oral instructions to test takers* and any other testing condition that may affect the test results. When you are measuring emotional arousal, for example, the social density (crowds increase arousal) and noise level in the vicinity affects the test results. Hence, ideally the surrounding must also be standardized. Lighting, ventilation, freedom from discomfort and distractions are a few factors that can lead to errors in test results.

Norms

The goal of standardization is to enable the test-giver to compare the test-taker with others. There is no absolute standard in psychology. Hence, psychological tests measure individual's characteristics by comparing it with that of others. Since there is no absolute scale, you get a scale when you compare the individual's score with the average performance. The average performance is called the "normal" performance, or the **norm.** If your score deviates from the norm, the *extent of divergence* determines how abnormal your performance is. Hence, in an IQ test, 100 is the norm and IQ of 30 or 170 is abnormal (retarded and gifted, respectively).

So, how is the norm determined? If 10-year-old children normally (i.e., on an average) complete 15 out of 50 problems correctly on a test, the norm is 15. To determine the norm, the test constructor administers the test to a large, representative sample of the type of subjects the test is designed to assess. For example, if a test is constructed to assess the degree of cognitive deprivation in a child from slum background of urban India, the test constructor administers it to a 'representative sample', which may be children of a few slums of Delhi, Mumbai, Kolkata and some other cities. Then, the constructor maps the scores of the sample on a graph to determine the distribution of scores and the normal score.

Difficulty

Visualize a situation in which the test items on 'an intelligence test' are made too difficult. In such tests, the scores easily reflect the difference between people with IQ 120 and people with IQ 160. But, this test can't differentiate between people with IQ 40 and people with IQ 80. This is because, the test items are so difficult that an individual with IQ 80 scores zero; so also an individual with IQ 40. Then, can this test be used to assess the general population.

NO! For an engineering entrance exam (such as IIT, JEE), test items can be difficult, as such exams are meant to compare the ones with elite engineering acumen and rank them. Whatever the scores of those without the acumen doesn't matter. But, a psychological test can't be difficult, because then it wont be able to give accurate diagnosis for those at below normal level. Similarly, a very easy psychological test can't differentiate between two students with abilities much above normal.

A psychological test has to be of roughly average difficulty. The most likely score, obtained by the large number of subjects, usually corresponds to about 50% correct items. If the test is more or less difficult, the test results are skewed as under:

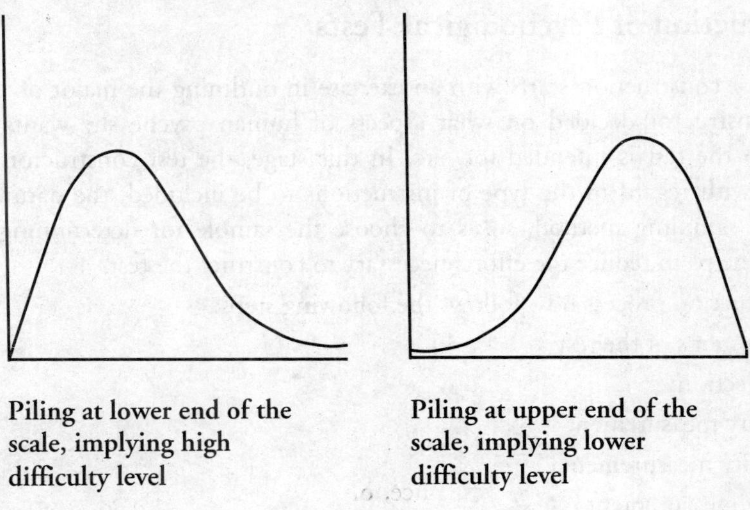

Piling at lower end of the scale, implying high difficulty level

Piling at upper end of the scale, implying lower difficulty level

Fig. 17.2 : A psychological test results.

Objectivity

Psychology is a science. Hence, psychological tests should ideally be objective. It means that the administration, scoring and interpretation of scores are not affected by subjective judgments of the individual examiner. Further, the test should give the same score every time it is administered and make objective assessment of the psychological variable in the individual, that the test seeks to measure.

Owing to the nature of psychology, absolute objectivity is only theoretically possible. In practice, the aim is to attain as much objectivity as possible.

There are three measures used by psychologists to study the extent of objectivity:

1. Reliability of scores
2. Validity of scores
3. Difficulty of the test

'Reliability' refers to the internal consistency and stability with which a measuring instrument performs its function. In the case of psychological tests, it refers to the consistency in test scores when measured again and again. If a test administration at one time gives a score of 90 and when administered at another time it gives a score of 150, it means the test is not reliable. For an individual, 90 and 150 cannot both be correct measures. We don't even know if any one of them is the correct measure. In short, the results are so subjective that we can't rely on the test.

Another measure of objectivity is 'validity'. An objective test should measure what it is supposed to measure. If a test is designed to measure intelligence and it ends up measuring some other characteristics, then the test is not valid.

17.3 Construction of Psychological Tests

The process of test construction starts with an exercise in outlining the major objectives of the test. The test constructor decided on what aspects of human psyche she wants to measure, which population the test is intended for, etc. In this stage, the test constructor has to make careful planning with regard to the type of instructions to be included, the nature of the test, the medium, the sampling method, so as to choose the sample for determining norms, etc. Careful planning helps to reduce the efforts necessary to construct the test.

The test construction process now follows the following steps:

1. Writing items of the test
2. Item selection
3. Difficulty measurement
4. Reliability measurement
5. Validity measurement
6. Standardization of preparation of norms

7. Preparation of manual

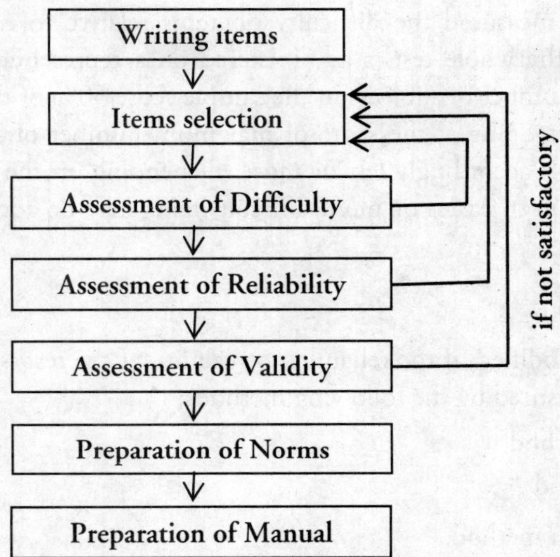

Fig. 17.3 : The psychological test construction process

Writing items of the test

After the test constructor has decided upon the medium of the test (verbal, performance, or audio-visual, etc.), the constructor starts writing the test items. Item writing is a creative process, in which the constructor brainstorms and creates items that she believes is relevant to the characteristics being tested. There is no specific guideline the constructor has to follow, but there are certain pre- requisites for writing good and relevant items:

- The constructor must have a thorough knowledge of the subject matter and the target population the test is intended for.
- The constructor must have a large vocabulary.
- The test items must be evaluated by a group of subject experts and their criticism and suggestions must be taken into consideration when modifying the test.

Item selection

Not every item generated by the item writer must be incorporated in the test. Indeed, how do you prepare a test of items you haven't yet checked on levels of difficulty, reliability and validity. The maximum that can be done at this stage is to make a tentative list of items, arrange them in increasing order of difficulty (difficulty has not yet been measured; difficulty here is the perceived difficulty) and then make preliminary administrations.

In preliminary administration, on a representative sample, the results say which items are more difficult and which are less. For example, if one item is answered by 10 of 20 people in the sample, it is more difficult than another item answered by 16 people. After this, the items are again re-arranged in order of increasing difficulty.

Assessment of difficulty

Till now, we have only measured the difficulty of items relative to each other, but not the overall difficulty. Now, the whole test is administered on a representative sample and results analysed. If the greatest number of subjects in the sample score 50% of the maximum score, the test is of optimal difficulty. But, if the score of maximum number of subjects is less or more than 50%, the difficulty is accordingly less or more. Depending on the type of deviation from normality (average difficulty), easier or more difficult items may be added or other items may be removed or modified.

Assessment of Reliability

Test items are again modified, if the reliability or validity of the test is not found satisfactory. Reliability of a test is measured by the following methods:

1. Test-re-test method
2. Split-half method
3. Equivalent form method

In the test-re-test method, a simple form of the test is administered twice on the sample with a reasonable time gap. The scores obtained at different points of time when correlated, give the value of reliability coefficient. This is obviously an easy and simple form of assessment of reliability. However, this form of assessment is prone to many errors. For instance, an examinee giving the testa second time is better equipped with practice and memory of the first administration of the same test.

In the **split-half** method, a single form of the test is constructed and split into two. The two halves are administered on the same individual and the scores obtained are correlated. The correlation gives the reliability coefficient. When splitting the test, the major aim is to ascertain that the two halves have equivalent difficulty. Hence, most often, the odd-even method is used, i.e., odd numbered items are put in one half and even numbered items in another half. Since the items are arranged in order of increasing difficulty, the two split halves have similar difficulty levels. This method's obvious advantage is that it eliminates the variables affecting re-test after a specific period. A single administration of the test on the subject is needed and the time taken is less.

Yet another choice at the disposal of the test constructor to measure reliability is the **equivalent** form **method.** In the above two methods, we used a single form of a test, but here we use two forms of the same test. Two equivalent forms are constructed. One form is administered at one point of time and another form after a reasonable time gap. The scores of the two results are correlated to get the reliability coefficient. This method counters some of the prime concerns of earlier methods. It is acknowledged that this is a better method to assess reliability than the earlier methods. However, it is a much costly method, given that the test constructor has to make two forms of the test.

Assessment of Validity

The most common way to measure the validity of a test is to compare it with a criterion. This is called **criterion validity.** Suppose you want to select candidates for the job of shop floor worker. How do you know the test you have constructed will select the most deserving candidates? Simply you administer the test to criterions – employees who have already done the job of shop-floor worker successfully. Those who have shown their performance become 'criterions' (or criteria) to evaluate those whose future performance you wish to predict. If the successful employees score high on the test and unsuccessful employees score low, the test is valid. It has high validity.

But, a criterion is not always available. So you go for construct validity. In construct validity, you check if the test measures what it is supposed to measure as per a theoretical stance. For example, psycho-analytic theory speaks about projection as a defense mechanism. Projective tests, like TAT, have high construct validity because they seek to follow the theoretical paradigm to evaluate the human characteristics.

Preparation of Norms

The scores obtained by an individual in a test hold no meaning by themselves. They derive their meaning from the comparison of their performance with average performance of the population. The average performance of the population is called norm. To prepare the norms, you don't administer the test on the whole population, but on a representative sample of the population. Sampling is a challenge here. Suppose you want to develop a test for male, North India population from a specific community. You need to do sampling, taking care of the variety of the population in terms of age, sex, tribes and their population, geographical spread, etc.

The three commonly used norms are:

1. Age-equivalent norm
2. Grade-equivalent norm
3. Percentage norm

Age equivalent norm is the average performance of a representative sample of people belonging to an age group. For example, if maximum number of 8-year-old children who are administered the test score 15 out of 50, 15 is the age-equivalent norm. Grade-equivalent norm, on the other hand, is the average performance of a representative sample of a certain grade or class.

Percentage norms are in the form of a series of raw scores. For each raw score, the number of subjects who lie below that score, as a percentage of total number of subjects in the representative sample is provided. You must have encountered percentage norms in exams, like CAT, MAT and XAT.

Manual Preparation

The psychological tests we are discussing are standardized, objective tests. Hence, the test administration should follow a standardized procedure, so that the subjective judgments of the test administered don't affect the evaluation process; the constructor should prepare a manual where detailed procedure to administer the test are given. Other details, like norms, precautions and interpretation of results should also be incorporated in the manual.

17.4 Types of Psychological Tests

There are some myriad ways in which psychological tests are classified. This is because, such tests vary on a number of aspects. In this section, we will investigate into the major classifications of psychological tests:

1. Speed and power test

A pure speed test is one in which individual differences are measured exclusively from the speed of performance. Some major features of speed tests are:

- The items in the test are of uniformly low difficulty level.
- The time limit is so short that no one could finish all the items.
- Each test taker's score reflects her speed of performance.

On the other hand, a power test is one where the difficulty of items is steeply graded and there are some items that are too difficult for anyone to solve.

Major features of a pure power test are:

- The time limit is long enough to permit every test taker to attempt every question.
- Some items are so difficult that no one can get a perfect score.

Most tests in practice are not pure speed tests or pure power tests. They depend upon both speed and power, in varying proportion.

2. Individual and Group Tests

Individual tests are administered singly to one participant, as in the case of Stanford-Binet test. Group tests, such as the Block test, Otis inventory for screening military personnel, etc., permit mass testing. There is some relative advantage of both types of tests. For example, in individual tests:

- The examiner is highly trained and he can make many valuable auxillary observations regarding the subject.
- Better rapport exists between the examiner and the subject. As a result, the examiner can obtain the cooperation of the subject and maintain his interest in the test.
- Individual tests have higher reliability and validity than group tests.
- The subject can easily clarify any doubts he has.

On the other hand,

- Group tests are cheaper.
- In some occasions, individual testing is just not practically possible. For instance, when screening thousands of applications for recruitment into military, group tests are the only practical option.
- There is more uniformity of procedure in group tests. The subjects can be compared among themselves.

3. Aptitude and Achievement tests

As per the Oxford dictionary of Psychology (2006), an aptitude test is designed to measure aptitude. Aptitude is the suitability, natural ability or the capacity to learn. In psychology, it means the potential, rather than existing capacity to perform some functions after necessary education or training is imparted. An achievement test on the other hand, is a test of acquired ability or skill. For example, SAT or the Scholastic Achievement Test.

Hence, aptitude tests only predict future performance after some form of training. But, achievement tests assess the present level of performance. If you seek to conduct a training (or an educational course) for an engineering skill, for instance, the steps are as follows:

1. Conduct an aptitude test to know who have the aptitude to acquire the skill.
2. Select the ones with aptitude and train them.
3. Assess, if they really have acquired the skill using achievement tests.

4. Classification based on testing medium

A distinction is made between paper-and-pencil tests and performance tests based on the medium of test administration. In the paper-and-pencil tests, all items are printed and responses are written by the subject. On the other hand, performance tests require the individual to manipulate objects, pictures or blocks, etc., and she may have to perform some complex activity.

The advantage of performance tests over paper-and-pencil tests is that performance tests are more culture neutral than paper-and-pencil tests. Paper-and-pencil tests are basically tests that require the individual to be literate, that too in the language in which the tests are administered. Further, language proficiency acts as an extraneous variable, thus affecting the test scores. Another advantage of performance tests is that they can be replicated, with some caution, across cultures. This is not so in the case of paper-and-pencil tests. Often, translated paper-and-pencil tests don't have the desired psychometric properties (such as, standardization, validity, reliability, etc.)

5. General classification versus differential aptitude

General classical tests are those that provide a very general description of individual differences. For example, we know that there are many different components of intelligence. Most recent theories have shown that what we call intelligence is actually different aptitudes tests, like the

IQ test, that try to give a general classification of intelligence. A major drawback of such tests is that they don't reflect upon the differential aptitudes or so to say all dimensions of individual differences the test seeks to measure. On the other hand, tests like the Differential Aptitude Test (DAT) and other such batteries permit differentiation among the individual's special assets and liabilities. Tests of special aptitudes focus on highly specialized areas, such as musical, artistic and mechanical aptitudes.

17.5 Ethical considerations in Psychological testing

Ethics refers to issues or practices (usually with reference to professionals) that are considered morally 'right' and 'fair'. Being professionals who intervene in the affairs of individuals, psychologists also have certain ethical standards. These standards are especially rigorous when the service period to the client is psychological testing.

Many professional associations have forwarded codes of ethics, regarding the professional behaviour of psychologists. The American Psychological Association (APA), the most popular of the professional organisation, sets the following five principles (APA2002) of professional behaviour of psychologists:

A. *Beneficence and non-maleficence:* Psychologists should strive to benefit their client and not to harm them.

B. *Fidelity and responsibility:* Psychologists should establish relationships of trust and be aware of their professional and scientific responsibilities to society.

C. *Integrity:* Psychologists should promote accuracy, honesty and truthfulness in lathe science, teaching and practice of psychology.

D. *Justice:* Psychologists should let all persons have access tot their services and provide equal quality of service to all the clients. A client who is politically important, or from the same community for example should not be given any preferential treatment.

E. *Respect for people's rights and dignity:* Psychologists should respect the dignity and worth of all individuals and their right to privacy, confidentiality and self-determination. (referred from McIntere & Miller, 1999)

Now, that we have discussed general ethical guidelines, let us investigate some ethical issues specific to psychological testing.

1. Test Publishers' Responsibilities

The test publisher has to follow many guidelines in order not to let the test's psychometric properties be diluted. Also, the test publisher should make all efforts to make all necessary psychometric information available.

Some general guidelines for the test publisher are:

- Tests should be sold only to qualified users.
- No tall claims should be made during marketing tests. The publisher needs to be truthful when marketing his products.

- The publisher should ensure test security, which means not disclosing the contents of the test. If the content becomes public, it harms the psychometric properties of the test, and invalidates the test for future use.
- The publisher should provide all necessary information to the test user. There should be a test manual that details the procedure for testing, and guides the; user in inferring the test scores. The test norms and other data should be provided such that the user doesn't find them confusing.

17.6 Test User Responsibility

A test user is anyone who purchases and administers the test and interprets the results of the test. Test-taker is the person whose behaviour is being measured.

Some major functions of the test user are:

1. He determines the need for psychological testing.
2. He selects the test or tests to use.
3. He administers the test to the test-taker.
4. He scores the test.
5. He interprets the test scores. (McIntire and Miller, 1999)

Owing to the varied functions that the test user performs, his role is crucial. He has to maintain certain ethical standards, such as:

- He needs to be well-qualified to perform the task. Training and experience are factors that affect the test user's skills. There are certain organisations that provide certification for test user.
- He should respect the test taker's rights (which are discussed separately below).
- He shouldn't misuse the information he gets from the assessment process.
- He should explain the test results to the participant in a language that the layman test-taker understands.

Test-taker's rights

There are certain rights for the individuals taking the test possess. The test publisher, test user and any other professional involved should respect and uphold these rights.

A few fundamental rights of the test-taker is:

1. *Right to privacy:* All the information that the client discloses should be kept private and not be disclosed without her explicit permission. This aspect of the psychologist's duty is called *confidentiality.* Another related concept is *anonymity.* Sometimes, the test-taker doesn't want to reveal his/her identity to the test user. The test user needs to understand and respect the test-taker's need for anonymity.

2. *Right to informed consent:* The test taker has the right to self-determination. He is entitled to full explanations of why he is being tested, how the test data will be used and what test scores mean. Sometimes, researchers conduct tests as part of surveys to understand prevalence of some behaviour in a population, so that their research is not influenced by the test-taker's expectations. They are tempted not to provide full information about the test. But, this is unethical.
3. The test-taker has a right to know and understand results. He is entitled to a non-technical explanation of test scores.

Testing Special Populations

Special provisions must be made when testing special populations, such as minority ethnic groups, students with learning disabilities, people with mental retardation, etc. For instance, the tribal groups of India have very different cultures from that of mainstream groups. If the test designed for mainstream groups are administered to them, the results are inaccurate. Hence, the testing itself is unethical. Similarly, special provisions should be made to test people with learning disabilities, given that they have problems in reading test items. Physically and mentally challenged individuals need to be administered special tests that overcome their disabilities and measure the intended skills.

■■■

REFERENCES

A. Agarwal (1995) Mass Media and Health Promotion in Indian Villages. Psychology and Developing Societies, Vol. 7, No.2, p. 217-236

A.K. Singh (1988) Intergroup Relations and Social Tension, in Janak Pandey (Ed.), Psychology in India: State-of the- Art. Sage: New Delhi

Adorno, T.W., Frenkel-Brunswik, E., Levinson, D.J., & Sanford, R.N. (1950) The Authoritarian Personality. Harper: New York

Allport, G.W. (1954). The nature of prejudice. Doubleday Books: New York

American Psychological Association (2002) ETHICAL PRINCIPLES OF PSYCHOLOGISTS AND CODE OF CONDUCT, retrieved on 10th December, 2008 from http://www.apa.org/ethics/code2002.html

Anantharaman, R.N. (1980) A study of institutionalized and noninstitutionalized older people. Psychological studies, Vol.25, p.31-33

Anastasi, A. (1954 [2008]) Psychological Testing, 7th edition. Pearson Education India: New Delhi

Anderson, C. A., Carnagey, N. L., & Eubanks, J. (2003). Exposure to violent media: The effects of songs with violent lyrics on aggressive thoughts and feelings. Journal of Personality and Social Psychology, 84, 960–971

Antoni, M. H., Baggett, L., Ironson, G., LaPerriere, A., August, S., Klimas, N., Schneiderman, N., & Fletcher, M.(1991) Cognitive-behavioral stress management intervention buffers distress responses and immunologic changes following notification of HIV-1 seropositivity. Journal of Consulting and Clinical Psychology, 59, 906-915

Argyle, M.(1999) Causes and correlates of happiness, in D.Kahneman & E.Deiner (Eds.), Well-being: The foundations of hedonic psychology (p.353-373). Russell Sage Foundation: New York

Atkinson, J.W.(1957) Motivational determinants of risktaking behaviour. Psychological Review, Vol.64, p.359-372

Balog, J.E. (1981) The concept of health and the role of health education. The Journal of School Health, Vol.9, p.462-464

Bandura, A. (1977) Social Learning Theory. New York: General Learning Press

Barak, A. & Suler, J. (2008) Reflections on the psychology and social science of Cyberspace. Retrieved on 2nd April, 2009 from http://construct.haifa.ac.il/~azy/01-Barak&Suler.pdf

Barak, A. (1999) Psychological Applications on the internet: A discipline on the threshold of a new millennium. Applied and Preventive Psychology, Vol. 8, p. 231- 245

Barak, A. (2004) Internet Counselling. Encyclopaedia of Applied psychology. Elsevier Academic Press: London

Bargh, J.A. & McKenna, K.Y.A. (2004) The Internet and Social Life. Annual Review of Psychology, Vol.55, p.573-590

Barlow, D.H. (2002) Anxiety and its disorders: The nature and treatment of anxiety and panic. Guilford Press: New York

Baron, R.A., & Bryne, D. (1991) Social Psychology: Understanding human interaction (6th ed.). Allyn and Bacon: Needham Heights, MA

Beck, A.T. (1964) Thinking and depression: 2. Theory and therapy. Archives of General Psychiatry, Vol.10, p.561- 571

Benokraitis, N.V. (1997) Subtle Sexism: Current Practice and Prospects for Change. Sage: CA

Berkowitz, L. (1984) Some effects of thoughts on anti- and prosocial influences of media events: A cognitiveneoassociation analysis. Psychological Bulletin, 95, 110-427

Bharat, Shalini (2000) On the Periphery: Psychology of Gender, in Janak Pandey (Ed.) Psychology in India Revisited: Development in the Discipline, Vol-3 (ICSSR Decade Review in Psychology). Sage: New Delhi

Bhatia, S & Sethi, N (2007) *History and Theory of Community Psychology in India: An International Perspective*, in Reich, S.M., Riemer, M., Prilleltensky, I. & Montero, M. (2007) International Community Psychology: History and Theories

Bhattacharjee, S. (1990) Motherhood in ancient India. Economic and political weekly, 25, p.42-43, WS 50-57

Borgen, F.H. (2004) Vocational Interests. Encyclopaedia of Applied psychology. Elsevier Academic Press: London

Boruchovitch, E. & Mednick, B.R. (2002) The meaning of Health and Illness: some considerations for Health Psychology. PsicoUSF, Vol.7, No.2

Borum, R (2004) *Psychology of Terrorism*. Mental Health Law & Policy Faculty Publications, University of South Florida, available online at: https://scholarcommons.usf.edu/cgi/viewcontent.cgi?referer=https://www.google.com/&httpsredir=1&article=1570&context=mhlp_facpub

Brown, M.J. & Cody, M.J. (1991) Effects of a Prosocial Television Soap Opera in Promoting Women's Status. Human Communication Research, Vol.18, No.1, p.114- 144

Carey, M.P. & Vanable, P.A. (2004) AIDS/HIV. Encyclopaedia of Applied psychology. Elsevier Academic Press: London

Chaffee, S.H., & McLeod, J.M. (1972) Adolescent television use in the family context, in G.A.Comstock & E.A.Rubinstein (Eds.) Television and social behaviour: Vol3, Television and adolescent aggressiveness (p.149- 172). US Government Printing Office: Washington D.C.

Chakraborty, Sujata (2001) Entrepreneurship development among women in the low income group: Scope and Constraints. Unpublished PhD thesis, Tata Institute of Social Sciences: Bombay

Chambless, D.L. & Hollon, S.D. (1998) Defining Empirically Supported Therapies. Journal of Consulting and Clinical Psychology, Vol.66, No.1, p.7-18

Christensen, I, Wagner, H.I., & Halliday, M. (2001) Instant Notes: Psychology. Viva Books: New Delhi

Coleman, J.C. (1969) Psychology and Effective Behaviour. Scott Foresman: Glenview, IL

Conger, J.A. and Kanungo, R.N. (1998) Charismatic Leadership in Organizations. Sage: Thousand Oaks, CA

Dalal, A.K. (2000) Health Psychology, in Janak Pandey (Ed.) Psychology in India Revisited: Development in the Discipline, Vol-2 (ICSSR Decade Review in Psychology). Sage: New Delhi

Das, J.P. (1973) Cultural Deprivation and Cognitive Competence, in Ellis, N.R. (Ed.), International Review of Research in Mental Retardation, Vol.6, p.1-53. Academic Press: New York

Das, J.P., Jachuck, K., & Panda, T.P. (1970) Caste, Cultural Deprivation and cognitive Growth, in H.C. Haywood (Ed.), Social-Cultural aspects of mental retardation. Appleton: New York

Davar, B.V. (1999). Mental Health of Indian Woman. Sage: New Delhi

Davison, K. P., Pennebaker, J. W. and Dickerson, S. S. (2000) Who talks? The social psychology of illness support groups. American Psychologist, Vol.55, p.205–217

Deci, E. L. & Ryan, R. (1985) Intrinsic motivation and selfdetermination in human behaviour. Plenum: New York

DeFleur, M.L. and Ball-Rokeach, S. (1989) Theories of Mass Communication. White Plains, NY: Longman

Denmark, F.L. (2004) Gender, overview. Encyclopaedia of Applied psychology. Elsevier Academic Press: London

deRidder, R., & Tripathi, R.C. (1992) Norm violation and inter-group relations. Chrendon Press: Oxford

Devos, G.A. (1968) Achievement and innovation in culture and personality, in E.Norbeck, D.Price-Williams, & W.M.McCord (Eds.) The study of personality: an interdisciplinary approach. Holt: New York

Dewe, P. (2004) Job stress and burnout. Encyclopaedia of Applied psychology. Elsevier Academic Press: London

Diener, E. & Diener, C. (1996) Most people are happy. Psychological Science, retrieved on 5th November, 2008 from http://education.ucsb.edu/ janeconoley/ ed197/ documents/Dienersmostpeoplearehappy.pdf

Diener, E. & Suh, E.M. (1999) Well-being: The foundations of hedonic psychology. Russel Sage Foundation: New York

Diener, E., Oishi, S. & Lucas, R.E. (2002) Subjective Well- Being: The Science of Happiness and Life Satisfaction, in Snyder, C.R. & Lopez, S.J. (ed) Oxford Handbook of Positive Psychology. Oxford University Press: New York

Diener, E., Sandvik, E., Seidlitz, L., & Diener, M. (1993) The relationship between income and subjective wellbeing: Relative or absolute? Social Indicators Research, Vol.28, No.3, p.195-223

Dodgen, C.E. (2004) Drug Abuse. Encyclopaedia of Applied psychology. Elsevier Academic Press: London

Dollard, J., Doob, L.W., Miller, N.E., Mowrer, O.H., & Sears, R.R. (1939) Frustration and Aggression. Yale University Press: New Haven

Donnerstein, E. & Smith, S.L. (1997) Impact of media violence on children, adolescents, and adults, in S.Kirschner & D.A. Kirschner (Eds.) Perspectives on psychology and the media(p.29-68). Americal Psychological Association: Washington (DC)

Donnerstein, E., Slaby, R. G., & Eron, L. D. (1994). The mass media and youth aggression; in L. D. Eron, J. H. Gentry, & P. Schlegel (Eds.) Reason to hope: A psychological perspective on violence and youth. Americal Psychological Association: Washington (DC)

Dweck, C.S. (1986) Motivational processes affecting learning. American Psychologist, Vol. 41, pp 1040 – 1048

Dwivedi, R.S. (1995) Human Relations and Organisational Behaviour: A global perspective. MacMillan:1995

Eagly, A.H., & Johannesen-Schmidt, M.C. (2002) The Leadership Styles of Women and Men, in L.L. Carli & A.H.Eagly (Eds.) Gender, hierarchy, and leadership. Wiley Blackwell: US

Eagly, A.H., & Johnson, B.T. (1990) Gender and leadership style: A meta-analysis. Psychological Bulletin, Vol. 108, No.2, p.233-256

Entwistle, N. & Peterson, E. (2004) Learning styles and approaches to learning. Encyclopaedia of Applied psychology. Elsevier Academic Press: London

Entwistle, N.J. (2000). Approaches to studying and levels of understanding: the influences of teaching and assessment. in Smart, J.C. (ed.), Higher education: Handbook of theory and research (Vol. XV). New York: Agathon Press, pp. 156 - 218

Esser, V.M. & Semenya, A.H. &Stelzl, M. (2004) Prejudice and Discrimination. Encyclopaedia of Applied psychology. Elsevier Academic Press: London

Eysenck, H. J. (1967). The biological basis of personality. Charles C. Thomas : Springfield, IL

Eysenck, H. J. (1998). Intelligence: A new look. New Brunswick, NJ: Transaction Publishers

Fassinger, R.E. (2008) Workplace Diversity and Public Policy: Challenges and Opportunity for Psychology. American Psychologist, Vol. 63, No.4, p. 252-264

Feldhusen, J.F. (2004) Gifted students. Encyclopaedia of Applied psychology. Elsevier Academic Press: London

Ferguson, Christopher; Garza, Adolfo (2011). "Call of (civic) duty: Action games and civic behavior in a large sample of youth". Computers in Human Behavior. 27 (2): 770–775

Fiedler, F. E. (1967). A Theory of Leadership Effectiveness. McGraw-Hill: New York

Fitzduff, M. (2006) Ending Wars: Development, Theories, and Practice, in Fitzduff & Stout (ed.), The Psychology of resolving global conflicts: From war to peace. Greenwood Publishing Group: Westport

Flora, J.A., & Thoreson, C.E. (1988) Reducing the risk of AIDS in adolescents. American Psychologist, Vol.43, p.965-970

Fondacaro, M.R. & Weinberg, D. (2002) Concepts of social justice in Community Psychology: Toward a social ecological epistemology. American Journal of Community Psychology, 30, 473–92

Fouad, N.A. (2007) Work and Vocational Psychology: Theory, Research and Applications. Annual Review of Psychology, Vol. 58, p.543-564

Friedman, D.E. (1988) Why the glass ceiling? Across the board, Vol.25, p.32-37

Furnham, A. (1997) The Psychology of behaviour at work: The individual in the organization. Psychology Press: London

Garcia, Julio and Cohen, Geoffrey Lawrence (2011) A Social Psychological Perspective on Educational Intervention (August 15, 2011). THE BEHAVIORAL FOUNDATIONS OF POLICY, E. Shafir, ed. Available at SSRN: https://ssrn.com/abstract=1910232

Gentile, D.A., Lynch, P.J., Linder, J.R., & Walsh, D.A. (2004) The effects of violent video game habits on adolescent hostility, aggressive behaviors, and school performance. Journal of Adolescence, Vol.27, No.1, p.5-22

Ghosh, E.S.K., & Huq, M.M. (1985) A study of the social identity of two ethnic groups in India and Bangladesh. Journal of Multilingual and Multicultural Development, Vol.6, p.239-251

Ghufran, M. & Qadri, A.J. (1988) Factors contributing to communal harmony and disharmony: A sociopsychological analysis, in Qadri, A.J. (Ed.), Intra-social Tension and National Integration: Psychological Assessment. Concept: New Delhi

Gillem, A.R., Sehgal, R. & Forcet, S. (2000) Understanding Prejudice and Discrimination, in Biaggio & Hersen (Eds.) Issues in the Psychology of Women. Springer: London

Greenfield, Patricia Marks (1984): Mind and Media: The Effects of Television, Computers and Video Games. Fontana: London

Gross, R. (2005) Psychology: the science of mind and behaviour. Hodder: London

Grossman, David (1996). On Killing: The Psychological Cost of Learning to Kill in War and Society. Little, Brown and Co: Boston

Hacker, Frederick J (1983). "Dialectical Interrelationships of Personal and Political Factors in Terrorism." Pages 19-32 in Lawrence Zelic Freedman and Yonah Alexander, eds., Perspectives on Terrorism. Wilmington, Delaware: Scholarly Resources

Hammen, C. (1991) Depression runs in families: The social context of risk and resilience in children of depressed mothers. Springer-Verlag: New York

Harpaz, I. (2002) Advantages and disadvantages of telecommuting for the individual, organization and society. Work Study, Vol.51, No.2, p.74-80

Heppner, M.J. & Heppner, P.P. (2004) Career Counselling. Encyclopaedia of Applied psychology. Elsevier Academic Press: London

Herriot, P. (1989) Attribution theory and interview decisions, in Eder, R.W., Ferris, G.R. (Eds),The Employment Interview: Theory, Research and Practice. Sage: Newbury Park, CA

Hersey, P. and Blanchard, K. H. (1977) The Management of Organizational Behaviour 3e. Prentice Hall: Upper Saddle River N. J.

Hodges, C.B. (2004) Designing to Motivate: Motivational Techniques to Incorporate in E-Learning Experiences. The Journal of Interactive Online Learning, Vol.2, No.3

Holahan, C.J. & Moos, R.H. (1990) Life stressors, resistance factors, and improved psychological functioning: an extension of the stress resistance paradigm. J Pers Soc Psychol, Vol. 58, No.5, p. 909-917

Holland, John. L. (1997) Making Vocational Choices: A Theory of Vocational Personalities and Work Environments. Psychological Assessment Resources Inc

Hollingworth, L. S. (1926) Gifted children: Their nature and nurture. The Macmillan Company: New York

Horgan, D. (1989) A cognitive learning perspective on women becoming expert managers. Journal of Business and Psychology, Vol.3, p.299-313

House, Robert J. (1971) A path-goal theory of leader effectiveness. Administrative Science Quarterly Vol.16: 321-339

Hussain, A. (1984) Ingroup-Outgroup perceptions of Hindus and Muslims on needs affiliation and aggression. Perspectives in Psychological Researches, Vol.7, No.1, p.25-29

Hutnik, Nimmi (2004) An intergroup perspective on ethnic minority identity, in Janak Pandey (Ed.) Psychology in India Revisited –Developments in the Discipline. Sage: New Delhi

Inglehart, R. (1990) Culture Shift in Advanced Industrial Society. Princeton University Press: Princeton, NJ

Irwin, A.R. & Gross, A.M. (1995) Cognitive tempo, violent video games, and aggressive behavior in young boys. Journal of Family Violence, Vol.10, No.3, p.1573-2851

Jain, Swatantra (2004) Bringing the adolescent criminals in the mainstream: A meditative approach. Journal of Psychological Researches, Vol.48, No.1, p.25-32

Jain, U. & Misra,G. (1990) The Experience and Consequences of Crowding, in Giriswar Misra(ed.) Applied Social Psychology in India (p.201-219). Sage: New Delhi

Jessup, G. and Jessup, H. (1971) Validity of the Eysenck Personality in pilot selection. Occupational Psychology. 45, 111-123

Jowett, G. S., & O'Donnell, V. (1992). Propaganda and persuasion (2nd ed). Beverly Hills, CA: Sage

Jung, C.G. (1954). Concerning the archetypes, with special reference to the anima concept, in collected works, p.54-72

Kakar, Sudhir (1978) The Inner World: A Psychoanalytic study of Childhood and Society in India. OUP: New Delhi

Kakar, Sudhir (1990) Some unconscious aspects of ethnic violence in India, in V.Das (Ed.), Mirrors of Violence: Communities, riots and survivors in South Asia. OUP: New Delhi

Kakar, Sudhir (2008) Teach your children that compassion is above justice. Times of India, 02.10.2008

Kang, J. (2000) Cyber-race. Harvard Law Review, Vol.113, No.5, p.1130-1208

Kellen, K. (1979) Terrorists –What are they like. Rand: Santa Monica, CA

Keller, J. M. (1987b) The systematic process of motivational design. Performance & Instruction, 26(9), 1–8

Keller, J.M. & Suzuki, K. (2004) Learner motivation and Elearning design: a multinationally validated process. Journal of Educational Media, Vol.29, No.3

Kelly, J.A., Lawrence, J.S., Diaz, Y.E., Stevenson, L.Y. et al(1991) HIV Risk Behaviour Reduction Following Intervention with Key Opinion Leaders of Population: An Experimental Analysis. American Journal of Public Health, Vol.81, No.2, p.168-171

Khan, S.R. (1988) A study of communal stereotypes among the Hindus and Muslims. Advances in Psychology, Vol.3, No.2, p.93-99

Kirk, S.A. (1962) Educating exceptional children. Houghton Mifflin: Boston

Knight, B.G. & David, S. (2004). Psychotherapy in older adults. Encyclopaedia of Applied psychology. Elsevier Academic Press: London

Kohlberg, L., & Mayer, R. (1972) Development as the aim of education. Harvard Educational Review Vol. 42, p.449-96

Kolb, D. A. (1984) Experiential Learning. Prentice Hall: Englewood Cliffs, NJ

Kool, V.K., & Agrawal, R. (2006) Applied Social Psychology: A global perspective. Atlantic: New Delhi

Kovalski, T., & Horan, J. J. (1998) Internet-cognitiverestructuring's impact on career beliefs of adolescent girls. Paper presented at the annual Meeting of the American Psychological Association, San Francisco

Kraut, R. E., Patterson, M., Lundmark, V., Kiesler, S., Mukhopadhyay, T., & Scherlis, W. (1998) Internet paradox: A social technology that reduces social involvement and psychological well-being? American Psychologist, Vol.53, No.9, p.1017-1032

Kraut, R.E., Fish, R.S., Root, R.W., Chalfonte, B.L., & Oskamp, I.S. (1990) Informal Communication in Organizations: Form, Function, and Technology. Retrieved on 10th February, 2009 from http://www.cs.cmu.edu/~kraut/RKraut.site.files/articles/kraut90-InformalCommInOrgs.pdf

Kraut, R.E., Kiesler, S., Boneva, B., Cummings, J.N., Helgeson, V., & Crawford, A.M. (2002) Internet paradox revisited. Journal of social issues, Vol.58, p.49- 74

Laak, J. And deGoede, M. (2004) Education and child assessment. Encyclopaedia of Applied psychology. Elsevier Academic Press: London

LaFrance, M., & Woodzicka, J.A. (1998) No laughing matter: Women's verbal and nonverbal reactions to sexist humor, in J. Swim & C. Stangor(Eds.) Prejudice: The Target's Perspective (pp. 61-80). Academic Press: Boston

Langer, K.G. (2004) Psychological Rehabilitation Therapies. Encyclopaedia of Applied psychology. Elsevier Academic Press: London

Lavalekar, A. (2000) Social Awareness in Relation to Media among high school students. Psychological Studies, Vol. 45, No.3, p.139-144

Lemma-Wright, A. (1995). Invitation to psychodynamic psychology. Whurr: London

Levinson, E.M. & Christy, A.B. & Maus, M.R. (2004) Vocational Assessment in School. Encyclopaedia of Applied psychology. Elsevier Academic Press: London

Lovaas, O.I. (1977) The autistic child: Language development through behavioural modification. Irvington: Oxford, UK

Lowerison, G., Cote, R., Abrami, P.C., and Lavoie, M. (2008) Revisiting Learning Theory for e-Learning, in Saul Carliner, Patti Shank (Eds.), The E-Learning Handbook: Past Promises, Present Challenges. John Wiley and Sons

Lucas, R.E., Diener, E., & Suh, E. (1996) Discriminant validity of well-being measures. Journal of Personality and Social Psychology, Vol. 71, p.616-628

Lykken, D. & Tellegen, A. (1996) Happiness is a stochastic phenomenon. Psychological Science, Vol.7, p.186-189

Lynton & Pareek (1967) Training for Development. Irwin: Homewood, IL

Majeed, A., & Ghosh, E.S.K. (1981) Ingroup and outgroup evaluation in intergroup conflict. Psychological Studies, Vol.26, No.1, p.34-40

Malamuth, N.M., Addison, T., & Koss, M. (2000) Pornography and secual aggression: Are there reliable effects and how might we understand them? Annual Review of Sex Research, Vol.11, p.26-91

Manasian, D. (2003) Digital dilemmas: A survey of the Internet society. Economist, Jan. 25, p.1–26

Martın-Baro, I. (1994) Writings for a Liberation Psychology, edited by A. Aron and S. Corne. Cambridge, MA: Harvard University Press

Martlett, G.A. & Gordon, J.R. (1985) Relapse prevention: Maintenance strategies in the treatment of addictive behaviours. Guilford Press: New York

McClelland, D.C. & Winter, D.G. (1969) Motivating Economic Achievement. Free Press: New York

McClelland, D.C. (1961) The achieving society. Van Nostrand: New York

McIntire, S.A. & Miller, L.A. (1999) Foundations of Psychological Testing: A Practical Approach. Sage Publications: CA

McKenna, K.Y.A., Green, A.S., & Gleason, M.E.J. (2002) Relationship formation on the internet: what's the big attraction? Journal of Social Issues, Vol.58, No.1, p.9- 31

Mehta, P. (1966) Managing Motivation in Education. Sahitya Mudranalaya: New Delhi

Mehta, P. (1968) A report on achievement motivation development for educational growth. Journal of General and Applied Psychology, Vol.1, p.28-32

Mehta, P. (1969) Achievement motive in high school boys. NCERT: New Delhi

Milgram, Stanley. (1974) The Perils of Obedience. Harper's Magazine, retrieved on 5th January, 2009 from http://home.swbell.net/revscat/perilsOf Obedience.html

Mishra, H. &Kiran Kumar, S.K. (1993) Clinical Applications of Biofeedback and Behaviour Therapy. Indian Journal of Applied Psychology, Vol. 30, No.2, p.17-23

Misra, G. (1982) Deprivation and cognitive competence. In D. Sinha, R.C. Tripathi, & G. Misra (Eds.) Deprivation: Its social roots and psychological consequences. (pp. 151-175). Concept: New Delhi

Misra, G. (1982) Experiential deprivation and development of representational competence. In R. Rath, H.S. Asthana, D. Sinha, & J.B.P. Sinha (Eds.) Diversity and unity in cross-cultural psychology, (pp. 70-77). Swets and Zeitlinger, B.V.: Netherlands

Misra, G. (Ed.) (1990) Applied social psychology in India. Sage Publications: New Delhi

Misra, G., & Mohanty, A.K. (2000) Consequences of poverty and disadvantage: A review of Indian studies. In A.K. Mohanty & G. Misra (Eds.), Psychology of poverty and disadvantage (pp. 121-148) Concept Publishing Company: New Delhi

Misra, G., & Mohanty, A.K. (2000) Poverty and disadvantage: Issues in retrospect. In A.K. Mohanty & G. Misra (Eds.), Psychology of poverty and disadvantage (p. 261-284). Concept Publishing Company: New Delhi

Misra, G., & Tripathi, L.B. (1980) Psychological consequences of prolonged deprivation. National Psychological Corporation: Agra

Mohanty, A. K. & Misra, G. (Ed.) (2001) Psychology of poverty and social disadvantage. Concept Publishing Company: New Delhi

Moore, M.G. & Kearsley, G. (1996) Distance Education: A Systems View. Wadsworth Pub. Co: Belmont, CA

Morrison, A.M., White, R.P., & Van Velsor, E., & the Center for Creative Leadership(1987) Breaking the glass ceiling: Can women reach the top of America's largest corporations? Addison-Wesley: Reading, MA

Mowen, J.C. (1989) Consumer Psychology, in L. Gregory & G. Burroughs (Eds.), Introduction to Applied Psychology (p.181-210). Scott Foresman: Glenview, IL

Munduate, L. & Medina, F.J. (2004) Power, Authority and Leadership. Encyclopaedia of Applied psychology. Elsevier Academic Press: London

Muttayya, B.C. (2008) Dynamics of Rural Development, in Pandey, J. (ed.), Psychology in India: State-of-the- Art. Sage: New Delhi

Myers, D.G. (1992) The pursuit of happiness: Who is happy – and why. William Morrow: New York

Myers, D.G., & Diener, E. (1995) Who is happy? Psychological Science, Vol.6, p.10-19

Nafziger, E.W. (1975) Class, Caste and Community of South Indian Industrialists: An Examination of the Horatio Alger Model. The journal of Developmental Studies, Vol.11, No.2, p.131-148

Nag, M. (2002). Empowering female sex workers for AIDS prevention and far beyond: Sonagachi shows the way. Indian Journal of Social Work, 63(3), 473-501

Naidu, R.K. (2000) Personality, Self and Life Events, in Janak Pandey (Ed.) Psychology in India Revisited: Development in the Discipline, Vol-2 (ICSSR Decade Review in Psychology). Sage: New Delhi

Om Prakash. (1984) Achievement and failures of an experiment in rural development. Social Change, Vol.14, p.16-24.

Ones, D. S., Viswesvaran, C. , & Schmidt, F. L. (1993) Comprehensive meta-analysis of integrity test validities: Findings and implications for personnel selection and theories of job performance. Journal of Applied Psychology (Monograph), Vol. 78, p. 679- 703

Orford, J (2008) Community Psychology: Challenges, Controversies and Emerging Consensus. John Wiley & Sons Ltd, England

Osgood, C.E. (1962) An Alternative To War Or Surrender. University of Illinois Press: Urbana

Ostrov, Jamie M.; Gentile, Douglas A.; Crick, Nicki R. (2003). "Media, Aggression and Pro-social Behavior" (PDF). Social Development

Ostrow, D. (1989) AIDS prevention through effective education. Dedalus, Vol.118, p.233-254

Ownes, R.L., & Nandy, A. (1977) The new vaishyas. Allied: New Delhi

Oxendine, J.B. (1970) Emotional Arousal and Motor Performance. Quest, Vol. 13, p.23 – 32

Pandya, Sunil K. (2001) Human Behaviour. National Book Trust: New Delhi

Paranjpe, A.C. (1970) Caste, prejudice, and the individual. Lalvani Publishing House: New Delhi

Parasher, R.P. (2000) Lifestyle for perfect health. Psychological Studies, Vol.45, No.3, p.139-144

Pareek, U. (1967) A motivational Paradigm of Development. Indian Educational Review, Vol.2, p.105-111

Pareek, U. (1991) HRD in India: Prospect and Retrospect. The Indian Journal of Social Work, Vol. L. ii No.4, p. 457-474

Parikh, I.J., & Shah, N.A. (1994) Woman managers in transition: From homes to corporate office. Indian Journal of Social Work, Vol.2, p.143-160

Parsons, F. (1909) Choosing a vocation. Houghton Mifflin: Boston

Paul, G.L. & Lentz, R.J. (1977) Psychosocial treatment of chronic mental patients: Milieu versus social-learning programs. Harvard University Press: Cambridge, MA

Peterson, C., Park, N., & Seligman, M.E.P. (2005) Orientations to happiness and life satisfaction: the full life versus the empty life. Journal of Happiness Studies, Vol.6, No.1, p.25-41

Picano, J.J. & Williams, T.J. & Roland, R.R. (2006) Assessment and selection of high-risk operational personnel, in Carrie H.Kennedy, Eric Zillmer (eds.) Military Psychology: clinical and operational applications. Guilford Press: London

Post, J.M. (1984) Notes on a psychodynamic theory of terrorist behaviour. Terrorism: An International Journal, Vol.7, p.241-256

Prem Prakash (2004) Introduction to Psychology. Arya publications: New Delhi

Prochaska, J. O., J. C. Norcross, et al. (1994) Changing for Good. William Morrow: New York

Quick, J.C. & Macik-Frey, M. & Nelson, D.L. (2004) Job Stress. Encyclopaedia of Applied psychology. Elsevier Academic Press: London

Ragins, B. R., & Sundstrom, E. (1989) Gender and power in organizations: A longitudinal perspective. Psychological Bulletin, Vol.105, p.5188

Raine, A., Mellingen, K., Liu, J., Venables, P., & Mednick, S.A. (2003) Effects of Environmental Enrichment at Ages 3-5 Years on Schozotypal Personality and Antisocial Behavior at Ages 17 and 23 Years. American Journal of Psychiatry, Vol.160, p.1627-1635

Raine, A., Venables, P.H. and Williams, M. (1996) Better autonomic conditioning and faster electrodermal halfrecovery time at age 15 years as possible protective factors against crime at age 29 years. Developmental Psychology, Vol.32, p.624-630

Rajwade, Shweta (2005). The Indian feminine: An exploration in the feminine identity. Psychological Studies, Vol.50, No.2-3, p.166-170

Ranganathan, N., Bohet, A.K., & Wadhwa, T. (2008) Beyond the Prison Walls: Reforming through silence. Psychological Studies, Vol.53, no.1, p.54-63

Rao, T.V., & Pareek, U. (1978) Developing Entrepreneurship: A Handbook. Learning System: New Delhi

Rath, R., Dash, A.S. and Dash, U.N. (1979) Cognitive abilities and school achievement of the socially disadvantaged children in primary schools. Allied: Bombay

Ray, J. (1983) Ambition and dominance among parsees in India. Journal of Social Psychology, Vol.119, p.173- 179

Rogers, C. & Dorfman, E. (1976) Client-Centered Therapy: its current practice, implications and theory. Constable: London

Rosenhan, D.D. & Seligman, M.P. (1989) Abnormal Psychology: Second Edition. W.W.Norton: New York

Rosenthal, R., & Jacobson, L. (1968) Pygmalion in the classroom. Holt, Rinehart & Winston: New York

Rubin, A. M., West, D .V. & Mitchell, W. S. (2001). Differences in aggression, attitudes toward women, and distrust as reflected in popular music preferences. Media Psychology, 3, 25–42

Russell, D.E.H. (1984) Sexual exploitation: rape, child sexual abuse, and workplace harassment. Sage: CA

Sageman, M. (2006) The Psychology of Al Qaeda terrorists, in Carrie H.Kennedy, Eric Zillmer (Eds.) Military Psychology: clinical and operational applications. Guilford Press: London

Saraswathi, T.S. & Dutta, R. (1990) Poverty and Human Development: Socialization of Girls Among the Urban and Rural Poor, in Giriswar Misra(ed.) Applied Social Psychology in India (p.201-219). Sage: New Delhi

Schmeck, R.R. (1988) Learning Strategies and Learning Styles. Springer: London

Schultz, D. & Schultz, S.E. (2002) Psychology and Work Today: International Edition. Pearson Higher Education

Schwitzgebel, R.K. & Kolb, D.A. (1974). Changing Human Behaviour: Principles of plammed intervention. McGraw-Hill: New York

Seligman, M.E.P. & Parks, A.C. & Steen, T. (2004) A Balanced Psychology and Full Life. Phil. Trans. R. Soc. Lond. B., Vol.359, p.1379-1381

Sen, A.K. (2000) Research in Mental Retardation in India: Challenges and Opportunities. Psychological Studies, Vol. 45, No.3, p.139-144

SETHI, R., & ALLEN, M.J. (1988) Sex role stereotypes in. Northern India and the United States. Sex Roles, Vol.8, p.24-32

Sharma, I. & Agnihotri, S.S. (1982) Yoga therapy in psychiatric disorders: risks and difficulties. Indian Journal of Medical Sciences, Vol.36, No.7-8, p.138-41

Sharma, P., Michael, A., Reddy, M.V., & Gehlot, P.S. (1985) Migration and mental illness. Indian Journal of Psychological Medicine, Vol. 8, p.47-52

Sharma, Sagar & Sharma, Monica (2008). Stress induced psychological vital signs in Military domain. Psychological studies, Jan 2008, Vol. 53, No.1, p. 7-19

Sherif, M., Harvey, O.J., White, B.J., Hood, W.R., & Sherif, C.W. (1961) Intergroup conflict and cooperation: The robber's cave experiment. Octagon Books: New York

Shukla, A. (1988) A comparative study of high and low casteprejudiced college girls in respect of their reaction to frustration. Indian Psychological Review, Vol.33, No.6- 7, p.5-9

Shukla, K.S. (1977). Adolescent Thieves. Leela Devi Publication: New Delhi

Siegel, S. (1984) Pavlovian Conditioning and Heroin Overdose: Reports by Overdose Victims. Bulletin of the Psychonomic Society, Vol. 22, p. 428-430

Silber, Norman I (1990) Observing Reasonable Consumers: Cognitive Psychology, Consumer Behavior and Consumer Law, available online at: https://pdfs.semanticscholar.org/5f2b/2fc4da9db61f178e8acde018edbf5d47c796.pdf

Singer-Dudek, Jessica(2004) Exceptional students. Encyclopaedia of Applied psychology. Elsevier Academic Press: London

Singh, A.K. (1983) Parental support and academic achievement. Social Change, Vol.10, p.9-14

Singh, K.P. (1993) Women Entrepreneurs: Their profile and motivation. Journal of Entrepreneurship, Vol.2, p.47- 58

Singhal, R. & Misra, G. (1990) The Challenge of Achievement, in Giriswar Misra(Ed.) Applied Social Psychology in India (p.201-219). Sage: New Delhi

Sinha, D. (1969) Indian villages in transition: A Motivational analysis. Associated Publishing House

Sinha, D. (1984) Reflections on the measurement of human motivation in India. Psychological Studies, Vol.29, p.197-206

Sinha, J.B.P. (1985) Collectivism, social energy, and development in India, in A.R.Langunes & Y.H.Poortinga (Eds.) From a different perspective: Studies of behaviour across cultures. Swets and Zeitlinger: Lisse

Smith, J.A. (1981) The idea of health: a philosophical enquiry. Advances in nursing science, Vol.3, p. 43-50

Sonalkar, W. (1975) Women can affect social change. National Labour Institute Bulletin, Vol.1, No.4, p.6-7

Sprafkin, J.N., Liebert, R.M., & Poulos, R.W. (1975) Effects of a prosocial televised example on children's helping. Journal of Experimental Child Psychology, 20, 119-126

Sproull, I. & Kiesler, S. (1985) Reducing social context cues: Electronic mail in organizational communication. Management science, Vol.11, p.1492-1512

Sridhara, A. (1984) A study of language stereotypes in children. Journal of Psychological Researches, Vol.28, No.1, p.45-51

Sternberg, R.J. & Zhang, L. (2001) Perspectives on Thinking, Learning, and Cognitive Styles. Lawrence Erlbaum Associates: Philadelphia

Suedfeld, P., & Steel, G.D. (2000) The environmental psychology of capsule habitats. Annual Review of Psychology, Vol. 51, p. 227-253

Sugarman, K. (1999) Winning the Mental Way. Retrieved on 2nd of December, 2008 from http://www.psychwww.com/sports/index.htm

Suler, John (1996 – 2008) The Psychology of Cyberspace. Retrieved on 10th of November 2008 from http://wwwusr. rider.edu/~suler/psycyber/psycyber.html

Super, D.E. (1957) The psychology of careers. Harper: New York

Swain, Smarak (2009) An Enquiry into the Functionality of the Dominant Ideology of Gender in Traditional Hindu Society. Journal of Alternative Perspectives in the Social Sciences, Vol.1, No.2, p.435-448

Tajfel, H. (1981) Human groups and social categories. Cambridge University Press: Cambridge

Tamhankar, A., Barnes, B. & Pereira, J. (2005) Personality predisposition and prognosis of Alcoholics after therapeutic intervention. Psychological studies, vol. 50, No. 2-3, p.277-280

Tandon AK, Bajpai M, Tandon RK, Shukla R. (1978) Aggressive behaviour disorders of juvenile delinquents. J Assoc Physicians India, vol. 26(9), p. 787-92

Taran, C. (2005) Motivation Techniques in eLearning. Proceedings of the fifth IEEE International Conference on Advanced Learning Technologies

Terman, L.M. (1925) Mental and physical traits of a thousand gifted children. Stanford University Press: Stanford, CA

Thomas, E.L., Robinson H.A. (1982) Improving Reading in Every Class. Alyn and Bacon: Boston

Tilly III, W.D. (2004) Learning Disabilities. Encyclopaedia of Applied psychology. Elsevier Academic Press: London

Timpe, Klaus-Peter and Giesa, Hans-Gerhard, and Seifert, Katharina(2004) Engineering Psychology. Encyclopaedia of Applied psychology. Elsevier Academic Press: London

Tipathi, R.C., & Srivastava, R. (1981) Relative deprivation and inter-group attitudes. European Journal of Social Psychology, Vol.11, p.313-318

Toffler, A. (1970) Future Shock. Random House: New York

TOI (2008) Terror anxiety cases up by 50%: psychiatrist. By Nandita Sengupta, 07.10.2008

Tripathi, R.C. (1988) Applied Social Psychology, in Janak Pandey(ed), Psychology in India: The state-of-theart. Sage: New Delhi

Truscott, S.D. & Berry, R.A.W. & Lee, K. (2004) Special Education. Encyclopaedia of Applied psychology. Elsevier Academic Press: London

Varma, A., & Stroh, L. K. (2001) Different perspectives on selection for international assignments: the impact of LMX and gender. Cross Cultural Management, Vol.8, p.85-97

Venkatasubrahmanyan, T.R. (1973) Group Prejudices in India: Experiments in learning theory. Sri Ram Centre for Industrial Relations and Human Resources: New Delhi

Vindhya, U. (2005) Western feminism and Indian womanhood: In search of a middle path. Psychological Studies, Vol.50, No.2-3, p.160-165

Vindhya, U. (2007) Quality of Women's lives in India: Some findings from two decades of Psychological research on gender. Feminist & Psychology, Vol. 17(3), p.337- 356

Vroom, V.H. and Yelton, P.W. (1973) Leadership and decision-making. University of Pittsburg Press: Pittsburg

Vyas, S.K. (1973) The origin of prejudice in children. Research in Personality and Social Problems, Madras University

Wallace, R.K. (1970) Physiological Effects of Transcendental Meditation. Science, Vol. 167, No. 3926, p. 1751-1754

Weiner, B. (1974) Achievement motivation and attribution theory. General Learning Press: Morristown, N.J.

Weitten, Wayne (2004) Psychology: Themes and Variations: Sixth Edition. Wadsworth Publishing Company

Wells, B. E., & Twenge, J. M. (2005). Changes in young people's sexual behavior and attitudes, 1943–1999: A cross-temporal meta-analysis. Review of General Psychology, 9, 249–261

Wilson, Barbara J. (2008). "Media and Children's Aggression, Fear, and Altruism". Children and Electronic Media. 18 (1): 7

Winterbottom, M.R. (1953) The relation of childhood training in independence to achievement motivation. Unpublished doctoral dissertation, University of Michigan, Ann Arbor

Wirth, L. (2001) Breaking through the glass ceiling: Women in management. International Labour Office, retrieved on 5th March, 2009 from http://www-ilomirror. cornell.edu/public/english/support/publ/pdf/ women.pdf#page=248

Wlodkowski, R. J. (1985) Enhancing adult motivation to learn. Jossey-Bass: San Francisco

Woods, B. (1998) Applying Psychology to Sports. Hodder Educational: London

Young, K.S. (1996) Internet addiction: The emergence of a new clinical disorder. CyberPsychology and Behaviour, Vol.1, No.3, p.237-244, retrieved on 10th February, 2009 from http://www.netaddiction.com/ articles/ newdisorder.htm

Yuki, G. (2003) Leadership in Organizations. Prentice Hall: Upper Saddle River, NJ

Zaccaria, J.S. (1970) Theories of occupational choice and vocational development. Houghton Mifflin: Boston

Zillmann, D. & Bryant, J. (1982) Pornography, sexual callousness, and the trivialization of rape. Journal of Communication, Vol.33, No.4, p.111-114

Zillmann, D. & Bryant, J. (1989) Pornography: Research Advances and Policy Considerations. Lawrence Erlbaum Associates: Hillsdale, NJ

Zillmann, D. (1971) Excitation transfer in communicationmediated aggressive behavior. Journal of Experimental Social Psychology, Vol.7, p.419-434

Zillmer, E.A. (2006) The Psychology of Terrorists: Nazi Perpetrators, the Baader-Meinhof ang, War criminals in Bosnia, and Suicide Bombers, in Carrie H.Kennedy, Eric Zillmer (eds.) Military Psychology: clinical and operational applications. Guilford Press: London

Zimbardo, P.G. (1972) The psychology of imprisonment: privation, power and pathology. Stanford University: Stanford

Zimmerman, M.A. (1995) Psychological Empowerment: Issues and Illustrations. American Journal of Community Psychology, 23, 581–99 (cited by Dalton et al., 2001)

■ ■ ■